# MASS TORT LITIGATION

## CASES AND MATERIALS

### Third Edition

■ ■ ■

### Linda S. Mullenix

*Morris and Rita Atlas Chair in Advocacy*
*University of Texas School of Law*

**AMERICAN CASEBOOK SERIES®**

WEST
ACADEMIC
PUBLISHING

*American Casebook Series* is a trademark registered in the U.S. Patent and Trademark Office.

COPYRIGHT © 1996 WEST PUBLISHING CO.
© 2008 Thomson/West
© 2017 LEG, Inc. d/b/a West Academic
    444 Cedar Street, Suite 700
    St. Paul, MN 55101
    1-877-888-1330

West, West Academic Publishing, and West Academic are trademarks of West Publishing Corporation, used under license.

Printed in the United States of America

**ISBN:** 978-1-63460-681-3

*This book is dedicated to the next generation: Rob, Joyce, Jack, Laura, and Will; and grandchildren Amy, Chris, Ned, and Ben*

# PREFACE TO THE THIRD EDITION

This third edition of MASS TORT LITIGATION is a radically revised edition from the first and second editions of this casebook. As such, it reflects the both the changing landscape of mass tort litigation over the past four decades, as well as the changing circumstances of contemporary legal education. Thus, the ambitious first and second editions of this book, running in excess of 1500 pages, has been shortened to accommodate the more realistic expectations of students and professors engaged in a one-semester survey course in mass tort litigation.

The phenomenon of mass tort litigation now spans forty years. It is perhaps difficult today to realize that, prior to the mid-1970s, mass tort litigation had not yet appeared as a distinct sub-field of legal enterprise or jurisprudential study. Indeed, the term "mass tort litigation" had not yet been created or recognized in the legal lexicon. There were no "mass tort" lawyers and no law school offered a course in mass tort litigation. There certainly was no casebook addressing issues and problems related to mass tort litigation.

All this changed in the late 1970s, with the emergence of several first-generation, seminal mass torts: complex litigation involving Agent Orange, asbestos, the Dalkon Shield, Bendectin, and DES. By the mid-1980s—with the proliferation of mass tort litigation congesting federal and state court dockets—institutional reform groups, attorneys, judges, and commentators realized that mass tort litigation presented a new and unique litigation phenomenon. The first decade of mass tort litigation, then, reflected the novel litigation challenges raised by mass tort litigation. Against this backdrop, institutional reform organizations, scholars, and the judiciary formulated numerous reform proposals and innovative techniques for handling these new cases.

The first edition of this casebook was published in 1995 and it was the first and only casebook devoted solely to mass tort litigation. As such, that first edition reflected the state of mass tort litigation then; the casebook attempted to organize a newly emerging field of substantive and procedural law. The book was ambitious in its scope and detail. The book was intended to provide a comprehensive historical and contemporary examination of all issues relating to mass tort litigation. In addition, that book incorporated many of the pending institutional reform proposals addressing the challenges of mass tort litigation. For those familiar with mass tort litigation, it is sobering to reflect that the first edition of the casebook was published prior to the Supreme Court's landmark settlement class action decisions in *Amchem Products v. Windsor* (1997) and *Ortiz v. Fibreboard* (1999).

As it turned out, mass tort litigation proved to be an enduring and rapidly changing, dynamic area of law. The 1995 edition quickly became dated in its exposition of judicial decisions and secondary source materials. The second edition, published in 2008, updated and reorganized the casebook to reflect experience with three decade of mass tort litigation and the changing mass tort landscape. New materials on settlement classes, collateral attack; medical monitoring classes, punitive damage classes, personal and subject matter jurisdiction, mass tort bankruptcy, federalism issues, substantive tort law, and choice of law problems were added to the casebook. Materials relating to peripheral interests, such as the use of special masters and alternative claims facilities, were eliminated. Nonetheless, the second edition, in effort to provide the definitive text on mass tort litigation, was driven by a principle of inclusiveness that resulted in a revised 1500 page casebook.

This third edition takes a different approach to providing a casebook for students wishing to study mass tort litigation. This edition no longer attempts to provide a definitive text or a comprehensive examination of every possible problem relating to mass tort litigation. Instead, the casebook has been reconfigured to provide a one-semester survey course addressing the major issues of mass tort litigation. In addition, the text is updated with the recent decisions reflecting current mass tort practice.

Two principles guided reconfiguration of the casebook. First, the book aims to afford students a fundamental exposure to the major issues and precedents relating to mass tort litigation that one needs to practice in this field. As such, the book is organized around the concept that there now is a "canon" of mass tort cases that every student and practitioner should to be conversant with to be an educated mass tort attorney.

Second, the book has been organized to conform to a one-semester, fourteen-week survey course. Therefore, the casebook has been organized into fourteen compact chapters comprised of fewer cases. This edition also has eliminated all secondary source materials, as well as notes, comments, and questions. There are now hundreds of academic articles on mass tort litigation, and much of this material becomes dated fairly rapidly.

Some foundational materials from the casebook's first two editions have been retained in the belief that knowledgeable attorneys need to know the historical, landmark mass tort cases from the first three decades of mass tort litigation. The landmark cases that continue to be cited today have been retained in the text. The casebook's first seven chapters largely retain the same conceptual framework and materials as the original text, but the second half of the book is reconfigured with substantially new materials.

Chapters 1 and 2 from the previous editions have been preserved. Chapter 1 encourages students to address the threshold question of defining a mass tort, as well as the jurisprudential debate embedded in the continuing controversy over the appropriate means for resolving these complex aggregative litigations. Chapter 2 introduces students to the continuing ethical challenges raised by mass tort litigation and the obligations of attorneys to their clients in mass tort litigation.

Chapters 3 and 4 have also been retained from the first and second editions. Theses chapters introduce students to the problems relating to resolving mass tort litigation through the class action Rule 23. These chapters set forth the landmark historical class action decisions, which are still cited today, that chart the federal judiciary's ever-evolving views over three decades. These materials focus on the concept of mass tort litigation classes. Chapter 5 concentrates on the possibility of medical monitoring as a particular approach to resolving certain types of mass torts. Finally, Chapter 6 focuses on the problem of settlement classes, providing the historical background to understanding the debate over settlement classes, and the Supreme Court's resolution of these issues in the landmark *Amchem* and *Ortiz* decisions.

The remaining seven chapters are comprised of almost entirely new cases and reflect the reality of contemporary mass tort litigation. Thus, these chapters first address the question of the resolution of mass tort litigation in a post-*Amchem* and *Ortiz* litigation arena. Second, these chapters indicate the ways in which mass tort litigation is now resolved through multidistrict litigation auspices, non-class aggregative settlements, and alternative fund approaches.

Chapters 7 and 8, respectively, deal with the persistence of mass tort litigation and settlement classes in a post-*Amchem/Ortiz* world. Consequently, these chapters set forth illustrative cases decided after *Amchem* and *Ortiz* that illuminate the ways in which mass tort class actions have both receded and survived the Court's two major mass tort decisions in the late 1990s.

Chapters 9 and 10 turn attention to the burgeoning use of the multidistrict litigation statute and MDL auspices to resolve mass tort litigation. These materials document the federal judiciary's sea-change in attitude towards creating mass tort MDLs. In addition, this chapter contains new material on the emergence of the "quasi class action," bellwether trials, non-class aggregate settlements, the fiduciary duties of attorneys representing clients in non-class aggregate settlements, and the continuing problem of attorney fees in mass tort litigation.

Chapters 11 and 12 focus attention on a series of challenging issues that continue to persist in the mass tort litigation arena. Thus, this chapter addresses problems relating to damage sampling and statistic proof, limited issues classes, multiphase trial plans and sub-classing of claimants, and the res judicata implications resulting from bifurcated trials.

Chapter 13 includes new materials on the Class Action Fairness Act of 2005, with its creation of the concept of a "mass action." This chapter surveys the interesting development of state court mass actions that some attorneys now deploy as a means to avoid the problems of resolving mass torts in the federal judicial system.

Finally, Chapter 14 sets forth materials relating to the possible resolution of mass torts through non-adjudicative fund approaches. This chapter focuses on two such auspices: the September 11th World Trade Center Disaster Fund, and the Gulf Coast Claims Facility, both overseen by special master and administrator Kenneth Feinberg.

As indicated above, this third edition is revised to reflect developments in mass tort litigation since the second edition. To this end, materials have been added concerning expanded use of MDL auspices, bellwether trials, non-class aggregate settlements, the quasi-class action, the aggregate settlement rule, and the ethical duties of attorneys with clients in MDL and non-class proceedings. In addition, new cases have been added that reflect resolution of various pharmaceutical mass torts (Vioxx and Zyprexa); personal injury mass torts (the NFL and Collegiate Athletes concussion litigation); products liability mass torts (the Ford and GMC Ignition Switch litigations; heart-valve cases; tobacco litigation; the moldy washer cases); natural and man-made environmental disasters (the Hurricane Katrina and BP Gulf Oil Spill litigation), and the World Trade Center events.

Some final comments concerning the editorial decisions made in comprising the text. Judicial decisions in mass tort cases often run to dozens of pages (and in some instances, more than 100 pages). Editing mass tort cases in a manageable but comprehensible fashion continues to be a challenge. Thus, large portions of the judicial decisions have been heavily edited, with entire sections eliminated. All footnotes have been excised. In addition, to make the cases more readable, almost all supporting citation has been eliminated, except where major precedential authority is cited or necessary to retain meaning. In addition, all Notes, Comments, and Questions in the first two editions have been eliminated. Finally, as indicated above, all secondary source academic commentary has been excised.

LINDA S. MULLENIX

July 2016

# ACKNOWLEDGMENTS

I am indebted to the copyright holders identified below for permission to reprint excerpts from the following copyrighted materials. Except for granting me permission to reprint in this book, the following copy- right holders have retained all rights:

American Law Institute, Complex Litigation: Statutory Recommendations and Analysis, copyright © 1994 by the American Law Institute. Reprinted with the permission of the American Law Institute.

American Law Institute, Enterprise Responsibility for Personal Injury, Reporter's Study (1991), copyright © 1991 by the American Law Institute. Reprinted with the permission of the American Law Institute.

Brodeur, Outrageous Misconduct: The Asbestos Industry on Trial (1985), copyright © 1985, by Paul Brodeur. Reprinted by permission of Pantheon Books, a division of Random House, Inc.

Hensler, Resolving Mass Toxic Torts: Myths and Realities, 1989 U.Ill.L. Rev. 89 (1989), copyright © 1989, by Deborah Hensler and the Board of Trustees of the University of Illinois.

Mintz, At Any Cost: Corporate Greed, Women, and the Dalkon Shield (1985), copyright © 1985, by Morton Mintz. Reprinted by permission of Pantheon Books, a division of Random House, Inc.

Peterson and Selvin, Resolution of Mass Torts: Toward a Framework for Evaluation of Aggregative Procedures (1988), copyright © RAND, N–2805–ICJ, 1988. Reprinted by permission of RAND and the Institute for Civil Justice.

Schuck, Agent Orange on Trial: Mass Toxic Disasters in the Courts (1986), copyright © 1986, 1987 by Mary Schuck Trust. Reprinted by permission of the publishers, Cambridge, Mass.: Harvard University Press.

Transgrud, Mass Trials in Mass Tort Cases: A Dissent, 1989 U.Ill.L. Rev. 69 (1989), copyright © 1989, by Roger H. Transgrud and the Board of Trustees of the University of Illinois.

Weinstein, Ethical Dilemmas in Mass Tort Litigation, 88 Nw.U.L.Rev. 469 (1994), copyright © 1994, by Hon. Jack B. Weinstein.

# SUMMARY OF CONTENTS

# TABLE OF CONTENTS

# TABLE OF CASES

The principal cases are in bold type.

---

# TABLE OF AUTHORITIES

# MASS TORT LITIGATION
## CASES AND MATERIALS

## Third Edition

# CHAPTER 1

# INTRODUCTION TO THE PROBLEM OF MASS TORT LITIGATION

■ ■ ■

## A. CASE STUDIES IN MASS TORT LITIGATION: THE SEMINAL CASES

### MORTON MINTZ, AT ANY COST: CORPORATE GREED, WOMEN, AND THE DALKON SHIELD*

New York: Pantheon Books (1985) at 3–8.

In January 1971, the A.H. Robins Company began to sell the Dalkon Shield, promoting it as the "modern, superior," "second generation," and—most importantly—"safe" intrauterine device for birth control. Robins, a major pharmaceutical manufacturer in Richmond, Virginia, distributed 4.5 million of the IUDs in eighty countries before halting sales in the mid-1970s. There followed a catastrophe without precedent in the annals of medicine and law.

The seriously injured victims number in the tens of thousands. Nearly all suffered life-threatening forms of infections known as pelvic inflammatory disease (PID). In the United States alone, PID killed at least eighteen women who had been wearing Shields. Most of the infections impaired or destroyed the women's ability to bear children.

Not only was the Shield unsafe, it was surprisingly ineffective. The number of wearers who became pregnant with the devices in place was on the order of 110,000, or 5 percent—a rate nearly five times the one falsely claimed in advertising and promotion to physicians and women, and a rate sharply higher than that for many other IUDs. More than ordinary commercial puffery, the exaggerated and bogus claims led women to reject more effective birth control in favor of the Shield; and this led directly to consequences far worse than unwanted pregnancies. Statistically, half of all women who became pregnant with an IUD miscarry. But in fact, of the estimated 110,000 women who conceived while wearing the Dalkon Shield, 66,000—or 60 percent—miscarried. Most suffered the previously rare miscarriages called *spontaneous abortions* in either the first or second trimester. Others, in the fourth to sixth months of pregnancy, experienced

---

the still rarer infected miscarriages, or *septic spontaneous abortions.* By the count of the Food and Drug Administration, 248 women just in this country endured this dangerous, Shield-related complication; for 15 of them, these septic abortions were fatal.

Moreover, hundreds of women throughout the world who conceived while wearing the Shield gave birth prematurely, in the final trimester, to children with grave congenital defects including blindness, cerebral palsy, and mental retardation, or that were stillborn. No one can pinpoint the exact number of such women, partly because no one knows how many times women or their doctors failed to make a proper connection between the Shield and the premature birth of a defective baby.

Robins distributed about 2.86 million Shields in the United States, and doctors implanted them, by the company's estimate, in 2.2 million women. Abroad, Robins distributed about 1.7 million Shields, and in June 1974 it estimated that 800,000 to one million were implanted. The Agency for International Development (AID) brought more than 697,000 Shields for use in the Third World, slightly more than half of them for the International Planned Parenthood Federation and most of the rest for the Pathfinder Fund, the Population Council, and the Family Planning International Assistance. AID said in a report in 1985 that nearly half of the Shields it had bought were returned unused to Robins and that a review of cables to the agency left the impression "that very few Dalkon Shield insertions were made." But whatever the precise numbers of Shield insertions in African, Asian, Middle Eastern, Caribbean, Latin American, and South American countries, poor medical conditions made lethal complications more likely. My guess is that Shield-related PID killed hundreds—possibly thousands—of women outside of the United States. Dr. Richard P. Dickey, a former member of the Food and Drug Administration's obstetrical and gynecological devices advisory panel, has seen at first hand the conditions faced by a woman who suffers PID. An infected Shield wearer, "where there are no doctors, no antibiotics, she's going to die," he told me.

In 1974, increasing numbers of Shield-related spontaneous septic abortions became known to the FDA, and the agency asked Robins to suspend Shield sales in the United States. It did so on June 28, 1974. After the sales suspension, the company retrieved unsold Shields from supply channels in this country. Plaintiffs' lawyer Dale I. Larson asked company chairman E. Claiborne Robins why this had been done. Because "it was the proper thing to do," the chairman swore. Larson, trying to find out if the retrieved devices may have been exported, asked if the Shields had been destroyed, and how and when—and why "the proper thing" had not also been done for less-developed countries—where product liability lawsuits and adverse publicity about a defective product are rarities. To all such questions the chairman's answer was that he did not know.

In fact, after halting domestic sales, the company continued to distribute Shields abroad for as long as nine months—"at the request of specific governments," Robins swore at a deposition in January 1984. Asked who had told him that, he replied, "I don't know that. It seems to me I saw a memo somewhere, but I don't remember when or where."

In El Salvador in 1975—a year after the suspension of Shield sales here—Martine Langley was a volunteer in a family-planning clinic. Now a lawyer in Austin, Texas, she recalls that the only IUD the clinic's doctors were inserting was the Shield, and that some clinics in El Salvador continued to implant Shields until 1980. "Sometimes the doctor would say to the patient, 'This is from the United States and it's very good,' " Langley told David Phelps, a Washington correspondent for the *Minneapolis Star and Tribune*. Then, she said, the doctor would motion toward her and tell the woman, "She is from the United States and people there use it."

Today, more than a decade after Shield sales officially ended, legacies of death, disease, injury, and pain persist. Even women who have had the Shield removed are not out of danger. Because PID is not an affliction that is simply treated and is then over and done with, large numbers of former Dalkon Shield wearers suffer chronic pain and illness, sometimes requiring repeated hospitalizations and surgery; many have waged desperate battles to bear children despite severe damage to their reproductive systems. More cheerless news came in April 1985 from two studies funded by the National Institutes of Health. They showed that childless IUD wearers who have had PID run a far higher risk of infertility if their devices were Shields than if they were other makes. Not even women who currently wear the Shield with no apparent problem are safe: they run the risk of suddenly being stricken by PID. In the words of Judge Lord, they are wearing "a deadly depth charge in their wombs, ready to explode at any time."

The exact number of women still wearing the Shield is unknown. By early 1983, some Food and Drug Administration officials and OB-GYNs were confident that few American women, probably only hundreds, still used it. Other qualified observers, however, were estimating the figure to be much higher, anywhere from 80,000 to more than half a million. Certainly the response to Robin's own call-back campaign of October 1984 suggests that the higher figures are closer to the mark. By February 1985, a $4-million advertising drive, which urged women still wearing the Shields to have them removed at Robins's expense, had drawn more than 16,000 phone calls on toll-free hotlines; by the end of March 4,437 women had filed claims for Shield removals. The claims were flowing in at the dramatic rate of more than one hundred a week.

And what of women in the seventy-nine other countries where the Shield was distributed? The company told the FDA that it had notified first the countries' ambassadors in Washington and then their senior health officials at home of its Shield-removal campaign in the United States, and had "sought direction on whether a similar program would be appropriate in those countries." By early April 1985, Australia, Canada, and the United Kingdom had requested, and the company had put into effect, one or another kind of removal program. New Zealand, too, was considering a program. Sixteen other countries had simply acknowledged receipt of Robins's letter. Eight others—Denmark, Mexico, Norway, Pakistan, the Philippines, South Africa, Tanzania, and Zambia—had declined any removal program. From the rest of the countries, of which there were fifty-one, Robins had received no response almost a half-year after inviting one. If this record suggests indifference to the health and safety of women, at least a partial explanation may be found in the company's adamant refusal to admit to the special dangers inherent in its device. "Robins believes that serious scientific questions exist about whether the Dalkon Shield poses a significantly different risk of infection than other IUDs," it said in an interim report to the FDA.

Another measure of the extent of the damage is provided by the lawsuits and unlitigated claims filed by Shield wearers in the United States. Nearly all of these women had suffered PID followed by damage to or loss of their ability to bear children. The large majority had not been pregnant when stricken. Through June 30, 1985, by the company's own count, the total number of cases was 14,330, and new ones were being filed at a rate of fifteen a day. The company continues to experience a dramatic upsurge in the number of new Shield claims, president E. Claiborne Robins, Jr., told the annual stockholders' meeting on May 30, 1985. "I want to emphasize that the company anticipates that a substantial number of new claims will be filed in the future," he said. Through June 30, 1985, Robins and its former Shield insurer, Aetna Life & Casualty Company, had paid out $378.3 million to dispose of cases, plus $107.3 million in legal expenses. Juries have awarded $24.8 million in punitive or exemplary damages, which are intended to punish wanton or reckless behavior and to deter it repetition or emulation.

Still, no summary of suits and claims can come close to accounting for the total number of Shield injuries. By Robins's own conservative estimate in April 1985, 4 percent of the wearers were injured—that is, nearly 90,000 women in the United States alone. Of course, only a fraction of these will file suit. It is conventional wisdom among medical scientists that adverse reactions to drugs are always grossly underreported, and this is surely true of Shield injuries, too. Also, some Shield victims who stood to win substantial damages chose not to sue, either because they wanted to put a horrifying experience behind them, or because they placed a higher value on avoiding public disclosure of a matter as private and sensitive as the impairment or destruction of their ability to bear children. Other victims did not know or had forgotten the makes of their IUDs, as confirmed by Robins in its report to the FDA. By January 17, 1985, it said, 3,939 calls had come in on its special phone lines "from women presently wearing an IUD but of unknown type."

Furthermore, some of the women who might have sought compensation were certainly intimidated by Robins's brutal invasions of privacy and courtroom techniques. Judge Lord charged:

> When the time came for these women to make their claims against your company, you attacked their characters. You inquired into their sexual practices and into the identity of their sex partners. You exposed these women—and ruined families and reputations and careers—in order to intimidate those who would raise their voices against you. You introduced issues that had no relationship whatsoever to the fact that you planted in the bodies of these women instruments of death, of mutilation, of disease.

Again, if the claims against Robins in the United States represent only a fraction of the incidence of injury, they represent an even smaller fraction worldwide, since figures are simply unavailable from most of the countries where the Shield was used.

## PAUL BRODEUR, OUTRAGEOUS MISCONDUCT: THE ASBESTOS INDUSTRY ON TRIAL*
New York: Pantheon Books (1985) at 3–6.

When the Manville Corporation, the world's largest asbestos company, with twenty-five thousand employees and more than fifty factories and mines in the United States and Canada, filed a debtor's petition for reorganization and protection under Chapter 11 of the federal Bankruptcy Code, on August 26, 1982, it did so in order to force a halt to thousands of lawsuits that had been brought against it by workers who claimed that they had developed lung cancer and other diseases as a result of their exposure to asbestos in Manville's insulation products, and who were alleging that the company had failed to warn them of the dangers involved. The story made the front page of virtually every major newspaper in the country, because Manville (formerly the Johns-Manville Corporation) was not only the largest American industrial company ever to file under Chapter 11—at the time, it ranked 181st on *Fortune's* list of the nation's 500 leading industrial corporations—but, with assets of more than $2 billion, was also one of the most financially healthy companies ever to take such action. In a full-page statement that appeared on August 27 in the New York *Times*, the Washington *Post,* the *Wall Street Journal*, and other leading papers, John A. McKinney, Manville's chairman and chief executive officer, announced that the company was "overwhelmed by 16,500 lawsuits related to the health effects of asbestos." McKinney said

---

that lawsuits were being brought against Manville at a rate of 500 a month, and that the company could expect to be named as a defendant in at least 52,000 asbestos-disease lawsuits before the litigation ran its course. He estimated that at present settlement cost of about $40,000 per case the lawsuits would create a potential liability of $2 billion, requiring Manville to set aside a reserve fund that would wipe out most of its net worth and cripple its operation. For these reasons, he declared, the company's board of directors had decided to file for relief in the hope of establishing an effective system for handling the asbestos claims under Chapter 11.

In his statement, McKinney took pains to point out those people whom he considered responsible for Manville's predicament. He began by blaming the federal government for refusing to admit responsibility for asbestos disease that had developed among Second World War shipyard workers, who made up half the plaintiffs in the lawsuits brought against Manville. He criticized Congress for failing to enact a statutory compensation program for the victims of asbestos disease "so that the thousands of citizens and voters caught up in this problem will be spared the expensive, inefficient, and haphazard litigation system we have been saddled with." In addition, he castigated the insurance companies with which Manville had been doing business over the years for refusing to pay claims against product-liability policies totaling hundreds of millions of dollars. As for any responsibility that Manville might have incurred for the plight of the insulation workers, McKinney implied that the company was not at fault because "not until 1964 was it known that excessive exposure to asbestos fiber released from asbestos-containing insulation products can sometimes cause certain lung diseases." Since the mid-1970s, he said, Manville had disposed of some thirty-five hundred lawsuits by settlement or trial, and in a significant number of the cases that had gone to trial, he said, "juries have found that we are not at fault and acted responsibly in light of then existing medical knowledge."

In many ways, McKinney's statement was more revealing for its omissions than for what it contained. By neglecting to mention that Manville and its insurance carriers had settled out of court approximately thirty-four hundred of the thirty-five hundred lawsuits it had disposed of, and that it had paid out some $50 million in doing so, he ignored the extent to which his company had already acknowledged responsibility for the incidence of asbestos disease in insulation workers. In claiming that insulation materials containing asbestos were not known to be dangerous until 1964—an assertion that had constituted Manville's chief legal defense for many years—he ignored the fact that this defense had been rejected by juries across the country, and had recently been struck down by the New Jersey Supreme Court. Far and away the most self-serving of the omissions in McKinney's statement, however, was his failure to go beyond a bare mention of the fact that punitive damages had been awarded against Manville. Not only had juries found Manville liable for punitive damages in ten of some sixty-five asbestos lawsuits involving the company that had been tried in the United States during 1981 and the first half of 1982, but the average amount of punitive damages in the first six months of 1982 was about $600,000 a case. It is usually not possible to insure against punitive damages, which are assessed for outrageous and reckless misconduct, and McKinney could not have been unaware of their potential effect upon his company, for the simple reason that the likelihood of their being awarded in subsequent trials had been listed as a chief reason for Manville's financially uncertain future in a sworn affidavit that Manville's treasurer had submitted to the United States Bankruptcy Court of the Southern District of New York on the previous day. Moreover, in testimony given before the Senate Committee on Labor and Human Resources two years earlier, McKinney himself had underscored the devastating implications of punitive damages when, in order to substantiate his denial of the charge that employers had knowingly exposed workers to the hazards of excessive asbestos dust, he had pointed out that in all the litigation to date there had not been a single instance in which a jury or a trial judge had awarded punitive damages against any asbestos company. "I can think of no greater demonstration that the cover-up charge is a complete fabrication," he declared.

By and large, the newspaper stories that appeared on August 27 tended to describe Manville as a beleaguered giant reeling under the burden of mass litigation, and to portray McKinney as an embattled business manager fighting for his company's survival. Few of them reported the fact that juries had assessed punitive damages against Manville after hearing evidence that the company had engaged in a cover-up of the asbestos hazard for nearly five decades. The *Times,* for example, not only neglected to tell its readers initially that punitive damages had been assessed but also ran an editorial that compared the suffering of asbestos workers with the fiscal woes afflicting the asbestos companies. "Asbestos is a tragedy, most of all for the victims and their families but also for the companies, which are being made to pay the price for decisions made long ago," the editorial read. The editorial warned Congress to address the asbestos problem "before more victims die uncompensated and other companies follow Manville into the bankruptcy courts."

During the remainder of August and in the first part of September, the economic, legal, and political ramifications of Manville's Chapter 11 petition received daily attention in the press, which speculated at length on the dilemma it presented to Manville's stockholders and creditors, on the problems it posed for bankruptcy court, and on the pressure it placed on Congress to enact legislation that would help Manville overcome its financial difficulties. Considerably less attention was given to a grim prediction made by Dr. Irving J. Selikopff, who was director of the Environmental Sciences Laboratory at the Mount Sinai School of Medicine, in New York, and was widely acknowledged as the world's leading expert on asbestos disease. Selikopff estimated that among the twenty-one million living American men and women who had been occupationally exposed to asbestos between 1940 and 1980 there would be between eight and ten thousand deaths from asbestos-related cancer each year for the next twenty years. As for the culpability of Manville and other leading asbestos companies in helping to create this immense human tragedy, it either went unreported or was mentioned only in passing. By the last week of September, when the story of Manville's Chapter 11 petition had dropped from the headlines, few people were aware that the bankruptcy filing was simply the latest episode in a fifty-year history of corporate malfeasance and inhumanity to man that is unparalleled in the annals of the private enterprise system.

## PETER H. SCHUCK, AGENT ORANGE ON TRIAL: MASS TOXIC DISASTERS IN THE COURTS*

The Belknap Press of Harvard University Press (1986).
3–6; 10–12, 13–15.

This is about two urgent social problems and about the extraordinary lawsuit they have spawned.

The first problem arose from the smoldering ashes of Vietnam. For many of the millions of American soldiers who returned home from that charnel house, the future was filled with bitterness, dread, controversy, and debilitating illness. In 1978 the veterans sued a number of chemical manufacturers, blaming them for various diseases and traumas that they and their families had allegedly suffered because of exposure to Agent Orange, a herbicide the United States Army had used to defoliate Vietnam's luxuriant jungle cover. The law, the veterans hoped, would assuage their pain and vindicate their sacrifices. Today, almost a decade later, they are still waiting. For many of them, the law has become a mockery of justice, an object of derision.

The second problem arose from a very different set of social facts. We live in the midst of a burgeoning technological revolution. For several decades a torrent of new synthetic chemicals has cascaded out of our laboratories. Complex industrial processes have been developed, and intricate patterns of distribution, consumption, and disposal have evolved. These innovations have benefited American society enormously, but they have also created new kinds of risks. Agent Orange, originally hailed by some environmentalists and even by one of the veterans' lawyers as a model herbicide, was later found to harbour insidious dangers as well; in this respect it was a characteristic product of the great scientific advance.

It might seem surprising that these two disparate social problems—the one produced by unspeakable human suffering, the other by unparalleled human ingenuity—came together in a courtroom. On the surface, each of these problems seems quite unsuited to resolution at the instance of private parties wrangling before a judge. War, after all, leaves many bitter legacies; distributing its burdens is ordinarily the stuff of national politics, not of private litigation. By the same token, environmental risk management is an immensely complex technical task; controlling such risks is usually the responsibility of legislatures and regulatory agencies, not of courts.

Students of the contemporary legal system, however, know better. Times have changed. Traditionally, tort (personal injury) cases were generally regarded as essentially isolated disputes in which the law's role was simply to allocate losses between putative injurers and victims according to a moral conception that Aristotle called corrective justice; the law required that a wrongdoer return to a victim, typically in the form of money damages, what the former had "taken" from the latter. Such disputes were readily managed by the parties and the court system. Typically, the parties would adduce a relatively simple, comprehensible body of evidence before a detached arbiter, usually a jury. Applying general and familiar norms of conduct to the facts of the case, the jury would reach a decision, one that bound the parties but, because it was so fact-specific and was not explained by the jury, had little precedential effects on other cases.

Today, the law books abound with tort cases, especially in the product liability area, that involve not a few individuals but large aggregations of people and vast economic and social interests. These cases are not preoccupied with corrective justice between individuals concerned solely with past events. Instead, they concern the public control of large-scale activities and the distribution of social power and values for the future. The court and the jury in these cases do not simply prescribe and apply familiar norms to discrete actions; they function as policy-oriented risk regulators, as self-conscious allocators of hard-to-measure benefits and risks, and as social problem solvers.

The *Agent Orange* case carries this trend to its logical (or, as we shall see, perhaps illogical) extreme. Apart from its locus in a courtroom, its bears little resemblance to traditional tort adjudication. Its magnitude and complexity beggar imagination, as a few crude numerical indicators will suggest. The case is actually a consolidation into one class action of more than 600 separate actions originally filed by more than 15,000 named individuals throughout the United States, and almost 400 individual cases not included in the class action ("opt out" cases). The parties in these consolidated actions consist of some 2.4 million Vietnam veterans, their wives, children born and unborn, and soldiers from Australia and New

Zealand; a small number of civilian plaintiffs; seven (originally twenty-four) corporate defendants; and the United States government.

In a typical case litigated in the federal district court in which the *Agent Orange* case was heard, the docket sheet is one or two pages long and contains perhaps sixty individual entries, each representing a filed document. The *Agent Orange* docket sheet in the district court alone is approximately 425 single-spaced pages long. It contains over 7,300 individual entries, many representing documents that are hundreds of pages long. The files of briefs, hearing transcripts, court orders, affidavits, and other court documents in the case were so voluminous that the already cramped clerk's office had to take the unprecedented step of devoting an entire room, staffed by two special clerks, to house them.

The financial and personnel demands of the case are even more staggering. The plaintiffs are represented by a network of law firms that numbered almost 1,500 by May 1984, located in every region of the country; the documented cost of their activities to date certainly exceeds $10 million and increases daily. It has been estimated that defendants spent roughly $100 million merely to prepare for the trial, utilizing hundreds of lawyers and corporate staff in their Herculean effort.

The court has also borne an enormous administrative burden. The current district court judge—the second to preside over the *Agent Orange* case—had to create a considerable bureaucracy within its chambers simply to enable him to run it, employing additional law clerks and paralegals. And although it is highly unusual for a judge to appoint even one special master to handle particular aspects of a litigation for him, this judge used no fewer than six special masters (four or five of them simultaneously) plus a federal magistrate, and they in turn sometimes hired consultants to assist them.

Finally, the case resulted in the largest tort settlement in history. That settlement, reached in May 1984 after almost six years of litigation, created a fund of $180 million; with accrued interest, it now totals more than $200 million, increasing at the rate of more than $40,000 each day. The case is now on appeal; since the settlement has been challenged, the court will not be in a position to begin distributing that fund for years, even if the plan is ultimately upheld. Nevertheless, simply to maintain the fund, the court has already been obliged to disburse more than two million dollars. For example, it had to create an *Agent Orange* computer center to process the almost 250,000 claims that class members have filed against the fund.

But the significance of the Agent Orange case is not confined to the features that have been mentioned—its symbolic reenactment of the war, its heralding of a new role for courts and juries, or its gigantic dimensions. Even more important is what the case reveals about a new and far-reaching legal and social phenomenon—the "mass toxic tort"—and society's response to it. The *Agent Orange* case is not the first mass toxic tort litigation (the diethylstilbestrol, or DES, and asbestos litigations began earlier), but it is probably the most revealing and perplexing example of the legal genre. In the *Agent Orange* case, we confront an unprecedented challenge to our legal system: a future in which the law must grapple with the chemical revolution and help us live comfortably with it.

The mass toxic tort has only become possible in recent years, as a vibrant chemical technology converged with mass distribution techniques and mass markets. We have not yet grasped its full meaning and implications. To begin to understand what is truly distinctive about it, we must isolate the three constitutive elements—mass, toxic, and tort.

The *Agent Orange* case dramatically illustrates each of these distinctive characteristics of mass toxic tort litigation. Its *mass* aspect, as we have already seen, is especially striking, creating the prospect of ruinous liability for defendants, stupefying organizational complexity for plaintiffs, and unprecedented problems of procedural, evidentiary, and substantive law for the court.

Even more than the mass character of the claims, however, the *toxic* nature of the injury in *Agent Orange* defines the case as extraordinary. This is especially evident when Agent Orange is compared with the two most important and difficult toxic tort litigations that had been brought previously, those involving asbestos and DES. Although each of these litigations presented its own unique array of complications, the issue that would prove most perplexing in *Agent Orange*—the question of whether the chemical caused plaintiffs' injuries—was far more straightforward in the asbestos and DES cases. First, the objective symptoms of asbestosis and mesothelioma, the two most common asbestos-related diseases, and the vaginal adenocarcinoma caused by DES, are relatively exposure-and-disease-specific, distinctive, and easily observed. Second, the long latency periods for those diseases (often twenty years or more) had already run their courses by the time many of the cases reached trial. Third, the exposure levels of asbestos workers and of women who had ingested DES during pregnancy were relatively high and sustained.

None of these conditions obtained in the case of Agent Orange: the cancers and birth defects that it allegedly caused were not distinctive; the exposures had occurred less than fifteen years earlier and thus may not yet have fully revealed their toxic effects; and the levels of dioxin (the highly toxic contaminant of Agent Orange) to which the veterans were exposed were generally quite low. For these and other reasons, the obstacles to establishing general causation and damage, easily overcome in the earlier toxic tort cases, would prove decisive in shaping the *Agent Orange* litigation and settlement and the public reaction to them.

By the same token, the task of establishing the liability of particular defendants was far more daunting in the *Agent Orange* case. The DES cases presented the indeterminate defendant problem; the pills, although manufactured by many different drug companies, were fungible and had been consumed long ago. Some asbestos cases presented the problem of indeterminate plaintiffs; certain injuries, especially cancer, were not asbestos-specific.

The *Agent Orange* case, however, presented both the indeterminate defendant and indeterminate plaintiff problems and in extreme forms. The Agent Orange was produced by different companies, but their formulations were mixed together in non-identifiable steel drums before being sent to Vietnam. The most serious injuries of which the veterans complained apparently are not dioxin-specific. And although in the asbestos cases the issue of which particular firms were liable was sometimes complicated by a number of variables (type of asbestos, condition of packaging and handling, use of respirators) that were not usually relevant to *Agent Orange,* the issues of which individuals were exposed and at what levels were even more difficult in *Agent Orange.*

But this case also reveals in an unusually clear and arresting form the distinctive moral dilemma that characterizes tort disputes. From the perspective of the veterans who sued, the case's significance lay less in large questions of public policy, such as the conduct of the Vietnam War and the social control of toxic substances, than in their claim to what tort law has traditionally promised—corrective justice. The veterans viewed the case as their opportunity to settle accounts, to recover from the government and the chemical manufacturers some portion of what the Vietnam War had taken from them in the name of duty: their youth, their vigor, and their future. The case came to symbolize their most human commitments and passions: their insistence upon respect and recognition, their hope for redemption and renewal, and their hunger for vindication and vengeance. For them, it was a searing morality play projected onto a national stage. These deeply personal aspirations pervaded the case, influencing the strategies of plaintiffs' counsel, shaping certain issues, and casting a shadow over the negotiated settlement that would obscure its legal status for years to come.

*Agent Orange*, however, is more than a paradigm of a particularly difficult kind of mass toxic tort case. It also exemplifies a long historical development in the structure and underlying assumptions of tort law generally. This development consists of three interwoven themes. First, tort law has moved from an individualistic grounding toward a more collective one. In defining the parties' legal rights and duties, tort law has come to be concerned with them less as discrete, idiosyncratic actors than as relatively interchangeable units of large, impersonal aggregations— broadly defined classes, epidemiological populations, or stochastic events. Second, the criteria for evaluating the parties' behavior have moved from moral categories to more functional ones. Evaluations of conduct based on fault, specific causation, and corrective justice norms have increasingly given way to considerations of compensation, deterrence, and administrative efficiency. Third, tort law has come to legitimate a judicial role that is less arbitral and more managerial in nature. Today's judge does not simply decide between the competing proofs and legal theories offered by the parties; he or she is also widely expected to administer large-scale litigation with an eye to achieving broad social purposes. The judge is supposed to allocate scarce resources wisely, develop legal rules that advance sound public policy, ensure that lawyers adequately represent their clients, and consider the social and political implications of settlements.

But for all its unique features, it would be profoundly mistaken to regard the case as only an interesting oddity, a sort of legal sideshow of interest to veterans, to be sure, but without larger significance for American society generally. In reality, the Agent Orange litigation prefigures a grim dimension of our future; it is a harbinger of mass toxic tort cases yet to come. Future disputes will surely possess their own idiosyncratic elements; for example, they may involve pharmaceuticals, food additives, industrial compounds, pollutants, toxic wastes deposited in landfills, radiation, or some other effusion of modern technology. The causal linkages between toxic agents, exposure levels, and pathological symptoms may be more or less elusive than was true of *Agent Orange*. The injurers' identity and responsibility may be more or less determinate than in this case. The judges who adjudicate future cases may have very different conceptions of the court's role and of the nature of mass toxic tort litigation than did Judges Pratt and Weinstein. Other differences will surely exist. The contours of the new cases are no more predictable today than the *Agent Orange* case was twenty-five years ago.

But emphasizing the case's significance as a lodestar for future litigants and judges is to miss what in the end may be an even more profound lesson. The *Agent Orange* case is not simply a response to the veterans' anguish and to the social risks from toxic chemicals. It is, most pointedly, an attempt to solve these problems in a particular way. Tort litigation is an exceedingly valuable mechanism of social integration and control, a mechanism of which Americans appear to be unusually fond. But it is by no means our only, or necessarily our most promising, remedy for mass toxic harms. It is only one in a repertoire of policy instruments, including regulation, administrative compensation schemes, collective bargaining, and insurance, by which society can attempt to control risks and compensate harms.

It may seem odd to close this introduction by emphasizing the particularized, idiosyncratic, human dimension of the *Agent Orange* case. After all, it has been stressed that its causes, character, and consequences are firmly rooted in technological developments, fundamental legal structures, and large historical and political forces. These are social phenomena in which the role of individuals might seem insignificant or at most merely epiphenomenal. Yet the truth is that almost every aspect of the *Agent Orange* litigation has been influenced by contingent human choices. Dedicated but deeply divided veterans; flamboyant trial lawyers; class-action financial entrepreneurs; skillful, Machiavellian special masters; a Naderesque litigation organizer; a brilliant, crafty judge—these forceful personalities continually collided in a kind of Brownian motion of strategic choice, high idealism, seat-of-the-pants innovation, and human folly. Seldom has the contradiction between the popular, intuitive aspiration for law and its technical, formal reality been more vividly revealed. The *Agent Orange* case reminds us that the great historic developments not only play upon, but may also be the playthings of, ordinary men and women who are sometimes capable of doing extraordinary things.

# B. DEFINING MASS TORT LITIGATION: ANALYTICAL FRAMEWORKS

## THE AMERICAN LAW INSTITUTE, COMPLEX LITIGATION: STATUTORY RECOMMENDATIONS AND ANALYSIS
### (1994) at 7–18.

### THE PROBLEM OF COMPLEX LITIGATION

*a.   Introduction.* "Complex litigation" has no uniform definition, and the term sometimes is used to refer to litigation that concerns complex issues even if the dispute takes place only between two parties in a single forum. As used in this Project, however, "complex litigation" refers exclusively to multiparty, multiforum litigation; it is characterized by related claims dispersed in several forums and often over long periods of time and presents one of the greatest problems our courts currently confront. Repeated litigation of the common issues in a complex case unduly expends the resources of attorney and client, clogs already over-crowded dockets, delays recompense for those in need, and brings our legal system into general disrepute. Creative lawyers and judges have shown that both justice and efficiency can be achieved by those willing to stretch the bounds of the existing procedural scheme, but as Congress, the profession, and newspaper journalists have noted, we are in urgent need of procedural reform to meet the exigencies of the complex litigation problem.

Complex cases may arise under state or federal law and in the courts of either system. They are generated by a variety of circumstances—from a single mass disaster such as the collapse of a Hyatt Hotel skywalk, from myriad individual contacts with a hazardous product such as asbestos, or from allegations of antitrust violations committed by one of the world's largest corporations or a number of small ones. The claims in a complex case may accrue all at once as in an air crash, or they may be latent for generations and mature at different times, as in the case of DES. But complex cases share two defining characteristics: they all involve duplicative relitigation of identical or nearly identical issues, and consequently, they all involve the enormous expenditure of resources.

b. *A description of the history of complex litigation.* The history of complex litigation is a litany of gargantuan and often well-known cases that have posed unprecedented challenges for the courts. An outline of some of the most important developments in that history follows and illustrates the current problem posed by this form of litigation.

In the early 1960s, as the House Judiciary Committee has noted, "following the successful Government prosecution of the electrical equipment manufacturers for antitrust law violations, more than 1,800 separate damage actions were filed in 33 federal district courts. This wave of litigation threatened to engulf the courts." As a result, a Coordinating Committee for Multiple Litigation was established, without whose efforts, in the late Chief Justice Earl Warren's view, "district court calendars throughout the country could well have broken down." Congress eventually responded to the electrical equipment cases by creating the Judicial Panel on Multidistrict Litigation, *see* 28 U.S.C. § 1407, one of the most important tools for processing complex litigation that the federal system has developed to date. As of December 31, 1987, after two decades of operation, the Multidistrict Litigation Panel had consolidated 16,173 separate civil actions for pretrial proceedings.. Despite the Multidistrict Litigation Panel's past success and undoubted future potential, however, the much-criticized provisions that limit its authority to consolidation for pretrial purposes have prevented it from serving as anything like a comprehensive solution for the complex litigation problem.

After a 1963 grand jury indictment charged the Wm. Merrell Company with falsifying data submitted to the Food and Drug Administration, fifteen hundred plaintiffs brought suit claiming injuries due to MER/29. MER/29 cases "were begun in almost every state and in many different courts, both state and federal, within most states." MER/29 was one of the great success stories of voluntary cooperation among litigants—a lawyers' committee was able to consolidate pretrial discovery effectively, and because there was only a single defendant, the few cases that went to trial served as test cases that facilitated settlement. The lawyers even established a MER/29 "school" to train plaintiffs' attorneys in the facts of the case. Nevertheless, MER/29 was the type of exception that proves a rule—altogether extraordinary effort, trust, and good faith were necessary to prevent the disintegration of the litigation into a fight to the last ditch that could have generated immense legal fees at the expense of the tort victims and the defendant.

The giant of complex litigation has been and continues to be asbestos. Asbestos litigation on a large scale began in the mid-1970s and has continued to grow. As a result, so many asbestos-related personal injury claims now have been brought that, in 1986, "approximately 20,000 damage actions by asbestos disease victims, mostly workers, [were] pending in state and federal courts across the country, and the number [was] increasing by several hundred new claims each month." An even larger estimate was suggested in a 1987 study for the Federal Judicial Center: "Exact counts of pending asbestos cases are impossible to find. Recent estimates range from about 33,000 to 50,000. New cases continue to be filed, and Johns-Manville estimates that it will have to pay between 83,000 and 100,000 personal injury claims." Asbestos also has spawned a great number of ancillary suits seeking to determine responsibility for removing the substance from buildings or to apportion blame among defendants. It should not be surprising, therefore, that "the estimated legal bill for all facets of the asbestos litigation easily exceeds a billion dollars." Many complex cases over the past three decades have arisen from single mass catastrophes. United States Circuit Judge Alvin Rubin provides a simple but moving catalog:

> We all know of the Bhopal disaster in which, as a result of the release of noxious chemicals from a Union Carbide plant in Bhopal, India, more than 1700 persons were killed and 200,000 were injured. When a Pan American Boeing 727 crashed into a residential area near the New Orleans airport on July 9, 1982, 179 people died. The collapse of a skywalk at the Hyatt Regency Hotel in Kansas City in 1981 resulted in 114 deaths and hundreds of injuries. In 1985, 500 people died in an airline crash in Japan, 174 in a Delta Airlines crash at the Dallas airport, and 57 persons in a crash of a Midwestern Airlines plane.

Because catastrophes like these invariably raise complex issues of fact, they can have a much greater impact on the courts than the small number of the cases suggests. It is not uncommon that cases may be dispersed in both the state and federal judicial systems. For example, after the Hyatt Hotel skywalk collapse, hundreds of virtually identical lawsuits were filed in state court as well as before United States District Court Judge Scott Wright.

In the early 1980's, *Agent Orange* was perhaps the most highly visible complex case in the federal system. After more than 600 individual suits were filed, first Judge Pratt and then Chief Judge Jack Weinstein of the United States District Court for the Eastern District of New York certified a plaintiff class containing an estimated 2.4 million members. Efficient handling of the case was made more difficult by the decision of 2,440 individuals to opt out of the plaintiff class, although 600 of them later asked to be reinstated. The controversy over Judge Weinstein's aggressive management of this case, his tactics in achieving settlement, and the adequacy of the settlement he obtained, may not abate for years to come.

Nevertheless, a seemingly hopeless litigation morass was resolved. The case is a perfect example of the inadequacy of our traditional procedural system to cope with mass disasters or the demands of modern substantive law.

The sometimes devastating impact of complex litigation is suffered by large defendants, as well as individual plaintiffs. This fact was underscored recently when two mass tort defendants, asbestos producer Johns-Manville and Dalkon Shield manufacturer A.H. Robins, resorted to bankruptcy in order to resolve the outstanding tort claims against them. Although the invocation of bankruptcy procedures may be one method of achieving the consolidated adjudication of a complex case, it is by no means obvious that it is the optimal means for handling mass tort claims. Indeed, the very propriety of using bankruptcy in this setting has proved extremely controversial. Serious questions also can be raised as to whether bankruptcy courts can cope with the massive litigation ancillary to a complex case, or can achieve equity between early-and-late filing claimants.

At times the complexity of some cases goes beyond what appears on the surface of the litigation. For example, in massive environmental clean-up litigation what already is a highly complex basic dispute is compounded by the complexity of deciding the applicability of insurance coverage as well as assigning the liability among multiple insurers.

Even this brief summary suffices to show that huge multiparty, multiforum disputes have become a recurring feature of modern litigation. In many cases systemic resources have been saved and costs reduced by good sense, procedural creativity, and judge or lawyer initiative. Nevertheless, the time has come to replace ad hoc innovation with procedures developed specifically for complex cases. This is especially true because the essential features of complex litigation are predictable, and the number of cases is bound to increase.

    *c.*    *Cost of duplicative litigation.* Rule 1 of the Federal Rules of Civil Procedure specifies a tripartite goal for the federal procedural system: "the just, speedy, and inexpensive determination of every action." Unfortunately, complex litigation can yield determinations that are slow, enormously expensive, and potentially unjust.

Complex litigation as defined in this proposal is not limited to cases involving complex substantive issues. Rather, it is characterized by the wasteful multiplication of proceedings, needless costs, and the likelihood of injustice resulting from inconsistent adjudications. Judicial overload also leads to delay and costs throughout the entire judicial system. It is worth stressing, however, that the effect of long court delays does not fall equally on all members of society—although a large corporation may be able to wait many years to obtain a tort or contract recovery, or may be content to defer liability for that length of time, someone who is poor and seriously injured may find that justice delayed is indeed, as the saying goes, justice denied.

Duplicative litigation of the issues in a complex case also can lead to injustice in more direct ways. "Beyond the sheer economy of not having to litigate the same matters twice," authors Rowe and Sibley point out, "consolidation of related proceedings can reduce such problems as inconsistent outcomes, whipsawing (from the ability of defendants in separate litigation to point to a nonparty as the one truly liable), and uncoordinated scrambles for the assets of a limited fund." The ultimate result of an "uncoordinated scramble," of course, can be a defendant's bankruptcy before all potential plaintiffs have been paid, and this risk particularly is plausible in cases allowing plaintiffs to obtain large and often widely differing punitive damage awards. In addition, consolidation of related claims can ensure that people with modest means or those with relatively small claims can gain access to justice; forcing individual litigation of propositions that are true but expensive to demonstrate can be tantamount to barring the courthouse doors.

Finally, the most striking problem caused by complex litigation is its enormous cost. That cost cannot be measured precisely, but every indication is that it is staggering.

> Even saving one week of judicial time per case would, as most trial judges know, be substantial. In the Dalkon Shield litigation, the record disclosed that, if the usual percentage (90) of the 100 members [in a] statewide class settled their cases, the savings of judicial resources in the trial of the remaining 100 would amount to 400 weeks, or, roughly eight years of trial time. In addition, there would be an estimated savings of $26 million in litigation expense to the parties and $7 million of court expenses.

If a 90% settlement rate in a single thousand-member portion of a nationwide complex case can achieve savings of $33 million plus eight years of judicial time, it seems clear that the savings from a carefully planned consolidation procedure for all types of complex litigation might prove to be billions of dollars. This conclusion is reinforced by the fact that the legal bill for asbestos cases alone already has been estimated at over $1 billion.

The economic expense of complex litigation also can be estimated by tabulating the cost of its component parts. As of 1982, an hour of judicial time cost approximately $600. In addition, studies have shown that each dollar of plaintiff recovery typically costs two dollars in attorney's fees. Thus, assume that the crash of a small plane injured ten plaintiffs and that the litigation brought by each cost the defendant $100,000 in legal fees and compensation after an individual ten-hour trial. Based on that, and even without adjusting the estimated system costs to take into account of cost-of-living increases in judicial salaries, it can be estimated that the plaintiffs will take $333,000, the lawyers $666,000, and the court system $60,000. In other words, it will have cost $726,000 to generate only $333,000 in plaintiff recovery.

This example of a ten-person air crash, a case almost certainly too small to be considered complex and consolidated by current procedures, demonstrates that a two-thirds reduction in court and lawyer time would save almost $500,000, or half of the total costs of compensation. Equally, a reduction in litigation time of only fifty percent would save $363,000, or 36% of the costs of compensation. Moreover, because this estimate is based on only three assumptions—that legal services take two-thirds of compensation costs, that court time costs $600 per hour, and the claims will require on average one hour per $10,000 to litigate—it should be subject to generalization. That is, so long as a case requires about one hour of court time per $10,000 of compensation, any consolidation that cuts legal time in half will save an average of 37% of the total costs of compensation, and this is true even if the parties' own expenditure of time and effort is left out of the equation. Thus, to the extent that empirical data are available, they provide a dramatic confirmation of Professor Chafee's statement that "in matters of justice, the benefactor is he who makes one lawsuit grow where two grew before."

## AMERICAN LAW INSTITUTE, ENTERPRISE RESPONSIBILITY FOR PERSONAL INJURY (REPORTERS' STUDY 1991)

389–93.

From the process perspective, the salient defining characteristics of a mass tort include:

(1) numerous victims who have filed or might file damage claims against the same defendant(s);

(2) claims arising from a single event or transaction, or from a series of similar events or transactions spread over time;

(3) questions of law and fact that are complex and expensive to litigate and adjudicate—frequently questions that are scientific and technological in nature;

(4) important issues of law and fact which are identical or common to all or substantial subgroups of the claims;

(5) injuries that are widely dispersed over time, territory, and jurisdiction;

(6) causal indeterminacy—especially in cases involving toxic substance exposure—that precludes use of conventional procedures to determine and standards to measure any causal connection between the plaintiff's injury and the defendant's tortious conduct;

(7) disease and other injuries from long delayed latent risks, especially in cases involving toxic substance exposure.

The standard lawsuit embodies the ideal of individual justice through its strong procedural preference for adjudicating tort claims de novo, one by one, and for customizing judgments according to the particular facts and circumstances of each case. Yet, as Holmes put it, this ideal may be more consistent with, if not largely the creation of, "our law of torts from the old days." In contrast to the bygone era "of isolated, ungeneralized wrongs, assaults, slanders, and the like," modern tort law is primarily concerned with the "incidents of certain well known businesses injuries to person or property by railroads, factories, and the like." Since Holmes's observations nearly a century ago, substantive tort rules have undergone major reforms that take account of the systemic and statistically predictable risks created by business activity.

Tort process, however, remains largely unchanged. In mass tort cases the wholesale infliction of injury is still redressed at retail. Adjudicating mass torts on an individual basis entails great costs that may preclude or disable the effective preparation and prosecution of a large number of claims. This means that many claims are redressed at a steep—and, in fact, standardized—discount, while a substantial number are not redressed at all. Consequently, standard tort process not only sacrifices potential gains in compensation, prevention, and administrative efficiency, but also undermines its patron norm of individual justice.

## MARK A. PETERSON AND MOLLY SELVIN, RESOLUTION OF MASS TORTS: TOWARD A FRAMEWORK FOR EVALUATION OF AGGREGATIVE PROCEDURES

Rand, The Institute for Civil Justice (1988) at vii, 31–37.

Mass tort litigation presents unique problems for courts and litigants:

- The large number of litigants, plaintiffs as well as defendants, makes mass litigation burdensome. These large numbers significantly complicate the processing and resolution of litigation with procedures that evolved primarily for "simple" lawsuits—i.e., those involving one or two parties on each side.

- Mass tort litigation can involve enormous personal, financial, and political stakes for parties on all sides. It also imposes large burdens on the court system in terms of both public costs and concentration of cases within particular jurisdictions.

- Timing is critical for plaintiffs with significant disabilities and expenses. Yet as the number of claims increases, the need of plaintiffs for prompt compensation becomes harder to satisfy. The complex issues and larger numbers of parties can result in long delays in processing and resolving cases.

- Litigation involving toxic torts presents particular difficulties centering on issues, both technical and legal, about the causation and documentation of injuries and diseases. The frequently long latency period between exposure to a toxic substance and injury, together with the need to identify the products to which exposure occurred, further complicates legal and technical issues.

- Finally, mass litigation presents special threats to the fairness of our justice system, raising the possibilities that outcomes will be inconsistent; that defendants faced with a great number of claims may be forced to make significant settlements even when liability is unlikely; that defendants can avoid responsibility by aggressively pursuing litigation; that compensation is not related to the seriousness of injuries; and that the burdens on defendants might not accurately reflect their relative culpability.

## CONCEPTUAL OVERVIEW OF MASS TORT LITIGATION

The impact aggregative procedures is both complex and significant, primarily because of the complexity of mass tort litigation. Each instance of mass personal injury litigation involves a multitude of parties and a maze of issues, procedures, and strategies, and each can lead to outcomes that can have varying effects on hundreds or thousands of participants. The overview also provides a common way of looking across various instances of mass tort litigation so that inferences can be drawn about similarities and differences in the effects of aggregative procedures.

The overview is primarily intended as a means for organizing elements of mass tort litigation by grouping those elements in the following manner:

### Characteristics

What is the litigation about?

Who are the participants?

What are the objectives and strategies of the participants, and what are the relationships among them?

### Approach

What is the formal organization of the litigation?

What aggregative procedures are used?

What are the features of those aggregative procedures?

### Course of the litigation

What procedural actions have been taken?

How have those actions been carried out?

What informal actions have been taken, such as negotiations and contacts among parties?

## Outcomes

Has the litigation been resolved?

Was the resolution comprehensive—i.e., did it include all issues and all parties?

How was compensation distributed among plaintiffs?

What were defendants' relative contributions?

How satisfied are the parties with the outcome?

How much did the litigation cost? What were the transaction costs?

How long did the litigation take?

### FIGURE 2—GENERAL OVERVIEW OF MASS TORT LITIGATION

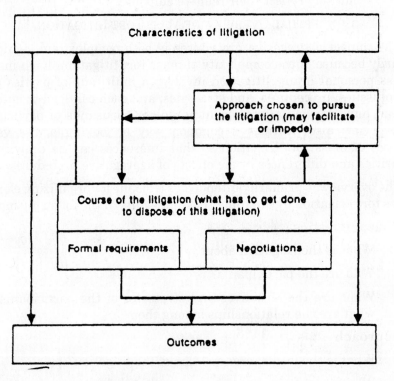

Figure 3 provides a working list of elements. Some of the characteristics listed are obvious determinants of the course and outcomes of litigation, while others have been deemed important in previous discussions of mass litigation. This overview lists characteristics that are particularly critical to mass litigation—i.e., traits that seem to have a direct effect on the course and outcomes of mass litigation or that interact with aggregative procedures to have such effects. Figure 3 lists these characteristics, grouping them as "issues," "participants," and "organization of litigation." We used these groupings to stress relationships among various characteristics rather than to draw sharp definitional lines for each group.

In addition to listing elements important to mass litigation, the overview serves as a kind of flow chart; the arrows on the overview suggest relationships among the elements in mass litigation. For example, the course of litigation, subsuming both informal and formal (procedural) activities, contributes to the determination of outcomes. In turn, the activities of litigation are affected by the characteristics of that litigation, such as the nature and strength of liability claims or the relative resources of the parties. The course of litigation is also affected by the approach toward handling the litigation—i.e., whether it is handled through traditional means or through specific types of aggregation.

While some of the relationships shown on the overview are obvious, others are more complex. For example, the choice of approach to handling mass litigation—traditional case-by-case litigation or the type of aggregative procedure, if any,—is driven by characteristics of the litigation, particularly the complexity of issues and number of parties. Decisions bearing on whether to aggregate and on the type of aggregative procedure to apply will also be affected by the progress of the litigation. Different types of aggregative procedures have been used at different stages of the same mass litigation.

Issues and participants can combine in several ways to change the nature of litigation. For example, mass toxic litigation in which there are questions about exposure to a toxic agent—or about injury causation or latency—may pose the problem of "indeterminate plaintiffs." Plaintiff indeterminacy makes it difficult to fashion aggregative procedures that will produce comprehensive and final resolution.

FIGURE 3—DETAILED OVERVIEW OF MASS TORT LITIGATION

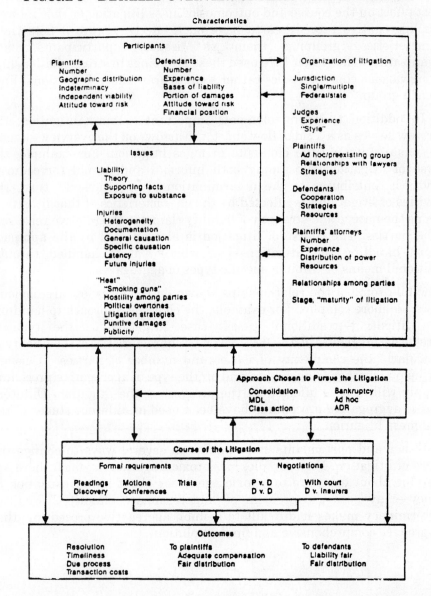

The characteristics of litigation will affect the impact of aggregative procedures. Differences among claims may diminish the effectiveness of aggregative procedures. Issues of liability and injuries usually vary among plaintiffs so that there is a distribution in the strength of claims. This distribution affects matters of cooperation and power among plaintiffs' attorneys as well as their likely response to aggregative procedures. The distribution of injuries—i.e., the relative number of plaintiffs with weak as opposed to strong claims—may markedly affect the success of aggregative procedures. Aggregative procedures can be frustrated if the strength of claims is varied and plaintiffs with strong claims choose not to cooperate in the aggregative procedure, as in the Hyatt Skywalk case.

The overview illustrates the complex relationships among the characteristics of mass litigation. Issues and litigants' characteristics not only shape but can also be affected by the organization of litigation. In Fig. 3, for example, we have described a set of issues as "heat": emotional matters that can inflame jurors, producing extreme verdicts, and that can upset litigants, making settlement difficult. Emotional issues might arise with (or even before) the filing of claims (as occurred following the 1984 Union Carbide gas leak at Bhopal, India) or they may grow out of the process of litigation (as in the discovery of incriminating documents or attempts to frustrate litigation). Heat might also be generated, however, by the manner in which litigation is organized or carried out. Much of the fervor among plaintiffs and plaintiffs' lawyers in the Dalkon Shield litigation grew out of an aggressive litigation strategy by the defendant that included thorough investigation and trial of claimants' sexual histories.

The general overview also identifies several other hypotheses that will be explored. We expect to find that the approach adopted to handle mass litigation—the type of aggregative procedure—affects many of the litigation outcomes. Aggregative procedures are employed to change litigation activities and are intended to change some outcomes, such as faster resolution of claims or comprehensive resolution of all claims, but the procedures may also change substantive results. For example, a given aggregative procedure might affect the comprehensiveness of resolution. Bankruptcy and class actions are both methods that might be used to resolve all claims. In contrast, MDL (multidistrict litigation procedure) has no formal legal provisions for comprehensive resolution of claims.

Another hypothesis of our studies is that aggregative procedures and characteristics interact to determine the course and outcome of mass litigation; the characteristics of litigation will influence how those aggregative procedures affect the course and outcome.

A third hypothesis is that aggregative procedures can change other important characteristics of litigation—e.g., redefining and adding issues, adding or subtracting parties, changing jurisdictions or judges, or altering the organization of litigants and their lawyers.

Observations and hypotheses suggested by the arrows indicate the complex relationships between aggregative procedures and characteristics that complicate our research. Since each aggregative procedure is used in distinctive litigation, we must understand the central characteristics of that litigation, how those characteristics shape the litigation in their own right, how they affect the consequences of the aggregative procedure, and how aggregative procedures in turn reshape the characteristics.

## C. THE JURISPRUDENTIAL DEBATE: LITIGANT AUTONOMY VERSUS AGGREGATIVE JUSTICE

### MERTENS V. ABBOTT LABORATORIES

United States District Court, District of New Hampshire, 1983.
99 F.R.D. 38.

This action was brought by twelve Plaintiffs. Eight of them are women who allege that by reason of exposure to diethystilbestrol (hereinafter referred to as DES) *in utero*, they suffered various injuries, including cancerous or pre-cancerous conditions, repeated pregnancy losses, infertility, incomplete, defective or abnormal development of their reproductive tracts and other adverse effects. They seek damages and a variety of other forms of relief, including the establishment of a fund, treatment facilities for themselves and persons who in the future might suffer similar injury. The eight female Plaintiffs contend that they have sustained a variety of injuries by reason of their in utero exposure to DES. One of these eight Plaintiffs seeks damages for multiple surgeries to eradicate adenocarcinoma and sterility. The other seven seek damages for the following, respectively: genital tract abnormalities requiring frequent medical procedures; spontaneous abortions, tubal pregnancy and uterine and cervical adenosis; chronic cervicitis dysplasia with foci of carcinoma in situ requiring frequent medical procedures; irregular cervix necessitating surgery and the development of tissue abnormalities; adenosis in the genital tract and deformed cervix; irregular cervix; and hyperkeratosis and glycogenital squamous epithelium of the genital tract.

Defendants are eleven firms that allegedly manufactured DES. They assert that the companies which manufactured DES numbered in the hundreds. Some of the Plaintiffs can produce evidence to identify a specific Defendant as manufacturer of the product that allegedly harmed them. In other claims, the manufacturer is probably either one of two Defendants, and in still other actions the manufacturer of the DES is not and cannot be identified.

Plaintiffs seek a determination that this action can be maintained as a class action.

Rule 23(b) (3) requires a finding "that the questions of law or fact common to the members of the class predominate over any questions affecting only individual members, and that a class action is superior to other available methods for the fair and efficient adjudication of the controversy. The matters pertinent to the findings include: (A) the interest of members of the class in individually controlling the prosecution or defense of separate actions; (B) the extent and nature of any litigation concerning the controversy already commenced by or against members of the class; (C) the desirability or undesirability of concentrating the litigation of the claims in the particular forum; (D) the difficulties likely to be encountered in the management of a class action."

While there are enough common issues of law and fact in this action to satisfy the 23(a) analysis, 23(b) (3) requires that these common questions predominate over individual issues. In *Ryan v. Eli Lilly & Co.*, the court observed:

> Apparently it is not sufficient that common questions merely exist, rather the common issues must outweigh the individual ones in terms of quantity or quality. In deciding the issue of predominance this Court must predict the evidence likely to be introduced at trial.

In a sense, Plaintiffs would have the question of global liability be the predominant one in this litigation. They seek a blanket determination that DES causes injury to a female *in utero*, and believe that this common issue predominates over any questions affecting only individual class members. The telling inquiry is what would such a determination do to advance the cause of the class members as a group?

It is this Court's view that a mere finding that DES causes injury in utero would do substantially nothing to advance the common cause of class members. In light of the varied degrees of use, exposure and harm in each Plaintiff's case, a determination in principle would serve no useful purpose in resolving the individual claims made in this action. As in *Ryan*,

> The mothers of the proposed plaintiffs each used a synthetic estrogen; however, the length of exposure, the reason for the drug's use, the specific chemical formulation of the drug, the state of the art at the time of consumption or the manufacturer's knowledge of synthetic estrogen's carcinogenic effect and possible medical result in the absence of the estrogens are all specific points going toward proximate causation which will require proof for each individual class member.

Although common questions need not be dispositive of the entire class action, their resolution should at least provide a definite signal of the beginning of the end. This is not the type of litigation, however, that lends itself to establishing a global result that a product causes harm with details merely to be tidied up thereafter. The importance of the "details" in each individual claim would clearly outweigh the single determination that DES causes injury.

If the damages question were the only one to be determined on an individual basis for each class member, bifurcating the trial as to liability and damages would be a practical consideration. It is clear, however, that a per se rule that DES causes injury could not possibly result in a per se rule of liability. The liability issue would require separate and individual proof for each claimant and therefore could not be the predominant issue in the proposed class action. In *Yandle v. PPG Industries, Inc.*, former employees and survivors of former employees of the defendant's asbestos plant, sought class certification. Like that case, the litigation presently before this Court,

> is very different from the single mass accident case that have in the past allowed a class action to proceed on the liability issues. Those cases have normally involved a single tragic happening which caused physical harm or property damage to a group of people, and affirmative defenses are absent. Usually, one set of operative facts will establish liability. The Court is in agreement with the defendant that there is not a single act of negligence or proximate cause which would apply to each potential class member and each defendant.

The difficulties with a class determination of the liability issue weight heavily in a consideration of the prerequisite of predominance from the Defendant's perspective as well. Although there may be some advantage to litigation which establishes what the industry manufacturing DES knew at specified intervals of time concerning the deleterious effects of the drug, there is nothing to show that knowledge at a given point in time essentially settles anything with respect to liability to a particular claimant. Moreover, the manufacturers are so disparately situated in terms of market participation that little, if anything, would be accomplished except as to those specifically identified.

What has already been said about the individual nature of proof in the context of predominance applies with equal force to the issue of superiority. In addition, the Court notes that this is not a situation involving a large number of small claims which would otherwise not be brought since it is unlikely that any claim for DES inflicted injury would have an ad damnum of less than $10,000. Nor is this a situation where the "floodgate" argument is appropriate. If thousands of claims are brought, they will be dealt with in the same fashion as any other litigation. Indeed, judicial resources applied to each claim on an individual basis would doubtless be effective than a general pronouncement applied to all cases without any real effect. These factors militate against a finding that the proposed class action in these circumstances is superior to other available methods of adjudication.

The advantage of certifying a class in this action is at best obscure, and the gain difficult to perceive. Other than the possibility of seeking to commit the law of New Hampshire in a particular direction, it is unlikely that anything of real value could be determined that would aid in the resolution of the claims of any individual Plaintiff.

# CIMINO V. RAYMARK INDUSTRIES, INC.

United States District Court, Eastern District of Texas.
Order, December 29, 1989.

On October 26, 1989, this Court consolidated 3031 asbestos cases for resolution of the state of the art and punitive damages issues. The Court also certified, under Fed.R.Civ.P. 23(b)(3), a class of plaintiffs in personal injury asbestos cases pending in the Beaumont Division of the Eastern District of Texas as of February 1, 1989, for a determination of the exposure and actual damage issues. The Defendants informed the Court of their desire to respond to the certification Order. For reasons given below, the Defendants' objections are overruled. . . .

[The Order set forth a three-phase trial procedure, with phases one and two to be tried before a jury, and phase three without a jury. In phase one the jury was to try the issue of gross negligence and formulate a multiplier for each defendant for which the jury returned an affirmative finding. In phase two, the court was to try the cases of the class representatives. In addition, the plaintiffs and the defendants would be allowed to introduce evidence as to fifteen claimants, chosen by that side. The jury was to make classwide findings on the issues of exposure and actual damages, and would be able to award lump sum punitive damages in place of the multiplier in phase one. In phase three, the court was to distribute the jury's award of actual and punitive damages. The defendants objected to this trial plan on a number of grounds, including applicable law under *Erie* doctrine; use of statistical evidence; class action and mass tort case law precedents; court-supervised distribution; statute of limitations; amount in controversy; punitive damages; and violation of the Rules Enabling Act. The following deals solely with the defendants' objections based on Seventh Amendment grounds.—*ed.*]

## DEFENDANTS' RIGHTS TO A JURY TRIAL

The Defendants' position is that the Court's plan for the disposition of these cases violates the Defendants' right to a jury trial. Contrary to the Defendants' belief, the Court's procedure more than adequately protects the Defendants' right to a Jury trial. First, by trial date, the defendants will have performed 45-minute depositions of all 3031 Plaintiffs in this consolidated action and class action. With respect to the eleven class representatives and the thirty illustrative Plaintiffs, the defendants will have conducted full, extensive depositions. The Defendants will have also completed medical examinations on all 3031 Plaintiffs. Due to the need to bring these cases to trial once and for all, the discovery in this action will have some restrictions. Nevertheless, as explained in the Discovery Plan and Schedule, the defendants will have had a reasonable opportunity to conduct discovery in this action.

By deposing and testing every member of this consolidated action and class action, the defendants will be able to gather all the necessary information for their defense of this action. Specifically, this information will form the basis of the Defendants' expert testimony at trial. By having looked at and investigated each and every one of the Plaintiffs in this action, the Defendants will be able to expose the Jury to the full range of defenses contained in the class.

The Defendants will have the chance to contest each one of the cases of the eleven class representatives in this action. The Defendants will have the opportunity to expose the Jury to the weaknesses of the representatives' cases.

The Jury will hear the testimony of thirty illustrative Plaintiffs (fifteen chosen by each side) in addition to the testimony of the class representatives. In selecting fifteen Plaintiffs, the Defendants will once again have the opportunity to ensure that a variety of defenses are exposed to the Jury. In addition, by cross-examining the Plaintiffs' fifteen witnesses, the Defendants will once again have the chance of showing the weaknesses in the Plaintiffs' claims.

Given these procedural safeguards, the Court finds that its certification Order does not violate the Defendants' right to a Jury trial. Nevertheless, the defendants urge that they have the right to contest each one of these 3031 cases on an individual basis. Trial of these cases individually or by a procedure of mini-trials would only serve to violate the Plaintiffs' right to a jury trial. The Court does not have the resources to utilize such an alternative procedure. Many plaintiffs would simply wait in vain for their day in court.

These cases have been pending for over three years. The Defendants would have this Court delay these cases for another day. Yet many of the class members are ill; some of them have died since the filing of this action. Any procedure other than a single adjudication of these cases can by no means protect the Plaintiffs' right to a jury trial. This Court can see no justice in denying the Plaintiffs their day in court in the interest of providing Defendants with a procedure for the repetitive assertion of their defenses.

The Defendants' opposition to the Court's plan lies in their hope that these cases will eventually just "go away." The "Defendants enjoy all the advantages, and the Plaintiffs incur the disadvantages, of this class action—with one exception: the cases are to be brought to trial." The defense costs attributable to trying these cases individually or in groupings would be astronomical. Attorneys' fees for the Defendants, as well as for the individual Plaintiffs, will be greatly reduced under this plan as the Court will control the fees collected from all class members. The Court's Order protects the Defendants' right to a trial by jury while ensuring that the Plaintiffs receive their day in court.

## IN RE FIBREBOARD CORPORATION

United States Court of Appeals, Fifth Circuit, 1990.
893 F.2d 706.

Defendants Fibreboard Corporation and Pittsburgh Corning Corporation, joined by other defendants, petition for a writ of mandamus, asking that we vacate pretrial orders consolidating 3,031 asbestos cases for trial entered by Judge Robert Parker, Eastern District of Texas.

In 1986 there were at least 5,000 asbestos-related cases pending in this circuit. We then observed that "because asbestos-related diseases will continue to manifest themselves for the next fifteen years, filings will continue at a steady rate until the year 2000." That observation is proving to be accurate. In *Jenkins v. Raymark,* we affirmed Judge Parker's certification of a class of some 900 asbestos claimants, persuaded that the requirements of Rule 23(b)(3) were met for the trial of certain common questions including the "state of the art" defense. After that order and certain settlements, approximately 3,031 asbestos personal injury cases accumulated in the Eastern District of Texas.

The petitions for mandamus attack the district court's effort to try these cases in a common trial.

Defendants find numerous flaws in the procedures set for Phase II of the trial. They argue with considerable force that such a trial would effectively deny defendants' rights to a jury trial under the seventh amendment, would work an impermissible change in the controlling substantive law of Texas, would deny procedural due process under the fifth amendment of the United States Constitution, and would effectively amend the rules of civil procedure contrary to the strictures of the enabling acts.

The contentions that due process would be denied, the purposes of *Erie* would be frustrated, and the seventh amendment circumvented are variations of a common concern of defendants. Defendants insist that one-to-one adversarial engagement or its proximate, the traditional trial, is secured by the seventh amendment and certainly contemplated by Article III of the Constitution itself. Defendants point out, and the plaintiffs quickly concede, that under Phase II there will inevitably be individual class members whose recovery will be greater or lesser than it would have been if tried alone. Indeed, with the focus in Phase II upon the "total picture", with arrays of data that will attend the statistical presentation, persons who would have had their claims rejected may recover. Plaintiffs say that "such discontinuities" would be reflected in the overall omnibus figure. Stated another way, plaintiffs say that so long as their mode of proof enables the jury to decide the total liability of defendants with reasonable accuracy, the loss of one-to-one engagement infringes no right of defendants. Such unevenness, plaintiffs say, will be visited upon them, not the defendants.

With the procedures described at such a level of abstraction, it is difficult to describe concretely any deprivation of defendants' rights. Of course, there will be a jury, and each plaintiff will be present in a theoretical, if not practical, sense. Having said this, however, we are left with a profound disquiet. First, the *assumption* is that its proof of omnibus damages is in fact achievable; that statistical measures of representativeness and commonality will be sufficient for the jury to make informed decisions concerning damages. We are pointed to our experience in the trial of Title VII cases and securities cases involving use of fraud on the market concepts and mathematical constructs for examples of workable trials of large numbers of claims. We find little comfort in such cases. It is true that there is considerable judicial experience with such techniques, but it is also true we have remained cautious in their use.

We are also uncomfortable with the suggestion that a move from one-on-one "traditional" modes is little more than a move towards modernity. Such traditional ways of proceeding reflect far more than habit. They reflect the very culture of the jury trial and the case and controversy requirement of Article III. It is suggested that the litigating unit is the class and, hence, we have the adversarial engagement or that all are present in a "consolidated" proceeding. But, this begs the very question of whether these 3,031 claimants are sufficiently situated for class treatment; it equally begs the question whether they are actually before the court under Fed.R.Civ.P. Rules 23 and 42(b) in any more than a fictional sense. Ultimately, these concerns find expression in defendants' right to due process.

We are told that Phase II is the only realistic way of trying these cases; that the difficulties faced by the courts as well as the rights of the class members to have their cases tried cry powerfully for innovation and judicial creativity. The arguments are compelling, but they are better addressed to the representative branches—Congress and the State Legislature. The Judicial Branch can offer the trial of lawsuits. It has no power or competence to do more. We are persuaded on reflection that the procedures here called for comprise something other than a trial within our authority. It is called a trial, but it is not.

We admire the work of our colleague, Judge Robert Parker, and are sympathetic with the difficulties he faces. This grant of the petition for writ of mandamus should not be taken as a rebuke of an able judge, but rather as another chapter in an ongoing struggle with the problems presented by the phenomenon of mass torts. The petitions for writ of mandamus are granted. The order for Phase II trial is vacated and the cases are remanded to the district court for further proceedings.

## IN RE COPLEY PHARMACEUTICAL, INC., "ALBUTEROL" PRODS. LIAB. LITIG.

United States District Court for the District of Wyoming, 1995.
161 F.R.D. 456.

[The facts and decision in *In re Copley Pharmaceutical* are set forth in Chapter 4. The following portion of the court's decision sets forth its policy reasons for denying the Defendant's motion for decertification of the class action that the court had previously approved.—*ed.*]

### POLICY REASONS SUPPORTING A CLASS ACTION

In its Order Granting Partial Class Certification, this Court stated that the most convincing reason for certification was not offered by Plaintiffs' lead counsel, but by a single attorney in less than a minute. During oral arguments concerning class certification, one attorney approached the Court from the back of the courtroom. He succinctly stated that he had six clients, none of whom had large claims against Copley. He said that without class certification his clients would essentially lose their claims because neither he nor his clients had the resources to sue a large defendant like Copley.

Seven months later, after hearing the arguments on decertification, the compelling argument made by this attorney still rings true in the Court's ears. Plaintiffs' counsel repeated this point when they suggested that the real motivation behind Copley's motion to decertify was to cripple the claims brought by individual plaintiffs with less experienced counsel. Copley may or may not have such a goal, but the Court agrees that if the class is decertified, the courthouse door could be slammed on a great many plaintiffs.

Given Judge Posner's recent decision in *Rhone-Poulenc*, it is ironic that over fifty years ago, it was the Seventh Circuit which recognized,

> to permit the defendant to contest liability with each claimant in a single separate suit would, in many cases, give defendants an advantage which would almost be equivalent to closing the door of justice to small claimants. This is what we think the class suit practice was to prevent.

Today, in the era of "mass torts" many commentators agree that class actions are necessary to protect the interests of individual plaintiffs. One such commentator has observed,

> The case by case mode of adjudication magnifies this burden of litigating complex issues by requiring the parties and courts to reinvent the wheel for each claim. The merits of each case are determined de novo even though the major liability issues are common to every claim arising from the mass tort accident, even though they may have been previously determined several times

by full and fair trials. These costs exclude many mass tort victims from the system and sharply reduce the recovery for those who gain access. Win or lose, the system's private law process exacts a punishing surcharge from defendant firms as well as plaintiffs.

In addition, the case-by-case, individualized processing of the mass tort claims that are filed confers a strategic edge upon defendant firms. While it prevents victims from deriving the benefits of a concerted action, the traditional process has no similar effect on the capacity of the defendant firms to spread litigation costs and prepare the common questions efficiently for a once-and-for-all basis.

Class treatment, moreover, has been extended solely to common questions of law and fact concerning liability, preserving the right to an individual trial on damages. In some cases courts have gone slightly beyond the conventional bifurcation of liability and damage elements of the tort cause of action. They have instead designated certain common liability issues for class treatment, while remanding the remaining liability questions related to the circumstances of each member to an individual trial before, or along with, determination of damages.

Numerous other commentators have recognized the benefit of class certification for common issues of liability. Some practitioners have also observed the value of use of class actions to conserve the resources of plaintiffs, defendants and the courts.

Finally, Copley directs the Court to the infamous Advisory Committee Note to Fed.R.Civ.Pro. 23. That advisory note, a favorite among class action defendants, states, "A 'mass accident' resulting in injuries to numerous persons is ordinarily not appropriate for class action." However, this note was written nearly thirty years ago, before the advent of most "mass tort" litigation. As the Plaintiffs point out, even one of the authors of that note has repudiated it:

> I was an ex-officio member of the Advisory Committee on Civil Rules when Rule 23 was amended, which came out with an Advisory Committee Note saying mass torts are inappropriate for class certification. I thought then that was true. Unless we can use the class action and devices built on the class action, our judicial system is simply not going to be able to cope with the challenge of the mass repetitive wrong that we see in this case and so many others that have been mentioned this morning and afternoon.

In the world of practice, it is now generally accepted that the committee's note is outdated.

After many months of discovery, the able litigators on both sides of this case are well-versed in Copley's Albuterol and its contamination. Just as Copley will have the best counsel available, the Plaintiffs deserve to have counsel who are familiar with Albuterol, its manufacture and its contamination. In this way the truth about the common issues liability may be decided in one class trial.

## ROGER H. TRANGSRUD, MASS TRIALS IN MASS TORT CASES: A DISSENT

1989 U. Ill. L. Rev. 69, 74–76 (1985).

In the last decade, mass trials have come to be seen in much of the academic literature as the proper and efficient answer to mass torts in our mass society. Burdened by lengthening dockets, federal judges have begun to experiment with mass trials to try many claims at once. In this way, we appear ready to reject a centuries old tradition of individual claim autonomy in tort litigation involving substantial personal injuries or wrongful death. Insufficient attention has been paid, however, to the impact of mass trials on the fairness of such proceedings to individual plaintiffs, on the relationship of counsel to client, on the role of the judge in coercing settlement, and on the temptation to distort substantive law to skirt important procedural obstacles to mass trial. As explained below, all of these concerns argue against using mass trials to adjudicate mass tort cases. The better course is to coordinate and consolidate pretrial discovery and motions practice but then individually try the tort cases in an appropriate venue. After a number of cases have been tried substantial incentives will operate to encourage the private settlement of many of the remaining claims.

### THE TRADITIONAL JUSTIFICATIONS FOR INDIVIDUAL CLAIM AUTONOMY REMAIN IMPORTANT IN MASS TORT CASES

The English and American judicial systems have long favored individual control and disposition of substantial personal injury and wrongful death claims for several reasons. Such claims usually involve incidents of tremendous importance to the individual plaintiff or the plaintiff's family. A mother who perishes in a hotel fire or airplane crash, a father who works in a trade for many years and now has terminal lung cancer, or a child born with foreshortened limbs are catastrophic human tragedies of the first order. Until recently, our system treated such incidents and the tort claims they created with uncompromised due process. This we should continue to do.

The purpose of our civil justice system is and should be to offer corrective justice in disputes arising between private parties. While today we burden our courts with many claims arising out of government regulatory and entitlement programs and even ask our judges to manage prisons, mental health institutions, and schools, we should not let these cases obscure the original and first purpose of our civil courts—to adjudicate justly disputes between individuals. Among such private disputes, cases involving substantial personal injury or wrongful death claims are as important, or more important, than any other. Regardless of the burden of such claims put on the judicial resources of our courts, we ought not to compromise in the quality of process we afford these tort plaintiffs.

Underlying our tradition of individual claim autonomy in substantial tort cases is the natural law notion that this is an important personal right of the individual. While much less celebrated than other natural rights, such as the right to practice one's own religion or to think and speak freely, the right to control personally the suit whereby a badly injured persons seeks redress from the alleged tortfeasor has long been valued both here and in England. The responsibility for asserting such a claim rested with the injured individual or his family, and the exercise of this right was protected. It was not the duty of the government or some third party to initiate such a suit, nor could the government or some third party interfere in the prosecution of the action.

This jealous protection of the individual's absolute right to control his own tort claim was respected for practical as well as philosophical reasons. For example, English and American courts have held for many years that a tort action for personal injury is not assignable before judgment. Limiting ownership and control of such claims to the injured party was believed to be important for several reasons that remain important today. Unless control of such tort claims was left with the injured party, a "litigious person could harass and annoy others if allowed to purchase claims for pain and suffering and pursue the claims in court as assignees." There was also the risk of overreaching, deception, and other misconduct by the party seeking to acquire the right to bring a tort claim on another's behalf. These remain major concerns today, as evidenced by the methods used by attorneys to solicit clients in mass tort cases and to obtain control over the cases of non-clients by bringing class actions or becoming lead counsel in huge consolidated tort cases. The attorney's fees at stake in mass tort cases are so high as to strain the norms that ought to govern professional conduct. The questionable activities of many of the counsel in the Agent Orange litigation, for example, has been well documented in Professor Schuck's history of that case.

Our traditional justifications for individual claim autonomy remain important today in mass tort cases. From a purely economic point of view, our system operates mainly on the assumption that economic decisions are best made by the true owner of property rather than by any other person. Control and disposition of a valuable piece of property, such as a substantial tort claim, ought to rest with its owner, the injured party or his family, and not with some stranger such as a class representative or lead counsel in a mass tort case consolidated in a common venue. In addition, parties often wish to settle or litigate claims based upon a variety of personal economic considerations and intangible personal beliefs or concerns which are unique to them. If the plaintiffs enjoy autonomy over the settlement or trial of their particular claim, they can obtain the outcome best suited to their personal views on the proper disposition of this property. If others assume control over their claim, then this is less likely to happen because these strangers will often not be aware of the special circumstances attending this claim or will have a divided loyalty because the stranger will often be responsible for many other substantial tort claims as well.

Traditionally, our civil justice system avoided mass trials of mass tort claims for another reason grounded in efficiency. The more parties and claims lumped together in a single proceeding, the greater the procedural and substantive complexity of the litigation. While the repetitious trial of common fact issues is regularly deplored today, less concern is voiced about the enormous additional costs created by consolidation and mass trials. Large numbers of plaintiffs and defendants often create a matrix of cross-claims, a web of choice-of-law issues, and a host of peripheral and satellite litigation that would never exist if the claims had been tried separately.

These and other concerns argue strongly against the use of mass trials in mass tort cases and help explain the nearly unbroken tradition of individual claim autonomy in substantial tort cases that characterized Anglo-American litigation until the last decade.

## DEBORAH R. HENSLER, RESOLVING MASS TOXIC TORTS: MYTHS AND REALITIES

1989 U. Ill. L. Rev. 89, 91–97 (1989).

### II.   THE TRADITIONAL TORT VERSION OF REALITY

Beliefs about the traditional tort approach relate to both process and outcomes. As Professor Schuck indicates, the version of legal reality implicit in the traditional tort approach assumes that "private litigant control of litigation" and "intimate contact and consultation" between litigants and lawyers "force lawyers to educate their clients, respond to their wishes, and litigate faithfully and vigorously." The quite widely noted lawyer opposition to class actions for tort claims partly derives from concern that aggregating cases will "corrode the individual attorney-client relationship," which, it is assumed, would otherwise exist. According to Schuck, Judge Weinstein told one of the leading Agent Orange litigators that in class actions "the nominal representative plaintiffs are only names and the case is turned over to the lawyers." Implicit in this admonition is the notion that such a state of affairs would not exist, absent a class action.

Although the "sanctity and indissolubility of the conventional attorney-client relationship" is one of the primary underpinnings of the tort process, there are other important elements. Trial by jury and general adjudication hold out the promise that parties will be fairly treated, carefully, and with dignity.

Just as traditional tort process values are highly individualistic in nature, so are criteria for judging the outcomes of the system. Each individual possesses an absolute right to the integrity of his or her personhood. If injured, he or she possesses the right to recover damages that compensate not simply for out-of-pocket expenses and other economic losses wrongfully caused by the defendants but for invasion of dignitary and other subjective interests, particularly pain and suffering.

Another argument against class actions for tort claims is motivated by concern about "the inequities of subjecting all individuals to uniform class treatment leading to settlement funds which when distributed on a wholesale basis are almost certain to result in a lower recovery than some individuals (especially the most seriously injured) would receive by litigating on their own."

According to the traditional tort approach, fair outcomes not only require adequate compensation and similar levels of compensation for similarly situated plaintiffs but also proper attention to defendants' varying degrees of fault. More generally, the deterrence objective of the tort system can only be satisfied, according to modern economic theory, if the full losses of plaintiffs are imposed upon negligent defendants.

### III. PROCEDURAL REALITIES

Systematic empirical research on litigation suggests that the tort process in practice diverges substantially from the picture painted above. Although most of the research concerns routine litigation, some involves mass torts. The version of legal reality drawn from this research posits a litigation process in which (1) lawyer-client relations are more often perfunctory and superficial than intimate; (2) the locus of control is shifted towards lawyers rather than clients; (3) lawyers educate their clients to a view of the legal process that serves the lawyer's interests as much, if not more than clients' interests; (4) litigants are frequently only names to both lawyers and court personnel; and (5) trial is rarely desired, except perhaps by litigants, or delivered.

### A.  *Lawyer-Client Relations and Litigant Control*

One of the first researchers to document the character of lawyer-client relations was Douglas Rosenthal, who surveyed a small number of litigants in routine tort cases. Within his sample, he found that most lawyers spent little time with their clients and that most clients had little control over the progress or outcomes of their cases.

In a more recent and larger survey of litigants in personal injury cases involving amounts up to $50,000, respondents were asked how many times they met in person with their lawyer and how many times they talked to their lawyer on the telephone. Twenty-five percent either never met with their lawyers or met with them only once, and thirty-two percent talked by telephone fewer than three times. Because this survey deliberately overrepresented litigants whose cases were resolved after some sort of court intervention (e.g., arbitration, judicial settlement conference, or trial) these numbers may overestimate the average time spent by lawyers with clients whose cases are more typically resolved through bilateral bargaining. Some support for this caveat is provided by the pattern of interaction for only those litigants whose cases were bargained to resolution. Although significant fractions of litigants do interact multiple times with their attorneys, a sizeable number would seem to have little opportunity to establish the "intimate" relationship envisioned by the traditional tort version of reality. Data from several other studies documenting the modest number of hours attorneys typically spend on civil cases bolster this interpretation. For example, the Civil Litigation Research Project (CLRP) estimated that lawyers spend an average of about forty-five to fifty hours on a typical case. Not surprisingly, the range of hours spent on cases was large, with very high stakes cases receiving more effort. A study of 222 New Jersey lawyers who handle routine automobile personal injury cases found the median number of billable hours spent on such cases was twenty.

The New Jersey survey of tort litigants' experiences also inquired into their perceptions of their control over the litigation process. Researchers asked a number of questions about the litigants' role in key decisions in the litigation process. Litigants described the decision to file the lawsuit rather than settle out of court. About half of the litigants saw filing the lawsuit as mainly the lawyer's decision. Litigants' views of their role varied across different decisions (e.g., to settle or appeal), but for most decisions, only a minority of litigants viewed themselves as the dominant decision maker.

Litigants summarized their role in the litigation process. A majority of litigants felt they had little or no control over how their cases were handled. About half of those who felt relatively lacking in control attributed this to their lawyers; only a few litigants said they exercised little control by choice.

The New Jersey study did not inquire into the content of litigant-attorney interactions, but recent research by Sarat and Felstiner suggests that educating the client to the attorney's version of legal reality is an important dimension of the litigation process, at least in family law cases. Felstiner and Sarat's analysis of transcripts of lawyer-client conversations depicts a process where lawyers gradually wean clients from their views of what the justice system ought to provide in the way of equitable dispute resolution to a more realistic—or even, cynical—view of the systems's goals and operations, a view that serves both the lawyer's and the legal order's interests. This type of education does not appear to accord well with the idealized education process envisaged in the traditional tort version of reality.

None of the research described above deals with mass toxic tort cases, and no one has yet surveyed litigants in these cases. However, descriptions of the mass tort litigation process give little reason to believe that the traditional tort approach to such cases provides more interaction between lawyers and clients, more intimate relations between lawyers and clients, or more opportunity for clients rather than lawyers to control the litigation process. In fact, the reverse is likely to be true: when lawyers handle cases individually, the already tenuous client relationship described above is attenuated further by the press of the sheer number of claims. More frequently, cases are aggregated *informally*, despite strictures against such groupings.

The Rand Corporation's Institute for Civil Justice first studied asbestos litigation practices during a period when no formal aggregative procedures were in place and found plaintiff attorneys with inventories of several hundred to several thousand claimants per firm. In the Dalkon Shield litigation, two plaintiff attorneys represented nine hundred clients over a relatively brief time. In asbestos litigation, initial lawyer contacts with claimants often involved mass meetings or bureaucratic intake procedures rather than intimate conversations between lawyer and client. Pleadings and discovery were highly standardized, and rulings made in a single case were often applied by judicial order to hundreds of other cases. By the time of the Rand study, many law firms were so overburdened with asbestos suits—or their staffs were so "burned out"—that junior attorneys were assigned to important pretrial activities and opportunities for settling cases expeditiously were lost. Some courts with large mass tort caseloads encouraged or ordered plaintiff and defense attorneys to group cases for pretrial preparation and settlement discussions. Where courts were able to provide a credible threat of trial, attorneys with large caseloads were forced to settle on different grounds from those possible with a real option of trial. Litigants were rarely, if ever, included in the settlement discussions directed by the court.

In his description of another mass litigation, DDT cases in Alabama, Brazil notes that several hundred named DDT claimants could not be located by the court for discovery purposes "suggesting that attorney-client communication left something to be desired." In these and other examples of mass litigation conducted under apparently traditional formal procedures, the pressures to aggregate cases informally are so great that it is difficult to discern a qualitative difference between litigant-attorney relations in such situations and the relationships that typically exist under formal class actions. In the latter, however, by reviewing settlements and fees, the court is assigned the role of protecting clients' interests. In the former, the court performs no such review.

# CHAPTER 2

---

# PROBLEMS IN PROFESSIONAL RESPONSIBILITY

■ ■ ■

## A.  SOLICITATION

### MUSSLEWHITE V. THE STATE BAR OF TEXAS
Texas Court of Appeals, 1990.
786 S.W.2d 437.

Benton Musslewhite appeals from a judgment revoking his probation and suspending him from the practice of law for three years. In twenty-three points of error he claims the court erred in finding he had violated a disciplinary rule and in finding he had taken on a new client during the year in which he was prohibited from doing so. Musslewhite also asserts certain procedural errors. We affirm.

[In an earlier disciplinary action, Musslewhite signed an agreed judgment suspending him from practice and placing him on probation for three years. Beginning on January 31, 1988 he was prohibited from committing professional misconduct as defined by state bar rules, and from accepting new employment until November 1, 1988. The court permitted him to refer potential clients to other attorneys. The court further ordered that "should Respondent violate any of the terms or conditions of probation, the Court may revoke such probation and impose a suspension from the practice of law for a period not to exceed three years." In September 1988, the State Bar of Texas filed a motion to revoke Musslewhite's probation on two grounds. The excerpted decision relates to only one of these grounds, the improper solicitation of clients.—*ed.*]

### THE PIPER ALPHA ALLEGATIONS

An off-shore oil platform, known as the Piper Alpha, exploded in the North Sea on July 6, 1988. Beginning at approximately 10:30 that morning, Musslewhite began making telephone calls to Scottish solicitors to discuss a potential lawsuit. On July 15, 1988, Musslewhite made arrangements to go to Scotland to obtain cases arising out of the Piper Alpha tragedy. Before going to Scotland, Musslewhite talked with John O'Quinn about referring to O'Quinn any cases he obtained in Scotland. Musslewhite also spoke with Kelly Newman to obtain his assistance in working on the Piper Alpha cases. Musslewhite gave Newman a list of solicitors and asked him to go to Scotland and telephone them.

When Newman arrived in Scotland he began to telephone the Scottish solicitors. When talking with the solicitors, Newman identified himself as working with "some of the best trial lawyers in Houston" who were investigating the Piper Alpha tragedy. He told them he was talking to solicitors about possible referral of cases for filing in the United States. He told them Musslewhite would be there in a few days to talk with them in person. Newman did not tell the solicitors that Musslewhite was prohibited from accepting new clients until November 1, 1988, or that he would be suspended from practicing law between November 1, 1988, and January 30, 1989.

When Musslewhite arrived in Scotland, two days later, he and Newman hired a public relations consultant named John MacDonald. MacDonald prepared a press release that day and issued it for Musslewhite. The press release referred to Musslewhite as the team's lead counsel, and stated that the team would be working with Scottish solicitors. The release described the unnamed members of the team as "internationally-renowned."

After the press release was issued, Musslewhite left for London while Newman stayed behind. Newman sent a letter addressed to "all victims or families of victims of the Occidental Petroleum Platform disaster." That letter said that Newman was acting on behalf of a "group of internationally renowned trial lawyers in the United States," and stated:

> The purpose of this letter is to ask that if you have already retained a solicitor to let us know who that solicitor is so we can discuss the suit that we are bringing in the United States with him. If you have not retained a solicitor then we would advise that you do so as a matter of urgency and ask him to contact us so that we can discuss the action in the United States.

McDonald, the public relations consultant, prepared the letter and prepared a newspaper advertisement for Musslewhite's group. Musslewhite knew about both communications and discussed them over the telephone with Newman. The advertisement McDonald prepared stated that the team was willing to talk to "victims, families of victims, and their solicitors."

In its motion to revoke probation the State Bar claims that, by issuing the press release, the letters, and the advertisement, Musslewhite violated DR 2–101 because certain statements in those communications were false and misleading. DR 2–101 provides:

> (A) A lawyer shall not make, on behalf of himself, his partner, associate, or any other lawyer, any false or misleading communication about the lawyer or the lawyer's services. A communication is false or misleading if it:

(1)  Contains a material misrepresentation of fact or law, or omits a fact necessary to make the statement considered as a whole not materially misleading;

(2)  Contains a statement of opinion as to the quality of legal services;

(3)  Contains a representation or implication regarding the quality of legal services which is not susceptible to reasonable verification by the public;

(4)  Contains predictions of future success;

(5)  Contains statistical data which is not susceptible to reasonable verification by the public;

(6)  Contains other information based on past performance which is not susceptible to reasonable verification by the public;

(7)  Contains a testimonial about or endorsement of a lawyer;

(8)  Is intended or is likely to create an unjustified expectation about results the lawyer can achieve.

SUPREME COURT OF TEXAS, RULES GOVERNING THE STATE BAR OF TEXAS art. 10, § 9 (Code of Professional Responsibility) DR 2–101.

The trial court found the press release, letters, and advertisement were false and misleading because they failed to identify the lawyers, because no team existed, because the communications suggested that Musslewhite already had Piper Alpha clients, because they did not disclose that Musslewhite could not take any cases, because Musslewhite predicted high recoveries in Texas courts, and because the advertisement did not contain a disclaimer stating that Musslewhite was not certified by the Texas Board of Legal Specialization.

In point of error one, Musslewhite contends the press release, letters, and advertisement were directed to solicitors, not the public; therefore, he did not violate DR 2–101. Musslewhite's contention is simply not true. The letters were mailed to the victims of the Piper Alpha tragedy and were addressed to "All Victims or Families of Victims of the Occidental Petroleum Platform Disaster." Further, the advertisement stated, "We respectfully suggest it is in your interest to have your solicitor call us immediately or that you call us immediately and give us the name, address and phone number of your solicitor or the solicitor you propose to employ." Clearly, the press release, letters, and advertisement were directed to the victims of the tragedy, not their solicitors. Point of error one is overruled.

In points of error two and three Musslewhite claims DR 2–101 is unconstitutionally vague. A regulation that "either forbids or requires the doing of an act in terms so vague that men of common intelligence must necessarily guess at its meaning and differ as to its application, violates the first essential of due process of law." The Fourteenth Amendment's Due Process Clause insists that laws give persons of ordinary intelligence a reasonable opportunity to know what is prohibited, so that he may act accordingly. This requirement applies with particular force in review of laws dealing with speech. These guidelines apply fully to attorney disciplinary proceedings.

Appellant claims that DR 2–101 is unconstitutionally vague because it does not advise the attorney that he may be prevented from advertising to other lawyers in other countries. We do not find that DR 2–101 is unconstitutionally vague. It does not forbid conduct in terms that are so vague that people of common intelligence must guess at its meaning. The rule does not regulate communication with other lawyers. Contrary to appellant's contentions, he was not disciplined for communications with other lawyers, he was disciplined for false communications to victims of the Piper Alpha tragedy. That activity is clearly prohibited by DR 2–101.

Moreover, the Supreme Court adopted DR 2–101 and the other State Bar rules as advertising guidelines to remove the uncertainty and confusion surrounding attorney advertising, solicitation, and trade names in the aftermath of *Bates v. State Bar of Arizona*. We presume the court intended that DR 2–101 comply with the restraints constitutionally permitted to prevent false, deceptive, or misleading advertising. Accepting the supreme court's inherent power to adopt the rule, it is not our function as an intermediate appellate court to nullify or alter it, for once the court decides on a rule of law, the decision is, in the absence of a controlling decision by the United States Supreme Court, binding on lower courts until the court changes the rule.

In points of error four through nine and eleven Musslewhite claims the evidence was insufficient to support findings that the press release, letters, and advertisement were false and misleading. He also claims that Newman acted alone in publishing the advertisement and mailing the letters.

First, Musslewhite claims the evidence does not show that the press release, letters, and advertisement were false and misleading. With regard to the press release, the recitation that a "team of internationally renowned U.S. Lawyers based in Houston, Texas" is misleading because it fails to identify any of the lawyers. Further, Musslewhite admitted that anyone reading the press release would not know who the team was. The release also states that the team "would be working with United Kingdom solicitors to represent the victims or families of victims involved in the Piper Alpha tragedy." That statement is false and misleading because it suggests that Musslewhite, or the team, already had Piper Alpha clients, when they did not. The release refers to Musslewhite as the "team's lead counsel." That is misleading because the release does not disclose that the agreed judgment prevented Musslewhite from accepting new employment by clients and that he would be suspended for ninety days in the future. Finally, DR 2–101 requires a lawyer who publishes, advertises, or broadcasts with regard to any area of law to include a disclaimer stating that he is not certified by the Texas Board of Legal Specialization. The press release fails to include such a disclaimer.

The letter sent to the victims of the Piper Alpha tragedy also refers to a "group of internationally renowned trial lawyers in the United States" and is misleading because it does not identify the lawyers. Further, the statement that the team is "currently having discussions with a number of United Kingdom solicitors with a view to filing suit in the state court of Texas to obtain maximum damages" is false and misleading because it suggests that the "team" already had Piper Alpha clients when it did not.

The advertisement that was published in the local Aberdeen paper contains similar misrepresentations. Again, the reference to a "team of internationally renowned American lawyers experienced in handling damage claims in mass disaster in the United States of America and Europe" is misleading because it never identifies the lawyers and is not susceptible to reasonable verification by the public. The advertisement similarly does not contain a disclaimer. We find sufficient evidence that the press release, letters, and advertisement contained false and misleading statements.

Musslewhite also contends that Newman acted alone when in Scotland and, specifically, with regard to the running of the advertisement and the mailing of the letters to the victims. The evidence shows, however, that Musslewhite telephoned Newman and asked that Newman work with him on the project. Musslewhite provided Newman with a list of solicitors and potential clients to telephone once he arrived. Musslewhite admitted that Newman discussed the advertisement with him over the telephone and that Newman showed him the letter before it was mailed. Newman testified that MacDonald drafted the advertisement based on information provided by Newman and Musslewhite. We find the evidence sufficient to show that Newman was working with Musslewhite when he published the advertisement and mailed the letters. Points four through nine and eleven are overruled.

### ERIC S. ROTH, CONFRONTING SOLICITATION OF MASS DISASTER VICTIMS*

26 Geo. L.J. 967, 971–74, 968–71 (1989).

#### EXAMPLES OF IMPROPER ATTORNEY CONDUCT AND INSURANCE COMPANY TACTICS

Notwithstanding the rules against in-person solicitation, some lawyers are driven by the opportunity to make money. Some mass disasters represent the potential for an attorney to earn a considerable amount of money. With recovery in these cases almost certain, often the only unknown is how much will be recovered. Thus whether it is the explosion of an oil refinery or the crash of a commercial airliner, the victims and their relatives are routinely "hustled by a whole gaggle of plaintiff's lawyers because mere rules will not keep a lawyer without qualifications from going out and touting himself as an expert and getting retained."

The instances of direct attorney solicitation after mass disasters are numerous. Specific examples of solicitation, however, are difficult to find because of the private nature of the act of solicitation. The only witnesses of the solicitation are usually the solicitor and the solicitee. This makes in-person solicitation very hard to prove as compared to solicitation by mail, which often occurs after a mass disaster. An attorney solicits business by obtaining a list of the victims and mailing out letters to individuals or relatives detailing the lawyer's past experience in disasters. Here the letter is physical evidence of solicitation.

In 1978, after the crash of a PSA jet which had hit a private plane in San Diego, the widow of a man killed in the collision reported that she had been contacted by no less than twenty attorneys. After the recent crash of Pan Am flight 103 in Scotland, one victim's widow reported that she was solicited "by no less than 30 attorneys" within 24 hours of the crash. In the Arrow Air disaster in Gander, Newfoundland on December 12, 1985, 248 American servicemen were killed. All of the victims had been stationed at Fort Campbell, Kentucky and many lived there. The families proved to be a significant target for soliciting attorneys. One Washington, D.C. law firm managed to get the names of the victims and to have a non-lawyer employee of the firm call the families of the victims. He would call them and begin the conversation by saying, "Are you the wife or mother of Sgt. _____? I was sorry to learn of the accident." One widow reported she had received telephone calls from lawyers on Christmas Day, and another widow, in a radio interview, complained that she had been called at least fifty times by attorneys whom she did not know.

Perhaps the most outrageous example of solicitation occurred after the crash of a Northwest airliner in Detroit on August 16, 1987. Shortly after

---

    *    Reprinted with the permission of the publisher, The Georgetown Law Journal © 1989 & Georgetown University.

the accident, a man posing as a Catholic priest, Father John Irish, appeared on the scene to console the families of the victims. He "hugged crying mothers and talked with grieving fathers of God's rewards in the hereafter. He even sobbed along with dazed families. Then he would pass out the business card of a Florida attorney and repeatedly urge them to call the lawyer."

While many mass disasters are the result of airplane crashes, there are other types of disasters as well. Probably the most well-known incident occurred in Bhopal, India at the Union Carbide chemical plant. Over 2,000 people were killed in the accident and thousands of others were injured. American lawyers rushed to India in an attempt to retain clients and in their zeal brought shame and discredit to the American bar. Many attorneys engaged in unprofessional activity using various methods of solicitation while in India. Indications are that lawyers paid claimants who signed retainer agreements, set up booths on the streets, and held receptions for the victims at which the media were present. Not only were these actions morally reprehensible, but they were contrary to the rules of professional conduct prohibiting in-person solicitation.

Another well publicized disaster occurred at the Dupont Plaza Hotel fire in San Juan, Puerto Rico on New Year's Eve, 1986, in which ninety-six people were killed. The aftermath of the hotel fire was particularly notorious for the wide range of misconduct by attorneys and the presence of insurance adjusters. A member of the Puerto Rican Bar Association likened the presence of American lawyers to that of "vultures," while a hospitalized victim complained that lawyers and hotel representatives solicited her in the hospital. One attorney on the scene said he saw numerous incidents of attorneys directly soliciting families of victims and victims themselves both at the scene and at hospitals. Guerry Thornton, an Atlanta attorney, reported that he observed another attorney directly soliciting a survivor of the fire. Thornton said that the soliciting attorney, in an effort to impress the potential client, boasted about his success in the Bhopal, India tragedy claiming that he was responsible for $380 million in settlements. Thornton noted that not only was the attorney engaging in unethical direct solicitation, but factual misrepresentation as well because American lawyers were dismissed when the case was transferred to India. He commented that attorney misrepresentation was widespread in the aftermath of the tragedy as attorneys scrambled to get clients and media exposure.

One tactic used by attorneys was to arrive at the scene and announce he had been retained by a victim to file suit and to investigate the accident when in fact he had no client. The purpose of such misrepresentation was to get media exposure which ensured the attorney that clients would contact him. In fact, one attorney had announced within twenty-four hours of the fire that he had nine cases and was preparing to file complaints using pleadings from the 1980 MGM Hotel fire in Las Vegas. In the rush to file as quickly as possible, some attorneys simply ignored Puerto Rican law and others were not even knowledgeable as to Puerto Rican law. This led some attorneys to file suits against the wrong parties as they did not yet know who was liable. Thornton also charged that some attorneys attempted to control the litigation in what he described as a monopolistic fashion. The same attorneys engaging in-person solicitation and misrepresentation were acting in concert under an agreement in an attempt to control the Multi-District Litigation Council and threatened to "cut out" any attorneys who did not cooperate with them. Moreover, some American firms hired local attorneys to refer cases to them for a fee, in direct violation of the *Model Rules.*

The Dupont Plaza fire is also notable for the actions of insurance adjusters. Representing the hotel, they sought out victims and the families of victims offering them immediate cash settlements in exchange for a waiver of their right to sue. Lawyers complained that the insurance companies were offering sums substantially less than what the individuals could expect to recover in court. The explosion at the Shell Oil refinery in Norco, Louisiana on May 5, 1988 was also the source of many complaints of attorney solicitation. Some reports claimed attorneys were roaming neighborhoods in "Lincolns and limousines" in an effort to contact potential clients. Complaints were filed with the St. Charles Parish Sheriff's Department alleging that attorneys were going door-to-door soliciting prospective clients. One attorney, after associating himself with another attorney who had a client who had been injured in the explosion, managed to get a television appearance as a part of his effort to receive publicity in order to attract clients.

### Rules of Attorney Conduct and Solicitation

The Model Rules of Professional Conduct expressly prohibit in-person solicitation "when a significant motive for doing so is the lawyer's pecuniary gain." Such a prohibition against in-person solicitation is based on the presumption that, whether or not actual harm results, the potential for attorneys exerting pressure on prospective clients to retain the attorney is inherent in such instances where an attorney knows a prospective client is in need of legal services. In the aftermath of a mass disaster, the potential for abuse is increased as the prospective client has likely been so shocked by the event that he is less able to reason fully or to protect his own interests, especially when confronted by an attorney, one who is trained in the art of persuasion.

The conduct of a lawyer is restrained further by the requirement that any statements a lawyer makes about his services must not be misleading or misrepresentative of the services he provides. Any statements a lawyer makes about his services should be truthful and "special care should be taken by lawyers to avoid misleading the public." Little justification is needed for such basic guidelines for professional conduct. At a very minimum, it is in the best interests of the profession to deal honestly with the public.

Although it is easy to repeat the standards of permissible solicitation, it is difficult to delineate the limits of acceptable attorney behavior following a mass disaster. Clearly, if any attorney approaches a potential client at the scene of the accident or at the hospital shortly after the event, the individual, still under the influence of the event, is susceptible to undue pressure. But is this danger so great that attorneys should be prohibited from communicating with the victims in any manner? Before answering yes, one must remember that insurance company representatives are given free rein to exert their own pressures on the survivors and the families of the victims. While one may argue whether a soliciting attorney has a potential client's best interest in mind, it is certain that an airline's insurance company has primarily its financial interest in mind when is seeks to communicate with victims or their families.

A valuable service may be rendered to the victims and their families when they are informed of their legal rights and of their legal options. Thus to prohibit attorneys from any contact with the victims may work to the victims' detriment. Conversely, to allow an attorney merely to inform the individual of his or her legal rights and then to allow the attorney to represent that individual would be improper because it is unprofessional for attorneys to solicit business for themselves. The Model Rules of Professional Conduct and the Model Code of Professional Responsibility prohibit any contact by an attorney in which a significant motive for the lawyer's conduct is pecuniary gain. Furthermore, if the attorney gives unsolicited advice that the individual should obtain legal advice or take legal action, the attorney shall not accept employment as a result of giving such advice.

Several problems exist with these rules. First, "a significant motive for pecuniary gain" is hard to identify and nearly impossible to prove. Second, the rules falsely assume that individuals are knowledgeable about legal rights. By prohibiting solicitation, the rules cut off a means by which the victims of mass disasters and their relatives can become informed of their legal rights or their legal options. If these people remain uniformed, they might be vulnerable to insurance company abuse. Lastly, varying degrees of construction of the rules makes objective determination of when a violation occurs difficult to determine. Certain conduct by one attorney may be viewed as a liberal construction or a bending of the rules while another attorney may consider the same conduct as constituting a breach of the rules.

## FLORIDA BAR V. WENT FOR IT, INC.

Supreme Court of the United States, 1995.
515 U.S. 618, 115 S.Ct. 2371, 132 L.Ed.2d 541.

JUSTICE O'CONNOR delivered the opinion of the Court.

Rules of the Florida Bar prohibit personal injury lawyers from sending targeted direct-mail solicitations to victims and their relatives for 30 days following an accident or disaster. This case asks us to consider whether such rules violate the First and Fourteenth Amendments of the Constitution. We hold that in the circumstances presented here, they do not.

### I.

In 1989, the Florida Bar completed a 2-year study of the effects of lawyer advertising on public opinion. After conducting hearings, commissioning surveys, and reviewing extensive public commentary, the Bar determined that several changes to its advertising rules were in order. In late 1990, the Florida Supreme Court adopted the Bar's proposed amendments with some modifications. Two of these amendments are at issue in this case. Rule 4–7.4(b) (1) provides that "a lawyer shall not send, or knowingly permit to be sent, a written communication to a prospective client for the purpose of obtaining professional employment if: (A) the written communication concerns an action for personal injury or wrongful death or otherwise relates to an accident or disaster involving the person to whom the communication is addressed or a relative of that person, unless the accident or disaster occurred more than 30 days prior to the mailing of the communication." Rule 4–7.8(a) states that "a lawyer shall not accept referrals from a lawyer referral service unless the service: (1) engages in no communication with the public and in no direct contact with prospective clients in a manner that would violate the Rules of Professional Conduct if the communication or contact were made by the lawyer." Together, these rules create a brief 30-day blackout period after an accident during which lawyers may not, directly or indirectly, single out accident victims or their relatives in order to solicit their business.

In March 1992, G. Stewart McHenry and his wholly owned lawyer referral service, Went For It, Inc., filed this action for declaratory and injunctive relief in the United States District Court for the Middle District of Florida challenging Rules 4.7–4(b) (1) and 4.7–8 as violative of the First and Fourteenth Amendments to the Constitution. McHenry alleged that he routinely sent targeted solicitations to accident victims or their survivors within 30 days after accidents and that he wished to continue doing so in the future. Went For It, Inc. represented that it wished to contact accident victims or their survivors within 30 days of accidents and to refer potential clients to participating Florida lawyers. In October 1992, McHenry was disbarred for reasons unrelated to this suit.

The District Court referred the parties' competing summary judgment motions to a Magistrate Judge, who concluded that the Florida Bar had substantial government interests, predicated on a concern for professionalism, both in protecting the personal privacy and tranquility of recent accident victims and their relatives and in ensuring that these individuals do not fall prey to undue influence or overreaching. Citing the Florida Bar's extensive study, the Magistrate Judge found that the rules directly serve those interests and sweep no further than reasonably necessary. The Magistrate recommended that the District Court grant the Florida Bar's motion for summary judgment on the ground that the rules pass constitutional muster.

The District Court rejected the Magistrate Judge's report and recommendations and entered summary judgment for the plaintiffs, relying on *Bates v. State Bar of Arizona* and subsequent cases. The Eleventh Circuit affirmed. The panel noted, in its conclusion, that it was "disturbed that *Bates* and its progeny require the decision" that it reached. We granted certiorari, and now reverse.

II.

A.

Constitutional protection for attorney advertising, and for commercial speech generally, is of recent vintage. Until the mid-1970s, we adhered to the broad rule laid that, while the First Amendment guards against government restriction of speech in most contexts, "the Constitution imposes no such restraint on government as respects purely commercial advertising." In 1976, the Court changed course. In *Virginia State Bd. of Pharmacy v. Virginia Citizens Consumer Council, Inc.*, we invalidated a state statute barring pharmacists from advertising prescription drug prices. At issue was speech that involved the idea that "I will sell you the X prescription drug at the Y price." Striking the ban as unconstitutional, we rejected the argument that such speech "is so removed from 'any exposition of ideas,' and from 'truth, science, morality, and arts in general, in its diffusion of liberal sentiments on the administration of Government,' that it lacks all protection."

In *Virginia State Board*, the Court limited its holding to advertising by pharmacists, noting that "physicians and lawyers do not dispense standardized products; they render professional services of almost infinite variety and nature, with the consequent enhanced possibility for confusion and deception if they were to undertake certain kinds of advertising." One year later, however, the Court applied the Virginia State Board principles to invalidate a state rule prohibiting lawyers from advertising in newspapers and other media. In *Bates*, the Court struck a ban on price advertising for what it deemed "routine" legal services: "the uncontested divorce, the simple adoption, the uncontested personal bankruptcy, the change of name, and the like." Expressing confidence that legal advertising would only be practicable for such simple, standardized services, the Court rejected the State's proffered justifications for regulation.

Nearly two decades of cases have built upon the foundation laid by *Bates*. It is now well established that lawyer advertising is commercial speech and, as such, is accorded a measure of First Amendment protection. Such First Amendment protection, of course, is not absolute. We have always been careful to distinguish commercial speech from speech at the First Amendment's core. " 'Commercial speech enjoys a limited measure of protection, commensurate with its subordinate position in the scale of First Amendment values,' and is subject to 'modes of regulation that might be impermissible in the realm of noncommercial expression.' " We have observed that " 'to require a parity of constitutional protection for commercial and noncommercial speech alike could invite dilution, simply by a leveling process, of the force of the Amendment's guarantee with respect to the latter kind of speech.' "

Mindful of these concerns, we engage in "intermediate" scrutiny of restrictions on commercial speech, analyzing them under the framework set forth in *Central Hudson Gas & Electric Corp. v. Public Service Comm'n of N.Y.* Under *Central Hudson*, the government may freely regulate commercial speech that concerns unlawful activity or is misleading. Commercial speech that falls into neither of those categories, like the advertising at issue here, may be regulated if the government satisfies a test consisting of three related prongs: first, the government must assert a substantial interest in support of its regulation; second, the government must demonstrate that the restriction on commercial speech directly and materially advances that interest; and third, the regulation must be " 'narrowly drawn.' "

### B.

"Unlike rational basis review, the *Central Hudson* standard does not permit us to supplant the precise interests put forward by the State with other suppositions." The Florida Bar asserts that it has a substantial interest in protecting the privacy and tranquility of personal injury victims and their loved ones against intrusive, unsolicited contact by lawyers. This interest obviously factors into the Bar's paramount (and repeatedly professed) objective of curbing activities that "negatively affect the administration of justice." Because direct mail solicitations in the wake of accidents are perceived by the public as intrusive, the Bar argues, the reputation of the legal profession in the eyes of Floridians has suffered commensurately. The regulation, then, is an effort to protect the flagging reputations of Florida lawyers by preventing them from engaging in conduct that, the Bar maintains, " 'is universally regarded as deplorable and beneath common decency because of its intrusion upon the special vulnerability and private grief of victims or their families.' "

We have little trouble crediting the Bar's interest as substantial. On various occasions we have accepted the proposition that "States have a compelling interest in the practice of professions within their boundaries, and as part of their power to protect the public health, safety, and other valid interests they have broad power to establish standards for licensing practitioners and regulating the practice of professions." Our precedents also leave no room for doubt that "the protection of potential clients' privacy is a substantial state interest." In other contexts, we have consistently recognized that "the State's interest in protecting the well-being, tranquility, and privacy of the home is certainly of the highest order in a free and civilized society." Indeed, we have noted that "a special benefit of the privacy all citizens enjoy within their own walls, which the State may legislate to protect, is an ability to avoid intrusions."

Under *Central Hudson's* second prong, the State must demonstrate that the challenged regulation "advances the Government's interest 'in a direct and material way.'" That burden, we have explained, " 'is not satisfied by mere speculation and conjecture; rather, a governmental body seeking to sustain a restriction on commercial speech must demonstrate that the harms it recites are real and that its restriction will in fact alleviate them to a material degree.'" In *Edenfield*, the Court invalidated a Florida ban on in-person solicitation by certified public accountants (CPAs). We observed that the State Board of Accountancy had "presented no studies that suggest personal solicitation of prospective business clients by CPAs creates the dangers of fraud, overreaching, or compromised independence that the Board claims to fear." Moreover, "the record did not disclose any anecdotal evidence, either from Florida or another State, that validated the Board's suppositions." In fact, we concluded that the only evidence in the record tended to "contradict rather than strengthen the Board's submissions." Finding nothing in the record to substantiate the State's allegations of harm, we invalidated the regulation

The direct-mail solicitation regulation before us does not suffer from such infirmities. The Florida Bar submitted a 106-page summary of its 2-year study of lawyer advertising and solicitation to the District Court. That summary contains data—both statistical and anecdotal—supporting the Bar's contentions that the Florida public views direct-mail solicitations in the immediate wake of accidents as an intrusion on privacy that reflects poorly upon the profession. As of June 1989, lawyers mailed 700,000 direct solicitations in Florida annually, 40% of which were aimed at accident victims or their survivors. A survey of Florida adults commissioned by the Bar indicated that Floridians "have negative feelings about those attorneys who use direct mail advertising." Fifty-four percent of the general population surveyed said that contacting persons concerning accidents or similar events is a violation of privacy. A random sampling of persons who received direct-mail advertising from lawyers in 1987 revealed that 45% believed that direct-mail solicitation is "designed to take advantage of gullible or unstable people"; 34% found such tactics "annoying or irritating"; 26% found it "an invasion of your privacy"; and 24% reported that it "made you angry." Significantly, 27% of direct-mail recipients reported that their regard for the legal profession and for the judicial process as a whole was "lower" as a result of receiving the direct mail.

The anecdotal record mustered by the Bar is noteworthy for its breadth and detail. With titles like *"Scavenger Lawyers"* (The Miami Herald, Sept. 29, 1987) and *"Solicitors Out of Bounds"* (St. Petersburg Times, Oct. 26, 1987), newspaper editorial pages in Florida have burgeoned with criticism of Florida lawyers who send targeted direct mail to victims shortly after accidents. The study summary also includes page upon page of excerpts from complaints of direct-mail recipients. For example, a Florida citizen described how he was " 'appalled and angered by the brazen attempt' " of a law firm to solicit him by letter shortly after he was injured and his fiancee was killed in an auto accident. Another found it " 'despicable and inexcusable' " that a Pensacola lawyer wrote to his mother three days after his father's funeral. Another described how she was " 'astounded' " and then " 'very angry' " when she received a solicitation following a minor accident. Still another described as " 'beyond comprehension' " a letter his nephew's family received the day of the nephew's funeral. One citizen wrote, " 'I consider the unsolicited contact from you after my child's accident to be of the rankest form of ambulance chasing and in incredibly poor taste. I cannot begin to express with my limited vocabulary the utter contempt in which I hold you and your kind.' "

In light of this showing—which respondents at no time refuted, save by the conclusory assertion that the rule lacked "any factual basis,"—we conclude that the Bar has satisfied the second prong of the *Central Hudson* test. Nothing in *Edenfield,* a case in which the State offered no evidence or anecdotes in support of its restriction, requires more. After scouring the record, we are satisfied that the ban on direct-mail solicitation in the immediate aftermath of accidents, unlike the rule at issue in *Edenfield,* targets a concrete, non-speculative harm.

In reaching a contrary conclusion, the Court of Appeals determined that this case was governed squarely by *Shapero v. Kentucky Bar Assn.* Making no mention of the Bar's study, the court concluded that " 'a targeted letter does not invade the recipient's privacy any more than does a substantively identical letter mailed at large. The invasion, if any, occurs when the lawyer discovers the recipient's legal affairs, not when he confronts the recipient with the discovery.' " In many cases, the Court of Appeals explained, "this invasion of privacy will involve no more than reading the newspaper." While some of *Shapero's* language might be read to support the Court of Appeals' interpretation, Shapero differs in several fundamental respects from the case before us. First and foremost, *Shapero's* treatment of privacy was casual. Second, in contrast to this case,

*Shapero* dealt with a broad ban on all direct-mail solicitations, whatever the time frame and whoever the recipient. Finally, the State in *Shapero* assembled no evidence attempting to demonstrate any actual harm caused by targeted direct mail. The Court rejected the State's effort to justify a prophylactic ban on the basis of blanket, untested assertions of undue influence and overreaching. Because the State did not make a privacy-based argument at all, its empirical showing on that issue was similarly infirm.

We find the Court's perfunctory treatment of privacy in *Shapero* to be of little utility in assessing this ban on targeted solicitation of victims in the immediate aftermath of accidents. While it is undoubtedly true that many people find the image of lawyers sifting through accident and police reports in pursuit of prospective clients unpalatable and invasive, this case targets a different kind of intrusion. The Florida Bar has argued, and the record reflects, that a principal purpose of the ban is "protecting the personal privacy and tranquility of Florida's citizens from crass commercial intrusion by attorneys upon their personal grief in times of trauma." The intrusion targeted by the Bar's regulation stems not from the fact that a lawyer has learned about an accident or disaster (as the Court of Appeals notes, in many instances a lawyer need only read the newspaper to glean this information), but from the lawyer's confrontation of victims or relatives with such information, while wounds are still open, in order to solicit their business. In this respect, an untargeted letter mailed to society at large is different in kind from a targeted solicitation; the untargeted letter involves no willful or knowing affront to or invasion of the tranquility of bereaved or injured individuals and simply does not cause the same kind of reputational harm to the profession unearthed by the Florida Bar's study.

Nor do we find *Bolger v. Youngs Drug Products Corp.*, dispositive of the issue, despite any superficial resemblance. In *Bolger*, we rejected the Federal Government's paternalistic effort to ban potentially "offensive" and "intrusive" direct-mail advertisements for contraceptives. Minimizing the Government's allegations of harm, we reasoned that "recipients of objectionable mailings may 'effectively avoid further bombardment of their sensibilities simply by averting their eyes.'" We found that the "'short, though regular, journey from mail box to trash can is an acceptable burden, at least so far as the Constitution is concerned.'" Concluding that citizens have at their disposal ample means of averting any substantial injury inhering in the delivery of objectionable contraceptive material, we deemed the State's intercession unnecessary and unduly restrictive.

Here, in contrast, the harm targeted by the Florida Bar cannot be eliminated by a brief journey to the trash can. The purpose of the 30-day targeted direct-mail ban is to forestall the outrage and irritation with the state-licensed legal profession that the practice of direct solicitation only days after accidents has engendered. The Bar is concerned not with citizens' "offense" in the abstract, but with the demonstrable detrimental effects that such "offense" has on the profession it regulates. Moreover, the harm posited by the Bar is as much a function of simple receipt of targeted solicitations within days of accidents as it is a function of the letters' contents. Throwing the letter away shortly after opening it may minimize the latter intrusion, but it does little to combat the former. We see no basis in *Bolger,* for dismissing the Florida Bar's assertions of harm, particularly given the unrefuted empirical and anecdotal basis for the Bar's conclusions.

Passing to *Central Hudson's* third prong, we examine the relationship between the Florida Bar's interests and the means chosen to serve them. With respect to this prong, the differences between commercial speech and noncommercial speech are manifest. In *Fox*, we made clear that the "least restrictive means" test has no role in the commercial speech context. "What our decisions require," instead, "is a 'fit' between the legislature's ends and the means chosen to accomplish those ends, a fit that is not necessarily perfect, but reasonable; that represents not necessarily the single best disposition but one whose scope is 'in proportion to the interest served,' that employs not necessarily the least restrictive means but a means narrowly tailored to achieve the desired objective."

Respondents levy a great deal of criticism, at the scope of the Bar's restriction on targeted mail. "By prohibiting written communications to all people, whatever their state of mind," respondents charge, the rule "keeps useful information from those accident victims who are ready, willing and able to utilize a lawyer's advice."  This criticism may be parsed into two components. First, the rule does not distinguish between victims in terms of the severity of their injuries. According to respondents, the rule is unconstitutionally over-inclusive insofar as it bans targeted mailings even to citizens whose injuries or grief are relatively minor. Second, the rule may prevent citizens from learning about their legal options, particularly at a time when other actors—opposing counsel and insurance adjusters—may be clamoring for victims' attentions. Any benefit arising from the Bar's regulation, respondents implicitly contend, is outweighed by these costs.

We are not persuaded by respondents' allegations of constitutional infirmity. We find little deficiency in the ban's failure to distinguish among injured Floridians by the severity of their pain or the intensity of their grief. Indeed, it is hard to imagine the contours of a regulation that might satisfy respondents on this score. Rather than drawing difficult lines on the basis that some injuries are "severe" and some situations appropriate (and others, presumably, inappropriate) for grief, anger, or emotion, the Florida Bar has crafted a ban applicable to all post-accident or disaster solicitations for a brief 30-day period. Unlike respondents, we do not see "numerous and obvious less-burdensome alternatives" to Florida's short temporal ban. The Bar's rule is reasonably well-tailored to its stated objective of eliminating targeted mailings whose type and timing are a source of distress to Floridians, distress that has caused many of them to lose respect for the legal profession.

Respondents' second point would have force if the Bar's rule were not limited to a brief period and if there were not many other ways for injured Floridians to learn about the availability of legal representation during that time. Our lawyer advertising cases have afforded lawyers a great deal of leeway to devise innovative ways to attract new business. Florida permits lawyers to advertise on prime-time television and radio as well as in newspapers and other media. They may rent space on billboards. They may send untargeted letters to the general population, or to discrete segments thereof. There are, of course, pages upon pages devoted to lawyers in the Yellow Pages of Florida telephone directories. These listings are organized alphabetically and by area of specialty. These ample alternative channels for receipt of information about the availability of legal representation during the 30-day period following accidents may explain why, despite the ample evidence, testimony, and commentary submitted by those favoring (as well as opposing) unrestricted direct-mail solicitation, respondents have not pointed to—and we have not independently found—a single example of an individual case in which immediate solicitation helped to avoid, or failure to solicit within 30 days brought about, the harms that concern the dissent. In fact, the record contains considerable empirical survey information suggesting that Floridians have little difficulty finding lawyers when they need one. Finding no basis to question the commonsense conclusion that the many alternative channels for communicating necessary information about attorneys are sufficient, we see no defect in Florida's regulation.

## III.

Speech by professionals obviously has many dimensions. There are circumstances in which we will accord speech by attorneys on public issues and matters of legal representation the strongest protection our Constitution has to offer. This case, however, concerns pure commercial advertising, for which we have always reserved a lesser degree of protection under the First Amendment. Particularly because the standards and conduct of state-licensed lawyers have traditionally been subject to extensive regulation by the States, it is all the more appropriate that we limit our scrutiny of state regulations to a level commensurate with the "'subordinate position'" of commercial speech in the scale of First Amendment values.

We believe that the Florida Bar's 30-day restriction on targeted direct-mail solicitation of accident victims and their relatives withstands scrutiny under the three-part Central Hudson test that we have devised for this context. The Bar has substantial interest both in protecting injured Floridians from invasive conduct by lawyers and in preventing the erosion of confidence in the profession that such repeated invasions have engendered. The Bar's proffered study, unrebutted by respondents below, provides evidence indicating that the harms it targets are far from illusory. The palliative devised by the Bar to address these harms is narrow both in scope and in duration. The Constitution, in our view, requires nothing more.

The judgment of the Court of Appeals, accordingly, is reversed.

# B. ADEQUATE REPRESENTATION

## MEKDECI V. MERRELL NATIONAL LABORATORIES

United States Court of Appeals, Eleventh Circuit, 1983.
711 F.2d 1510.

### I.

In 1975, Elizabeth Mekdeci gave birth to a son, David. The child suffered from a combination of birth defects, which included malformed and missing fingers and a missing pectoral muscle. Thereafter, she extensively investigated the possible origin of her son's injury and became convinced that a drug she had ingested for nausea during the pregnancy was the cause. That drug, Bendectin, is manufactured by the defendant.

Based on that conclusion, the Mekdecis, both individually and on behalf of their son, instituted the present suit against Merrell. In their complaint, they alleged Florida causes of action for strict liability, negligence, breach of warranty and fraud. At the end of a two month trial, the jury appeared to be deadlocked in its deliberations. The district court gave the jury further instruction, and soon afterward, the jury returned a verdict awarding the "plaintiff" $20,000.00, the amount stipulated by the parties as compensation for the parents' medical expenses. The verdict, however, denied any recovery on the child's individual cause of action. For that reason, the plaintiffs sought a new trial limited to a determination of damages. Declaring the jury's award to be a compromise verdict, the district court ordered a new trial on all issues.

Prior to the second trial, the plaintiffs' attorneys made several unsuccessful attempts to withdraw as counsel for the Mekdecis and to obtain a continuance. The second trial proceeded as scheduled and resulted in a verdict absolving the defendant of all liability. The district court entered a judgment in conformance with the verdict and taxed the costs incurred by Merrell in both trials against the plaintiffs. This appeal followed.

### III.

The plaintiff's next assignment of error involves the persistent efforts of their original lawyers to withdraw as counsel for the Mekdecis. During the nine month interim between the two trials, the six attorneys of record made various attempts to abandon the case and, failing that, to obtain a continuance. Finding no compelling justification for the lawyers' requests, the district court denied the motions. In addition, the court refused to grant the six month continuance requested by another law firm, who sought to replace the recalcitrant attorneys but conditioned their entry into the case on the court's willingness to delay the proceedings. On appeal, the plaintiffs attack those rulings and urge that the presentation of their case by unwilling counsel deprived them of a fair trial.

A.

The events giving rise to these allegations present an extraordinary tale. The story begins with the extensive efforts of Mrs. Mekdeci, following the birth of her son, to discover the possible cause of his defects. During the course of her investigation, she talked with many medical experts and examined numerous documents, including government studies of Bendectin. After several years, she collected sufficient information to convince her that the drug had caused David's injury. At that point, she contacted Melvin Belli in San Francisco about legal representation. Belli reviewed the materials she had assembled, and then consented to accept the case.

The agreement with Belli evidently called for him to serve as trial counsel. He also referred the Mekdecis to a Florida attorney, Gerald Tobin. Tobin brought in one of his associates, Arthur Tifford, as well as two local attorneys, Arthur Cohen and George Kokus. The arrangement contemplated that Cohen and Kokus would orchestrate the discovery, and that Belli would conduct the trial. A trial date was originally set for July, 1979. Apparently at Belli's request, the district court granted a continuance until January, 1980. However, just several weeks before the scheduled date, Belli informed the Florida attorneys that he would not appear as counsel. Consequently, the other lawyers, with the assistance of Allen Eaton, a Washington, D.C. attorney specializing in food and drug regulation, prepared to litigate the case themselves.

At a May hearing following the first trial, the judge informed the parties that the second trial would begin in January, 1981. During that spring, Belli and several of the Florida attorneys capitalized on the claimed victory in the first trial in a rather obvious effort to attract other Bendectin clients. They traveled both in this country and Europe, trumpeting their participation in that trial and advertising for Bendectin mothers to contact them, ostensibly for statistical studies. Although the record does not reveal the exact number of cases they have obtained, it is clear that the attorneys now represent plaintiffs in numerous Bendectin cases, presumably as a result of this publicity.

In the summer of 1980, the first signs appeared that the lawyers might be abandoning the Mekdecis. The *London Observer* quoted Belli as saying that Mrs. Mekdeci was too difficult to work with, that her case was not that strong, and that he was turning his attention to two hundred similar cases. About the same time, on July 24, 1980, all of the attorneys of record moved to withdraw, citing an alleged "irreconcilable conflict" with the clients as the basis for the motion. The district court held a hearing on the matter on July 29, 1980. There, Mrs. Mekdeci disclosed her complete surprise over the attorneys' motion as well as the allegation of an irreconcilable conflict. She denied any such disagreement. The court postponed any resolution of the issue so that the attorneys could apprise the Mekdecis of their reasons for seeking withdrawal. [The Mekdecis then unsuccessfully attempted to retain successor counsel, after the court denied a continuance of the case.— *ed.*]

After denying the continuance, the court turned to a consideration of the motion to withdraw. In the letter of explanation requested earlier by the court, the attorneys basically cited differences of opinion between them and the Mekdecis over trial strategy. The Mekdecis informed the court that they did not consider the disagreements insurmountable, that they were willing to cooperate fully with the lawyers, and that they wished to continue with their original attorneys. Mrs. Mekdeci also suggested that the real dispute centered on her reluctance to acquiesce in the attorneys' preference to delay the trial until after the trial of another Bendectin case. Based on the plaintiffs' assurances, the district court denied the motion to withdraw, admonishing all of the parties to work together toward their common purpose.

The court's order did not even momentarily deter the attorneys' attempts to extricate themselves from the case. Less than a month later, Cohen, Kokus, Tifford and Eaton renewed their motion to withdraw. They based the request on the same conclusory allegation of an "irreconcilable conflict." They also emphasized that their motion did not include Belli, therefore leaving him to represent the plaintiffs. The Mekdecis opposed the motion. In a brief order, the district court denied the request, observing that

> good grounds have not been shown as to why it would be in the interest of justice for this Court to permit the Florida attorneys and the Washington, D.C. attorney, Allen, to abandon the plaintiffs to rely upon a California attorney who has not actively participated in this case, nor indicated a firm resolve to do so, and further, who is reported to have stated that he has no further interest in the case.

Even the district court's adherence to its original ruling and the Fifth Circuit's denial of extraordinary relief did not end the attorneys' maneuvers. On December 31, 1980, less than one month before the scheduled trial date, the attorneys renewed their request still again, this time in alternative motions to withdraw, for a continuance or stay of proceedings pending the disposition of their appeal. For the first time, they suggested that they lacked sufficient funds to finance the costs of the second trial. The court held a hearing on January 12, 1980 to consider those motions. During that hearing, Kokus asserted every conceivable basis for delaying the proceedings. He primarily attempted to convince the court that extensive discovery remained to be accomplished and that the lawyers could not afford a retrial at that time. The court noted the complete absence of any proof substantiating the lawyers' alleged inability to advance costs. Moreover, while acknowledging that the family could not cover expenses, Mrs. Mekdeci expressed her disbelief of the allegation and her determination to obtain funds to assure the presence of their chief expert witness. She also emphasized her preference to proceed to trial as scheduled, if at all possible.

The court also observed that the attorneys' assertions appeared to contradict their position in another Bendectin case pending in the United States District Court for the District of Columbia. During a hearing held only a month earlier in that case, Eaton had urged that court to set a trial date as early as June. Merrell's attorney protested that the intervening Mekdeci trial might make it impossible to complete discovery in the other case by June. In a statement that perhaps shed more light than intended on the attorneys' motivations in the Mekdeci case, Eaton recounted numerous problems in the Mekdeci lawsuit and said,

> that being the case, we have a group of people—a group of attorneys who have agreed that, in order to start afresh and develop the issues properly, that the Koller case in our opinion represents perhaps the cleanest case of all the cases and the clearest one.
>
> We have a nurse here who ingested Bendectin, and only Bendectin. She ingested it during the critical period. And little Anne Koller has no arms and she has only a left leg which has a club foot on it.
>
> We figure this was a clear case in order to litigate the issues properly.

Even though they urged an early trial date in *Koller*, the attorneys adhered to their contention that they could not afford a trial in the Florida case. In fact, they threatened the court that they would not present any live witnesses if they were unable to procure a continuance. Still, based on all of the circumstances and the plaintiffs' desire to proceed, the district court denied the request.

The second trial was the final chapter in this saga. The attorneys to some extent made good their threat, at least initially, by offering an essentially "paper" case. Midway through the proceedings, Belli sent $25,000.00 for use to pay the expenses of several live witnesses. In any event, the two witnesses which the plaintiffs primarily relied upon in the first trial did not appear in person. Several weeks into the trial, the district court learned of the brief filed on behalf of the Mekdecis, in the attorneys' appeal pending before the Fifth Circuit. The brief suggested that the trial court erred in its handling of the lawyers' repeated motions, especially in its refusal to grant the last request for a continuance. Chief Judge Young was amazed, to say the least, over the plaintiffs' position, since they had consistently conveyed their preference to proceed to trial.

## C.

After the district court denied the motion for a continuance, the Mekdecis consistently urged the court to reject the various requests by their original attorneys to withdraw from the case. Nonetheless, they now argue in this appeal that the district court erred in not granting the motion permitting the lawyers to withdraw. To justify this change in position, the plaintiffs suggest that they only opposed the motions in the trial court because that court erroneously denied a continuance for successor counsel, therefore placing them in the predicament of choosing between retaining their reluctant counsel or facing trial with the possibility of no representation. However, because we find that the district court acted within its discretion by refusing a continuance, we conclude that the choice presented them was proper. Thus, the only remaining question is whether compelling ethical considerations mandated withdrawal from the case regardless of the clients' stated preference to keep their attorneys.

Local Rule 2.03(b) of the United States District Court for the Middle District of Florida prohibits the withdrawal of counsel without the court's approval. Additionally, Local Rule 2.03(c) states that the court will not grant permission "absent compelling ethical considerations, if such withdrawal would likely cause continuance or delay." In this court, the plaintiffs advance two reasons why withdrawal was purportedly mandated under the Code of Professional Responsibility, which, if true, would obviously constitute "compelling ethical considerations" under the Local Rule.

First, they maintain that the attorney-client relationship was indeed plagued by an "irreconcilable conflict." This allegation directly contradicts their repeated assurances to the district court that such enmity did not exist. Moreover, the record does not support such a claim. As the representations of Mrs. Mekdeci and the lawyers to the district court illustrated, their past disagreement basically centered on strategic choices made at the first trial. At the time they sought to be excused from the case, their only apparent dispute with the plaintiffs concerned Mrs. Mekdeci's refusal to acquiesce in their desire to obtain a continuance. Such a difference of opinion, standing alone, falls fall short of establishing an irreconcilable conflict. As the former Fifth Circuit Court of Appeals has recognized, a client by virtue of a contract with his attorney is not made an indentured servant, a puppet on counsel's string, nor a chair in the courtroom. Counsel should advise, analyze, argue, and recommend, but his role is not that of an imperator whose edicts must prevail over the client's desire.

The record does not contain evidence of a conflict in the attorney-client relationship of such proportions as would require an ethically-mandated withdrawal of counsel.

The plaintiffs next allege that the attorneys had an improper financial stake in the outcome of the second trial, which ethically precluded their continued representation under D.R. 5–101 and 5–103. They claim that the lawyers' obligation to advance costs created such an unlawful proprietary interest. To the contrary, D.R. 5–103(B) specifically states that "a lawyer may advance or guarantee the expenses of litigation, including court costs, expenses of investigation, expenses of medical examination, and costs of obtaining and presenting evidence, provided the client remains ultimately liable for such expenses." Hence, the attorneys' initial responsibility for trial expenses does not amount to a mandatory ground for withdrawal.

In summary, the plaintiffs' lawyers did not present the court with any compelling ethical consideration demanding their withdrawal. Absent such a reason, the court had the discretion to deny the withdrawal motion. When making its decision, the district court faced the emphatic insistence of the plaintiffs that it deny the withdrawal motion. The Mekdecis cannot now complain that the district court erred by assenting to their wishes.

### D.

Underlying each of the plaintiffs' specific contentions pertaining to the attorneys' conduct is their belief that counsel ultimately performed ineffectively at the second trial. Essentially, the fundamental premise of their argument is that they were denied a fair trial, in violation of their right to due process, because of the alleged inadequacy of the representation. Based on that perception, they suggest that the prejudice which purportedly resulted therefrom renders the trial court's rulings on the motions for a continuance and for withdrawal erroneous. While we are not unsympathetic, we find a critical flaw in their reasoning.

In effect, the plaintiffs assume that they have a protected right to competent representation in their lawsuit. Simply stated, however, "there is no constitutional or statutory right to effective assistance of counsel on a civil case." The sixth amendment standards for effective counsel in criminal cases do not apply in the civil context for that reason, "a party does not have any right to a new trial in a civil suit because of inadequate counsel, but has as its remedy a suit against the attorney for malpractice."

Our conclusion in no way suggests that we condone the conduct of the plaintiffs' original attorneys. On the contrary, we agree that the present record raises disturbing questions on the propriety of the lawyers' actions. The attorneys' various antics create an impression that they may have been more concerned with bettering their position in other Bendectin cases, rather than with fulfilling their professional responsibilities to the Mekdecis, who ironically made it possible for the lawyers to obtain the other cases in the first place. Additionally, there are indications that several, if not all, of the attorneys may have breached their contractual obligations to the plaintiffs. Consequently, we do not necessarily discount the Mekdecis' claim that they have been aggrieved by the conduct of their lawyers.

## STEPHENSON V. DOW CHEMICAL CO.

United States Court of Appeals for the Second Circuit, 2001.
273 F.3d 249.

This appeal requires us to determine the effect of the Supreme Court's landmark class action decisions in *Amchem Products, Inc. v. Windsor* and *Ortiz v. Fibreboard Corp.* on a previously settled class action concerning exposure to Agent Orange during the Vietnam War. Daniel Stephenson and Joe Isaacson are two Vietnam War veterans who allege that they were injured by exposure to Agent Orange while serving in the military in Vietnam. In the late 1990s, Stephenson and Isaacson (along with their families) filed separate lawsuits against manufacturers of Agent Orange. These lawsuits were eventually transferred to Judge Jack B. Weinstein in the Eastern District of New York by the Judicial Panel on Multidistrict Litigation (MDL Panel).

In 1984, however, some twelve years before these suits, virtually identical claims against these defendants, brought by a class of military personnel who were exposed to Agent Orange while in Vietnam between 1961 and 1972, were globally settled. The Isaacson and Stephenson actions were brought in 1998 and 1999 respectively. Judge Weinstein, who presided over the 1984 settlement, dismissed the claims of Stephenson and Isaacson, concluding that the prior settlement barred their suits. On appeal, plaintiffs chiefly contend, citing *Amchem* and *Ortiz,* that they were inadequately represented and, therefore, due process considerations prevent the earlier class action settlement from precluding their claims. Because we agree that *Amchem* and *Ortiz* prevent applying res judicata to bar plaintiffs' claim, we vacate the district court's dismissal and remand for further proceedings.

### I.  BACKGROUND

#### A.  *Prior Agent Orange Litigation*

The Agent Orange class action litigation has a lengthy and complicated history, which we set forth in some detail below in order to convey the magnitude of this decision.

The first Agent Orange litigation began in the late 1970s, when individual veterans and their families filed class action suits in the Northern District of Illinois and Southern and Eastern Districts of New York, alleging that exposure to Agent Orange caused them injury. By order of the MDL Panel, these actions were transferred to the Eastern District of New York and consolidated for pretrial purposes. Plaintiffs asserted claims of negligent manufacture, strict liability, breach of warranty, intentional tort and nuisance.

In 1983, the district court certified the following class under Federal Rule of Civil Procedure 23(b)(3):

> those persons who were in the United States, New Zealand or Australian Armed Forces at any time from 1961 to 1972 who were injured while in or near Vietnam by exposure to Agent Orange or other phenoxy herbicides, including those composed in whole or in part of 2, 4, 5-trichlorophenoxyacetic acid or containing some amount of tetrachlorodibenzo-p-dioxin. The class also includes spouses, parents, and children of the veterans born before January 1, 1984, directly or derivatively injured as a result of the exposure.

To support class certification, the district court specifically found: (1) that the affirmative defenses (including the "military contractor" defense) and the question of general causation are common to the class, (2) that those questions predominate over any questions affecting individual members, and (3) given the enormous potential size of plaintiffs' case and the judicial economies that would result from a class trial, a class action is superior to all other methods for a "fair and efficient adjudication of the controversy." The court also ordered notice by mail, print media, radio and television to be provided to class members, providing in part that persons who wished to opt out must do so by May 1, 1984.

Trial of the class claims was to begin on May 7, 1984. On the eve of trial, the parties reached a settlement. The settlement provided that defendants would pay $180 million into a settlement fund, $10 million of which would indemnify defendants against future state court actions alleging the same claims. The settlement provided that "the Class specifically includes persons who have not yet manifested injury." Additionally, the settlement specifically stated that the district court would "retain jurisdiction over the Fund pending its final disposition."

The district court held fairness hearings throughout the country, and approved the settlement as fair, reasonable and adequate. The court rejected the motion to certify a subclass of those class members who objected to terms of the settlement. The court concluded that "no purpose would have been served by appointing counsel for a subclass of disappointed claimants except to increase expenses to the class and delay proceedings."

Seventy-five percent of the $180 million was to be distributed directly " 'to exposed veterans who suffer from long-term total disabilities and to the surviving spouses or children of exposed veterans who have died.' " "A claimant would qualify for compensation by establishing exposure to Agent Orange and death or disability not 'predominately' caused by trauma." Payments were to be made for ten years, beginning January 1, 1985 and ending December 31, 1994:

> No payment will be made for death or disability occurring after December 31, 1994. Payment will be made for compensable deaths occurring both before and after January 1, 1985. Payments will be made for compensable disability to the extent that the period of disability falls within the ten years of the program's operation.

Most of the remaining 25% of the settlement fund established the Agent Orange Class Assistance Program, which made grants to agencies serving Vietnam veterans and their families. Explaining the creation of this kind of fund, Judge Weinstein stated that it was "the most practicable and equitable method of distributing benefits to" those claimants who did not meet eligibility criteria for cash payments.

We affirmed class certification, settlement approval and much of the distribution plan. We rejected challenges to class certification, concluding that "class certification was justified under Rule 23(b)(3) due to the centrality of the military contractor defense." We specifically rejected an attack based on adequacy of representation, again based on the military contractor defense which, we reasoned, "would have precluded recovery by all plaintiffs, irrespective of the strengths, weaknesses, or idiosyncrasies of their claims." We additionally concluded that the notice scheme devised by Judge Weinstein was the "best notice practicable" under Federal Rule of Civil Procedure 23(c)(2). Finally, we affirmed the settlement as fair, reasonable and adequate, given the serious weaknesses of the plaintiffs' claims.

In 1989 and 1990, two purported class actions, *Ivy v. Diamond Shamrock Chemicals Co.* and *Hartman v. Diamond Shamrock Chemicals Co.*, were filed in Texas state courts. These suits, on behalf of Vietnam veterans exposed to Agent Orange, sought compensatory and punitive damages against the same companies as in the settled suit. The plaintiffs alleged that their injuries manifested only after the May 7, 1984 settlement. Additionally, the *Ivy/Hartman* plaintiffs expressly disclaimed any reliance on federal law, asserting only state law claims. Nonetheless, the defendants removed the actions to federal court on the grounds that these claims had already been asserted and litigated in federal court. The MDL Panel transferred the actions to Judge Weinstein in the Eastern District of New York.

The district court rejected plaintiffs' motion to remand, reasoning that it had jurisdiction over the class action because it "had authority to ensure that its prior orders and the Settlement Agreement were enforced," especially given the injunction it issued enjoining all class members from commencing any action arising out of Agent Orange exposure. In support of its decision, the district court cited the All-Writs Act, 28 U.S.C. § 1651, which authorizes writs "necessary or appropriate" in aid of its jurisdiction.

The district court then turned to the plaintiffs' substantive arguments that it was unfair to bind them to the settlement when their injuries were not manifested until after the settlement had been reached. The district court rejected this argument, based on the following reasoning:

> All of the courts which considered the *Agent Orange* Settlement were fully cognizant of the conflict arguments now hypothesized by the plaintiffs and took steps to minimize the problem in the way they arranged for long-term administration of the Settlement Fund.
>
> In many cases the conflict between the interests of present and future claimants is more imagined than real. In the instant case, for example, the injustice wrought upon the plaintiffs is nonexistent. *These plaintiffs, like all class members who suffer death or disability before the end of 1994, are eligible for compensation from the Agent Orange Payment Fund.* The relevant latency periods and the age of the veterans ensure that almost all valid claims will be revealed before that time.
>
> Even when it is proper and necessary for the courts to be solicitous of the interests of future claimants, the courts cannot ignore the interests of presently injured plaintiffs as well as defendants in achieving a settlement. Class action settlements simply will not occur if the parties cannot set definitive limits on defendants' liability. Making settlement of Rule 23 suits too difficult will work harms upon plaintiffs, defendants, the courts, and the general public.

The district court therefore dismissed the *Ivy/Hartman* litigation.

We affirmed the district court's dismissal. We then addressed plaintiffs' argument that they were not members of the prior class, because they were not "injured" as the term was used in the class definition. We concluded that, for the purposes of the Agent Orange litigation, "injury occurs when a deleterious substance enters a person's body, even though its adverse effects are not immediately apparent." We emphasized that the plaintiffs in the original suit had sought to include such "at-risk" plaintiffs, over defendants' objections, and that we had already affirmed the inclusion of these plaintiffs in the class.

We likewise rejected plaintiffs' argument that their due process rights were violated because they were denied adequate representation and adequate notice in the prior action. We reasoned that "providing individual notice and opt-out rights to persons who are unaware of an injury would probably do little good." We concluded that the plaintiffs were adequately represented in the prior action, and that a subclass of future claimants was unnecessary " 'because of the way the settlement was structured to cover future claimants.' "

Shortly before our decision in *Ivy/Hartman II,* the $10 million set aside for indemnification from state court Agent Orange judgments was transferred to the Class Assistance Program, because the district court deemed such a fund unnecessary. The distribution activities had begun in 1988, and concluded in June 1997. During the ten year period of the settlement, $196.5 million was distributed as cash payments to approximately 52,000 class members. The program paid approximately $52 million to "after-manifested" claimants, whose deaths or disabilities occurred after May 7, 1984. Approximately $71.3 million of the fund was distributed through the Class Assistance Program.

### B.   The Instant Litigation

#### 1.   The Parties

Daniel Stephenson served in Vietnam from 1965 to 1970, serving both on the ground in Vietnam and as a helicopter pilot in Vietnam. He alleges that he was in regular contact with Agent Orange during that time. On February 19, 1998, he was diagnosed with multiple myeloma, a bone marrow cancer, and has undergone a bone marrow transplant.

Joe Isaacson served in Vietnam from 1968 to 1969 as a crew chief in the Air Force, and worked at a base for airplanes which sprayed various herbicides, including Agent Orange. In 1996, Isaacson was diagnosed with non-Hodgkins lymphoma.

Defendants are chemical manufacturers who produced and sold to the United States Government the herbicide Agent Orange during the Vietnam War.

#### 2.   Proceedings Below

In August 1998, Isaacson filed suit in New Jersey state court, asserting claims only under state law. Defendants quickly removed the case to federal court and Isaacson's subsequent motion to remand was denied by Chief Judge Anne Thompson in the District of New Jersey. Thereafter, Isaacson's case was transferred to Judge Weinstein by the MDL Panel.

Stephenson filed his suit *pro se* in the Western District of Louisiana in February 1999, but he soon retained his current counsel. In April 1999, defendants moved for and were granted a Conditional Transfer Order by the MDL Panel, transferring this action to Judge Weinstein. After Stephenson's case was transferred, it was consolidated with the Isaacson case.

Defendants moved to dismiss under Federal Rule of Civil Procedure 12(b)(6), asserting that plaintiffs' claims were barred by the 1984 class action settlement and subsequent final judgment. Judge Weinstein granted this motion from the bench following argument, rejecting plaintiffs' argument that they were inadequately represented and concluding that plaintiffs' suit was an impermissible collateral attack on the prior settlement.

Because we disagree with this conclusion, based on the Supreme Court's holdings in *Amchem* and *Ortiz,* we must vacate the district court's dismissal and remand for further proceedings.

## II.  DISCUSSION

### B.  *Collateral Attack*

The parties devote much energy to debating the permissibility of a collateral attack in this case. Plaintiffs assert that, since the Supreme Court's decision in *Hansberry v. Lee,* courts have allowed collateral attacks on class action judgments based upon due process concerns. Defendants strenuously disagree and contend that to allow plaintiffs' suit to go forward, in the face of the 1984 global settlement, would "violate defendants' right to due process of law." Defendants likewise strenuously argue that the district court's injunction against future litigation prevents these appellants from maintaining their actions. While it is true that "an injunction must be obeyed until modified or dissolved, and its unconstitutionality is no defense to disobedience," defendants' injunction-based argument misses the point. The injunction was part and parcel of the judgment that plaintiffs contend failed to afford them adequate representation. If plaintiffs' inadequate representation allegations prevail, as we so conclude, the judgment, which includes the injunction on which defendants rely, is not binding as to these plaintiffs.

Defendants contend that Supreme Court precedent permits a collateral attack on a class action judgment "only where there has been no prior determination of absent class members' due process rights." According to defendants, because the "due process rights of absent class members have been extensively litigated in the *Agent Orange* litigation," these plaintiffs cannot now attack those prior determinations. We reject defendants' arguments and conclude that plaintiffs' collateral attack, which seeks only to prevent the prior settlement from operating as res judicata to their claims, is permissible.

First, even if, as defendants contend, collateral attack is only permitted where there has been no prior determination of the absent class members' rights, plaintiffs' collateral attack is allowed. It is true that, on direct appeal and in the *Ivy/Hartman* litigation, we previously concluded that there was adequate representation of all class members in the original *Agent Orange* settlement. However, neither this Court nor the district court has addressed specifically the adequacy of representation for those members of the class whose injuries manifested after depletion of the settlements funds. Therefore, even accepting defendants' argument, plaintiffs' suit can go forward because there has been no prior adequacy of representation determination with respect to individuals whose claims arise after the depletion of the settlement fund.

Second, the propriety of a collateral attack such as this is amply supported by precedent. In *Hansberry v. Lee,* the Supreme Court entertained a collateral attack on an Illinois state court class action judgment that purported to bind the plaintiffs. The Court held that class action judgments can only bind absent class members where "the interests of those not joined are of the same class as the interests of those who are, and where it is considered that the latter fairly represent the former in the prosecution of the litigation." Additionally, we have previously stated that a "judgment in a class action is not secure from collateral attack unless the absentees were adequately and vigorously represented."

Allowing plaintiffs' suit would be consistent with many other circuit decisions recognizing the ability of later plaintiffs to attack the adequacy of representation in an earlier class action. For example, the Fifth Circuit holds:

> To answer the question whether the class representative adequately represented the class so that the judgment in the class suit will bind the absent members of the class requires a two-pronged inquiry: (1) Did the trial court in the first suit correctly determine, initially, that the representative would adequately represent the class? and (2) Does it appear, after the termination of the suit, that the class representative adequately protected the interest of the class? The first question involves us in a *collateral review* of the trial court's determination to permit the suit to proceed as a class action with the named plaintiff as the representative, while the second involves a review of the class representative's conduct of the entire suit-an inquiry which is not required to be made by the trial court but which is appropriate in a collateral attack on the judgment.

Defendants' citation to *Federated Department Stores, Inc. v. Moitie* is unavailing. According to that case, a "judgment merely voidable because based upon an erroneous view of the law is not open to collateral attack, but can be corrected only by a direct review and not by bringing another action upon the same cause of action." Defendants' reliance on this case misperceives plaintiffs' argument. Plaintiffs do not attack the merits or finality of the settlement itself, but instead argue that they were not proper parties to that judgment. If plaintiffs were not proper parties to that judgment, as we conclude below, res judicata cannot defeat their claims. Further, such collateral review would not, as defendants maintain, violate defendants' due process rights by exposing them to double liability. Exposure to liability here is not duplicative if plaintiffs were never proper parties to the prior judgment in the first place.

We therefore hold that a collateral attack to contest the application of res judicata is available. We turn next to the merits of this attack.

### C.   Due Process Considerations and Res Judicata

The doctrine of res judicata dictates that "a final judgment on the merits of an action precludes the parties or their privies from relitigating issues that were or could have been raised in that action." Res judicata ordinarily applies "if the earlier decision was (1) a final judgment on the merits, (2) by a court of competent jurisdiction, (3) in a case involving the same parties or their privies, and (4) involving the same cause of action."

Plaintiffs' argument focuses on element number three in the res judicata analysis: whether they are parties bound by the settlement. Plaintiffs rely primarily on the United States Supreme Court's decisions in *Amchem Products, Inc. v. Windsor* and *Ortiz v. Fibreboard Corp.*

In *Amchem,* the Supreme Court confronted, on direct appeal, a challenge to class certification for settlement purposes in an asbestos litigation. The class defined in the complaint included both individuals who were presently injured as well as individuals who had only been exposed to asbestos. The Supreme Court held that this "sprawling" class was improperly certified under Federal Rules of Civil Procedure 23(a) and (b). Specifically, the Court held that Rule 23(a)(4)'s requirement that the named parties " 'will fairly and adequately protect the interests of the class' " had not been satisfied. The Court reasoned that "named parties with diverse medical conditions sought to act on behalf of a single giant class rather than on behalf of discrete subclasses. In significant respects, the interests of those within the single class are not aligned. Most saliently, for the currently injured, the critical goal is generous immediate payments. That goal tugs against the interest of exposure-only plaintiffs in ensuring an ample, inflation-protected fund for the future."

*Amchem* also implied, but did not decide, that the notice provided to exposure-only class members was likewise inadequate. The Court stated that, because many exposure-only individuals, may not be aware of their exposure or realize the ramifications of exposure, "those without current afflictions may not have the information or foresight needed to decide, intelligently, whether to stay in or opt out."

In *Ortiz,* the Supreme Court again addressed a settlement-only class action in the asbestos litigation context. *Ortiz,* however, involved a settlement-only limited fund class under Rule 23(b)(1)(B). The Supreme Court ultimately held that the class could not be maintained under Rule 23(b)(1)(B), because "the limit of the fund was determined by treating the settlement agreement as dispositive, an error magnified" by conflicted counsel. In so holding, *Ortiz* noted that "it is obvious after *Amchem* that a class divided between holders of present and future claims (some of the latter involving no physical injury and attributable to claimants not yet born) requires division into homogeneous subclasses under Rule 23(c)(4)(B), with separate representation to eliminate conflicting interests of counsel."

Res judicata generally applies to bind absent class members except where to do so would violate due process. Due process requires adequate representation "at all times" throughout the litigation, notice "reasonably calculated to apprise interested parties of the pendency of the action," and an opportunity to opt out. Both Stephenson and Isaacson fall within the class definition of the prior litigation: they served in the United States military, stationed in Vietnam, between 1961 and 1972, and were allegedly injured by exposure to Agent Orange. However, they both learned of their allegedly Agent Orange-related injuries only after the 1984 settlement fund had expired in 1994. Because the prior litigation purported to settle all future claims, but only provided for recovery for those whose death or disability was discovered prior to 1994, the conflict between Stephenson and Isaacson and the class representatives becomes apparent. No provision was made for post-1994 claimants, and the settlement fund was permitted to terminate in 1994. *Amchem* and *Ortiz* suggest that Stephenson and Isaacson were not adequately represented in the prior Agent Orange litigation. Those cases indicate that a class which purports to represent both present and future claimants may encounter internal conflicts.

Defendants contend that there was, in fact, no conflict because all class members' claims were equally meritless and would have been defeated by the "military contractor" defense. This argument misses the mark. At this stage, we are only addressing whether plaintiffs' claims should be barred by res judicata. We are therefore concerned only with whether they were afforded due process in the earlier litigation. Part of the due process inquiry (and part of the Rule 23(a) class certification requirements) involves assessing adequacy of representation and intra-class conflicts. The ultimate merits of the claims have no bearing on whether the class previously certified adequately represented these plaintiffs.

Because these plaintiffs were inadequately represented in the prior litigation, they were not proper parties and cannot be bound by the settlement. We therefore must vacate the district court's dismissal and remand for further proceedings. We, of course, express no opinion as to the ultimate merits of plaintiffs' claims.

## III. CONCLUSION

For the foregoing reasons, we hold that the prior *Agent Orange* settlement does not preclude these plaintiffs from asserting their claims alleging injury due to Agent Orange exposure. Because these plaintiffs were inadequately represented in the prior litigation, based on the

Supreme Court's teaching in *Amchem* and *Ortiz,* they were not proper parties to the litigation. We therefore vacate the district court's dismissal and remand the case to the district court for further proceedings consistent with this opinion.

# C. FIDUCIARY DUTIES TO THE CLIENT: MDL NON-CLASS AGGREGATE SETTLEMENTS

## IN RE GUIDANT CORP. IMPLANTABLE DEFIBRILLATORS PRODS. LIAB. LITIG.

United States District Court, 2009.
2009 WL 5195841.

### ORDER SANCTIONING PATRICK J. MULLIGAN, ESQ.

#### INTRODUCTION

There is no wonder why the general public has such a poor perception of attorneys when one examines the conduct of Patrick J. Mulligan, Esq., in this litigation. Mr. Mulligan's conduct has added to the common detriment of this MDL and sullied the legal profession for us all.

On May 7, 2009, the Court held a status conference with Mr. Mulligan to discuss a variety of communications the Court had received from some of Mr. Mulligan's MDL clients. As discussed in the Court's previous Orders concerning Mr. Mulligan, these clients had contacted the Court directly about the Mulligan Law Firm's lack of communication with them and, more importantly, the fact that the Mulligan Law Firm never communicated the projected range of the clients' proposed settlement awards at the time that the clients were asked to sign settlement documents. After the status conference, the Court asked for more information from Mr. Mulligan and reserved the right to formally sanction Mr. Mulligan for his actions in this MDL.

After reviewing the information submitted and for the reasons stated below, the Court fines Mr. Mulligan $50,000 for his contribution to the common detriment of this MDL. In addition, the Court will forward a copy of this Order to the Minnesota Office of Lawyers Professional Responsibility, the Office of Chief Disciplinary Counsel for State Bar of Texas, and to the appropriate ethics boards in all states or territories in which a Guidant MDL client of Mr. Mulligan's resides.

#### BACKGROUND

#### I.   GENERAL BACKGROUND

The background of this MDL is set forth more fully in the Court's previous orders. Briefly, this MDL commenced in November 2005 when the Judicial Panel on Multidistrict Litigation consolidated certain actions and transferred them to the District of Minnesota for pre-trial proceedings against Defendants Guidant Corporation, Guidant Sales Corporation, and Cardiac Pacemakers, Inc. Individual claimants commenced these actions against Guidant for injuries alleged to have been caused by certain defective implantable defibrillator devices and pacemakers manufactured by Guidant.

From early 2006 through July 2007, the parties conducted extensive discovery, engaged in motion practice, and prepared for five bellwether trials. Shortly before the first bellwether trial was to begin in July 2007, the parties entered into a proposed settlement. Later, the parties signed a term sheet with a negotiated settlement fund of $195 million. Soon thereafter, the parties commenced a renegotiation process that lasted approximately four months. The renegotiation process resulted in a new term sheet, increasing the total settlement fund to $240 million. Nearly five months after the first proposed settlement was reached, the parties finally entered into a confidential Master Settlement Agreement (MSA) on December 10, 2007. Since that time, the parties have been working through the claims administration process. To date, the vast majority of participating claimants have received at least a partial payment for their claims.

### III. MR. MULLIGAN'S COMMUNICATIONS WITH HIS CLIENTS

The Court asked Mr. Mulligan to submit copies of all standard or form communications he sent to his clients and to provide the Court with a spreadsheet listing each of his clients who are Guidant claimants by name and the dates on which those clients signed their settlement documents. Mr. Mulligan did so, explaining that he was providing the Court with copies of all communications his firm made to claimant Robert Pena Ayala because Mr. Ayala's file was representative of the standard communications Mr. Mulligan had with his clients.

On July 20, 2007, Mr. Mulligan first announced a tentative Guidant settlement to his clients. He explained that the exact settlement amounts would be determined by an allocation process headed by the Special Masters: "The mechanism's details are currently being developed, but rest assured that adequate and timely data will be available to you so that you can make an informed decision regarding whether or not to accept that settlement offer that will eventually be made to you."

On February 22, 2008, Mr. Mulligan sent another letter to his clients concerning the Guidant settlement. In it, Mr. Mulligan explained that a recent United States Supreme Court decision, *Riegel,* "severely limited the ability to bring lawsuits for personal injuries against makers of medical devices," and as a result, he informed clients that they "will lose the ability to ever receive monetary damages relating to a Guidant heart device" if they did not participate in the settlement. With respect to settlement awards, Mr. Mulligan stated "the exact settlement amount for your claim will be determined through an allocation process headed by the Special

Masters" and that "we anticipate this process to take two to three months to complete, and we will present you with your individual settlement award at that time." Mr. Mulligan attached copies of the claimants' settlement documents and the MSA, together with a copy of the Confidentiality Order entered in the Guidant MDL and asked that those documents be completed and returned to him by mid-March 2008.

Mr. Mulligan specifically instructed his staff to respond to any inquiries following the February 22, 2008 letter by not discussing the individual settlement awards and instead only communicating the final settlement award of $240 million for all 8,550 claimants ("my office staff is instructed to not discuss settlement awards or offers until they are final. The only settlement amounts given were $240 million for all 8,550 participating claimants and eventually their individual award amount"). On this information, the majority of Mr. Mulligan's clients who decided to participate in the settlement signed the appropriate settlement documents between March and May 2008.

Six months after receiving the court-approved settlement allocation plan that contained base allocation awards, Mr. Mulligan sent his clients a Guidant Settlement Update Letter dated September 19, 2008. In that letter, Mr. Mulligan expressed his frustration with the length of the settlement process and discussed certain terms of the settlement related to participation rates that could impact the final settlement award. With respect to settlement award allocations, Mr. Mulligan stated that the process would not begin until after Guidant makes certain settlement determinations, after which "the Settlement will proceed to award allocation by the Special Masters after which claimants' counsel will be notified of the award allocations for their individual claimants and we will notify you of your original award as soon as we receive that information."

Mr. Mulligan began distributing settlement awards to his clients in January 2009, after the Court issued its first and second allocation orders. In addition to sending a check to his clients, Mr. Mulligan sent a letter to his clients explaining that this Court had ordered that 75% of the settlement awards allocated by the Special Masters be distributed to claimants. Included with each letter was a "Settlement Sheet," which showed the amount of attorney fees and costs deducted from a claimant's settlement allocation. The comments section of the Settlement Sheet stated, among other things, that by cashing the settlement check, the claimant releases "Patrick J. Mulligan and The Mulligan Law Firm, the Special Master and all co-counsel from any and all liability result from or in association with the aforementioned settlement as I fully understand the terms of the settlement and have accepted same." According to Mr. Mulligan's records, this is the first time that his clients were made aware of the monetary amount of their settlement award.

Shortly after the May 7, 2009 status conference, Mr. Mulligan sent another letter to his clients, distancing himself from the allocation process and explaining that the claimants' gross awards may be reduced by a small percentage related to participation-related provisions in the MSA and because of third-party payer liens. Specifically, in a letter dated May 29, 2009, Mr. Mulligan stated:

> The settlement was negotiated by the Plaintiffs' Lead Counsel Committee, also appointed by the Court, in the gross amount of $240 million dollars for 8550 claimants. Our office did not participate in the negotiation of the settlement and was not involved in the allocation of settlement awards. All settlement awards were made by the Special Masters, who were appointed by the Court to make settlement allocations and awards independently and free of any potential conflicts of interest. To date, we have not been provided the individual settlement awards for all 8550 claimants as those are under seal by court order.

## IV. THE COURT'S INTERACTIONS WITH MR. MULLIGAN AND HIS CLIENTS

### *Mr. Mulligan's Complaints About Contingency Fee Cap*

On March 7, 2008, the Court entered an Order that determined the amount of the common benefit attorney fee and capped individual attorney fees. In that Order, the Court allowed a procedure by which individual attorneys could petition the Special Masters for an upward departure from the cap, after which the Court would either approve or decline the Special Masters' recommendation. Mr. Mulligan submitted a petition to the Special Masters dated May 1, 2008. In it, Mr. Mulligan argued that he was entitled to an upward departure because, among other things, "it is important to note that 353 individual Mulligan claimants, accounting for 26% of the Mulligan Docket, are projected to be allocated settlement amounts of no greater that $500 each." When the Special Masters did not recommend a large enough upward departure, Mr. Mulligan submitted an objection to this Court dated July 15, 2008. In that objection, Mr. Mulligan again used the fact that a large percentage of his clients were going to receive a small monetary recovery to support his objection.

### *Complaints by Mr. Mulligan's Clients*

The Court scheduled the May 7, 2009 status conference in response to numerous complaints it had received from Mr. Mulligan's clients. The Court received some of these complaints in response to letters the Court sent to claimants after Mr. Mulligan sought to withdraw as their counsel. A provision in the MSA required Mr. Mulligan to withdraw as counsel in certain circumstances. In response to the Court's letters, some claimants complained that Mr. Mulligan never sent them any correspondence or responded to their letters or telephone calls. The Court previously sanctioned Mr. Mulligan for that behavior in November 2008.

Other clients complained that Mr. Mulligan failed to inform them of their settlement allocation award before they signed the settlement documents or that they were misled into believing that the $240 million settlement was to be divided equally by, at a minimum, 8,550 claimants. As discussed above, Mr. Mulligan admitted to the Court that he and his staff only informed his clients of the aggregate settlement award of $240 million and that he and his staff never gave his clients individual settlement amounts before they signed the releases and bound themselves to participate in the settlement.

Although Mr. Mulligan has repeatedly admitted withholding the settlement ranges from his clients, Mr. Mulligan maintained at the status conference that he was confident that his clients were given "full disclosure" before they signed the releases and that the clients signed the releases with "informed consent." He also stated that the "Texas Ethics Board" had issued an Ethics Opinion approving of his practice of not disclosing settlement ranges to his Guidant MDL clients. Later (but only in response to a question from the Court as to whether Mr. Mulligan had informed the Texas Ethics Board that he had access to projected ranges of settlements that he did not share with his clients), Mr. Mulligan indicated that the Texas Ethics Board had merely dismissed a complaint filed against him. When the board dismissed the complaint, it did not know that Mr. Mulligan had been given a court-approved settlement allocation plan in March 2008.

## DISCUSSION

### Standard of Review

Under its inherent authority noted in a prior Order, the Court reserved the right to sanction certain individual attorneys and/or their firms to pay fees to the common benefit fund if the Court determines that they contributed to the "common detriment of the MDL." An MDL creates a unique situation in which a court may create a common fund from which attorney fees will be paid for those attorneys who have worked for the common benefit of all plaintiffs. An MDL also creates a unique situation in which one attorney's actions can contribute to the common detriment of the MDL by, among other things, damaging the public's trust and confidence in the effectiveness and fairness of the MDL. For this reason and under its inherent authority, the Court reserved the right to sanction an attorney for contributing to the common detriment on the Guidant MDL.

The existence in the federal courts of an inherent power "necessary to the exercise of all others" is firmly established. The inherent power of the federal courts includes the power to "control admission to its bar and to discipline attorneys who appear before it." A court must exercise such power with great caution when fashioning an appropriate sanction, and a court must ensure that an individual receives notice and an opportunity to be heard before imposing any sanction. The Eighth Circuit Court of

Appeals has held that a showing of bad faith is not necessary to support a monetary sanction against counsel, and it has recognized that the bad faith requirement does not extend "to every possible disciplinary exercise of the court's inherent power, especially because such an extension would apply the requirement to even the most routine exercises of inherent power."

The current issue before the Court is whether Mr. Mulligan has contributed to the common detriment of this MDL by, among other things, failing to disclose the allocation plan to his clients. With great caution and after much deliberation, the Court concludes that he has.

In a 14-page memorandum to the Court, Mr. Mulligan provided the Court with "additional information and analysis on the issue of informed consent." In his filings to the Court, Mr. Mulligan improperly assumes, without discussion, that the only issue before the Court is that of "informed consent" and that only the Texas Disciplinary Rules of Professional Conduct apply to his actions. Mr. Mulligan is incorrect on both accounts. First, as discussed above, the Court may impose sanctions against Mr. Mulligan based on its inherent authority. Second, the Minnesota Rules of Professional Responsibility apply to Mr. Mulligan's actions.

The Minnesota Rules of Professional Responsibility, as adopted by the Minnesota Supreme Court, apply to attorneys practicing before this Court. D. Minn. L.R. 83.6(d)(2). "Whenever an attorney applies to be admitted or is admitted to this Court for purposes of a particular proceeding (pro hac vice,) the attorney shall be deemed thereby to have conferred disciplinary jurisdiction upon this Court for any alleged misconduct of that attorney arising in the course of or in the preparation for such proceeding." D. Minn. L.R. 83(h). Mr. Mulligan has been admitted to practice pro hac vice in this Court. Therefore, while Mr. Mulligan may be bound by other states' ethical rules, he is also bound by the Minnesota Rules of Professional Responsibility.

Traditional legal ethic rules are based on the one-attorney, one-client model. But as several commentators have discussed, it is impossible for attorneys representing numerous mass tort victims to have the same type of relationship with their clients as do attorneys who represent only one client in one particular case. While the Court recognizes that an MDL alters the traditional relationship by placing different pressures on attorneys, it does not believe that participation in an MDL excuses an attorney from serving the best interests of his or her clients.

Mr. Mulligan's actions implicate, at a minimum, Minnesota Rules of Professional Responsibility 1.4 and 1.8. Those rules govern communication and conflicts of interest between an attorney and his or her client. Specifically, in relevant part, those rules provide:

Rule 1.4. Communication

(a)  A lawyer shall

(1) promptly inform the client of any decision or circumstance with respect to which the client's informed consent is required by these Rules;

(3)  keep the client reasonably informed about the status of the matter; and

(4) promptly comply with reasonable requests for information;

(b)  A lawyer shall explain a matter to the extent reasonably necessary to permit the client to make informed decisions regarding the representation.

Rule 1.8. Conflict of Interest: Current Clients: Specific Rules

(g)  A lawyer who represents two or more clients shall not participate in making an aggregate settlement of the claims of or against the clients unless each client gives informed consent in a writing signed by the client. The lawyer's disclosure shall include the existence and nature of all the claims involved and of the participation of each person in the settlement.

Minn. Code of Prof. Responsibility 1.4, 1.8; *see also* Minn. Code of Prof. Responsibility 1.4 cmt. 7 (stating that an attorney "may not withhold information to serve the lawyer's own interests or convenience or interests of another person"). While the Court believes that Mr. Mulligan may have violated the Minnesota Rules of Professional Responsibility, it does not reach that precise issue because it is imposing sanctions against Mr. Mulligan under its inherent authority.

*Mr. Mulligan's Rationale*

In his submissions to the Court, Mr. Mulligan explained "the analytical thought process he undertook in deciding how best to communicate with his clients regarding the MDL settlement and why he believed at the time (and still believes today) that his communications were sufficient." In essence, Mr. Mulligan justified his actions by claiming that they "were driven by the particular facts and circumstances of the settlement reached by the PLCC, combined with the Supreme Court's decision in *Riegel v. Medtronic*." He conceded, however, that he does not believe that his disclosures in this case would necessarily be appropriate in another MDL.

Mr. Mulligan gave five reasons for not informing his clients about the settlement allocation plan. First, he claimed that it would have been misleading to do so when there were not assurances that such ranges would be accurate, given the possibility that the settlement awards could be reduced either by the Special Masters or by other provisions in the MSA. Second, based on his experience representing personal injury clients, Mr. Mulligan asserted that he believed that the more conservative route was to give his clients no range, rather than having them feel that they were mislead into a settlement if the projected range turned out to be inaccurate. Third, based on the terms of the MSA, Mr. Mulligan believed that his clients needed only to know that they were agreeing to release their claims in exchange for an award to be determined by the Court-appointed Special Masters. Fourth, because of *Riegel,* Mr. Mulligan explained that he thought providing a range of settlement values would not have been meaningful because the clients' only choice was to participate in the settlement or receive nothing. Fifth, Mr. Mulligan noted that "as a practical matter," he did not provide settlement ranges because "the proposed settlement allocation plan was not referenced in the MSA or any other settlement documents."

Mr. Mulligan believes that his clients gave informed consent to participate in the Guidant settlement because he explained the material terms of the settlement to his clients and told them that the Special Masters, in their sole discretion, would determine each client's individual awards. Mr. Mulligan alleges that because he did not know a meaningful dollar range at the time he asked his clients to enter into the settlement, "communicating a dollar range that turned out to be inaccurate likely would have been far more misleading than no dollar range at all," especially because he believed that *Riegel* foreclosed any possibility of his clients having viable claims outside of the settlement. Mr. Mulligan explains that he did not provide his clients with estimates of their awards because, "as best as he could determine," there were no "final allocations and awards in place that his clients could effectively and meaningfully rely upon in evaluating the settlement proposal." According to Mr. Mulligan, his clients "were not being asked to consent to receiving certain dollar amounts or ranges thereof in exchange for a release but instead were being asked to agree to be a part of a process whereby their dollar recovery (if any) would be determined by the Special Masters."

Mr. Mulligan further believes that his actions were in compliance with the Texas State Bar Rules because the Office of Chief Disciplinary Counsel for State Bar of Texas dismissed a complaint against him. Robert Pena Ayala, a relative of a Guidant device recipient, filed a complaint against Mr. Mulligan, claiming that Mr. Mulligan never informed him as to the amount he might recover as a Guidant claimant and stating that he never would have gone through the settlement process for his somewhat small recovery amount. The Office of Chief Disciplinary Counsel for State Bar of Texas dismissed Mr. Ayala's complaint for failure to allege "a professional misconduct or disability." The Supreme Court of Texas Board of Disciplinary Appeals later affirmed that dismissal.

*Court's Analysis*

The Court disagrees with Mr. Mulligan. By signing the Release, Mr. Mulligan's clients agreed and acknowledged that the settlement was "fair" and "reasonable." Without knowing whether he or she was to receive $1, $500, or $240 million, a client could not agree that a settlement was fair and reasonable. Mr. Mulligan's failure to understand the mechanics of the MSA, in particular the difference between eligible, participating and payment-eligible claimants, and the mechanics of the settlement process does not excuse his actions. Indeed, most of Mr. Mulligan's rationale is based on his erroneous interpretation of the MSA and his complaint that he had no control over the settlement process.

Mr. Mulligan knew as of January 2008 whether his clients were eligible to participate in the settlement, and he knew as of March 2008 the base allocation amounts. Those base allocation amounts were calculated using fixed factors that Mr. Mulligan should have known about each of his clients. Nevertheless, Mr. Mulligan states that he did not inform his clients of the base allocation amounts because those amounts will be reduced by a provision in the MSA that reduces the $240 million settlement fund when there are fewer than 8,400 "participating claimants" in the settlement. It is true that individual base allocation awards will be reduced slightly because there will be fewer than 8,400 participating claimants in the settlement. This slight reduction, however, does not justify Mr. Mulligan's decision to withhold all information from his clients about the base allocation awards. Mr. Mulligan chose to ignore known facts about the settlement process in his communications with his clients, yet he used those same facts in his communications to the Court concerning contingency fees. Mr. Mulligan's use of the settlement allocation plan as both a sword and a shield belies any argument he may have had regarding his lack of knowledge about base settlement awards.

Moreover, Mr. Mulligan's argument that giving a range of recovery to his clients would give them unjustified expectations is untenable. Repeatedly at the status conference, Mr. Mulligan said that he "tried to answer all of our client's questions and give them the best information based on informed consent and I think we did that in this case." Specifically, Mr. Mulligan explained:

> And I think you can do it either one of two ways. You can do it the way the other lawyers may have done it by giving them a proposed range, but that presents problems, or you can specifically tell the clients up front that you are going into an aggregate settlement. The Court is supervising this. The money is going to be split—is going to be determined fairly by a Special Master. You always have a lot of problems that I have found in settlements, that if you give ranges, the clients always stick on the top, on the largest number. They always think they have the worst case and they

should get the highest number. And in addition, at this point we didn't have any EIF awards.

At least with respect to some claimants, however, Mr. Mulligan's actions created grossly distorted expectations because they were only told of the $240 million amount. Mr. Mulligan would have lowered expectations if he would have used the allocation plan and explained to his clients that he could not give them a range for recoveries from the EIF. In general, early communication about the criteria used to evaluate awards helps to manage expectations, rather than to inflate them.

Presumably, Mr. Mulligan did not provide his clients with a settlement range because some claimants would have chosen not to participate in the settlement for nominal awards. Mr. Mulligan's own self-interest would not have been served if all of his clients did not join the settlement, and as a result, he refused to inform his clients of the settlement allocation plan.

Finally, the decision in *Riegel* does not justify his actions. The Court acknowledges that most plaintiffs' lawyers believed at the time of settlement that *Riegel* was the death knell for claims such as those at issue in this MDL. Whether this will hold true for the claims of MDL claimants not participating in the settlement is a matter yet to be decided by the Court, especially in light of the recent announcement that Guidant will plead guilty to two misdemeanor charges related to failure to include information in reports to the U.S. Food and Drug Administration and that Boston Scientific will pay $296 million on behalf of Guidant. Regardless of developments post-*Riegel,* there is nothing in that case that erases Mr. Mulligan's obligations to give his clients the information that was readily available and that was needed to make decisions with respect to participation in the settlement.

In light of the foregoing, and with great caution, the Court concludes that Mr. Mulligan's actions have contributed to the common detriment of this MDL. Mr. Mulligan's actions created situations in which his clients signed the claimants' settlement documents without having all available settlement information given to them. Withholding available information was misleading, and doing so damaged both the integrity of the Guidant MDL and the overall system of justice. Mr. Mulligan's actions contributed to the common detriment of this MDL by, among other things, eroding his clients' trust and confidence in the MDL process and damaging the public's image of the legal profession and the court system. In addition, Mr. Mulligan contributed to the common detriment by causing the PLCC to incur significant additional costs as a result of Mr. Mulligan's actions. Specifically, the PLCC was forced to research and respond to a large number of inquiries from Mr. Mulligan's enraged and bewildered clients and also to work extensively with the many pro se claimants who were Mr. Mulligan's former clients. Ultimately, Mr. Mulligan's conduct contributed to a delay in the disbursement of settlement proceeds for all claimants.

As discussed in previous Orders, the Court has been and continues to be concerned with protecting claimants and the system of justice in this MDL. Lawyers are public servants who are given the privilege, not the right, to practice law. With that privilege, lawyers have a public responsibility to serve the interests of justice. Mr. Mulligan's actions are not compatible with the interests of justice. For these reasons and under its inherent authority, the Court fines Mr. Mulligan $50,000. In addition, the Court will forward a copy of this Order to the Minnesota Office of Lawyers Professional Responsibility, the Office of Chief Disciplinary Counsel for State Bar of Texas, and to the appropriate ethics boards in all states or territories in which a Guidant MDL client of Mr. Mulligan's resides.

## CONCLUSION

Mr. Mulligan founded the Mulligan Law Firm on the philosophy that "every individual client's case is extremely important." The Mulligan Law Firm summarizes its commitment to its clients as follows: "You, the client, are our priority." Unfortunately in the Guidant MDL, Mr. Mulligan has neither abided by his firm's philosophy nor made his clients a priority.

As the Court stated at the May 7, 2009 status conference, it is a sad day for the legal profession (in particular those that practice in the area of mass torts) if Mr. Mulligan's conduct towards his clients is the norm. Indeed, if such a practice were the norm, the Court concludes that multi-district litigation would not serve the interests of litigants or justice and should be discontinued. Luckily, based on the Court's interaction with other claimants' lawyers in this MDL, the Court believes that Mr. Mulligan's conduct is the exception, rather than the rule.

# CHAPTER 3

RESOLVING MASS TORTS THROUGH RULE 23 LITIGATION CLASSES: HISTORICAL BACKGROUND (I)

■ ■ ■

## A.  THE CLASS ACTION RULE AND MASS TORTS

### Federal Rule of Civil Procedure 23

**(a)  Prerequisites.** One or more members of a class may sue or be sued as representative parties on behalf of all members only if:

**(1)** the class is so numerous that joinder of all members is impracticable;

**(2)** there are questions of law or fact common to the class;

**(3)** the claims or defenses of the representative parties are typical of the claims or defenses of the class; and

**(4)** the representative parties will fairly and adequately protect the interests of the class.

**(b)  Types of Class Actions.** A class action may be maintained if Rule 23(a) is satisfied and if:

**(1)** prosecuting separate actions by or against individual class members would create a risk of:

**(A)** inconsistent or varying adjudications with respect to individual class members that would establish incompatible standards of conduct for the party opposing the class; or

**(B)** adjudications with respect to individual class members that, as a practical matter, would be dispositive of the interests of the other members not parties to the individual adjudications or would substantially impair or impede their ability to protect their interests;

**(2)** the party opposing the class has acted or refused to act on grounds that apply generally to the class, so that final injunctive relief or corresponding declaratory relief is appropriate respecting the class as a whole; or

**(3)** the court finds that the questions of law or fact common to class members predominate over any questions affecting only individual members, and that a class action is superior to other available methods for fairly and efficiently adjudicating the controversy. The matters pertinent to these findings include:

> **(A)** the class members' interests in individually controlling the prosecution or defense of separate actions;
>
> **(B)** the extent and nature of any litigation concerning the controversy already begun by or against class members;
>
> **(C)** the desirability or undesirability of concentrating the litigation of the claims in the particular forum; and
>
> **(D)** the likely difficulties in managing a class action.

**(c) Certification Order; Notice to Class Members; Judgment; Issues Classes; Subclasses.**

> **(1)** *Certification Order.*
>
> > **(A)** *Time to Issue.* At an early practicable time after a person sues or is sued as a class representative, the court must determine by order whether to certify the action as a class action.
> >
> > **(B)** *Defining the Class; Appointing Class Counsel.* An order that certifies a class action must define the class and the class claims, issues, or defenses, and must appoint class counsel under Rule 23(g).
> >
> > **(C)** *Altering or Amending the Order.* An order that grants or denies class certification may be altered or amended before final judgment.
>
> **(2)** *Notice.*
>
> > **(A)** *For (b)(1) or (b)(2) Classes.* For any class certified under Rule 23(b)(1) or (b)(2), the court may direct appropriate notice to the class.
> >
> > **(B)** *For (b)(3) Classes.* For any class certified under Rule 23(b)(3), the court must direct to class members the best notice that is practicable under the circumstances, including individual notice to all members who can be identified through reasonable effort. The notice must clearly and concisely state in plain, easily understood language:
> >
> > > **(i)** the nature of the action;
> > >
> > > **(ii)** the definition of the class certified;
> > >
> > > **(iii)** the class claims, issues, or defenses;

**(iv)** that a class member may enter an appearance through an attorney if the member so desires;

**(v)** that the court will exclude from the class any member who requests exclusion;

**(vi)** the time and manner for requesting exclusion; and

**(vii)** the binding effect of a class judgment on members under Rule 23(c)(3).

**(3)** *Judgment.* Whether or not favorable to the class, the judgment in a class action must:

**(A)** for any class certified under Rule 23(b)(1) or (b)(2), include and describe those whom the court finds to be class members; and

**(B)** for any class certified under Rule 23(b)(3), include and specify or describe those to whom the Rule 23(c)(2) notice was directed, who have not requested exclusion, and whom the court finds to be class members.

**(4)** *Particular Issues.* When appropriate, an action may be brought or maintained as a class action with respect to particular issues.

**(5)** *Subclasses.* When appropriate, a class may be divided into subclasses that are each treated as a class under this rule.

**(d)** **Conducting the Action.**

**(1)** *In General.* In conducting an action under this rule, the court may issue orders that:

**(A)** determine the course of proceedings or prescribe measures to prevent undue repetition or complication in presenting evidence or argument;

**(B)** require—to protect class members and fairly conduct the action—giving appropriate notice to some or all class members of:

**(i)** any step in the action;

**(ii)** the proposed extent of the judgment; or

**(iii)** the members' opportunity to signify whether they consider the representation fair and adequate, to intervene and present claims or defenses, or to otherwise come into the action;

**(C)** impose conditions on the representative parties or on intervenors;

**(D)** require that the pleadings be amended to eliminate allegations about representation of absent persons and that the action proceed accordingly; or

**(E)** deal with similar procedural matters.

**(2)** *Combining and Amending Orders.* An order under Rule 23(d)(1) may be altered or amended from time to time and may be combined with an order under Rule 16.

**(e) Settlement, Voluntary Dismissal, or Compromise.** The claims, issues, or defenses of a certified class may be settled, voluntarily dismissed, or compromised only with the court's approval. The following procedures apply to a proposed settlement, voluntary dismissal, or compromise:

**(1)** The court must direct notice in a reasonable manner to all class members who would be bound by the proposal.

**(2)** If the proposal would bind class members, the court may approve it only after a hearing and on finding that it is fair, reasonable, and adequate.

**(3)** The parties seeking approval must file a statement identifying any agreement made in connection with the proposal.

**(4)** If the class action was previously certified under Rule 23(b)(3), the court may refuse to approve a settlement unless it affords a new opportunity to request exclusion to individual class members who had an earlier opportunity to request exclusion but did not do so.

**(5)** Any class member may object to the proposal if it requires court approval under this subdivision (e); the objection may be withdrawn only with the court's approval.

**(f) Appeals.** A court of appeals may permit an appeal from an order granting or denying class-action certification under this rule if a petition for permission to appeal is filed with the circuit clerk within 14 days after the order is entered. An appeal does not stay proceedings in the district court unless the district judge or the court of appeals so orders.

**(g) Class Counsel.**

**(1)** *Appointing Class Counsel.* Unless a statute provides otherwise, a court that certifies a class must appoint class counsel. In appointing class counsel, the court:

**(A)** must consider:

**(i)** the work counsel has done in identifying or investigating potential claims in the action;

**(ii)** counsel's experience in handling class actions, other complex litigation, and the types of claims asserted in the action;

**(iii)** counsel's knowledge of the applicable law; and

**(iv)** the resources that counsel will commit to representing the class;

**(B)** may consider any other matter pertinent to counsel's ability to fairly and adequately represent the interests of the class;

**(C)** may order potential class counsel to provide information on any subject pertinent to the appointment and to propose terms for attorney's fees and nontaxable costs;

**(D)** may include in the appointing order provisions about the award of attorney's fees or nontaxable costs under Rule 23(h); and

**(E)** may make further orders in connection with the appointment.

**(2)** *Standard for Appointing Class Counsel.* When one applicant seeks appointment as class counsel, the court may appoint that applicant only if the applicant is adequate under Rule 23(g)(1) and (4). If more than one adequate applicant seeks appointment, the court must appoint the applicant best able to represent the interests of the class.

**(3)** *Interim Counsel.* The court may designate interim counsel to act on behalf of a putative class before determining whether to certify the action as a class action.

**(4)** *Duty of Class Counsel.* Class counsel must fairly and adequately represent the interests of the class.

**(h)** **Attorney's Fees and Nontaxable Costs.** In a certified class action, the court may award reasonable attorney's fees and nontaxable costs that are authorized by law or by the parties' agreement. The following procedures apply:

**(1)** A claim for an award must be made by motion under Rule 54(d)(2), subject to the provisions of this subdivision (h), at a time the court sets. Notice of the motion must be served on all parties and, for motions by class counsel, directed to class members in a reasonable manner.

**(2)** A class member, or a party from whom payment is sought, may object to the motion.

**(3)** The court may hold a hearing and must find the facts and state its legal conclusions under Rule 52(a).

**(4)** The court may refer issues related to the amount of the award to a special master or a magistrate judge, as provided in Rule 54(d)(2)(D).

**Supplementary Note of the Advisory
Committee Regarding This Rule,
1966 Amendment**

**Subdivision (b)(3).** The court is required to find, as a condition of holding that a class action may be maintained under this subdivision, that the questions common to the class predominate over the questions affecting individual members. It is only where this predominance exists that economies can be achieved by means of the class-action device. In this view, a fraud perpetrated on numerous persons by the use of similar misrepresentations may be an appealing situation for a class action, and it may remain so despite the need, if liability is found, for separate determination of the damages suffered by individuals within the class. On the other hand, although having some common core, a fraud case may be unsuited for treatment as a class action if there was material variation in the representations made or in the kinds or degrees of reliance by the persons to whom they were addressed. A "mass accident" resulting in injuries to numerous persons is ordinarily not appropriate for a class action because of the likelihood that significant questions, not only of damages but of liability and defenses of liability, would be present, affecting the individuals in different ways. In these circumstances an action conducted nominally as a class action would degenerate in practice into multiple lawsuits separately tried. Private damage claims by numerous individuals arising out of concerted antitrust violations may or may not involve predominating common questions.

## B.  MAPPING POSSIBLE APPROACHES TO RESOLVING MASS TORT LITIGATION

### IN RE AGENT ORANGE PROD. LIAB. LITIG.

United States District Court, Eastern District New York, 1980.
506 F.Supp. 762.

Plaintiffs, Vietnam war veterans and members of their families claiming to have suffered damage as a result of the veterans' exposure to herbicides in Vietnam, commenced these actions against the defendant chemical companies. Defendants, seeking indemnification or contribution in the event they are held liable to plaintiffs, then served third party complaints against the United States. Five motions are now considered: (1) the government's motion to dismiss the third party complaint on grounds of sovereign immunity; (2) plaintiffs' motion for class action certification; (3) defendants' motion for summary judgment; (4) plaintiffs' motion to proceed with "serial trials," and (5) plaintiffs' motion to serve and file a fifth amended verified complaint.

### I.  SUMMARY OF CLAIMS

There are four groups of plaintiffs: Vietnam veterans, their spouses, their parents, and their children. They assert numerous theories of liability, including strict products liability, negligence, breach of warranty, intentional tort and nuisance. Plaintiff veterans seek to recover for personal injuries caused by their exposure to Agent Orange. The family members seek to recover on various derivative claims; some of the children assert claims in their own right for genetic injury and birth defects caused by their parents' exposure to the Agent Orange; and some of the veterans' wives seek to recover in their own right for miscarriages. In their third party complaints against the government defendants allege negligence, misuse of product, post-discharge failure to warn, implied indemnity, denial of due process and failure to comply with herbicide registration laws.

### III. THE CASE MANAGEMENT PLAN

There have been pending for some time motions by various parties urging the court to make various orders affecting the overall management of this action, including such matters as class action treatment, summary judgment, discovery, and division of the action into various parts for pretrial and trial purposes. The court has reserved decision on all these motions pending resolution of two major questions that greatly affect how the case might be managed efficiently: (1) whether the United States was to be a party to the action, and (2) whether jurisdiction lies under federal common law or whether the principles and consequences of diversity jurisdiction must be considered. Now that both of these questions have been answered, it is time to get on with orderly discovery and ultimate disposition of the litigation.

In developing the case management plan described in this section, the court has weighed and considered many problems presented by this litigation. Some of them are:

1.    There are a large number of plaintiffs and potential plaintiffs who claim to have been injured by exposure to Agent Orange. There are now approximately 167 suits pending in the Eastern District of New York involving over 3,400 plaintiffs. The court has been informed that there are many thousands more who have, at the court's request and pending decision of the class action motion, refrained from bringing individual actions.

2.    There are numerous chemical companies named as defendants. The fact that they may have had differing degrees of involvement in manufacturing and supplying Agent Orange for the government may or may not cause differing levels of responsibility for the effects of Agent Orange on plaintiffs.

3.    The present plaintiffs come from most of the 50 states and from Australia. This may require consideration of varying standards of conduct, rules of causation and principles of damages that may substantially affect the results in individual cases.

4.    The causation issues are difficult and complex. Clearly this is not the "simple" type of "disaster" litigation such as an airplane crash involving a single incident, having a causation picture that is readily grasped through conventional litigation techniques, and presenting comparatively small variations among the claimants as to the effects upon them of the crash. With the Agent Orange litigation, injuries are claimed to have

resulted from exposure to a chemical that was disseminated in the air over Southeast Asia during a period of several years. Each veteran was exposed differently, although undoubtedly patterns of exposure will emerge. The claimed injuries vary significantly. Moreover, there is a major dispute over whether Agent Orange can cause the injuries in question, and there are separate disputes over whether the exposure claimed in each case did cause the injuries claimed. The picture is further complicated by the use in Vietnam of other chemicals and drugs that also are claimed to be capable of causing many of the injuries attributed to Agent Orange.

5.   The litigation presents numerous questions of law that lie at the frontier of modern tort jurisprudence. Among them are questions of enterprise liability, strict products liability, liability for injuries that appear long after original exposure to the offending substance, and liability for so-called genetic injuries.

6.   Many of the people exposed to Agent Orange may not even yet have experienced the harm it may cause.

7.   Numerous scientific and medical issues are presented, and there are serious questions of whether there is adequate data to reach scientifically sound conclusions about them. There is the further question of whether legally permissible conclusions may nevertheless be reached on data that would not permit "scientific" conclusions.

8.   Various agencies of the government have expressed concern but as yet have shown little tangible action about the problems claimed to have been caused by the government's use of Agent Orange.

9.   There are important and conflicting public policies that run as crosscurrents through many phases of both the substantive and procedural problems of this litigation.

10.  There is a wide choice available among the many procedural devices that could be used for addressing and ultimately deciding this controversy. All of these problems are compounded by the practical realities of having on one side of the litigation plaintiffs who seek damages, but who have limited resources with which to press their claims and whose plight becomes more desperate and depressing as time goes on, and having on the other side defendants who strenuously contest their liability, who have ample resources for counsel and expert witnesses to defend them, and who probably gain significantly, although immeasurably, from every delay that they can produce. Overarching the entire dispute is a feeling on both sides that whatever existing law and procedures may technically require, fairness, justice and equity in this unprecedented controversy demand that the government assume responsibility for the harm caused our soldiers and their families by its use of Agent Orange in Southeast Asia.

Out of these and other problems it is this court's task as the transferee judge in this multidistrict litigation to supervise and manage the action so as to bring it to a "just, speedy and inexpensive determination," Fed.R.Civ.P. Rule 1, either in this court, or if that is not possible, then in the transferor courts after completion here of as much of the litigation as may fairly and reasonably be resolved under the supervision of this single judge. With the foregoing and other problems in mind, the court has considered a variety of possibilities for managing this multidistrict litigation. Each possibility has both advantages and disadvantages. Among the numerous possibilities are the following:

1.    Transfer all actions to the Eastern District of New York for trial before this court.

a.    *Advantages:* All parties would know precisely where they stand, and how the action would be handled. There would tend to be consistency in the results to the extent permitted by the varying applicable laws.

b.    *Disadvantages:* Handling the cases would take the full time of this court, which would be able to handle no other cases, a result that would be unfair not only to the other judges in the Eastern District of New York who are already overburdened with one of the heaviest criminal workloads in the nation, but also to other civil litigants in the Eastern District, who would be further delayed in getting their cases to trial. Moreover, to separately try these actions would take far too long a time; probably neither the litigants nor this court would live long enough to see the last case tried.

2.    Supervise all discovery, prepare a pretrial order, and then remand the cases for separate trials in the transferor districts around the country.

a.    *Advantages:* This is by far the easiest course of action for this court to take. In many MDL cases this is an acceptable and proper technique and achieves all of the MDL benefits available to those cases. It accomplishes coordinated discovery, a single plan for processing up through the pretrial order, and a shared workload in the actual trial of the individual actions.

b.    *Disadvantages:* This technique would require separate trials of each action in the transferor courts, a technique that would be repetitious and wasteful with respect to the issues that are common to all actions. Although testimony of key expert witnesses might be made available to each of the transferor courts through use of videotape so that the need for those witnesses to personally appear at each trial would thereby be eliminated, the opportunity to cross-examine the experts on special problems that relate to the individual plaintiffs would still be lost. The greatest disadvantage of this method is that it would place unnecessary burdens on each of the transferor judges, each of whom would have to struggle with identical legal and factual issues, and it would thus fail to reach the level of judicial efficiency and economy that MDL procedures were designed to achieve.

3.    Coordinate discovery and other pretrial work, consolidate the actions for trial of the common issues of fact and law, and then remand to

the transferor districts for separate trials of the individual issues such as specific causation and damages.

*a.    Advantages:* A single trial of common issues has obvious benefits in economy and efficiency. Spreading to other courts the workload of trying individual cases at least makes a judicial solution to this litigation possible in terms of time and workloads.

*b.    Disadvantages:* The consolidation technique addresses only the pending actions, that is, it involves those situations where the plaintiff has seized the initiative and brought suit. However, there are many people with valid claims who for one reason or another have not asserted them by bringing suit and who would therefore not recover for damages inflicted, including damages of which they might not yet even be aware.

4.    Certify the litigation as a class action, using all the flexibility of that device, including subclasses, to determine common issues before this court and ultimately determine the individual issues either under the direct supervision of this court or after remand to other courts.

*a.    Advantages:* Class action treatment would give this court full control over the entire litigation. Any determinations reached in the class action would bind all defendants as well as all members of the class except those who chose to opt out, and as to them, their suits could be consolidated for joint trial with the class action. By use of subclasses to be certified as the need later arises, additional trials on issues common to identified subclasses may be conducted either here in the Eastern District of New York, or by the transferor courts after remand, or by a combination of both. This method provides the greatest flexibility and the greatest opportunity for judicial efficiency and economy of time and money.

*b.    Disadvantages:* The disadvantages with class action treatment lie largely in technical and procedural problems that have arisen with the class action device in other contexts. Such problems have proved particularly troublesome in the context of mass tort cases. Having considered carefully the nature of those technical problems, this court is satisfied that they can be overcome by following the case management plan described in this section and the steps described under the section entitled "Class Action". After considering the submissions and arguments of the parties and after weighing all of the foregoing and many other considerations, the court has developed the following plan for management of the Agent Orange litigation assigned to it under MDL No. 381:

1.    Class action. The *Agent Orange* litigation will be certified as a class action under Fed.R.Civ.P. 23(b)(3).

## IV.  CLASS ACTION

Contending that many of the issues here presented are best determined by class action to avoid duplicitous litigation by the individual members of the proposed class, plaintiffs have moved for a conditional order pursuant to Fed.R.Civ.P. 23 permitting the suit to proceed as a class action on behalf of all persons exposed to Agent Orange and various members of their families. Under Rule 23(c)(1) and 23(d), the order would be subject to such later modification as the court may find appropriate and necessary in light of future developments in the case.

Before a class action may be maintained under Rule 23, the action must meet the prerequisites of Rule 23(a) and one set of the alternate requirements of Rule 23(b). Defendants oppose class treatment, but continue to advance some outrageous arguments in the name of advocacy; detracting from whatever valid arguments they might otherwise have, they argue that plaintiffs fail to satisfy even one of the elements necessary under Rule 23. Plaintiffs, equally undiscriminating in their advocacy, argue that every element of every alternative of Rule 23 is met here.

The court has carefully read and considered the voluminous submissions of the parties and has heard and considered oral arguments of counsel on this issue. After due consideration, the court determines that plaintiffs have demonstrated that a class action is appropriate under Rule 23(b)(3). Accordingly, plaintiffs' motion for conditional class action certification is granted as herein provided. Certain specific findings are required.

### A.   The Prerequisites of Rule 23(a)

#### 1.   Numerosity

The members of the plaintiff class here are so numerous that joinder of all members of the class in the same action is impracticable. Rule 23(a)(1). Indeed, if the only members of the class were the plaintiffs in the 167 actions now pending in this court, "numerosity" would be satisfied.

#### 2.   Commonality

Rule 23(a)(2) states that a class action may only be maintained if "there are questions of law or fact common to the class." Here, the action raises numerous questions of law and fact common to the class. Whatever may be the individual questions relating to the manner and extent of each veteran's exposure to Agent Orange, and relating to the particular effects of Agent Orange on the veteran when considered along with his/her medical history, circumstances, lifestyle and other unique conditions, all of these claims share a common ground when proceeding through the many factual and legal issues relating to the government contract defense, negligence by the defendants, whether Agent Orange was a "defective product," and the many questions embodied in the concept of "general causation." In part, the requirement of commonality is one aimed at determining whether there is a need for combined treatment and a benefit to be derived therefrom. Here the need is compelling, and the benefits are substantial.

### 3.  Typicality

Rule 23(a)(3) requires that in a class action "the claims or defenses of the representative parties be typical of the claims or defenses of the class." As already noted, plaintiffs' claims of negligence, products liability and general causation, as well as the defendants' government contract defense are not just "typical" of the entire class, they are identical. In a few areas, such as the rules governing liability and the application of various statutes of limitations, the claims may fall into groups that are "typical," but even there the different groups' claims can be efficiently managed either on a subclass basis or directly by way of separately determining the issues. Although the named plaintiffs for purposes of the class action are yet to be designated, the court is satisfied that out of the extremely large pool available representative plaintiffs can be named who will present claims typical of those of the class. As already indicated, the issues of specific causation and damages will, of course, ultimately require individual consideration, but until that point in the litigation is reached, a class action appears to be the only practicable means for managing the lawsuit.

### 4.  Adequacy

Rule 23(a)(4) provides that a class action may only be maintained if "the representative parties will fairly and adequately protect the interests of the class." Adequacy of representation depends on the qualifications and interests of counsel for the class representatives, the absence of antagonism or conflicting interests, and a sharing of interests between class representatives and absentees. Here, the court will select from among the hundreds of plaintiffs representative persons who have a substantial stake in the litigation, who lack conflicts, antagonisms or reasons to be motivated by factors inconsistent with the motives of absentee class members, and who will fairly and adequately protect the interests of the class. Further the class will be represented by experienced, capable counsel, Yannacone & Associates, who have shown themselves willing to undertake the considerable commitment of time, energy and money necessary for the vigorous prosecution of the claims here asserted.

### 5.  Additional Requirements

Courts have implied two additional prerequisites to class action certification that are not specifically mentioned in Rule 23: (1) there must be an identifiable class, and (2) the class representatives must be members of the class. Here, the plaintiff class can be readily identified; they are persons who claim injury from exposure to Agent Orange and their spouses, children and parents who claim direct or derivative injury therefrom. The court has intentionally defined the class in broad terms consistent with the demands of this litigation. If we begin with the broadest possible class, the issues common to all members of that class can be resolved. It may later prove advantageous to create subclasses for various purposes, e.g., for resolving statute of limitations claims, for determining liability in "negligence" as opposed to "product liability" states, and finally, perhaps, for preserving the class action format prior to remand to the transferor judges so as to provide them with the greatest possible flexibility in ultimately determining the issues remaining after multidistrict treatment has ended.

### B.   The Requirements of Rule 23(b)

Plaintiffs seek certification of a plaintiff class under Rule 23(b)(1)(A), (b)(1)(B), (b)(2) and (b)(3). For the reasons set forth below, however, the court concludes that class certification is appropriate only under Rule 23(b)(3).

### 1.   Rule 23(b)(1)

Rule 23(b)(1), the "prejudice" class action provision, authorizes class action treatment if some prejudice would result to any party if members of the class were required to litigate their claims in a series of individual actions, and the resulting prejudice can be obviated by using a class action. The provision is broken down into two separate clauses. Rule 23(b)(1)(A) authorizes a class action when the prosecution of separate actions would create a risk of "inconsistent or varying adjudications with respect to individual members of the class which would establish incompatible standards of conduct for the party opposing the class." This section focuses on the difficulties that class action certification may visit on the party opposing the class action. It is designed to prevent situations in which different courts establish "incompatible standards of conduct" for that party. Rule 23(b)(1)(A) is not meant to apply, however, where the risk of inconsistent results in individual actions is merely the possibility that the defendants will prevail in some cases and not in others, thereby paying damages to some claimants and not others. "The risk of paying money damages to some and not others is not what the rule-makers intended by the words 'incompatible standards of conduct.'" Since the only effect of inconsistent decisions here would be the payment of damages to some claimants and not others, class certification under Rule 23(b)(1)(A) would be inappropriate.

Rule 23(b)(1)(B) authorizes a class action when separate actions would create a risk of "adjudications with respect to individual members of the class which would as a practical matter be dispositive of the interest of the other members not parties to the adjudications or substantially impair or impede their ability to protect their interest." This rule emphasizes possible undesirable effects on the class members, rather than on the opposing party, and permits a class action if separate suits might have undesirable effects on the class members. "The paradigm Rule 23(b)(1)(B) case is one in which there are multiple claimants to a limited fund and there is a risk that if litigants are allowed to proceed on an individual basis those who sue first will deplete the fund and leave nothing for the late-comers."

However large the potential damages may appear here, plaintiffs offer no evidence of the likely insolvency of defendants and apparently do not, in defendant Dow's words, "have the temerity to argue that the aggregate claims of the purported class exceed the total assets of the five named defendants." For good measure, Dow adds "such an argument would be ludicrous on its face." As one court has noted, "without more, numerous plaintiffs and a large *ad damnum* clause should not guarantee (b)(1)(B) certification." Thus, certification under Rule 23(b)(1)(B) is not appropriate.

### 2.   Rule 23(b)(2)

Rule 23(b)(2) authorizes class action treatment where "the party opposing the class has acted or refused to act on grounds generally applicable to the class, thereby making appropriate final injunctive relief or corresponding declaratory relief with respect to the class as a whole." This subdivision "does not extend to cases in which the appropriate final relief relates exclusively or predominately to money damages;" rather, it applies when injunctive relief or declaratory relief on which injunctive relief could be based is proper. Here, the relief requested relates predominately to money damages so the class may not be certified under Rule 23(b)(2).

### 3.   Rule 23(b)(3)

Rule 23(b)(3) authorizes a class action when the court finds "that the questions of law or fact common to the members of the class predominate over any questions affecting only individual members, and that a class action is superior to all other available methods for the fair and efficient adjudication of the controversy." The rule lists four matters pertinent to a consideration of these issues:

> (A) the interest of members of the class in individually controlling the prosecution or defense of separate actions; (B) the extent and nature of any litigation concerning the controversy already commenced by or against members of the class; (C) the desirability or un-desirability of concentrating the litigation of the claims in the particular forum; (D) the difficulties likely to be encountered in the management of a class action.

Considering the circumstances of this action, and bearing in mind the manner in which the class action will proceed, the court determines that the interest of class members in individually controlling the prosecution of separate actions is minimal, especially at this early stage of the litigation when the issues under consideration concern the relationship between the defendants and the government, issues that impact equally on every plaintiff's claim. Rule 23(b)(3)(A). Later stages of this litigation, especially those concerned with individual causation and damages, may require reconsideration of this element and possibly decertification, but at this stage, individual class members have almost no interest in individually controlling the prosecution of separate actions. Indeed, the problems inherent in every one of the individual actions are so great that it is doubtful if a single plaintiff represented by a single attorney pursuing an individual action could ever succeed.

With respect to the extent and nature of currently pending litigation, almost all the *Agent Orange* litigation currently pending is before this court under the multidistrict litigation procedures. All those cases are advancing simultaneously, and certification of a class action will serve the goals of judicial economy and reduce the possibility of multiple lawsuits. Rule 23(b)(3)(B). In addition, it will significantly expedite final resolution of this controversy. With respect to the desirability of concentrating the litigation of the claims in this forum, the actions have already been concentrated before this court through the use of MDL procedures. Allowing it to proceed as a class action will minimize the hazards of duplicate efforts and inconsistent results. Moreover, given the location of present counsel and the widely varying citizenships of the interested parties, this court is as appropriate a place to settle the controversy as any. Rule 23(b)(3)(C).

With respect to the difficulties likely to be encountered in the management of a class action, the court has carefully and humbly considered the management problems presented by an action of this magnitude and complexity, and concluded that great as they are, the difficulties likely to be encountered by managing these actions as a class action are significantly outweighed by the truly overwhelming problems that would attend any other management device chosen. While the burdens on this court might be lessened by denying class certification, those imposed collectively on the transferor courts after remand of the multidistrict cases would be increased many times. Having carefully considered the above factors and all other circumstances of this action, the court is satisfied that at this time the questions of law and fact common to the members of the class predominate over questions of law or fact affecting only individual members, and that a class action is superior to any other available method for the fair and efficient adjudication of the controversy.

Because over a year ago this court requested plaintiffs not to file actions pending decision on the class action motion, because the facts and issues in all of the pending and future cases are to a great degree identical, or at least parallel, and because this action presents a variety of questions in relatively untested areas of the law, this court sees the objectives of Fed.R.Civ.P. Rule 1 and Rule 23, as well as the interests of justice, best served by determining here, and for all parties, as many legal and factual issues as may properly be decided. To achieve those ends the court will certify this to be a class action under Fed.R.Civ.P. 23(c). Formal certification will be by separate order to be processed under the court's instructions.

# C.  HISTORICAL RESISTANCE TO MASS TORT LITIGATION CLASSES

## YANDLE V. PPG INDUSTRIES, INC.

United States District Court, Eastern District of Texas, 1974.

65 F.R.D. 566.

This is a massive tort action brought by former employees and survivors of former employees of the Pittsburgh Corning Corporation asbestos plant that was located in Tyler, Texas. The question before the Court is whether this case should proceed as a class action under the provisions of Rule 23(b)(3). Before passing on this question, it will be necessary for the Court to review the background of this litigation and the law on the use of class actions in mass tort cases.

By the way of history, Pittsburgh Corning purchased the plant in question from Union Asbestos and Rubber Company and began operations in 1962, producing asbestos insulation materials. The plant continued operations over a ten year period through February of 1972, when it closed its doors forever. The records of Pittsburgh Corning Corporation show that during the plant's existence some 570 employees were exposed to asbestos dust and these employees may be broken down into the following categories. These persons were employed in several different positions at the plant and they were, therefore, exposed to varying concentrations of asbestos dust during their periods of employment.

Suit was brought originally against nine defendants in January, 1974, by six former employees and one survivor of a former employee of Pittsburgh Corning on behalf of themselves and others similarly situated. These plaintiffs allege that due to exposure to asbestos fibers over a lengthy period of time that they "suffer from various stages of asbestosis and/or lung cancer and/or other pulmonary disease."

Different theories of recovery were asserted against the various defendants. Negligence is attributed to PPG Industries and Corning Glass Works for failing to correct the deficiencies at the Tyler plant and in failing to warn the employees of the danger of asbestos exposure. Additionally, plaintiffs contend that Dr. Lee Grant, as an agent or employee of PPG, knew the hazards posed to the workers' health, yet he failed to advise such workers of the hazards and was therefore negligent. Essentially the same allegations are made against the Industrial Health Foundation. As to the defendant, Asbestos Textile Institute, plaintiffs claim that this unincorporated association was negligent because it impeded the flow of information about the health hazards involved in asbestos manufacturing. These plaintiffs claim that all of these actions constituted gross negligence on the part of each defendant.

The plaintiffs assert a strict liability theory against North American Asbestos, E.G.N.E.P. Limited, and Cape Asbestos Company. They allege that these defendants were in the business of mining and selling raw amosite-asbestos to Pittsburgh Corning and they failed to warn the plaintiffs of the danger, thereby rendering them strictly liable. Finally, as to the plaintiffs' employer, Pittsburgh Corning, it is alleged that they are liable for exemplary damages under the Texas Workmen's Compensation Act to all statutory beneficiaries of deceased employees who died as a result of their alleged gross negligence. Plaintiffs allege total actual and exemplary damages for the class to be at least one hundred million dollars.

In passing upon the class action question presented herein, the Court will confine its discussion to the liability issues, since the plaintiffs appear to have conceded at the December 17, 1974, hearing on this question that the damage issues are not proper for class treatment because they require individualized determination.

Class actions have had limited application in the past in mass tort cases, partially due to the recommendation of the Advisory Committee on Rules. In its 1966 revision of Rule 23, the Advisory Committee stated:

> A mass accident's resulting in injuries to numerous persons is ordinarily not appropriate for a class action because of the likelihood that significant questions, not only of damages but of liability and defenses of liability, would be present, affecting the individuals in different ways. In these circumstances an action conducted nominally as a class action would degenerate in practice into multiple lawsuits separately tried.

The policy reasons for the disallowance of class actions in mass tort cases generally fall into three categories. First of all there is the general feeling that when personal injuries are involved that each person should have the right to prosecute his own claim and be represented by the lawyer of his choice. Secondly, that the use of this procedure may encourage solicitation of business by attorneys. And finally that individual issues may predominate because the tortfeasor's defenses may depend on facts peculiar to each plaintiff.

There are situations where the class action device may properly be used in mass accident cases, at least for the common questions that will apply to each class member equally. Thus, in *Hernandez v. Motor Vessel Skyward*, the court utilized it to try a single issue only: Whether the defendant was negligent in preparing the food and water that caused the passengers on the M/V SKYWARD to become ill. The court found that the plaintiff's other theories, breach of contract, negligence in medical care and implied warranty of fitness, as well as the question of proximate causation were not proper for class treatment. In *American Trading and Production Corp. v. Fischbach & Moore, Inc.*, the court allowed a class action to be maintained on the liability issues and reserved the damage questions for individual treatment. That case involved a suit by some 1200 exhibitors of housewares who suffered losses because of a fire at the exhibition hall. The Court said that class treatment would be proper on the liability issue because identical evidence would be required to establish the origin of the fire, the parties responsible, and proximate cause. A similar opinion was expressed by the court in *Petition of Gabel*, a case which involved a collision between an airliner and a military jet. In that case the court stated that the liability issues could expeditiously be treated as a class action because there was one common set of operative facts and a single wrongful invasion of a single primary right was involved. The damage issues were to be tried separately because there was "a peculiar and different set of facts applicable to the amount of damages of each different plaintiff in the class."

Other courts facing this question have reached contrary conclusions and have refused to allow a class action to be maintained on any of the issues in the case. In *Hobbs v. Northeast Airlines, Inc.*, some 32 persons were killed in an air crash which also left ten survivors. In deciding that common questions of law and fact did not predominate over questions affecting the individual members, the Court said:

> But irrespective of similarities or dissimilarities in the legal standards to be applied to a particular defendant, it is clear that each claimant in this situation may properly be regarded as having a legitimate interest in litigating independently. Not only do the claims vitally affect a significant aspect of the lives of the claimants (unlike the usual class action, where individual claims are usually somewhat peripheral to the lives of the claimants), but there is a wide range of choice of the strategy and tactics of the litigation. Some claimants may well evaluate their chances against certain potential defendants as better than against others.

The Court went on to say that the class action device would not be superior to other available methods because persons wishing to join the litigation could intervene if they wished and the case would proceed under the Multidistrict Litigation Statute. In a case which involved the crash of a school bus, the court in *Daye v. Commonwealth of Pennsylvania* held that although liability would be a common issue, that the cause could not be maintained as a class action. After taking note of the advisory committee recommendation on the use of class actions in mass accident cases, the court concluded that in view of the fact that there were two actions presently pending and that there would be personal injury and death claims involving different measure of damages, a class action would be improper under Rule 23(b)(3).

Setting this problem aside and assuming for the purpose of argument that the plaintiffs have established the four requirements set forth in Rule 23(a), the court is of the opinion that this case is not proper for (b)(3) class certification because the plaintiffs have not shown that the questions common to the class predominate over the questions that affect the individual members. Further, the court is of the opinion that a class action is simply not the superior method for adjudication of this cause.

### THE COMMON QUESTIONS DO NOT PREDOMINATE

As noted previously, the Pittsburgh Corning plant was in operation in Tyler for a ten year period, during which some 570 persons were employed for different periods of time. These employees worked in various positions at the plant, and some were exposed to greater concentrations of asbestos dust than were others. Of these employees it is only natural that some may have had occupational diseases when they entered their employment for Pittsburgh Corning. There are other issues that will be peculiar to each plaintiff and will predominate in this case, such as: The employee's knowledge and appreciation of the danger of breathing asbestos dust and further, whether the employee was given a respirator and whether he used it or refused to use it. Additionally, as to the defendant, Pittsburgh Corning, the only persons who could maintain an action would be the survivors of employees who were employed by that company. These are individual questions peculiar to each potential class member. Additionally, the plaintiffs have asserted various theories of recovery against the defendants, and the nine defendants have alleged differing affirmative defenses against the plaintiffs. For example, the statute of limitations may bar some plaintiffs, but not others. During the ten year period the state of medical knowledge was changing, which has a significant bearing on the defendants' duty to warn of dangers. Taking all these factors into consideration, the court is convinced that the number of uncommon questions of law and fact would predominate over the common questions, and the case would therefore "degenerate into multiple lawsuits separately tried."

This case is very different from the single mass accident cases that have in the past allowed a class action to proceed on the liability issues. Those cases have normally involved a single tragic happening which caused physical harm or property damage to a group of people, and affirmative defenses are absent. Usually, one set of operative facts will establish liability. Here we have two lawsuits covering a ten year span of time in which the nine defendants acted differently at different times. The court is in agreement with the defendant that there is not a single act of negligence or proximate cause which would apply to each potential class member and each defendant in this case.

The plaintiffs placed great reliance at the hearing on this question on the case of *Biechele v. Norfolk & Western Railway Co.* which they contended was very similar to the instant case because it involved a continuing tort over a period of years. In *Biechele* a group of landowners brought an action for injunctive relief and damages against the defendant for operating its coal loading facilities as a nuisance. The *Biechele* case was brought under the provisions of 23(b)(1) and (2) for damages and injunctive relief, unlike the present case which is a (b)(3) damage case only. In the *Biechele* case the court began its inquiry by first assuming that the injunctive and damage claims were both certifiable class actions. After stating this, the court concluded that it would assume jurisdiction over the principal claim, which was injunctive in nature, and then, in the interest of judicial efficiency, the court found that it would retain jurisdiction over the damage claims. As was pointed out by the Court in *Boring,* "the *Biechele* precedent nevertheless is based on discretionary jurisdiction applied if the court certifies the injunction as a class action." There is no injunctive relief requested in this case.

## A CLASS ACTION IS NOT THE SUPERIOR METHOD

There are several reasons why this court feels that a class action would not be the superior method for adjudication of this cause. A class action certification would entail costly and time consuming notice procedures and record keeping on those who would wish to "opt-out." Further, because of the nature of the injuries claimed, there may be persons that might neglect to "opt-out" of the class, and then discover some years in the future that they have contracted asbestosis, lung cancer or other pulmonary disease. These persons would be bound by decision rendered in this litigation. Finally, the court finds that the members of the purported class have a vital interest in controlling their own litigation because it involves serious personal injuries and death in some cases. This is demonstrated by the fact that there are presently four sets of plaintiffs' attorneys in two ongoing cases and the plaintiffs in the *Kay* case strongly oppose the class action certification.

## CONCLUSION

In conclusion, the court is of the opinion that this case should not be certified as a class action under Rule 23(b)(3), because the questions of law or fact that are common to the class as a whole do not predominate over individual questions and further because the class action device is not the superior method for adjudicating the claims presented herein. The court is of the opinion that the superior method for adjudication of this case is to continue allowing intervention freely for those who wish to join and to maintain firm control over this litigation by utilizing the tools set forth in the MANUAL FOR COMPLEX AND MULTIDISTRICT LITIGATION.

It is, therefore, ordered that the plaintiffs' Motion for Class Action Status be, and the same is hereby in all things denied, and that the class action allegations be stricken from the plaintiffs' complaints.

## IN RE NORTHERN DISTRICT OF CALIFORNIA, DALKON SHIELD IUD PRODS. LIAB. LITIG.

United States Court of Appeals, Ninth Circuit, 1982.
693 F.2d 847.

Plaintiffs appeal from a district court order conditionally certifying their claims as: (1) a nationwide class action on the issue of punitive damages pursuant to Federal Rule of Civil Procedure 23(b)(1)(B); and (2) a statewide (California) class action on the issue of liability pursuant to Rule 23(b)(3).

All plaintiffs claim to have been injured by the Dalkon Shield intrauterine device. All of those plaintiffs who have joined in this appeal challenge class certification. Defendant A.H. Robins also opposes certification of the California 23(b)(3) class. Defendant Hugh J. Davis opposes certification of both classes.

Between June 1970 and June 1974, approximately 2.2 million Dalkon Shields were inserted in women in the United States. Many users sustained injuries. Complaints include uterine perforations, infections, ectopic and uterine pregnancies, spontaneous abortions, fetal injuries and birth defects, sterility, and hysterectomies. Several deaths also were reported. On June 28, 1974, Robins withdrew the Dalkon Shield from the market.

By May 31, 1981, approximately 3,258 actions relating to the Dalkon Shield had been filed, and 1,573 claims were pending. The claims are based on various theories: negligence and negligent design, strict products liability, breach of express and implied warranty, wanton and reckless conduct, conspiracy, and fraud. Most plaintiffs seek both compensatory and punitive damages.

Some plaintiffs joined Robins, Davis, and Irwin W. Lerner as defendants, as well as their own doctors or medical practitioners who recommended and inserted the Dalkon Shield, and local suppliers. Many plaintiffs sued fewer defendants.

In 1975 all actions then pending in federal district courts alleging damages from the use of the Dalkon Shield were transferred by the Judicial Panel on Multidistrict Litigation to the District of Kansas for consolidated pretrial proceedings. After four years of consolidated discovery, the Judicial Panel began vacating its conditional transfer orders and remanded the cases to their respective transferor courts. State courts have also received a number of Dalkon Shield cases. The results have been mixed. Some plaintiffs have recovered substantial verdicts. Others have recovered nothing. Many cases have been settled.

Approximately 166 Dalkon Shield cases were pending in the Northern District of California. After one jury that lasted nine weeks, Judge Williams consolidated all Dalkon Shield cases pending in that district and ordered briefing on the feasibility of a class action. All but one of California plaintiffs' counsel opposed class certification. Out-of-state plaintiffs were not notified of the briefing request and did not participate in the status conferences held to discuss the class action proposal. All defendants at that time opposed class certification.

On June 25, 1981, Judge Williams entered an order conditionally certifying a nationwide class, under Fed.R.Civ.P. 23(b)(1)(B), consisting of all persons who filed actions for punitive damages against Robins. Judge Williams also conditionally certified a California statewide subclass under Rule 23(b)(3) consisting of plaintiffs who have filed actions against Robins in California. This California class is limited to the question of Robins' liability arising from the manufacture and sale of the Dalkon Shield. Any plaintiff may opt out of this class, whereas all plaintiffs in the nation would be bound by the determination on punitive damages.

Plaintiffs from California, Oregon, Ohio, Florida, and Kansas moved to decertify the punitive damages class.

THE RULE 23(b)(1)(B) NATIONWIDE PUNITIVE DAMAGES CLASS

A.   Rule 23(a) Prerequisites

1.   Commonality.

The district court held that the punitive damages class presented common questions about Robins' knowledge of the safety of its product at material times while the Shield was on the market. What Davis, Lerner, and Robins knew about the Dalkon Shield, when they knew it, what information they withheld from the public, and what they stated in their advertising to doctors and in their product instructions during various time periods may all be common questions. These questions are not entirely common, however, to all plaintiffs.

Moreover, as the plaintiffs correctly argue, the 50 jurisdictions in which these cases arise do not apply the same punitive damages standards. Punitive damages standards can range from gross negligence to reckless disregard to various levels of willfulness and wantonness. If commonality were the only problem in this case, it might be possible to sustain some kind of a punitive damage class. But difficulties remain with other certification requirements.

2.   Typicality.

Typicality, while it may not be insurmountable, remains a significant problem. The district court order recites that representative parties have been selected. However, all of the appealing plaintiffs assert that no plaintiff has accepted the role, and that no single plaintiff or group of plaintiffs could be typical of the numerous persons who might have claims. No plaintiff has appeared in this appeal in support of class certification. Again, while typicality alone might not be an insurmountable problem, it helps make the overall situation difficult to rationalize as proper for class treatment.

### 3. Adequacy of Representation.

The court designated lead counsel for the nationwide class, but he has resigned. New counsel has been designated but has not yet started to represent the class. Apparently none of the attorneys already involved in the case is willing to serve as class counsel. The district judge may well be better able to choose a good lawyer than some of the plaintiffs may be, but the rights of litigants to choose their own counsel is a right not lightly to be brushed aside.

The plaintiffs argue that newly appointed, even if expert counsel, may not litigate the action as vigorously as counsel selected by plaintiffs. This court is hesitant to force unwanted counsel upon plaintiffs on the assumption that appointed counsel will be adequate. Even if the class were otherwise acceptable, it would have to be certified if adequate lead counsel turned out to be unavailable.

We are not necessarily ruling out the class action tool as a means for expediting multi-party product liability actions in appropriate cases, but the combined difficulties overlapping from each of the elements of Rule 23(a) preclude certification in this case.

## IN RE FEDERAL SKYWALK CASES

United States Court of Appeals, Eighth Circuit, 1982.
680 F.2d 1175.

This action challenges the validity of a mandatory class certification order rendered by the United States District Court for the Western District of Missouri during the course of litigation arising out of the collapse of two skywalks at the Hyatt Regency Hotel in Kansas City, Missouri in July, 1981. The class was certified on the issues of liability for compensatory and punitive damages and amount of punitive damages, and includes all business invitees at the hotel during the disaster.

Two objecting plaintiffs (objectors) now petition this court to vacate the order. Alternatively, the class representative argues that the federal district judge did not abuse his discretion in certifying the class and further that the class is appropriate. For the reasons discussed below, we conclude that the order must be vacated because it violates the Anti-Injunction Act, 28 U.S.C. § 2283.

On July 17, 1981, two skywalks in the central lobby of the Hyatt Regency Hotel in Kansas City, Missouri, collapsed killing 114 persons and injuring hundreds of others. Following the disaster numerous individual lawsuits were filed in both the Circuit Court for Jackson County, Missouri (state court), and the United States District Court for the Western District of Missouri (district court). The federal district court jurisdiction was based on 28 U.S.C. § 1332, diversity of citizenship.

The state court cases were consolidated and assigned to Judge Timothy O'Leary. The federal cases were also consolidated and assigned to Judge Scott O. Wright. Shortly after the first cases were filed, the state and district court consolidated their respective cases for discovery. Each court appointed a Plaintiffs' Liaison Committee to aid in discovery and other matters. In addition, the two courts appointed a joint state-federal Plaintiffs' Liaison Committee to aid in the consolidated discovery.

Prior to the class certification, the Plaintiffs' Liaison Committee accomplished substantial discovery and trial preparation on behalf of all plaintiffs. The accomplishments included nearly completing the interrogatory phase of discovery and serving requests for production upon the defendants. In addition, the committee collected approximately 300,000 documents pertaining to the litigation and had arranged for a document depository available to all plaintiffs' counsel. The committee had also arranged for the testing of the skywalk materials by the National Bureau of Standards.

On October 27, 1981, Molly Riley, a district court plaintiff, filed a motion for class certification. The motion sought class certification under Fed.R.Civ.P. 23(b)(1)(B), or in the alternative under 23(b)(3), as to the issues of liability for compensatory and punitive damages and the amount of punitive damages. The basis for requesting class certification was Riley's concern that there would be inadequate funds available to pay all claims for compensatory and punitive damages. Riley also moved that her counsel be appointed as lead counsel for the class.

Several federal and state court plaintiffs filed pleadings in opposition to Riley's motion. The objecting plaintiffs challenged Riley's and her attorney's qualifications to represent the class. They also challenged the need for and desirability of class action treatment arguing that there was no evidence of insufficient funds to satisfy all claims. A hearing was held before Judge Wright on December 10, 1981.

On January 25, 1982, Judge Wright entered the order appealed from in which he (1) denied Riley's motion for class certification because her citizenship was not diverse from all defendants, (2) certified a class action under Rule 23(b)(1)(A) on the issues of liability for compensatory and punitive damages, (3) certified a class action under Rule 23(b)(1)(B) on the issues of liability for punitive damages and the amount of punitive damages.

In support of its order the district court found that the general prerequisites for class actions prescribed by Rule 23(a) were satisfied and that the specific requirements of Rule 23(b)(1) were also satisfied. The court stressed that the "interests of all parties concerned" would best be served by "the avoidance of wasteful, repetitive litigation," and that such litigation could be avoided by "trying the issues of liability for compensatory damages, liability for punitive damages and amount of punitive damages only once." In support of the Rule 23(b)(1)(A) class the court found that individual suits on the issues of liability for compensatory and punitive damages would create a risk of inconsistent results.

In support of the Rule 23(b)(1)(B) class the court relied on three considerations. First, the defendants held liable for punitive damages might lack the funds to pay the full amount of such damages. Second, individual suits for punitive damages would create a risk of unfairness to the other claimants because "there is some uncertainty under Missouri law as to whether a single defendant can be liable for more than one award of punitive damages." Third, the court noted that the prosecution of individual punitive damage actions could create an ethical problem for counsel representing more than one victim in that the counsel would be forced to decide which suit to bring first.

On February 9, 1982, the objectors filed their notice of appeal and petition for mandamus.

Our initial inquiry must be whether the order is appealable. Recognizing that the order is interlocutory, we would nevertheless have appellate jurisdiction under 28 U.S.C. § 1292(a)(1) if that order is injunctive in character. Therefore, resolution of this issue depends upon the nature of the order. The objectors argue that the order enjoins them from prosecuting their state court actions for punitive damages. In response the class argues that the order is not an injunction because it does not use injunction terminology and, more importantly, it does not enjoin the objectors from settling their claims. The class characterizes the order as follows:

> the motion concerns only whether the defendants can use individual punitive damage settlements as evidence to defeat or diminish the recovery of punitive damages in the classwide trial on that issue. *The representative plaintiff and the class have never sought to enjoin any member of the class from entering into an individual settlement of any claim.*

We do not agree with that characterization and conclude that we do have jurisdiction under 28 U.S.C. § 1292(a). (1) The determination of whether an order is an injunction depends upon the substantial effect of the order rather than its terminology. (2) In the present case, contrary to the class's assertion, the district court expressly prohibited class members from settling their punitive damage claims:

> Legitimate claimants may negotiate and execute settlements with those defendants who have vociferously urged this court to allow the settlement process to continue. *Those claimants who want to*

*exact payment for allegedly punishable acts must forego the
settlement process and await the trial of the punitive damage
issues.*

In addition, the substantial effect of the order also enjoined the state
plaintiffs from pursuing their pending state court actions on the issues of
liability for compensatory and punitive damages and the amount of
punitive damages.

At oral argument counsel for the class argued that 28 U.S.C.
§ 1292(a)(1) should not be construed to apply to class certification because
the inevitable effect of a mandatory class is an injunction against state
court actions on class issues. We conclude that the argument is not
persuasive on the facts before us.

It is true that parties to a mandatory class are not free to initiate
actions in other courts to litigate class certified issues. However, in the
present case the objectors had commenced their state court actions before
the motion for class certification had been filed in district court. The state
court cases had been filed, consolidated, and discovery had begun.

Our conclusion that the order enjoins pending state proceedings
necessitates an inquiry as to the propriety of that order under the Anti-
Injunction Act, 28 U.S.C. § 2283. The Act provides that "a court of the
United States may not grant an injunction to stay proceedings in a state
court except as expressly authorized by Act of Congress, or where necessary
in aid of its jurisdiction, or to protect or effectuate its judgment."

In *Atlantic Coast Line R.R. v. Locomotive Engineers*, the Supreme
Court recognized that the Act imposes a flat and positive prohibition:

> On its face the present Act is an absolute prohibition against
> enjoining state court proceedings, unless the injunction falls
> within one of three specifically defined exceptions. The
> respondents here have intimated that the Act only establishes a
> "principle of comity," not a binding rule on the power of the federal
> courts. The argument implies that in certain circumstances a
> federal court may enjoin state court proceedings even if that
> action cannot be justified by any of the three exceptions. We
> cannot accept any such contention. In 1955 when this Court
> interpreted this statute, it stated: "This is not a statute conveying
> a broad general policy for appropriate ad hoc application.
> Legislative policy is here expressed in a clear-cut prohibition
> qualified only by specifically defined exceptions."

In the present case the class has an uncertain claim for punitive
damages against defendants who have not conceded liability. The claim
does not qualify as a limited fund which is a jurisdictional prerequisite for
federal interpleader. Without the limited fund there is no analogy to an

interpleader and no reason to treat the class action as an interpleader for purposes of the Anti-Injunction Act.

The class proposes a second analogy between the order and several earlier decisions which allowed an injunction when an insurance company brought a federal suit for a declaratory judgment that a particular policy was invalid and the beneficiary subsequently sues in state court to recover under the policy. We conclude that the analogy is not persuasive. Initially we note that the most recent case cited by class was decided in 1940, long before the enactment of the current Anti-Injunction Act. We also note that even the commentator cited by the class acknowledges:

> it seems probable that a federal court would not be warranted in enjoining the prosecution of a pending state action on the policy, where it is brought during the contestable period and there is an opportunity to set up the defense of fraud in the state court.

In addition, the cited cases are distinguishable on the basis that they involved situations in which identical parties were litigating mutually exclusive theories concerning their rights in the same policy in different forums. Such is not the case here. Furthermore, as conceded by the class, the cases involved injunctions against subsequent state actions. In contrast, the injunction in the present case was against pending state actions.

Next the class argues that allowing individual actions in state court will nullify the purpose of the class. The Supreme Court has narrowly interpreted the "necessary in aid of jurisdiction" exception, and a pending state suit must truly interfere with the federal court's jurisdiction. As the objectors correctly point out, a plurality of the Supreme Court reaffirmed in *Vendo Co.* its earlier holdings that a simultaneous *in personam* state action does not interfere with the jurisdiction of a federal court in a suit involving the same subject matter.

In *Toucey v. New York Life Ins. Co.* we acknowledged the existence of a historical exception to the Anti-Injunction Act in cases where the federal court has obtained jurisdiction over *res*, prior to the state-court action. Although the "necessary in aid of" exception to § 2283 may be fairly read as incorporating this historical *in rem* exception, the federal and state actions here are simply *in personam*. The traditional notion is that *in personam* actions in federal and state court may proceed concurrently, without interference from either court, and there is no evidence that the exception to § 2283 was intended to alter this balance. We have never viewed parallel *in personam* actions as interfering with the jurisdiction of either court; as we stated in *Kline v. Burke Construction Co.*:

> An action brought to enforce a personal liability *does not tend to impair or defeat the jurisdiction* of the court in which a prior action for the same cause is pending. Each court is free to proceed in its

own way and in its own time, without reference to the proceedings in the other court. Whenever a judgment is rendered in one of the courts and pleaded in the other, the effect of that judgment is to be determined by the application of the principles of *res adjudicata*.

In the present case the federal and state actions are *in personam* claims for compensatory and punitive damages. Therefore, based on the foregoing principles, we are compelled to hold that despite Judge Wright's legitimate concern for the efficient management of mass tort litigation, the class certification order must be vacated. Mr. Justice Black's concluding words in *Atlantic Coast Line* are particularly apt here:

> This case is by no means an easy one. The arguments in support of the union's contentions are not insubstantial. But whatever doubts we may have are strongly affected by the general prohibition of § 2283. Any doubts as to the propriety of a federal injunction against state court proceedings should be resolved in favor of permitting the state courts to proceed in an orderly fashion to finally determine the controversy. The explicit wording of § 2283 itself implies as much, and the fundamental principle of a dual system of courts leads inevitably to that conclusion.

The order of the district court is vacated.

# IN RE BENDECTIN PRODS. LIAB. LITIG.

United States Court of Appeals, Sixth Circuit, 1984.
749 F.2d 300.

Petitioners seek a writ of mandamus ordering the district court to vacate its order certifying a class action pursuant to Federal Rule of Civil Procedure 23(b)(1). For the reasons stated below, the petition shall be granted, and the writ shall be issued.

## I.

This case is just one stage in a massive products liability lawsuit against Merrell Dow Pharmaceuticals, Inc., the manufacturer of the drug Bendectin. Bendectin is a prescription drug developed to relieve morning sickness in pregnant women. Numerous plaintiffs have filed claims in both federal and state court alleging that they suffer from birth defects as a result of their *in utero* exposure to Bendectin.

The present controversy has its roots in a transfer order of the Judicial Panel on Multidistrict Litigation in early 1982. Pursuant to that order, all Bendectin actions pending in federal courts were transferred to the Southern District of Ohio for consolidated pretrial proceedings. Shortly after the transfer, a five-person Plaintiffs' Lead Counsel Committee was formed to coordinate discovery efforts for all plaintiffs in federal court. Over the next year, many other cases were transferred to the Southern District of Ohio, and many more cases were filed in that court as original actions. In September 1983, the district judge issued an order to show cause why the cases should not be certified as a class action under Federal Rule of Civil Procedure 23 or, in the alternative, be consolidated for trial on common issues of liability pursuant to Federal Rule of Civil Procedure 42. After the parties responded to this order, the district judge held in November 1983 that the action was not appropriate for class certification and instead consolidated the cases for trial pursuant to Rule 42. The consolidation order, however, only included those cases that had been filed in Ohio federal courts, and the cases that had been transferred to the Southern District were to be returned to their original venue for trial unless the plaintiffs agreed to the consolidated trial.

The consolidated trial began June 11, 1984, and a jury was impaneled. Because of serious settlement negotiations between the Plaintiffs' Lead Counsel Committee and Merrell Dow, the district court recessed the trial on June 18 and certified a class for settlement purposes under Federal Rule of Civil Procedure 23(b). Merrell Dow has apparently made a settlement offer of $120 million, and a majority of the Plaintiffs' Lead Counsel Committee tentatively favor the settlement offer. A hearing is scheduled for October 31, 1984, to determine the proper allocation of the settlement among subclasses, and a fairness hearing on the settlement is scheduled for November 30.

In the order certifying the class, the district judge found that all four requirements of Rule 23(a) were easily met. The court also found that the requirements of Rule 23(b)(1)(A) and (B) were met. With respect to Rule 23(b)(1)(A), the district court stated that "continued case by case determinations will inevitably result in varying adjudications which will impose inconsistent standards of conduct upon the defendant." The district judge found 23(b)(1)(B) to have been met because "there is a risk that a limited fund may exist from which judgments can be satisfied." The district judge then certified a "non-opt out" class for settlement purposes of all persons exposed to Bendectin.

## II.

Rule 23(b)(1)(A) provides that class actions are maintainable if a separate action would create a risk of "inconsistent or varying adjudications with respect to individual members of the class which would establish incompatible standards of conduct for the party opposing the class." The fact that some plaintiffs may be successful in their suits against a defendant while others may not is clearly not a ground for invoking Rule 23(b)(1)(A). The class certification in this case therefore cannot stand on this ground.

The district judge, however, apparently did not rely solely on the possibility of varying adjudications because he also cited *Hernandez v. Motor Vessel Skyward* to support his conclusion as to Rule 23(b)(1)(A). In

*Hernandez,* the district judge certified a class under Rule 23(b)(1)(A) on the ground that the doctrine of collateral estoppel might bind the defendant on issues of liability if any plaintiff were to win a suit against it. Irrespective of the merits of this argument as a ground for Rule 23(b)(1)(A) certification, this concern has been eliminated by the Supreme Court's curtailment of the use of offensive collateral estoppel in *Parklane Hosiery Co. v. Shore.* The district court therefore failed to establish any grounds for certification under Rule 23(b)(1)(A).

With respect to Rule 23(b)(1)(B), the district judge stated that there was a limited fund from which the plaintiffs could be compensated for their claims and therefore adjudications by earlier plaintiffs could "as a practical matter be dispositive of the interests of the other members of the class not parties to the adjudications." Fed.R.Civ.P. 23(b)(1)(B). This limited fund theory has been endorsed by several courts. The district court was therefore not clearly erroneous as a matter of law to hold that a limited fund is a justification for a class action under a Rule 23(b)(1)(B).

The district court, however, was clearly erroneous as a matter of law in the method it used to determine that there was a limited fund. The certification order states without support "that there is a risk that a limited fund may exist from which judgments can be satisfied." No findings were made on the record as to this conclusion, and the petitioners in this case were given no opportunity to dispute whether there was a limited fund. In deciding whether a limited fund would subvert the rights of some plaintiffs, the courts have differed over whether the proponent of the class certification must show that a limited fund will "necessarily" affect the plaintiffs' claims, or whether a "substantial probability" will suffice. Irrespective of the proper test, the district court, as a matter of law, must have a fact-finding inquiry on this question and allow the opponents of class certification to present evidence that a limited fund does not exist. Because the district judge in this case failed to make any such finding, the certification was clearly erroneous as a matter of law.

The final guideline is whether the district court's order raises issues of first impression and creates new and important problems. Several of the issues raised by the class certification are of first impression in this Circuit. This Court has never been faced with a non-opt out class certification for settlement purposes only. Moreover, the sheer magnitude of the case makes the disposition of these issues crucial as several hundred litigants are waiting for a decision before proceeding with their cases.

Based on these guidelines, we find that the issuance of a writ of mandamus is appropriate in this case. Although we shall issue the writ, we realize that the district judge has been faced with some very difficult problems in this case, and we certainly do not fault him for attempting to use this unique and innovative certification method. On pure policy grounds, the district judge's decision may be commendable, and several commentators have argued that Rule 23 should be used in this manner. Because of the situation presented by this case, however, we conclude that a writ of mandamus vacating the certification order of the district court should be issued. So ordered.

## IN RE AMERICAN MEDICAL SYSTEMS, INC.
United States Court of Appeals, Sixth Circuit, 1996.
75 F.3d 1069.

Petitioners American Medical Systems (AMS) and Pfizer, Inc., defendants below, both seek a writ of mandamus directing the district court to vacate orders conditionally certifying a class in a products liability suit involving penile prostheses. This court has held that class certification is generally not the kind of subject matter for which mandamus relief is available on the grounds that class certification decisions are reviewable on direct appeal. However, on the extraordinary facts of this case we find that the district judge's disregard of class action procedures was of such severity and frequency so as to warrant its issuance here.

I.

Since 1973, AMS, a wholly-owned subsidiary of Pfizer, has manufactured and marketed penile prostheses, which are used to treat impotence. The plaintiffs, respondents in this proceeding, all use or have used AMS' products. Plaintiff Paul Vorhis was implanted with an AMS penile prosthesis on April 25, 1989. It failed to function in January of 1993, and Vorhis had the prosthesis replaced with an AMS 700 Ultrex prosthesis in May 1993. This second prosthesis caused him pain and discomfort, and plaintiff had it removed in August of 1993 and replaced with a third AMS prosthesis, with which he is presently satisfied.

Vorhis filed this action against defendant AMS in the Southern District of Ohio on December 5, 1994, individually and on behalf of others similarly situated who suffered damages as a result of the implantation of penile prostheses manufactured by AMS. The complaint alleges strict product liability, negligence, breach of implied and express warranties, fraud and punitive damages, and seeks a declaratory judgment for medical monitoring.

On December 29, 1994, Vorhis filed a motion for class certification. On February 28, 1995, the district judge issued a two-page order stating, "based upon the information currently available to it, that class certification appears to be the most efficient and appropriate manner in which to handle this matter," and promised a "further order outlining the reasoning supporting that conclusion" to follow. The order was conditional, subject to decertification at any time, and conditioned further "upon class counsel acting to amend the complaint within thirty (30) days in order to add additional plaintiffs who qualify as appropriate class representatives and who are free of the alleged infirmities on which Defendant's objections to the suitability of the current Plaintiff/class representative are premised." Subsequently the district judge certified the class as:

> All persons residing in the United States, who have had inflatable penile prostheses developed, manufactured and/or sold by Defendant American Medical Systems, Inc. and/or Defendant Pfizer, Inc. implanted in their bodies.

### III.

### A.

We begin our analysis by considering whether the lower court committed patent error. We address in tandem petitioners' contentions that the lower court disregarded the standards for class certification and certified a class despite the absence of an adequate factual record establishing the elements of Rule 23.

The Supreme Court has required district courts to conduct a "rigorous analysis" into whether the prerequisites of Rule 23 are met before certifying a class. *General Tel. Co. v. Falcon.* A class is not maintainable as a class action by virtue of its designation as such in the pleadings. Although a hearing prior to the class determination is not always required, "it may be necessary for the court to probe behind the pleadings before coming to rest on the certification question." This court has stated that:

> Mere repetition of the language of Rule 23(a) is not sufficient. There must be an adequate statement of the basic facts to indicate that each requirement of the rule is fulfilled. Maintainability may be determined by the court on the basis of the pleadings, if sufficient facts are set forth, but ordinarily the determination should be predicated on more information than the pleadings will provide. The parties should be afforded an opportunity to present evidence on the maintainability of the class action.

The party seeking the class certification bears the burden of proof. Subsection (a) of Rule 23 contains four prerequisites which must all be met before a class can be certified. We shall examine each of these factors individually.

### 1.

The first subdivision of Rule 23(a)(1) requires that the class be "so numerous that joinder of all members is impracticable." "The reason for the impracticability requirement is obvious. Only when joinder is impracticable is there a need for a class action device." There is no strict numerical test for determining impracticability of joinder. Rather, "the numerosity requirement requires examination of the specific facts of each case and imposes no absolute limitations." When class size reaches substantial proportions, however, the impracticability requirement is usually satisfied by the numbers alone.

In the original complaint, Vorhis alleged that although he was unable to state the exact size of the class, "members of the class number at least in the thousands." The first amended complaint modified that estimate to "over 150,000." The district judge's finding of a class of 15,000 to 120,000 persons may not be unreasonable, especially since AMS has been producing penile prostheses for over twenty years, and has the largest share of the penile implant market (district judge may consider reasonable inferences drawn from facts before him at early stage in proceedings in determining whether class is sufficiently numerous to make joinder impracticable). Defendant, moreover, does not contest this factor. Although the district judge made no findings but merely rubberstamped the plaintiffs' assertions that such potential class members truly exist, we do not hold that this factor is not established because petitioners do not contest it.

2.

Rule 23(a)(2) requires that for certification there must be "questions of law or fact common to the class." The commonality requirement is interdependent with the impracticability of joinder requirement, and the "tests together form the underlying conceptual basis supporting class actions." For in such cases, "the class-action device saves the resources of both the courts and the parties by permitting an issue potentially affecting every class member to be litigated in an economical fashion under Rule 23." The commonality test "is qualitative rather than quantitative, that is, there need be only a single issue common to all members of the class" ("mere fact that questions peculiar to each individual member of the class remain after the common questions of the defendant's liability have been resolved does not dictate the conclusion that a class action is impermissible"). Plaintiffs' complaint and class certification motion simply allege in general terms that there are common issues without identifying any particular defect common to all plaintiffs. Yet AMS introduced uncontradicted evidence that since 1973 AMS has produced at least ten different models, and that these models have been modified over the years. Plaintiffs' claims of strict liability, fraudulent misrepresentation to both the FDA and the medical community, negligent testing, design and manufacture, and failure to warn will differ depending upon the model and the year it was issued.

Proofs as to strict liability, negligence, failure to warn, breach of express and implied warranties will also vary from plaintiff to plaintiff because complications with an AMS device may be due to a variety of factors, including surgical error, improper use of the device, anatomical incompatibility, infection, device malfunction, or psychological problems. Furthermore, each plaintiff's urologist would also be required to testify to determine what oral and written statements were made to the physician, and what he in turn told the patient, as well as to issues of reliance, causation and damages (on issues of negligence, strict products liability, adequacy of warnings, fraud and conspiracy, "commonality begins to be obscured by individual case histories).

The amended complaint reflects that the plaintiffs received different models and have different complaints regarding each of those models. In the absence of more specific allegations and/or proof of commonality of any factual or legal claims, plaintiffs have failed to meet their burden of proof on Rule 23(a)(2).

This failure of proof highlights the error of the district judge. Despite evidence in the record presented by the nonmoving party that at least ten different models existed, testimony from a urologist that there is no "common cause" of prostheses malfunction, and conclusory allegations by the party with the burden of proof on certification, we find not even the hint of any serious consideration by the judge of commonality. Moreover, although not dispositive, it is noteworthy that a Judicial Panel on Multidistrict Litigation denied consolidation of all federal AMS penile prostheses case pursuant to 28 U.S.C. § 1407, concluding that "the degree of factual commonality among the actions in this litigation does not rise to a level that warrants Section 1407 transfer." The district judge was made aware of this ruling, and still did not give the question of commonality any discernible degree of scrutiny.

3.

Rule 23(a)(3) requires that "claims or defenses of the representative parties be typical of the claims or defenses of the class." Typicality determines whether a sufficient relationship exists between the injury to the named plaintiff and the conduct affecting the class, so that the court may properly attribute a collective nature to the challenged conduct. In other words, when such a relationship is shown, a plaintiff's injury arises from or is directly related to a wrong to a class, and that wrong includes the wrong to the plaintiff. Thus, a plaintiff's claim is typical if it arises from the same event or practice or course of conduct that gives rise to the claims of other class members, and if his or her claims are based on the same legal theory ("typicality requirement is said to limit the class claims to those fairly encompassed by the named plaintiffs' claims"); ("to be typical, a representative's claim need not always involve the same facts or law, provided there is a common element of fact or law"). A necessary consequence of the typicality requirement is that the representative's interests will be aligned with those of the represented group, and in pursuing his own claims, the named plaintiff will also advance the interests of the class members.

Vorhis' claim relates to a previous AMS penile prosthesis which, several years after insertion, allegedly could not be inflated due to a possible leak in the input tube of a CX device. This in turn may have been caused by rear-tip extender surgery Vorhis had in 1990, in an attempt to increase penile length that was lost through surgery to correct a curvature of his penis. Based on what little we have to go on, it is hard to imagine that Vorhis' claim is typical of the class certified in this case. Because the district judge issued its amended order of certification before discovery of the plaintiffs other than Vorhis, we have less information about them. However, we know from the amended complaint that each plaintiff used a different model, and each experienced a distinct difficulty. York claims that his 700 inflatable penile prosthesis fails to fully inflate. Kennedy alleges that his Ultrex inflatable penile prosthesis malfunctioned because the cylinders and pump leaked. Finally, Gordy maintains that his Hyrdoflex failed, and that his current implant, the Dynaflex prosthesis, inflates on one side only. These allegations fail to establish a claim typical to each other, let alone a class.

Once again, it should have been obvious to the district judge that it needed to "probe behind the pleadings" before concluding that the typicality requirement was met. Instead, the district judge gave no serious consideration to this factor, but simply mimicked the language of the rule. This was error. (reversing certification for failure of proof on typicality element, holding that it was error for district court to presume that respondent's claim was typical of other claims against petitioner).

4.

Rule 23(a)(4) allows certification only if "the representative parties will fairly and adequately protect the interests of the class." Fed.R.Civ.P. 23(a). This prerequisite is essential to due process, because a final judgment in a class action is binding on all class members. *Hansberry v. Lee* ("no class should be certified where the interests of the members are antagonistic, because the preclusive effect of the verdict may deprive unnamed class members of their right to be heard").

We articulated two criteria for determining adequacy of representation: "1) the representative must have common interests with unnamed members of the class, and 2) it must appear that the representatives will vigorously prosecute the interests of the class through qualified counsel" (Rule 23(a)(4) tests "the experience and ability of counsel for the plaintiffs and whether there is any antagonism between the interests of the plaintiffs and other members of the class they seek to represent"). *See also Falcon* ("adequacy of representation requirement also raises concerns about the competency of class counsel and conflicts of interest"). The adequate representation requirement overlaps with the typicality requirement because in the absence of typical claims, the class representative has no incentives to pursue the claims of the other class members.

Although the district judge considered the qualifications of plaintiff's counsel, he made no finding on the first criterion, and did not consider whether Vorhis or the other plaintiffs would "vigorously prosecute the interests of the class." AMS raised a serious question as to Vorhis' suitability to serve as a class representative given his history of psychological problems. At the hearing, the judge made no finding regarding plaintiff, but remarked that:

> I don't think he is going to control anything. I don't think a client in a class action ever controls anything. And if you want my feeling on it, he is a name. He's a symbol. I just want to make sure there aren't defenses against that symbol that would then be transmitted against the class.

This statement is clearly contrary to our holding.

The district judge's February 28 and March 16 orders compound the problem. In the first order the judge again deferred making a finding, referring to plaintiff's "alleged infirmities," and allowing the addition of other class representatives. In the March 16 order the judge not only again failed to make an explicit decision regarding Vorhis, but added three additional class representatives without a record and without any meaningful findings of fact.

As amply illustrated, plaintiffs' complaint and class certification motion simply allege the elements of Rule 23(a) in conclusory terms without submitting any persuasive evidence to show that these factors are met. Because the plaintiffs did not create a factual record, and petitioners have demonstrated that the products at issue are very different and that each plaintiff's claim is unique, class certification was inappropriate.

[Discussion of failure to satisfy Rule 23(b)(3) requirements omitted— *ed.*]

## IV.

Under the various formulations of the writ, we conclude that petitioners have met their heavy burden. For all the foregoing reasons, the petitions for writ of mandamus are granted, and the district judge is directed to decertify the plaintiff class.

# CHAPTER 4

---

# RESOLVING MASS TORTS THROUGH RULE 23 LITIGATION CLASSES: HISTORICAL BACKGROUND (II)

■ ■ ■

## A. INROADS AND SUCCESSES

### JENKINS V. RAYMARK INDUSTRIES
United States Court of Appeals, Fifth Circuit, 1986.
782 F.2d 468.

In this interlocutory appeal, the thirteen defendants challenge the decision of District Judge Robert M. Parker to certify a class of plaintiffs with asbestos-related claims. We affirm.

### I. BACKGROUND TO JUDGE PARKER'S PLAN

Experts estimate that at least 21 million American workers have been exposed to "significant" amounts of asbestos at the workplace since 1940; other millions have been exposed through environmental contact or contact with relatives who have worked with the products. Because of its injurious propensities, such exposure, in human terms, has meant that literally tens of thousands of people fall ill or die from asbestos-related diseases every year. In legal terms, it has translated into thousands of lawsuits, over 20,000 as of 1983, centered mainly in industrialized areas along the country's coasts.

Courts, including those in our own circuit, have been ill-equipped to handle this "avalanche of litigation." Our numerous opinions in asbestos-related cases have repeatedly recognized the dilemma confronting our trial courts, and expressed concern about the mounting backlog of cases and inevitable, lengthy trial delays.

About 5,000 asbestos-related cases are pending in this circuit. Much, though by no means all, of the litigation has centered in the Eastern District of Texas. Nearly nine hundred asbestos-related personal injury cases, involving over one thousand plaintiffs, were pending there in December of 1984. Despite innovative streamlined pretrial procedures and large-scale consolidated trials of multiple plaintiffs, the dockets of that district's courts remained alarmingly backlogged. Plaintiffs had waited years for trial, some since 1979—and new cases were (and still are) being filed every day. It is predicted that, because asbestos-related diseases will continue to manifest themselves for the next 15 years, filings will continue at a steady rate until the year 2000.

In early 1985, ten of these plaintiffs responded by moving to certify a class of all plaintiffs with asbestos-related personal injury actions pending in the Eastern District on December 31, 1984. These plaintiffs hoped to determine in the class action one overarching issue—the viability of the "state of the art" defense. Because the trial of that issue consistently consumed substantial resources in every asbestos trial, and the evidence in each case was either identical or virtually so, they argued, a class determination would accelerate their cases.

## II.   THE PLAN

Following copious briefing and several hearings, the district court granted the motion. In his order of October 16, 1985, Judge Parker carefully considered the request under Rule 23(a), (b)(1) and (b)(3) of the Federal Rules of Civil Procedure. Finding a "limited fund" theory too speculative, he refused to certify the class under Rule 23(b)(1); by contrast, he found all of the elements for a 23(b)(3) action present. Drawing on his past experience, the judge concluded that evidence concerning the "state of the art" defense would vary little as to individual plaintiffs while consuming a major part of the time required for their trials. Considerable savings, both for the litigants and for the court, could thus be gained by resolving this and other defense and defense-related questions, including product identification, product defectiveness, gross negligence and punitive damages, in one class trial. The court further found that the named representatives had "typical" claims, and that they and their attorneys would adequately represent the other class members. Accordingly, it certified the class as to the common questions, ordering them resolved for the class by a class action jury. The class jury would also decide all the individual issues in the class representatives' underlying suits; individual issues of the unnamed members would be resolved later in "mini-trials" of seven to ten plaintiffs. Although the class action jury would evaluate the culpability of defendants' conduct for a possible punitive damage award, any such damages would be awarded only after class members had won or settled their individual cases. The court subsequently appointed a special master to survey the class and prepare a report, detailing the class members and their claims, to apprise the jury of the gravity and extent of the absent members' claims and the typicality of the representatives' claims.

On appeal, defendants challenge the court's decision on three grounds: (1) the class fails to meet the requirements of Rule 23; (2) Texas law proscribes a bifurcated determination of punitive damages and actual damages; and (3) the contemplated class format is unconstitutional.

### III. DISCUSSION

The purpose of class actions is to conserve "the resources of both the courts and the parties by permitting an issue potentially affecting every class member to be litigated in an economical fashion." To ensure that this purpose is served, Rule 23 demands that all class actions certified under Rule 23(b)(3) meet the requirements of both 23(a): numerosity, commonality, typicality, and adequacy of representation; and 23(b)(3): predominance and superiority. The district court has wide discretion in deciding whether or not to certify a proposed class. Assuming the court considers the Rule 23 criteria, we may reverse its decision only for abuse of discretion.

### IV. RULE 23

Defendants argue that this class meets none of the Rule 23 requirements, except "numerosity." There is no merit to this argument.

The threshold of "commonality" is not high. Aimed in part at "determining whether there is a need for combined treatment and a benefit to be derived therefrom," the rule requires only that resolution of the common questions affect all or a substantial number of the class members. Defendants do not claim that they intend to raise a "state of the art" defense in only a few cases; the related issues are common to all class members.

The "typicality" requirement focuses less on the relative strengths of the named and unnamed plaintiffs' cases than on the similarity of the legal and remedial theories behind their claims (both commonality and typicality "serve as guideposts for determining whether maintenance of a class action is economical and whether the named plaintiff's claim and the class claims are so interrelated that the interests of the class members will be fairly and adequately protected in their absence"). Defendants do not contend that the named plaintiffs' claims rest on theories different from those of the other class members.

The "adequacy" requirement looks at both the class representatives and their counsel. Defendants have not shown that the representatives are "inadequate" due to an insufficient stake in the outcome or interests antagonistic to the unnamed members. Neither do they give us reason to question the district court's finding that class counsel is "adequate" in light of counsel's past experience in asbestos cases, including trials involving multiple plaintiffs.

We similarly find no abuse in the court's determination that the certified questions "predominate," under Rule 23(b)(3). In order to "predominate," common issues must constitute a significant part of the individual cases. It is difficult to imagine that class jury findings on the class questions will not significantly advance the resolution of the underlying hundreds of cases.

Defendants also argue that a class action is not "superior;" they say that better mechanisms, such as the Wellington Facility and "reverse bifurcation," exist for resolving these claims. Again, however, they have failed to show that the district court abused its discretion by reaching the contrary conclusion. We cannot find that the Wellington Facility, whose merits we do not question, is so superior that it must be used to the exclusion of other forums. Similarly, even if we were prepared to weigh the merits of other procedural mechanisms, we see no basis to conclude that this class action plan is an abuse of discretion.

Courts have usually avoided class actions in the mass accident or tort setting. Because of differences between individual plaintiffs on issues of liability and defenses of liability, as well as damages, it has been feared that separate trials would overshadow the common disposition for the class. See Advisory Committee Notes to 1966 Amendment to Fed.R.Civ.P. 23(b)(3). The courts are now being forced to rethink the alternatives and priorities by the current volume of litigation and more frequent mass disasters. If Congress leaves us to our own devices, we may be forced to abandon repetitive hearings and arguments for each claimant's attorney to the extent enjoyed by the profession in the past. Be that as time will tell, the decision at hand is driven in one direction by all the circumstances. Judge Parker's plan is clearly superior to the alternative of repeating, hundreds of times over, the litigation of the state of the art issues with, as that experienced judge says, "days of the same witnesses, exhibits and issues from trial to trial."

This assumes plaintiffs win on the critical issues of the class trial. To the extent defendants win, the elimination of issues and docket will mean a far greater saving of judicial resources. Furthermore, attorneys' fees for all parties will be greatly reduced under this plan, not only because of the elimination of so much trial time but also because the fees collected from all members of the plaintiff class will be controlled by the judge. From our view it seems that the defendants enjoy all of the advantages, and the plaintiffs incur the disadvantages, of the class action—with one exception: the cases are to be brought to trial. That counsel for plaintiffs would urge the class action under these circumstances is significant support for the district judge's decision.

Necessity moves us to change and invent. Both the *Agent Orange* and the *Asbestos School* courts found that specific issues could be decided in a class "mass tort" action—even on a nationwide basis. We approve of the district court's decision in finding that this "mass tort" class could be certified.

## IN RE SCHOOL ASBESTOS LITIG.

United States Court of Appeals, Third Circuit, 1986.
789 F.2d 996.

In an effort to reach an equitable result in these asbestos property damage cases brought by school authorities, the district court certified a nationwide mandatory class for punitive damages and an opt-out class for compensatory damages. We conclude that the mandatory class cannot be approved because of a lack of necessary findings and for the additional reason that the class, being under-inclusive, cannot in the circumstances here accomplish the objectives for which it was created. We will, however, affirm the denial of a (b)(2) class and despite misgivings on manageability, will affirm the district court's conditional certification of a Rule 23(b)(3) opt-out class on compensatory damages.

The district court invoked Fed.R.Civ.P. 23(b)(1)(B) in entering the certification order designating a mandatory class for school districts seeking punitive damages and followed Rule 23(b)(3) in forming a class for those seeking compensatory damages. A request for class certification under Rule 23(b)(2) was denied.

The court certified that the order constituting the 23(b)(1)(B) class raised a controlling question of law respecting possible violation of the Anti-Injunction Act, 28 U.S.C.A. § 2283. Various parties have appealed, challenging not only that phase of the case but also the propriety of the (b)(3) certification as well as the denial of the (b)(2) request.

This litigation began with the filing of class action complaints in the Eastern District of Pennsylvania by several Pennsylvania school districts and the Barnwell, South Carolina School District. The cases were consolidated soon after filing. Defendants, numbering approximately fifty, are associated with the asbestos industry as miners, bulk suppliers, brokers, assemblers, manufacturers, distributors, and at least one contractor.

As a result of federal legislation and regulation, plaintiffs are required to test for the presence of asbestos in schools. The complaints seek compensatory and punitive damages as well as injunctive relief stemming from compliance with the federal legislation and the alleged need to remove or treat materials containing asbestos. The claims are based on theories of negligence, strict liability, intentional tort, breach of warranty, concert of action, and civil conspiracy.

After a group of plaintiffs presented a motion for the formation of classes under section (b)(1) and (b)(2) of Rule 23, the court issued an order certifying such classes but limited them to claims against three defendants which had agreed not to oppose that action. This ruling led to objections by various other plaintiffs and defendants, and the court later vacated the order in part. Arguments were then heard from all parties who split, not along the usual plaintiff-defendant lines, but into a number of unusual alignments as dictated by their perceived interests. The eventual certification order included the claims against all defendants.

In conditionally creating a mandatory class under (b)(1)(B) on the punitive damage claims, the court found "a substantial possibility that early awards of punitive damages in individual cases would impair or impede the ability of future claimants to obtain punitive damages." Although plaintiffs had advanced the argument that the defendants' funds would be exhausted before all claimants were paid, no substantive evidence was presented demonstrating that those assets would be insufficient, and accordingly the district judge declined to address that issue.

The court believed that a mandatory class would create an opportunity for parity of treatment by bringing all injured parties into the same forum. Nevertheless, any plaintiff who opted out of the (b)(3) class would be permitted to settle a punitive damage claim with defendants. Additional support for certification was found in the strong "federal interest inherent in asbestos abatement" and the minimal intrusion on the interests of the school districts.

Class certification under 23(b)(2), however, was denied. The court commented that "despite the ingenuity of plaintiffs' claims for limited equitable remedies, this case remains at bottom, one for legal damages." Although recognizing the possibility that at some point there might be "an incidental need for equitable relief," the court concluded that such a potential could not sustain certification under 23(b)(2).

The court directed the certification of a 23(b)(3) class, finding the numerosity requirement satisfied by estimates that friable asbestos is present in approximately 14,000 of the nation's schools, about 8,500 of which have an abatement problem. Commonality existed in an underlying core of issues identified as: "(a) The general health hazards of asbestos; (b) defendants' knowledge or reason to know of the health hazards of asbestos; (c) defendants' failure to warn/test; and (d) defendant's concert of action and/or conspiracy involving formation of and adherence to industry practices." Those elements could "be established by common proof, which, although it may be complex, does not vary from class-member school to class-member school."

The typicality requirement was satisfied because the plaintiffs' theories of liability were harmonious, and the named plaintiffs stood in a position similar to other members of the class. Some of the parties had obliquely questioned the adequacy of representation, but the court concluded that the class was represented by counsel "very experienced with class action litigation and thoroughly familiar with property damage and mass disaster litigation."

In considering the specific requirements for a (b)(3) certification, the court noted that the presence of asbestos in school buildings had a similar impact on each member of the class. Additionally, the question of proximate cause was a legal one which could be resolved on a class-wide basis without involving individualized member-by-member proof.

Addressing the requirement of superiority, the court emphasized that in resolving "at least some of the issues" on a class basis potential savings in expense would result, a consideration particularly important in asbestos litigation with its staggering costs. Moreover, because all claims were for property damage, the level of concern for the plaintiffs' right to choose individual forums and counsel was reduced.

The district judge conceded that the manageability aspect was not "wholly without difficulty," but stated "at this point I believe the management problems can be overcome." The court was convinced that although the substantive tort law of many jurisdictions might be applicable, the basic variations could be reduced to a reasonable number and subclasses could be created to accommodate those differences. Furthermore, plaintiffs represented to the trial judge that they would "direct discovery and trial briefs to meet the most stringent test of liability."

Notwithstanding the difficulties, the court determined that the class action was superior to the only existing alternative—repetitious individual litigation.

## I.

This appeal must be decided against the background of the asbestos scene, an unparalleled situation in American tort law. To date, more than 30,000 personal injury claims have been filed against asbestos manufacturers and producers. An estimated 180,000 additional claims of this type will be on court dockets by the year 2010. Added to those monumental figures are the claims for property damage—the cost of removing or treating asbestos-based materials used in building construction. Some indication of the magnitude of that potential liability may be gleaned from the fact that the property damage claims filed in the Johns-Manville bankruptcy proceedings stood at $69 billion as of June 1985.

The procedures of the traditional tort system proved effective in unearthing the hazards of asbestos to workers and the failure of its producers to reduce the risk. However, the undeniable limitations of the "one-on-one" approach in coping with the massive onset of claims now in the courts have caused serious and justified concern.

A report compiled by the Rand Corporation paints a gloomy picture. It points out the high cost and inefficiencies in handling these individual claims as well as the uneven, inconsistent, and unjust results often achieved. Perhaps the least flattering statistic is the high cost of processing these claims: "On the average, the total cost to plaintiffs and defendants of litigating a claim was considerably greater than the amount paid in compensation."

Inefficiency results primarily from relitigation of the same basic issues in case after case. Since a different jury is empaneled in each action, it must hear the same evidence that was presented in previous trials. A clearer example of reinventing the wheel thousands of times is hard to imagine.

Apparent inconsistency of jury verdicts has often been a reflection of the ability of the system to sort out individual differences and tailor redress to precise circumstances. In the asbestos litigation field, however, the variation in jury awards has led to complaints that injustice rather than careful apportionment has resulted. The problems are complicated by the variations and permutations of state law that govern tort liability.

The national dimensions of the problem have led to calls for congressional action. Although the subject has attracted the attention of individual representatives and senators, no legislative response has garnered enough support to be enacted.

III.

THE 23(b)(1)(B) CERTIFICATION

Rule 23(b)(1)(B) applies where there is a risk that "adjudications with respect to individual members of the class would as a practical matter be dispositive of the interests of the other members not parties to the adjudications or substantially impair or impede their ability to protect their interests."

Because plaintiffs had presented no evidence that the defendants' available assets would be insufficient to pay all claims, the district court did not rely on a "limited fund" theory as a basis for class certification. The proponents of the mandatory class, however, asserted "the very real possibility" that late-coming plaintiffs would be unable to receive punitive damages if a court decided in the future that defendants had been punished enough. In short, at some point punitive damages might be prohibited because they would amount to overkill. Finding a "substantial possibility" of the overkill scenario, the district court determined that creation of a (b)(1)(B) class was warranted as a measure to promote "equality of treatment for all litigants."

The demands for punitive damages have propelled this action into the controversy over awarding exemplary damages in successive mass tort cases arising from the same wrongful act. Problems in this area have been created by the failure of some courts to recognize the reasons underlying punitive damages.

In the era when most tort suits were "one-against-one" contests, a single act triggered a single punishment. The increasingly prevalent mass tort situation, however, exposes a defendant to repetitious punishment for the same culpable conduct. The parallels between the assessment of exemplary damages and a fine levied in criminal courts have led to suggestions that the concepts of double jeopardy and excessive punishment should be invoked in the civil field as well.

Similar concerns have prompted highly respected judges to comment on the possibility that the due process clause might contain some constitutional limitation on the amount of exemplary damages to be awarded. In addition to a possible federal constitutional limitation, state substantive tort law could place restraints on repetitive punitive damage awards. This concept, aimed at the prevention of "overkill" has been labeled the "limited generosity" theory by some of the parties to this case.

Thus powerful arguments have been made that, as a matter of constitutional law or of substantive tort law, the courts shoulder some responsibility for preventing repeated awards of punitive damages for the same acts or series of acts. Preliminarily we will assume, without deciding, that these arguments might provide a threshold justification for the exercise of discretion in certifying a nationwide (mandatory) Rule 23(b)(1)(B) class for punitive damages. We nonetheless hold that the district court abused its discretion in certifying the 23(b)(1)(B) class here because neither the record nor the court's findings are adequate to support the procedure.

The district court made no factual findings at all as to the potential amount and scope of punitive damages. The most the district court mustered here was its conclusion that: "It is apparent that there is a substantial possibility that early awards of punitive damages in individual cases will impair or impede the ability of future claimants to obtain punitive damages. The reality of such impairment has been recognized by commentators and courts."

Some basic considerations expose a critical flaw in the district court's analysis. The class certified does not even include all property damage claimants. Claims for repair of municipal buildings, for instance, are omitted, as are those of homeowners. Within a few weeks after oral argument in this appeal, a jury awarded $6 million in a property damage case brought as a result of the presence of asbestos products in a city hall. Added to the recovery was $2 million in punitive damages.

There is some evidence that the school claims make up a significant portion of the total property damage alleged. Clearly, however, this aspect of the litigation transcends the nation's classrooms and extends to municipal buildings, homes, and other structures.

Far more significant are the tens of thousands of personal injury suits in which punitive damage verdicts have been and continue to be assessed. These claims are satisfied from the same pool of assets to which the school districts now look. If a limit is ever placed on the total punitive damages to be imposed on the asbestos defendants, then that limit probably would apply to all claims whether they arise in property damage or personal injury suits. The school claims would be but a small portion of this total.

Assuming that the record supported the "limited generosity" theory, we would nonetheless decertify the class on the ground that it is under-inclusive. Since the purpose of a 23(b)(1)(B) class is to avoid a judgment that "while not technically concluding the other members, might do so as a practical matter," *id.*, all persons with claims upon the "limited fund" should be included in the 23(b)(1)(B) class.

Thus, because all awards must come from the same defendants, a mandatory class predicated on a potential legal limit to punitive damages would logically include all litigants who seek such awards. From that standpoint, the (b)(1)(B) class certified here is under-inclusive with the result that separate actions by those who should properly be included in the class will go forward. However, the suppression of such separate actions is described in the advisory committee note as "the reason for and the principal key to the propriety and value" of a 23(b)(1) class.

The effect of the mandatory class has been to single out the school districts for special and possibly disadvantageous treatment. They have been forced to litigate in a jurisdiction and under a class procedure that many districts do not desire, and their punitive damage claims have been put "on hold" while the protracted class certification procedure runs its course. Because of this delay, this class could end up in a detrimental position if punitive damage awards are precluded because of a future judicial ruling.

Since the thousands of other claimants who seek exemplary damages from the asbestos defendants need not operate within the confines of a mandatory class procedure, the quest for punitive damages remains for them a race to the courthouse door. Consequently, if the district court proves correct in its theory that at some point a limit on all punitive damage awards will be established, the school districts may be prejudiced in their opportunity to share in the available funds in the meantime.

We do not hold that under-inclusiveness is necessarily fatal to a class created under 23(b)(1)(B); rather, each case requires a careful assessment of the factors mentioned in Rule 19. Courts should give particular attention to the possibility of prejudice either to those omitted from the class or to those within it. In the circumstances here, we conclude that under-inclusiveness does pose an obstacle.

A certain inherent prejudice exists when a litigant is forced to participate in an undesired mandatory class action. That result may be acceptable where the class device will serve the worthwhile goal of protecting the interests of all litigants to a potentially limited fund, but is hard to justify where only a small number of potential claimants can be included in the mandatory action.

## IV.

### DENIAL OF 23(b)(2) CERTIFICATION

The district court concluded that despite the plaintiffs' ingenuity the claims in this suit were essentially for damages. The judge pointed to the advisory committee notes accompanying Rule 23(b)(2), which state that it "does not extend to cases in which the appropriate final relief relates exclusively or predominantly to money damages." The district court did not rule out the possible application of equitable remedies at some stage of the proceeding but concluded that a (b)(2) certification was not appropriate at this time.

Precedent supports the district court's view that an action for money damages may not be maintained as a Rule 23(b)(2) class action. We see no justification for overturning the district judge's evaluation of the realities of the litigation before him. Counsel's desire to have a mandatory class is understandable, but the case for such a certification has not been established.

We find neither error of law nor abuse of discretion in the judge's ruling, and consequently will affirm the denial of a (b)(2) class.

## V.

### THE 23(b)(3) CERTIFICATION

The advisory committee notes to (b)(3) state that a "mass accident" causing injuries to numerous persons is generally not appropriate for class action treatment because "significant questions, not only of damages but of liability and defenses of liability, would be present, affecting the individuals in different ways." If such an action were conducted as a class action, it "would degenerate in practice into multiple lawsuits separately tried."

Although that statement continues to be repeated in case law, there is growing acceptance of the notion that some mass accident situations may be good candidates for class action treatment. An airplane crash, for instance, would present the same liability questions for each passenger, although the damages would depend on individual circumstances. Determination of the liability issues in one suit may represent a substantial savings in time and resources. Even if the action thereafter "degenerates" into a series of individual damage suits, the result nevertheless works an improvement over the situation in which the same separate suits require adjudication on liability using the same evidence over and over again.

Reassessment of the utility of the class action in the mass tort area has come about, no doubt, because courts have realized that such an action need not resolve all issues in the litigation. *See* Fed.R.Civ.P. 23(c)(4)(A). If economies can be achieved by use of the class device, then its application must be given serious and sympathetic consideration.

Part of the reluctance to apply the class action to mass torts is rooted in the notion that individual plaintiffs have the right to select their own counsel and forum, particularly in personal injury actions. That factor has little, if any, relevance in this case because the claims are limited to property damage, and school districts are unlikely to have strong emotional ties to the litigation. Furthermore, the school districts have the right to opt out, and some have stated their intention to do so.

In short, the trend has been for courts to be more receptive to use of the class action in mass tort litigation.

The only serious challenge raised to the 23(a) ruling is the argument that no "questions of law or fact common to the class" exist. Noting that the complaints allege claims for damages based on negligence, strict liability, breach of warranty, intentional tort, concert of action and civil conspiracy, the district court explained that all these claims "arise out of the same common nucleus of operative facts relating to defendants' conduct and the nature of asbestos products."

The district judge identified common factual issues as the health hazards of asbestos, the defendants' knowledge of those dangers, the failure to warn or test, and the defendants' concert of action or conspiracy in the formation of and adherence to industry practices. The court also believed that the proof of these matters would not vary widely from one class member to another. While harboring some reservations as to the breadth of the district court's analysis, we agree with its determination that Rule 23(a)(2) is satisfied.

Plaintiffs contend that the presence of any airborne asbestos fibers in a school presents an unacceptable hazard. Whether that is true or whether only a higher concentration creates a danger is an issue common to all members of the plaintiff class. Ascertaining the danger point is critical to the determination of whether class members have sustained a legal injury and also is pertinent in establishing the existence of a defective product.

The plaintiffs' contention that defendants knew of the dangers of asbestos and failed to warn is also common to the members of the class. The opponents assert that the defendants' knowledge cannot be proved on a common basis because medical understanding of the effects of asbestos exposure has "changed markedly" over the years. The focus, however, must be on whether the fact to be proved is common to the members of the class, not whether it is common to all the defendants. Similarly, proof of concert of action or conspiracy by the defendants (or some of them) involves common questions.

We find ourselves in substantial agreement with the reasoning of the Court of Appeals for the Fifth Circuit which, in upholding a (b)(3) class action of 893 asbestos personal injury claims, noted that the "threshold of commonality is not high." *Jenkins v. Raymark Indus. Inc.*

Once the mandates of Rule 23(a) are satisfied, certification may be upheld when common issues predominate over individual ones and the class method of adjudication is superior to existing alternatives. There may be cases in which class resolution of one issue or a small group of them will so advance the litigation that they may fairly be said to predominate. Resolution of common issues need not guarantee a conclusive finding on liability, nor is it a disqualification that damages must be assessed on an individual basis.

Experience shows that in the asbestos litigation arena redundant evidence is the rule rather than the exception. In case after case, the health issues, the question of injury causation, and the knowledge of the defendants are explored, often by the same witnesses. Efforts to achieve expeditious disposition of the cases by invocation of stare decisis and collateral estoppel have been largely unsuccessful.

The use of the class action device appears to offer some hope of reducing the expenditure of time and money needed to resolve the common issues which are of substantial importance. As the *Jenkins* court commented, "It is difficult to imagine that class jury findings on the class questions will not significantly advance the resolution of the underlying hundreds of cases."

In some ways, *Jenkins* presented more difficult problems because of the complexity of the causation questions in personal injury suits; that phase of a property damage claim is more straightforward. However, the *Jenkins* class action is confined to claims arising under the law of a single state. Here the court is confronted with the substantive law of many states.

To meet the problem of diversity in applicable state law, class plaintiffs have undertaken extensive analysis of the variances in products liability among the jurisdictions. That review separates the law into four categories. Even assuming additional permutations and combinations, plaintiffs have made a creditable showing, which apparently satisfied the district court, that class certification does not present insuperable obstacles. Although we have some doubt on this score, the effort may nonetheless prove successful.

As we see it, at the present stage, manageability is a serious concern. In a sense, a whole industry is on trial, presenting a likelihood that defendants occupying various positions in the distribution chain could bear differing degrees of responsibility for the alleged injury to the class. For example, two of the common questions are the defendants' knowledge of the dangers of asbestos and the existence of an industry-wide conspiracy to suppress that knowledge. Although the plaintiffs' proof on those points would not differ from class member to class member, certain defendants may respond on an individual basis as to their lack of culpability. The potential for individualized defenses does not detract from the commonality of the questions as viewed from the standpoint of the class members, but the problem clearly poses significant case management concerns.

Manageability is a practical problem, one with which a district court generally has a greater degree of expertise and familiarity than does an appellate court. Hence, a district court must necessarily enjoy wide discretion, and we are not inclined to reverse a certification before the district judge has had an opportunity to put the matter to a test. We point out the critical fact that certification is conditional. When, and if, the district court is convinced that the litigation cannot be managed, decertification is proper.

As the case goes forward, the district court may well find other important common issues, perhaps even more critical for resolution than those sorted out at this early stage. We are unwilling to foreclose that possibility. Nor do we limit the option of the district court to decertify if the issues it has classified as substantial later appear insufficient to justify the class procedure.

We acknowledge that our reluctance to vacate the (b)(3) certification is influenced by the highly unusual nature of asbestos litigation. The district court has demonstrated a willingness to attempt to cope with an unprecedented situation in a somewhat novel fashion, and we do not wish to foreclose an approach that might offer some possibility of improvement over the methods employed to date.

Accordingly, the order certifying a (b)(3) class will be affirmed as will the order denying a (b)(2) certification. The order granting a (b)(1)(B) class will be vacated.

## IN RE AGENT ORANGE PROD. LIAB. LITIG.

United States Court of Appeals, Second Circuit, 1987.
818 F.2d 145.

This is the first of nine opinions, all filed on this date, dealing with appeals from various decisions in this multidistrict litigation and class action. The present opinion also contains our rulings regarding the certification of a class action and the approval of the settlement between the plaintiff class and the defendant chemical companies.

### I.   OVERVIEW AND SUMMARY OF RULINGS

By any measure, this is an extraordinary piece of litigation. It concerns the liability of several major chemical companies and the United States government for injuries to members of the United States, Australian, and New Zealand armed forces and their families. These injuries were allegedly suffered as a result of the servicepersons' exposure to the herbicide Agent Orange while in Vietnam.

Agent Orange, which contains trace elements of the toxic by-product dioxin, was purchased by the United States government from the chemical companies and sprayed on various areas in South Vietnam on orders of United States military commanders. The spraying generally was intended to defoliate areas in order to reduce the military advantage afforded enemy forces by the jungle and to destroy enemy food supplies.

We are a court of law, and we must address and decide the issues raised as legal issues. We do take note, however, of the nationwide interest in this litigation and the strong emotions these proceedings have generated among Vietnam veterans and their families. The correspondence to the court, the extensive hearings held throughout the nation by the district court concerning the class settlement with the chemical companies, and even the arguments of counsel amply demonstrate that this litigation is viewed by many as something more than an action for damages for personal injuries. To some, it is a method of public protest at perceived national indifference to Vietnam veterans; to others, an organizational rallying point for those veterans. Thus, although the precise legal claim is one for damages for personal injuries, the district court accurately noted that the plaintiffs were also seeking "larger remedies and emotional compensation" that were beyond its power to award.

Central to the litigation are the many Vietnam veterans and their families who have encountered grievous medical problems. It is human nature for persons who face cancer in themselves or serious birth defects in their children to search for the causes of these personal tragedies. Well-publicized allegations about Agent Orange have led many such veterans and their families to believe that the herbicide is the source of their current grief. That grief is hardly assuaged by the fact that contact with the herbicide occurred while they were serving their country in circumstances that were unpleasant at best, excruciating at worst.

When the case is viewed as a legal action for personal injury sounding in tort, the most noticeable fact is the pervasive factual and legal doubt that surrounds the plaintiffs' claims. Indeed, the clear weight of scientific evidence casts grave doubt on the capacity of Agent Orange to injure human beings. Epidemiological studies of Vietnam veterans, many of which were undertaken by the United States, Australian, and various state governments, demonstrate no greater incidence of relevant ailments among veterans or their families than among any other group. To an individual plaintiff, a serious ailment will seem highly unusual. For example, the very existence of a birth defect may persuade grieving parents as to Agent Orange's guilt. However, a trier of fact must confront the statistical probability that thousands of birth defects in children born to a group the size of the plaintiff class might not be unusual even absent exposure to Agent Orange. A trier of fact must also confront the fact that there is almost no evidence, even in studies involving animals, that exposure of males to dioxin causes birth defects in their children.

Both the Veterans' Administration and the Congress have treated the epidemiological studies as authoritative. Although such studies do not exclude the possibility of injury and settle nothing at all as to future effects, they offer little scientific basis for believing that Agent Orange caused any injury to military personnel or their families. The scientific basis for the plaintiffs' case consists of studies of animals and industrial accidents involving dioxin. Differences in the species examined and nature of exposure facially undermine the significance of these studies when compared with studies of the veterans themselves.

Proving that the ailments of a particular individual were caused by Agent Orange is also extremely difficult. Indeed, in granting summary judgment against those plaintiffs who opted out of the class action (the "opt-outs"), the district court essentially held that such proof was presently impossible. The first evidentiary hurdle for such an individual is to prove exposure to Agent Orange, an event years past that at the time did not carry its current significance. Such evidence generally consists only of oral testimony as to an individual's remembering having been sprayed while on the ground and/or having consumed food and water in areas where spraying took place. The second and, in the view of the district court, insurmountable hurdle is to prove that the individual's exposure to Agent Orange caused the particular ailment later encountered. Plaintiffs do not claim that Agent Orange causes ailments that are not found in the population generally and that cannot result from causes known and unknown other than exposure to dioxin. Plaintiffs' proof of causation would consist largely of inferences drawn from the existence of an ailment, exposure to Agent Orange, and medical opinion as to a causal relationship. However, the difficulties in excluding known causes, such as undetected exposure to the same or similar toxic substances in civilian life, and the conceded existence of unknown causes might make it difficult for any plaintiff to persuade a trier of fact as to Agent Orange's guilt. Causation is nevertheless an absolutely indispensable element of each plaintiff's claim.

The plaintiffs' claims are further complicated by the fact that an individual's exposure to Agent Orange cannot be traced to a particular defendant because the military mixed the Agent Orange produced by various companies in identical, unlabeled barrels. No one can determine, therefore, whether a particular instance of spraying involved a particular defendant's product. In addition, the Agent Orange produced by some defendants had a considerably higher dioxin content than that produced by others. Because the alleged ailments may be related to the amount of dioxin to which an individual was exposed, it is conceivable that if Agent Orange did cause injury, only the products of certain companies could have done so.

Difficult legal problems also arise from the considerable uncertainty as to which product liability rules and statutes of limitations apply to the various plaintiffs. The plaintiffs come from throughout the United States, Australia, and New Zealand, and each would face difficult choice of law problems that might be resolved adversely to their claims.

Finally, doubt about the strength of the plaintiffs' claims exists because of the so-called military contractor defense. The chemical companies sold Agent Orange to the United States government, which used it in waging war against enemy forces seeking control of South Vietnam. It would be anomalous for a company to be held liable by a state or federal court for selling a product ordered by the federal government, particularly when the company could not control the use of that product. Moreover, military activities involve high stakes, and common concepts of risk averseness are of no relevance. To expose private companies generally to lawsuits for injuries arising out of the deliberately risky activities of the military would greatly impair the procurement process and perhaps national security itself.

The procedural aspects of this litigation are also extraordinary. Chief Judge Weinstein certified it as a class action at the behest of most of the plaintiffs and over the objections of all of the defendants. Certain issues, such as the damage suffered by each plaintiff, were not, of course, to be determined in the class action. Instead, they were to be left to individual trials if the outcome of the class action proceedings was favorable to the plaintiffs. Some plaintiffs opted out of the class action, but their cases remained in the Eastern District of New York as part of a multidistrict referral.

The class certification and settlement caused the number of claimants and the variety of ailments attributed to Agent Orange to climb dramatically. It also has caused disunity among the plaintiffs and increased the controversy surrounding this case. Correspondence to this court indicates that many of the original plaintiffs, most of whom joined the motions for class certification, were never advised that use of the class action device might lead to their being represented by counsel whom they did not select and who could settle the case without consulting them. In the midst of this litigation, original class counsel, Yannacone & Associates, asked to be relieved for financial reasons. Control of the class action soon passed to the PMC. Six of the nine members of the PMC advanced money for expenses at a time when the plaintiffs' case, already weak on the law and the facts, was near collapse for lack of resources. This money was furnished under an agreement that provided that three times the amount advanced by each lawyer would be repaid from an eventual fee award.

These payments would have priority, moreover, over payments for legal work done on the case.

The trial date set by Chief Judge Weinstein put the parties under great pressure, and just before the trial was to start, the defendants reached a $180 million settlement with the PMC. The size of the settlement seems extraordinary. However, given the serious nature of many of the various ailments and birth defects plaintiffs attributed to Agent Orange, the understandable sympathy a jury would have for the particular plaintiffs, and the large number of claimants, 240,000, the settlement was essentially a payment of nuisance value. Although the chances of the chemical companies' ultimately having to pay any damages may have been slim, they were exposed potentially to billions of dollars in damages if liability was established and millions in attorneys' fees merely to continue the litigation.

The district judge approved the settlement. It is clear that he viewed the plaintiffs' case as so weak as to be virtually baseless. Indeed, shortly after the settlement, he granted summary judgment against the plaintiffs who opted out of the class action on the grounds that they could not prove that a particular ailment was caused by Agent Orange and that their claims were barred by the military contractor defense.

In addition, Chief Judge Weinstein awarded counsel fees in an amount that was considerably smaller than had been requested by the attorneys involved. The size of the award was clearly influenced by his skepticism about whether the case should ever have been brought.

The final extraordinary aspect of this case is the scheme adopted by Chief Judge Weinstein to distribute the class settlement award. That scheme, which is described as "compensation-based" rather than "tort-based," allows veterans who served in areas in which the herbicide was sprayed and who meet the Social Security Act's definition of disabled to collect benefits up to a ceiling of $12,000. Smaller payments are provided to the survivors of veterans who served in such areas. No proof of causation by Agent Orange is required, although benefits are available only for non-traumatic disability or death. The distribution scheme also provides for the funding of a foundation to undertake projects thought to be helpful to members of the class.

Many of the decisions of the district court were appealed, and we summarize our rulings here. In this opinion, we reject the various challenges to the certification of a class action. Although we share the prevalent skepticism about the usefulness of the class action device in mass tort litigation, we believe that its use was justified here in light of the centrality of the military contractor defense to the claims of all plaintiffs. We also approve the settlement in light of both the pervasive difficulties faced by plaintiffs in establishing liability and our conviction that the military contractor defense absolved the chemical companies of any liability. A third opinion affirms the grant of summary judgment against the opt-out plaintiffs based on the military contractor defense. On two grounds we hold that the chemical companies did not breach any duty to inform the government of Agent Orange's hazardous properties. First, at the times relevant here, the government had as much information about the potential hazards of dioxin as did the chemical companies. Second, the weight of present scientific evidence does not establish that Agent Orange caused injury to personnel in Vietnam. The chemical companies did not breach any duty to inform the government and are therefore not liable to the opt-outs.

### III. CLASS MEMBERS' OBJECTIONS TO THE SETTLEMENT

#### *Class Certification*

Appellants argue that the district court erred in certifying the Rule 23(b)(3) class action.

Existence of the first Rule 23(a) prerequisite in this case is undisputed. Whether there are problems regarding typicality and adequacy of representation depends upon the nature of the questions of law or fact common to the class. Our view of the existence of the third and fourth prerequisites is thus influenced by our view of the second.

The comment to Rule 23(b)(3) explicitly cautions against use of the class action device in mass tort cases ("A 'mass accident' resulting in injuries to numerous persons is ordinarily not appropriate for a class action because of the likelihood that significant questions, not only of damages but of liability and defenses of liability, would be present, affecting the individuals in different ways."). Moreover, most courts have denied certification in those circumstances.

The present litigation justifies the prevalent skepticism over the usefulness of class actions in so-called mass tort cases and, in particular, claims for injuries resulting from toxic exposure. First, the benefits of a class action have been greatly exaggerated by its proponents in the present matter. For example, much ink has been spilled in this case over the distinction between generic causation—whether Agent Orange is harmful at all, regardless of the degree or nature of exposure, and what ailments it may cause—and individual causation—whether a particular veteran suffers from a particular ailment as a result of exposure to Agent Orange. It has been claimed that the former is an issue that might appropriately be tried in a class action, notwithstanding that individual causation must be tried separately for each plaintiff if the plaintiff class prevails.

We do not agree. The generic causation issue has three possible outcomes: 1) exposure to Agent Orange always causes harm; 2) exposure to Agent Orange never causes harm; and 3) exposure to Agent Orange may or may not cause harm depending on the kind of exposure and perhaps on other factors. It is indisputable that exposure to Agent Orange does not automatically cause harm. The relevant question, therefore, is not whether Agent Orange has the capacity to cause harm, the generic causation issue, but whether it *did* cause harm and to whom. That determination is highly individualistic, and depends upon the characteristics of individual plaintiffs (*e.g.* state of health, lifestyle) and the nature of their exposure to Agent Orange. Although generic causation and individual circumstances concerning each plaintiff and his or her exposure to Agent Orange thus appear to be inextricably intertwined, the class action would have allowed generic causation to be determined without regard to those characteristics and the individual's exposure.

The second reason for our skepticism is that, with the exception of the military contractor defense, there may be few, if any, common questions of law. Although state law governs the claims of the individual veterans, Chief Judge Weinstein decided that there were common questions of law because he predicted that each court faced with an Agent Orange case would resort to a national consensus of product liability law. Chief Judge Weinstein's analysis of the choice of law issues in this action, with which we assume familiarity, is bold and imaginative. However, in light of our prior holding that federal common law does not govern plaintiffs' claims, every jurisdiction would be free to render its own choice of law decision, and common experience suggests that the intellectual power of Chief Judge Weinstein's analysis alone would not be enough to prevent widespread disagreement.

Third, the dynamics of a class action in a case such as this may either impair the ability of representative parties to protect the interests of the class or cause the inefficient use of judicial resources. These undesirable results stem from the fact that potential plaintiffs in toxic tort cases do not share common interests because of differences in the strength of their claims. Before the class is certified, it is usually some of the plaintiffs who seek certification and defendants who resist. This is so because many of the plaintiffs' counsel will perceive in a class action efficiencies in discovery, legal and scientific research, and the funding of expenses. When counsel can reasonably expect to become counsel for the class and to share in a substantial award of fees, the incentive to seek certification is greatly enhanced. Defendants will resist certification, hoping to defeat the plaintiffs individually through application of their greater resources.

All plaintiffs may not desire class certification, however, because those with strong cases may well be better off going it alone. The drum-beating that accompanies a well-publicized class action claiming harm from toxic exposure and the speculative nature of the exposure issue may well attract excessive numbers of plaintiffs with weak to fanciful cases. For example, notwithstanding the grave doubt surrounding the factual basis of the plaintiffs' case, some 240,000 veterans and family members alleging hundreds of different ailments, including many that are both minor and commonplace, have filed claims for payment out of the settlement fund.

If plaintiffs with strong claims remain members of the class, they may see their claims diluted because a settlement attractive to the defendants will in all likelihood occur. Weak plaintiffs, who may exist in very large numbers, stand to gain from even a small settlement. Moreover, once a significant amount of money is on the table, the class attorneys will have an incentive to settle. They may well anticipate that the percentage of this money likely to be awarded as counsel fees will decline after a certain point. If they go to trial, on the other hand, they run the risk of losing the case and receiving no compensation for what may have been an enormous amount of work. There is thus great pressure to settle. Indeed, a settlement in a case such as the instant litigation, dramatically arrived at just before dawn on the day of trial after sleepless hours of bargaining, seems almost as inevitable as the sunrise. Such a settlement, however, is not likely to lead to a fund that can be distributed among the large number of class members who will assert claims and still compensate the strong plaintiffs for the value of their cases.

Moreover, the ability of the district court to scrutinize the fairness of the settlement is greatly impaired where the legal and factual issues to be determined in the class action are as numerous and complex as they were under the district court's order in the instant case. Similarly, the fashioning of a distribution plan that is both fair to the strong plaintiffs and efficient in adjudicating the large number of claims may be impossible. Only the weakness of the evidence of causation as to all plaintiffs and the strength of the military contractor defense enabled the district court to evaluate the settlement accurately and to fashion an appropriate distribution scheme in the instant matter. We regard those factors as largely coincidental and not to be expected in all toxic exposure cases.

If the strong plaintiffs opt out, however, the efficiencies of a class action may be negative. The class would then consist largely of plaintiffs with weak cases, many or most of which should never have been brought. The defendants would be unlikely to settle with the class because such a settlement with the class would not affect their continuing exposure to large damage awards in the individual cases brought by strong plaintiffs. Both the class action and the strong cases would then have to be tried.

Were this an action by civilians based on exposure to dioxin in the course of civilian affairs, we believe certification of a class action would have been error. However, we return to the cardinal fact we noted in denying the petition for writ of mandamus, namely that "the alleged damage was caused by a product sold by private manufacturers under contract to the government for use in a war."

In our view, class certification was justified under Rule 23(b)(3) due to the centrality of the military contractor defense. First, this defense is common to all of the plaintiffs' cases, and thus satisfies the commonality requirement of Rule 23(a)(2). Second, because the military contractor defense is of central importance in the instant matter for reasons explained in our subsequent discussion of the fairness of the settlement and in our separate opinion affirming the grant of summary judgment against the opt-outs, this issue is governed by federal law, and a class trial in a federal court is a method of adjudication superior to the alternatives. If the defense succeeds, the entire litigation is disposed of. If it fails, it will not be an issue in the subsequent individual trials. In that event, moreover, the ground for its rejection, such as a failure to warn the government of a known hazard, might well be dispositive of relevant factual issues in those trials.

Appellants argue that the diverse interests of the class make adequate representation virtually impossible. We disagree. If defendants had successfully interposed the military contractor defense, they would have precluded recovery by all plaintiffs, irrespective of the strengths, weaknesses, or idiosyncrasies of their claims. Similarly, the typicality issue disappears because of the virtual identity of all of the plaintiffs' cases with respect to the military contractor defense.

It is true that some of the dynamics that generate pressure for an undesirable settlement will continue to operate in a class action limited to the military contractor defense. We believe, however, that a district court's ability to scrutinize the fairness of a class settlement is greatly enhanced by narrowing the legal and factual issues to this defense. We are confident, moreover, that such scrutiny will be informed by the court's awareness of the danger of such a settlement occurring. It is also true that the difficulty in fashioning a distribution scheme that does not overcompensate weak claimants and undercompensate strong ones is not alleviated by limiting the class certification to the military contractor defense. However, on balance we believe use of the class action was appropriate, although many potential difficulties were avoided only because all plaintiffs had very weak cases on causation and the military contractor defense was so strong.

We thus conclude that certification of the Rule 23(b)(3) class action was proper. Because our disposition of the appeals from the approval of the settlement and from the grant of summary judgment against the opt-outs excludes any possibility of an award of punitive damages, we need not address the propriety of the certification of a mandatory class under Rule 23(b)(1)(B).

# B.  SETBACKS AND RETREAT

## IN RE FIBREBOARD CORP.

United States Court of Appeals, Fifth Circuit, 1990.
893 F.2d 706.

### I.

On September 20, 1989, Professor Jack Ratliff of the University of Texas Law School filed his special master's report in *Cimino v. Raymark*. The special master concluded that it was "self-evident that the use of one-by-one individual trials is not an option in the asbestos cases." The master recommended four trial phases: I (classwide liability, class representatives' cases), II (classwide damages), III (apportionment) and IV (distribution). On October 26, the district court entered the first of the orders now at issue. The district court concluded that the trial of these cases in groups of 10 would take all of the Eastern District's trial time for the next three years, explaining that it was persuaded that "to apply traditional methodology to these cases is to admit failure of the federal court system to perform one of its vital roles in our society an efficient, cost-effective dispute resolution process that is fair to the parties." The district court then consolidated 3,031 cases under Fed.R.Civ.P. 42(a) "for a single trial on the issues of state of the art and punitive damages and certified a class action under rule 23(b)(3) for the remaining issues of exposure and actual damages." The consolidation and certification included all pending suits in the Beaumont Division of the Eastern District of Texas filed as of February 1, 1989, by insulation workers and construction workers, survivors of deceased workers, and household members of asbestos workers who were seeking money damages for asbestos-related injury, disease, or death.

Phase I is to be a single consolidated trial proceeding under Rule 42(a). It will decide the state of the art and punitive damages issues. By its order of December 29, 1989, the district court explained that "the jury may be allowed to formulate a multiplier for each defendant for which the jury returns an affirmative finding on the issue of gross negligence."

The district court also described the proceedings for Phase II in its October 26 order. In Phase II the jury is to decide the percentage of plaintiffs exposed to each defendant's products, the percentage of claims barred by statutes of limitation, adequate warnings, and other affirmative defenses. The jury is to determine actual damages in a lump sum for each disease category for all plaintiffs in the class. Phase II will include a full trial of liability and damages for 11 class representatives and such evidence as the parties wish to offer from 30 illustrative plaintiffs. Defendants will choose 15 and plaintiffs will choose 15 illustrative plaintiffs, for a total of 41 plaintiffs. The jury will hear opinions of experts from plaintiffs and defendants regarding the total damage award. The basis for the jury's judgment is said to be the 41 cases plus the data supporting the calculation of the experts regarding total damages suffered by the remaining 2,990 class members.

## II.

Plaintiffs deny that Phase II would deny defendants any right. Plaintiffs argue that every plaintiff is effectively before the court; that the evidence to be offered by their experts is more the use of summary evidence under Rule 1006 of the Federal Rules of Evidence than the use of math models to extrapolate total damages from sample plaintiffs. Plaintiffs concede that the contemplated trial is extraordinary, but argue that extraordinary measures are necessary if these cases are to be tried at all. While extraordinary, the measures are no more than a change in the mode of proof, plaintiffs say. The argument continues that Rule 23 is not the necessary vehicle for the ordered trial, but will sustain it, if the "consolidation" is viewed as a class. We turn to these arguments.

The plaintiffs' answers to interrogatories and the depositions already conducted have provided enough information to show that if, as plaintiffs contend, the representative plaintiffs accurately reflect the class, it is a diverse group. The plaintiffs' "class" consists of persons claiming different diseases, different exposure periods, and different occupations. The depositions of ten tentative class representatives indicate that their diseases break down into three categories: asbestosis (pleural and pulmonary)—eight representatives; lung cancer—three representatives; and Mesothelioma—one representative.

We are also uncomfortable with the suggestion that a move from one-on-one "traditional" modes is little more than a move to modernity. Such traditional ways of proceeding reflect far more than habit. They reflect the very culture of the jury trial and the case and controversy requirement of Article III. It is suggested that the litigating unit is the class and, hence, we have the adversarial engagement or that all are present in a "consolidated" proceeding. But, this begs the very question of whether these 3,031 claimants are sufficiently situated for class treatment; it equally begs the question of whether they are actually before the court under Fed.R.Civ.P. Rules 23 and 42(b) in any more than a fictional sense. Ultimately, these concerns find expression in defendants' right to due process.

The 2,990 class members cannot be certified for trial as proposed under Rule 23(b)(3), Fed.R.Civ.P. Rule 23(b)(3) requires that "the questions of law or fact common to the members of the class predominate over any questions affecting individual members." There are too many disparities among the various plaintiffs for their common concerns to predominate. The plaintiffs suffer from different diseases, some of which are more likely to have been caused by asbestos than others. The plaintiffs were exposed to asbestos in various manners and to varying degrees. The plaintiffs' lifestyles differed in material respects. To create the requisite commonality for trial, the discrete components of the class members' claims and the asbestos manufacturers' defenses must be submerged. The procedures for Phase II do precisely that, but, as we have explained, do so only by reworking the substantive duty owed by the manufacturers. At the least, the enabling acts prevent that reading.

Finally, it is questionable whether defendants' right to trial by jury is being faithfully honored, but we need not explore this issue. It is sufficient now to conclude that Phase II cannot go forward without changing Texas law and usurping legislative prerogatives, a step federal courts lack authority to take.

### III.

We admire the work of our colleague, Judge Robert Parker, and are sympathetic with the difficulties he faces. This grant of the petition for writ of mandamus should not be taken as a rebuke of an able judge, but rather as another chapter in an ongoing struggle with the problems presented by the phenomenon of mass torts. The petitions for writ of mandamus are granted. The order for Phase II trial is vacated and the cases are remanded to the district court for further proceedings. We find no impediment to the trial of Phase I should the district court wish to proceed with that trial. We encourage the district court to continue its imaginative and innovative efforts to confront these cases. We also caution that defendants are obligated to cooperate in the common enterprise of obtaining a fair trial.

## IN THE MATTER OF RHONE-POULENC RORER, INC.

United States Court of Appeals, Seventh Circuit, 1995.
51 F.3d 1293.

Drug companies that manufacture blood solids are the defendants in a nationwide class action brought on behalf of hemophiliacs infected by the AIDS virus as a consequence of using the defendants' products. The defendants have filed with us a petition for mandamus, asking us to direct the district judge to rescind his order certifying the case as a class action. We have no appellate jurisdiction over that order. Mandamus has occasionally been granted to undo class certifications, and we are not aware that any case has held that mandamus will never be granted in such cases. The present case, as we shall see, is quite extraordinary when all its dimensions are apprehended.

The suit to which the petition for mandamus relates arises out of the infection of a substantial fraction of the hemophiliac population of this country by the AIDS virus because the blood supply was contaminated by the virus before the nature of the disease was well understood or adequate methods of screening the blood supply existed. The AIDS virus (HIV— human immunodeficiency virus) is transmitted by the exchange of bodily fluids, primarily semen and blood. Hemophiliacs depend on blood solids that contain the clotting factors whose absence defines their disease. These blood solids are concentrated from blood obtained from many donors. If just one of the donors is infected by the AIDS virus the probability that the blood solids manufactured in part from his blood will be infected is very high unless the blood is treated with heat to kill the virus.

First identified in 1981, AIDS was diagnosed in hemophiliacs beginning in 1982, and by 1984 the medical community agreed that the virus was transmitted by blood as well as by semen. That year it was demonstrated that treatment with heat could kill the virus in the blood supply and in the following year a reliable test for the presence of the virus in blood was developed. By this time, however, a large number of hemophiliacs had become infected. Since 1984 physicians have been advised to place hemophiliacs on heat-treated blood solids, and since 1985 all blood donated for the manufacture of blood solids has been screened and supplies discovered to be HIV-positive have been discarded. Supplies that test negative are heat-treated, because the test is not infallible and in particular may fail to detect the virus in persons who became infected within six months before taking the test.

The plaintiffs have presented evidence that 2,000 hemophiliacs have died of AIDS and that half or more of the remaining U.S. hemophiliac population of 20,000 may be HIV-positive. Unless there are dramatic breakthroughs in the treatment of HIV or AIDS, all infected persons will die from the disease. The reason so many are infected even though the supply of blood for the manufacture of blood solids (as for transfusions) has been safe since the mid-80s is that the disease has a very long incubation period; the median period for hemophiliacs may be as long as 11 years. Probably most of the hemophiliacs who are now HIV-positive, or have AIDS, or have died of AIDS were infected in the early 1980s, when the blood supply was contaminated.

Some 300 lawsuits, involving some 400 plaintiffs, have been filed, 60 percent of them in state courts, 40 percent in federal district courts under the diversity jurisdiction, seeking to impose tort liability on the defendants for the transmission of HIV to hemophiliacs in blood solids manufactured by the defendants. Obviously these 400 plaintiffs represent only a small fraction of the hemophiliacs (or their next of kin, in cases in which the hemophiliac has died) who are infected by HIV or have died of AIDS. One of the 300 cases is *Wadleigh,* filed in September 1993, the case that the district judge certified as a class action. Thirteen other cases have been tried already in various courts around the country, and the defendants have won twelve of them. All the cases brought in federal court—cases brought under the diversity jurisdiction—have been consolidated for pre-trial discovery in the Northern District of Illinois by the panel on multidistrict litigation.

The plaintiffs advance two principal theories of liability. The first is that before anyone had heard of AIDS or HIV, it was known that Hepatitis B, a lethal disease though less so than HIV-AIDS, could be transmitted either through blood transfusions or through injection of blood solids. The plaintiffs argue that due care with respect to the risk of infection with Hepatitis B required the defendants to take measures to purge that virus from their blood solids, whether by treating the blood they bought or by screening the donors—perhaps by refusing to deal with paid donors, known to be a class at high risk of being infected with Hepatitis B. The defendants' failure to take effective measures was, the plaintiffs claim, negligent. Had the defendants not been negligent, the plaintiffs further argue, hemophiliacs would have been protected not only against Hepatitis B but also, albeit fortuitously or as the plaintiffs put it "serendipitously," against HIV.

The plaintiffs' second theory of liability is more conventional. It is that the defendants, again negligently, dragged their heels in screening donors and taking other measures to prevent contamination of blood solids by HIV when they learned about the disease in the early 1980s. The plaintiffs have other theories of liability as well, including strict products liability, but it is not necessary for us to get into them.

The district judge did not think it feasible to certify *Wadleigh* as a class action for the adjudication of the entire controversy between the plaintiffs and the defendants. The differences in the date of infection alone of the thousands of potential class members would make such a procedure infeasible. Hemophiliacs infected before anyone knew about the contamination of blood solids by HIV could not rely on the second theory of liability, while hemophiliacs infected after the blood supply became safe (not perfectly safe, but nearly so) probably were not infected by any of the defendants' products. Instead the judge certified the suit "as a class action with respect to particular issues" only. Fed.R.Civ.P. 23(c)(4)(A). He explained this decision in an opinion which implied that he did not envisage the entry of a final judgment but rather the rendition by a jury of a special verdict that would answer a number of questions bearing, perhaps decisively, on whether the defendants are negligent under either of the theories sketched above. If the special verdict found no negligence under either theory, that presumably would be the end of all the cases unless other theories of liability proved viable. If the special verdict found negligence, individual members of the class would then file individual tort suits in state and federal district courts around the nation and would use the special verdict, in conjunction with the doctrine of collateral estoppel, to block relitigation of the issue of negligence.

With all due respect for the district judge's commendable desire to experiment with an innovative procedure for streamlining the adjudication of this "mass tort," we believe that his plan so far exceeds the permissible bounds of discretion in the management of federal litigation as to compel us to intervene and order decertification.

Nevertheless we shall assume that eventually there will be a final judgment to review. Only it will come too late to provide effective relief to the defendants; and this is an important consideration in relation to the first condition for mandamus, that the challenged ruling of the district court have inflicted irreparable harm, which is to say harm that cannot be rectified by an appeal from the final judgment in the lawsuit. The reason that an appeal will come too late to provide effective relief for these defendants is the sheer magnitude of the risk to which the class action, in contrast to the individual actions pending or likely, exposes them. Consider the situation that would obtain if the class had not been certified. The defendants would be facing 300 suits. More might be filed, but probably only a few more, because the statutes of limitations in the various states are rapidly expiring for potential plaintiffs. The blood supply has been safe since 1985. That is ten years ago. The risk to hemophiliacs of having become infected with HIV has been widely publicized; it is unlikely that many hemophiliacs are unaware of it. Under the usual discovery statute of limitations, they would have to have taken steps years ago to determine their infection status, and having found out file suit within the limitations period running from the date of discovery, in order to preserve their rights.

Three hundred is not a trivial number of lawsuits. The potential damages in each one are great. But the defendants have won twelve of the first thirteen, and, if this is a representative sample, they are likely to win most of the remaining ones as well. Perhaps in the end, if class-action treatment is denied (it has been denied in all the other hemophiliac HIV suits in which class certification has been sought), they will be compelled to pay damages in only 25 cases, involving a potential liability of perhaps no more than $125 million altogether. These are guesses, of course, but they are at once conservative and usable for the limited purpose of comparing the situation that will face the defendants if the class certification stands. All of a sudden they will face thousands of plaintiffs. Many may already be barred by the statute of limitations, as we have suggested, though its further running was tolled by the filing of *Wadleigh* as a class action.

Suppose that 5,000 of the potential class members are not yet barred by the statute of limitations. And suppose the named plaintiffs in *Wadleigh* win the class portion of this case to the extent of establishing the defendants' liability under either of the two negligence theories. It is true that this would only be prima facie liability, that the defendants would have various defenses. But they could not be confident that the defenses would prevail. They might, therefore, easily be facing $25 billion in potential liability (conceivably more), and with it bankruptcy. They may not wish to roll these dice. That is putting it mildly. They will be under intense pressure to settle. If they settle, the class certification—the ruling that will have forced them to settle—will never be reviewed. Judge Friendly, who was not given to hyperbole, called settlements induced by a small probability of an immense judgment in a class action "blackmail settlements." Judicial concern about them is legitimate, not "sociological," as it was derisively termed in *In re Sugar Antitrust Litigation.*

We do not want to be misunderstood as saying that class actions are bad because they place pressure on defendants to settle. That pressure is a reality, but it must be balanced against the undoubted benefits of the class action that have made it an authorized procedure for employment by federal courts. We have yet to consider the balance. All that our discussion to this point has shown is that the first condition for the grant of mandamus—that the challenged ruling not be effectively reviewable at the end of the case—is fulfilled. The ruling will inflict irreparable harm; the next question is whether the ruling can fairly be described as usurpative. We have formulated this second condition as narrowly, as stringently, as can be, but even so formulated we think it is fulfilled. We do not mean to suggest that the district judge is engaged in a deliberate power-grab. We have no reason to suppose that he wants to preside over an unwieldy class action. We believe that he was responding imaginatively and in the beast of faith to the challenge that mass torts, graphically illustrated by the avalanche of asbestos litigation, pose for the federal courts. But the plan that he has devised for the HIV-hemophilia litigation exceeds the bounds of allowable judicial discretion. Three concerns, none of them necessarily sufficient in itself but cumulatively compelling, persuade us to this conclusion.

The first is a concern with forcing these defendants to stake their companies on the outcome of a single jury trial, or be forced by fear of the risk of bankruptcy to settle even if they have no legal liability, when it is entirely feasible to allow a final, authoritative determination of their liability for the colossal misfortune that has befallen the hemophiliac population to emerge from a decentralized process of multiple trials, involving different juries, and different standards of liability, in different jurisdictions, and when, in addition, the preliminary indications are that the defendants are not liable for the grievous harm that has befallen the members of the class. These qualifications are important. In most class actions—and those the ones in which the rationale for the procedure is most compelling—individual suits are infeasible because the claim of each class member is tiny relative to the expense of litigation. That plainly is not the situation here. A notable feature of this case, and one that has not been remarked upon or encountered, so far as we are aware, in previous cases, is the demonstrated great likelihood that the plaintiffs' claims, despite their human appeal, lack legal merit. This is the inference from the defendants' having won 92.3 percent (12/13) of the cases to have gone to judgment. Granted, thirteen is a small sample and further trials, if they are held, may alter the pattern that the sample reveals. But whether they do or not, the result will be robust if these further trials are permitted to go forward, because the pattern that results will reflect a consensus, or at least a pooling of judgment, of many different tribunals.

For this consensus or maturing of judgment the district judge proposes to substitute a single trial before a single jury instructed in accordance with no actual law of any jurisdiction—a jury that will receive a kind of Esperanto instruction, merging the negligence standards of the 50 states and the District of Columbia. One jury, consisting of six persons (the standard federal civil jury nowadays consists of six regular jurors and two alternates), will hold the fate of an industry in the palm of its hand. This jury, jury number fourteen, may disagree with twelve of the previous thirteen juries—and hurl the industry into bankruptcy. That kind of thing can happen in our system of civil justice (it is not likely to happen, because the industry is likely to settle—whether or not it really is liable) without violating anyone's legal rights. But it need not be tolerated when the alternative exists of submitting an issue to multiple juries constituting in the aggregate a much larger and more diverse sample of decision-makers. That would not be a feasible option if the stakes to each class member were too slight to repay the cost of suit, even though the aggregate stakes are very large and would repay the costs of a consolidated proceeding. But this is not the case with regard to the HIV-hemophilia litigation. Each plaintiff if successful is apt to receive a judgment in the millions. With the aggregate stakes in the tens or hundreds of millions of dollars, or even in the billions, it is not a waste of judicial resources to conduct more than one trial, before more than six jurors, to determine whether a major segment of the international pharmaceutical industry is to follow the asbestos manufacturers into Chapter 11.

We have hinted at the second reason for questioning whether the district judge did not exceed the bounds of permissible judicial discretion. He proposes to have a jury determine the negligence of the defendants under a legal standard that does not actually exist anywhere in the world. One is put in mind of the concept of "general" common law that prevailed in the era of *Swift v. Tyson*. The assumption is that the common law of the 50 states and the District of Columbia, at least so far as bears on a claim of negligence against drug companies, is basically uniform and can be abstracted in a single instruction. It is no doubt true that at some level of generality the law of negligence is one, not only nationwide but worldwide. Negligence is a failure to take due care, and due care a function of the probability and magnitude of accident and the costs of avoiding it. A jury can be asked whether the defendants took due care. And in many cases such differences as there are among the tort rules of the different states would not affect the outcome. The Second Circuit was willing to assume *dubitante* that this was true of the issues certified for class determination in the *Agent Orange* litigation.

We doubt that it is true in general, and we greatly doubt that it is true in a case such as this in which one of the theories pressed by the plaintiffs, the "serendipity" theory, is novel. If one instruction on negligence will serve to instruct the jury on the legal standard of every state of the United States applicable to a novel claim, implying that the claim despite its controversiality would be decided identically in all 50 states and the District of Columbia, one wonders what the Supreme Court thought it was doing in the *Erie* case when it held that it was unconstitutional for federal courts in diversity cases to apply general common law rather than the common law of the state whose law would apply if the case were being tried in state rather than federal court. The law of negligence, including subsidiary concepts such as duty of care, foreseeability, and proximate cause, may as the plaintiffs have argued forcefully to us differ among the states only in nuance, (though we think not, for a reason discussed later). But nuance can be important, and its significance is suggested by a comparison of differing state pattern instructions on negligence and differing judicial formulations of the meaning of negligence and the subordinate concepts. The voices of the quasi-sovereigns that are the states of the United States sing negligence with a different pitch.

The "serendipity" theory advanced by the plaintiffs in *Wadleigh* is that if the defendants did not do enough to protect hemophiliacs from the risk of Hepatitis B, they are liable to hemophiliacs for any consequences—including infection by the more dangerous and at the time completely unknown AIDS virus—that proper measures against Hepatitis B would, all unexpectedly, have averted. This theory of liability dispenses, rightly or wrongly from the standpoint of the Platonic form of negligence, with proof of foreseeability, even though a number of states, in formulating their tests for negligence, incorporate the foreseeability of the risk into the test. These states follow Judge Cardozo's famous opinion in *Palsgraf v. Long Island R.*, under which the HIV plaintiffs might (we do not say would—we express no view on the substantive issues in this litigation) be barred from recovery on the ground that they were unforeseeable victims of the alleged failure of the defendants to take adequate precautions against infecting hemophiliacs with Hepatitis B and that therefore the drug companies had not violated any duty of care to them.

The plaintiffs' second theory focuses on the questions when the defendants should have learned about the danger of HIV in the blood supply and when, having learned about it, they should have taken steps to eliminate the danger or at least warn the hemophiliacs or their physicians of it. These questions also may be sensitive to the precise way in which a state formulates its standard of negligence. If not, one begins to wonder why this country bothers with different state legal systems.

Both theories, incidentally, may be affected by differing state views on the role of industry practice or custom in determining the existence of negligence. In some states, the standard of care for a physician, hospital, or other provider of medical services, including blood banks, is a professional standard, that is, the standard fixed by the relevant profession. In others, it is the standard of ordinary care, which may, depending on judge or jury, exceed the professional standard. Which approach a state follows, and whether in those states that follow the professional-standard approach manufacturers of blood solids would be assimilated to blood banks as providers of medical services entitled to shelter under the professional standard, could make a big difference in the liability of these manufacturers. We note that persons infected by HIV through blood transfusions appear to have had little better luck suing blood banks than HIV-positive hemophiliacs have had suing the manufacturers of blood solids.

The diversity jurisdiction of the federal courts is, after *Erie,* designed merely to provide an alternative forum for the litigation of state-law claims, not an alternative system of substantive law for diversity cases. But under the district judge's plan the thousands of members of the plaintiff class will have their rights determined, and the four defendant manufacturers will have their duties determined, under a law that is merely an amalgam, an averaging, of the non-identical negligence laws of 51 jurisdictions. No one doubts that Congress could constitutionally prescribe a uniform standard of liability for manufacturers of blood solids. It might we suppose promulgate pertinent provisions of the RESTATEMENT (SECOND) OF TORTS. The point of *Erie* is that Article III of the Constitution does not empower the federal courts to create such a regime for diversity cases.

The plaintiffs argue that an equally important purpose of the class certification is to overcome the shyness or shame that many people feel at acknowledging that they have AIDS or are HIV-positive even when the source of infection is not a stigmatized act. That, the plaintiffs tell us, is why so few HIV-positive hemophiliacs have sued. We do not see how a class action limited to a handful of supposedly common issues can alleviate that problem. Any class member who wants a share in any judgment for damages or in any settlement will have to step forward at some point and identify himself as having AIDS or being HIV-positive. He will have to offer jury findings as collateral estoppel, overcome the defendants' defenses to liability (including possible efforts to show that the class member became infected with HIV through a source other than the defendants' product), and establish his damages. If the privacy of these class members in these follow-on proceedings to the class action is sought to be protected by denominating them "John Does," that is something that can equally well be done in individual lawsuits. The "John Doe" device—and with it the issue of privacy—is independent of class certification.

The third respect in which we believe that the district judge has exceeded his authority concerns the point at which his plan of action proposes to divide the trial of the issues that he has certified for class-action treatment from the other issues involved in the thousands of actual and potential claims of the representatives and members of the class. Bifurcation and even finer divisions of lawsuits into separate trials are authorized in federal district courts. Fed.R.Civ.P. 42(b). And a decision to employ the procedure is reviewed deferentially. However, as we have been at pains to stress recently, the district judge must carve at the joint. Of particular relevance here, the judge must not divide issues between separate trials in such a way that the same issue is reexamined by different juries. The problem is not inherent in bifurcation. It does not arise when the same jury is to try the successive phases of the litigation. But most of the separate "cases" that compose this class action will be tried, after the initial trial in the Northern District of Illinois, in different courts, scattered throughout the country. The right to a jury trial in federal civil cases, conferred by the Seventh Amendment, is a right to have juriable issues determined by the first jury impaneled to hear them (provided there are no errors warranting a new trial), and not reexamined by another finder of fact. This would be obvious if the second finder of fact were a judge. But it is equally true if it is another jury. In this limited sense, a jury verdict can have collateral estoppel effect.

The plan of the district judge in this case is inconsistent with the principle that the findings of one jury are not to be reexamined by a second, or third, or nth jury. The first jury will not determine liability. It will determine merely whether one or more of the defendants was negligent under one of the two theories. The first jury may go on to decide these additional issues with regard to the named plaintiffs. But it will not decide them with regard to the other class members. Unless the defendants settle, a second (and third, and fourth, and hundredth, and conceivably thousandth) jury will have to decide, in individual follow-on litigation by class members not named as plaintiffs in the *Wadleigh* case, such issues as comparative negligence—if any class members knowingly continued to use unsafe blood solids after they learned or should have learned of the risk of contamination with HIV—and proximate causation. Both issues overlap the issue of the defendants' negligence. Comparative negligence entails, as the name implies, a comparison of the degree of negligence of plaintiff and defendant. Proximate causation is found by determining whether the harm to the plaintiff followed in some sense naturally, uninterruptedly, and with reasonable probability from the negligent act of the defendant. It overlaps the issue of the defendants' negligence even when the state's law does not (as many states do) make the foreseeability of the risk to which the defendant subjected the plaintiff an explicit ingredient of negligence. A second or subsequent jury might find that the defendants' failure to take precautions against infection with Hepatitis B could not be thought the proximate cause of the plaintiffs' infection with HIV, a different and unknown blood-borne virus. How the resulting inconsistency between juries could be prevented escapes us.

The protection of the right conferred by the Seventh Amendment to trial by jury in federal civil cases is a traditional office of the writ of mandamus. When the writ is used for that purpose, strict compliance with the stringent conditions on the availability of the writ (including the requirement of proving irreparable harm) is excused. But the looming infringement of Seventh Amendment rights is only one of our grounds for believing this to be a case in which the issuance of a writ of mandamus is warranted. The others as we have said are the undue and unnecessary risk of a monumental industry-busting error in entrusting the determination of potential multi-billion dollar liabilities to a single jury when the results of the previous cases indicate that the defendants' liability is doubtful at best and the questionable constitutionality of trying a diversity case under a legal standard in force in no state. We need not consider whether any of these grounds standing by itself would warrant mandamus in this case. Together they make a compelling case.

We know that an approach similar to that proposed by Judge Grady has been approved for asbestos litigation. *See* in particular *Jenkins v. Raymark Industries, Inc.*; *In re School Asbestos Litigation.* Most federal courts, however, refuse to permit the use of the class-action device in mass-tort cases, even asbestos cases. *cf. In re Fibreboard Corp.* Those courts that have permitted it have been criticized, and alternatives have been suggested which recognize that a sample of trials makes more sense than entrusting the fate of an industry to a single jury. The number of asbestos cases was so great as to exert a well-nigh irresistible pressure to bend the normal rules. No comparable pressure is exerted by the HIV-hemophilia litigation. That litigation can be handled in the normal way without undue inconvenience to the parties or to the state or federal courts.

The defendants have pointed out other serious problems with the district judge's plan, but it is unnecessary to discuss them. The petition for a writ of mandamus is granted, and the district judge is directed to decertify the plaintiff class.

## CASTANO V. THE AMERICAN TOBACCO CO.

United States Court of Appeals, Fifth Circuit, 1996.
84 F.3d 734.

In what may be the largest class action ever attempted in federal court, the district court in this case embarked "on a road certainly less traveled, if ever taken at all" (citing Edward C. Latham, THE POETRY OF ROBERT FROST, "*The Road Not Taken*"), and entered a class certification order. The court defined the class as:

   (a)  All nicotine-dependent persons in the United States who have purchased and smoked cigarettes manufactured by the defendants;

   (b)  the estates, representatives, and administrators of these nicotine-dependent cigarette smokers; and

   (c)  the spouses, children, relatives and "significant others" of these nicotine-dependent cigarette smokers as their heirs or survivors.

The plaintiffs limit the claims to years since 1943.

This matter comes before us on appeal of the class certification order. Concluding that the district court abused its discretion in certifying the class, we reverse.

## II.

A district court must conduct a rigorous analysis of the Rule 23 prerequisites before certifying a class. The decision to certify is within the broad discretion of the court, but that discretion must be exercised within the framework of Rule 23. The party seeking certification bears the burden of proof.

The district court erred in its analysis in two distinct ways. First, it failed to consider how variations in state law affect predominance and superiority. Second, its predominance inquiry did not include consideration of how a trial on the merits would be conducted.

Each of these defects mandates reversal. Moreover, at this time, while the tort is immature, the class complaint must be dismissed, as class certification cannot be found to be a superior method of adjudication.

### A.   *Variations in State Law*

Although Rule 23(c)(1) requires that a class should be certified "as soon as practicable" and allows a court to certify a conditional class, it does not follow that the rule's requirements are lessened when the class is conditional.

In a multi-state class action, variations in state law may swamp any common issues and defeat predominance. *See Georgine v. Amchem Prods.* (decertifying class because legal and factual differences in the plaintiffs' claims "when exponentially magnified by choice of law considerations, eclipse any common issues in this case."); *American Medical Sys.*, (granting mandamus in a multi-state products liability action, in part because "the district court failed to consider how the law of negligence differs from jurisdiction to jurisdiction"). Accordingly, a district court must consider how variations in state law affect predominance and superiority.

A district court's duty to determine whether the plaintiff has borne its burden on class certification requires that a court consider variations in state law when a class action involves multiple jurisdictions. "In order to make the findings required to certify a class action under Rule 23(b)(3) one must initially identify the substantive law issues which will control the outcome of the litigation."

A requirement that a court know which law will apply before making a predominance determination is especially important when there may be differences in state law. *See In re Rhone-Poulenc Rorer, Inc.* (comparing differing state pattern instructions on negligence and differing formulations of the meaning of negligence); *In re "Agent Orange" Prod. Liability Litig.,* (noting possibility of differences in state products liability law). Given the plaintiffs' burden, a court cannot rely on assurances of counsel that any problems with predominance or superiority can be overcome. The able opinion in *School Asbestos* demonstrates what is required from a district court when variations in state law exist. There, the court affirmed class certification, despite variations in state law.

A thorough review of the record demonstrates that, in this case, the district court did not properly consider how variations in state law affect predominance. The court acknowledged as much in its order granting class certification, for, in declining to make a choice of law determination, it noted that "the parties have only briefly addressed the conflict of laws issue in this matter." Similarly, the court stated that "there has been no showing that the consumer protection statutes differ so much as to make individual issues predominate."

The district court's review of state law variances can hardly be considered extensive; it conducted a cursory review of state law variations and gave short shrift to the defendants' arguments concerning variations. In response to the defendants' extensive analysis of how state law varied on fraud, products liability, affirmative defenses, negligent infliction of emotional distress, consumer protection statutes, and punitive damages, the court examined a sample phase 1 jury interrogatory and verdict form, a survey of medical monitoring decisions, a survey of consumer fraud class actions, and a survey of punitive damages law in the defendants' home states. The court also relied on two district court opinions granting certification in multi-state class actions.

The district court's consideration of state law variations was inadequate. The surveys provided by the plaintiffs failed to discuss, in any meaningful way, how the court could deal with variations in state law. The consumer fraud survey simply quoted a few state courts that had certified state class actions. The survey of punitive damages was limited to the defendants' home states. Moreover, the two district court opinions on which the court relied did not support the proposition that variations in state law could be ignored. Nothing in the record demonstrates that the court critically analyzed how variations in state law would affect predominance.

The court also failed to perform its duty to determine whether the class action would be manageable in light of state law variations. The court's only discussion of manageability is a citation to *Jenkins* and the claim that "while manageability of the liability issues in this case may well prove to be difficult, the Court finds that any such difficulties pale in comparison to the specter of thousands, if not millions, of similar trials of liability proceeding in thousands of courtrooms around the nation." The problem with this approach is that it substitutes case-specific analysis with a generalized reference to *Jenkins*. The *Jenkins court*, however, was not faced with managing a novel claim involving eight causes of action, multiple jurisdictions, millions of plaintiffs, eight defendants, and over fifty years of alleged wrongful conduct. Instead, *Jenkins* involved only 893 personal injury asbestos cases, the law of only one state, and the prospect of trial occurring in only one district. Accordingly, for purposes of the instant case, *Jenkins* is largely inapposite.

In summary, whether the specter of millions of cases outweighs any manageability problems in this class is uncertain when the scope of any manageability problems is unknown. Absent considered judgment on the manageability of the class, a comparison to millions of individual trials is meaningless.

## B. Predominance

The district court's second error was that it failed to consider how the plaintiffs' addiction claims would be tried, individually or on a class basis. The district court, based on *Eisen v. Carlisle & Jacquelin* and *Miller v. Mackey Int'l* believed that it could not go past the pleadings for the certification decision. The result was an incomplete and inadequate predominance inquiry.

A district court certainly may look past the pleadings to determine whether the requirements of Rule 23 have been met. Going beyond the pleadings is necessary, as a court must understand the claims, defenses, relevant facts, and applicable substantive law in order to make a meaningful determination of the certification issues.

The district court's predominance inquiry demonstrates why such an understanding is necessary. The premise of the court's opinion is a citation to *Jenkins* and a conclusion that class treatment of common issues would significantly advance the individual trials. Absent knowledge of how addiction-as-injury cases would actually be tried, however, it was impossible for the court to know whether the common issues would be a "significant" portion of the individual trials. The court just assumed that because the common issues would play a part in every trial, they must be significant. The court's synthesis of *Jenkins* and *Eisen* would write the predominance requirement out of the rule, and any common issue would predominate if it were common to all the individual trials.

The court's treatment of the fraud claim also demonstrates the error inherent in its approach. According to both the advisory committee's notes to Rule 23(b)(3) and this court's decision in *Simon v. Merrill Lynch, Pierce, Fenner & Smith, Inc.* a fraud class action cannot be certified when individual reliance will be an issue. The district court avoided the reach of this court's decision in *Simon* by an erroneous reading of *Eisen*; the court refused to consider whether reliance would be an issue in individual trials.

The problem with the district court's approach is that after the class trial, it might have decided that reliance must be proven in individual trials. The court then would have been faced with the difficult choice of decertifying the class after phase 1 and wasting judicial resources, or continuing with a class action that would have failed the predominance requirement of Rule 23(b)(3).

### III.

In addition to the reasons given above, regarding the district court's procedural errors, this class must be decertified because it independently fails the superiority requirement of Rule 23(b)(3). In the context of mass tort class actions, certification dramatically affects the stakes for defendants. Class certification magnifies and strengthens the number of unmeritorious claims. Aggregation of claims also makes it more likely that a defendant will be found liable and results in significantly higher damage awards.

In addition to skewing trial outcomes, class certification creates insurmountable pressure on defendants to settle, whereas individual trials would not. The risk of facing an all-or-nothing verdict presents too high a risk, even when the probability of an adverse judgment is low. *Rhone-Poulenc*. These settlements have been referred to as judicial blackmail.

It is no surprise then, that historically, certification of mass tort litigation classes has been disfavored. The traditional concern over the rights of defendants in mass tort class actions is magnified in the instant case. Our specific concern is that a mass tort cannot be properly certified without a prior track record of trials from which the district court can draw the information necessary to make the predominance and superiority requirements required by Rule 23. This is because certification of an immature tort results in a higher than normal risk that the class action may not be superior to individual adjudication.

We first address the district court's superiority analysis. The court acknowledged the extensive manageability problems with this class. Such problems include difficult choice of law determinations, sub-classing of eight claims with variations in state law, *Erie* guesses, notice to millions of class members, further sub-classing to take account of transient plaintiffs, and the difficult procedure for determining who is nicotine-dependent. Cases with far fewer manageability problems have given courts pause.

The district court's rationale for certification in spite of such problems—*i.e.,* that a class trial would preserve judicial resources in the millions of inevitable individual trials—is based on pure speculation. Not every mass tort is asbestos, and not every mass tort will result in the same judicial crises. The judicial crisis to which the district court referred is only theoretical.

What the district court failed to consider, and what no court can determine at this time, is the very real possibility that the judicial crisis may fail to materialize. The plaintiffs' claims are based on a new theory of liability and the existence of new evidence. Until plaintiffs decide to file individual claims, a court cannot, from the existence of injury, presume that all or even any plaintiffs will pursue legal remedies. Nor can a court make a superiority determination based on such speculation. *American Medical Sys.* (opining that superiority is lacking where judicial management crisis does not exist and individual trials are possible).

Severe manageability problems and the lack of a judicial crisis are not the only reasons why superiority is lacking. The most compelling rationale for finding superiority in a class action—the existence of a negative value suit—is missing in this case. *Accord Phillips Petroleum Co. v. Shutts*; *Rhone-Poulenc.*

As he stated in the record, plaintiffs' counsel in this case has promised to inundate the courts with individual claims if class certification is denied. Independently of the reliability of this self-serving promise, there is reason to believe that individual suits are feasible. First, individual damage claims are high, and punitive damages are available in most states. The expense of litigation does not necessarily turn this case into a negative value suit, in part because the prevailing party may recover attorneys' fees under many consumer protection statutes.

In a case such as this one, where each plaintiff may receive a large award, and fee shifting often is available, we find Chief Judge Posner's analysis of superiority to be persuasive. So too here, we cannot say that it would be a waste to allow individual trials to proceed, before a district court engages in the complicated predominance and superiority analysis necessary to certify a class.

The remaining rationale for superiority—judicial efficiency—is also lacking. In the context of an immature tort, any savings in judicial resources is speculative, and any imagined savings would be overwhelmed by the procedural problems that certification of a *sui generis* cause of action brings with it.

Even assuming arguendo that the tort system will see many more addiction-as-injury claims, a conclusion that certification will save judicial resources is premature at this stage of the litigation. Take for example the district court's plan to divide core liability from other issues such as comparative negligence and reliance. The assumption is that after a class verdict, the common issues will not be a part of follow-up trials. The court has no basis for that assumption.

It may be that comparative negligence will be raised in the individual trials, and the evidence presented at the class trial will have to be repeated. The same may be true for reliance. The net result may be a waste, not a savings, in judicial resources. Only after the courts have more experience with this type of case can a court certify issues in a way that preserves judicial resources. *See Jenkins* (certifying state of the art defense because experience had demonstrated that judicial resources could be saved by certification).

Even assuming that certification at this time would result in judicial efficiencies in individual trials, certification of an immature tort brings with it unique problems that may consume more judicial resources than certification will save. These problems are not speculative; the district court faced, and ignored, many of the problems that immature torts can cause. The primary procedural difficulty created by immature torts is the inherent difficulty a district court will have in determining whether the requirements of Rule 23 have been met. We have already identified a number of defects with the district court's predominance and manageability inquires, defects that will continue to exist on remand because of the unique nature of the plaintiffs' claim.

The district court's predominance inquiry, or lack of it, squarely presents the problems associated with certification of immature torts. Determining whether the common issues are a "significant" part of each individual case has an abstract quality to it when no court in this country has ever tried an injury-as-addiction claim. As the plaintiffs admitted to the district court, "we don't have the learning curb [sic] that is necessary to say to Your Honor 'this is precisely how this case can be tried and that will not run afoul of the teachings of the 5th Circuit.' "

Yet, an accurate finding on predominance is necessary before the court can certify a class. It may turn out that the defendant's conduct, while common, is a minor part of each trial. Premature certification deprives the defendant of the opportunity to present that argument to any court and risks decertification after considerable resources have been expended.

The court's analysis of reliance also demonstrates the potential judicial inefficiencies in immature tort class actions. Individual trials will determine whether individual reliance will be an issue. Rather than guess that reliance may be inferred, a district court should base its determination that individual reliance does not predominate on the wisdom of such individual trials. The risk that a district court will make the wrong guess, that the parties will engage in years of litigation, and that the class ultimately will be decertified (because reliance predominates over common issues) prevents this class action from being a superior method of adjudication.

The complexity of the choice of law inquiry also makes individual adjudication superior to class treatment. The plaintiffs have asserted eight theories of liability from every state. Prior to certification, the district court must determine whether variations in state law defeat predominance. While the task may not be impossible, its complexity certainly makes individual trials a more attractive alternative and, ipso facto, renders class treatment not superior.

Through individual adjudication, the plaintiffs can winnow their claims to the strongest causes of action. The result will be an easier choice of law inquiry and a less complicated predominance inquiry. State courts can address the more novel of the plaintiffs' claims, making the federal court's *Erie* guesses less complicated. It is far more desirable to allow state courts to apply and develop their own law than to have a federal court apply "a kind of Esperanto jury instruction." *Rhone-Poulenc.*

The full development of trials in every state will make sub-classing an easier process. The result of allowing individual trials to proceed is a more accurate determination of predominance. We have already seen the result of certifying this class without individual adjudications, and we are not alone in expressing discomfort with a district court's certification of a novel theory. *See Rhone-Poulenc.*

Another factor weighing heavily in favor of individual trials is the risk that in order to make this class action manageable, the court will be forced to bifurcate issues in violation of the Seventh Amendment. This class action is permeated with individual issues, such as proximate causation, comparative negligence, reliance, and compensatory damages. In order to manage so many individual issues, the district court proposed to empanel a class jury to adjudicate common issues. A second jury, or a number of "second" juries, will pass on the individual issues, either on a case-by-case basis or through group trials of individual plaintiffs.

The Seventh Amendment entitles parties to have fact issues decided by one jury, and prohibits a second jury from reexamining those facts and issues. Thus, Constitution allows bifurcation of issues that are so separable that the second jury will not be called upon to reconsider findings of fact by the first.

The Seventh Circuit recently addressed Seventh Amendment limitations to bifurcation. In *Rhone-Poulenc*, Chief Judge Posner described the constitutional limitation as one requiring a court to "carve at the joint" in such a way so that the same issue is not reexamined by different juries. "The right to a jury trial is a right to have juriable issues determined by the first jury impaneled to hear them (provided there are no errors warranting a new trial), and not reexamined by another finder of fact."

Severing a defendant's conduct from comparative negligence results in the type of risk that our court forbade in *Blue Bird*. Comparative negligence, by definition, requires a comparison between the defendant's and the plaintiff's conduct. *Rhone-Poulenc* ("Comparative negligence entails, as the name implies, a comparison of the degree of negligence of plaintiff and defendant."). At a bare minimum, a second jury will rehear evidence of the defendant's conduct. There is a risk that in apportioning fault, the second jury could reevaluate the defendant's fault, determine that the defendant was not at fault, and apportion 100% of the fault to the plaintiff. In such a situation, the second jury would be impermissibly reconsidering the findings of a first jury. The risk of such reevaluation is so great that class treatment can hardly be said to be superior to individual adjudication.

The plaintiffs' final retort is that individual trials are inadequate because time is running out for many of the plaintiffs. They point out that prior litigation against the tobacco companies has taken up to ten years to wind through the legal system. While a compelling rhetorical argument, it is ultimately inconsistent with the plaintiffs' own arguments and ignores the realities of the legal system. First, the plaintiffs' reliance on prior personal injury cases is unpersuasive, as they admit that they have new evidence and are pursuing a claim entirely different from that of past plaintiffs.

Second, the plaintiffs' claim that time is running out ignores the reality of the class action device. In a complicated case involving multiple jurisdictions, the conflict of law question itself could take decades to work its way through the courts. Once that issue has been resolved, discovery, sub-classing, and ultimately the class trial would take place. Next would come the appellate process. After the class trial, the individual trials and appeals on comparative negligence and damages would have to take place. The net result could be that the class action device would lengthen, not shorten, the time it takes for the plaintiffs to reach final judgment.

### IV.

The district court abused its discretion by ignoring variations in state law and how a trial on the alleged causes of action would be tried. Those errors cannot be corrected on remand because of the novelty of the plaintiffs' claims. Accordingly, class treatment is not superior to individual adjudication.

We have once before stated that "traditional ways of proceeding reflect far more than habit. They reflect the very culture of the jury trial." *In re Fibreboard Corp.* The collective wisdom of individual juries is necessary before this court commits the fate of an entire industry or, indeed, the fate of a class of millions, to a single jury. For the forgoing reasons, we reverse and remand with instructions that the district court dismiss the class complaint.

# C. MASS TORT CLASS ACTIONS SURVIVE

## IN RE COPLEY PHARMACEUTICAL, INC., ALBUTEROL PRODS. LIAB. LITIG.

United States District Court for the District of Wyoming, 1995.
161 F.R.D. 456.

The above-entitled matter comes before the Court on the Defendant's Motion to Decertify the Class and the Plaintiffs' opposition thereto, and the trial plans submitted by the parties, and the Court, having reviewed the relevant materials on file herein, having heard the oral arguments of the parties and being fully informed in the premises, finds and orders as follows.

### BACKGROUND

This case involves a national class action product liability lawsuit against Defendant Copley Pharmaceutical, Inc. Copley manufactures generic drugs including Albuterol, a bronchodilator prescription pharmaceutical. Copley's Albuterol was the subject of a nationwide recall in January 1994 after contamination was discovered in its Albuterol 0.5% solution. The exact nature, cause and extent of this contamination remains the subject of much controversy and is one of the issues pending before this Court.

Following the recall, Copley was named in a large number of lawsuits filed throughout the United States. Ultimately the Judicial Panel on Multidistrict Litigation consolidated all the federal cases brought against Copley in this Court. On July 18, 1994, this Court held an initial status conference in which it appointed a Plaintiffs' Steering Committee (PSC) to coordinate discovery with Copley. The PSC, with some dissention from other plaintiffs' counsel, filed an Amended Class Action Complaint and asked the Court to certify the case as a class action.

On October 28, 1994, the Court issued its Order Granting Partial Class Certification. In that order the Court recognized the presence of several common threshold issues affecting the class. The Court also held that individual issues of causation and damages were present and that those issues were not proper for class adjudication. Balancing these considerations under Fed.R.Civ.P. 23(c)(4)(A), the Court certified the class under Fed.R.Civ.P. 23(b)(3) for the following common issues of liability: strict liability, negligence, negligence per se, breach of warranties, and declaratory relief.

The Court's approach was influenced, in part, by a similar holding by Judge Grady in his certification of another partial class action brought by hemophiliacs against blood products manufacturers. In the intervening six and a half months, Copley neither appealed this Court's class certification nor moved for reconsideration.

Subsequent to the class certification, this action has moved forward with surprising speed and efficiency. For the most part, counsel on both sides have cooperated to coordinate discovery and minimize the delays that can plague national products liability actions.

Along with its trial plan, Copley filed the pending Motion to Decertify the Class. In that motion, Copley argues that the Court should decertify the class because the Seventh Circuit reversed Judge Grady's class certification in *Wadleigh*. Based largely on that decision, Copley has submitted two arguments for class decertification. First, Copley contends that its Seventh Amendment rights will be infringed by the Court's bifurcated trial plan. Second, Copley argues that the class is unmanageable because it is impossible for the Court to consider the laws of fifty-one different jurisdictions. Plaintiffs argue in reply that the class certified by the Court is not only constitutional and manageable, but is also the fairest way to resolve the common issues facing the class. Plaintiffs also suggest that the Defendant's motion is motivated by a desire to dissipate the resources of the Plaintiffs, thereby preventing many of them from pursuing claims.

After careful consideration of Copley's arguments, the *Rhone-Poulenc* decision, and the Court's fiduciary duty to the class, the Court is confident that its class certification remains legally sound. After dealing with this class over the last seven months, the Court is even more convinced that the class certification of some common issues is necessary and judicially efficient.

## I.  DEFENDANT COPLEY'S MOTION TO DECERTIFY THE CLASS

### B.  *The Applicability of the* Rhone-Poulenc *decision*

The *Rhone-Poulenc* decision contains a number of legal and logical inconsistencies that lessen its weight in this Court. For the reasons discussed below, the Court finds the *Wadleigh* case factually distinguishable from this case. The Court declines Copley's invitation to follow the Seventh Circuit's application of economic justice to the Federal Rules of Civil Procedure.

The first concern expressed by Judge Posner was the placement of the fate of an entire industry in the hands of a single jury and the apparent lack of merit of the plaintiffs' claims. First of all, as this Court observed last October, consideration of the merits of the plaintiffs' claims is expressly prohibited when deciding whether to certify a class. Second, Judge Posner's apprehension that a single jury "will hold the fate of an industry in the palm of its hand" simply is not a legal basis to deny class certification. Such economic reasoning may carry substantial weight in the Seventh Circuit, but this Court must look to Fed.R.Civ.P. 23 and its interpretation by courts to determine the appropriateness of class certification. In any event, in this case a single jury will determine the "fate" of a single company not an entire industry.

The second concern expressed in *Rhone-Poulenc* is the district court's manageability of the laws of various jurisdictions, especially in light of the plaintiffs' novel "serendipity" theory of liability. This Court notes that even Judge Posner conceded "that at some level of generality the law of negligence is one, not only nationwide but worldwide." Certainly difficulties will be encountered in trying to condense the negligence standards of different jurisdictions, but classes based on such standards have been certified before. *E.g. In re Asbestos School Litigation.* Most significantly, the plaintiffs in this case do not propose any novel theories of liability, and as will discussed below, many traditional strict liability and negligence defenses may be irrelevant in this case.

The Seventh Circuit's third "concern" is no more persuasive to this Court. Judge Posner reasoned that the class issue of the defendants' negligence was inseparable from the issues of proximate cause and comparative negligence. Unlike the *Wadleigh* case where some of the plaintiffs allegedly continued using blood products after the HIV danger was known, comparative negligence is unlikely to be a defense in this case. Unless a particular plaintiff used contaminated Albuterol after the recall, it is difficult to see how an individual plaintiff could be comparatively negligent by her use of Albuterol. Furthermore, Judge Posner's analysis effectively eviscerates Fed.R.Civ.P. 23(c)(4)(A). As this Court noted last October, the advisory note to that rule suggests the same separation of liability and injury issues proposed by the Court.

The majority's concerns are focused more on the soundness of Fed.R.Civ.P. 23(c)(4)(A) than on its application in *Wadleigh*. Unlike Judge Posner, this Court finds Fed.R.Civ.P. 23(c)(4)(A) a highly efficient way to preserve both judicial economy and the rights of the parties in the case. Judge Posner directs that, when separating out common issues, district courts must "carve at the joint." However, the effect of his decision takes away one of the sharpest instruments available to trial courts managing mass tort litigation.

Finally, this Court observes than many of the economic factors that seem to be the real driving force behind the *Rhone-Poulenc* decision are not present here. This case does not involve an entire industry and a wide range of products, but a single company and single product. This case does not involve novel theories of hindsight liability, but instead concerns a defendant who has admitted that some of its product was contaminated and that it is liable for any resulting injuries. Furthermore, even in October the Court noted that this case is not complicated by the foreseeability and professional standard of care issues present in *Wadleigh*. Simply put, this Court in unpersuaded by the decision in *Rhone-Poulenc*. On the contrary, seven months after its initial certification, the Court is even more convinced of its class certification of the common factual issues of liability.

### C.   Defendant Copley's Arguments in Favor of Decertification

#### 1.   Constitutional Concerns

##### a.   Generic Causation

Under the Court's trial plan, there will be two phases: (1) a trial of common underlying factual issues to determine Copley's liability, if any, to the class, and (2) separate trials in the transferor districts where Plaintiffs will have to prove, through a showing of individual causation, that they are in fact members of the class as defined by the Court.

Through this approach the Court recognizes that there are common issues concerning the extent, nature and dangerousness of the contamination in Copley's Albuterol. Even Copley's proposed trial plan admits this much. For example, a threshold common issue that will have to be proved by every Plaintiff is whether the contaminants in Albuterol are harmful to the human body. Defendant contends that it would be unconstitutional for one jury to consider whether its Albuterol can injure a user and a second jury to consider whether a particular Plaintiff was in fact so injured. The main authorities cited by Copley for this proposition are *Rhone-Poulenc* and *Gasoline Products*. In *Gasoline Products,* the Supreme Court held that under the Seventh Amendment, a second jury can consider an issue related to a prior jury's verdict only if it "is so distinct and separable from the others that a trial of it alone may be had without injustice." Therefore, the Court examines whether the general issues of causation are "distinct and separable" from the issues of individual causation.

At the outset, the Court observes that *Gasoline Products* predates the Federal Rules of Civil Procedure. Thus, one can conclude that the comments from the Fed.R.Civ.P. 23(c)(4)(A) and the MANUAL FOR COMPLEX LITIGATION endorsing the separate treatment of liability issues considered the requirements of *Gasoline Products*. The Court also recognizes that there are numerous cases where courts have separated out general issues of causation and liability from individual issues of injury and damages. These cases suggest that the Seventh Circuit's approach to Fed.R.Civ.P. 23(c)(4)(A) is the exception rather than the rule.

Perhaps the case most factually similar to the Court's trial plan is *Sterling v. Velsicol Chemical Corp.* In *Sterling* the plaintiffs brought a class action against a single defendant claiming that their land had been contaminated by toxins which had migrated from the defendant's landfill. The district court certified the class and held a bench trial on the claims of representative class members. Under the trial court's plan, it deferred individual issues of causation and injury of other class members for later hearings. After the district court held the defendant liable and awarded individual damages to the representative plaintiffs and punitive damages to the class, defendant Velsicol appealed. Among Velsicol's arguments on appeal were its contentions that common issues did not exist to justify class certification.

The Sixth Circuit observed that district courts enjoy broad discretion in certifying a class and that their plans should not be overturned absent an abuse of discretion. While this case involved a bench trial, this Court finds it significant that the Sixth Circuit did not even consider whether separate proceedings on general causation, individual causation, damages and injuries were constitutionally suspect.

This Court observes that there has been no intervening Supreme Court decisions or changes in the Federal Rules of Civil Procedure that could explain the Seventh Circuit's decision in *Rhone-Poulenc.* On the contrary, several other circuits have endorsed the separate treatment of class and individual issues. For example in *In re School Asbestos Litigation,* Judge Weis upheld a district court's certification of common issues of liability for a Rule 23(b)(3) class. Judge Weis reasoned that, "determination of liability issues in one suit may represent a substantial savings in time and resources." Finally, Judge Weis endorsed the trial court's view that common factual issues involving the health hazards of asbestos, "would not vary widely from one class member to another." As a result, class treatment of those issues was appropriate.

In *Jenkins v. Raymark Industries, Inc.,* the Fifth Circuit affirmed the trial court's decision to try common issues of liability followed by "mini-trials" representing the claims of individual plaintiffs. The court stated, "necessity moves us to change and invent. Both the *In re Agent Orange Product Liability Litigation,* and the *Asbestos School* courts found that specific issues could be decided in a class 'mass tort' action-even on a nationwide basis. We approve of the district court's decision in finding that this 'mass tort' class could be certified."

The Fourth Circuit took a similar approach in a case against the insurer of the manufacturer of the Dalkon Shield. After what may be the most comprehensive review of the law of class actions to be found in the *Federal Reporter,* the Fourth Circuit made several observations. Among these observations are that "the 'trend' is once again to give Rule 23 a liberal rather than restrictive construction" and "in order to promote the use of the class device and to reduce the range of disputed issues, courts should take full advantage of the provision in subsection (c)(4) permitting class treatment of separate issues in the case." After the broad endorsement of the innovative use of Rule 23, and after noting the "uniqueness" of the *Dalkon Shield* case, the court went on to affirm the district court's certification of a Rule 23(b)(1)(B) and (c)(4) class.

Apparently finding that *Dalkon Shield* was not so unique after all, the Fourth Circuit took a similar approach four years later. In that case the court affirmed a district court's certification of a class under Fed.R.Civ.P. 23(c)(4)(A) for issues common to a class of colleges and universities seeking damages from asbestos manufacturers. In fact, the court praised the district court's identification of common liability issues, stating, "significant economies may be achieved by relieving educational institutions of the need to prove over and over when defendants knew or should have known of asbestos' hazards, or whether defendants engaged in concerted efforts to conceal this knowledge."

Thus, between 1977 and 1993, the Third, Fourth, Fifth, Sixth and Ninth Circuits have all used class certification for common issues of liability as a step forward in managing "mass torts." Significantly, none of those courts held that such an approach had any constitutional infirmities whatsoever. This Court chooses to join those courts in their progressive treatment of mass torts and disagrees with the Seventh Circuit's decision to take a massive leap back to the time before Rule 23 class actions. The weight of the current law demonstrates that the Seventh Amendment is not violated by the separation of common issues of liability for class treatment.

### b.   Application of Different State's Laws

The heart of Copley's arguments concerning the application of laws from different jurisdictions comes in its argument that the class is unmanageable. However, Copley also contends that consideration of different standards of liability violates the Constitution. Despite *Rhone-Poulenc's* holding that Judge Grady's approach would be unconstitutional, in many of the cases discussed above the courts approved nationwide classes and did not find that the difference in state laws made such an approach unconstitutional. *E.g. In re Asbestos School Litigation* (holding that "substantial duplication" of negligence and strict liability laws in fifty-one jurisdictions make nationwide class manageable). For example, when presented with a nationwide class in *In re School Asbestos Litigation,* the Third Circuit did not even consider—much less agree with—an argument that the district court's approach was unconstitutional. Confident that the Seventh Circuit may be out of step with its sister circuits, this Court will turn to Copley's primary argument about differing state laws: that they make the class unmanageable.

### 2.   Manageability of the Class

Copley raises a very real concern that the laws of the different state jurisdictions make a trial unmanageable. In addition to the *Rhone-Poulenc* decision, Copley contends that states' differing approaches to products liability makes the certification of a nationwide class unmanageable.

For their part, the Plaintiffs give numerous examples of courts who were undeterred by the specter of differing standards of negligence and product liability. Most notable among these was *In re Asbestos School Litigation,* where Judge Kelly observed that "51 jurisdictions are in virtual agreement in that they apply the RESTATEMENT (SECOND) OF TORTS § 388" and "forty seven jurisdictions have adopted strict liability and all of them start with the concept of a defective product."

This differing authority leads the Court to conclude that the decision whether to attempt to manage a class under differing laws is committed to the discretion of the trial court. Furthermore, several factors make this class an excellent candidate for the application of law to a nationwide class. First, this case involves only one defendant manufacturer, Copley Pharmaceutical, and, at the present time, only one product, Albuterol 0.5%. Second, the product in question is safely manufactured by many other generic drug companies. Third, Copley, through its counsel, has admitted that at least some of its Albuterol was contaminated and that it is liable for any injuries such contamination may have caused.

Because of these facts, many of the "nuances" in state negligence and products liability laws may be irrelevant in this case. For example, comparative negligence, a defense that varies throughout the states, will only be relevant in the rare cases where a plaintiff used Albuterol after the recall. Similarly, the traditional strict liability defenses of risk/utility, state of the art and assumption of the risk are irrelevant because Copley has admitted that it is liable for any injuries caused by its Albuterol. As detailed in the Court's trial plan below, if an individual state's law is at variance with the general law on a relevant point of law, its residents may be removed from the class. Therefore, the Court is not intimidated by the parade of horribles presented by the Defendant.

Finally, Copley's counsel repeatedly argued that there was not a single case where a trial was held in a mass tort case which applied the laws of all fifty states. But the absence of an example does not prove that such classes are per se unmanageable. The fact is that most class actions settle and few go to trial whether the class is nationwide or statewide. This Court might indeed be the first to take such a class action to trial, but based on the policy reasons discussed below, the Court is ready to take on that challenge.

### 3. *Policy Reasons Supporting a Class Action*

In its Order Granting Partial Class Certification, this Court stated that the most convincing reason for certification was not offered by Plaintiffs' lead counsel, but by a single attorney in less than a minute. During oral arguments concerning class certification, one attorney approached the Court from the back of the courtroom. He succinctly stated that he had six clients, none of whom had large claims against Copley. He said that without class certification his clients would essentially lose their claims because neither he nor his clients had the resources to sue a large defendant like Copley.

Seven months later, after hearing the arguments on decertification, the compelling argument made by this attorney still rings true in the Court's ears. Plaintiffs' counsel repeated this point when they suggested that the real motivation behind Copley's motion to decertify was to cripple the claims brought by individual plaintiffs with less experienced counsel. Copley may or may not have such a goal, but the Court agrees that if the class is decertified, the courthouse door could be slammed on a great many plaintiffs.

Today, in the era of "mass torts" many commentators agree that class actions are necessary to protect the interests of individual plaintiffs. Numerous other commentators have recognized the benefit of class certification for common issues of liability. Some practitioners have also observed the value of use of class actions to conserve the resources of plaintiffs, defendants and the courts.

Finally, Copley directs the Court to the infamous Advisory Committee Note to Fed.R.Civ.Pro. 23. That advisory note, a favorite among class action defendants, states, "A 'mass accident' resulting in injuries to numerous persons is ordinarily not appropriate for class action." However, this note was written nearly thirty years ago, before the advent of most "mass tort" litigation. As the Plaintiffs point out, even one of the authors of that note has repudiated it. In the world of practice, it is now generally accepted that the committee's note is outdated.

After many months of discovery, the able litigators on both sides of this case are well-versed in Copley's Albuterol and its contamination. Just as Copley will have the best counsel available, the Plaintiffs deserve to have counsel who are familiar with Albuterol, its manufacture and its contamination. In this way the truth about the common issues liability may be decided in one class trial. The Court's October 28, 1994 Order Granting Partial Class Certification stands and the Defendant's Motion to Decertify the Class is denied.

# CHAPTER 5

---

# MEDICAL MONITORING CLASS ACTIONS

■ ■ ■

## A. STRUGGLING WITH THE CONCEPT

### IN RE TELECTRONICS PACING SYSTEMS, INC., ACCUFIX ATRIAL "J" LEADS PRODS. LIAB. LITIG.

United States District Court, S.D. Ohio, Western Division, 1997.
172 F.R.D. 271.

This matter is before the Court on Plaintiffs' Renewed Motion for Class Certification.

For the fourth time in little more than a year, this Court addresses the question whether class certification is appropriate in this case. There has been much discussion regarding the need to reform or improve how federal courts deal with mass tort litigation. While we agree changes might be appropriate, the district courts are left to fight the battles and resolve the Parties disputes' with the tools provided by Congress and our appellate courts. Thus, we must grant or deny certification on the basis of the federal rules as written today and interpreted by the Sixth Circuit and the Supreme Court.

In deciding this question, the Court is mindful of the applicable law and rules, the procedural and substantive legal rights of the Parties and the ethical concerns raised by adjudication of mass tort claims. Recently, several Circuit Court's have been highly critical of the use of class actions in mass tort and product liability cases. While we recognize the difficulties inherent in diversity based-class actions as outlined by the Circuit Courts, we continue to believe that class action provides the fairest, most efficient and economical means of dealing with these types of cases. We believe courts must play an important role in the efficient resolution of mass tort action. This is especially so where, as here, there is a danger that the expense of litigation and potential for large damage awards threaten to bankrupt the defendant and leave some class members without a remedy.

We also strongly disagree with those Circuit Courts which have allowed their apparent economic biases to influence their interpretation of the requirements of Rule 23. For example, in *Castano v. American Tobacco Co.*, the Fifth circuit found that class certification of all nicotine dependent individuals was not superior under Rule 23(b)(3) because of the strategic effect class certification has upon the defendants' chances.

In the context of mass tort class actions, certification dramatically affects the stakes for defendants. Class certification magnifies and strengthens the number of unmeritorious claims. Aggregation of claims also makes it more likely that a defendant will be found liable and results in significantly higher damage awards. *See also Matter of Rhone-Poulenc Rorer Inc.* To credit the Fifth Circuit's statement is to also state that its converse—denying class certification makes it less likely defendants will be found liable or responsible for lower damage awards—is true. Plaintiffs in individual actions will have to bear a greater share of the cost and risk for maintaining their action as compared to plaintiffs in a class action. Often an individual action pits a single plaintiff relying on his or her own resources to fund the litigation against the vast resources of a large manufacturer and the large law firms which represents it.

Obviously, the procedural rules affect the outcome of litigation. These Circuit Courts seemed to ignore the essence of Rule 23 because of their philosophical disagreement with the effects of Rule 23.

## I.

### BACKGROUND

#### A.  *The Parties*

This is a products liability action concerning pacemakers containing the Accufix Atrial "J" Lead. Plaintiffs in this action are recipients of the Accufix Atrial "J" Lead Pacemaker Model 330–801 and Model 329–701 (J Lead).

Defendant, TPLC, Incorporated (TPLC), is a Delaware corporation engaged in the business of designing, manufacturing, and marketing medical devices including the Accufix Atrial "J" Lead pacemakers at issue in this case. They manufactured the "J" Lead pacemakers Models 330–801 and 329–701 from 1988 until 1994. Defendant, Telectronics Pacing Systems, Incorporated ("TPSI"), is also a Delaware corporation. TPSI's sole business is to hold certain industrial property rights, real estate and the equity interest in TPLC.

#### B.  *The "J" Lead Controversy*

A pacemaker is a device that uses electrical impulses to reproduce or regulate the rhythms of the heart. It is driven by a battery and connected to the heart by leads and electrodes.

The heart pacing system at issue consists of three main parts: a pulse generator, leads, and a programmer. Pacemaker Models 330–801 and 329–701 utilize a retention wire to hold the atrial lead in the shape of a "J". The lead's retention wire is a filament of one of two metal alloys, Elgiloy or MP35N. Both Elgiloy and MP35N are nickel-cobalt based alloys which are "virtually equivalent in composition, chemical and physical properties."

The retention wire is encased in polyurethane insulation and bends back and forth within the system. The bending has caused the retention wire to break in some instances and poke through the polyurethane. The retention wire is not electrically active in the pacing circuit. Consequently, it has nothing to do with the conduction of the electrical signal or the operation of the pacing system. A fracture, however, can cause serious injury to the heart or blood vessels if it pokes through the polyurethane.

Approximately 25,000 pacemakers with "J" Leads were implanted in hearts of United States residents. Between December 1988 and February 1993, TPLC received reports of at least seven fractures of "J" Lead retention wires. On October 21, 1994, TPLC notified the Food and Drug Administration that it was recalling all unsold leads. Telectronics' President, James W. Dennis, then sent a letter to all doctors on November 3, 1994, notifying them that TPLC was voluntarily recalling all un-implanted Accufix Atrial "J" Lead pacemakers, Models 330–801 and 329–701.

By August 1996, TPLC had received notice of at least thirty-two injuries due to fractures, including six deaths. Additionally, eight others have died while having their lead extracted. On February 10, 1995, TPLC estimated the incidence of suspected fracture at 12%. Other TPLC documents indicate that the fracture rate may be as high as 20%.

In response to the fracture problem, TPLC has done three things to control the situation. First, TPLC has established the Accufix Research Institute (ARI) to manage the lead recall. The ARI communicates with doctors and patients concerning patient management recommendations. ARI is conducting a Multi-Center study (MCS) involving twelve hospitals to monitor a subset of leads over time. ARI analyzes the data from the MCS to assess the risk of injury from the "J" wire fracture as well as the risk of injury from lead extraction.

Secondly, TPLC formed a Physicians Advisory Committee ("PAC") to provide advice concerning clinical management of lead patients. The PAC reviews information from the MCS and other sources. The PAC then makes recommendations to the ARI concerning patient care. Upon the PAC's recommendation, Telectronics sent a letter to doctors advising them that implantees should receive screening for fractures every six months.

Finally, TPLC has agreed to "reimburse reasonable unreimbursed medical expenses for screening and Lead extraction that are consistent with patient management guidelines."

### C.  Procedural History

Plaintiffs, Elise and Eugene Owens, filed the lead action in this case on February 13, 1995, alleging injury due to a defective "J" lead. Plaintiffs allege that it was TPLC's negligent manufacture or design of the "J" Lead that causes the retention wire to fracture. The Panel on Multi-District

Litigation (MDL Panel) selected this Court as the transferee court for all claims involving the Accufix "J" Lead. Presently, over 400 cases are pending before this Court for pretrial proceedings.

The Court appointed a Plaintiffs' Steering Committee (PSC) to coordinate discovery and other pretrial proceedings on behalf of Plaintiffs in the cases transferred to this Court. The Court ordered the PSC to file a Master Complaint. On July 20, 1995, Plaintiffs filed an Amended and Consolidated Master Class Action Complaint asserting thirteen claims for relief: strict liability, negligence, failure to warn, breach of implied warranty, breach of express warranty, fear of future product failure, intentional infliction of emotional distress, negligent infliction of emotional distress, fraud, misrepresentation, medical monitoring, loss of consortium, and punitive damages.

The Court initially certified a worldwide class of all "J" Lead implantees for the common issues of medical monitoring, negligence, strict liability, fraud, misrepresentation, and breach of warranty. On February 23, 1996, the Court decertified the international class. TPLC moved to have the Court reconsider the class certification in light of the Sixth Circuit's decision in *In re American Medical Systems*. On July 16, 1996, the Court granted the motion to reconsider and decertified this case as a class action.

## D. Class Structure

Plaintiffs have now filed a Renewed Motion for Class Certification. Plaintiffs, however, have moved to certify only four causes of action as a class action: medical monitoring, negligence, strict liability and punitive damages. Plaintiffs seek to certify a nationwide class on claims of medical monitoring, negligence, strict liability and punitive damages.

First, Plaintiffs propose one nationwide subclass for all medical monitoring claims. It is defined as follows:

> Subclass One: all persons who have had the Accufix atrial "J" pacemaker leads, Model 330–801 and Model 329–701 placed in their bodies whose leads have not been explanted and who seek the establishment of a medical monitoring and research program.

The medical monitoring program which Plaintiffs seek would provide diagnostic testing for each class member, as well as conduct research on better methods of detecting fractured leads and determine safer methods for removing the fractured leads.

## II.

[The Court held that the proposed medical monitoring class satisfied the Rule 23(a) requirements for numerosity, commonality, typicality, and adequacy.—*ed.*]

ELEMENTS OF RULE 23(b) AND MEDICAL MONITORING CLASS

Having found the conditions of Rule 23(a) are met, we now move to whether the class proponent has shown that the proposed class satisfies at least one of the three subsections of Rule 23(b).

Turning to the requirements of Rule 23(b) as applied to the specific subclasses, we find that certifying a medical monitoring class is justified under both Rule 23(b)(1)(A) and 23(b)(3). "Certification under Rule 23(b)(1) is appropriate when a unitary decision is essential." "Rule 23(b)(1) classes are designed to avoid prejudice to the defendant or absent class members if individual actions were prosecuted in contrast to a class suit yielding a unitary adjudication." However, the possibility that some plaintiffs might recover and others might not does not justify class certification under Rule 23(b)(1)(A). *In re Bendectin Prod. Liability Lit.*

### A.   Class Certification of Medical Monitoring Pursuant to Rule 23(b)(1)(A)

Rule 23(b)(1)(A) states that class certification is proper if separate actions "would create a risk of inconsistent or varying adjudications with respect to individual members of the class which would establish incompatible standards of conduct for the party opposing the class." Fed.R.Civ.P. 23(b)(1)(A). "The phrase 'incompatible standards of conduct' is thought to refer to the situation where different results in separate actions would impair the opposing party's ability to pursue a uniform continuing course of conduct." "Subdivision (b)(1)(A) is applicable when practical necessity forces the opposing party to act in the same manner toward the individual class members and thereby makes inconsistent adjudications in separate actions unworkable or intolerable."

The medical monitoring claim here is an ideal candidate for class certification pursuant to Rule 23(b)(1)(A) because separate adjudications would impair TPLC's ability to pursue a single uniform medical monitoring program. *See Boggs v. Divested Atomic Corp.* (certifying claims remediation claims-medical monitoring, plant cleanup and nuisance abatement-under Rule 23(b)(1)(A)). Presently, TPLC is conducting a research program which is investigating the cause of the fractures, looking for better ways to detect the fractures and seeking safer methods of extracting the damaged leads. Plaintiffs seek the establishment of a medical monitoring program which would include diagnostic testing and research. TPLC asserts that medical monitoring beyond that recommended by TPLC's Physicians' Advisory Committee is not warranted. TPLC's research program is a uniform benefit to the class of "J" lead implantees as a whole. Any judicially-imposed modification of this program would then, by necessity, affect all of the "J" lead implantees. Furthermore, separate judicial orders pertaining to medical monitoring could require TPLC to institute differing types of monitoring programs which TPLC would have to reconcile.

TPLC argues that the recommendations of the Physicians' Advisory Committee are subject to approval by the FDA. TPLC insists that "the Court will have to reconcile its involvement in a medical monitoring program with FDA's statutorily mandated oversight function. The potential for unnecessary conflict and expense with no patient benefit is readily apparent, with TPLC caught in an impossible position between the judicial and executive branches of government." Whether FDA regulations preempt or otherwise limit state law tort claims for medical monitoring goes to the merits of the class claims and must be determined at a later date.

However, individual adjudication of implantees claims for medical monitoring would not alleviate TPLC's fear of conflicting standards of medical monitoring imposed by the judicial branch and executive branch. In fact, the danger of courts imposing conflicting duties upon Telectronics would only be compounded if the question of medical monitoring is not certified as a class action pursuant to Rule 23(b)(1)(A). Presently, there are over 400 individual actions consolidated before this Court by the Judicial Panel for Multidistrict Litigation. Certainly, a large number of similar cases are pending in state courts across the country. Thus, TPLC could still face multiple and conflicting orders rendered from different courts regarding the scope and necessity of a medical monitoring program which may also conflict with FDA imposed requirements. Accordingly, the Court certifies the medical monitoring subclass under Rule 23(b)(1)(A).

In addition to the danger of various courts mandating differing standards of conduct concerning monitoring, there are also significant policy reasons for requiring one medical monitoring class. Any research component should be coordinated in order to maximize resources and avoid duplication. To promote consistency in treatment, doctors should also be given one set of advice in terms of treatment options for their "J" lead patients.

### B.  Class Certification of Medical Monitoring Pursuant to Rule 23(b)(1)(B)

The argument for certification of a medical monitoring subclass is bolstered by the fact that separate adjudications may adversely affect other implantees' ability to recover anything. Under Rule 23(b)(1)(B), certification is justified if adjudications by individual class members might "as a practical matter be dispositive of the interests of the other members not parties to the adjudications or substantially impair or impede their ability to protect their interests." Fed.R.Civ.P. 23(b)(1)(B). The most common use of subsection (b)(1)(B) is in limited fund cases. "A limited fund exists when a fixed asset or piece of property exists in which all class members have a preexisting interest, and an apportionment or determination of the interests of one class member cannot be made without affecting the proportionate interests of other class members similarly situated." In the same limited circumstances, the potential or probable insolvency of the defendant due to a large number of pending tort actions can create a limited fund appropriate for adjudication under Rule 23(b)(1)(B). *See e.g., In re Asbestos Litigation*.

According to previous pleadings and the representations of counsel for both sides, TPLC has recently sold all of its assets to another corporation. Thus, TPLC is no longer an operating corporation. TPLC received approximately $105 million for all of its assets. TPLC also has a $25 million liability policy. This policy is a diminishing policy; that is defense costs are deducted from the total coverage. TPLC has depleted approximately $9 million of their insurance coverage to cover legal fees and medical monitoring expenses. Thus, TPLC currently has approximately $120 million in assets and insurance to cover its liabilities related to the "J" lead litigation.

In the United States, an estimated 25,000 individuals have had the "J" Lead implanted. Dividing $120 million by the number of implantees, TPLC has about $4800 to spend on each of the implantees for medical monitoring and any potential damage awards. TPLC has spent over $2.5 million on medical monitoring since it agreed to pay for the reasonable unreimbursed expenses of fluoroscopy and explantation. Because the Parties did not submit evidence regarding the potential cost of the medical monitoring program, the Court cannot determine whether TPLC faces insolvency as a result its expenses arising out of the "J" lead controversy. The possibility of the existence of a limited fund, however, lends further support to a conclusion that medical monitoring class should be certified under Rule 23(b)(1).

### C.    Class Certification of Medical Monitoring Pursuant to Rule 23(b)(3)

In addition, we note that a medical monitoring subclass also satisfies Rule 23(b)(3). Rule 23(b)(3) has two primary requirements: (1) that common issues predominate over individual issues, and (2) class treatment is superior to other methods of adjudication.

First, TPLC's defense to Plaintiffs' medical monitoring claim clearly predominates over any individual issues raised by the medical monitoring claims. TPLC acknowledges that all "J" lead implantees require medical monitoring to prevent injury due to fracture. Telectronics' primary defense to Plaintiffs' claims for additional or different medical monitoring than that offered by TPLC is that its medical monitoring program has been approved by the FDA and is the best program available under present research and technology. This defense is common to all implantees and is the predominant issue regarding the appropriateness of a court ordered medical monitoring program. *See Jenkins v. Raymark Industries* ("In order to 'predominate,' common issues must constitute a significant part of the individual cases."); *In re "Agent Orange" Product Liability Litigation* (finding common issues predominated where critical defenses affected all class members equally).

Second, class certification of a medical monitoring class is also the superior method of dealing with the medical monitoring claims. As pointed out in our discussion of Rule 23(b)(1), there is risk that TPLC could be ordered to conduct conflicting medical monitoring programs if individual implantees pursue medical monitoring claims in separate actions. In addition, practically speaking, for many of the "J" Lead recipients their only realistic claim may be for medical monitoring. This is not the type of claim that is likely to lead to large damage awards. While TPLC has to its credit instituted a significant medical monitoring program, Plaintiffs have every right to challenge the adequacy of this program. Thus, it appears that many of the proposed class members have small monetary claims that would be difficult to pursue in individual actions. *See In re Copley Pharmaceutical, Inc.* (finding that decertification of class involving relatively small claims would "slam" the courthouse door shut for many plaintiffs). The superiority prong of Rule 23(b)(3) is satisfied if aggregation of small monetary claims is required to ensure vindication of legal rights.

Defendants counter that class certification of a medical monitoring subclass is unmanageable in light of the variations in state law of medical monitoring. We disagree. TPLC acknowledges that all implantees require medical monitoring. The critical questions are whether the present monitoring program is adequate and whether Telectronics will be required to continue it. Thus, most variations in state law regarding medical monitoring are immaterial.

One major distinction in the law of medical monitoring is relevant in this situation. In some states, medical monitoring is only recoverable if the plaintiff shows physical injury. Without a fracture of the "J" Lead, class members in those states may be unable to pursue claims for monitoring even though TPLC concedes that monitoring is required. Thus, pursuant to Rule 23(c)(4), the Court will divide the medical monitoring class into two subclass: (1) implantees from states that do not require present physical injury to recover for medical monitoring, and (2) implantees from state that require present physical injury in order to recover for medical monitoring.

## CONCLUSION

Accordingly, the Court grants in part and denies in part Plaintiffs' Renewed Motion for Class Certification. The Court hereby certifies subclasses for medical monitoring.

# B. THE COHESIVENESS REQUIREMENT

## BARNES V. THE AMERICAN TOBACCO CO.

United States Court of Appeals, Third Circuit, 1998.
161 F.3d 127.

In this suit against the major American tobacco companies, we must decide whether a medical monitoring class should be certified under Federal Rule of Civil Procedure 23(b)(2). The District Court decertified a proposed class of cigarette smokers on the grounds that significant individual issues precluded certification. After finding the statute of limitations had run with respect to the claims of five named plaintiffs and the sixth had failed to establish the need for medical monitoring, the District Court granted defendants summary judgment. We will affirm the District Court's decertification order and its grant of summary judgment.

## I.

### FACTS AND PROCEDURAL HISTORY

Named plaintiffs William Barnes, Catherine Potts, Norma Rodweller, Barbara Salzman, Edward J. Slivak, and Ciaran McNally are Pennsylvania residents who began smoking cigarettes before the age of 15 and have smoked for many years. Plaintiffs filed suit against the defendant tobacco companies in the Court of Common Pleas of Philadelphia County. Defendants removed to the Eastern District of Pennsylvania, and plaintiffs filed an Amended Complaint asserting claims of intentional exposure to a hazardous substance, negligence, and strict products liability on behalf of a purported class of over one million Pennsylvania cigarette smokers. In their prayer for relief, plaintiffs asked (1) that defendants fund a court-supervised or court approved program providing medical monitoring to class members; (2) for punitive damages to create a fund for common class-wide purposes, including medical research, public education campaigns, and smoking cessation programs; and (3) for other monetary and injunctive relief the court deemed just and proper.

### A.

The District Court found the class did not meet the requirements of Rule 23(b)(2) or (b)(3). The District Court rejected Rule 23(b)(2) certification because plaintiffs had not primarily sought injunctive or equitable relief, finding that "plaintiffs' medical monitoring claim is merely a thinly disguised claim for future damages" and that "the overwhelming majority of the relief sought by plaintiffs in their entire complaint is monetary in nature." The court also found certification improper under Rule 23(b)(3) because issues common to the class did not predominate over plaintiffs' individual issues. In particular, the District Court found individual issues, such as addiction, causation, the need for medical monitoring, and affirmative defenses, made a class action unmanageable and not the superior method for fair and efficient adjudication of the case.

The District Court suggested, however, that plaintiffs' request for a court-supervised program of medical monitoring to detect the latent diseases caused by smoking was the "paradigmatic" request for injunctive relief under a medical monitoring claim. Specifically, the court stated:

> The Court finds that it may properly certify a medical monitoring claim under Rule 23(b)(2) when the plaintiffs seek such specific relief which can be properly characterized as invoking the court's equitable powers. In reaching this decision, the Court perforce rejects defendants' argument that a medical monitoring claim can never be characterized as injunctive.

The dispositive factor that must be assessed to determine whether a medical monitoring claim can be certified as a Rule 23(b)(2) class is—what type of relief do plaintiffs actually seek. If plaintiffs seek relief that is a disguised request for compensatory damages, then the medical monitoring claim can only be characterized as a claim for monetary damages. In contrast, if plaintiffs seek the establishment of a court-supervised medical monitoring program through which the class members will receive periodic medical examinations, then plaintiffs' medical monitoring claims can be properly characterized as claim seeking injunctive relief.

In *Day v. NLO, Inc.,* Judge Spiegel cogently articulates the fine distinction between a medical monitoring claim that seeks monetary relief in the form of compensatory damages and a medical monitoring claim that seeks injunctive relief in the form of a court-supervised medical monitoring program. Judge Spiegel explains:

> Relief in the form of medical monitoring may be by a number of means. First, a court may simply order a defendant to pay a plaintiff a certain sum of money. The plaintiff may or may not choose to use that money to have his medical condition monitored. Second, a court may order the defendants to pay the plaintiffs' medical expenses directly so that a plaintiff may be monitored by the physician of his choice. Neither of these forms of relief constitute injunctive relief as required by Rule 23(b)(2).

> However, a court may also establish an elaborate medical monitoring program of its own, managed by court-appointed court-supervised trustees, pursuant to which a plaintiff is monitored by particular physicians and the medical data produced is utilized for group studies. In this situation, a defendant, of course, would finance the program as well as being required by the Court to address issues as they develop during the program administration. Under these circumstances, the relief constitutes injunctive relief as required by Rule 23(b)(2).

Based on Judge Spiegel's insightful distinction, it is apparent that relief requested under a medical monitoring claim can be either injunctive or equitable in nature.

To determine whether the named plaintiffs in this case seek equitable relief under their medical monitoring claim, plaintiffs' specific request for relief under this claim must be closely scrutinized. Plaintiffs seek the establishment of a court-supervised program through which class members would undergo periodic medical examinations in order to promote the early detection of diseases caused by smoking. This portion of plaintiffs' request is the paradigmatic request for injunctive relief under a medical monitoring claim.

Accordingly, the District Court granted plaintiffs leave to file an amended complaint. In their Second Amended Complaint, plaintiffs brought only one claim against defendants—medical monitoring. Moreover, plaintiffs eliminated all requests for smoking cessation programs, medical treatment programs, punitive damages, and restitutional damages; the only relief they sought was a court-supervised fund that would pay for medical examinations designed to detect latent diseases caused by smoking. Plaintiffs sought certification under Rule 23(b)(2) for "all current residents of Pennsylvania who are cigarette smokers as of December 1, 1996 (the day the amended complaint was filed in federal court) and who began smoking before age 19, while they were residents of Pennsylvania."

The Second Amended Complaint alleged that plaintiffs and other class members had been exposed to proven hazardous substances through the intentional or negligent actions of the defendants and/or through defective products for which defendants are strictly liable. Plaintiffs alleged that as a proximate result of this exposure, they and other class members suffer significantly increased risks of contracting serious latent diseases and therefore need periodic diagnostic medical examinations. Specifically, plaintiffs contended that classwide expert evidence would prove that: (1) when cigarettes are used as defendants intended them to be used, the vast majority of those who use cigarettes become addicted and (2) cigarettes are the leading cause in the nation of cardiovascular disease, lung cancer, and chronic obstructive pulmonary disease, due to the exposure of the throat, heart, and lungs to tobacco smoke.

### III.

### DISCUSSION

#### A.   Medical Monitoring

The crucial issue is whether plaintiffs' medical monitoring claim requires inquiry into individual issues. We begin by briefly describing the evolution of this cause of action and its elements.

In *In re Paoli Railroad Yard PCB Litigation*, (*Paoli I*), we predicted the Pennsylvania Supreme Court would recognize a cause of action for medical monitoring. We reaffirmed that prediction in *In re Paoli Railroad Yard PCB Litigation* (*Paoli II*). The issue of medical monitoring first reached the Pennsylvania Supreme Court in *Simmons v. Pacor, Inc.,* where the unanimous court recognized medical monitoring as a viable cause of action under Pennsylvania law. In *Simmons,* the court permitted plaintiffs with asbestos-related asymptomatic pleural thickening to recover for medical monitoring. It was not until *Redland Soccer Club v. Department of the Army,* however, that the Pennsylvania Supreme Court had the opportunity to articulate the specific elements of a claim for medical monitoring. Building on this court's decisions in *Paoli I* and *Paoli II,* the Supreme Court found that plaintiffs must prove the following elements:

> (1) exposure greater than normal background levels; (2) to a proven hazardous substance; (3) caused by the defendant's negligence; (4) as a proximate result of the exposure, plaintiff has a significantly increased risk of contracting a serious latent disease; (5) a monitoring procedure exists that makes the early detection of the disease possible; (6) the prescribed monitoring regime is different from that normally recommended in the absence of the exposure; and (7) the prescribed monitoring regime is reasonably necessary according to contemporary scientific principles.

The injury in a cause of action for medical monitoring is the "costs of periodic medical examinations necessary to detect the onset of physical harm." It is evident that this injury is somewhat different from an injury in a traditional tort, which rests on physical harm. *See, e.g.,* RESTATEMENT SECOND OF TORTS § 402A (requiring plaintiff to prove in a products liability case "physical harm" which § 7 defines as "physical impairment of the human body").

In recognizing medical monitoring as a compensable injury, the Pennsylvania Supreme Court quoted at length from our distinction in *Paoli I* between a cause of action for increased risk of future harm and a cause of action for medical monitoring. We concluded that a claim for medical monitoring is different from a claim for increased risk of harm because the medical monitoring plaintiff has an identifiable rather than a speculative injury. We explained:

> The injury in an enhanced risk claim is the anticipated harm itself. The injury in a medical monitoring claim is the cost of the medical care that will, one hopes, detect that injury. The former is inherently speculative because courts are forced to anticipate the probability of future injury. The latter is much less speculative because the issue for the jury is the less conjectural question of whether the plaintiff needs medical surveillance.

In *Redland,* the court cited four important policy reasons for recognizing a cause of action for medical monitoring. First, medical monitoring promotes "early diagnosis and treatment of disease resulting from exposure to toxic substances caused by a tortfeasor's negligence." Second, "allowing recovery for such expenses avoids the potential injustice of forcing an economically disadvantaged person to pay for expensive diagnostic examinations necessitated by another's negligence," and "affords toxic-tort victims, for whom other sorts of recovery may prove difficult, immediate compensation for medical monitoring needed as a result of exposure." Third, medical monitoring "furthers the deterrent function of the tort system by compelling those who expose others to toxic substances to minimize risks and costs of exposure." Finally, such recovery is "in harmony with 'the important public health interest in fostering access to medical testing for individuals whose exposure to toxic chemicals creates an enhanced risk of disease.' "

## B.   Certification

[The Court upheld the District Court's findings that the proposed medical monitoring class satisfied Rule 23(a) requirements for numerosity, commonality, typicality, and adequacy.—*ed.*]

### *Fed.R.Civ.P. 23(b)(2)*

As noted, in its June 3, 1997 Order, the District Court found that under certain circumstances medical monitoring could constitute the injunctive relief required by Rule 23(b)(2). The District Court initially held that plaintiffs could not be certified under 23(b)(2) because most of the relief they sought was monetary in nature. In response to the court's analysis, plaintiffs amended their complaint so it contained only a claim for medical monitoring and asked only for the establishment of a court-supervised medical monitoring program.

Recently, the Supreme Court reexamined the requirements for Rule 23 certification in the context of mass tort class actions. In *Amchem Products, Inc. v. Windsor*, the Supreme Court affirmed our decision in *Georgine v. Amchem Products, Inc.* decertifying a settlement class of claimants exposed to asbestos. As in this case, the issue in *Amchem* was "whether the proposed classes were sufficiently cohesive to warrant adjudication by representation." We found that cohesiveness lacking and the Supreme Court agreed. Quoting Judge Becker's opinion, the Court noted: " 'Class members were exposed to different asbestos-containing products, for different amounts of time, in different ways, and over different periods. The exposure-only plaintiffs especially share little in common, either with each other or with the presently injured class members. They will also incur different medical expenses because their monitoring and treatment will depend on singular circumstances and individual medical histories.' " As we explained, such factual differences "translate into significant legal differences. Differences in amount of exposure and nexus between exposure and injury lead to disparate applications of legal rules, including matters of causation, comparative fault, and the types of damages available to each plaintiff." We also noted that "individualized issues can become overwhelming in actions involving long-term mass torts (*i.e.* those which do not arise out of a single accident)."

While *Amchem* involved a Rule 23(b)(3) class action, the cohesiveness requirement enunciated by both this court and the Supreme Court extends beyond Rule 23(b)(3) class actions. Indeed, (b)(2) class may require more cohesiveness than a(b)(3) class. This is so because in a (b)(2) action, unnamed members are bound by the action without the opportunity to opt out.

While 23(b)(2) class actions have no predominance or superiority requirements, it is well established that the class claims must be cohesive. Discussing the requirements for 23(b)(2) classes in *Wetzel v. Liberty Mutual Insurance Company* we noted, "by its very nature, a(b)(2) class must be cohesive as to those claims tried in the class action. Because of the cohesive nature of the class, Rule 23(c)(3) contemplates that all members of the class will be bound. Any resultant unfairness to the members of the class was thought to be outweighed by the purposes behind class actions: eliminating the possibility of repetitious litigation and providing small claimants with a means of obtaining redress for claims too small to justify individual litigation." In *Geraghty v. United States Parole Commission,* we again emphasized that a 23(b)(2) class must be cohesive, noting the District Court has the "discretion to deny certification in Rule 23(b)(2) cases in the presence of 'disparate factual circumstances.' " *See also Santiago v. City of Philadelphia* (holding that a "court should be more hesitant in accepting a(b)(2) suit which contains significant individual issues than it should under subsection 23(b)(3)."

In *Santiago,* the court recognized two reasons why courts must determine whether a proposed (b)(2) class implicates individual issues. First, unnamed members with valid individual claims are bound by the action without the opportunity to withdraw and may be prejudiced by a negative judgment in the class action. "Thus, the court must ensure that significant individual issues do not pervade the entire action because it would be unjust to bind absent class members to a negative decision where the class representatives's claims present different individual issues than the claims of the absent members present." Second, "the suit could become unmanageable and little value would be gained in proceeding as a class action if significant individual issues were to arise consistently."

In decertifying the class, the District Court decided that "too many individual issues exist which prevent this case from proceeding as a class action." As noted, the District Court found that addiction, causation, and affirmative defenses all presented individual issues not properly decided in a class action. We believe that addiction, causation, the defenses of comparative and contributory negligence, the need for medical monitoring and the statute of limitations present too many individual issues to permit certification. As in *Amchem,* plaintiffs were "exposed to different products, for different amounts of time, in different ways, and over different periods." These disparate issues make class treatment inappropriate.

### b.    The need for medical monitoring

We also believe the requirement that each class member demonstrate the need for medical monitoring precludes certification. In order to state a claim for medical monitoring, each class member must prove that the monitoring program he requires is "different from that normally recommended in the absence of exposure." To satisfy this requirement, each plaintiff must prove the monitoring program that is prescribed for the general public and the monitoring program that would be prescribed for him. Although the general public's monitoring program can be proved on a classwide basis, an individual's monitoring program by definition cannot. In order to prove the program he requires, a plaintiff must present evidence about his individual smoking history and subject himself to cross-examination by the defendant about that history. This element of the medical monitoring claim therefore raises many individual issues.

### IV.

For the foregoing reasons, we will affirm the judgment of the District Court.

## C.  MEDICAL MONITORING IN DISARRAY

### IN RE WELDING FUME PRODS. LIAB. LITIG.

United States District Court, N.D. Ohio, Eastern Division, 2007.
245 F.R.D. 279.

A number of plaintiff welders filed in California federal district court a lawsuit known as *Steele v. A.O. Smith Corp.* The *Steele* action was transferred to this Court as related to *In re: Welding Fume Products Liability Litigation,* MDL No. 1535. The plaintiffs in *Steele* now move for class certification. For the reasons stated below, the Court concludes this motion must be denied.

### I.    BACKGROUND

On June 23, 2003, the Judicial Panel on Multi-District Litigation (MDL Panel) conferred multi-district status on *"Welding Fume"* lawsuits filed in federal court, and transferred three such pending cases to this Court, pursuant to 28 U.S.C. § 1407. The MDL Panel concluded that the three *Welding Fume* cases each "presented claims of personal injuries allegedly caused by exposure to welding fumes. The actions thus share factual questions concerning, inter alia, whether exposure to welding fumes causes the conditions complained of by plaintiffs and whether defendants knew or should have known of any health risks associated with exposure to welding fumes."

Since that time, the MDL Panel has transferred to this Court about 9,750 related cases filed by plaintiffs around the country. Another 1,760 cases have been removed directly to, or filed directly in, this Court. By virtue of subsequent remands to state court, voluntary dismissals, and stipulated dismissals pursuant to a Tolling Agreement (and also two trials and a settlement), the number of active cases now pending in this *Welding Fume* MDL is about 1,775.

As a general matter, the plaintiffs in the *Welding Fume* cases all allege that: (1) they inhaled fumes given off by welding rods; (2) these fumes contained manganese; and (3) this manganese caused them permanent neurological injury and other harm. The *Welding Fume* plaintiffs name as defendants various manufacturers, suppliers, and distributors of welding rod products, and claim the defendants knew or should have known that the use of welding rods would cause these damages.

The plaintiffs generally bring claims sounding in strict product liability, negligence, fraud, and conspiracy. The gravamen of the complaints is that the defendants "failed to warn" the plaintiffs of the health hazards posed by inhaling welding rod fumes containing manganese and, in fact, conspired to affirmatively conceal these hazards from those engaged in the welding process.

## II.   THE STEELE CLASS ACTION COMPLAINT

One of the *Welding Fume* cases transferred more recently into this MDL is *Steele v. A.O. Smith Corp.* Like the other *Welding Fume* complaints, the *Steele* complaint names a large number of defendants that manufacture, supply, distribute, or consume welding rods. And, like the other *Welding Fume* complaints, the *Steele* complaint states claims for negligence, strict liability, fraud, and aiding and abetting. Unlike all of the other *Welding Fume* complaints, however, the 16 *Steele* plaintiffs do not allege they have suffered an *existing* physical injury caused by inhaling the manganese contained in welding fumes. Rather, the *Steele* plaintiffs allege that, as welders, they "have been exposed to welding fumes containing manganese in excess of the Threshold Limit Value and will continue to be exposed to manganese in welding fumes, and thereby suffer, and will continue to suffer, a significantly increased risk of serious neurological and neuropsychological injury."

Rather than seeking pure monetary damages, the 16 *Steele* plaintiffs pray for various types of injunctive and declaratory relief-primarily, a medical monitoring program to account for their allegedly increased risk of developing welding-fume-induced brain damage. Specifically, the *Steele* plaintiffs ask for:

creation of a comprehensive medical monitoring program, supervised by the Court, and funded by Defendants, that: (a) notifies individuals who have been exposed to manganese from welding rod fumes of the potential harm from such exposure and the need for periodic testing and examination; (b) provides periodic medical testing and examinations designed to facilitate early detection of toxic exposure to manganese from welding fumes; (c) provides early detection and treatment of neurological and neuropsychological diseases and injuries caused by exposure to welding fumes; (d) provides further observational epidemiological studies of steel welders that are sufficiently powered to assess the association between such welding and neurological and neuropsychological injury; (e) accumulates and analyzes relevant medical and exposure information from Class and Subclass members, and publishes findings; and (f) gathers and forwards to treating physicians information related to the diagnosis and treatment of neurological injuries and diseases which may result from exposure to welding fumes.

Finally, the *Steele* plaintiffs ask the Court to certify their lawsuit as a class action. Essentially, plaintiffs propose certification of eight, separate, state-wide classes, with two subclasses each—one sub-class of current welders, and one sub-class of former welders. As discussed below, the eight states listed each recognize the primary aspect of relief sought by the *Steele* plaintiffs—medical monitoring—as either a cause of action or an item of damages. Further, all eight states do *not* require that a plaintiff suffer an existing, physical injury to obtain medical monitoring.

The *Steele* plaintiffs explain that class certification is appropriate because "common questions of fact and law exist as to all members of each Class and Subclass." Plaintiffs assert that, among others, these "common legal and factual questions, which do not vary from member to member, and which may be determined without reference to the individual circumstances of any Subclass member," include: (a) "whether Defendants' conduct has caused, and/or continues to cause members to be exposed to manganese in welding fumes;" (b) "whether Defendants' conduct has caused, and/or continues to cause members to be at an increased risk of developing neurological injury or neuropsychological injury, relative to the non-welder population;" (c) "whether Defendants have intentionally or negligently failed, and/or continue to fail to adequately warn or disclose to members the true risks associated with exposure to manganese in welding fumes;" and (d) "whether Defendants engaged in a course of conduct to suppress, conceal or misrepresent facts relating to the dangers of exposure to manganese in welding fumes."

In support of their assertions that the defendants' conduct has put all class-member welders at increased risk of developing neurological injury, and that medical monitoring is an appropriate mechanism to address this increased risk, the *Steele* plaintiffs offer the following proven facts and allegations, which give context to the Court's class certification decision:

- manganese is a known neurotoxin;

- most welding rods contain manganese;

- when these welding rods are used, they produce fumes that contain manganese;

- during normal use of welding rods, welders often inhale these welding fumes in amounts exceeding safe levels;

- exposure to the manganese contained in welding fumes can cause brain damage, even after short periods of time;

- manufacturers of welding rods have known all of the above information for decades;. these manufacturers have insufficiently warned welders and their employers about the dangers of exposure to manganese in welding fumes; and

- these manufacturers have long acknowledged that, in light of the danger of exposure to manganese in welding fumes, regular medical monitoring of welders is necessary and appropriate.

## IV.

### B. *Rule 23(b)(2) and Rule 23(b)(3)*

Before turning to an analysis of whether the *Steele* plaintiffs meet the requirements for class certification, the Court examines the defendants' argument that, as a threshold matter, plaintiffs err in arguing that their class certification bid should be evaluated under Fed.R.Civ.P. 23(b)(2). Because the members of plaintiffs' proposed classes are not bound together by any legal relationship or trait and because the medical monitoring remedy plaintiffs seek is primarily monetary, as opposed to injunctive, in nature, their claims should be subject to the predominance, superiority and manageability requirements of Rule 23(b)(3).

Although the *Steele* plaintiffs assert in passing that class certification "could also be proper under Rule 23(b)(3)," they respond that they have invoked the proper subdivision of Rule 23 and should not have to meet "the relatively more stringent requirements of Rule 23(b)(3)." The Court agrees.

The MANUAL FOR COMPLEX LITIGATION observes that "courts are divided over whether Rule 23(b)(2) or 23(b)(3) is the appropriate vehicle for certifying a mass tort class for medical monitoring," but further notes that "Rule 23(b)(2) generally applies when the relief sought is a court-supervised program for periodic medical examination and research to detect diseases attributable to the product in question." If, instead, "money damages are the relief primarily sought in a medical monitoring class, as in programs that pay class members but leave it to the members to arrange for and obtain tests, certification must generally meet the Rule 23(b)(3) standards."

In this case, the *Steele* plaintiffs ask only for injunctive relief, in the form of a court-supervised medical monitoring program. The *Steele* plaintiffs do not ask for any money damages; indeed, the proposed class definition includes only welders "who are not presently asserting claims for manganese-related injury." Nor do the *Steele* plaintiffs ask that defendants simply be ordered to: (1) pay them "a certain sum of money" directly, which they then "may or may not choose to use" to monitor their medical condition; or (2) "pay their medical expenses directly so that they may be monitored by the physician of their choice."

Rather, the *Steele* plaintiffs ask the Court to "establish an elaborate medical monitoring program of its own, managed by court-appointed court-supervised trustees, pursuant to which a plaintiff is monitored by particular physicians and the medical data produced is utilized for group studies." Courts routinely find that, "under these circumstances, the requested relief constitutes injunctive relief as required by Rule 23(b)(2)." The *Steele* plaintiffs were careful to ask only for medical monitoring relief that is truly equitable in nature. Accordingly, it is the requirements of Rules 23(a) and 23(b)(2) that they must meet to obtain class certification.

[Following an extensive analysis of choice-of-law issues, the court held that choice-of-law issues raised no insuperable barrier to class certification.—*ed.*]

## VI. RULE 23(a)

[Holding that the proposed class satisfied the requirements of numerosity, commonality, and adequacy, the Court then turned to its analysis of typicality.—*ed.*]

### D.   Rule 23(a)(3)—Typicality

Although the two prerequisites of commonality and typicality are sometimes examined together, their foci are distinct: "commonality focuses on similarities, while typicality focuses on differences." More specifically, "under the commonality prong, a court must ask whether there are sufficient factual or legal questions *in common* among the class members' claims to make class certification economical and otherwise appropriate. In contrast, under the typicality prong, a court must ask whether, despite the presence of common questions, each class member's claim involves so many *distinct* factual or legal questions as to make class certification inappropriate." Although the "test for typicality, like commonality, is not demanding and does not require identicality," too many meaningful differences across the plaintiff class can preclude certification.

After having undertaken an exhaustive review of state and federal case law addressing class certification of medical monitoring claims, the Court concludes that, in fact, typicality is wanting in the *Steele* case. Given the large size of the class, the differences in defendants' conduct, and the variable working environments in which all of the welder plaintiffs performed, each class member's claims involve so many distinct factual questions that class certification becomes inappropriate.

### 1. A Matter of Perspective

As noted earlier, federal courts have "broad discretion in determining whether to certify a class." The same is invariably true for state courts. Thus, it is not surprising that there is no common set of factual circumstances predictive of whether a court will certify a medical monitoring class. It is easy to find cases, for example, where a court *granted* class certification to plaintiffs in a limited geographic region who sought medical monitoring after suffering single-source exposure to a toxin in their drinking water, and just as easy to find cases where a court *denied* certification under similar conditions—and there is no obvious or simple way to reconcile the two different results. Similarly, courts have ruled oppositely in different cases involving plaintiff classes seeking medical monitoring for illnesses allegedly caused by: (1) addiction to nicotine in the same brands of cigarette; and (2) adverse side effects of the same prescription drug.

Having pored over these cases seeking a unifying theme, the Court has noticed two factors worthy of mention. The first is that, when examining typicality, Courts tend to have one of two perspectives. Courts focus either on: (a) *the defendant's conduct,* and the degree to which it affected each plaintiff equally, or (b) *the effects on the plaintiff class* of the defendants' conduct, and the degree to which those effects are similar from plaintiff to plaintiff. Put more simply, the first focus is on what the defendants did; the second focus is on how the plaintiffs were affected by what defendants did. And because the latter is naturally more variable, this focus more often leads to denial of certification.

An example illustrates the point. In both *Scott v. American Tobacco Co.* and *Barnes v. American Tobacco Co.,* the plaintiffs sought to certify a statewide class of cigarette smokers, in order to obtain medical monitoring. In *Scott,* the court granted certification to a class of Louisiana smokers, and later denied a motion to decertify; in *Barnes,* the court initially granted certification to a class of Pennsylvania smokers, but later decertified the class. Most revealing are the views of the two courts regarding the "collective nature" of the plaintiffs' claims. In *Scott,* the court concluded that "certification of the class in this case is proper because it essentially boils down to one fundamental question: Is a cigarette that contains nicotine a defective product?" The answer to this "fundamental question," however, could focus on either the nature of *cigarettes*—that is the *defendants' product*—or the nature of *addiction*—that is, the *plaintiffs' responses* to cigarettes.

In contrast, the *Barnes* court focused more on the nature of the individual responses that the members of the proposed plaintiff class had to nicotine. Thus, while *Scott* focused on the universality of defendants' conduct toward the class, the *Barnes* court focused on the variety of plaintiffs' reactions to that same conduct. The rulings in other medical monitoring class certification cases also reflect this dichotomy.

The second factor worthy of mention is that state courts more often certify medical monitoring classes than do federal courts—as reflected in *Scott* (a state court case) and *Barnes* (a federal court case). To some extent, this is because the classes that state courts are asked to certify are more often single-state in scope, while federal court class certification requests are more often multi-state in scope; as a result, choice-of-law issues are more likely to derail a certification bid in federal court.

But it is not only the usually-smaller scope of the proposed class, and the concomitant smaller problem posed by choice-of-law issues, that make state courts more likely to certify medical monitoring classes. State courts generally have also been more willing than federal courts to look past individualized issues of proof in medical monitoring class actions. Again, an example proves the point. As noted above, most states that recognize a cause of action for medical monitoring include, as one of the essential elements of the claim, proof that exposure to the toxic substance "was caused by the defendant's negligence." Invariably, federal courts focus on this element and find it problematic. For example, in *In re Baycol Products Liability Litigation,* the court denied certification of a multi-state medical monitoring class because, among other things, the plaintiffs' entitlement to medical monitoring included the element of "negligence."

In other words, the syllogism goes: (1) a plaintiff's entitlement to medical monitoring requires proof of the defendant's negligence; (2) negligence proofs are highly individual as to each plaintiff; (3) therefore, medical monitoring claims are not suitable for class treatment. Carried to its logical extreme—which, in their arguments on brief and at oral argument, defendants push for, while plaintiffs ask the Court to guard against—medical monitoring classes should never be certified.

Of course, the individual issues that are "inextricably intertwined" with proof of negligence are present regardless of whether the medical monitoring class action is brought in a state or federal court. But state courts are more willing to discount these individual issues in the context of medical monitoring classes. For example, in *Lewis v. Bayer AG,* the Pennsylvania state court refused to certify a class composed of all Pennsylvanians who ingested the drug Baycol and wanted to pursue claims of *negligence.* The court reasoned that "the facts surrounding the class negligence claims demonstrates that proof as to one claimant would not be proof as to all. A myriad of individual causation inquiries exist." Yet the same court went on to certify a class composed of all Pennsylvanians who ingested the drug Baycol and wanted to pursue claims for *medical monitoring*-claims that incorporate, as an essential element, proof of the defendant's negligence. The *Lewis* court concluded that the common issues connected to all of the other elements of a medical monitoring claim—including the fact that "plaintiffs' claims arise out of similar conduct by the defendants"—outweighed the individual issues. Thus, even though the federal court refused to certify a medical monitoring class of Baycol users in *In re Baycol,* the state court granted certification to a medical monitoring class of Baycol users in *Lewis.* Generally, in state courts, the syllogistic inference is not as strong.

As plaintiffs pointed out in oral argument, this dichotomy between state and federal case law regarding medical monitoring class certification highlights a tension addressed by the *Erie* doctrine. "Under the *Erie* doctrine, federal courts sitting in diversity apply state substantive law and federal procedural law." Thus, this Court must apply Federal Rule of Civil Procedure 23 (as construed by federal courts) to determine whether certification of a class of plaintiffs bringing state-law medical monitoring claims (as construed by state courts) is appropriate. At the same time, a "federal court sitting in diversity should 'reach the same result as the state court would reach in deciding the identical issue.'" Apparently, however, it is not easy to do both. As discussed above, when faced with almost identical medical monitoring class certification motions, state courts are generally more amenable to granting certification than are federal courts.

### 2. Typicality Problems Exist from Any Perspective

To repeat, "under the typicality prong, a court must ask whether, despite the presence of common questions, each class member's claim involves so many *distinct* factual or legal questions as to make class certification inappropriate." To explain why the Court believes each class member's claim involves too many individualized questions of fact and law to allow for certification in *Steele,* the Court also repeats here the essential elements of a claim for medical monitoring, and focuses on the third and fourth elements:

(1) exposure

(2) to a toxic substance,

(3) which exposure was caused by the defendant's negligence,

(4) resulting in an increased risk

(5) of a serious disease, illness, or injury

(6) for which a medical test for early detection exists

(7) and for which early detection is beneficial, meaning that a treatment exists that can alter the course of the illness,

(8)  and which test has been prescribed by a qualified physician according to contemporary scientific principles.

For the sake of argument, the Court assumes that all except the third and fourth elements of this claim present questions common to all class members. That is, the Court assumes that whether manganese in welding fumes is a toxic substance (element two) is a fact question that all class members would attempt to prove with common evidence. Similarly, whether there exist medical tests capable of detecting Manganese-Induced Parkinsonism, as opposed to Parkinsonian symptoms induced by other causes for which defendants would not be liable (element six), is a fact question susceptible to proof through expert opinion that all class members will share.

The essential questions raised by the third and fourth elements of plaintiffs' medical monitoring claims, however, are problematic—even when viewed from the perspective of "what the defendants did," as opposed to "how the plaintiffs were affected by what defendants did." That is, even ignoring issues such as an individual plaintiff's age, medical history, lifestyle, susceptibility to Manganese-Induced Parkinsonism, and so on, the defendants' conduct in this case cannot be examined consistently across the class.

In medical monitoring cases stemming from toxic spills or radioactive releases, the question of negligence (element three) is virtually the same as the question of exposure—if the plaintiffs were exposed to a toxic material released by the defendant, then the defendant was negligent. In other words, if "what the defendants did" was to release a hazardous substance to which no person should normally ever be exposed, then the evidence going to the question of whether the defendant was negligent is common to all plaintiffs. This same reasoning may even be present in medical monitoring cases involving prescription drugs.

Similarly, in medical monitoring cases stemming from toxic spills or radioactive releases, the question of increased risk of injury (element four) is virtually the same as the question of exposure—if the plaintiffs were exposed to a toxic material released by the defendant, then their risk of illness is higher. Thus, for example, if a plaintiff would never normally use or consume the toxin TCE, the very fact of ingestion of TCE-laced drinking water virtually establishes an increase to his risk of illness caused by that toxin.

In this case, however, the allegedly hazardous substance to which the plaintiffs were exposed (manganese fumes) is released by a commonly-used and extremely useful product (welding rods), the sale and use of which requires no governmental dispensation. The parties experts agree, moreover, that not every exposure to manganese fumes is toxic; the level of exposure is critical to the question of whether an increased risk of illness occurs. And, the product came with warnings. Thus, whether the defendants were negligent (element three) depends not simply on whether any given plaintiff suffered exposure, but on whether the warning supplied by the defendant sufficiently apprised the plaintiff of the risk of exposure. Similarly, whether a given plaintiff suffers an increased risk of illness (element four) depends not simply on the fact of welding fume exposure, but on the *degree* of exposure, and whether there was more exposure than might have otherwise occurred *due to the failure of the warning*. These circumstances change dramatically the degree of typicality of evidence and issues among plaintiffs in this case, because of the great variety of products, manufacturers, warnings, employers, and workplaces involved.

The *Steele* plaintiffs have named as defendants about two dozen welding rod manufacturing companies. Each company produces a variety of welding rods and other welding consumables. Some of these welding rods have no manganese content, and some have high manganese content; some are consumed slowly during welding and produce little fume, and some are consumed quickly and produce copious fumes. These different products are sold with different warnings, and also with different cautionary statements contained in different Material Safety Data Sheets (MSDSs). Further, the warnings and MSDSs accompanying these products have changed over time, and the risks about which the defendants had to warn depended upon, among other things, the changing, then-current state of knowledge regarding the dangers posed by use of the product. Also, the workplace conditions where the plaintiffs use these welding rods are highly variable-some workplaces have state-of-the-art ventilation systems, while others are confined spaces with no source of fresh air. Finally, some plaintiffs work for sophisticated employers that have regular welding safety training programs and provide welders with filters, respirators, or other safety equipment; other plaintiffs work for employers who are far more laissez-faire.

Given all of these differences, no finder of fact can determine, on a class-wide basis, whether the defendants' conduct was "unreasonable" toward every plaintiff. For example, a jury could conclude a certain defendant was reasonable-not negligent-because it supplied a certain MSDS containing a certain warning to a certain sophisticated employer for whom a certain plaintiff worked, so that the plaintiff cannot prove the third element of his medical monitoring claim. And yet, the same jury could conclude it was not reasonable-it was negligent-for the same defendant to supply only certain other warnings to the employer of another plaintiff, whose training and working conditions were poor. Similarly, a jury could conclude that one plaintiff did not suffer any increased risk of illness resulting from a defendant's failure to warn, while another plaintiff did. Even if the Court ignores the individual, personal histories of the plaintiffs, the variety of contexts within which the defendants acted may yield different conclusions regarding liability. In light of the different welding products, warnings, employers, work environments, and so on, *there is ultimately no single course of conduct* by all of the defendants. In sum: there is insufficient typicality.

As a general matter, the undersigned finds that focusing on the universality of the defendant's conduct toward the class, rather than the variety of the plaintiffs' reactions to that conduct, tends to be more in keeping with the entire concept of whether certification of a medical monitoring class is appropriate. But no court-state or federal-has certified a medical monitoring class action as sprawling in scope as the one the *Steele* plaintiffs seek. In the case at hand, because the defendants' conduct (and, more particularly, the context in which the defendants acted) is not universal across the class, the Court cannot grant plaintiffs' motion for certification.

## VIII.          RULE 23(b)(2)

The Court sets out only a few additional comments regarding Rule 23(b)(2). In light of the Court's conclusion that the *Steele* plaintiffs do not satisfy all of the prerequisites of Rule 23(a), a more thorough examination of Rule 23(b)(2) would be superfluous.

In the 1990s, federal courts were more willing to certify medical monitoring cases under Rule 23(b)(2) than they are today. Generally, those courts that did so focused, again, on the defendant's conduct, as opposed to the varying effects this conduct had on the plaintiff class. Because the defendant's conduct was often an action or inaction "generally applicable to the [entire] class" and without regard to individual plaintiffs—conduct such as releasing toxins into the environment or marketing medical devices—courts were willing to find that Rule 23(b)(2) was satisfied.

Using this same logic, the *Steele* plaintiffs argue that Rule 23(b)(2) is satisfied in this case because the manufacturing defendants marketed their products, accompanied by allegedly insufficient warnings, to the entire class generally, without regard to any plaintiff's individual circumstances.

In 1998, however, the Third Circuit Court of Appeals affirmed denial of certification for a medical monitoring class in *Barnes v. American Tobacco Co.,* and used language that has since become widely adopted. In discussing Rule 23(b)(2), the *Barnes* court declared that "the cohesiveness requirement enunciated by both this court and the Supreme Court extends beyond Rule 23(b)(3) class actions. Indeed, a(b)(2) class may require more cohesiveness than a(b)(3) class. While 23(b)(2) class actions have no predominance or superiority requirements, it is well established that the class claims must be cohesive." This implicit "cohesiveness" requirement has since been cited by many other courts as one of their bases for denying medical monitoring class certification. Defendants argue in this case that the class proposed by the *Steele* plaintiffs is not cohesive, so certification under Rule 23(b)(2) is not appropriate.

This Court notes only that whether there is an implicit cohesiveness requirement within Rule 23(b)(2) is not settled within this Circuit. The Sixth Circuit Court of Appeals has never cited *Barnes,* nor used the term "cohesive" in any discussion of Rule 23(b)(2). And the Ninth Circuit Court of Appeals has pointedly "refused to read a 'cohesiveness' requirement into Rule 23(b)(2)."

It is impossible to know whether the apparent drop-off in certification of medical monitoring classes by federal courts in more recent years is due to adoption of the cohesiveness analysis set out in *Barnes,* or to the 1999 promulgation of Fed.R.Civ.P. 23(f) (which first permitted interlocutory appellate review of class certification orders), or to some other factor.

To a large degree, the cohesiveness requirement imposed by *Barnes* appears to duplicate aspects of the commonality and typicality requirements of Rule 23(a). Thus, this Court is not persuaded by the defendants' argument that certification under Rule 23(b)(2) must be denied for the *additional* reason of lack of class cohesiveness.

In any event, because the Court has already concluded that class certification is inappropriate for lack of typicality, the Court need not answer the question whether the plaintiff class in this case meets the requirements of Rule 23(b)(2).

## IX. CONCLUSION

As plaintiffs point out, many entities affiliated with the welding industry have publicly acknowledged, *outside of litigation,* that there is merit to plaintiffs' primary concern regarding possible dangerous health effects from exposure to welding fumes. Indeed, at least some defendants have recognized that some welder-plaintiffs: (1) are routinely exposed to manganese in welding fumes above safe threshold limits; (2) thereby suffer an increased risk of developing neurological illness due to exposure to welding fumes; and (3) should obtain medical monitoring to address this increased risk.

Further, members of the welding industry have recognized publicly that "long term overexposure to manganese compounds" can occur in as little as six months. That the industry has acknowledged, at least in part, the legitimacy of plaintiffs' prayer, however, is not tantamount to the existence of a basis upon which this Court can conclude that the plaintiffs are entitled to pursue their medical monitoring claims as a class. For the reasons stated above, the Court concludes that the *Steele* plaintiffs' motion for class certification does not meet all of the requirements of Federal Rule of Civil Procedure 23. This conclusion says nothing about the merits of the plaintiffs' claims, nor whether they can pursue medical monitoring on an individual basis, nor even whether a state court might allow a similar class action lawsuit to proceed. Nor does it say anything about the propriety of a common issues trial, pursuant to Fed R. Civ. P. 42(a). But it does mean that the *Steele* plaintiffs' motion to prosecute their case as a class action must be denied.

Having concluded that the *Steele* plaintiffs may not pursue their lawsuit as a class action, the question becomes: what may they do next? Even though the Court has denied the motion for class certification, it appears possible the plaintiffs may still be allowed to pursue their individual claims in this MDL court, because their jurisdictional basis for doing so (CAFA) remains valid. It also appears possible they may wish simply to dismiss their claims, as one of the bases for their motion for class certification was that the value of prosecuting "a medical monitoring claim is likely too small to merit an individual action."

# D. MEDICAL MONITORING RESURGENT

## IN RE NATIONAL COLLEGIATE ATHLETIC ASS'N STUDENT-ATHLETE CONCUSSION INJURY LITIGATION

United States District Court for the Northern District of Illinois, 2016.
314 F.R.D. 580.

Plaintiffs in this multi-district litigation are current and former collegiate athletes, who have sued the National Collegiate Athletic Association (NCAA) on a class-wide basis, asserting various contractual and common law claims arising from the manner in which the NCAA has handled student-athlete concussions and concussion-related risks over the years. After extensive discovery, the parties in the first-filed case commenced settlement negotiations with the assistance of two prominent retired federal judges. At around this time, a number of similar actions were filed on behalf of NCAA student-athletes nationwide, and those actions were consolidated by the Judicial Panel of Multidistrict Litigation before this Court.

After extensive, arms-length negotiations, the parties arrived at a settlement, and a number of the Plaintiffs submitted the settlement agreement to the Court for approval under Fed. R. Civ. P. 23(e). However, Anthony Nichols, the named Plaintiff in *Nichols v. NCAA*, opposed the settlement on various grounds.

On December 17, 2014, the Court declined to approve the settlement agreement, raising a number of significant concerns. Since that time, the Settling Plaintiffs and the NCAA have gone back to the drawing board to negotiate an amended settlement agreement in an effort to address these concerns. As part of this process, the Settling Plaintiffs also expanded the group of class representatives to include individuals who played non-contact sports at NCAA-affiliated schools. They did so in order to obtain the participation of non-contact sports athletes in the settlement process. After additional negotiations, the Settling Plaintiffs and the NCAA agreed on an amended settlement agreement.

As before, not all of the Plaintiffs are happy with the amended settlement. The Court again has permitted Nichols, whom the Court has appointed Interim Lead Objector, to file objections to the amended settlement. The Court also allowed Adrian Arrington, the former lead plaintiff in the *Arrington* case, to submit his objections as well.

Nichols directs his principal objection to the provision in the amended settlement agreement whereby the Settling Plaintiffs agree to release their right to pursue their personal injury claims on a class-wide basis. According to Nichols, these procedural rights are extremely valuable, and the benefits conferred upon the class members by the settlement pale in comparison.

After considering the voluminous materials submitted by the parties, the Court now preliminarily certifies the settlement class under Fed. R. Civ. P. 23(b)(2); orders the Settling Plaintiffs and the NCAA to provide notice to the settlement class, as well as an opportunity for individual class members to opt out of the class settlement; and finds that the amended settlement is within the range of possible approval. This approval, however, is subject to a number of modifications.

The first of these modifications limits the scope of the settlement class's release of class-wide personal injury claims to those instances where the plaintiffs or claimants seek a nationwide class or where the proposed class consists of student-athletes from more than one NCAA-affiliated school. The Court also has proposed a number of modifications to the notice program and the way in which certain settlement funds are to be utilized. To the extent that the Settling Plaintiffs and the NCAA are agreeable to these modifications or are otherwise able to address the Court's concerns, preliminary approval of the amended class settlement is granted.

## THE PROPOSED SETTLEMENT

First, the proposed Settlement Class is defined as: "All Persons who played an NCAA-sanctioned sport at an NCAA member institution on or prior to the Preliminary Approval Date."

As alleged in the complaint, each of the Settlement Class Representatives has played an NCAA sport during a time when the NCAA's concussion-management and return-to-play guidelines failed to meet the best practice consensus standards, and each is at risk for developing future symptoms related to concussions and/or the accumulation of sub-concussive hits.

As part of the settlement, the NCAA has agreed to the following terms. The NCAA and its insurers will pay $70 million to create a Medical Monitoring Fund. The Fund will be used to pay the expenses associated with the Medical Monitoring Program, including: Screening Questionnaires; Medical Evaluations; Notice and Administrative Costs;

Medical Science Committee Costs; approved Attorneys' Fees and Costs; and Class Representatives' Service Awards.

The Medical Monitoring Program will last for a period of fifty years. If the funding for the Medical Monitoring Program is depleted before the fifty-year period ends, the Settlement Class Members may pursue individual *or* class claims seeking medical monitoring, and the statute of limitations will be tolled during the fifty-year period. In addition, as part of the settlement, the NCAA also will provide $5 million in additional funds for concussion-related research over the course of the first ten years of the Medical Monitoring Period.

The Program itself contemplates two different assessment phases: screening and evaluation. In the screening phase, Class Members may seek an analysis of their symptoms by completing a Screening Questionnaire, in hard copy form or online, once every five years until age fifty and then not more than once every two years after the age of fifty. Their scores on the Screening Questionnaire will determine whether they qualify for a Medical Evaluation.

The standard for determining whether a Class Member qualifies for a Medical Evaluation will be set by the Medical Science Committee, which will consist of four medical experts, who have expertise in the diagnosis, care, and management of sports-related concussions and mid-to late-life neurodegenerative disease. These medical experts will be appointed jointly by the parties, and the Committee will be chaired by Special Master and retired United States District Judge Wayne R. Anderson. At the Court's request, a copy of the questionnaire and the parameters that will drive the Committee's review has been provided in the settlement materials.

Once the Committee reviews a Class Member's responses to the Screening Questionnaire, the Class Member will be notified whether he or she qualifies for a Medical Evaluation and instructed on where and how to obtain one. Medical Evaluations will be performed at thirty-three program locations nationwide. The Program Administrator will assist Class Members, who qualify for Medical Evaluations, find the most convenient location.

Class Members may qualify for up to two Medical Evaluations during the Medical Monitoring Period and may seek a third by submitting an appropriate request to the Committee. The Medical Evaluations will be submitted to a physician, who will provide a diagnosis as well as the results of the testing to the Class Member or his or her personal physician, at the option of the Class Member, within sixty days of the Medical Evaluation.

The Committee will determine the scope of the Medical Evaluations, which will be designed to assess symptoms related to persistent post-concussion syndrome, as well as cognitive, mood, behavioral, and motor problems associated with mid-to late-life onset diseases, such as Chronic

Traumatic Encephalopathy (CTE) and other disorders. The Committee also will review annually, and amend as needed, the Questionnaire and the scope of the Evaluations to reflect the then-current standard of care; oversee the performance of the Program Locations; provide an annual written report regarding their responsibilities and performance to the Court; and recommend how research funds should be expended. The Committee will be compensated at a reasonable hourly rate from the Fund by the Program Administrator.

In addition to the Medical Monitoring Program, the NCAA has agreed to continue implementing changes to its concussion-management and return-to-play policies to be consistent with consensus best practices. First, the NCAA has instituted a policy requiring all student-athletes to undergo pre-season baseline testing for each sport they play prior to the first practice or competition. Second, the NCAA has revised its return-to-play guidelines to provide that an NCAA student-athlete who has been "diagnosed with a concussion will be prohibited from returning to play or participation in any practice or game on the same day on which he or she sustained such concussion" and "must be cleared by a physician before being permitted to return to play in practice or competition." Third, medical personnel, who are trained in the diagnosis, treatment, and management of concussions, are required to be present at all games of Contact Sports—defined as football, lacrosse, wrestling, ice hockey, field hockey, soccer, and basketball—and are required to be available during all Contact Sports practices for Division I, II, and III schools. Fourth, the NCAA is instituting a uniform process for schools to report diagnosed concussions and their resolution, and for concerned persons to report potential problems directly to the NCAA. Fifth, NCAA-affiliated schools are required to provide approved concussion education and training to student-athletes, coaches, and athletic trainers prior to the start of each athletic season. Sixth, the NCAA is providing education for faculty with respect to accommodations for students suffering from concussions.

As consideration for the Settlement Terms outlined above, the Settlement Class Members agree to release any and all claims for "damages for medical monitoring, or other legal or equitable relief for medical monitoring, related to concussions or sub-concussive hits or contact arising from or relating to concussions or sub-concussive hits or contact sustained during participation in NCAA-sanctioned sports as an NCAA student-athlete." Furthermore, the Settlement Class Members agree to release any and all claims "brought or pursued on a class-wide basis and relating to concussions or sub-concussive hits or contact." However, they will retain the right to bring "individual personal or bodily injury claims" and "class claims that do not relate in any way to medical monitoring or medical treatment of concussions or sub-concussive hits or contact."

These releases would inure to the benefit of "the NCAA, its member institutions (past and present), its current and former officers, directors, employees, insurers, attorneys and agents." Additionally, the NCAA has agreed to toll the statute of limitations for all personal injury claims from September 12, 2011 through the date of the Court's final approval of the settlement.

The Settling Plaintiffs and the NCAA state that the issue of attorneys' fees was deferred until after an agreement on all other material terms had been reached during the mediation process. Since that time, the parties have arrived at an agreement as to the attorneys' fees and costs incurred by Lead Counsel. Specifically, the NCAA has agreed that it will not oppose a request for an award of attorneys' fees up to $15 million and out-of-pocket expenses up to $750,000. Any application for attorneys' fees and costs must be approved by the Court.

Because Class Counsel will have a continuing obligation to implement the terms of the settlement throughout the Medical Monitoring Period, the NCAA also has agreed not to object to applications from Lead Counsel and one member of the Plaintiffs' counsel Executive Committee for additional attorneys' fees, at a rate not to exceed $400 per hour, to a maximum of $500,000 for work performed after the first year from the Effective Date of Settlement. These requests also would be subject to court approval.

The Settling Plaintiffs also intend to apply to the Court for reasonable service awards for the Class Representatives in this matter, which will be paid from the Fund. The NCAA agrees not to object to Service Awards in the amount of $5,000 for the Class Representatives deposed in the *Arrington* matter and $2,500 for each Settlement Class Representative who has not been deposed.

Finally, the Amended Settlement Agreement provides that, if the Settlement Class is certified, the Court will appoint a Notice Administrator. The Notice Administrator will provide notice to the class and inform class members of the ability to opt out of the settlement.

## LEGAL STANDARD

"Federal Rule of Civil Procedure 23(e) requires court approval of any settlement that effects the dismissal of a class action." When parties seek preliminary approval of a class action settlement agreement and certification of a settlement class, the district court must undertake two essential inquiries.

First, "the court must conduct an independent class certification analysis." "This analysis 'demands undiluted, even heightened, attention' when applied to classes for which certification is sought for settlement purposes only." (quoting *Amchem Prods. Inc. v. Windsor*). This need for heightened attention is necessary because, when parties jointly seek approval of a class action settlement, the adversarial relationship between the plaintiffs and defendant may fall away, and potential conflicts of interest between class counsel and the class members may arise. To this end, the Seventh Circuit has gone so far as to describe "the district judge as a fiduciary of the class, who is subject therefore to the high duty of care that the law requires of fiduciaries."

Second, the district court must determine whether the proposed settlement is "within the range of possible approval." The purpose of this inquiry "is to ascertain whether there is any reason to notify the class members of the proposed settlement and to proceed with a fairness hearing." At this initial stage, the court is not "resolving the merits of the controversy or making a precise determination of the parties' respective legal rights." This is why some courts at this stage perform a summary version of the exhaustive final fairness inquiry.

In assessing a settlement's fairness, "relevant factors include: (1) the strength of the case for plaintiffs on the merits, balanced against the extent of settlement offer; (2) the complexity, length, and expense of further litigation; (3) the amount of opposition to the settlement; (4) the reaction of members of the class to the settlement; (5) the opinion of competent counsel; and (6) stage of the proceedings and the amount of discovery completed." "The most important factor relevant to the fairness of a class action settlement is the strength of plaintiff's case on the merits balanced against the amount offered in the settlement."

If the district court finds that the certification of the settlement class is appropriate and the proposed settlement is within the range of possible approval, the court will then order the plaintiffs to provide notice of the settlement to the class "in a reasonable manner" so that the class members can raise any objections to the settlement. Fed. R. Civ. P. 23(e)(1). Once the class is provided with notice of the settlement and an opportunity to object, the court conducts a final approval hearing to determine whether the settlement is "fair, reasonable, and adequate." Fed. R. Civ. P. 23(e)(2). If the district court is satisfied that the settlement meets these criteria, it will grant final approval of the settlement, which binds the defendant and all class members to the terms of the settlement.

It is worth noting that, at the preliminary approval stage, the extent of the district court's inquiry into the appropriateness of class certification and the reasonableness of the settlement terms depends, as it must, on the circumstances of the individual case. Where the size of the class is small, the cost of notice minimal, and the issues discrete, the court may be able to determine that class certification is proper and the settlement is "within the range of possible approval" with minimal fuss. But in a case such as this, where the putative class members range in the millions, the parties have completed extensive discovery, substantive objections are raised at the preliminary stage, and the costs and efforts to provide notice are substantial, it may be advisable for the court to engage in a more piercing and thorough analysis of the issues in the first instance, rather than waiting until the final approval hearing, in order promote the "just, speedy, and inexpensive" resolution of the case. Fed. R. Civ. P. 1.

## ANALYSIS

Although Nichols and Arrington object to a number of the substantive terms of the Amended Settlement Agreement, their primary argument is that the settlement impermissibly requires the putative class members to waive their ability to pursue personal injury claims on a class-wide basis under Fed. R. Civ. P. 23(b)(3) and 23(c)(4). According to Nichols, based upon the factual record, the personal injury claims brought by putative class members can (and should) be certified under Rule 23(b)(3) or 23(c)(4), and this in turn demonstrates that the Settling Plaintiffs and Lead Counsel have not adequately represented the interests of the class and renders the proposed settlement fundamentally unfair.

In response, the Settling Plaintiffs and the NCAA contend that the personal injury claims raise a host of individual issues and, therefore, are not amenable to class-wide treatment under Rule 23(b)(3) or 23(c)(4).

## I. STRENGTH OF CLASS CLAIMS FOR DAMAGES AGAINST THE NCAA AND WHETHER CERTIFICATION UNDER RULE 23(b)(3) OR RULE 23(c)(4) IS LIKELY

The Court finds that the likelihood that Plaintiffs would be able to obtain certification of their personal injury claims against the NCAA in this action pursuant to Rule 23(b)(3) and 23(c)(4) based upon the alleged claims of negligence and fraudulent concealment is minimal, at best. Accordingly, the Court finds that the ability of putative class members to assert these procedural claims in future proceedings provides them with minimal value.

### B.   Certification of the Putative Class Under Rule 23(b)(3)

Certification of a class under Rule 23(b)(3) is proper when "the questions of law or fact common to class members predominate over any questions affecting only individual members, and when a class action is superior to other available methods for fairly and efficiently adjudicating the controversy." Fed. R. Civ. P. 23(b)(3). Rule 23(b)(3) "tests whether proposed classes are sufficiently cohesive to warrant adjudication by representation" and is "far more demanding" than Rule 23(a)'s commonality requirement. *Amchem Prods.*

Predominance is not satisfied where liability determinations are individual and fact-intensive. Predominance also fails where "affirmative defenses will require a person-by-person evaluation of conduct to determine whether a defense precludes individual recovery." Nichols and Arrington lean heavily on Judge Anita Brody's certification of a Rule 23(b)(3) settlement class in *In re National Football League Players' Concussion Injury Litigation* (the NFL Litigation). In that multi-district litigation, a class of retired professional football players sued the NFL for negligence and fraudulent concealment, seeking declaratory relief, medical monitoring, and damages. The class members alleged that the NFL had breached its duty to protect players from short-term and long-term health risks associated with concussive and sub-concussive head injuries and fraudulently concealed those risks.

In granting certification, Judge Brody found that the NFL's alleged conduct injured the class members in the same, unvarying way: each class member "returned to play prematurely after head injuries and continued to experience concussive and sub-concussive hits." In addition, Judge Brody held that the NFL's alleged conduct raised "common and dispositive scientific questions" and that each class member "would have to confront the same causation issues in proving that repeated concussive blows give rise to long-term neurological damage." Accordingly, Judge Brody concluded that "resolution of these issues would so advance the litigation that they may fairly be said to predominate because the same set of core operative facts and theory of proximate cause apply to each member of the class."

There are stark contrasts, however, between the NFL Litigation and this case. That case involves approximately 20,000 former NFL football players. This case involves an estimated 4.4 million athletes in forty-three different men's and women's sports. The NFL Litigation involves roughly thirty-two NFL teams directly governed by the NFL's concussion policies. This case involves over a thousand NCAA member institutions, ranging from Division I schools to Division III schools, each of which has the option to adopt or reject the NCAA's concussion policies as well as the option to create its own concussion policies on a school-by-school, team-by-team, or coach-by-coach basis.

The examples provided by the Settling Plaintiffs starkly demonstrate how concussion education, evaluation, and treatment varied widely from one NCAA-affiliated school to another. Some schools warned student-athletes about the risks of head injuries, while others did not. Some schools administered baseline testing for concussions, while others did not. The evaluation and treatment that student-athletes received after a concussion event also varied from school to school and sometimes even within the same school. Each school also had different rules as to when an athlete could return to play after suffering a concussion. Because all of Plaintiffs' claims arise out of their experiences while in college, the nature and extent of the concussion protocols employed at individual schools play a critical role in the adjudication of Plaintiffs' claims against the NCAA.

Due to the unique circumstances of this case involving different schools, different sports, different coaches, and different concussion management practices, this Court cannot conclude, as Judge Brody did in *The NFL Litigation*, that the NCAA's alleged conduct injured the class members in the same, unvarying way. Rather, the facts produced in discovery present a multitude of potential permutations regarding whether the NCAA breached a duty to protect its athletes and caused any particular plaintiff injury. And the need to make individual, fact-intensive determinations as to liability with respect to each class member eclipses any common issues as to whether the NCAA had a duty to protect players from concussion-related risks, breached that duty, and fraudulently concealed those risks. Such individual issues also preclude a finding that class treatment would be the superior method of adjudicating such claims as compared to individual actions.

In addition, because the putative class members reside in all fifty states, any effort to certify a personal injury class under Rule 23(b)(3) would confront other serious hurdles. Because *Nichols* and *Arrington* were filed in Illinois, the Court must apply Illinois choice-of-law rules. "Under Illinois conflicts principles the law of the place of injury presumptively governs in a tort suit." Because the student-athletes allegedly were injured at their schools (or at another NCAA school if they were at an "away" game or meet), the Court would have to consider the law of virtually every state and territory in order to evaluate Plaintiffs' claims in these actions.

This is significant because, as the NCAA correctly notes, the law governing Plaintiffs' fraud and negligence claims, as well as the affirmative defenses of comparative negligence and assumption of risk, may vary materially by state. Accordingly, the Court concludes that it would be extremely difficult, if not impossible, for Plaintiffs to satisfy Rule 23(b)(3)'s requirements of superiority and predominance for their personal injury claims. *See In re Rhone-Poulenc Rorer, Inc.*

Furthermore, a Rule 23(b)(3) class of personal injury claimants would confront other manageability problems. For example, because of the indispensable role that the colleges played in this dispute, the NCAA would likely request (and the Court would likely grant) the joinder of the approximately six hundred and fifty non-governmental colleges and universities, as well as the conferences to which they belong, as necessary parties. The NCAA likely also would file third-party complaints against other potentially liable parties, including various equipment manufacturers and the trainers and physicians that treated some of the class members. As a result, thousands of additional parties would arrive at this Court's doorstep. Even when discounting for economies of scale, the sheer magnitude of discovery necessary to ascertain the efforts made (or not made) by these parties to warn of, prevent, evaluate, or treat concussions and concussion-related risks and symptoms would be unmanageable. And, no matter how imaginative an approach Nichols would have the Court take (and it is telling that Nichols does not detail any particular solutions himself), trying a nationwide class action seeking damages for personal injuries against the NCAA would require a multitude of mini-trials to adjudicate even basic liability issues, such as breach of duty and causation.

For all of these reasons, the Court finds it highly unlikely that Plaintiffs would be able to certify a nationwide personal injury class under Rule 23(b)(3) and concludes that this procedural right has little, if any, value. As such, Nichols and Arrington have not established that the Settlement Plaintiff's waiver of the right to pursue a class action for personal injury claims against the NCAA, in and of itself, demonstrates that Lead Counsel's representation of the putative class is inadequate.

### C.   Certification Under Rule 23(c)(4)

Nichols also argues that a nationwide personal injury class could be certified under Rule 23(c)(4). That rule provides that "when appropriate, an action may be brought or maintained as a class action with respect to particular issues." Under *In re Rhone-Poulenc Rorer Inc.*, however, certification of a nationwide personal injury damages class under Rule 23(c)(4) would likely be untenable.

The concerns expressed by Judge Posner in the *Rhone-Poulenc* case are equally applicable here. Nichols identifies three "core issues" upon which he argues Rule 23(c)(4) certification can be based: whether the NCAA owed class members a duty of care; the nature of that duty; and whether the NCAA breached that duty. This argument is unpersuasive.

First, like the defendants in *Rhone-Poulenc*, the NCAA would be forced to risk facing tremendous liability in a single proceeding "when it is entirely feasible to allow a final, authoritative determination of its liability from a decentralized process of multiple trials, involving different juries, and different standards of liability in different jurisdictions" and, with the participation of individual schools as likely co-defendants, that can provide additional particularized facts. Furthermore, like *Rhone-Poulenc*, this is not a situation where "individual suits are infeasible because the claim of each class member is tiny relative to the expense of litigation." In fact, numerous personal injury suits already have been filed by individual student-athletes, some seeking more than a million dollars in damages.

Additionally, Nichols' "core issues" class would include class members in all fifty states, and certification would require the Court to evaluate Nichols' "core issues" under "a kind of Esperanto" multi-state standard in contravention of *Erie. Rhone-Poulenc.* Again, such an exercise seems unnecessary and imprudent when injured student-athletes can seek damages in their respective forum based upon the particular forum's substantive law.

Lastly, limiting certification, as Nichols suggests, to the issues of duty and breach would violate the Seventh Amendment, which guarantees the putative class members and the NCAA the "right to have juriable issues determined by the first jury impaneled to hearing them and not reexamined by another finder of fact." *Rhone-Poulenc.*

Undeterred, Nichols argues that, because he is only seeking Rule 23(c)(4) certification as to the issues of duty and breach and not liability *per se*, he has properly "carved at the joint." Such a narrow approach may be permissible in some circumstances, but the crucial role that the individual schools play in this case not only makes it untenable, but impractical. For example, assume, again for the sake of argument, that the NCAA had a duty to safeguard student-athletes from concussions risks, but did not impose requirements on a particular school because it knew (or was told) that the school had its own concussion management protocols that met the prevailing standard of care. This is hypothetical, of course, but not implausible, and under this scenario the first empaneled jury would not be in a position to adjudicate the issues surrounding NCAA's breach without also evaluating the actions of the particular school and its interaction with the NCAA—the same issues that a subsequent jury would have to consider when deciding issues of causation and comparative negligence.

For all of these reasons, the Court concludes that Nichols' "core issues" class likely would not satisfy the requirements of Rule 23(c)(4) and has little, if any, value to the putative class members. Having determined, then, that Plaintiffs' personal injury damages class and "core issues" class likely would not satisfy Rule 23(b)(3) and Rule 23(c)(4), the Court now turns to the Settling Plaintiffs' request to certify the proposed settlement class under Rule 23(b)(2) and the reasonableness of the Amended Settlement Agreement.

## II.   THE PROPOSED SETTLEMENT CLASS SATISFIES RULE 23(b)(2)

The Settling Plaintiffs, along with the NCAA, move to certify the settlement class under Rule 23(b)(2) with notice to the class and the ability of class members to opt out of the class as provided under Rule 23(c)(2)(B). Under Rule 23(b)(2), a court may certify a class where "the party opposing the class has acted or refused to act on grounds that apply generally to the class, so that final injunctive relief or corresponding declaratory relief is appropriate respecting the class as a whole." Fed. R. Civ. P. 23(b)(2). "Colloquially, 23(b)(2) is the appropriate rule to enlist when the plaintiffs' primary goal is not monetary relief, but rather to require the defendant to do or not do something that would benefit the whole class."

Plaintiffs allege that the NCAA had a duty to protect the health and safety of student-athletes that played NCAA-sanctioned sports and knew the health risks associated with concussive and sub-concussive injuries. Despite this, according to Plaintiffs, the NCAA failed to promulgate and implement the rules and regulations necessary to safeguard student-athletes from sustaining such injuries and to diagnose them properly.

As remedy, Plaintiffs seek injunctive relief requiring the NCAA to adopt corrective measures, including "system-wide stepwise 'return to play' guidelines," protective treatment and eligibility requirements for injured student-athletes, and management and oversight by appropriate medical personnel. Plaintiffs also request "the establishment of a medical monitoring program that enables each class member to monitor whether he or she has any long-term effects or neurodegenerative conditions related to concussions or sub-concussive hits."

Here, the NCAA is alleged to have failed to act on grounds that apply generally to the class. Furthermore, Plaintiffs seek injunctive relief that would apply to the class as a whole, and the Medical Monitoring Program created by the settlement benefits the entire class. As such, if this were the extent of the settlement, the inquiry would end here, and the Court would readily find that the proposed settlement class meets the requirements of Rule 23(b)(2). But the proposed settlement goes further.

Although the Settling Plaintiffs seek certification under Rule 23(b)(2), the Amended Settlement Agreement also releases the right of class members to pursue their personal injury claims on a class-wide basis (presumably under Rule 23(b)(3), Rule 23(c)(4), or a similar state procedural rule). The question is whether such a release would preclude certification under Rule 23(b)(2). Put another way, can a settlement class that is certified under Rule 23(b)(2) release its rights to seek certification of their individual damages claims under Rule 23(b)(3)? Given the particular circumstances of this case, the ability of the class members to seek substantial damages on an individual basis, and the additional protections provided by the issuance of class notice and the ability of class members to opt-out of the settlement, the Court concludes that it can.

The Supreme Court discussed the boundaries separating Rule 23(b)(2) classes and Rule 23(b)(3) classes most recently in *Wal-Mart Stores, Inc. v. Dukes*: "Our opinion in *Ticor Title Ins. Co. v. Brown* expressed serious doubt about whether claims for monetary relief may be certified under that provision. We now hold that they may not, at least where (as here) the monetary relief is not incidental to the injunctive or declaratory relief." And, whatever this Court's views may be as to the fairness and reasonableness of the proposed settlement agreement, the Court must adhere mindfully to Rule 23's procedural requirements. *See Amchem.*

The appropriateness of certifying a class under Rule 23(b)(2) where the class also has asserted claims for individual damages has received various treatment by the Seventh Circuit over the years. The Seventh Circuit recently has endorsed the viability of [Rule 23(b)(2) class certification in *Johnson v. Meriter Health Services Employee Retirement Plan.* The Seventh Circuit affirmed, but because it was concerned that individual hearings may be required to determine the merits of each class member's individual damages claim, presented two permissible alternatives: "either the class members should be notified of the class action and allowed to opt out (and notice and opt out, we just said, are permitted in a (b)(2) class action even though not required), or the class should be bifurcated, which is to say divided into a trial on liability followed by a trial on damages if liability is found." The court continued that, "if the issues underlying the declaratory and damages claims overlapped," "the preferable alternative might be to stick with the (b)(2) certification but to require that the class members receive notice and have an opportunity to opt out of the class."

Here, the Settling Plaintiffs seek certification of their medical monitoring claims under Rule 23(b)(2) and also request that the Court exercise its discretion under Rule 23(d) to provide notice to the class and provide class members with an opportunity to opt out. The Court concludes that proceeding along these lines is consistent with the Seventh Circuit precedent discussed above. First, notice and the opportunity to opt out will safeguard the due process rights of the class members with respect to their personal injury claims. Furthermore, the settlement agreement does not entirely foreclose those claims, but expressly preserves the right of class members to pursue their damages claims against the schools and the NCAA on an individual basis, as many already have done. By permitting class members to litigate their individual damages claims in future proceedings and providing notice and the ability of class members to opt out of the settlement, this case is distinguishable from *Crawford* and does not raise the necessity of individual determinations underlying the Supreme Court's concerns in *Wal-Mart*.

It should also be noted that the law encourages the settlement of class actions. Thus, it would be strange to require the Settling Plaintiffs to obtain certification under Rule 23(b)(3) before it can waive that right in exchange for other benefits when negotiating a settlement, particularly where the record demonstrates that the likelihood of succeeding on such a motion is extremely low and class members are provided notice and the ability to opt out.

For these reasons, the Court grants the Settling Plaintiffs' request to conditionally certify the settlement class under Rule 23(b)(2). The Court also requires the parties to provide class members notice of the Amended Settlement Agreement and the opportunity to opt out pursuant to Rule 23(e)(1). Furthermore, exercising its discretion under Rule 23(d), the Court finds that "reasonable notice" in this case means "the best notice that is practicable under the circumstances, including individual notice to all members who can be identified through reasonable effort" as provided in Rule 23(c)(2)(B) and requires that the settlement class members be afforded an opportunity to opt out of the settlement as provided in Rule 23(c)(2)(B) and 23(c)(3). This procedure will give class members the opportunity to exclude themselves from the settlement and the settlement class.

Because adequate notice to the class is essential for this settlement, the Court has scrutinized the Settling Plaintiffs' notice program and has raised a number of concerns in its prior orders and during previous hearings. In response, the Settling Plaintiffs and the NCAA have performed additional investigations into the feasibility of direct notice and have provided additional support for their assertion that the proposed notice program will provide direct notice to fifty-nine to sixty-two percent of the settlement class members. Under the current proposal, the remaining settlement class members will receive indirect notice via national print publications (such as *ESPN The Magazine*, *Sports Illustrated*, and *USA Today*), the Settlement Class website, and a widely disseminated press release. Additionally, it is anticipated that class members will learn of the settlement through news coverage of the wide-reaching settlement.

The cost of these efforts is estimated to be $1.5 million, which is less than 2.2 percent of Medical Monitoring Fund, and an amount the Court deems reasonable. This multi-faceted notice plan is conservatively estimated to reach eighty percent of the settlement class, which is well within an acceptable range for class actions. In an effort to reach as many class members as possible, however, the Court also directs the parties to provide notice to the settlement class via the internet and social media using the NCAA's website, as well as the NCAA's Facebook pages and Twitter accounts. The Court does not anticipate that the costs of such additional efforts would be substantial, and they would provide additional publicity of the settlement to the class.

### III. WHETHER THE PROPOSED SETTLEMENT IS WITHIN THE RANGE OF POSSIBLE APPROVAL

Having conditionally certified the settlement class, the Court now must determine whether the proposed settlement is "within the range of possible approval." As previously noted, the "relevant factors include: (1) the strength of the case for plaintiffs on the merits, balanced against the extent of settlement offer; (2) the complexity, length, and expense of further litigation; (3) the amount of opposition to the settlement; (4) the reaction of members of the class to the settlement; (5) the opinion of competent counsel; and (6) stage of the proceedings and the amount of discovery completed."

In this case, the parties have already engaged in a lengthy mediation process and have conducted extensive discovery, including taking depositions, reviewing hundreds of thousands of documents, and consulting with leading medical experts in sports-related concussions. Litigation of this size and complexity takes many years to complete, at great expense to the class and great risk that affirmative defenses may thwart the class's legal theories. Balancing the fairness factors in a summary fashion as is appropriate on preliminary approval, the Court finds that, with the modifications required herein, the Amended Settlement Agreement is within the range of possible approval.

### A.   The Settlement's Benefits and the
### Release of Classwide Claims

The balancing of the settlement offer against the strength of Plaintiffs' case demonstrates that the settlement is within the range of possible approval. The settlement offer creates and funds a $70 million dollar Medical Monitoring Program that entitles all class members to be screened for symptoms of neurodegenerative diseases multiple times during a fifty-year period. The Screening Questionnaire incorporates questions based on scientifically and clinically accepted standardized scales and measures.

In those instances where the screening indicates that further assessment is necessary, a class member will qualify to receive up to two medical evaluations (or more with prior approval) that is fully funded by the Medical Monitoring Program. The medical evaluation would include a neurological examination, neuropsychological examination, mood and behavioral evaluation, and any necessary ancillary tests that comply with the then-current American Academy of Neurology clinical practice guidelines for the diagnosis and treatment of neurologic diseases. The breadth and extent of this program provides each class member an opportunity to monitor his or her own health at various times during the Medical Monitoring Period in order to assess whether the concussive or sub-concussive impacts the individual experienced as a student-athlete may have resulted in a neurologic condition.

The strength of settlement class's claims for medical monitoring depends upon a number of factors, including: whether the state, in which the class member resides, recognizes medical monitoring as an independent cause of action; whether the state recognizes medical monitoring as a form of injunctive relief; and whether the state allows medical monitoring as a form of relief in the absence of present physical injury. The laws of the various states differ with respect to these issues. Additionally, in order to prevail, Plaintiffs would have to overcome numerous defenses, such as statute of limitations and assumption of risk arguments, and likely incur hundreds of thousands, if not millions, of additional dollars in attorneys' fees and costs to pursue this litigation through trial and possible appeal. Given that it is far from certain that every student-athlete within the settlement class could obtain relief in the form of medical monitoring even after years of litigation, the fact that the settlement provides medical monitoring for *all* class members within ninety days of the Effective Date is a significant victory for the members of the settlement class.

Nichols and Arrington's primary objection is to the provision in the settlement agreement whereby the settling class members agree to release the NCAA and its affiliates from filing claims "pursued on a class-wide basis and relating to concussions or sub-concussive hits or contact" sustained during participating in collegiate sports as an NCAA student-athlete. But the Court has concluded that there is very little likelihood that a Rule 23(b)(3) or 23(c)(4) class for personal injury claims against the NCAA could be certified on a nationwide or multi-school basis. Furthermore, the settlement preserves the right of each class member to pursue his or her personal injury claims on an individual basis. Accordingly, the Court finds that the objections raised by Nichols and Arrington are not well-founded.

That said, Nichols correctly points out that the release provision in the Amended Settlement Agreement, on its face, appears to foreclose any and all class actions based on personal injury claims, regardless of the class definition, however focused or narrowly defined. As previously discussed, the Court lacks the factual record to evaluate the likelihood of class certification for a narrowly defined class action brought against a single school and the NCAA—such as a class of student-athletes who played a single sport, on the same team, during the same time, and who were subjected to the same concussion management protocols. Such a putative class still would face substantial barriers to certification for the reasons discussed above, but the record before the Court does not permit an evaluation of its merits. As a result, the Court cannot find that the release of personal injury claims on a class-wide basis is reasonable as it is currently set forth in the Amended Settlement Agreement. To the extent that the Settling Plaintiffs and the NCAA seek approval of such a provision, the scope of the release of class-wide personal injury claims must be limited to those instances where the plaintiffs or claimants seek a nationwide class or where the proposed class is comprised of student-athletes from more than one NCAA-affiliated school.

### B.   Other Objections Regarding Fairness of the Settlement

#### 1.   The Value of the Medical Monitoring Program

Nichols argues that the parties' estimation of the value of Medical Monitoring Program is greatly exaggerated. First, he contends that the questionnaire discourages class members from participating. Having reviewed the questionnaire, the Court does not find that answering its questions will be unduly onerous or invasive. Rather, the questions about family history, educational history, medical history, sports involvement, concussion history, and current symptoms are relevant to assessing a class member's health and well-being. Furthermore, to the extent that class members are unwilling to fill out the questionnaire, there will likely be a correlation between members who are not sufficiently motivated to fill out the questionnaire and those who are asymptomatic at that point in time such that an evaluation is likely unnecessary.

Second, Nichols contends that, because many class members have private health insurance, the ultimate benefit to the class member is the amount of his or her co-pay for the services provided. That argument assumes that a class member could go to a single doctor on a single visit to determine whether they have PCS or CTE. That also assumes that the Medical Monitoring Program requires class members to assert a claim of benefits against their private health insurance company to obtain the benefits of the settlement. Neither is accurate.

The benefit of the Medical Monitoring Program is the streamlining of a highly specialized and multi-step process necessary to obtain a medical evaluation designed to determine whether a class member is suffering from PCS or CTE. Many class members may not have any idea that they are experiencing symptoms caused by prior head injuries and, thus, may not seek an evaluation or the appropriate treatments required to ease their symptoms. Here, medical experts with specializing expertise in the diagnosis, care, and management of concussions in sport, as well as mid-to late-life neurodegenerative diseases, have created a screening questionnaire specifically designed to determine whether a class member is experiencing neurological symptoms caused by concussions. The experts also have created a standardized scoring protocol to determine whether additional evaluation is necessary in individual cases. Where additional evaluation is warranted, the class member will undergo a battery of neurologic, neurophysiological, mood, and behavioral tests. All of the information gathered from a Medical Evaluation will be collectively evaluated by a physician skilled in the diagnosis, treatment, and management of concussions, and the results will be communicated to the class member. Armed with the results, the Settlement Class Member will then be in a position to seek treatment appropriate to the diagnosis and be knowledgeable about the effects, if any, of concussions or sub-concussive hits he or she experienced while in college. Such a comprehensive assessment program has substantial value to the class.

Furthermore, a class member is not required to assert a claim of benefits to their insurance company in order to obtain a Medical Evaluation. ("In no event shall a Qualifying Class Member be responsible for making a claim on his or her insurance policy to receive or qualify for the benefits of the Settlement."). A class member would only pay a co-pay or deductible if a claim of benefits were being asserted against his or her own insurance company. Because such a claim is not required, there should never be a need for a class member to pay a co-pay or deductible.

That said, to the extent that the settlement agreement allows the Medical Monitoring Program Administrator to seek subrogation or reimbursement of the program costs from a class member's private insurance carrier, the Court rejects the provision as unreasonable. (providing that "the Program Administrator may pursue subrogation or reimbursement from Qualifying Class Members' private health insurance for the cost of Medical Evaluations, as long as doing so does not preclude the Qualifying Class Member from qualifying for at least one (1) examination under his or her health insurance plan in the two (2) year period following his or her Medical Evaluation"). Not only would such a provision shift the costs of the Medical Monitoring Program to the class member and his or her insurer, but the filing of such a claim would likely impact the availability of annual and lifetime benefits to the class member under the private plan, as well as the class member's ability to obtain health insurance in the future. The Court sees no difference between, on the one hand, forcing a class member to file a claim with her private insurer and, on the other hand, allowing the Program Administrator to assert subrogation rights against the same insurer.

Accordingly, as a condition of preliminary approval, the Court directs that the following provisions be omitted from the Settlement Agreement: (1) "Any deductible or co-pay required to be paid by a Qualifying Class Member in order to obtain reimbursement by the Program Administrator for a Medical Evaluation at a Program Location under the Medical Monitoring Program shall be paid from the Medical Monitoring Fund," and (2) "the Program Administrator may pursue subrogation or reimbursement from Qualifying Class Members' private health insurance for the cost of Medical Evaluations, as long as doing so does not preclude the Qualifying Class Member from qualifying for at least one (1) examination under his or her health insurance plan in the two (2) year period following his or her Medical Evaluation."

### 2.   Class Members Who Live More than 100 Miles Away

To address the Court's concerns regarding the scarcity of Program Locations, the Settling Plaintiffs and the NCAA have agreed to expand the number of Program Locations to thirty-three sites nationwide. Assuming that the geographic distribution of the class members approximates the general population, 50 percent of the class would be within fifty miles of a Program Location and 70 percent would be within one hundred miles of a Program Location. As explained in the Garretson Report, the Medical Science Committee concluded that the costs of adding more Program Locations at the present time would far outweigh any benefits, and the Court finds this conclusion reasonable.

Those class members who live more than one hundred miles from a Program Location would have two options. The class member could travel to the nearest Program Location and obtain reimbursement of reasonable travel expenses. Alternatively, in the event that travel to the nearest location is unduly burdensome, the class member could request that the Program Administrator qualify another medical institution or provider that is within 100 miles of the class member's residence to provide a Medical Evaluation in accordance with standards set forth in the Amended Settlement Agreement. The Program Administrator then would enter into a contact with the alternative medical institution or provider for those services.

Under the second scenario, the settlement agreement proposes to reimburse the class member "the lesser of (1) the average cost of the Medical Evaluation within the Medical Monitoring Program or (2) the Qualifying Class Member's actual out-of-pocket costs for the Medical Evaluation by the local physician." However, given that the provider would have to enter into a contract with the Program Administrator (which presumably would not only specify the services to be rendered, but also any fees), and the class member is not required to submit a claim to her private insurer, the provision should simply provide that the Program Administrator will pay the medical institution or physician for performing the Medical Evaluation pursuant to the negotiated contract.

### 3.    Funds Remaining at the Program's Expiration

Confirming the sufficiency of the $70 million Medical Monitoring Fund, Bruce Deal, the Settling Plaintiffs' economic expert, estimates that at least $2 million will be left over at the end of the fifty-year monitoring period based on conservative assumptions. Ross Mishkin, the economic expert offered by the NCAA, performed a different analysis and agrees that the funds are sufficient for the program, estimating that approximately $34 million (albeit, in 2066 dollars) will remain in the end of fifty years. The Amended Settlement Agreement provides that any remaining funds "shall be either used to extend the Medical Monitoring Program or donated to an institution or institutions selected by the Medical Science Committee to be used for concussion-related research or treatment." Nichols objects to this provision, arguing that the funds remaining at the expiration of the Medical Monitoring Period should benefit the class members rather than be donated for concussion research.

Provisions in class action settlements providing *cy pres* awards can be appropriate "if distribution to the class members is infeasible." Here, if sufficient funds remain at the end of the monitoring period to extend the Medical Monitoring Program, doing so would provide a direct benefit to class members, some of whom will only be in their late sixties or early seventies. Accordingly, the Court directs that one year prior to the expiration of the program, the Medical Science Committee should inform the Court whether sufficient funds remain to extend the Medical Monitoring Period for a period greater than six months; if such funds exist, the period should be so extended. If there are insufficient funds to extend the Medical Monitoring Period for six months, then the Medical Science Committee may elect to donate the remaining funds to an institution be used for concussion-related research or treatment, subject to approval by the Court at that time.

### 4.   The $5 Million Research Fund

Nichols argues that the NCAA's obligation under the Amended Settlement Agreement to contribute $5 million to concussion research provides no value to the class members. This value is illusory, according to Nichols, because NCAA member institutions already spend, and will continue to spend, millions on concussion-related research regardless of the settlement agreement, and, under the terms of the agreement, research conducted by any NCAA member institution is credited toward the $5 million. This point is well taken.

The research funds that have been or would have been spent in the absence of this settlement cannot be counted as a benefit arising from of the settlement itself. Accordingly, NCAA's $5 million contribution to concussion research must constitute *additional* funding for research that otherwise would not have occurred absent this settlement. And the following provision in the Amended Settlement Agreement should be deleted: "For purposes of this provision, research undertaken by NCAA member institutions with respect to the prevention, treatment and/or effects of concussions will be credited (as appropriate) toward the foregoing monetary requirement."

### 5.   The Ten-Year Publicity Campaign

In assessing the cost and effectiveness of the Medical Monitoring Program, Deal assumes there will be a publicity campaign ten years into the Medical Monitoring Period reminding class members of their eligibility for the Medical Monitoring Program. The Amended Settlement Agreement, however, does not require a second publicity campaign. The Court believes that additional publicity campaigns via relevant print publications, internet publications, and social media on the ten-year, twenty-year, thirty-year, and forty-year anniversaries of the commencement of the Medical Monitoring Program will be necessary to ensure that class members remain aware of the availability of the program.

### 6.   Duty to Report to the Court

As currently drafted, the parties are required to file with the Court the Medical Science Committee's annual report on the first day of each year during the Medical Monitoring Period. The agreement also should provide that the Court can request a report from the Medical Science Committee, the Program Administrator, the Notice Administrator, and/or the Special Master regarding the status of the Medical Monitoring Program at any time during the monitoring period.

### CONCLUSION

Subject to the modifications outlined herein, the Court grants the Joint Motion for Preliminary Approval of Amended Class Settlement and Certification of Settlement Class. The parties should discuss whether they are amenable to the Court's modifications and report on the status of these discussions at the next status hearing.

# CHAPTER 6

## RESOLVING MASS TORTS THROUGH SETTLEMENT CLASSES

■ ■ ■

## A. HISTORICAL ANTECEDENTS

### IN RE A.H. ROBINS CO.
United States Court of Appeals, Fourth Circuit, 1989.
880 F.2d 709.

This diversity suit by seven individual claimants, suing on their own behalf and as the proposed class representatives of all injured Dalkon Shield claimants, seeks recovery against Aetna Casualty and Surety Company for injuries resulting from the use of an allegedly defective intrauterine device known as the Dalkon Shield. Aetna was neither the manufacturer nor the vender of the device; it was the products liability insurance carrier of A.H. Robins Company, Inc. (Robins), the manufacturer and distributor of the device. It is the theory of the plaintiffs that Aetna's conduct, while acting in its role as insurance carrier, was such that it rendered itself liable as a joint tortfeasor with Robins for any injuries sustained by persons using the device. The plaintiffs sought class certification of the suit. During consideration whether to give final certification of the suit, the parties entered into a settlement of the action conditioned on certification. The District Court granted final class certification of the action and approval of the settlement of the action so certified. The appeal challenges the two orders. We affirm both the class certification and the settlement orders.

### XVI.

It is to be noted that a number of the decisions we have discussed involved settlements of the proposed class action. This raises the question whether class certification for settlement purposes is permissible under Rule 23. The appellants argue flatly that certification for such purposes is impermissible. However, despite this statement of appellants, certification for such purposes finds strong support in a number of various Law Review comments. Nielson, *Was the 1966 Advisory Committee Right?: Suggested Revisions of Rule 23 to Allow More Frequent Use of Class Actions in Mass Tort Litigation*, 25 Harv. J. Legislation 461, 480 (1988), for instance, recognized a "trend" in favor of such certification:

In recent years, several federal judges have explicitly recognized the effect of class certification on the likelihood of prejudgment settlement in mass-tort suits, and have apparently allowed such recognition to influence their decision to certify class actions.

Professor Trangsrud, though he took a somewhat skeptical view of mass-tort certifications generally, felt that certification "as a pretrial joinder device to facilitate group settlements was both proper and desirable," adding

> Its use is proper because Federal Rule of Civil Procedure 23 provides that the court may certify a common question class action when it will prove "superior to other available methods for the fair and efficient adjudication of the controversy." A judicially supervised and approved class action settlement, like a judicially supervised trial, is a means of hearing and determining judicially, in other words, "adjudicating," the value of claims arising from a mass tort. As a result, if conditional certification of the case as a common question class action for settlement purposes would enhance the prospects for a group settlement, then Rule 23 authorizes certification.

Recent court decisions have also spoken approvingly of the class certification of mass-tort actions for purposes of settlement in conformity with these academic comments. These decisions confirm that the promotion of settlement may well be a factor in resolving the issue of certification. Thus, in *Agent Orange,* Chief Judge Weinstein wrote:

> Finally, the court may not ignore the real world of dispute resolution. As already noted, a classwide finding of causation may serve to resolve the claims of individual members, in a way that determinations in individual cases would not, by enhancing the possibility of settlement among the parties and with the federal government.

Similarly, in In re School Asbestos Litigation, the Court said:

> Concentration of individual damage suits in one forum can lead to formidable problems, but the realities of litigation should not be overlooked in theoretical musings. Most tort cases settle, and the preliminary maneuverings in litigation today are designed as much, if not more, for settlement purposes than for trial. Settlements of class actions often result in savings for all concerned.

The only federal court decision which has actually granted class certification for settlement purposes in a mass-tort action is *In re Bendectin.* In that case, Judge Rubin, in granting certification for settlement purposes, said:

The *Bendectin* litigation is but one example of massive product liability lawsuits involving large numbers of plaintiffs, protracted trials and substantial litigation costs. The traditional court system is simply unequipped to handle such mass tort litigation in a conventional manner without materially depleting the judicial resources available for all other litigation. It is theoretically possible to assign sufficient judicial time to hear these cases promptly but only at the cost of further delay in an already overburdened system. The cost to the parties of litigating these cases under current procedures is such that few plaintiffs could afford the expense or the delay. Justice is not served by erecting tollgates at the courthouse door.

There is a solution. The resolution of disputes does not necessarily require trial. Within the judicial authority of this Court is a means whereby the parties might be assisted in reaching a prompt and equitable disposition of the entire problem. That solution involves limited use of Rule 23 of the Federal Rules of Civil Procedure. A class certification would enable any proposed settlement to be presented to all class members and by them either accepted or rejected.

On appeal, the certification was invalidated. The ground for denial was that the action failed to qualify for certification under (b)(1) because of the limitation in the use of the class action decision stated in *McDonnell Douglas,* and under the "limited fund" doctrine. The Court, however, was careful to point out that it was not determining that class certification for settlement purposes of the mass tort in that case was impermissible. To emphasize this fact, the Court declared:

> We do note that there is precedent for the proposition that a class can be certified for settlement purposes only. The *Beef Industry* case involved the certification of a temporary settlement class prior to certification of a class for trial. In this case, the District Judge certified a class for settlement purposes after having rejected the same class for trial purposes. The District Judge therefore implicitly held that the standards for certifying a class are different depending on whether the class is for settlement or whether it is for trial. Because we decide the case on other grounds, we do not consider whether this holding is correct.

As *Bendectin* had recognized, courts in cases involving numerous parties, though not mass-tort cases, had granted class certification for settlement purposes. Judge Wisdom in *In re Beef Industry Antitrust Litigation* carefully considered all angles of the question of class certification to promote settlement and, in his convincing opinion, found certification under proper circumstances to be in order. That decision has been followed in other cases, perhaps the most notable one being

*Weinberger v. Kendrick*, in which Judge Friendly, speaking for the court, said:

> The hallmark of Rule 23 is the flexibility it affords to the courts to utilize the class device in a particular case to best serve the ends of justice for the affected parties and to promote judicial efficiencies. Temporary settlement classes have proved to be quite useful in resolving major class action disputes. While their use may still be controversial, most Courts have recognized their utility and have authorized the parties to seek to compromise their differences, including class action issues through this means.

Though, as we have said, these cases were not mass-tort suits, there seems to be no real reason why the precedent established by the cases, just cited, should not be equally applicable to the mass-tort. If not a ground for certification per se, certainly settlement should be a factor, and an important factor, to be considered when determining certification. That is all the District Court did in this case. Its action in considering this circumstance would appear to have been appropriate.

## XVII.

In summary, we take it as the lessons to be gleaned from the authorities already cited and discussed to be a that the "trend" is once again to give Rule 23 a liberal rather than a restrictive construction, adopting a standard of flexibility in application which will in the particular case "best serve the ends of justice for the affected parties and promote judicial efficiency;" (b) that the Advisory Committee's Note suggestion that suit for damages is "not appropriate" for class certification has proved unworkable and is now increasingly disregarded; (c) that the theory that the Rule should be constrained by establishing judicially, without support in the Rule itself, limitations on its use has been outdated by the increasing phenomenon of the mass products tort action and by the growing body of recent class action decisions and comments favoring class actions in the mass tort context; (d) that, in order to promote the use of the class device and to reduce the range of disputed issues, courts should take full advantage of the provision in subsection (c)(4) permitting class treatment of separate issues in the case and, if such separate issues predominate sufficiently (i.e., is the central issue), to certify the entire controversy as in *Agent Orange;* and (e) that it is "proper" in determining certification to consider whether such certification will foster settlement of the case with advantage to the parties and with great saving in judicial time and services; and (f) that the mass tort action for damages may in a proper case be appropriate for class action, either partially on in whole.

# B.  SETTING THE DEBATE

## IN RE GENERAL MOTORS CORP. PICK-UP TRUCK FUEL TANK PRODS. LIAB. LITIG.

United States Court of Appeals, Third Circuit, 1995.
55 F.3d 768.

This is an appeal from an order of the District Court for the Eastern District of Pennsylvania approving the settlement of a large class action following its certification of a so-called settlement class. Numerous objectors challenge the fairness and reasonableness of the settlement. The objectors also challenge: (1) the district court's failure to certify the class formally; (2) its denial of discovery concerning the settlement negotiations; (3) the adequacy of the notice as it pertained to the fee request; and (4) its approval of the attorneys' fee agreement between the defendants and the attorneys for the class, which the class notice did not fully disclose, thereby (allegedly) depriving the class of the practical opportunity to object to the proposed fee award at the fairness hearing.

The class members are purchasers, over a 15 year period, of mid-and full-sized General Motors pick-up trucks with model C, K, R, or V chassis, which may have had a design defect in their location of the fuel tank. Objectors claim that the side-saddle tanks rendered the trucks especially vulnerable to fuel fires in side collisions. Many of the class members are individual owners (i.e., own a single truck), while others are "fleet owners," who own a number of trucks. Many of the fleet owners are governmental agencies. The negotiated settlement treats fleet owners quite differently from individual owners, a fact with serious implications for the fairness of the settlement and the adequacy of representation of the class.

While all the issues we have mentioned are significant, the threshold and most important issue concerns the propriety and prerequisites of settlement classes. The settlement class device is not mentioned in the class action rule, Federal Rule of Civil Procedure 23. Rather it is a judicially crafted procedure. Usually, the request for a settlement class is presented to the court by both plaintiffs and defendants; having provisionally settled the case before seeking certification, the parties move for simultaneous class certification and settlement approval. Because this process is removed from the normal, adversarial, litigation mode, the class is certified for settlement purposes only, not for litigation. Sometimes, as here, the parties reach a settlement while the case is in litigation posture, only then moving the court, with the defendants' stipulation as to the class's compliance with the Rule 23 requisites, for class certification and settlement approval. In any event, the court disseminates notice of the proposed settlement and fairness hearing at the same time it notifies class members of the pendency of class action determination. Only when the settlement is about to be finally approved does the court formally certify the class, thus binding the interests of its members by the settlement.

The first MANUAL FOR COMPLEX LITIGATION strongly disapproved of settlement classes. Nevertheless, courts have increasingly used the device in recent years, and subsequent manuals have relented, endorsing settlement classes under carefully controlled circumstances, but continuing to warn of the potential for abuse. This increased use of settlement classes has proven extremely valuable for disposing of major and complex national and international class actions in a variety of substantive areas ranging from toxic torts (*Agent Orange*) and medical devices (Dalkon Shield, breast implant), to antitrust cases (the beef or cardboard container industries). But their use has not been problem free, provoking a barrage of criticism that the device is a vehicle for collusive settlements that primarily serve the interests of defendants—by granting expansive protection from law suits—and of plaintiffs' counsel—by generating large fees gladly paid by defendants as a quid pro quo for finally disposing of many troublesome claims.

After reflection upon these concerns, we conclude that Rule 23 permits courts to achieve the significant benefits created by settlement classes so long as these courts abide by all of the fundaments of the Rule. Settlement classes must satisfy the Rule 23(a) requirements of numerosity, commonality, typicality, and adequacy of representation, as well as the relevant 23(b) requirements, usually (as in this case) the (b)(3) superiority and predominance standards. We also hold that settlement class status (on which settlement approval depends) should not be sustained unless the record establishes, by findings of the district judge, that the same requisites of the Rule are satisfied. Additionally, we hold that a finding that the settlement was fair and reasonable does not serve as a surrogate for the class findings, and also that there is no lower standard for the certification of settlement classes than there is for litigation classes. But so long as the four requirements of 23(a) and the appropriate requirement(s) of 23(b) are met, a court may legitimately certify the class under the Rule.

For the reasons that follow at some length, we conclude that, although settlement classes are valid generally, this settlement class was not properly certified. We therefore reverse the challenged order of the district court and remand for further proceedings.

## C.   *Arguments Favoring Settlement Classes*

Although settlement classes are vulnerable to potent criticisms, some important dynamics militate in favor of a judge's delaying or even substantially avoiding class certification determinations. Because certification so dramatically increases the potential value of the suit to the plaintiffs and their attorneys as well as the potential liability of the defendant, the parties will frequently contest certification vigorously. As a result, a defendant considering a settlement may resist agreeing to class certification because, if the settlement negotiations should fail, it would be left exposed to major litigation.

In mass tort cases, in particular, use of a settlement class can help overcome certain elements of these actions that otherwise can considerably complicate efforts to settle. These hurdles include "the large number of individual plaintiffs and lawyers; the existence of unfiled claims by putative plaintiffs; and the inability of any single plaintiff to offer the settling defendant reliable indemnity protection." By using the courts to overcome some of the collective action problems particularly acute in mass tort cases, the settlement class device can make settlement feasible. The use of settlement classes can thus enable both parties to realize substantial savings in litigation expenses by compromising the action before formal certification. Through settlement class certification, courts have fostered settlement of some very large, complex cases that might otherwise never have yielded deserving plaintiffs any substantial remuneration.

Settlement classes also increase the number of actions that are amenable to settlement by increasing the rewards of a negotiated solution, in at least four ways. First, the prospect of class certification increases a defendant's incentive to settle because the settlement would then bind the class members and prevent further suits against the defendant. Second, settlement classes may reduce litigation costs by allowing defendants to stipulate to class certification without forfeiting any of their legal arguments against certification should the negotiations fail. Third, because the payment of settlement proceeds, even relatively small amounts, may palliate class members, settlement can reduce differences among class members, and thus make class certification more likely, increasing the value of settlement to the defendant, since a larger number of potential claims can thus be resolved.

Fourth, the use of settlement classes reduces the probability of a successful subsequent challenge to the class-wide settlement. By treating the class as valid pending settlement, a temporary class facilitates notice to those persons whom the court might consider part of the class. The expanded notice afforded by access to the customary class action notification process protects both the absentees and the defendants by eliminating negotiations between the defendants and the named plaintiffs with respect to the class definition that could leave the defendant vulnerable to additional suits by absentees whose interests, a court later determines, were not adequately served or protected. Increasing the certainty that the settlement will be upheld augments the value of settling to the defendant and consequently the amount defendants will be willing to pay. Thus, delaying certification, in contravention of a strict reading of Rule 23, encourages settlement, an important judicial policy, by increasing the prospective gains to the defendant (and thus potentially to the plaintiffs as well) from exploring a negotiated solution.

Moreover, critics of settlement classes may underestimate the safeguards that still inhere. Although courts are often certifying settlement classes with sub-optimal amounts of information, and without the full benefit of the processes meant to protect the absentees' interests, the provisional certification of a settlement class does not finally determine the absentees' rights. When the simultaneous notice of the class and the settlement is distributed to the proposed class, objecting class members can still challenge the class on commonality, typicality, adequacy of representation, superiority, and predominance grounds—they are not limited to objections based strictly on the settlement's terms.

Furthermore, the view that, in settlement class cases, the court lacks the information necessary to fulfill its role as protector of the absentees, may reflect an assumption that the court's approval always comes early in the case. While it often does, the certification decision is sometimes made later in the case, when the parties have presumably developed the merits more fully (in discovery or in the course of wrangling over the settlement terms) and when prior governmental procedures or investigations might have also yielded helpful information. Whatever the timing of the certification ruling, the judge has the duty of passing on the fairness and adequacy of the settlement under Rule 23(e) and also of determining whether the class meets the Rule's requisites under 23(a). Whether or not the court certifies the class before settlement discussions, these duties are the same.

Although a judge cannot presume that the putative class counsel actively represented the absentees' interests, the court can still monitor the negotiation process itself to assure that both counsel and the settlement adequately vindicate the absentees' interests. Thus, there is no reason to inflexibly limit the use of settlement classes to any specified categories of cases (for example, those cases with few objectors, those which do not involve partial settlements, or those which do not involve an expanded class). Even apparently troublesome litigation activity, such as expanding the class just before settlement approval at the defendant's request, is no more free from judicial scrutiny in a settlement class context than it would be otherwise. The court still must give notice to the now-expanded class and satisfy itself that the requisites of class certification are met. Since the party advocating certification bears the burden of proving appropriateness of class treatment, where the procedural posture is such that the court lacks adequate information to make those determinations, it can and should withhold the relevant approvals.

But even if the use of settlement classes did reduce a judge's capacity to safeguard the class's interests, it does not necessarily impair the ability of absentees to protect their own interests. Individual class members retain the right to opt out of the class and settlement, preserving the right to pursue their own litigation. In fact, the use of the settlement class in some sense enhances plaintiffs' right to opt out. Since the plaintiff is offered the opportunity to opt out of the class simultaneously with the opportunity to accept or reject the settlement offer, which is supposed to be accompanied by all information on settlement, the plaintiff knows exactly what result he or she sacrifices when opting out.

In sum, settlement classes clearly offer substantial benefits. However, the very flexibility required to achieve these gains strains the bounds of Rule 23 and comes at the expense of some of the protections the Rule-writers intended to construct. As Judge Schwarzer has explained: "one way to see the settlement class is as a commendable example of the law's adaptability to meet the needs of the time-in the best tradition of the Anglo-American common law. But another interpretation might be that it is an unprincipled subversion of the Federal Rules of Civil Procedure. True, if it is a subversion, it is done with good intentions to help courts cope with burgeoning dockets, to enable claimants at the end of the line of litigants to recover compensation, and to allow defendants to manage the staggering liabilities many face. But as experience seems to show, good intentions are not always enough to ensure that all relevant private and public interests are protected. The siren song of Rule 23 can lead lawyers, parties and courts into rough waters where their ethical compass offers only uncertain guidance."

### D.   Are Settlement Classes Cognizable Under Rule 23?

Although not specifically authorized by Rule 23, settlement classes are not specifically precluded by it either; indeed, Judge Brieant has read subsection (d), giving the court power to manage the class action, as authorizing the creation of "tentative", "provisional", or "conditional" classes through its grant of power to modify or decertify classes as necessary. And because of the broad grant of authority in Rule 23(d), at least one commentator has noted that the validity of temporary settlement classes is usually not questioned. Courts apparently share this confidence. Indeed, one court believed that "it is clear that the Court may provisionally certify the Class for settlement purposes."

Alternatively, some courts have conceived of settlement classes as a "temporary assumption" by the court to facilitate settlement. The arguments of the late Herbert Newberg, one of the leading advocates of settlement classes, reflect an assumption that the Rule 23 determinations are merely postponed, not eliminated: "On analysis, however, it would appear that this argument that courts using settlement classes circumvent the need to test the propriety of the class action according to the specific criteria of Rule 23 may be rebutted by perceiving the temporary settlement class as nothing more than a tentative assumption indulged in by the court. The actual class ruling is deferred in these circumstances until after hearing on the settlement approval. At that time, the court in fact applies the class action requirements to determine whether the action should be maintained as a class action." Newberg posits, therefore, that the temporary assumption conception of the settlement needs no special authorization since the court eventually follows the ordinary certification process, only deferring it until the settlement approval stage.

Courts have also relied on the more general policies of Rule 23—promoting justice and realizing judicial efficiencies—to justify this arguable departure from the rule. The hallmark of Rule 23 is flexibility. Temporary settlement classes have proved to be quite useful in resolving major class action disputes. While their use may still be controversial, most Courts have recognized their utility and have authorized the parties to compromise their differences, including class action issues through this means.

It is noteworthy that resistance to more flexible applications of Rule 23 has diminished over time. The evolution of the reception accorded settlement classes has manifested itself in the successive versions of the MANUAL FOR COMPLEX LITIGATION. The first edition of the MANUAL criticized the initiation of settlement negotiations before certification, and discouraged all such negotiations. The second edition recognizes the potential benefits of settlement classes but still cautioned that "the court should be wary of presenting the settlement to the class." The draft third version acknowledges that "settlement classes offer a commonly used vehicle for the settlement of complex litigation" and aims only to supervise rather than discourage their use.

A survey of the case law confirms the impression that resistance to settlement classes has diminished: few cases since the late 1970's and early 1980's even bother to squarely address the propriety of settlement classes. Moreover, no court of appeals that has had the opportunity to comment on the propriety of settlement classes has held that they constitute a per se violation of Rule 23. But some courts recognize that this practice represents a significant departure from the usual Rule 23 scenario and thereby counsel that courts should scrutinize these settlements even more closely.

We acknowledge that settlement classes, conceived of either as provisional or conditional certifications, represent a practical construction of the class action rule. Such construction affords considerable economies to both the litigants and the judiciary and is also fully consistent with the flexibility integral to Rule 23. A number of other jurisdictions have already accepted settlement classes as a reasonable interpretation of Rule 23 and thereby achieved these substantial benefits. Although we appreciate the concerns raised about the device, we are confident that they can be addressed by the rigorous applications of the Rule 23 requisites by the courts at the approval stages, as we discuss at greater length herein. For these reasons, we hold that settlement classes are cognizable under Rule 23.

# C.  SETTLEMENT CLASSES: THE SUPREME COURT SPEAKS

## AMCHEM PRODS., INC. V. WINDSOR

Supreme Court of the United States, 1997.
521 U.S. 591, 117 S.Ct. 2231, 132 L.Ed.2d 689.

This case concerns the legitimacy under Rule 23 of the Federal Rules of Civil Procedure of a class-action certification sought to achieve global settlement of current and future asbestos-related claims. The class proposed for certification potentially encompasses hundreds of thousands, perhaps millions, of individuals tied together by this commonality: each was, or some day may be, adversely affected by past exposure to asbestos products manufactured by one or more of 20 companies. Those companies, defendants in the lower courts, are petitioners here.

The United States District Court for the Eastern District of Pennsylvania certified the class for settlement only, finding that the proposed settlement was fair and that representation and notice had been adequate. That court enjoined class members from separately pursuing asbestos-related personal-injury suits in any court, federal or state, pending the issuance of a final order. The Court of Appeals for the Third Circuit vacated the District Court's orders, holding that the class certification failed to satisfy Rule 23's requirements in several critical respects. We affirm the Court of Appeals' judgment.

### I.

### A.

The settlement-class certification we confront evolved in response to an asbestos-litigation crisis. A United States Judicial Conference Ad Hoc Committee on Asbestos Litigation, appointed by the Chief Justice in September 1990, described facets of the problem in a 1991 report: "This is a tale of danger known in the 1930s, exposure inflicted upon millions of Americans in the 1940s and 1950s, injuries that began to take their toll in the 1960s, and a flood of lawsuits beginning in the 1970s. On the basis of past and current filing data, and because of a latency period that may last as long as 40 years for some asbestos related diseases, a continuing stream of claims can be expected. The final toll of asbestos related injuries is unknown. Predictions have been made of 200,000 asbestos disease deaths before the year 2000 and as many as 265,000 by the year 2015. "The most objectionable aspects of asbestos litigation can be briefly summarized: dockets in both federal and state courts continue to grow; long delays are routine; trials are too long; the same issues are litigated over and over; transaction costs exceed the victims' recovery by nearly two to one; exhaustion of assets threatens and distorts the process; and future claimants may lose altogether." Real reform, the report concluded, required federal legislation creating a national asbestos dispute-resolution scheme. As recommended by the Ad Hoc Committee, the Judicial Conference of the United States urged Congress to act. To this date, no congressional response has emerged.

In the face of legislative inaction, the federal courts—lacking authority to replace state tort systems with a national toxic tort compensation regime—endeavored to work with the procedural tools available to improve management of federal asbestos litigation. Eight federal judges, experienced in the superintendence of asbestos cases, urged the Judicial Panel on Multidistrict Litigation (MDL Panel), to consolidate in a single district all asbestos complaints then pending in federal courts. Accepting the recommendation, the MDL Panel transferred all asbestos cases then filed, but not yet on trial in federal courts to a single district, the United States District Court for the Eastern District of Pennsylvania; pursuant to the transfer order, the collected cases were consolidated for pretrial proceedings before Judge Weiner. The order aggregated pending cases only; no authority resides in the MDL Panel to license for consolidated proceedings claims not yet filed.

B.

After the consolidation, attorneys for plaintiffs and defendants formed separate steering committees and began settlement negotiations. Ronald L. Motley and Gene Locks—later appointed, along with Motley's law partner Joseph F. Rice, to represent the plaintiff class in this action—co-chaired the Plaintiffs' Steering Committee. Counsel for the Center for Claims Resolution (CCR), the consortium of 20 former asbestos manufacturers now before us as petitioners, participated in the Defendants' Steering Committee. Although the MDL order collected, transferred, and consolidated only cases already commenced in federal courts, settlement negotiations included efforts to find a "means of resolving future cases" ("primary purpose of the settlement talks in the consolidated MDL litigation was to craft a national settlement that would provide an alternative resolution mechanism for asbestos claims," including claims that might be filed in the future).

In November 1991, the Defendants' Steering Committee made an offer designed to settle all pending and future asbestos cases by providing a fund for distribution by plaintiffs' counsel among asbestos-exposed individuals. The Plaintiffs' Steering Committee rejected this offer, and negotiations fell apart. CCR, however, continued to pursue "a workable administrative system for the handling of future claims."

To that end, CCR counsel approached the lawyers who had headed the Plaintiffs' Steering Committee in the unsuccessful negotiations, and a new round of negotiations began; that round yielded the mass settlement agreement now in controversy. At the time, the former heads of the Plaintiffs' Steering Committee represented thousands of plaintiffs with then-pending asbestos-related claims—claimants the parties to this suit call "inventory" plaintiffs. CCR indicated in these discussions that it would resist settlement of inventory cases absent "some kind of protection for the future" (CCR communicated to the inventory plaintiffs' attorneys that once the CCR defendants saw a rational way to deal with claims expected to be filed in the future, those defendants would be prepared to address the settlement of pending cases).

Settlement talks thus concentrated on devising an administrative scheme for disposition of asbestos claims not yet in litigation. In these negotiations, counsel for masses of inventory plaintiffs endeavored to represent the interests of the anticipated future claimants, although those lawyers then had no attorney-client relationship with such claimants.

Once negotiations seemed likely to produce an agreement purporting to bind potential plaintiffs, CCR agreed to settle, through separate agreements, the claims of plaintiffs who had already filed asbestos-related lawsuits. In one such agreement, CCR defendants promised to pay more than $200 million to gain release of the claims of numerous inventory plaintiffs. After settling the inventory claims, CCR, together with the plaintiffs' lawyers CCR had approached, launched this case, exclusively involving persons outside the MDL Panel's province—plaintiffs without already pending lawsuits.

C.

The class action thus instituted was not intended to be litigated. Rather, within the space of a single day, January 15, 1993, the settling parties—CCR defendants and the representatives of the plaintiff class described below—presented to the District Court a complaint, an answer, a proposed settlement agreement, and a joint motion for conditional class certification.

The complaint identified nine lead plaintiffs, designating them and members of their families as representatives of a class comprising all persons who had not filed an asbestos-related lawsuit against a CCR defendant as of the date the class action commenced, but who (1) had been exposed—occupationally or through the occupational exposure of a spouse or household member—to asbestos or products containing asbestos attributable to a CCR defendant, or (2) whose spouse or family member had been so exposed. Untold numbers of individuals may fall within this description. All named plaintiffs alleged that they or a member of their family had been exposed to asbestos-containing products of CCR defendants. More than half of the named plaintiffs alleged that they or their family members had already suffered various physical injuries as a result of the exposure. The others alleged that they had not yet manifested any asbestos-related condition. The complaint delineated no subclasses; all named plaintiffs were designated as representatives of the class as a whole.

The complaint invoked the District Court's diversity jurisdiction and asserted various state-law claims for relief, including (1) negligent failure to warn, (2) strict liability, (3) breach of express and implied warranty, (4) negligent infliction of emotional distress, (5) enhanced risk of disease, (6) medical monitoring, and (7) civil conspiracy. Each plaintiff requested unspecified damages in excess of $100,000. CCR defendants' answer denied the principal allegations of the complaint and asserted 11 affirmative defenses.

A stipulation of settlement accompanied the pleadings; it proposed to settle, and to preclude nearly all class members from litigating against CCR companies, all claims not filed before January 15, 1993, involving compensation for present and future asbestos-related personal injury or death. An exhaustive document exceeding 100 pages, the stipulation presents in detail an administrative mechanism and a schedule of payments to compensate class members who meet defined asbestos-exposure and medical requirements. The stipulation describes four categories of compensable disease: mesothelioma; lung cancer; certain "other cancers" (colon-rectal, laryngeal, esophageal, and stomach cancer); and "non-malignant conditions" (asbestosis and bilateral pleural thickening). Persons with "exceptional" medical claims—claims that do not fall within the four described diagnostic categories—may in some instances qualify for compensation, but the settlement caps the number of "exceptional" claims CCR must cover.

For each qualifying disease category, the stipulation specifies the range of damages CCR will pay to qualifying claimants. Payments under the settlement are not adjustable for inflation. Mesothelioma claimants— the most highly compensated category—are scheduled to receive between $20,000 and $200,000. The stipulation provides that CCR is to propose the level of compensation within the prescribed ranges; it also establishes procedures to resolve disputes over medical diagnoses and levels of compensation.

Compensation above the fixed ranges may be obtained for "extraordinary" claims. But the settlement places both numerical caps and dollar limits on such claims. The settlement also imposes "case flow maximums," which cap the number of claims payable for each disease in a given year.

Class members are to receive no compensation for certain kinds of claims, even if otherwise applicable state law recognizes such claims. Claims that garner no compensation under the settlement include claims by family members of asbestos-exposed individuals for loss of consortium, and claims by so-called "exposure-only" plaintiffs for increased risk of cancer, fear of future asbestos-related injury, and medical monitoring. "Pleural" claims, which might be asserted by persons with asbestos-related plaques on their lungs but no accompanying physical impairment, are also excluded. Although not entitled to present compensation, exposure-only claimants and pleural claimants may qualify for benefits when and if they develop a compensable disease and meet the relevant exposure and medical criteria. Defendants forgo defenses to liability, including statute of limitations pleas.

Class members, in the main, are bound by the settlement in perpetuity, while CCR defendants may choose to withdraw from the settlement after ten years. A small number of class members—only a few per year—may reject the settlement and pursue their claims in court. Those permitted to exercise this option, however, may not assert any punitive damages claim or any claim for increased risk of cancer. Aspects of the administration of the settlement are to be monitored by the AFL-CIO and class counsel. Class counsel are to receive attorneys' fees in an amount to be approved by the District Court.

## D.

On January 29, 1993, as requested by the settling parties, the District Court conditionally certified, under Federal Rule of Civil Procedure 23(b)(3), an encompassing opt-out class. Objectors raised numerous challenges to the settlement. They urged that the settlement unfairly disadvantaged those without currently compensable conditions in that it failed to adjust for inflation or to account for changes, over time, in medical understanding. They maintained that compensation levels were intolerably low in comparison to awards available in tort litigation or payments received by the inventory plaintiffs. And they objected to the absence of any compensation for certain claims, for example, medical monitoring, compensable under the tort law of several States. Rejecting these and all other objections, Judge Reed concluded that the settlement terms were fair and had been negotiated without collusion. He also found that adequate notice had been given to class members and that final class certification under Rule 23(b)(3) was appropriate.

Strenuous objections had been asserted regarding the adequacy of representation, a Rule 23(a)(4) requirement. Objectors maintained that class counsel and class representatives had disqualifying conflicts of interests. In particular, objectors urged, claimants whose injuries had become manifest and claimants without manifest injuries should not have common counsel and should not be aggregated in a single class. Furthermore, objectors argued, lawyers representing inventory plaintiffs should not represent the newly-formed class.

Satisfied that class counsel had ably negotiated the settlement in the best interests of all concerned, and that the named parties served as adequate representatives, the District Court rejected these objections. The objectors appealed. The United States Court of Appeals for the Third Circuit vacated the certification, holding that the requirements of Rule 23 had not been satisfied.

E.

The Court of Appeals, in a long, heavily detailed opinion by Judge Becker, first noted several challenges by objectors to justiciability, subject-matter jurisdiction, and adequacy of notice. These challenges, the court said, raised "serious concerns." However, the court observed, "the jurisdictional issues in this case would not exist but for the class action certification." Turning to the class-certification issues and finding them dispositive, the Third Circuit declined to decide other questions.

On class-action prerequisites, the Court of Appeals referred to an earlier Third Circuit decision, *In re General Motors Corp. Pick-Up Truck Fuel Tank Products Liability Litigation*, which held that although a class action may be certified for settlement purposes only, Rule 23(a)'s requirements must be satisfied as if the case were going to be litigated. The same rule should apply, the Third Circuit said, to class certification under Rule 23(b)(3). While stating that the requirements of Rule 23(a) and (b)(3) must be met "without taking into account the settlement," the Court of Appeals in fact closely considered the terms of the settlement as it examined aspects of the case under Rule 23 criteria.

The Third Circuit recognized that Rule 23(a)(2)'s "commonality" requirement is subsumed under, or superseded by, the more stringent Rule 23(b)(3) requirement that questions common to the class "predominate over" other questions. The court therefore trained its attention on the "predominance" inquiry. The harmfulness of asbestos exposure was indeed a prime factor common to the class, the Third Circuit observed. But uncommon questions abounded.

In contrast to mass torts involving a single accident, class members in this case were exposed to different asbestos-containing products, in different ways, over different periods, and for different amounts of time; some suffered no physical injury, others suffered disabling or deadly diseases. "These factual differences," the Third Circuit explained, "translated into significant legal differences." State law governed and varied widely on such critical issues as "viability of exposure-only claims and availability of causes of action for medical monitoring, increased risk of cancer, and fear of future injury." "The number of uncommon issues in this humongous class action," the Third Circuit concluded, barred a determination, under existing tort law, that common questions predominated.

The Court of Appeals next found that "serious intra-class conflicts precluded the class from meeting the adequacy of representation requirement" of Rule 23(a)(4). Adverting to, but not resolving charges of attorney conflict of interests, the Third Circuit addressed the question whether the named plaintiffs could adequately advance the interests of all class members. The Court of Appeals acknowledged that the District Court was certainly correct to this extent: " 'The members of the class are united in seeking the maximum possible recovery for their asbestos-related claims.' " "But the settlement does more than simply provide a general recovery fund," the Court of Appeals immediately added; "rather, it makes important judgments on how recovery is to be allocated among different kinds of plaintiffs, decisions that necessarily favor some claimants over others."

In the Third Circuit's view, the "most salient" divergence of interests separated plaintiffs already afflicted with an asbestos-related disease from plaintiffs without manifest injury (exposure-only plaintiffs). The latter would rationally want protection against inflation for distant recoveries. They would also seek sturdy back-end opt-out rights and "causation provisions that can keep pace with changing science and medicine, rather than freezing in place the science of 1993." Already injured parties, in contrast, would care little about such provisions and would rationally trade them for higher current payouts. These and other adverse interests, the Court of Appeals carefully explained, strongly suggested that an undivided set of representatives could not adequately protect the discrete interests of both currently afflicted and exposure-only claimants.

The Third Circuit next rejected the District Court's determination that the named plaintiffs were "typical" of the class, noting that this Rule 23(a)(3) inquiry overlaps the adequacy of representation question: "both look to the potential for conflicts in the class." Evident conflict problems, the court said, led it to hold that "no set of representatives can be 'typical' of this class."

The Court of Appeals similarly rejected the District Court's assessment of the superiority of the class action. The Third Circuit initially noted that a class action so large and complex "could not be tried." The court elaborated most particularly, however, on the unfairness of binding exposure-only plaintiffs who might be unaware of the class action or lack sufficient information about their exposure to make a reasoned decision whether to stay in or opt out. "A series of statewide or more narrowly defined adjudications, either through consolidation under Rule 42(a) or as class actions under Rule 23, would seem preferable," the Court of Appeals said.

The Third Circuit ultimately ordered decertification of the class and vacation of the District Court's anti-suit injunction.

We granted certiorari, and now affirm.

## II.

Objectors assert in this Court, as they did in the District Court and Court of Appeals, an array of jurisdictional barriers. As earlier recounted, the Third Circuit declined to reach these issues because they "would not exist but for the class action certification." We agree that "the class certification issues are dispositive," because their resolution here is logically antecedent to the existence of any Article III issues, it is appropriate to reach them first. We therefore follow the path taken by the Court of Appeals, mindful that Rule 23's requirements must be interpreted in keeping with Article III constraints, and with the Rules Enabling Act, which instructs that rules of procedure "shall not abridge, enlarge or modify any substantive right," 28 U.S.C. § 2072(b).

### III.

Among current applications of Rule 23(b)(3), the "settlement only" class has become a stock device. Although all Federal Circuits recognize the utility of Rule 23(b)(3) settlement classes, courts have divided on the extent to which a proffered settlement affects court surveillance under Rule 23's certification criteria.

In *GM Trucks*, and in the instant case, the Third Circuit held that a class cannot be certified for settlement when certification for trial would be unwarranted. Other courts have held that settlement obviates or reduces the need to measure a proposed class against the enumerated Rule 23 requirements.

A proposed amendment to Rule 23 would expressly authorize settlement class certification, in conjunction with a motion by the settling parties for Rule 23(b)(3) certification, "even though the requirements of subdivision (b)(3) might not be met for purposes of trial." In response to the publication of this proposal, voluminous public comments—many of them opposed to, or skeptical of, the amendment—were received by the Judicial Conference Standing Committee on Rules of Practice and Procedure. The Committee has not yet acted on the matter. We consider the certification at issue under the rule as it is currently framed.

### IV.

We granted review to decide the role settlement may play, under existing Rule 23, in determining the propriety of class certification. The Third Circuit's opinion stated that each of the requirements of Rule 23(a) and (b)(3) "must be satisfied without taking into account the settlement." That statement, petitioners urge, is incorrect.

We agree with petitioners to this limited extent: settlement is relevant to a class certification. The Third Circuit's opinion bears modification in that respect. But, as we earlier observed, the Court of Appeals in fact did not ignore the settlement; instead, that court homed in on settlement terms in explaining why it found the absentees' interests inadequately represented. The Third Circuit's close inspection of the settlement in that regard was altogether proper.

Confronted with a request for settlement-only class certification, a district court need not inquire whether the case, if tried, would present intractable management problems, *see* Fed. Rule Civ. Proc. 23(b)(3)(D), for the proposal is that there be no trial. But other specifications of the rule—those designed to protect absentees by blocking unwarranted or overbroad class definitions—demand undiluted, even heightened, attention in the settlement context. Such attention is of vital importance, for a court asked to certify a settlement class will lack the opportunity, present when a case is litigated, to adjust the class, informed by the proceedings as they unfold.

And, of overriding importance, courts must be mindful that the rule as now composed sets the requirements they are bound to enforce. Federal Rules take effect after an extensive deliberative process involving many reviewers: a Rules Advisory Committee, public commenters, the Judicial Conference, this Court, the Congress. The text of a rule thus proposed and reviewed limits judicial inventiveness. Courts are not free to amend a rule outside the process Congress ordered, a process properly tuned to the instruction that rules of procedure "shall not abridge any substantive right."

Rule 23(e), on settlement of class actions, reads in its entirety: "A class action shall not be dismissed or compromised without the approval of the court, and notice of the proposed dismissal or compromise shall be given to all members of the class in such manner as the court directs." This prescription was designed to function as an additional requirement, not a superseding direction, for the "class action" to which Rule 23(e) refers is one qualified for certification under Rule 23(a) and (b). Subdivisions (a) and (b) focus court attention on whether a proposed class has sufficient unity so that absent members can fairly be bound by decisions of class representatives. That dominant concern persists when settlement, rather than trial, is proposed.

The safeguards provided by the Rule 23(a) and (b) class-qualifying criteria, we emphasize, are not impractical impediments—checks shorn of utility—in the settlement class context. First, the standards set for the protection of absent class members serve to inhibit appraisals of the chancellor's foot kind—class certifications dependent upon the court's gestalt judgment or overarching impression of the settlement's fairness.

Second, if a fairness inquiry under Rule 23(e) controlled certification, eclipsing Rule 23(a) and (b), and permitting class designation despite the impossibility of litigation, both class counsel and court would be disarmed. Class counsel confined to settlement negotiations could not use the threat of litigation to press for a better offer, and the court would face a bargain proffered for its approval without benefit of adversarial investigation.

Federal courts, in any case, lack authority to substitute for Rule 23's certification criteria a standard never adopted—that if a settlement is "fair," then certification is proper. Applying to this case criteria the rulemakers set, we conclude that the Third Circuit's appraisal is essentially correct. Although that court should have acknowledged that settlement is a factor in the calculus, a remand is not warranted on that account. The Court of Appeals' opinion amply demonstrates why—with or without a settlement on the table—the sprawling class the District Court certified does not satisfy Rule 23's requirements.

A.

We address first the requirement of Rule 23(b)(3) that "common questions of law or fact predominate over any questions affecting only individual members." The District Court concluded that predominance was satisfied based on two factors: class members' shared experience of asbestos exposure and their common "interest in receiving prompt and fair compensation for their claims, while minimizing the risks and transaction costs inherent in the asbestos litigation process as it occurs presently in the tort system." The settling parties also contend that the settlement's fairness is a common question, predominating over disparate legal issues that might be pivotal in litigation but become irrelevant under the settlement.

The predominance requirement stated in Rule 23(b)(3), we hold, is not met by the factors on which the District Court relied. The benefits asbestos-exposed persons might gain from the establishment of a grand-scale compensation scheme is a matter fit for legislative consideration, but it is not pertinent to the predominance inquiry. That inquiry trains on the legal or factual questions that qualify each class member's case as a genuine controversy, questions that preexist any settlement.

The Rule 23(b)(3) predominance inquiry tests whether proposed classes are sufficiently cohesive to warrant adjudication by representation. The inquiry appropriate under Rule 23(e), on the other hand, protects unnamed class members "from unjust or unfair settlements affecting their rights when the representatives become fainthearted before the action is adjudicated or are able to secure satisfaction of their individual claims by a compromise." But it is not the mission of Rule 23(e) to assure the class cohesion that legitimizes representative action in the first place. If a common interest in a fair compromise could satisfy the predominance requirement of Rule 23(b)(3), that vital prescription would be stripped of any meaning in the settlement context.

The District Court also relied upon this commonality: "The members of the class have all been exposed to asbestos products supplied by the defendants." Even if Rule 23(a)'s commonality requirement may be satisfied by that shared experience, the predominance criterion is far more demanding. Given the greater number of questions peculiar to the several categories of class members, and to individuals within each category, and the significance of those uncommon questions, any overarching dispute about the health consequences of asbestos exposure cannot satisfy the Rule 23(b)(3) predominance standard.

The Third Circuit highlighted the disparate questions undermining class cohesion in this case: "Class members were exposed to different asbestos-containing products, for different amounts of time, in different ways, and over different periods. Some class members suffer no physical injury or have only asymptomatic pleural changes, while others suffer from lung cancer, disabling asbestosis, or from mesothelioma. Each has a different history of cigarette smoking, a factor that complicates the causation inquiry. "The exposure-only plaintiffs especially share little in common, either with each other or with the presently injured class members. It is unclear whether they will contract asbestos-related disease and, if so, what disease each will suffer. They will also incur different medical expenses because their monitoring and treatment will depend on singular circumstances and individual medical histories." Differences in state law, the Court of Appeals observed, compound these disparities.

No settlement class called to our attention is as sprawling as this one. Predominance is a test readily met in certain cases alleging consumer or securities fraud or violations of the antitrust laws. Even mass tort cases arising from a common cause or disaster may, depending upon the circumstances, satisfy the predominance requirement. The Advisory Committee for the 1966 revision of Rule 23, it is true, noted that "mass accident" cases are likely to present "significant questions, not only of damages but of liability and defenses of liability, affecting the individuals in different ways." And the Committee advised that such cases are "ordinarily not appropriate" for class treatment. But the text of the rule does not categorically exclude mass tort cases from class certification, and district courts, since the late 1970s, have been certifying such cases in increasing number. The Committee's warning, however, continues to call for caution when individual stakes are high and disparities among class members great. As the Third Circuit's opinion makes plain, the certification in this case does not follow the counsel of caution. That certification cannot be upheld, for it rests on a conception of Rule 23(b)(3)'s predominance requirement irreconcilable with the rule's design.

## B.

Nor can the class approved by the District Court satisfy Rule 23(a)(4)'s requirement that the named parties "will fairly and adequately protect the interests of the class." The adequacy inquiry under Rule 23(a)(4) serves to uncover conflicts of interest between named parties and the class they seek to represent. *See General Telephone Co. of Southwest v. Falcon.* "A class representative must be part of the class and 'possess the same interest and suffer the same injury' as the class members."

As the Third Circuit pointed out, named parties with diverse medical conditions sought to act on behalf of a single giant class rather than on behalf of discrete subclasses. In significant respects, the interests of those within the single class are not aligned. Most saliently, for the currently injured, the critical goal is generous immediate payments. That goal tugs against the interest of exposure-only plaintiffs in ensuring an ample, inflation-protected fund for the future.

The disparity between the currently injured and exposure-only categories of plaintiffs, and the diversity within each category are not made insignificant by the District Court's finding that petitioners' assets suffice to pay claims under the settlement. Although this is not a "limited fund" case certified under Rule 23(b)(1)(B), the terms of the settlement reflect essential allocation decisions designed to confine compensation and to limit defendants' liability. For example, as earlier described, the settlement includes no adjustment for inflation; only a few claimants per year can opt out at the back end; and loss-of-consortium claims are extinguished with no compensation.

The settling parties, in sum, achieved a global compromise with no structural assurance of fair and adequate representation for the diverse groups and individuals affected. Although the named parties alleged a range of complaints, each served generally as representative for the whole, not for a separate constituency. In another asbestos class action, the Second Circuit spoke precisely to this point: "Where differences among members of a class are such that subclasses must be established, we know of no authority that permits a court to approve a settlement without creating subclasses on the basis of consents by members of a unitary class, some of whom happen to be members of the distinct subgroups. The class representatives may well have thought that the Settlement serves the aggregate interests of the entire class. But the adversity among subgroups requires that the members of each subgroup cannot be bound to a settlement except by consents given by those who understand that their role is to represent solely the members of their respective subgroups." The Third Circuit found no assurance here—either in the terms of the settlement or in the structure of the negotiations—that the named plaintiffs operated under a proper understanding of their representational responsibilities. That assessment, we conclude, is on the mark.

C.

Impediments to the provision of adequate notice, the Third Circuit emphasized, rendered highly problematic any endeavor to tie to a settlement class persons with no perceptible asbestos-related disease at the time of the settlement. Many persons in the exposure-only category, the Court of Appeals stressed, may not even know of their exposure, or realize the extent of the harm they may incur. Even if they fully appreciate the significance of class notice, those without current afflictions may not have the information or foresight needed to decide, intelligently, whether to stay in or opt out.

Family members of asbestos-exposed individuals may themselves fall prey to disease or may ultimately have ripe claims for loss of consortium.

Yet large numbers of people in this category—future spouses and children of asbestos victims—could not be alerted to their class membership. And current spouses and children of the occupationally exposed may know nothing of that exposure.

Because we have concluded that the class in this case cannot satisfy the requirements of common issue predominance and adequacy of representation, we need not rule, definitively, on the notice given here. In accord with the Third Circuit, however, we recognize the gravity of the question whether class action notice sufficient under the Constitution and Rule 23 could ever be given to legions so unselfconscious and amorphous.

## V.

The argument is sensibly made that a nationwide administrative claims processing regime would provide the most secure, fair, and efficient means of compensating victims of asbestos exposure. Congress, however, has not adopted such a solution. And Rule 23, which must be interpreted with fidelity to the Rules Enabling Act and applied with the interests of absent class members in close view, cannot carry the large load CCR, class counsel, and the District Court heaped upon it. As this case exemplifies, the rulemakers' prescriptions for class actions may be endangered by "those who embrace Rule 23 too enthusiastically just as they are by those who approach the rule with distaste."

For the reasons stated, the judgment of the Court of Appeals for the Third Circuit is affirmed.

JUSTICE BREYER, with whom JUSTICE STEVENS joins, concurring in part and dissenting in part.

Although I agree with the Court's basic holding that "settlement is relevant to a class certification," I find several problems in its approach that lead me to a different conclusion. First, I believe that the need for settlement in this mass tort case, with hundreds of thousands of lawsuits, is greater than the Court's opinion suggests. Second, I would give more weight than would the majority to settlement-related issues for purposes of determining whether common issues predominate. Third, I am uncertain about the Court's determination of adequacy of representation, and do not believe it appropriate for this Court to second-guess the District Court on the matter without first having the Court of Appeals consider it. Fourth, I am uncertain about the tenor of an opinion that seems to suggest the settlement is unfair. And fifth, in the absence of further review by the Court of Appeals, I cannot accept the majority's suggestions that "notice" is inadequate.

These difficulties flow from the majority's review of what are highly fact-based, complex, and difficult matters, matters that are inappropriate for initial review before this Court. The law gives broad leeway to district courts in making class certification decisions, and their judgments are to be reviewed by the Court of Appeals only for abuse of discretion. Indeed, the District Court's certification decision rests upon more than 300 findings of fact reached after five weeks of comprehensive hearings. Accordingly, I do not believe that we should in effect set aside the findings of the District Court. That court is far more familiar with the issues and litigants than is a court of appeals or are we, and therefore has "broad power and discretion with respect to matters involving the certification" of class actions.

## II.

The issues in this case are complicated and difficult. The District Court might have been correct. Or not. Subclasses might be appropriate. Or not. I cannot tell. And I do not believe that this Court should be in the business of trying to make these fact-based determinations. That is a job suited to the district courts in the first instance, and the courts of appeal on review. But there is no reason in this case to believe that the Court of Appeals conducted its prior review with an understanding that the settlement could have constituted a reasonably strong factor in favor of class certification. For this reason, I would provide the courts below with an opportunity to analyze the factual questions involved in certification by vacating the judgment, and remanding the case for further proceedings.

## ORTIZ V. FIBREBOARD CORP.
United States Supreme Court, 1999.
527 U.S. 815, 119 S.Ct. 2295, 144 L.Ed.2d 715.

This case turns on the conditions for certifying a mandatory settlement class on a limited fund theory under Federal Rule of Civil Procedure 23(b)(1)(B). We hold that applicants for contested certification on this rationale must show that the fund is limited by more than the agreement of the parties, and has been allocated to claimants belonging within the class by a process addressing any conflicting interests of class members.

## I.

Like *Amchem Products, Inc. v. Windsor*, this case is a class action prompted by the elephantine mass of asbestos cases, and our discussion in *Amchem* will suffice to show how this litigation defies customary judicial administration and calls for national legislation. In 1967, one of the first actions for personal asbestos injury was filed in the United States District Court for the Eastern District of Texas against a group of asbestos manufacturers. In the 1970s and 1980s, plaintiffs' lawyers throughout the country, particularly in East Texas, honed the litigation of asbestos claims to the point of almost mechanical regularity, improving the forensic identification of diseases caused by asbestos, refining theories of liability, and often settling large inventories of cases.

Respondent Fibreboard Corporation was a defendant in the 1967 action. Although it was primarily a timber company, from the 1920's through 1971 the company manufactured a variety of products containing asbestos, mainly for high-temperature industrial applications. As the tide of asbestos litigation rose, Fibreboard found itself litigating on two fronts. On one, plaintiffs were filing a stream of personal injury claims against it, swelling throughout the 1980s and 1990s to thousands of new claims for compensatory damages each year. On the second front, Fibreboard was battling for funds to pay its tort claimants. From May, 1957, through March, 1959, respondent Continental Casualty Company had provided Fibreboard with a comprehensive general liability policy with limits of $1 million per occurrence, $500,000 per claim, and no aggregate limit. Fibreboard also claimed that respondent Pacific Indemnity Company had insured it from 1956 to 1957 under a similar policy. Beginning in 1979, Fibreboard was locked in coverage litigation with Continental and Pacific in a California state trial court, which in 1990 held Continental and Pacific responsible for indemnification as to any claim by a claimant exposed to Fibreboard asbestos products prior to their policies' respective expiration dates. The decree also required the insurers to pay the full cost of defense for each claim covered. The insurance companies appealed.

With asbestos case filings continuing unabated, and its secure insurance assets almost depleted, Fibreboard in 1988 began a practice of "structured settlement," paying plaintiffs 40 percent of the settlement figure up front with the balance contingent upon a successful resolution of the coverage dispute. By 1991, however, the pace of filings forced Fibreboard to start settling cases entirely with the assignments of its rights against Continental, with no initial payment. To reflect the risk that Continental might prevail in the coverage dispute, these assignment agreements generally carried a figure about twice the nominal amount of earlier settlements. Continental challenged Fibreboard's right to make unilateral assignments, but in 1992 a California state court ruled for Fibreboard in that dispute.

Meanwhile, in the aftermath of a 1990 Federal Judicial Center conference on the asbestos litigation crisis, Fibreboard approached a group of leading asbestos plaintiffs' lawyers, offering to discuss a "global settlement" of its asbestos personal-injury liability. Early negotiations bore relatively little fruit, save for the December 1992 settlement by assignment of a significant inventory of pending claims. This settlement brought Fibreboard's deferred settlement obligations to more than $1.2 billion, all contingent upon victory over Continental on the scope of coverage and the validity of the settlement assignments.

In February 1993, after Continental had lost on both issues at the trial level, and thus faced the possibility of practically unbounded liability, it too joined the global settlement negotiations. Because Continental conditioned its part in any settlement on a guarantee of "total peace," ensuring no unknown future liabilities, talks focused on the feasibility of a mandatory class action, one binding all potential plaintiffs and giving none of them any choice to opt out of the certified class. Negotiations continued throughout the spring and summer of 1993, but the difficulty of settling both actually pending and potential future claims simultaneously led to an agreement in early August to segregate and settle an inventory of some 45,000 pending claims, being substantially all those filed by one of the plaintiffs' firms negotiating the global settlement. The settlement amounts per claim were higher than average, with one-half due on closing and the remainder contingent upon either a global settlement or Fibreboard's success in the coverage litigation. This agreement provided the model for settling inventory claims of other firms.

With the insurance companies' appeal of the consolidated coverage case set to be heard on August 27, the negotiating parties faced a motivating deadline, and about midnight before the argument, in a coffee shop in Tyler, Texas, the negotiators finally agreed upon $1.535 billion as the key term of a "Global Settlement Agreement." $1.525 billion of this sum would come from Continental and Pacific, in the proportion established by the California trial court in the coverage case, while Fibreboard would contribute $10 million, all but $500,000 of it from other insurance proceeds. The negotiators also agreed to identify unsettled present claims against Fibreboard and set aside an as-then unspecified fund to resolve them, anticipating that the bulk of any excess left in that fund would be transferred to class claimants. The next day, as a hedge against the possibility that the Global Settlement Agreement might fail, plaintiffs' counsel insisted as a condition of that agreement that Fibreboard and its two insurers settle the coverage dispute by what came to be known as the "Trilateral Settlement Agreement." The two insurers agreed to provide Fibreboard with funds eventually set at $2 billion to defend against asbestos claimants and pay the winners, should the Global Settlement Agreement fail to win approval.

On September 9, 1993, as agreed, a group of named plaintiffs filed an action in the United States District Court for the Eastern District of Texas, seeking certification for settlement purposes of a mandatory class comprising three groups: all persons with personal injury claims against Fibreboard for asbestos exposure who had not yet brought suit or settled their claims before the previous August 27; those who had dismissed such a claim but retained the right to bring a future action against Fibreboard; and "past, present and future spouses, parents, children, and other relatives" of class members exposed to Fibreboard asbestos. The class did not include claimants with actions presently pending against Fibreboard or claimants "who filed and, for cash payment or some other negotiated value, dismissed claims against Fibreboard, and whose only retained right is to sue Fibreboard upon development of an asbestos-related malignancy." The complaint pleaded personal injury claims against Fibreboard, and, as justification for class certification, relied on the shared necessity of ensuring insurance funds sufficient for compensation. After Continental and Pacific had obtained leave to intervene as party-defendants, the District Court provisionally granted class certification, enjoined commencement of further separate litigation against Fibreboard by class members, and appointed a guardian ad litem to review the fairness of the settlement to the class members.

As finally negotiated, the Global Settlement Agreement provided that in exchange for full releases from class members, Fibreboard, Continental, and Pacific would establish a trust to process and pay class members' asbestos personal injury and death claims. Claimants seeking compensation would be required to try to settle with the trust. If initial settlement attempts failed, claimants would have to proceed to mediation, arbitration, and a mandatory settlement conference. Only after exhausting that process could claimants go to court against the trust, subject to a limit of $500,000 per claim, with punitive damages and prejudgment interest barred. Claims resolved without litigation would be discharged over three years, while judgments would be paid out over a 5-to-10-year period. The Global Settlement Agreement also contained spendthrift provisions to conserve the trust, and provided for paying more serious claims first in the event of a shortfall in any given year.

After an extensive campaign to give notice of the pending settlement to potential class members, the District Court allowed groups of objectors, including petitioners here, to intervene. After an 8-day fairness hearing, the District Court certified the class and approved the settlement as "fair, adequate, and reasonable," under Rule 23(e). Satisfied that the requirements of Rule 23(a) were met, the District Court certified the class under Rule 23(b)(1)(B), citing the risk that Fibreboard might lose or fare poorly on appeal of the coverage case or lose the assignment-settlement dispute, leaving it without funds to pay all claims. The "allowance of individual adjudications by class members," the District Court concluded, "would have destroyed the opportunity to compromise the insurance coverage dispute by creating the settlement fund, and would have exposed the class members to the very risks that the settlement addresses." In response to intervenors' objections that the absence of a "limited fund" precluded certification under Rule 23(b)(1)(B), the District Court ruled that although the subdivision is not so restricted, if it were, this case would qualify. It found both the "disputed insurance asset liquidated by the $1.535 billion Global Settlement," and, alternatively, "the sum of the value of Fibreboard plus the value of its insurance coverage," as measured by the insurance funds' settlement value, to be relevant "limited funds."

On appeal, the Fifth Circuit affirmed both as to class certification and adequacy of settlement. In re Asbestos Litigation, supra. Agreeing with the District Court's application of Rule 23(a), the Court of Appeals found that there was commonality in class members' shared interest in securing and equitably distributing maximum possible settlement funds, and that the representative plaintiffs were sufficiently typical both in sharing that interest and in basing their claims on the same legal and remedial theories that absent class members might raise. The Fifth Circuit also thought that there were no conflicts of interest sufficiently serious to undermine the adequacy of class counsel's representation. As to Rule 23(b)(1)(B), the Court approved the class certification on a "limited fund" rationale based on the threat to "the ability of other members of the class to receive full payment for their injuries from Fibreboard's limited assets." The Court of Appeals cited expert testimony that Fibreboard faced enormous potential liabilities and defense costs that would likely equal or exceed the amount of damages paid out, and concluded that even combining Fibreboard's value of some $235 million with the $2 billion provided in the Trilateral Settlement Agreement, the company would be unable to pay all valid claims against it within five to nine years. Judge Smith dissented, arguing among other things that the majority had skimped on serious due process concerns, had glossed over problems of commonality, typicality, and adequacy of representation, and had ignored a number of justiciability issues.

Shortly thereafter, this Court decided *Amchem* and proceeded to vacate the Fifth Circuit's judgment and remand for further consideration in light of that decision. On remand, the Fifth Circuit again affirmed, in a brief per curiam opinion, distinguishing *Amchem* on the grounds that the instant action proceeded under Rule 23(b)(1)(B) rather than (b)(3), and did not allocate awards according to the nature of the claimant's injury. Again citing the findings on certification under Rule 23(b)(1)(B), the Fifth Circuit affirmed as "incontestable" the District Court's conclusion that the terms of the subdivision had been met. The Court of Appeals acknowledged *Amchem's* admonition that settlement class actions may not proceed unless the requirements of Rule 23(a) are met, but noted that the District Court had made extensive findings supporting its Rule 23(a) determinations. Judge Smith again dissented, reiterating his previous concerns, and argued specifically that the District Court erred in certifying the class under Rule 23(b)(1)(B) on a "limited fund" theory because the only limited fund in the case was a creature of the settlement itself.

We granted certiorari and now reverse.

## II.

The nub of this case is the certification of the class under Rule 23(b)(1)(B) on a limited fund rationale, but before we reach that issue, there are two threshold matters. First, petitioners call the class claims non-justiciable under Article III, saying that this is a feigned action initiated by Fibreboard to control its future asbestos tort liability, with the "vast majority" of the "exposure-only" class members being without injury in fact and hence without standing to sue. Ordinarily, of course, this or any other

Article III court must be sure of its own jurisdiction before getting to the merits. But the class certification issues are, as they were in Amchem, "logically antecedent" to Article III concerns, and themselves pertain to statutory standing, which may properly be treated before Article III standing. Thus the issue about Rule 23 certification should be treated first, "mindful that the Rule's requirements must be interpreted in keeping with Article III constraints." *Amchem.*

Petitioners also argue that the Fifth Circuit on remand disregarded *Amchem* in passing on the Rule 23(a) issues of commonality, typicality, and adequacy of representation. We agree that in reinstating its affirmance of the District Court's certification decision, the Fifth Circuit fell short in its attention to *Amchem's* explanation of the governing legal standards. Two aspects in particular of the District Court's certification should have received more detailed treatment by the Court of Appeals. First, the District Court's enquiry into both commonality and typicality focused almost entirely on the terms of the settlement. Second, and more significantly, the District Court took no steps at the outset to ensure that the potentially conflicting interests of easily identifiable categories of claimants be protected by provisional certification of subclasses under Rule 23(c)(4), relying instead on its post-hoc findings at the fairness hearing that these subclasses in fact had been adequately represented. As will be seen, however, these points will reappear when we review the certification on the Court of Appeals's "limited fund" theory under Rule 23(b)(1)(B). We accordingly turn directly to that.

III.

A.

Although representative suits have been recognized in various forms since the earliest days of English law, class actions as we recognize them today developed as an exception to the formal rigidity of the necessary parties rule in equity. From these roots, modern class action practice emerged in the 1966 revision of Rule 23. In drafting Rule 23(b), the Advisory Committee sought to catalogue in "functional" terms "those recurrent life patterns which call for mass litigation through representative parties."

Rule 23(b)(1)(B) speaks from "a vantage point within the class, from which the Advisory Committee spied out situations where lawsuits conducted with individual members of the class would have the practical if not technical effect of concluding the interests of the other members as well, or of impairing the ability of the others to protect their own interests." Thus, the subdivision provides for certification of a class whose members have no right to withdraw, when "the prosecution of separate actions would create a risk" of "adjudications with respect to individual members of the class which would as a practical matter be dispositive of the interests of the other members not parties to the adjudications or substantially impair or impede their ability to protect their interests." Classic examples of such a risk of impairment may, for example, be found in suits brought to reorganize fraternal-benefit societies; actions by shareholders to declare a dividend or otherwise to "fix their rights,"; and actions charging "a breach of trust by an indenture trustee or other fiduciary similarly affecting the members of a large class" of beneficiaries, requiring an accounting or similar procedure "to restore the subject of the trust." In each of these categories, the shared character of rights claimed or relief awarded entails that any individual adjudication by a class member disposes of, or substantially affects, the interests of absent class members.

Among the traditional varieties of representative suit encompassed by Rule 23(b)(1)(B) were those involving "the presence of property which called for distribution or management." One recurring type of such suits was the limited fund class action, aggregating "claims made by numerous persons against a fund insufficient to satisfy all claims" ("Classic" limited fund class actions "include claimants to trust assets, a bank account, insurance proceeds, company assets in a liquidation sale, proceeds of a ship sale in a maritime accident suit, and others"). As the Advisory Committee recognized, equity required absent parties to be represented, joinder being impractical, where individual claims to be satisfied from the one asset would, as a practical matter, prejudice the rights of absent claimants against a fund inadequate to pay them all.

## B.

The cases forming this pedigree of the limited fund class action as understood by the drafters of Rule 23 have a number of common characteristics, despite the variety of circumstances from which they arose. The points of resemblance are not necessarily the points of contention resolved in the particular cases, but they show what the Advisory Committee must have assumed would be at least a sufficient set of conditions to justify binding absent members of a class under Rule 23(b)(1)(B), from which no one has the right to secede.

The first and most distinctive characteristic is that the totals of the aggregated liquidated claims and the fund available for satisfying them, set definitely at their maximums, demonstrate the inadequacy of the fund to pay all the claims. The concept driving this type of suit was insufficiency, which alone justified the limit on an early feast to avoid a later famine. The equity of the limitation is its necessity.

Second, the whole of the inadequate fund was to be devoted to the overwhelming claims. It went without saying that the defendant or estate or constructive trustee with the inadequate assets had no opportunity to benefit himself or claimants of lower priority by holding back on the amount distributed to the class. The limited fund cases thus ensured that the class as a whole was given the best deal; they did not give a defendant a better deal than seriatim litigation would have produced.

Third, the claimants identified by a common theory of recovery were treated equitably among themselves. The cases assume that the class will comprise everyone who might state a claim on a single or repeated set of facts, invoking a common theory of recovery, to be satisfied from the limited fund as the source of payment. In these cases the hope of recovery was limited, respectively, by estate assets, the residuum of profits, and the amount of the bond. Once the represented classes were so identified, there was no question of omitting anyone whose claim shared the common theory of liability and would contribute to the calculated shortfall of recovery. The plaintiff appeared on behalf of all similarly situated parties; thus, the creditors' bill was brought on behalf of all creditors, the constructive trust was asserted on behalf of all victims of the fraud, and the surety suit was brought on behalf of all entitled to a share of the bond. Once all similar claims were brought directly or by representation before the court, these antecedents of the mandatory class action presented straightforward models of equitable treatment, with the simple equity of a pro rata distribution providing the required fairness.

In sum, mandatory class treatment through representative actions on a limited fund theory was justified with reference to a "fund" with a definitely ascertained limit, all of which would be distributed to satisfy all those with liquidated claims based on a common theory of liability, by an equitable, pro rata distribution.

## C.

The Advisory Committee, and presumably the Congress in approving subdivision (b)(1)(B), must have assumed that an action with these characteristics would satisfy the limited fund rationale cognizable under that subdivision. The question remains how far the same characteristics are necessary for limited fund treatment. While we cannot settle all the details of a subdivision (b)(1)(B) limited fund here (and so cannot decide the ultimate question whether settlements of multitudes of related tort actions are amenable to mandatory class treatment), there are good reasons to treat these characteristics as presumptively necessary, and not merely sufficient, to satisfy the limited fund rationale for a mandatory action. At the least, the burden of justification rests on the proponent of any departure from the traditional norm.

It is true, of course, that the text of Rule 23(b)(1)(B) is on its face open to a more lenient limited fund concept, just as it covers more historical antecedents than the limited fund. But the greater the leniency in departing from the historical limited fund model, the greater the likelihood of abuse in ways that will be apparent when we apply the limited fund criteria to the case before us. The prudent course, therefore, is to presume that when subdivision (b)(1)(B) was devised to cover limited fund actions, the object was to stay close to the historical model. As will be seen, this limiting construction finds support in the Advisory Committee's expressions of understanding, minimizes potential conflict with the Rules Enabling Act, and avoids serious constitutional concerns raised by the mandatory class resolution of individual legal claims, especially where a case seeks to resolve future liability in a settlement-only action.

To begin with, the Advisory Committee looked cautiously at the potential for creativity under Rule 23(b)(1)(B), at least in comparison with Rule 23(b)(3). Although the committee crafted all three subdivisions of the Rule in general, practical terms, without the formalism that had bedeviled the original Rule 23, the Committee was consciously retrospective with intent to codify pre-Rule categories under Rule 23(b)(1), not forward-looking as it was in anticipating innovations under Rule 23(b)(3). Thus, the Committee intended subdivision (b)(1) to capture the "standard" class actions recognized in pre-Rule practice.

Consistent with its backward look under subdivision (b)(1), as commentators have pointed out, it is clear that the Advisory Committee did not contemplate that the mandatory class action codified in subdivision (b)(1)(B) would be used to aggregate unliquidated tort claims on a limited fund rationale. None of the examples cited in the Advisory Committee Notes or by Professor Kaplan in explaining Rule 23(b)(1)(B) remotely approach what was then described as a "mass accident" case. While the Advisory Committee focused much attention on the amenability of Rule 23(b)(3) to such cases, the Committee's debates are silent about resolving tort claims under a mandatory limited fund rationale under Rule 23(b)(1)(B). It is simply implausible that the Advisory Committee, so concerned about the potential difficulties posed by dealing with mass tort cases under Rule 23(b)(3), with its provisions for notice and the right to opt out, *see* Rule 23(c)(2), would have uncritically assumed that mandatory versions of such class actions, lacking such protections, could be certified under Rule 23(b)(1)(B). We do not, it is true, decide the ultimate question whether Rule 23(b)(1)(B) may ever be used to aggregate individual tort claims. But we do recognize that the Committee would have thought such an application of the Rule surprising, and take this as a good reason to limit any surprise by presuming that the Rule's historical antecedents identify requirements.

The Rules Enabling Act underscores the need for caution. As we said in *Amchem*, no reading of the Rule can ignore the Act's mandate that "rules of procedure 'shall not abridge, enlarge or modify any substantive right,' " *Amchem* (quoting 28 U.S.C. § 2072(b)); Petitioners argue that the Act has been violated here, asserting that the Global Settlement Agreement's priorities of claims and compromise of full recovery abrogated the state law that must govern this diversity action. Although we need not grapple with the difficult choice-of-law and substantive state-law questions raised by petitioners' assertion, we do need to recognize the tension between the limited fund class action's pro rata distribution in equity and the rights of individual tort victims at law. Even if we assume that some such tension is acceptable under the Rules Enabling Act, it is best kept within tolerable limits by keeping limited fund practice under Rule 23(b)(1)(B) close to the practice preceding its adoption.

Finally, if we needed further counsel against adventurous application of Rule 23(b)(1)(B), the Rules Enabling Act and the general doctrine of constitutional avoidance would jointly sound a warning of the serious constitutional concerns that come with any attempt to aggregate individual tort claims on a limited fund rationale. First, the certification of a mandatory class followed by settlement of its action for money damages obviously implicates the Seventh Amendment jury trial rights of absent class members. By its nature, however, a mandatory settlement-only class action with legal issues and future claimants compromises their Seventh Amendment rights without their consent.

Second, and no less important, mandatory class actions aggregating damage claims implicate the due process "principle of general application in Anglo-American jurisprudence that one is not bound by a judgment in personam in a litigation in which he is not designated as a party or to which he has not been made a party by service of process," *Hansberry v. Lee*, it being "our 'deep-rooted historic tradition that everyone should have his own day in court.'" Although "'we have recognized an exception to the general rule when, in certain limited circumstances, a person, although not a party, has his interests adequately represented by someone with the same interests who is a party,'" or "where a special remedial scheme exists expressly foreclosing successive litigation by non-litigants, as for example in bankruptcy or probate," the burden of justification rests on the exception.

The inherent tension between representative suits and the day-in-court ideal is only magnified if applied to damage claims gathered in a mandatory class. Unlike Rule 23(b)(3) class members, objectors to the collectivism of a mandatory subdivision (b)(1)(B) action have no inherent right to abstain. The legal rights of absent class members (which in a class like this one would include claimants who by definition may be unidentifiable when the class is certified) are resolved regardless either of their consent, or, in a class with objectors, their express wish to the contrary. And in settlement-only class actions the procedural protections built into the Rule to protect the rights of absent class members during litigation are never invoked in an adversarial setting, *see Amchem*.

IV.

The record on which the District Court rested its certification of the class for the purpose of the global settlement did not support the essential premises of mandatory limited fund actions. It failed to demonstrate that the fund was limited except by the agreement of the parties, and it showed exclusions from the class and allocations of assets at odds with the concept of limited fund treatment and the structural protections of Rule 23(a) explained in *Amchem*.

## A.

The defect of certification going to the most characteristic feature of a limited fund action was the uncritical adoption by both the District Court and the Court of Appeals of figures agreed upon by the parties in defining the limits of the fund and demonstrating its inadequacy. When a district court, as here, certifies for class action settlement only, the moment of certification requires "heightened attention," *Amchem*, to the justifications for binding the class members. This is so because certification of a mandatory settlement class, however provisional technically, effectively concludes the proceeding save for the final fairness hearing. And, as we held in *Amchem*, a fairness hearing under Rule 23(e) is no substitute for rigorous adherence to those provisions of the Rule "designed to protect absentees," among them subdivision (b)(1)(B). Thus, in an action such as this the settling parties must present not only their agreement, but evidence on which the district court may ascertain the limit and the insufficiency of the fund, with support in findings of fact following a proceeding in which the evidence is subject to challenge.

We have already alluded to the difficulties facing limited fund treatment of huge numbers of actions for unliquidated damages arising from mass torts, the first such hurdle being a computation of the total claims. It is simply not a matter of adding up the liquidated amounts, as in the models of limited fund actions. Although we might assume arguendo that prior judicial experience with asbestos claims would allow a court to make a sufficiently reliable determination of the probable total, the District Court here apparently thought otherwise, concluding that "there is no way to predict Fibreboard's future asbestos liability with any certainty." Nothing turns on this conclusion, however, since there was no adequate demonstration of the second element required for limited fund treatment, the upper limit of the fund itself, without which no showing of insufficiency is possible.

The "fund" in this case comprised both the general assets of Fibreboard and the insurance assets provided by the two policies (describing fund as Fibreboard's entire equity and $2 billion in insurance assets under the Trilateral Settlement Agreement). As to Fibreboard's assets exclusive of the contested insurance, the District Court and the Fifth Circuit concluded that Fibreboard had a then-current sale value of $235 million that could be devoted to the limited fund. While that estimate may have been conservative, at least the District Court heard evidence and made an independent finding at some point in the proceedings. The same, however, cannot be said for the value of the disputed insurance.

The insurance assets would obviously be "limited" in the traditional sense if the total of demonstrable claims would render the insurers insolvent, or if the policies provided aggregate limits falling short of that total; calculation might be difficult, but the way to demonstrate the limit would be clear. Neither possibility is presented in this case, however. Instead, any limit of the insurance asset here had to be a product of potentially unlimited policy coverage discounted by the risk that Fibreboard would ultimately lose the coverage dispute litigation. This sense of limit as a value discounted by risk is of course a step removed from the historical model, but even on the assumption that it would suffice for limited fund treatment, there was no adequate finding of fact to support its application here. Instead of undertaking an independent evaluation of potential insurance funds, the District Court (and, later, the Court of Appeals), simply accepted the $2 billion Trilateral Settlement Agreement figure as representing the maximum amount the insurance companies could be required to pay tort victims, concluding that "where insurance coverage is disputed, it is appropriate to value the insurance asset at a settlement value."

Settlement value is not always acceptable, however. One may take a settlement amount as good evidence of the maximum available if one can assume that parties of equal knowledge and negotiating skill agreed upon the figure through arms-length bargaining, unhindered by any considerations tugging against the interests of the parties ostensibly represented in the negotiation. But no such assumption may be indulged in this case, or probably in any class action settlement with the potential for gigantic fees. In this case, certainly, any assumption that plaintiffs' counsel could be of a mind to do their simple best in bargaining for the benefit of the settlement class is patently at odds with the fact that at least some of the same lawyers representing plaintiffs and the class had also negotiated the separate settlement of 45,000 pending claims, the full payment of which was contingent on a successful global settlement agreement or the successful resolution of the insurance coverage dispute (either by litigation or by agreement, as eventually occurred in the Trilateral Settlement Agreement). Class counsel thus had great incentive to reach any agreement in the global settlement negotiations that they thought might survive a Rule 23(e) fairness hearing, rather than the best possible arrangement for the substantially unidentified global settlement class. The resulting incentive to favor the known plaintiffs in the earlier settlement was, indeed, an egregious example of the conflict noted in *Amchem* resulting from divergent interests of the presently injured and future claimants.

We do not, of course, know exactly what an independent valuation of the limit of the insurance assets would have shown. It might have revealed that even on the assumption that Fibreboard's coverage claim was sound, there would be insufficient assets to pay claims, considered with reference to their probable timing; if Fibreboard's own assets would not have been enough to pay the insurance shortfall plus any claims in excess of policy limits, the projected insolvency of the insurers and Fibreboard would have indicated a truly limited fund. (Nothing in the record, however, suggests that this would have been a supportable finding.) Or an independent valuation might have revealed assets of insufficient value to pay all projected claims if the assets were discounted by the prospects that the insurers would win the coverage cases. Or the Court's independent valuation might have shown, discount or no discount, the probability of enough assets to pay all projected claims, precluding certification of any mandatory class on a limited fund rationale. Throughout this litigation the courts have accepted the assumption that the third possibility was out of the question, and they may have been right. But objecting and unidentified class members alike are entitled to have the issue settled by specific evidentiary findings independent of the agreement of defendants and conflicted class counsel.

B.

The explanation of need for independent determination of the fund has necessarily anticipated our application of the requirement of equity among members of the class. There are two issues, the inclusiveness of the class and the fairness of distributions to those within it. On each, this certification for settlement fell short.

The definition of the class excludes myriad claimants with causes of action, or foreseeable causes of action, arising from exposure to Fibreboard asbestos. While the class includes those with present claims never filed, present claims withdrawn without prejudice, and future claimants, it fails to include those who had previously settled with Fibreboard while retaining the right to sue again "upon development of an asbestos related malignancy," plaintiffs with claims pending against Fibreboard at the time of the initial announcement of the Global Settlement Agreement, and the plaintiffs in the "inventory" claims settled as a supposedly necessary step in reaching the global settlement. The number of those outside the class who settled with a reservation of rights may be uncertain, but there is no such uncertainty about the significance of the settlement's exclusion of the 45,000 inventory plaintiffs and the plaintiffs in the unsettled present cases, estimated by the Guardian Ad Litem at more than 53,000 as of August 27, 1993. It is a fair question how far a natural class may be depleted by prior dispositions of claims and still qualify as a mandatory limited fund class, but there can be no question that such a mandatory settlement class will not qualify when in the very negotiations aimed at a class settlement, class counsel agree to exclude what could turn out to be as much as a third of the claimants that negotiators thought might eventually be involved, a substantial number of whom class counsel represent.

Might such class exclusions be forgiven if it were shown that the class members with present claims and the outsiders ended up with comparable benefits? The question is academic here. On the record before us, we cannot speculate on how the unsettled claims would fare if the Global Settlement were approved, or under the Trilateral Settlement. As for the settled inventory claims, their plaintiffs appeared to have obtained better terms than the class members. They received an immediate payment of 50 percent of a settlement higher than the historical average, and would get the remainder if the global settlement were sustained (or the coverage litigation resolved, as it turned out to be by the Trilateral Settlement Agreement); the class members, by contrast, would be assured of a 3-year payout for claims settled, whereas the unsettled faced a prospect of mediation followed by arbitration as prior conditions of instituting suit, which would even then be subject to a recovery limit, a slower payout and the limitations of the trust's spendthrift protection. Finally, as discussed below, even ostensible parity between settling non-class plaintiffs and class members would be insufficient to overcome the failure to provide the structural protection of independent representation as for subclasses with conflicting interests.

On the second element of equity within the class, the fairness of the distribution of the fund among class members, the settlement certification is likewise deficient. Fair treatment in the older cases was characteristically assured by straightforward pro rata distribution of the limited fund. While equity in such a simple sense is unattainable in a settlement covering present claims not specifically proven and claims not even due to arise, if at all, until some future time, at the least such a settlement must seek equity by providing for procedures to resolve the difficult issues of treating such differently situated claimants with fairness as among themselves.

First, it is obvious after *Amchem* that a class divided between holders of present and future claims (some of the latter involving no physical injury and to claimants not yet born) requires division into homogeneous subclasses under Rule 23(c)(4)(B), with separate representation to eliminate conflicting interests of counsel. *See Amchem* (class settlements must provide "structural assurance of fair and adequate representation for the diverse groups and individuals affected"); As we said in *Amchem*, "for the currently injured, the critical goal is generous immediate payments," but "that goal tugs against the interest of exposure-only plaintiffs in ensuring an ample, inflation-protected fund for the future." *Amchem.* No such procedure was employed here, and the conflict was as contrary to the equitable obligation entailed by the limited fund rationale as it was to the requirements of structural protection applicable to all class actions under Rule 23(a)(4).

Second, the class included those exposed to Fibreboard's asbestos products both before and after 1959. The date is significant, for that year saw the expiration of Fibreboard's insurance policy with Continental, the one which provided the bulk of the insurance funds for the settlement. Pre-

1959 claimants accordingly had more valuable claims than post-1959 claimants, the consequence being a second instance of disparate interests within the certified class. While at some point there must be an end to reclassification with separate counsel, these two instances of conflict are well within the requirement of structural protection recognized in *Amchem*.

It is no answer to say, as the Fifth Circuit said on remand, that these conflicts may be ignored because the settlement makes no disparate allocation of resources as between the conflicting classes. The settlement decides that the claims of the immediately injured deserve no provisions more favorable than the more speculative claims of those projected to have future injuries, and that liability subject to indemnification is no different from liability with no indemnification. The very decision to treat them all the same is itself an allocation decision with results almost certainly different from the results that those with immediate injuries or claims of indemnified liability would have chosen.

Nor does it answer the settlement's failures to provide structural protections in the service of equity to argue that the certified class members' common interest in securing contested insurance funds for the payment of claims was so weighty as to diminish the deficiencies beneath recognition here. This argument is simply a variation of the position put forward by the proponents of the settlement in *Amchem*, who tried to discount the comparable failure in that case to provide separate representatives for subclasses with conflicting interests. The current position is just as unavailing as its predecessor in *Amchem*. There we gave the argument no weight, observing that "the benefits asbestos-exposed persons might gain from the establishment of a grand-scale compensation scheme is a matter fit for legislative consideration," but the determination whether "proposed classes are sufficiently cohesive to warrant adjudication" must focus on "questions that preexist any settlement." Here, just as in the earlier case, the proponents of the settlement are trying to rewrite Rule 23; each ignores the fact that Rule 23 requires protections under subdivisions (a) and (b) against inequity and potential inequity at the pre-certification stage, quite independently of the required determination at post-certification fairness review under subdivision (e) that any settlement is fair in an overriding sense. A fairness hearing under subdivision (e) can no more swallow the preceding protective requirements of Rule 23 in a subdivision (b)(1)(B) action than in one under subdivision (b)(3).

## C.

A third contested feature of this settlement certification that departs markedly from the limited fund antecedents is the ultimate provision for a fund smaller than the assets understood by the Court of Appeals to be available for payment of the mandatory class members' claims; most notably, Fibreboard was allowed to retain virtually its entire net worth. Given our treatment of the two preceding deficiencies of the certification, there is of course no need to decide whether this feature of the agreement would alone be fatal to the Global Settlement Agreement. To ignore it entirely, however, would be so misleading that we have decided simply to identify the issue it raises, without purporting to resolve it at this time.

Fibreboard listed its supposed entire net worth as a component of the total (and allegedly inadequate) assets available for claimants, but subsequently retained all but $500,000 of that equity for itself. On the face of it, the arrangement seems irreconcilable with the justification of necessity in denying any opportunity for withdrawal of class members whose jury trial rights will be compromised, whose damages will be capped, and whose payments will be delayed. With Fibreboard retaining nearly all its net worth, it hardly appears that such a regime is the best that can be provided for class members. Given the nature of a limited fund and the need to apply its criteria at the certification stage, it is not enough for a District Court to say that it "need not ensure that a defendant designate a particular source of its assets to satisfy the class' claims; but only that the amount recovered by the class be fair."

The District Court in this case seems to have had a further point in mind, however. One great advantage of class action treatment of mass tort cases is the opportunity to save the enormous transaction costs of piecemeal litigation, an advantage to which the settlement's proponents have referred in this case. Although the District Court made no specific finding about the transaction cost saving likely from this class settlement, estimating the amount in the "hundreds of millions," it did conclude that the amount would exceed Fibreboard's net worth as the Court valued it (Fibreboard's net worth of $235 million "is considerably less than the likely savings in defense costs under the Global Settlement"). If a settlement thus saves transaction costs that would never have gone into a class member's pocket in the absence of settlement, may a credit for some of the savings be recognized in a mandatory class action as an incentive to settlement? It is at least a legitimate question, which we leave for another day.

## V.

Our decision rests on a different basis from the ground of JUSTICE BREYER'S dissent, just as there was a difference in approach between majority and dissenters in *Amchem*. The nub of our position is that we are bound to follow Rule 23 as we understood it upon its adoption, and that we are not free to alter it except through the process prescribed by Congress in the Rules Enabling Act. Although, as the dissent notes, the revised text adopted in 1966 was understood (somewhat cautiously) to authorize the courts to provide for class treatment of mass tort litigation, it was also the Court's understanding that the Rule's growing edge for that purpose would be the opt-out class authorized by subdivision (b)(3), not the mandatory class under subdivision (b)(1)(B). While we have not ruled out the possibility under the present Rule of a mandatory class to deal with mass tort litigation on a limited fund rationale, we are not free to dispense with the safeguards that have protected mandatory class members under that theory traditionally.

Apart from its effect on the requirements of subdivision (a) as explained and held binding in *Amchem*, the dissent would move the standards for mandatory actions in the direction of opt-out class requirements by according weight to this "unusual limited fund's witching hour," in exercising discretion over class certification. It is on this belief (that we should sustain the allowances made by the District Court in consideration of the exigencies of this settlement proceeding) that the dissent addresses each of the criteria for limited fund treatment (demonstrably insufficient fund, intra-class equity, and dedication of the entire fund).

As to the calculation of the fund, the dissent believes an independent valuation by the District Court may be dispensed with here in favor of the figure agreed upon by the settling parties. The dissent discounts the conflicts on the part of class counsel who negotiated the Global Settlement Agreement by arguing that the "relevant" settlement negotiation, and hence the relevant benchmark for judging the actual value of the insurance amount, was the negotiation between Fibreboard and the insurers that produced the Trilateral Settlement Agreement. This argument, however, minimizes two facts: (1) that Fibreboard and the insurers made this separate, backup agreement only at the insistence of class counsel as a condition for reaching the Global Settlement Agreement; (2) even more important, that "the Insurers were adamant that they would not agree to pay any more in the context of a backup agreement than in a global agreement," a principle "Fibreboard acceded to" on the day the Global Settlement Agreement was announced "as the price of permitting an agreement to be reached with respect to a global settlement," Under these circumstances the reliability of the Trilateral Settlement Agreement's figure is inadequate as an independent benchmark that might excuse the want of any independent judicial determination that the Global Settlement Agreement's fund was the maximum possible. In any event, the dissent says, it is not crucial whether a $30 claim has to settle for $15 or $20. But it is crucial. Conflict-free counsel, as required by Rule 23(a) and *Amchem*, might have negotiated a $20 figure, and a limited fund rationale for mandatory class treatment of a settlement-only action requires assurance that claimants are receiving the maximum fund, not a potentially significant fraction less.

With respect to the requirement of intra-class equity, the dissent argues that conflicts both within this certified class and between the class as certified and those excluded from it may be mitigated because separate counsel were simply not to be had in the short time that a settlement agreement was possible before the argument (or likely decision) in the coverage case. But this is to say that when the clock is about to strike midnight, a court considering class certification may lower the structural requirements of Rule 23(a) as declared in *Amchem*, and the parallel equity requirements necessary to justify mandatory class treatment on a limited fund theory.

Finally, the dissent would excuse Fibreboard's retention of virtually all its net worth, and the loss to members of the certified class of some 13 percent of the fund putatively available to them, on the ground that the settlement made more money available than any other effort would likely have done. But even if we could be certain that this evaluation were true, this is to reargue *Amchem*: the settlement's fairness under Rule 23(e) does not dispense with the requirements of Rule 23(a) and (b).

We believe that if an allowance for exigency can make a substantial difference in the level of Rule 23 scrutiny, the economic temptations at work on counsel in class actions will guarantee enough exigencies to take the law back before *Amchem* and unsettle the line between mandatory class actions under subdivision (b)(1)(B) and opt-out actions under subdivision (b)(3).

## VI.

In sum, the applicability of Rule 23(b)(1)(B) to a fund and plan purporting to liquidate actual and potential tort claims is subject to question, and its purported application in this case was in any event improper. The Advisory Committee did not envision mandatory class actions in cases like this one, and both the Rules Enabling Act and the policy of avoiding serious constitutional issues counsel against leniency in recognizing mandatory limited fund actions in circumstances markedly different from the traditional paradigm. Assuming arguendo that a mandatory, limited fund rationale could under some circumstances be applied to a settlement class of tort claimants, it would be essential that the fund be shown to be limited independently of the agreement of the parties to the action, and equally essential under Rule 23(a) and (b)(1)(B) that the class include all those with claims unsatisfied at the time of the settlement negotiations, with intra-class conflicts addressed by recognizing independently represented subclasses. In this case, the limit of the fund was determined by treating the settlement agreement as dispositive, an error magnified by the representation of class members by counsel also representing excluded plaintiffs, whose settlements would be funded fully upon settlement of the class action on any terms that could survive final fairness review. Those separate settlements, together with other exclusions from the claimant class, precluded adequate structural protection by subclass treatment, which was not even afforded to the conflicting elements within the class as certified.

The judgment of the Court of Appeals, accordingly, is reversed, and the case is remanded for further proceedings consistent with this opinion.

It is so ordered.

CHIEF JUSTICE REHNQUIST, with whom JUSTICE SCALIA and JUSTICE KENNEDY join, concurring.

JUSTICE BREYER'S dissenting opinion highlights in graphic detail the massive impact of asbestos-related claims on the federal courts. Were I devising a system for handling these claims on a clean slate, I would agree entirely with that dissent, which in turn approves the near-heroic efforts of the District Court in this case to make the best of a bad situation. Under the present regime, transactional costs will surely consume more and more of a relatively static amount of money to pay these claims.

But we are not free to devise an ideal system for adjudicating these claims. Unless and until the Federal Rules of Civil Procedure are revised, the Court's opinion correctly states the existing law, and I join it. But the "elephantine mass of asbestos cases," cries out for a legislative solution.

JUSTICE BREYER, with whom JUSTICE STEVENS joins, dissenting.

This case involves a settlement of an estimated 186,000 potential future asbestos claims against a single company, Fibreboard, for approximately $1.535 billion. The District Court, in approving the settlement, made 446 factual findings, on the basis of which it concluded that the settlement was equitable, that the potential claimants had been well represented, and that the distinctions drawn among different categories of claimants were reasonable. The Court of Appeals, dividing 2 to 1, held that the settlement was lawful. I would not set aside the Court of Appeals' judgment as the majority does. Accordingly, I dissent.

I.

A.

Four special background circumstances underlie this settlement and help to explain the reasonableness and consequent lawfulness of the relevant District Court determinations. First, as the majority points out, the settlement comprises part of an "elephantine mass of asbestos cases," which "defies customary judicial administration." An estimated 13 to 21 million workers have been exposed to asbestos. Eight years ago the Judicial Conference spoke of the mass of related cases having "reached critical dimensions," threatening "a disaster of major proportions." In the Eastern District of Texas, for example, one out of every three civil cases filed in 1990 was an asbestos case. In the past decade nearly 80,000 new federal asbestos cases have been filed; more than 10,000 new federal asbestos cases were filed last year.

The Judicial Conference found that asbestos cases on average take almost twice as long as other lawsuits to resolve. Judge Parker, the experienced trial judge who approved this settlement, noted in one 3,000-member asbestos class action over which he presided that 448 of the original class members had died while the litigation was pending. *Cimino v. Raymark Industries, Inc.* And yet, Judge Parker went on to state, if the district court could close "thirty cases a month, it would still take six and one-half years to try these cases and due to new filings there would be pending over 5,000 untouched cases" at the end of that time. His subsequent efforts to accelerate final decision or settlement through the use of sample cases produced a highly complex trial (133 trial days, more than 500 witnesses, half a million pages of documents) that eventually closed only about 160 cases because efforts to extrapolate from the sample proved fruitless. The consequence is not only delay but also attorney's fees and other "transaction costs" that are unusually high, to the point where, of each dollar that asbestos defendants pay, those costs consume an estimated 61 cents, with only 39 cents going to victims.

Second, an individual asbestos case is a tort case, of a kind that courts, not legislatures, ordinarily will resolve. It is the number of these cases, not their nature, that creates the special judicial problem. The judiciary cannot treat the problem as entirely one of legislative failure, as if it were caused, say, by a poorly drafted statute. Thus, when "calls for national legislation" go unanswered, judges can and should search aggressively for ways, within the framework of existing law, to avoid delay and expense so great as to bring about a massive denial of justice.

Third, in that search the district courts may take advantage of experience that appellate courts do not have. Judge Parker, for example, has written of "a disparity of appreciation for the magnitude of the problem," growing out of the difference between the trial courts' "daily involvement with asbestos litigation" and the appellate courts' "limited" exposure to such litigation in infrequent appeals. *Cimino.*

Fourth, the alternative to class-action settlement is not a fair opportunity for each potential plaintiff to have his or her own day in court. Unusually high litigation costs, unusually long delays, and limitations upon the total amount of resources available for payment, together mean that most potential plaintiffs may not have a realistic alternative. And Federal Rule of Civil Procedure 23 was designed to address situations in which the historical model of individual actions would not, for practical reasons, work.

For these reasons, I cannot easily find a legal answer to the problems this case raises by referring, as does the majority, to "our 'deep-rooted historic tradition that everyone should have his own day in court.'" Instead, in these circumstances, I believe our Court should allow a district court full authority to exercise every bit of discretionary power that the law provides. And, in doing so, the Court should prove extremely reluctant to overturn a fact-specific or circumstance-specific exercise of that discretion, where a court of appeals has found it lawful. This cautionary principle of review leads me to an ultimate conclusion different from that of the majority.

### B.

Because I believe that all three of the majority's conditions are satisfied, and because I see no fatal conceptual difficulty, I would uphold the determination, made by the District Court and affirmed by the Court of Appeals, that the insurance policies (along with Fibreboard's net value) amount to a classic limited fund, within the scope of Rule 23(b)(1)(B).

### III.

Petitioners raise additional issues, which the majority does not reach. I believe that respondents would likely prevail were the Court to reach those issues. That is why I dissent. But, as the Court does not reach those issues, I need not decide the questions definitively.

In some instances, my belief that respondents would likely prevail reflects my reluctance to second-guess a court of appeals that has affirmed a district court's fact- and circumstance-specific findings.

In other instances, my belief reflects my conclusion that class certification here rests upon the presence of what is close to a traditional limited fund. And I doubt that petitioners' additional arguments that certification violates, for example, the Rules Enabling Act, the Bankruptcy Act, the Seventh Amendment, and the Due Process Clause, are aimed at or would prevail against a traditional limited fund (e.g., "trust assets, a bank account, insurance proceeds, company assets in a liquidation sale, proceeds of a ship sale in a maritime accident suit"). Regardless, I need not decide these latter issues definitively now, and I leave them for another day. With that caveat, I respectfully dissent.

# CHAPTER 7

---

# MASS TORT CLASS ACTIONS POST-*AMCHEM* AND *ORTIZ*

■ ■ ■

## A. LITIGATION CLASSES DISAPPROVED

### IN RE ST. JUDE MEDICAL, INC.
United States Court of Appeals for the Eighth Circuit, 2005.
425 F.3d 1116.

St. Jude Medical, Inc. (SJM) produced the Silzone prosthetic heart valve. A test conducted by SJM showed a slightly higher risk of paravalvular leaks at the site where the valves were implanted. SJM thereafter recalled all unimplanted Silzone valves. Numerous suits were then filed across the nation, and the cases were later consolidated in Minnesota. On motions by the plaintiffs, the district court issued three orders that collectively had the result of certifying two subclasses-one seeking damages based on Minnesota's consumer protection statutes, and another seeking primarily injunctive relief. SJM appeals these two class certifications. We reverse and remand.

### I. BACKGROUND

SJM received approval from the Food and Drug Administration (FDA) for the Silzone Heart Valve. The valve had as a unique characteristic a sterile, antimicrobial silver coating on the valve's polyester sewing cuff where the valve connected to a patient's heart tissue. Months after receiving FDA approval, SJM sponsored a random, controlled study comparing patient experience with Silzone- and non-Silzone-coated heart valves. The study data showed a statistically significant 2% increase for patients implanted with Silzone-coated valves over those implanted with non-Silzone-coated valves in the incidence of paravalvular leaks severe enough to require valve explanation.

SJM immediately recalled all unimplanted Silzone valves. Following the recall, plaintiffs sued SJM in courts across the nation. The cases were consolidated for pretrial proceedings in Minnesota pursuant to the Judicial Panel on Multidistrict Litigation. Eventually, five plaintiffs filed a consolidated amended class action complaint, claiming to represent over 11,000 Silzone valve recipients. The plaintiffs alleged common law strict liability, breach of implied and express warranties, negligence and medical monitoring, and claims under various Minnesota consumer statutes-the

False Advertising Act, the Consumer Fraud Act, the Unlawful Trade Practices Act, and the Uniform Deceptive Trade Practices Act. The plaintiffs moved for class certification of an injunctive class, called the "medical monitoring class," and a personal injury class seeking money damages, although both classes made many of the same claims under the same legal theories noted above. The district court found both proposed classes met the threshold requirements of Federal Rule of Civil Procedure 23(a), then conditionally certified the common-law claims in both classes under Rule 23(b)(3) and (c)(4). The court also conditionally certified the medical monitoring class under Rule 23(b)(2) and (c)(4). Finally, the court concluded common issues of law and fact predominated over plaintiffs' claims under Minnesota's consumer protection and deceptive trade practices acts, and a class action was the superior method to adjudicate those claims. The court unconditionally certified a consumer protection class under those statutes pursuant to Rule 23(b)(3).

As to the common law claims, the district court "envisioned a minimal number of subclasses, and found that only significant variations in state law will be sufficient to require different subclasses," then requested briefing from the parties with regard to subclasses in the conditionally certified classes. After receiving briefing, the court decertified the personal injury class, citing *Erie Railroad v. Tompkins* and *Castano v. American Tobacco Co.,* wherein the Fifth Circuit reversed a district court's class certification order because the district court failed to consider how the variations in state law would affect predominance and superiority. The district court found no two states' laws were substantially alike, which, in the court's estimation, would require management of at least 25 subclasses. The court again conditionally certified the medical monitoring class, subject to the plaintiffs submitting to the court the identities of suitable class representatives and a manageable trial plan. After reviewing the laws of different states with regard to medical monitoring, the court observed it would apply the medical monitoring law of different states, conditionally certifying the class only as to "those plaintiffs whose valves were implanted in states that recognize a stand-alone cause of action for medical monitoring, absent proof of injury." The court concluded the elements of medical monitoring claims in states that recognize such claims "appeared to be the same." In a third order, the court added plaintiffs from more states (for a total of 17) to the list of those presenting medical monitoring claims. Following the third order, two certified subclasses remain: the class based on Minnesota's consumer protection statutes, and the medical monitoring class.

## II.  DISCUSSION

"We review a district court's ruling granting or denying class certification for abuse of discretion." "The district court's rulings on issues of law are reviewed de novo, and the court abuses its discretion if it commits an error of law." "Thus, even under the abuse of discretion standard, a district court's rulings on issues of law are reviewed de novo."

To be certified as a class, plaintiffs must meet all of the requirements of Rule 23(a) and must satisfy one of the three subsections of Rule 23(b). *Amchem Prods., Inc. v. Windsor.* The district court certified the class based on Minnesota's consumer protection statutes using Rule 23(b)(3), which provides that a class action may be maintained if the court finds the questions of law or fact common to members of the class predominate over the questions affecting only individual class members, and a class action is the superior method for fair and efficient adjudication of the dispute. The district court certified the medical monitoring class under Rule 23(b)(2), which provides a class action is appropriate if "the party opposing the class has acted or refused to act on grounds generally applicable to the class, thereby making appropriate final injunctive relief or corresponding declaratory relief with respect to the class as a whole."

### A.   Consumer Protection Class

The district court concluded it would apply Minnesota law to the consumer protection statutes class because the Minnesota statutes permit "any person" to bring suit thereunder. The court conducted a cursory conflict-of-laws analysis as to the application of the Minnesota consumer protection statutes. The court concluded applying Minnesota law was proper because the parties, particularly SJM, had significant contacts with Minnesota, including SJM being headquartered in Minnesota, and the fact that "much of the conduct relevant" to the claims "occurred or emanated from Minnesota."

SJM makes numerous assertions of error regarding the district court's order certifying the consumer protection class. SJM argues the U.S. Constitution does not permit a nationwide personal injury class action using the consumer protection law of one state to the exclusion of all other states. SJM claims the nationwide class violates the Constitution's Commerce Clause, the Due Process Clause, the Full Faith and Credit Clause, the *Erie* doctrine, and the Rules Enabling Act. SJM also argues the nationwide consumer protection class violates Federal Rule of Civil Procedure 23, questioning the manageability of the class, the adequacy of the class representatives, and the typicality of their claims. Finally, SJM argues the plaintiffs cannot meet the predominance or superiority requirements of Rule 23(b)(3).

Addressing the class certification issues only with regard to the Due Process and Full Faith and Credit Clauses, we conclude the district court did not conduct a sufficient conflicts-of-law analysis. The due process and full faith and credit issues "are dispositive, and we believe it prudent not to decide issues unnecessary to the disposition of the case," especially given the numerous constitutional issues implicated in such an analysis. See

Georgine v. Amchem Prods., Inc., aff'd sub nom., Amchem Prods., Inc. v. Windsor.

The district court's class certification was in error because the district court did not conduct a thorough conflicts-of-law analysis with respect to each plaintiff class member before applying Minnesota law. The Supreme Court has held an individualized choice-of-law analysis must be applied to each plaintiff's claim in a class action. Phillips Petroleum Co. v. Shutts. There is, of course, no constitutional injury to out-of-state plaintiffs in applying Minnesota law unless Minnesota law is in conflict with the other states' laws. Therefore, we must first decide whether any conflicts actually exist. The district court certified a class of over 11,000 Silzone valve recipients, assumedly residing in numerous states. We deem it unnecessary here to review each state's consumer protection laws, and rather rely on our sister circuit's conclusion that "state consumer-protection laws vary considerably, and courts must respect these differences rather than apply one state's law to sales in other states with different rules." In re Bridgestone/Firestone, Inc.

"For a State's substantive law to be selected in a constitutionally permissible manner, that State must have a significant contact or significant aggregation of contacts, creating state interests, such that choice of its law is neither arbitrary nor fundamentally unfair." Allstate Ins. Co. v. Hague. Here, we cannot determine whether the district court's choice of Minnesota law was arbitrary or unfair, because the court did not analyze the contacts between Minnesota and each plaintiff class member's claims. Application of Minnesota law to all plaintiffs' claims ultimately may be proper, although we suspect Minnesota lacks sufficient contacts with all the parties' claims, and the different states have material variances between their consumer protection laws and Minnesota's. There is no indication out-of-state parties "had any idea that Minnesota law could control" potential claims when they received their Silzone-coated valves. Regardless, protection of out-of-state parties' constitutional rights requires an inquiry into their claims' contacts with Minnesota and their individual state laws before concluding Minnesota law may apply.

The district court justified its decision not to conduct a conflicts analysis by relying on section 8.31 of the Minnesota Statutes. The district court essentially attempted to preempt the Due Process and Full Faith and Credit Clauses with state standing statutes. This opposes basic constitutional law and is error. State consumer protection standing statutes do not extinguish federal constitutional rights or relieve courts from performing the analysis required to safeguard those rights. We therefore conclude the district court should have conducted the proper choice-of-law analysis and we reverse and remand for that analysis.

## B.   Medical Monitoring Class

SJM also asserts the district court erred in certifying the medical monitoring class. SJM argues this class defies *Erie's* command that federal courts refrain from altering or creating new state law. SJM further argues certification of this class as one seeking injunctive relief under Rule 23(b)(2) violates the Due Process Clause. Finally, SJM argues certification of this class is improper due to diverse legal and factual issues that would make a classwide trial inefficient and unmanageable. We conclude the diverse legal and factual issues preclude class certification, and we reverse on this ground. As this ground again is dispositive, we do not address the *Erie* and due process arguments.

Class certification under Rule 23(b)(2) is proper only when the primary relief sought is declaratory or injunctive. Although Rule 23(b)(2) contains no predominance or superiority requirements, class claims thereunder still must be cohesive. *Barnes v. Am. Tobacco Co.* Because "unnamed members are bound by the action without the opportunity to opt out" of a Rule 23(b)(2) class, even greater cohesiveness generally is required than in a Rule 23(b)(3) class. A "suit could become unmanageable and little value would be gained in proceeding as a class action if significant individual issues were to arise consistently." "At base, the (b)(2) class is distinguished from the (b)(3) class by class cohesiveness. Injuries remedied through (b)(2) actions are really group, as opposed to individual injuries. The members of a (b)(2) class are generally bound together through 'preexisting or continuing legal relationships' or by some significant common trait such as race or gender."

Proposed medical monitoring classes suffer from cohesion difficulties, and numerous courts across the country have denied certification of such classes. Quoting the Third Circuit, the Supreme Court in *Windsor* listed some of the individual variations precluding class certification: "Exposure-only plaintiffs will also incur different medical expenses because their monitoring and treatment will depend on singular circumstances and individual medical histories." Differences in state laws on medical monitoring further compound these disparities.

In this case, like in *Windsor,* each plaintiff's need (or lack of need) for medical monitoring is highly individualized. Every patient in the 17-state class who has ever been implanted with a mechanical heart valve already requires future medical monitoring as an ordinary part of his or her follow-up care. A patient who has been implanted with the Silzone valve may or may not require additional monitoring, and whether he or she does is an individualized inquiry depending on that patient's medical history, the condition of the patient's heart valves at the time of implantation, the patient's risk factors for heart valve complications, the patient's general health, the patient's personal choice, and other factors. The plaintiffs concede the states recognizing medical monitoring claims as a separate cause of action have different elements triggering culpability. Simply put, the medical monitoring class presents a myriad of individual issues making class certification improper. For the same reasons the district court decertified the personal injury tort class, the medical monitoring class was certified incorrectly.

Bolstering our conclusion is the fact the plaintiffs never demonstrated to the district court they "would sue for the medical monitoring program sought here even in the absence of a claim for damages." As the Southern District of New York ruled, a district court certifying a medical monitoring class must be satisfied that a reasonable plaintiff, based on a medical and economic calculus, would have sued solely for a medical monitoring program, not merely that a lawyer could have been found who would have located a plaintiff and brought a class action in the hope of a fee, else the test would be meaningless:

> Plaintiffs have not persuaded the Court that this criterion has been satisfied here. Neither the American Diabetes Association nor the American Association of Clinical Endocrinologists, which promulgate guidelines for the care and treatment of diabetics, nor any public health agency or professional medical society or institution, has recommended special monitoring for patients who formerly took Rezulin.

While every mechanical heart valve patient will require follow-up care in connection with the implant, the question of additional monitoring above that required for normal mechanical heart valve implantation is not clear.

For the above reasons, we conclude class certification of the medical monitoring class was an abuse of discretion. We reverse the district court's certification of this class.

## STEERING COMMITTEE V. EXXON MOBIL CORP.

United States Court of Appeals for the Fifth Circuit, 2006.
461 F.3d 598.

Plaintiff-Appellants, members of a purported class alleging claims against Defendant-Appellee Exxon Mobil Corporation arising out of a fire in an Exxon Mobil facility, appeal the district court's order denying certification of a Rule 23(b)(3) plaintiff class in this mass tort action. A panel of this court granted Appellants' petition for permission to appeal. Finding no abuse of discretion by the district court, we affirm the denial of class certification.

I.

On August 8, 1994, a recently installed control valve in Exxon Mobil's Baton Rouge Chemical Plant failed, resulting in sponge oil leaks. The oil ignited, and although the fire was controlled quickly, it burned until its fuel source was exhausted, sometime on the morning of August 11, 1994. During the time the fire was burning, the wind carried the smoke plume to the southwest and across the Mississippi River. Exxon Mobil conducted air monitoring both inside and outside the facility, and in the surrounding community during the time of the fire.

Hundreds of suits were soon filed against Exxon Mobil, alleging various causes of action including personal injury, personal discomfort and annoyance, emotional distress resulting from knowledge of exposure to hazardous substances, fear of future unauthorized exposures, and economic harm including damage to business and property, among others.

After the suits were consolidated, Appellants proposed class certification under Rule 23(b)(3) for all issues and with the following class definition:

> All persons or entities residing or located, or owning property or operating businesses in East Baton Rouge Parish or West Baton Rouge Parish at the time of the incident at the Exxon Chemical Plan, Exxon Refinery, in Baton Rouge, Louisiana, on August 8, 1994, and who sustained legally cognizable damages, including but not limited to all claims for exemplary or punitive damages as provided for in LSA-C.C. art. 2314.3, property damage, business loss, and all personal injury claims, and who have not settled their claims in full, and who have complied with and comply with all further orders of the court in this class action.

Following a hearing but before the court ruled on class certification, the court granted summary judgment to Exxon Mobil on certain categories of claims. First, the court granted summary judgment to Exxon Mobil on all claims for physical injuries and non-intentional emotional distress brought by individual plaintiffs who were located outside the geographic area that the air modeling experts agreed was affected by the plume. Second, the court granted summary judgment to Exxon Mobil on all claims for intentional infliction of emotional distress.

Following the entry of its summary judgment, the court denied Appellants' motion for class certification, concluding that Appellants failed to satisfy the typicality and adequacy requirements of Rule 23(a), as well as the predominance and superiority requirements of Rule 23(b)(3). This appeal followed.

## II.

### A.

We review the denial of class certification for abuse of discretion. Because, however, a court by definition abuses its discretion when it applies an incorrect legal standard, we review such errors *de novo*. Moreover, although the district court has substantial discretion, the "district court must conduct a rigorous analysis of the rule 23 prerequisites before certifying a class." *Castano v. American Tobacco Co.* Additionally, a "party seeking certification bears the burden of proof."

The district court in this case assumed for purposes of its order that the plaintiffs could satisfy the numerosity and commonality questions, but concluded that plaintiffs failed to satisfy the typicality, adequacy, predominance, or superiority requirements. We agree that plaintiffs failed to demonstrate either predominance or superiority, and because failure on those two requirements dooms class certification under Rule 23(b)(3), we decline to address the remaining requirements.

### B.

The predominance inquiry requires that questions of law or fact common to the members of the class "predominate over any questions affecting only individual members." The cause of action as a whole must satisfy Rule 23(b)(3)'s predominance requirement. *Castano.* This requirement, although similar to the commonality requirement of Rule 23(a), is "far more demanding" because it "tests whether proposed classes are sufficiently cohesive to warrant adjudication by representation." (quoting *Amchem*).

Appellants argue that the district court erred in concluding that the proposed class definition failed to satisfy the predominance requirement. Appellants argue that because the alleged injuries all arise from the single incident at the Exxon Mobil plant, the issues relating to Exxon Mobil's liability predominate over individual issues of causation and damages. Appellee argues that the district court correctly concluded that the individualized medical causation, injury, and damages issues were the predominant issues in the case, and therefore that a class action was an inappropriate vehicle for resolution.

The district court heard from experts who opined that the primary issues left to be resolved would turn on location, exposure, dose, susceptibility to illness, nature of symptoms, type and cost of medical treatment, and subsequent impact of illnesses on individuals. Moreover, in addition to the personal injury claims, separate types of proof would be necessary for the property damage, devaluation, and business loss claims. The district court observed that each plaintiff's claims will be highly individualized with respect to proximate causation, including individual issues of exposure, susceptibility to illness, and types of physical injuries. As a result, the district court found that "individual issues surrounding exposure, dose, health effects, and damages will dominate at the trial." The district court concluded that "one set of operative facts would not establish liability and that the end result would be a series of individual mini-trials which the predominance requirement is intended to prevent."

As Appellants argue, the necessity of calculating damages on an individual basis will not necessarily preclude class certification. However, where individual damages cannot be determined by reference to a mathematical or formulaic calculation, the damages issue may predominate over any common issues shared by the class.

It is clear from the record that the damages claims in this case are not subject to any sort of formulaic calculation. Instead, each individual plaintiff suffered different alleged periods and magnitudes of exposure and suffered different alleged symptoms as a result. Some plaintiffs allege both personal and property injuries, while others allege only one or the other. Moreover, many plaintiffs allege as part of their claim for compensatory damages emotional and other intangible injuries. "The very nature of these damages, compensating plaintiffs for emotional and other intangible injuries, necessarily implicates the subjective differences of each plaintiff's circumstances; they are an individual, not class-wide, remedy. The amount of compensatory damages to which any individual class member might be entitled cannot be calculated by objective standards."

Appellants rely principally on two cases in which mass tort classes were certified. However, Appellants do no more than recite the disposition in each of those cases; little effort is made to relate the results in those cases to the facts of the case now before this court. Indeed, Appellants' citation does little more than prove that it is theoretically possible to satisfy the predominance and superiority requirements of Rule 23(b)(3) in a mass tort or mass accident class action, a proposition this court has already accepted. *See, e.g., Watson v. Shell Oil Co.* (affirming class certification of claims arising from refinery explosion).

Importantly, the court in *Sala* determined that the claims in that case involved injuries sustained from a single cause: the collision and derailment of the train on which they were riding. Thus, causation could be adjudicated on a class-wide basis. In this case, although the alleged cause of the injuries is also a single accident—a refinery fire—the causal mechanism for plaintiff's injuries—alleged exposure or fear of exposure to toxic substances—is not so straightforward. While it is certainly true that the cause of the fire itself is an issue common to the class, each individual plaintiff must meet his or her own burden of medical causation, which in turn will depend on any number of the factors enumerated by the experts who testified at the class certification hearing.

Appellants argue, and Appellee appears to agree, that the issue of liability, i.e., Appellee's negligence or strict liability for improperly installing the valve and causing the fire, can be determined on a class-wide basis. Appellants' argument, however, does no more than prove that some common issues exist across the class. The predominance inquiry, however, is more rigorous than the commonality requirement. Appellee argues that the cause of the fire and related liability issues are relatively straightforward, and Appellants do little to dispute that claim. Based on the evidence presented to the district court regarding the complexity of the medical causation and damages issues, and with little evidence that the liability issues are similarly complex, it was not an abuse of its discretion for the district court to conclude that Appellants had failed to demonstrate that the class issue of Appellee's negligence or strict liability predominates over the vastly more complex individual issues of medical causation and damages.

Notably, moreover, the class certified in *Sterling* was bifurcated, with class treatment limited to certain class-wide liability issues. Similarly, the court in *Sala* acknowledged that individualized damages issues "will have to be determined on an individual basis." This court has likewise approved mass tort or mass accident class actions when the district court was able to rely on a manageable trial plan—including bifurcation and/or subclasses—proposed by counsel. *See, e.g., Watson.*

Although Appellants' counsel during oral argument to this court briefly suggested subclasses or bifurcation as a remedy for the obstacles preventing a finding of predominance in this case, the record does not reflect that counsel made such a proposal to the district court. Certainly, when the parties moving for class certification have full opportunity to present to the district court proposals for their preferred form of class treatment, the district court is under no obligation to *sua sponte* consider other variations not proposed by any party. We need not now consider whether bifurcation or subclasses would remedy Appellants' difficulties in this case, because Appellants' counsel never proposed either. We agree with the district court that Appellants have not met their burden of demonstrating that common issues predominate over the significant individual issues in the case, including medical causation, injury, and damages.

## C.

Appellants also argue that the district court erred in concluding that the proposed class action did not provide a superior vehicle for resolving the suits. The district court concluded that because of the predominance of individual causation and damage issues, it would not be efficient to certify a class. The district court also noted that the case has already been streamlined using other case management tools, including narrowing the claims and potential plaintiffs through summary judgment, and facilitating the disposition of the remaining plaintiffs' claims through issuance of a *Lone Pine* order.

Because all Rule 23 class-action requirements must be satisfied, and we hold the predominance factor is not, we need not address the superiority factor. However, we address this requirement to demonstrate the interrelationship between predominance and superiority. The Advisory

Committee's notes to Rule 23(b)(3) comment on the impact of the predominance inquiry on superiority in mass tort cases.

Appellants have not demonstrated that this mass tort has any exceptional features that warrant departing from the general rule and treating it as a class action.

As this court has noted, the predominance of individual issues relating to the plaintiffs' claims for compensatory and punitive damages detracts from the superiority of the class action device in resolving these claims. *See Castano.* Particularly in this case, where the district court has been careful to manage the litigation efficiently through the judicious use of consolidated summary judgments and other tools, we will not second-guess the district court's discretionary judgment that a class action would not provide a superior method of adjudication.

## III.

Because we agree that Appellants failed to demonstrate that their proposed class satisfied either the predominance or superiority requirements of Rule 23(b)(3), we affirm the district court's denial of class certification.

## MADISON V. CHALMETTE REFINING, LLC

United States Court of Appeals for the Fifth Circuit, 2011.
637 F.3d 551.

This is an interlocutory appeal under Rule 23(f) of the Federal Rules of Civil Procedure. Defendant-Appellant Chalmette Refining, LLC, appeals the district court's order certifying a class alleging claims arising out of a petroleum coke dust release from its refinery. For the following reasons, we reverse the district court's order granting class certification and remand this case for further proceedings.

### FACTS AND PROCEEDINGS

On January 12, 2007, a number of schoolchildren, chaperoned by parents and teachers, participated in a historical reenactment at the Chalmette National Battlefield, "the site along the Mississippi River where Andrew Jackson gave the British their comeuppance." Adjacent to the battlefield is the Chalmette Refinery. In the early afternoon, the Chalmette Refinery released an amount of petroleum coke dust that Plaintiffs-Appellees attendees and parents of attendees of the reenactment, allege migrated over the battlefield. Plaintiffs filed suit, seeking to sue on behalf of themselves and all other individuals who were exposed to the coke dust on the battlefield. They sought a variety of damages, including personal injury, fear, anguish, discomfort, inconvenience, pain and suffering, emotional distress, psychiatric and psychological damages, evacuation, economic damages, and property damages.

The district court allowed the parties to conduct discovery on the issue of class certification, "as it is encouraged to do." Chalmette Refining deposed each of the five named class representatives; Plaintiffs apparently conducted no discovery. Plaintiffs then moved for class certification under Rule 23(b)(3), asserting that this lawsuit is a type of action where "questions of law or fact common to class members predominate over any questions affecting only individual members, and that a class action is superior to other available methods for fairly and efficiently adjudicating the controversy." The proposed class consisted of

> all persons entities (sic) located at the Chalmette National Battlefield in St. Bernard Parish, Louisiana, in the early afternoon of Friday, January 12, 2007 and who sustained property damage, personal injuries, emotional, mental, or economic damages and/or inconvenience or evacuation as a result of the incident.

Chalmette Refining opposed the motion.

Over two years later, the district court held a hearing on the motion to certify the class. At the conclusion of that hearing and without any evidence being introduced, the district court orally granted Plaintiffs' motion. Fourteen days later, Chalmette Refining petitioned this court for permission to take an appeal pursuant to Rule 23(f). We granted the petition. The district court later stayed proceedings pending the resolution of this appeal.

## DISCUSSION

### III. ANALYSIS

"Recognizing the important due process concerns of both plaintiffs and defendants inherent in the certification decision, the Supreme Court requires district courts to conduct a rigorous analysis of Rule 23 prerequisites." Where the plaintiff seeks to certify a class under Rule 23(b)(3), the Rules demand "a close look at the case before it is accepted as a class action." *Amchem*. "We stress that it is the party seeking certification who bears the burden of establishing that the requirements of Rule 23 have been met."

Although class certification hearings "should not be mini-trials on the merits of the class or individual claims going beyond the pleadings is necessary, as a court must understand the claims, defenses, relevant facts, and applicable substantive law in order to make a meaningful determination of the certification issues." (citing *Castano*). The "close look" demanded by *Amchem* requires examination of both "the parties' claims and evidence." "The plain text of Rule 23 requires the court to 'find,' not merely assume, the facts favoring class certification."

The crux of this appeal lies in the legal basis for and sufficiency of evidence supporting the district court's findings of superiority and predominance under Rule 23(b)(3). Before certifying a class under Rule 23(b)(3), a court must determine that "questions of law or fact common to the members of the class predominate over any questions affecting only individual members and that a class action is superior to other available methods for fairly and efficiently adjudicating the controversy." Determining whether the plaintiffs can clear the predominance hurdle set by Rule 23(b)(3) requires district courts to consider "how a trial on the merits would be conducted if a class were certified." *Sandwich Chef of Texas, Inc. v. Reliance Nat'l Indem. Ins. Co.* This, in turn, "entails identifying the substantive issues that will control the outcome, assessing which issues will predominate, and then determining whether the issues are common to the class," a process that ultimately "prevents the class from degenerating into a series of individual trials." Determining whether the superiority requirement is met requires a fact-specific analysis and will vary depending on the circumstances of any given case.

In *Steering Committee v. Exxon Mobil Corp.,* this court found no abuse of discretion and affirmed a district court's denial of class certification in a case arising out of a fire at Exxon's Baton Rouge chemical plant. We noted that "the district court found that 'individual issues surrounding exposure, dose, health effects, and damages will dominate at the trial' and the district court concluded that 'one set of operative facts would not establish liability and that the end result would be a series of individual mini-trials which the predominance requirement is intended to prevent.'" Chalmette Refining argues that this case is nearly identical to *Steering Committee* and, as such, the class certification decision should be reversed. Chalmette Refining also relies heavily on an advisory committee note to Rule 23(b)(3), which has been cited numerous times by this court as highlighting the "relationship between predominance and superiority in mass torts." *See Castano v. American Tobacco Co.*

The district court determined that Rule 23(b)(3)'s predominance requirement was satisfied because "there is one set of operative facts that will determine liability. Plaintiffs were either on the battlefield and exposed to the coke dust or they were not. This case only deals with actual exposure and not fear of exposure. This class deals with a narrow window of exposure, in a narrow area, and to a narrow group of individuals." We hold that the district court abused its discretion by failing to afford its predominance determination the "rigorous analysis" that Rule 23 requires.

The district court did not meaningfully consider how Plaintiffs' claims would be tried. The two cases relied upon by the district court in conducting its conclusory inquiry are instructive. In *Watson v. Shell Oil,* this court affirmed a district court's decision to certify a class of over 18,000 plaintiffs seeking damages stemming from an explosion at a Shell plant. Whether

*Watson* has survived later developments in class action law—embodied in *Amchem* and its progeny—is an open question, but even in *Watson,* the district court had "issued orders detailing a four-phase plan for trial." That plan allowed the district court to adjudicate common class issues in the first phase and then later adjudicate individualized issues in other phases. In *Turner v. Murphy Oil USA, Inc.,* the district court granted class certification to a class of plaintiffs who suffered damages resulting from a post-Hurricane Katrina oil storage tank spill. Critical to the court's predominance inquiry was the fact that "Plaintiffs submitted a proposed trial plan to the Court. The plan provides for a three-phase trial." "The Court believes that the existence of a trial plan, and the potential for bifurcation of the issues of liability and damages, will address the Defendant's concern that individualized inquiries will be needed to determine damage amounts in these cases."

In stark contrast to the detailed trial plans in *Watson* and *Turner,* the district court simply concluded that "the common liability issues can be tried in a single class action trial with any individual issues of damages reserved for individual treatment." The district court failed to consider whether this case could be "streamlined using other case management tools, including narrowing the claims and potential plaintiffs through summary judgment, or facilitating the disposition of the remaining plaintiffs' claims through issuance of a Lone Pine order." *Steering Comm.* Indeed there was no "analysis or discussion regarding how it would administer the trial."

The court failed to identify "the substantive issues that will control the outcome, assess which issues will predominate, and then determine whether the issues are common to the class." Absent this analysis, "it was impossible for the court to know whether the common issues would be a 'significant' portion of the individual trials," *Castano,* much less whether the common issues predominate. The opinion is also silent as to the relevant state law that applies to Plaintiffs' claims and what Plaintiffs must prove to make their case. The district court characterized the issue of liability as "Plaintiffs were either on the battlefield and exposed to the coke dust or they were not," but this oversimplifies the issue. Chalmette Refining correctly notes that, even among the named class representatives, significant disparities exist, in terms of exposure, location, and whether mitigative steps were taken. As in *Steering Committee,* "primary issues left to be resolved would turn on location, exposure, dose, susceptibility to illness, nature of symptoms, type and cost of medical treatment, and subsequent impact of illnesses on individuals."

We must reverse because, "in its certification order, the district court did not indicate that it had seriously considered the administration of the trial. Instead, it appears to have adopted a figure-it-out-as-we-go-along approach that *Castano* criticized and that other Fifth Circuit cases have not endorsed." By failing to adequately analyze and balance the common issues against the individualized issues, the district court abused its discretion in determining that common issues predominated and in certifying the class. We do not suggest that class treatment is necessarily inappropriate. As Chalmette Refining acknowledged at oral argument, class treatment on the common issue of liability may indeed be appropriate. But our precedent demands a far more rigorous analysis than the district court conducted.

## CONCLUSION

The district court's class certification order is reversed and this case is remanded to the district court for further proceedings.

## NOLAN V. EXXON MOBIL CORP.

United States District Court for the Middle District of Louisiana, 2015.
2015 WL 2338336.

This case is before the Court on a Motion to Certify Class brought by the plaintiffs. The defendants filed an opposition, and on February 4–5, 2015, the Court held a hearing on the matter.

### BACKGROUND

The plaintiffs are a group of individuals who live near the Exxon refinery plant near the Mississippi River and Scenic Highway in Baton Rouge, Louisiana. They filed suit against Exxon Mobil Corporation (Exxon) and several associated entities; Exxon removed the case to this Court in July of 2013. In their petition, the plaintiffs allege that the refinery repeatedly failed to meet regulatory standards, resulting in numerous leaks—roughly 145—of chemicals such as, hydrogen sulfide, and they also complain about three specific incidents: a naptha leak on June 14, 2012; an HCI release on November 20, 2012; and, finally, a sulfur dioxide leak on May 23, 2012. These incidents, according to the plaintiffs, caused many physical issues and problems associated with nuisance. Their complaints included, among others, sinus irritation, post-nasal drip, odors, and persistent cough. In November of 2014, the plaintiffs filed a motion to certify class, and the Court held on a hearing on that motion on February 4–5, 2015.

### I.    PROPOSED CLASS REPRESENTATIVES

The plaintiffs' proposed class is defined as all individuals living within a certain geographic area near the refinery from June 2012 to the present, though not all proposed class representatives lived in this area for the entire time period. Before the hearing, the plaintiffs moved to remove Tonga Nolan and her minor children as class representatives, and the Court granted that motion. The remaining class representatives include residents who assert several, if not all, of the complaint's grievances—

odors, cough, sinus irritation, and lack of enjoyment of their property, for example. These proposed representatives have lived in the area for varying amounts of time, from decades to a few short months; several no longer live there but did during at least a portion of the identified time period. The proposed representatives who testified at the hearing all indicated that they were willing and able to participate in the litigation.

### A.  Representatives Absent from the Hearing

The first proposed representative, Lawrence J. Alexander (Alexander), lives at 2848 Jessamine Avenue in Baton Rouge, which is within the defined geographic area proposed by the plaintiffs. He has lived in his home for over twenty-five years, so the entirety of the class definition period, and complains of rashes, eye irritation, asthma, headaches, respiratory problems, fatigue, and memory issues. At the certification hearing, he did not testify.

Flora Dupree (Dupree) also did not testify at certification hearing. She lived at 2723 Arbutus Avenue in Baton Rouge, within the proposed class area, from before June 2012 until some point in 2013. Her symptoms included nausea, diarrhea, vomiting, burning eyes, and dizziness. Dupree also complained of the odor, indicating that it frequently overwhelmed her and forced her inside.

### B.  Representatives at the Hearing

Mary and Preston George, the next proposed class representatives, did testify at the hearing. They live at 2683 Linwood Drive in Baton Rouge, within the proposed class area, and they have lived there for the entire class definition period. Mrs. George testified that she experienced burning in her eyes, watery eyes, a cough, bronchitis, and sinus issues. She also indicated that she avoided spending too much time outside due to odors. Mr. George complained of similar health issues, though he also testified that he suffered a major vascular infection in 2013. Like his wife, Mr. George indicated that he limited his time outdoors. Further, on cross examination, Mr. George claimed that he believed the leaks and emissions from the Exxon refinery were at least partially responsible for the multiple roof replacements that his home required.

The next proposed class representative, Gussie Johnson, has lived for over three years, so the entirety of the class definition period, at 1501 Seneca Street in Baton Rouge, which is within the proposed class area. She testified at the hearing and complained of headaches, rashes, sinus issues, and being far more fatigued at home than away from home. On cross, she admitted to being a regular smoker for years until recently quitting, though she maintained that her symptoms appeared after moving to her current home. Her children and fiancé, she claimed, suffered similar symptoms. Johnson also complained about the odor, identifying it as rotten and persistent, and indicated that it made her uncomfortable having guests and hosting social events.

Keisha Smith, the last representative to testify at the hearing, lived at 2621 Lupine Avenue in Baton Rouge, within the proposed class area, from February 2013 to May 2013—not the entire class definition period. She, and her children, according to her testimony, suffered a decreased quality of life due to the odors—which prevented them from enjoying the home— and physical symptoms, which included sinus issues, watery eyes, and headaches. Ultimately, Smith broke her lease early and moved away due to her symptoms.

## II.   PROPOSED CLASS

The proposed class is defined as those who lived within a defined geographic area from June 2012 to the present. According to the plaintiffs' experts, all individuals within this area were exposed to sufficient levels of particulate matter and hydrogen sulfide to cause noticeable effects, and they all were exposed to sufficient amounts of naptha, HCl, and sulfur dioxideto suffer effects. At the hearing, the plaintiffs' experts—Dr. William Sawyer and Mr. William Auberle—focused on hydrogen sulfide, and they asserted that they compared models of exposure to a particular study indicating at what level exposure to hydrogen sulfide could produce effects for most individuals, also known as its "odor threshold." Further, according to Mr. Auberle, the modeling data accounted for other factors, such as terrain and atmospheric conditions—though he did acknowledge that he did not account for other possible sources of the chemicals, he still claimed that least 80% came from Exxon—ensuring a more precise measurement when evaluating the class area. These exposure levels, according to the plaintiffs, are also sufficient to invoke nuisance issues, such as offensive odors, within the area outlined. Although the measurements were for a twenty-four hour period of "theoretical" exposure that would not be uniform within the area, the plaintiffs' experts maintained the effects, across the board, would exist; they might be more intense in certain areas, but that would be addressed by the plaintiff's proposed bifurcated trial.

At the hearing, the defense experts challenged the findings and opinions of the plaintiffs' experts. Mr. Gale Hoffnagle, the first defense expert, testified that the odor threshold of hydrogen sulfide varies widely among individuals, and he also noted that the Louisiana Department of Environmental Quality (DEQ) air monitors showed lower concentrations in the area generally than those suggested by the plaintiffs. Their other expert, Dr. John Kind, testified that the isopleths chosen by the plaintiffs' experts were inappropriate, as there were too many variables involved, and he claimed that their methodology did not allow for measuring individual or even group exposure.

### III. BIFURCATED TRIAL PROPOSAL

Although the plaintiffs maintain that class action is appropriate, they acknowledge that questions of damages would vary among class members. To solve this, they propose a bifurcated trial where fault and causation would be addressed first, with a more individually tailored process for determining damages. Essentially, the questions of causation and fault are fit for the class action format, according to the plaintiffs, while the damages due to the harm that the class members suffered require more individual attention. The latter, damages phase would only occur if Exxon were found liable in the first stage. Exxon opposes this approach, claiming that the plaintiffs are trying to manufacture the elements necessary for a class action where they do not exist.

### ANALYSIS

Class certification requires satisfying all elements of Federal Rule of Civil Procedure 23(a) and at least one of the scenarios in Rule 23(b). When a party seeks certification of a class, it must "must affirmatively demonstrative its compliance with the Rule." The plaintiffs argue that they meet the standards for Rule 23(a) and 23(b)(3): predominance and superiority. When considering whether a case satisfies each element, "questions may be considered to the extent that they are relevant to determining whether the Rule 23 perquisites are satisfied."

### A.   Numerosity

The first element requires that the proposed class be "so numerous that joinder of all members is impractical." To establish this element, plaintiffs "must ordinarily demonstrate some evidence or reasonable estimate of the number of purported class members." The plaintiffs indicate that their chosen geographic area included over 7,000 residents as of the 2010 census, but the defense counters that the plaintiffs have not made an effort to clarify which of these individuals have experienced any of the physical symptoms or nuisance issues claimed in the suit.

Although the plaintiffs have not ascertained exactly who these individuals are, their models and data, along with public records, have pinpointed a time and area. This means their number almost certainly meets the numerosity requirement, even if all 7,000 people do not complain of symptoms or allege nuisance-related issues. The exact threshold for numerosity is not easily defined, but if even one-third of the people have complaints, their number certainly satisfies the numerosity requirement. Their complaints may differ in severity and potential cause, affecting their membership in the proposed class, but that is a predominance and/or superiority issue.

### B.   Commonality

To establish the second element, the party seeking certification must establish that "there are questions of law or fact common to the class." For commonality, that the parties suffered a common injury is important, though this "can be satisfied by an instance of the defendant's injurious conduct, even when the resulting injurious effects—the damages—are diverse." *In re Deepwater Horizon.* Significantly, these common questions of law or fact must be "central to the validity of each of the class member's claims." The plaintiffs argue that there are numerous questions of law and fact common to the parties, primarily those concerning causation and fault. For example, they argue that whether refinery leaks caused the purported high levels of hydrogen sulfide and whether Exxon was at fault in those leaks are questions common to all the claims, even if the level of damage and harm caused by the leaks may vary. Exxon claims that because there are three main events, and that these events occurred under different weather conditions, lasted for different amounts of time, and occurred at different times, commonality should fail; Exxon also applies to this logical generally, noting that beyond the three referenced leaks, there are claims for general exposure and regular, minor leaks that are also subject to different conditions depending on timing, weather, and, significantly, who among the class members was actually present at the time of exposure.

Exxon has correctly indicated that there are differences among the claims of the proposed class members, but these differences are insufficient to defeat commonality. Among the questions of law and fact common to the parties are factual questions concerning the size, timing, and location of the leaks, as well as questions concerning the ability of the leaks to cause symptoms and/or invoke nuisance concerns. The common question asserted to satisfy commonality for this class is not whether Exxon was at fault for the leaks but instead whether these leaks were sufficient to cause symptoms and nuisance issues. That question is the reason the experts plotted exposure data and testified about the threshold regarding hydrogen sulfide, and it is central to each claim, even if damages and other issues may differ among class members. Consequently, the plaintiffs have met their burden regarding Rule 23(a)(2).

### C.   Typicality

The next element that the party seeking certification must prove is that "the claims of the representatives are typical of the claims of the class. Typicality requires that "the class representative's claims have the same essential characteristics of those of the putative class," meaning the claims need to be rooted in similar actions and rely on similar legal theories. According to the plaintiffs, the representatives live and/or own property in the area—at least during the time frame—and, also like the members of the class, have a variety of health complaints and nuisance complaints due to the refinery's leaks and releases. Exxon, however, focuses on the variance in the types of harm, both health-related and property-related, that the proposed class members may have suffered.

According to the plaintiffs, the representatives allege a variety of similar complaints related to physical symptoms—including sinus issues, headaches, and eye irritation—and nuisance issues—including loss of enjoyment of property and malodorous scents. There are some differences among the representatives, but they are thorough and cover both nuisance and physical symptoms. Although the class members, like the representatives, might vary somewhat in their complaints, the essential characteristics of the claims are the same as those of the representatives. Primarily, all must prove what caused their symptoms and nuisance-related complaints, and they all must prove that Exxon is at fault for these symptoms and complaints.

### D.  Adequacy

Finally, regarding Rule 23(a), the parties seeking certification must show that "the representative parties will fairly and adequately protect the interests of the class." The adequacy requirement considers whether the attorneys are appropriately zealous and competent, whether the representatives are capable of taking an active role in pursuit of the claims, and whether there are any conflicts of interest among class members. Although Exxon does not challenge the competency of the plaintiffs' lawyers, they reiterate their belief that the claims and damages are different, and they argue that this presents potential conflicts of interests. The plaintiffs note that their lawyers are experienced in class action litigation, that the representatives testified that they would actively participate in the litigation, and that the claims are sufficiently similar to avoid any conflicts of interest.

As Exxon does not dispute the competency of the plaintiffs' lawyers, and because all representatives testified that they were willing and able to participate in the litigation, the main concern is a potential conflict of interest. Exxon argues that the differences in the claims present a potential conflict of interest, but these differences do not create a zero sum game among class members. Further, given the wide breadth of complaints that the proposed representatives have, from rashes and headaches to inability to hold outdoor gatherings or do yardwork, it is unlikely that a potential complaint of the class is uncovered. The experts did not agree on the reliability of the exposure data or that it showed enough exposure to cause symptoms, but they did not appear to disagree on the possible symptoms from exposure. This indicates that whether class members suffer sinus issues or headaches, rashes or gastrointestinal symptoms, their interests will be covered by the class representatives. Consequently, the proposed class representatives would adequately represent the interests of the class.

## II.  RULE 23(b)(3)

Rule 23(b)(3) requires that "questions of law or fact common to class members predominate over any questions affecting only individual methods, and that a class action is superior to other available methods for fairly and efficiently adjudicating the controversy." This presents a two-step inquiry: first, whether the questions of law or fact common to class members predominate; and second, whether the class action superior to other methods for addressing the controversy.

### A.  Predominance

Predominance requires that the Court identify "the substantive issues that will control the outcome, assess which issues will predominate, and then determine whether the issues are common to the class." Generally, class actions in mass tort cases are not favored, and certification should only be granted if there are "exceptional features" that justify deviating from the "general rule." In these instances, there are typically differences regarding damages, liability, and defenses with respect to those individuals affected, and this presents a high likelihood of a class action devolving into numerous individual lawsuits. Other cases also indicate similar issues with "air emission mass tort" suits due to "significant disparities in terms of exposure, location, and whether mitigative steps were taken." In a similar vein, the Louisiana Supreme Court has noted that nuisance claims tend to require individualized evaluation—particularly due to the "mere inconvenience" defense—making class actions disfavored for these claims as well.

Several cases, however, have discussed bifurcation in the context of class actions and the predominance issue. These cases agree that bifurcation cannot be used to separate common and divergent issues and create predominance; the case must satisfy predominance as a whole before any severance and trial management tinkering may occur. *See, e.g. Castano v. American Tobacco Co.* However, as the plaintiffs point out, courts have used bifurcation in class actions. *See, e.g., In re Deepwater Horizon.* The plaintiffs argue that they have demonstrated sufficient similarities such that the common issues of law and fact predominate as a whole; these common issues are, according to the plaintiffs, the factual and legal questions concerning Exxon's fault and the effects these leaks can cause on people and property. They also point to the *Deepwater Horizon* litigation to support their assertion that a court can use bifurcation to ameliorate concerns about divergent issues of law and fact regarding damages. Exxon argues, however, that this case is similar to mass tort cases where courts rejected certification, and in fact, to the extent that it is different, it differs in a way that more strongly supports denying certification: in the mass tort cases that they cited, there was one event; here, there are at least three major leaks at issue, along with numerous smaller leaks. According to Exxon, bifurcation here is inappropriate, and they distinguish *In re Deepwater Horizon* on the basis that it was a settlement class action, neutralizing potential issues with differences in questions concerning fault and causation.

The Court finds that there are some common issues of fact among the class members, but the plaintiffs have failed to establish that these questions predominate. As Exxon points out, certification is not favored in mass tort cases, and there are numerous cases rejecting certification with one event; the plaintiffs here seek certification relating to three separate leaks over an extended time period, as well as 145 smaller leaks. Here, there are simply too many variant questions as to each class member for the common issues that do exist to predominate. For example, at least one of the representatives, Gussie Johnson, smokes, so whether the purported leaks cause her symptoms, and to what extent, would be evaluated differently than those in the class who do not smoke and/or do not live with smokers. Questions like this, as well as questions of "location, exposure, dose, and susceptibility to illness" undercut the plaintiffs' case for predominance, and given the jurisprudence on mass tort cases rejecting certification with one event, this case, with three events, presents an even wider array of variant questions and issues, and certification is inappropriate.

The plaintiffs suggest that bifurcation can remedy these problems by separating damages from causation and fault, but the variant questions and issues extend well into the issues of fault and causation; this is unlike the *Deepwater Horizon* case, which involved a single event and was a settlement, leaving only damages to be decided. In that case, there were common questions such as "BP's involvement in the well design, explosion, discharge of oil, and cleanup efforts," and, the Fifth Circuit noted, " 'virtually every issue prior to damages was a common issue.' " *Deepwater Horizon*. Here, that is not the case; primarily, the influence of other factors on the alleged injuries varies among the class members. The symptoms of which the representatives complain can be caused by numerous factors, including allergies, other irritants (such as smoking), and illness. Although Exxon's fault in the three major leaks and other actions alleged may be a common question, it does not predominate over the questions of causation and damages together.

## B. Superiority

As the plaintiffs have failed to establish that the common questions of law or fact predominate, it is unnecessary to evaluate whether a class action is superior to other methods for addressing this controversy.

## CONCLUSION

Although the plaintiffs have satisfied the requirements of Rule 23(a), they have failed to establish those of Rule 23(b). Their proposed class is sufficiently numerous, there are common questions of law or fact among them, the claims of the representatives are typical of those of the class, and the class representatives and their lawyers would adequately represent the interests of the class. However, the common issues of law and fact do not predominate over other questions. There are at least three major events, along with numerous other, smaller events, and the questions of which class members were present, where within the proposed class area they were present, and for how long they were present would differ among the members of the class, and these questions would affect degree and nature of exposure. Other divergent questions exist as well, such as the role that certain habits, including smoking, have on some of the symptoms that the class members experienced.

For the foregoing reasons, the plaintiffs' Motion to Certify Class is denied. Signed in Baton Rouge, Louisiana, on May 13, 2015.

# B. LITIGATION CLASSES APPROVED

## TURNER V. MURPHY OIL USA, INC.

United States District Court for the Eastern District of Louisiana, 2006.
234 F.R.D. 597.

Before the Court is the Plaintiffs' Motion for Class Certification. The Court received evidence and argument regarding this motion in a two-day hearing that commenced on January 12, 2006. For the following reasons, Plaintiffs' Motion for Class Certification is hereby granted.

### I.   FACTUAL AND PROCEDURAL BACKGROUND

These twenty-seven consolidated class actions filed on behalf of several thousand people claiming damages arise from an incident in St. Bernard Parish, Louisiana, that occurred during the week following the landfall of Hurricane Katrina in 2005. On September 3, 2005, Defendant Murphy Oil USA, Inc. notified the federal government that an oil spill had been detected at their Meraux Refinery in St. Bernard Parish. According to Defendant, approximately 25,110 barrels of crude oil escaped from a 250,000-barrel above-ground storage tank on Murphy Oil's property. Some of this oil traveled into the neighborhoods surrounding the refinery. Plaintiffs are homeowners and business owners in St. Bernard Parish who claim they have suffered damage as a result of the oil spill.

Since the spill, Defendant Murphy Oil has worked with the Environmental Protection Agency and Louisiana Department of Environmental Quality (LDEQ) to assess the scope of the damage and to recover the oil that was spilled. Additionally, Murphy has developed a "settlement zone" and has undertaken a massive settlement program with residents of the area near the spill. Murphy has also begun cleanup and remediation efforts in public areas and for homeowners who have settled their claims with Murphy. In addition, the EPA has designated its own "oil-plume perimeter" which delineates the EPA's findings on oil contamination in the neighborhood. The EPA further classifies the oil contamination as either heavy, medium, or light within the perimeter. The EPA revised its initial oil spill boundary in early December 2005, and cautioned that the boundary was subject to change depending upon ongoing sampling and testing in the area.

The first suit of these consolidated class actions was filed on September 9, 2005. In separate Orders dated October 4 and October 5, 2005, this Court granted Plaintiffs' Motion to Consolidate Cases and provided that all future cases would be automatically consolidated. On October 12, 2005, the Court designated Plaintiffs' and Defendant's Liaison Counsel and established Plaintiffs' Executive and Steering Committees to manage the litigation. Plaintiffs subsequently petitioned the Court for supervision of Murphy Oil's settlement program, and their motion was granted in part on November 10, 2005. The Court restricted Murphy's communications with putative class members regarding their settlement program.

At the request of the Court, Plaintiffs and Defendant jointly compiled an Administrative Master Complaint, which was filed on November 28, 2005. This complaint consolidates all claims raised by Plaintiffs in the various pending lawsuits. In December 2005, Defendant filed several motions to dismiss portions of the master complaint, and the Court granted those motions in part.

On November 22, 2005, Plaintiffs urged the Court to set a hearing date for their Motion for Class Certification. Plaintiffs seek certification of Counts I through V and Count VII of the Administrative Master Complaint, as well as their Prayer for Relief and damage requests. These claims are as follows: Count I (negligence pursuant to Louisiana Civil Code article 2315), Count II (absolute liability pursuant to Louisiana Civil Code articles 667 and 2315), Count III (negligence, intentional conduct, and strict liability pursuant to common law), Count IV (strict liability pursuant to Louisiana Civil Code articles 2317 and 2322), Count V (nuisance and trespass pursuant to Louisiana Civil Code articles 3421 and 3425), and Count VII (groundwater contamination pursuant to Louisiana Revised Statutes Section 30:2015.1). Plaintiffs seek the following types of damages under these counts: actual and punitive damages pursuant to common law (Count III), damages or payments for remediation of groundwater (Count VII), compensatory damages and attorneys' fees for injuries including contamination of property, cost of homogeneous restoration, loss of use of property, increased living expenses, extended displacement costs, diminution of property value, ecological damages, loss of income, lest profits, lost business opportunity, inconvenience, mental anguish, emotional distress, bodily harm, past and future medical expenses, and injunctive relief.

Plaintiffs have further identified six potential class representatives. The potential class representatives allege that all of these properties were contaminated by the Murphy Oil spill. Four class representatives allege personal injuries from returning to their properties, and three allege business and/or rental losses as a result of the spill.

The class certification hearing was set for January 12, 2006. The parties engaged in discovery, conducted testing, and took depositions for class certification purposes. A two-day hearing was held at which counsel presented their evidence for and against class certification. The Court now considers the Plaintiffs' Motion.

## II.  PLAINTIFF'S MOTION FOR CLASS CERTIFICATION

### A.  Standard of Review

The proponents of the class bear the burden of demonstrating that the case is appropriate for class treatment. Class certification is soundly within the district court's discretion, and this decision is essentially a factual inquiry. The class certification decision should not reach the merits of the plaintiffs' claims. *Castano v. Am. Tobacco Co.* However, in some cases it is necessary for a district court to go beyond the pleadings to understand the claims, defenses, substantive law, and relevant facts in order to make a meaningful certification decision. The district court must make specific findings regarding how the case satisfies or fails to satisfy the requirements of Rule 23 of the Federal Rules of Civil Procedure.

### B.  Class Certification

Plaintiffs seek certification of their claims as a class action under Rule 23(a) and 23(b)(3) of the Federal Rules of Civil Procedure. Thus, read in combination, Rule 23(a) and 23(b)(3) provide six requirements for a group of claims to be certified as a class action—numerosity, commonality, typicality, adequacy, predominance, and superiority. These requirements shall be addressed in turn.

### 1.  Numerosity—Rule 23(a)(1)

To demonstrate numerosity, Plaintiffs must establish that joinder is impracticable through "some evidence or reasonable estimate of the number of purported class members." "Although the number of members of any proposed class is not determinative of whether joinder is impracticable," the Fifth Circuit has generally set the threshold of 100 to 150 people as satisfying the numerosity requirement. *Mullen v. Treasure Chest Casino LLC.*

The Agency for Toxic Substances and Disease Registry (ATSDR), a federal agency providing health consultations on the Murphy Oil spill, estimated in December 2005 that approximately 1,800 homes and an as-yet-undetermined number of other structures have been affected by the oil spill. Currently, there are 113 named plaintiffs in this litigation. However,

Defendant argues that its Settlement Program has greatly reduced the number of potential class members, and that joinder of the existing plaintiffs is not impracticable.

Contrary to Defendant's assertions, Rule 23(a)'s numerosity requirement is clearly met in this litigation. The number of impacted properties alone exceeds 1,800, and individual property owners are too numerous to make joinder feasible in this case. Also, the affected St. Bernard Parish residents are still dispersed throughout the country after Hurricane Katrina: it appears that very few, if any, have returned to the parish to live. The geographical displacement of potential plaintiffs further justifies the Court's finding that joinder would be impracticable in this case.

### 2.    Commonality—Rule 23(a)(2)

Rule 23(a)(2) requires that there be issues of law or fact common to the class. The commonality requirement is satisfied if at least one issue's resolution will affect all or a significant number of class members. There is a low threshold for commonality, and the fact that some plaintiffs have different claims or require individualized analysis does not defeat commonality.

Defendant argues that, particularly from the standpoint of damages, Plaintiffs' claims do not meet the Rule 23 commonality requirement. According to Defendant, Plaintiffs' homes and businesses received varying degrees of damage from the hurricane, and received different amounts of oil contamination. In addition, Defendant argues that the proof required for Plaintiffs' personal injury and mental anguish claims is such that their claims do not share common issues of law or fact: each Plaintiff learned of the damage at different times, returned to the area at different times, and suffered different levels of exposure to the crude oil. Murphy Oil argues that these differences compel the Court to find that the commonality requirement has not been met.

The Court disagrees with Defendant. Rule 23(a)(2) only requires that one issue's resolution will affect all or most of the potential class members. That requirement is clearly met in this case, which involves a single accident. These are just a few of the central issues that will affect all or most of the class members: whether Murphy Oil failed to properly maintain Tank 250–2, whether Murphy Oil had adequate hurricane safety plans and whether those plans were carried out during Hurricane Katrina, and whether the affected area will experience any long-term contamination. While Plaintiffs' claims will involve some individualized determinations regarding the amount of damage suffered, if any, there are enough common issues regarding Defendant's liability that class treatment would be appropriate under Rule 23.

### 3. Typicality—Rule 23(a)(3)

Rule 23(a)(3) requires that the claims of the class representatives are typical of the class's claims or defenses. Again, the threshold for typicality is low: class representatives must show similarity between their legal and remedial theories and the theories of the rest of the class. Typicality does not require that the claims of the class are identical, but rather that they share the same essential characteristics—a similar course of conduct, or the same legal theory.

Plaintiffs have identified six class representatives. All six allege either business or residential property damage as a result of the discharge of oil from Murphy's refinery, and several allege personal injury. Upon reviewing the various complaints in these consolidated cases, it is clear that the class representatives' claims and alleged damages are fairly similar, if not identical, to the claims of other plaintiffs. The theories of liability among property owners in the affected area are alike: they are suing for negligence, strict liability, and absolute liability under the Louisiana Civil Code, among other claims. In addition, the claims of the class representatives share essential characteristics in this case because they are based upon the same series of events—the natural disaster that befell St. Bernard Parish, the alleged negligence of the Defendant that led to the oil spill, and the remediation that has occurred since the spill. There may be differences in the types of damages, depending on the degree of contamination and depending upon whether the property was used as a residence or business. However, these differences do not relate to the Plaintiffs' legal theories regarding liability and causation. Again, the consolidated cases involve a single accident, and central issues of fact and law are shared among the group of Plaintiffs in the affected area. Because the class representatives share legal theories and the same course of conduct with other plaintiffs, the Court finds that the typicality requirement of Rule 23(a) is met.

### 4. Adequacy of Representation—Rule 23(a)(4)

Rule 23(a)(4) demands that the named class representatives fairly and adequately represent the claims of the other class members. There can be differences between the position of class representatives and other class members so long as these differences do not "create conflicts between the named plaintiffs' interests and the class members' interests." A district court should evaluate whether the class representatives have a sufficient stake in the outcome of the litigation, and whether the class representatives have interests antagonistic to the unnamed class members. In addition, the district court should inquire into the zeal and competence of the class representatives' counsel and into the class representatives' willingness to take an active role in the litigation and to protect the interests of absentees.

None of the six proposed class representatives appear to have interests that would be counter to those of other plaintiffs in this matter. Rather, the six class representatives' claims appear to be fairly representative of those raised by the plaintiffs in these cases, including personal property losses, business losses, personal injuries, and emotional distress. Moreover, all six class representatives have executed affidavits stating that they intend to vigorously prosecute their claims on behalf of the proposed class. In addition, counsel for the six class representatives have filed affidavits stating the number of clients they represent in this litigation: these affidavits satisfy the Court that counsel are committed enough to these cases so that they will litigate them zealously. (Plaintiffs' Exhibit P88). The Court finds that the six class representatives can fairly and adequately represent a proposed class of plaintiffs in this matter under Rule 23(a)(4).

5. *Predominance—Rule 23(b)(3)*

Rule 23(b)(3) requires that the class share common issues of law or fact that predominate over the questions affecting individual class members. In general, in order to predominate, common issues must form a significant part of individual cases. Specifically, a district court should consider how the cases would proceed to trial, that is, whether any cases would require individual trials on particular issues. *See Castano* (finding that certification was inappropriate where individual trials would be necessary to determine an element of the plaintiffs' fraud claims).

This element of the Rule 23 analysis requires the Court to examine each of Plaintiffs' claims individually, as the Court must determine how these claims would be tried. It is important that the same substantive law will apply to all Plaintiffs' claims in these cases: this is not a case in which the varying laws of different states create the need for state subclasses or individual trials. All of Plaintiffs' claims except one, Count III, arise under Louisiana law.

It is also important to note that, at least as far as the Plaintiffs' property damage claims are concerned, Plaintiffs' claims share large areas of fact in common. For example, it is safe to assume that few, if any, of the Plaintiffs were present at the time of the oil spill. All of the homes at issue were damaged by the same natural event, Hurricane Katrina, prior to the spill. Moreover, Plaintiffs' claims all have in common the circumstances surrounding the leak in Tank 250–2—how the leak physically occurred, what steps Murphy took or might have taken to contain the oil, and what steps Murphy took or might have taken to prevent the leak.

Defendant argues that the oil did not spread uniformly throughout the affected area, and that different homes in the area received differing degrees, if any, of oil contamination. However, the central factual basis for all of Plaintiffs' claims is the leak itself—how it occurred, and where the oil went. There is a large area of factual overlap in the Plaintiffs' causes of action.

Moreover, on January 19, 2006, Plaintiffs submitted a proposed trial plan to the Court. The plan provides for a three-phase trial. Phase One would concern common issues of liability for compensatory damages and the amount of damages for trial plaintiffs, Phase Two would address common issues regarding punitive damages, and Phase Three would involve compensatory damages for remaining members of the Plaintiff Class. As will be discussed, this trial plan will need revision in light of the instant ruling. However, the Court believes that the existence of a trial plan, and the potential for bifurcation of the issues of liability and damages, will address the Defendant's concern that individualized inquiries will be needed to determine damage amounts in these cases. The Fifth Circuit has repeatedly upheld the decisions of district courts to bifurcate class action trials into liability and damages phases. *See Mullen* (affirming a bifurcated plan and citing other instances of bifurcated class action trials).

6.    *Superiority—Rule 23(b)(3)*

Under Rule 23(b)(3), a district court must evaluate four factors to determine whether the class action format is superior to other methods of adjudication: the class members' interest in individually controlling their separate actions, the extent and nature of existing litigation by class members concerning the same claims, the desirability of concentrating the litigation in the particular forum, and the likely difficulties in class management.

Defendant argues that this element of the Rule 23 analysis is not met because Murphy's private settlement program is a superior method of resolving this dispute. However, the merits of Murphy's settlement program aside, Murphy's argument confuses the superiority standard under Rule 23. The analysis is whether the class action format is superior to other methods of *adjudication,* not whether a class action is superior to an out-of-court, private settlement program. When evaluated under those terms, the Court finds that the class action format would be superior to consolidation of individual cases in this matter. Both Murphy and Plaintiffs have expressed a desire for quick resolution of these cases, and the class action format could streamline this litigation. In addition, there appears to be little existing litigation of these claims outside of the lawsuits filed in this Court, so class certification would act to centralize these proceedings. Also, given the strains on the state judicial system after Hurricane Katrina, the federal forum appears to be preferable to state court at this time. Although the concerns raised by the Fifth Circuit in *Castano* with regard to the economic pressure placed on a litigant to settle are present here as they are in any mass tort litigation, the Court believes the pressures on the Defendant created by class certification would not be extreme in this case. Murphy Oil is already conducting an extensive settlement program with residents of St. Bernard Parish: class certification will not greatly exacerbate the pressure upon Murphy to settle these claims. The benefits of the class action format in case management and speed of resolution support class certification in this case. Accordingly, the Court finds that the superiority requirement of Rule 23(b)(3) has been met.

In summary, the Court finds that the requirements of Rule 23(a) and Rule 23(b)(3) have been met in these cases. As such, the pending consolidated cases shall be certified as a class action. The Court now must address the issues of class counsel, and, most importantly, the boundaries of the affected area.

### D.  Definition of Class to Be Certified—The Affected Area

One of the unwritten requirements of Rule 23 is that the class to be certified must be "adequately defined and clearly ascertainable." A precise definition is essential to identify those entitled to notice and those bound by a judgment.

In this case, in the fall of 2005, Murphy Oil designated an area to the west of the Meraux refinery that it has used for settlement purposes. This area is smaller than, but overlaps significantly with, the oil-plume perimeter established by the EPA. Plaintiffs have asked the Court to certify a much-larger expanse that covers areas farther to the west and east of the refinery.

Defendant has argued that the Court's only options are to certify Plaintiffs' proposed boundary or not to certify a class at all. However, the Fifth Circuit has stated recently that district courts enjoy discretion to "limit or modify class definitions to provide the necessary precision." That court recognized that class definition is a process of "ongoing refinement and give-and-take," and, as such, a district court's role is to define a precise class.

After reviewing the evidence and expert opinions offered by the parties, the Court elects to designate a class boundary somewhat smaller than that suggested by the Plaintiffs, and somewhat larger than Defendant's settlement zone.

Given that the Court cannot reach the merits of the dispute, the Court expresses no opinion upon when the oil leak into the surrounding neighborhoods stopped.

It is important to note that the above-stated class definition does not end the Court's involvement in this issue. The fact that a particular plaintiff resides outside the class area does not preclude that plaintiff from bringing an individual suit. Conversely, the fact that a plaintiff resides in the class area does not automatically entitle him or her to recovery. Also, the Court reserves the right to expand or reduce the class area, depending upon the results of further testing and discovery. The Court has endeavored to certify this area based upon the strongest evidence presented by the parties, given the ongoing testing and investigation in St. Bernard Parish.

### III. CONCLUSION—CERTIFICATION ORDER

Having considered the evidence, memoranda, and arguments of counsel at the January 12, 2006 class certification hearing, and, for the reasons stated above,

It is ordered, adjudged, and decreed that the prerequisites to a class action set forth in Rule 23(a) are satisfied, inasmuch as the class is so numerous that joinder of all plaintiffs is impracticable, there are questions of law and fact common to the class, the claims and defenses of the class representatives are typical of the claims of the class as a whole, and the class representatives for plaintiffs will fairly and adequately protect the interests of the proposed class.

## BUTLER V. SEARS, ROEBUCK AND CO.
United States Court of Appeals for the Seventh Circuit, 2013.
727 F.3d 796.

The Supreme Court has vacated our judgment in this class action suit and remanded the case to us for reconsideration in light of *Comcast Corp. v. Behrend.*

This suit, a diversity suit based on the breach-of-warranty laws of six states, is really two class actions because the classes have different members and different claims, though both arise from alleged defects in Kenmore brand Sears washing machines sold in overlapping periods beginning in 2001 and 2004. One class action complains of a defect that causes mold (the "mold claim"), the other of a defect that stops the machine inopportunely (the "control-unit claim"). The district court denied certification of the class complaining about the defect that causes mold and granted certification of the class complaining about the defect that causes the sudden stoppage. The plaintiffs asked us to reverse the denial, and we did so; Sears asked us to reverse the grant, and we refused.

Sears asks us to remand the case to the district court for a fresh ruling on certification in light of *Comcast,* or alternatively to deny certification in both class actions. The plaintiffs ask us to reinstate our judgment, granting certification in both.

Sears' request for a remand to the district court is based to a significant degree on new evidence that has come to light since the district court ruled on certification in September 2011. But the case remains pending in the district court, and, as Sears itself emphasizes, rulings on certification in class action suits are tentative and can be revisited by the district court as changed circumstances require. Fed.R.Civ.P. 23(c)(1)(C).

What could it mean to remand a case to a court before which the case is pending?

The question presented by the Supreme Court's remand is one of law—whether the *Comcast* decision cut the ground out from under our decision ordering that the two classes be certified. There is no point in delaying our decision on remand to await consideration by the district court of factual issues that may be moot on the basis of the *Comcast* decision.

The claim in the mold class action is that because of the low volume and temperature of the water in the front-loading machines compared to its volume and temperature in the traditional top-loading machines, they don't clean themselves adequately and as a result mold accumulates that emits bad odors. Traditional household cleaners do not eliminate the molds or the odors. Roughly 200,000 of these Kenmore-brand machines are sold each year and there have been many thousands of complaints of bad odors by the machines' owners.

Sears contends that Whirlpool (the manufacturer of the washing machines) made a number of design modifications, and as a result different models are differently defective; Sears does not contend that any of the design changes eliminated the odor problem, only that they diminished it. The basic question presented by the mold claim—are the machines defective in permitting mold to accumulate and generate noxious odors?—is common to the entire mold class, although damages are likely to vary across class members (the owners of the washing machines). A class action is the efficient procedure for litigation of a case such as this, a case involving a defect that may have imposed costs on tens of thousands of consumers, yet not a cost to any one of them large enough to justify the expense of an individual suit. A determination of liability could be followed by individual hearings to determine the damages sustained by each class member. The parties probably would agree on a schedule of damages based on the cost of fixing or replacing class members' mold-contaminated washing machines. In that event the hearings would be brief; indeed the case would probably be quickly settled.

We added that if it turned out as the litigation unfolded that there were large differences in the mold problem among the differently designed washing machines, the district judge might decide to create subclasses (and for the further reason that Sears' liability might vary across the states embraced by the class action because of differences among those states' laws), but that this possibility was not an obstacle to certification of a single mold class at the outset.

Sears argued that most members of the plaintiff class had not experienced any mold problem. But if so, we pointed out, that was an argument not for refusing to certify the class but for certifying it and then entering a judgment that would largely exonerate Sears—a course it should welcome, as all class members who did not opt out of the class action would be bound by the judgment.

The second class action involves a computer device that gives instructions to a washing machine's various moving parts. In 2004 the company that supplied these control units in Kenmore washing machines altered its manufacturing process in a way that caused some control units mistakenly to "believe" that a serious error had occurred and therefore to order the machine to shut down, though actually there had been no error. The plaintiffs allege that Sears knew about the problem yet charged each owner of a defective machine hundreds of dollars to repair the central control unit, and that after the defect was corrected in 2005, Sears continued to ship machines containing the earlier-manufactured, defective units.

The principal issue in the control-unit class action is whether the control unit is indeed defective. The only individual issues concern the amount of harm to particular class members, and we pointed out that it was more efficient for the principal issue—common to all class members— to be resolved in a single proceeding than for it to be litigated separately in hundreds of different trials. But we added that, as with the mold class action, the district court would want to consider whether to create different subclasses of the control unit class for the different states because of different state laws.

So how does the Supreme Court's *Comcast* decision bear on the rulings, just summarized, in our first decision?

*Comcast* holds that a damages suit cannot be certified to proceed as a class action unless the damages sought are the result of the class-wide *injury* that the suit alleges. *Comcast* was an antitrust suit, and the Court said that "if the plaintiffs prevail on their claims, they would be entitled only to damages resulting from reduced over-builder competition, since that is the only theory of antitrust impact accepted for class-action treatment by the District Court. It follows that a model purporting to serve as evidence of damages in this class action must measure only those damages attributable to that theory. If the model does not even attempt to do that, it cannot possibly establish that damages are susceptible of measurement across the entire class for purposes of Rule 23(b)(3)." "A methodology that identifies damages *that are not the result of the wrong*" is an impermissible basis for calculating class-wide damages. "For all we know, cable subscribers in Gloucester County may have been overcharged because of petitioners' alleged elimination of satellite competition (*a theory of liability that is not capable of classwide proof*)." And on the next page of its opinion the Court quotes approvingly from Federal Judicial Center, REFERENCE MANUAL ON SCIENTIFIC EVIDENCE, that "the first step in a damages study is the translation of the *legal theory of the harmful event* into an analysis of the economic impact *of that event*." None of the parties had even challenged the district court's ruling that class certification required "that the damages resulting from the antitrust violation were measurable 'on a class-wide basis' through use of a 'common methodology.'"

Unlike the situation in *Comcast*, there is no possibility in this case that damages could be attributed to acts of the defendants that are not challenged on a class-wide basis; all members of the mold class attribute their damages to mold and all members of the control-unit class to a defect in the control unit.

Sears argues that *Comcast* rejects the notion that efficiency is a proper basis for class certification, and thus rejects our statement that "predominance" of issues common to the entire class, a requirement of a damages class action under Rule 23(b)(3), "is a question of efficiency." But in support of its argument Sears cites only the statement in the *dissenting* opinion in *Comcast* that "economies of time and expense" favor class certification, a statement that the majority opinion does not contradict. Sears is wrong to think that anything a dissenting opinion approves of the majority *must* disapprove of.

Sears compares the design changes that may have affected the severity of the mold problem to the different antitrust liability theories in *Comcast*. But it was not the existence of multiple theories in that case that precluded class certification; it was the plaintiffs' failure to base all the damages they sought on the antitrust impact—the injury—of which the plaintiffs were complaining. In contrast, any buyer of a Kenmore washing machine who experienced a mold problem was harmed by a breach of warranty alleged in the complaint.

Furthermore and fundamentally, the district court in our case, unlike *Comcast*, neither was asked to decide nor did decide whether to determine damages on a class-wide basis. As we explained in *McReynolds v. Merrill Lynch, Pierce, Fenner & Smith, Inc.*, distinguishing *Wal-Mart Stores, Inc. v. Dukes*, a class action limited to determining liability on a class-wide basis, with separate hearings to determine—if liability is established—the damages of individual class members, or homogeneous groups of class members, is permitted by Rule 23(c)(4) and will often be the sensible way to proceed.

But if we are right that this is a very different case from *Comcast*, why did the Supreme Court remand the case to us for reconsideration in light of that decision? The answer must lie in the emphasis that the majority opinion places on the requirement of predominance and on its having to be satisfied by proof presented at the class certification stage rather than deferred to later stages in the litigation. The Court doesn't want a class action suit to drag on for years with the parties and the district judge trying to figure out whether it should have been certified. Because the class in *Comcast* was (in the view of the majority) seeking damages beyond those flowing from the theory of antitrust injury alleged by the plaintiffs, the possibility loomed that "questions affecting only individual members" of the class would predominate over questions "common to class members," rather than, as Rule 23(b)(3) requires, the reverse.

Sears argued passionately in its petition for certiorari that we had failed to make a sufficiently rigorous inquiry into predominance in allowing the two classes (the mold class and the control-unit class) to be certified. The petition was filed before the Supreme Court issued its decision in *Comcast,* and the Court may have felt that Sears should be allowed to amend its submission in light of *Comcast* and submit its amended argument to us in the first instance.

Sears thinks that predominance is determined simply by counting noses: that is, determining whether there are more common issues or more individual issues, regardless of relative importance. That's incorrect. An issue "central to the validity of each one of the claims" in a class action, if it can be resolved "in one stroke," can justify class treatment. *Wal-Mart Stores, Inc. v. Dukes*. That was said in the context of Rule 23(a)(2), the rule that provides that class actions are permissible only when there are issues common to the members of the class (as of course there are in this case). But predominance requires a qualitative assessment too; it is not bean counting. In *Amgen Inc. v. Connecticut Retirement Plans & Trust Funds* the Court said that the requirement of predominance is not satisfied if "individual questions overwhelm questions common to the class," and in *Amchem Products, Inc. v. Windsor* it said that the "predominance inquiry tests whether proposed classes are sufficiently cohesive to warrant adjudication by representation." And in *In re Inter-Op Hip Prosthesis Liability Litigation* we read that "common issues need only predominate, not outnumber individual issues." Or as we put it in *Messner v. Northshore University Health System*, "Under the district court's approach, Rule 23(b)(3) would require not only common evidence and methodology, but also common results for members of the class. That approach would come very close to requiring common proof of damages for class members, which is not required. To put it another way, the district court asked not for a showing of common questions, but for a showing of common answers to those questions. Rule 23(b)(3) does not impose such a heavy burden."

It would drive a stake through the heart of the class action device, in cases in which damages were sought rather than an injunction or a declaratory judgment, to require that every member of the class have identical damages. If the issues of liability are genuinely common issues, and the damages of individual class members can be readily determined in individual hearings, in settlement negotiations, or by creation of subclasses, the fact that damages are not identical across all class members should not preclude class certification. Otherwise defendants would be able to escape liability for tortious harms of enormous aggregate magnitude but so widely distributed as not to be remediable in individual suits. As we noted in *Carnegie v. Household Int'l., Inc.* "the more claimants there are, the more likely a class action is to yield substantial economies in litigation. It would hardly be an improvement to have in lieu of this single class 17 million suits each seeking damages of $15 to $30. The *realistic* alternative to a class action is not 17 million individual suits, but zero individual suits, as only a lunatic or a fanatic sues for $30." The present case is less extreme: tens of thousands of class members, each seeking damages of a few hundred dollars. But few members of such a class, considering the costs and distraction of litigation, would think so meager a prospect made suing worthwhile.

There is a single, central, common issue of liability: whether the Sears washing machine was defective. Two separate defects are alleged, but remember that this class action is really two class actions. In one the defect alleged involves mold, in the other the control unit. Each defect is central to liability. Complications arise from the design changes and from separate state warranty laws, but can be handled by the creation of subclasses. These are matters for the district judge to consider in the first instance, and Sears will be able to present to her the evidence it's obtained since the district judge ruled on certification almost two years ago.

One last point. Shortly before our original decision, the Sixth Circuit had upheld the certification of a single mold class in a case identical to this one (the defendant, Whirlpool, was the manufacturer of the defective Kenmore-brand washing machines), except that it did not involve the other claim in our case, the control unit claim. *In re Whirlpool Corp. Front-Loading Washer Products Liability Litigation*. Whirlpool sought certiorari, and the Supreme Court granted it, vacated the court of appeals' judgment, and remanded the case, just as in our case. On remand the Sixth Circuit, denying as we have done the defendant's motion to remand to the district court, and interpreting *Comcast* as we do, concluded that the requirement of predominance had been satisfied. The concordance in reasoning and result of our decision and the Sixth Circuit's decision averts an inter-circuit conflict.

Our judgment of November 13, 2012, is hereby reinstated.

## C. LIMITED FUND AND PUNITIVE DAMAGE CLASS ACTIONS

### IN RE SIMON II LITIG.

United States Court of Appeals, Second Circuit, 2005.
407 F.3d 125.

Defendant-appellant tobacco companies appeal from the September 19, 2002, order and October 22, 2002, supplemental memorandum and order of the United States District Court for the Eastern District of New York, Jack B. Weinstein, Judge, which certified a nationwide non-opt-out class of smokers seeking only punitive damages under state law for defendants' alleged fraudulent denial and concealment of the health risks posed by cigarettes. Having granted permission to appeal pursuant to Federal Rule of Civil Procedure 23(f), we must decide whether the district court properly certified this class under Rule 23(b)(1)(B).

Defendant-appellants challenge the propriety of certifying this action as a limited fund class action pursuant to a "limited punishment" theory. The theory postulates that a constitutional limit on the total punitive damages that may be imposed for a course of fraudulent conduct effectively limits the total fund available for punitive awards.

We hold that the order certifying this punitive damages class must be vacated because there is no evidence by which the district court could ascertain the limits of either the fund or the aggregate value of punitive claims against it, such that the postulated fund could be deemed inadequate to pay all legitimate claims, and thus plaintiffs have failed to satisfy one of the presumptively necessary conditions for limited fund treatment under *Ortiz v. Fibreboard Corp.*

While we expressly limit our holding to the conclusion that class certification is incompatible with *Ortiz,* the circumstances warrant some discussion of whether the order is incompatible with the Supreme Court's intervening decision in *State Farm Mutual Automobile Insurance Co. v. Campbell.* As we discuss it appears that the order fails to ensure that a potential punitive award in this action would bear a sufficient nexus, and be both reasonable and proportionate, to the harm or potential harm to the plaintiff class and to the general damages to be recovered, as required by *State Farm.*

We vacate the district court's certification order and remand for further proceedings.

## FACTS AND PROCEDURAL HISTORY

The district court certified the class proposed by the Third Amended Consolidated Class Action Complaint filed on July 26, 2002.

Plaintiffs sought certification to determine defendants' fraudulent course of conduct and total punitive damages liability to a class consisting of those who suffered from, or had died from, diseases caused by smoking. Plaintiffs did not seek a class-wide determination or allocation of compensatory damages or seek certification of subclasses. The certification followed extensive briefing and argument, not to mention numerous iterations of both the complaint and the proposed class.

A

The industry conspiracy prompting this litigation is described briefly in the allegations of the Third Amended Complaint and in considerable detail in the Certification Order. We will simply excerpt a relevant portion of the district court's description of the allegations:

> Plaintiffs allege, and can provide supporting evidence, that, beginning with a clandestine meeting in December 1953 at the Plaza Hotel in New York City among the presidents of Philip Morris, R.J. Reynolds, American Tobacco, Brown & Williamson, Lorillard and U.S. Tobacco, tobacco companies embarked on a systematic, half-century long scheme to (a) stop competing with each other in making or developing less harmful cigarettes; (b) continue knowingly and willfully to engage in misrepresentations and deceptive acts by, among other things, denying knowledge that cigarettes caused disease and death and agreeing not to disseminate harmful information showing the destructive effects of nicotine and tobacco consumption; (c) shut down research efforts and suppress medical information that appeared to be adverse to the Tobacco Companies' position that tobacco was not harmful; (d) not compete with respect to making any claims relating to the relative health-superiority of specific tobacco products; and (e) to confuse the public about, and otherwise distort, whatever accurate information about the harmful effects of their products became known despite their "efforts to conceal such information."

In 1999, a group of cigarette smokers filed a class action captioned *Simon v. Philip Morris Inc.*, (*Simon I*), on behalf of 20-pack-year smokers. They sought a determination of both compensatory and punitive damages for personal injury or wrongful death caused by lung cancer. Plaintiffs limited the class to 20-pack-year smokers because their medical and scientific experts had determined that, for that class, general and specific causation merged, and both could be proved class-wide without individual trials.

The *Simon I* class moved for certification in April 2000. Without ruling on the certification motion, the district court issued an order on April 18, 2000, consolidating *Simon I* and seven other tobacco-related suits pending before it "for purposes of settlement and for no other purpose." Following a discussion in chambers among counsel concerning possible settlement, the district court issued an order on May 9, 2000, that raised questions for continued discussion, including whether there was a limited fund for punitive damages, given the actual and potential individual and class action punitive damages sought, and whether a final punitive award, rather than multiple repeated punitive awards, would be equitable.

On September 6, 2000, individual and representative plaintiffs in ten existing actions filed a consolidated class action complaint, *In re Simon (II) Litigation (Simon II)*, on behalf of a proposed comprehensive nationwide class seeking, pursuant to Fed.R.Civ.P. 42(a) and (b) and Fed.R.Civ.P. 21, a joint trial of the common questions of law and fact determining defendants' total liability for punitive damages on all claims and theories of relief. Plaintiffs also sought declaratory judgment to determine and provide for the equitable allocation of a punitive damages award. The complaint listed six "Class Claims Supporting and/or Serving As Compensatory Predicates for Punitive Damages," namely, a claim for fraud or fraudulent concealment, a claim of civil conspiracy, a claim for unjust enrichment, restitution and disgorgement, a claim for violations of New York or other states' consumer protection laws, and two federal civil RICO claims.

On December 22, 2000, plaintiffs filed the First Amended Consolidated Class Action Complaint in *Simon II* and moved for class certification. The district court had denied the pending class certification motion in *Simon I* by order filed November 6, 2000, stating that "even though *Simon I* is a viable class action," denial of certification "would better preserve court resources to certify the broader *Simon II* class for trial."

Following an April 30, 2002, status conference, plaintiffs decided to narrow *Simon II* to include only the three cigarette smoker class actions and accordingly filed the Second Amended Consolidated Class Action Complaint on May 28, 2002. In the Second Amended Complaint, plaintiffs asserted a total of seven "Class Claims": four for product liability (design defect, failure to warn, negligent design, and negligent failure to warn), one for fraudulent concealment or conduct, one for conspiracy, and another for unjust enrichment. Balancing the approaches taken in *Simon I* and initially in *Simon II,* the amended and renewed motion for class certification of May 28, 2002, sought certification on behalf of two classes: a class of 20-pack-year smokers with lung cancer to be certified for all purposes, including compensatory and punitive damages, and a broader disease-based class solely for purposes of determining class-wide punitive damages. The first was to be an opt-out class under Rule 23(b)(3) and the latter a non-opt-out punitive damages class under Rule 23(b)(1)(B). Following briefing and oral argument, the district court reserved decision and suggested class counsel revise their class proposal.

During a July 2, 2002, hearing on the certification motion, the district court expressed reservations about plaintiffs' proposal to limit a smokers' class to persons with lung cancer only or to persons with a 20-pack-year history of cigarette smoking only. The district court indicated that it was not inclined to certify a portion of the class for compensatory damages purposes, but that the majority of the class could be certified for punitive damages only.

On July 26, 2002, Plaintiffs filed the Third Amended Complaint and an accompanying amended and renewed motion for class certification, which precipitated the Certification Order at issue here. Plaintiffs sought certification of a single class of smokers suffering from various diseases which the medical community attributes to smoking, including 20-pack-year smokers with lung cancer, for the sole purpose of determining defendants' total liability for punitive damages.

B

Upon considering the class proposed by plaintiffs' Third Amended Complaint and the motion for certification, the district court certified a punitive damages non-opt-out class pursuant to Rule 23(b)(1)(B). The class definition included current and former smokers of defendants' cigarettes who are U.S. residents, or who resided in the U.S. at time of death, and were first diagnosed between April 9, 1993, and the date of dissemination of class notice, with one or more of the following diseases: lung cancer, laryngeal cancer, lip cancer, tongue cancer, mouth cancer, esophageal cancer, kidney cancer, pancreatic cancer, bladder cancer, ischemic heart disease, cerebrovascular heart disease, aortic aneurysm, peripheral vascular disease, emphysema, chronic bronchitis, or chronic obstructive pulmonary disease. The class excluded persons who had obtained judgment or settlement against any defendant, persons against whom defendants had obtained judgment, members of the certified class in *Engle v. R.J. Reynolds Tobacco Co.*, No., persons who reasonably should have realized they had the disease prior to April 9, 1993, and persons whose diagnosis or reasonable basis for knowledge predated tobacco use.

The district court determined that the class action would proceed in three stages. In the first stage, a jury would make "a class-wide determination of liability and estimated total value of national undifferentiated compensatory harm to all members of the class." The sum of compensatory harm would "not be awarded but will serve as a predicate in determining non-opt-out class punitive damages." The same jury would determine compensatory awards, if any, for individual class representatives, although the class itself did not seek compensatory damages. In the second stage, the same jury would determine whether defendants engaged in conduct that warrants punitive damages. In the third stage, the same jury would determine the amount of punitive damages for the class and decide how to allocate damages on a disease-by-disease basis. The court would then distribute sums to the class on a pro-rata basis by disease to class members who submit appropriate proof. Any portion not distributed to class members would be "allocated by the court on a *cy pres* basis to treatment and research organizations working in the field of each disease on advice of experts in the fields." The order specified that the jury would apply New York law according to conflicts of laws principles, and reiterated that the court was not presented with and did not rule upon a compensatory class. The district court noted that although plaintiffs chose the more limited course in pursuing a punitive class only, certification "for determination of compensatory damages to be distributed using an appropriate matrix would be possible and might be desirable in coordination with the class now certified."

## II.

### DISCUSSION

#### A. Standard of Review

We note that this case raises issues of first impression insofar as this Circuit has never squarely passed on the validity of certifying a mandatory, stand-alone punitive damages class on the proposed "limited punishment" theory.

#### C. Standards for Maintaining a Class Action Under Rule 23(b)(1)

Plaintiffs in this case sought certification under Rule 23(b)(1)(B), for which the relevant inquiry is whether separate actions by individual members of the class create a risk that individual adjudications would as a practical matter dispose of other class members' interests in punitive damages or substantially impair or impede their ability to protect their interests.

Suits under Rule 23(b)(1) are often referred to as "mandatory" class actions because they are not subject to the Rule 23(c) provision for notice to absent class members or the opportunity for potential class members to opt out of membership as a matter of right. *See Ortiz v. Fibreboard Corp.*

#### D. Limited Fund Class Action Based on the "Limited Punishment" Theory

The district court, in certifying the punitive damages class under Rule 23(b)(1)(B), cited recent scholarship and court decisions that "have concluded that the theory of limited punishment supports a punitive damages class action." "Under this theory," the district court stated, "the limited fund involved would be the constitutional cap on punitive damages, set forth in *BMW v. Gore*, and related cases."

The premise for this theory is that there is a constitutional due process limitation on the total amount of punitive damages that may be assessed against a defendant for the same offending conduct. Whether the limitation operates to prejudice the respective parties, it seems, turns on two contrary assumptions. For the potential plaintiff, piecemeal individual actions or successive class actions for punitive damages would operate to his disadvantage if punitive awards in earlier-filed suits subtract from the constitutional total and thereby reduce or preclude punitive damages for future claimants. This proposition assumes that courts identify and successfully enforce the postulated total limit, and that plaintiffs have an interest in a ratable portion of the permissible damages. For defendants, piecemeal individual or successive class actions would pose a threat of excessive punishment in violation of their due process rights if successive juries assess awards that exceed the limit of what is necessary for deterrence and retribution. This proposition, to the contrary, assumes that early suits exhaust or exceed the constitutional limit and successive trial or appellate courts fail to enforce it by either reducing or barring awards. It is not clear whether the theory supposes that successive individual awards, which considered alone may be constitutionally permissible if they are reasonable and proportionate to the given plaintiff's harm and bear a sufficient nexus to that harm, may reach a point where the goals of punitive damages have been served, and successive victims of the same tortious course of conduct by the tortfeasor should be unable to recover punitive damages.

The notion of a constitutional cap on total allowable aggregate punitive damages awards, or on the number of times punitive awards can be made, has never been squarely articulated by the Supreme Court, but is said to derive from its precedents regarding punitive damages. In the Supreme Court's most recent punitive damages decision, *State Farm Mutual Automobile Insurance Co. v. Campbell,* Justice Kennedy, writing for the majority, reiterated what the Court's precedents had made clear: "While States possess discretion over the imposition of punitive damages, it is well established that there are procedural and substantive constitutional limitations on these awards. The Due Process Clause of the Fourteenth Amendment prohibits the imposition of grossly excessive or arbitrary punishments on a tortfeasor." The Court pointed to concerns voiced in earlier cases: "To the extent an award is grossly excessive, it furthers no legitimate purpose and constitutes an arbitrary deprivation of property." *State Farm* (quoting Justice O'Connor's dissent in *Haslip* ("Punitive damages are a powerful weapon. Imposed wisely and with restraint, they have the potential to advance legitimate state interests. Imposed indiscriminately, however, they have a devastating potential for harm. Regrettably, common-law procedures for awarding punitive damages fall into the latter category.")).

"Punitive damages have long been a part of traditional state tort law," and Congress has provided for punitive damages in a number of statutes. *Haslip.* While compensatory damages "are intended to redress the concrete loss that the plaintiff has suffered by reason of the defendant's wrongful conduct," punitive damages, "which have been described as 'quasi-criminal,' operate as 'private fines' intended to punish the defendant and to deter future wrongdoing." *Cooper Indus.*; *see also BMW v. Gore* (punitive damages may further a "State's legitimate interests in punishing unlawful conduct and deterring its repetition"). In addition to serving the goals of punishment and deterrence, punitive damages have been "justified as a 'bounty' that encourages private lawsuits seeking to assert legal rights."

Despite the long-recognized possibility that defendants may be subjected to large aggregate sums of punitive damages if large numbers of victims succeed in their individual punitive damages claims, *see, e.g., Roginsky v. Richardson-Merrell, Inc.* ("We have the gravest difficulty in perceiving how claims for punitive damages in such a multiplicity of actions throughout the nation can be so administered as to avoid overkill."), the United States Supreme Court has not addressed whether successive individual or class action punitive awards, each passing constitutional muster under the relevant precedents, could reach a level beyond which punitive damages may no longer be awarded.

### E.    The Traditional "Limited Fund" Class Action Under Ortiz v. Fibreboard Corp.

This brings us to appellants' chief argument—that class certification under Rule 23(b)(1)(B) is precluded by the Supreme Court's decision in *Ortiz v. Fibreboard Corp.,* because the proposed class plaintiffs have failed to demonstrate what the Supreme Court identified as the "presumptively necessary" conditions for certification in limited fund cases. Although *Ortiz* considered a set of circumstances quite unlike those in the instant case when it reviewed the certification of a Rule 23(b)(1)(B) mandatory settlement class on a limited fund theory, it identified, in the historical antecedents to Rule 23, the characteristic conditions that justified binding absent class members. It summarized those characteristics as "a 'fund' with a definitely ascertained limit, all of which would be distributed to satisfy all those with liquidated claims based on a common theory of liability, by an equitable, pro rata distribution." Given the presumptive necessity of these characteristics, "the burden of justification rests on the proponent of any departure from the traditional norm."

The first characteristic, a fund "with a definitely ascertained limit," usually entailed a situation where "the totals of the aggregated liquidated claims and the fund available for satisfying them, set definitely at their maximums, demonstrate the inadequacy of the fund to pay all the claims." "The concept driving this type of suit was insufficiency, which alone justified the limit on an early feast to avoid a later famine." The second characteristic required that "the whole of the inadequate fund was to be devoted to the overwhelming claims." In other words, the defendant with the inadequate fund "had no opportunity to benefit himself or claimants of lower priority by holding back on the amount distributed to the class," thus ensuring that the limited fund case "did not give a defendant a better deal than *seriatim* litigation would have produced." The third characteristic required that "the claimants identified by a common theory of recovery were treated equitably among themselves. The cases assume that the class will comprise everyone who might state a claim on a single or repeated set of facts, invoking a common theory of recovery, to be satisfied from the limited fund as the source of payment."

While neither the Rule itself, nor the Advisory Notes accompanying it, purports to delineate the outer limits of the Rule's application in the particular subset of "limited fund" cases, the Supreme Court in *Ortiz* has read the "limited fund" case as being moored to the Rule's historical antecedents, describing the classic actions as involving, for instance, "claimants to trust assets, a bank account, insurance proceeds, company assets in a liquidation sale, proceeds of a ship sale in a maritime accident suit, and others." In these cases, "equity required absent parties to be represented, joinder being impractical, where individual claims to be satisfied from the one asset would, as a practical matter, prejudice the rights of absent claimants against a fund inadequate to pay them all."

The *Ortiz* Court sounded a number of cautionary notes, expressing its extreme hesitation to apply Rule 23 in ways that would have been beyond the contemplation of the drafters of the Advisory Committee Notes. ("the Advisory Committee looked cautiously at the potential for creativity under Rule 23(b)(1)(B), at least in comparison with Rule 23(b)(3)," and was "consciously retrospective with intent to codify pre-Rule categories under Rule 23(b)(1), not forward looking as it was in anticipating innovations under Rule 23(b)(3)").

Keeping in mind that the Court has thus counseled "against leniency in recognizing mandatory limited fund actions in circumstances markedly different from the traditional paradigm," we hold that the first fundamental requisite for limited fund treatment is lacking here, because there was no "evidence on which the district court may ascertain the limit and the insufficiency of the fund."

The proposed fund in this case, the constitutional "cap" on punitive damages for the given class's claims, is a theoretical one, unlike any of those in the cases cited in *Ortiz,* where the fund was either an existing res or the total of defendants' assets available to satisfy claims. The fund here is-in essence-postulated, and for that reason it is not easily susceptible to proof, definition, or even estimation, by any precise figure. It is therefore fundamentally unlike the classic limited funds of the historical antecedents of Rule 23.

Not only is the upper limit of the proposed fund difficult to ascertain, but the record in this case does not evince a likelihood that any given number of punitive awards to individual claimants would be constitutionally excessive, either individually or in the aggregate, and thus overwhelm the available fund.

Without evidence indicating either the upper limit or the insufficiency of the posited fund, class plaintiffs cannot demonstrate that individual plaintiffs would be prejudiced if left to pursue separate actions without having their interests represented in this suit, as Rule 23(b)(1)(B) would require.

Defendant-appellants also argue that there are two ways in which the class certified fails to exhibit the third presumptively necessary characteristic of a limited fund case, namely, that "the claimants identified by a common theory of recovery were treated equitably among themselves." First, they argue that the class is fatally under-inclusive, and, second, they argue that the Certification Order fails to provide for equitable treatment among class members. The *Ortiz* Court found that these same two issues undermined the requirement of equity among class members for the settlement class in that case. Because we de-certify the class on other grounds, we need not resolve the equity question, which would be relevant only if the class were going forward as certified.

### F.   Punitive Awards After State Farm Mutual Automobile Life Ins. Co. v. Campbell

While our holding in this case rests exclusively on the conclusion that certification is incompatible with *Ortiz,* we have an additional concern that warrants some discussion. It seems that a punitive award under the circumstances articulated in the Certification Order is likely to run afoul of the Supreme Court's admonitions in *State Farm,* a decision handed down several months after the Certification Order issued. *See State Farm Mut. Auto. Ins. Co.* In certifying a class that seeks an assessment of punitive damages prior to an actual determination and award of compensatory damages, the district court's Certification Order would fail to ensure that a jury will be able to assess an award that, in the first instance, will bear a sufficient nexus to the actual and potential harm to the plaintiff class, and that will be reasonable and proportionate to those harms.

In *State Farm,* the Supreme Court held that the state appellate court erred in reinstating a $145 million punitive damages award that the jury had assessed for an automobile liability insurer's bad faith refusal to settle an accident claim on behalf of the Campbells, its insureds. The Court held that the excessive punitive award violated due process where compensatory damages were $1 million and evidence of out-of-state conduct unrelated to the insureds' specific harm permitted the jury to condemn State Farm for its nationwide policies. Although the Court was considering an award in an individual, not a class, action, it noted that punishment on any basis that does not have a nexus to the specific harm suffered by the plaintiff "creates the possibility of multiple punitive damages awards for the same conduct; for in the usual case nonparties are not bound by the judgment some other plaintiff obtains." In addressing the punitive award to the Campbells, the Court stated, "we have been reluctant to identify concrete constitutional limits on the ratio between harm, or potential harm, to the plaintiff and the punitive damages award. We decline again to impose a bright-line ratio which a punitive damages award cannot exceed." Recognizing that "there are no rigid benchmarks," the Court noted that greater ratios may be warranted "where a particularly egregious act has resulted in only a small amount of economic damages" or "where the injury is hard to detect or the monetary value of noneconomic harm might have been difficult to determine." "In sum," the Court concluded, "courts must ensure that the measure of punishment is both reasonable and proportionate to the amount of harm to the plaintiff and to the general damages recovered."

Furthermore, with respect to the evidence to be considered at the punitive damages stage, *State Farm* indicates that a jury could not consider acts of as broad a scope as the district court in this case anticipated. The Certification Order in this case provides:

> This class action is intended to cover all punitive damages nationwide. This could include punitive damages due to outrageous conduct by defendants towards non-class members. The punitive function served by this certified class could be utilized in part for persons outside the class as, for example, passive breathers of the smoke exuded by others, those with diseases other than those represented by this certified class, and future diseased persons. Allowing the jury to consider evidence of damage to others at this stage in setting the punitive award is appropriate in a nationwide class action where a portion of the harmful behavior may not be correlatable with class members.

*State Farm* made clear that conduct relevant to the reprehensibility analysis must have a nexus to the specific harm suffered by the plaintiff, and that it could not be independent of or dissimilar to the conduct that harms the plaintiff. Harmful behavior that is not "correlatable" with class members and the harm or potential harm to them would be precluded under *State Farm*.

### G.  Defendant-Appellants' Other Arguments

Defendant-appellants also contend the Certification Order runs afoul of the Rules Enabling Act, 28 U.S.C. § 2072(b), because, on a number of counts, it alters or abridges the parties' substantive rights. Defendant-appellants challenge the imposition of class-wide liability for punitive damages in the absence of individualized proof of the elements of the causes of action on which punitive damages would be predicated. They also claim that the trial plan to resolve individual compensatory claims in separate follow-on actions to the class-wide punitive damages determination would subject the facts underlying the compensatory claims to re-examination by successive juries in violation of the Seventh Amendment.

## III.
### CONCLUSION

The proposed class having failed to satisfy the threshold requirements for certification set forth in *Ortiz* and Rule 23(b)(1)(B), we must vacate the district court's certification order and remand for further proceedings.

## IN RE AMTRAK TRAIN DERAILMENT IN PHILADELPHIA, PA. ON MAY 12, 2015
United States District Court for the Eastern District of Pennsylvania, 2016.
2016 WL 1359725.

Before this Court is plaintiffs Mark and Nicola Tulks' motion for preliminary settlement class certification pursuant to Federal Rule of Civil Procedure 23(b)(1)(B). For the reasons discussed below, this motion is denied.

### I. FACTUAL BACKGROUND

On May 12, 2015, at approximately 9:21 P.M., Amtrak Train No. 188 suddenly and violently derailed near Frankford Junction, in Philadelphia, Pennsylvania. At the time of the derailment, the train was travelling in excess of 100 miles per hour as it approached a curve subject to a fifty-mile-per-hour speed limit. The train was carrying 238 people. As a result of the derailment, eight people perished, twenty to twenty-five people sustained catastrophic injuries, and numerous others suffered a range of injuries.

Soon after the derailment, lawsuits against the National Railroad Passenger Corporation (Amtrak) were filed in multiple federal jurisdictions. To bring order to the litigation, a group of plaintiffs sought the formation of an MDL. On October 13, 2015, the Judicial Panel on Multidistrict Litigation established MDL 2654 as the procedural framework for coordinating all pre-trial proceedings arising from the derailment. The JPML assigned the MDL to this Court.

At the time of this order, the parties estimate lawsuits on behalf of roughly 119 passengers have been filed, including all wrongful-death claims and all catastrophic-injury claims. Amtrak has acknowledged that the train was travelling above the allowable speed, and has admitted liability for compensatory damages arising from the incident.

Plaintiffs' claims in this matter are subject to a liability cap imposed by the Amtrak Reform and Accountability Act of 1997. At the time of the derailment, the liability cap was $200 million. On December 4, 2015, President Obama signed the Fixing America's Surface Transportation Act, which raised the cap to $295 million as it applies to this derailment. Amtrak has settled certain smaller claims, but has not resolved the claims in their entirety, and has not agreed that the aggregate compensatory damages for this matter exceed the $295 million liability limit.

## II.   PROCEDURAL BACKGROUND

Plaintiffs Mark and Nicola Tulk, through their counsel Evan K. Aidman, initially filed a complaint against Amtrak with no class claims. On August 6, 2015, the Tulks filed a separate class action. In the class complaint, the Tulks contend that this action is properly maintained as a class action under Rule 23(b)(1)(A), 23(b)(1)(B), and 23(b)(3), and request damages in the amount of one billion dollars. Despite these claims, the Tulks did not file any objections to the ongoing MDL proceedings. On February 2, 2016, after MDL 2654 had been established, the Tulks filed a motion to certify a mandatory, non-opt out, settlement class pursuant to Federal Rule of Civil Procedure 23(b)(1)(B).

The Tulks move for an order certifying a Settlement Class pursuant to Rule 23(b)(1)(B), "for the purpose of facilitating class-wide settlement discussions" with Amtrak. The certification is styled as preliminary. They argue that certification is appropriate because it will allow for class-wide negotiations, prevent individual plaintiffs from seeking to diminish the proceeds available for all claims, and permit notification to all potential class members who may be unaware of their potential claims. The Tulks maintain that if settlement is reached, plaintiffs will receive approximately $50 to $70 million more of the $295 million available, as a result of reduced legal fees. If the settlement class is preliminarily certified, the Tulks request that the Court temporarily enjoin putative class members from pursuing individual claims, to eliminate the risk that the limited funds available for class-wide settlement will be reduced. If settlement is reached, the parties will notify the Court and seek approval of the settlement and final class certification, with any evidentiary showing necessary to support such motions. If no settlement is reached, the Tulks state that the certification order will be automatically vacated, and the parties will retain all their rights with respect to class certification and the merits of the actions.

As the Tulks' motion was filed only in their individual docket, the Court ordered that all parties to the MDL respond to the motion for class certification. A consolidated brief in opposition to the motion was filed on behalf of counsel from 80 of the then 88 cases coordinated in the MDL. Consolidated Plaintiffs vigorously oppose certification and argue that the Tulks have failed to establish the predicates for a class action under Rule 23(b)(1)(b) and 23(a) and, further, that the MDL procedure is appropriate and sufficient to currently manage this litigation. Defendant Amtrak also filed a response deferring to the Court and plaintiffs as to whether certification is the most fair and efficient way to resolve this case. No plaintiffs filed a response in support of the Tulks' motion.

On March 14, 2016, the Tulks re-filed their initial class certification motion on the MDL docket, and then filed a reply in support of settlement class certification. In response to this Court's Order directing the parties to furnish recommendations for the structure and management of the litigation, the Tulks also filed recommendations that further flesh out how this litigation would proceed if class certification were preliminarily approved. The Tulks' motion is now ripe for decision.

III. DISCUSSION

a.   Class Settlement Certification

The Federal Rules of Civil Procedure do not expressly provide for certification of a class for settlement purposes only. In *GM Trucks,* the Third Circuit extensively reviewed class action law and the use of class action settlements, and found that the certification of a settlement class can be appropriate, provided that the court ensures that the class meets the requirements of Rule 23. This model, in which the plaintiffs and defendants involved in the litigation first reach a settlement before moving for class certification, is ubiquitous in settlement class certifications. The standard procedure in these instances is for courts to 1) provisionally certify the class, such that proper notifications can be disseminated to the class at large, and then 2) hold a final fairness hearing in order to issue a final class certification and approve the settlement. Thus, in the normal course of events, "by the time the court considers certification, the defendant has essentially stipulated to the existence of the class requirements since it now has an interest in binding an entire class with its proffered settlement." *GM Trucks.*

The posture of the Tulks' motion diverges from this model. The Tulks cite to language in *GM Trucks* to support their position that a class may be provisionally certified so that parties can negotiate a settlement, and then proceed with formal certification However, the Tulks cite that portion of the *GM Trucks* which explains typical class certification procedure, in which a class complaint is filed, certification is delayed pending settlement discussions amongst the parties, and only after the success of the negotiations does the court conditionally certify the class for settlement purposes. That is not the case here. *GM Trucks* does not support the Tulks' assertion that their motion is routine. In fact, the Tulks' motion glosses over its atypical nature and does not cite a single case where a settlement class was certified before a settlement had been negotiated, or even formally discussed. In essence, the Tulks' motion does not seek settlement class certification, as it is traditionally defined and used, but rather requests preliminary class certification in order to conduct settlement negotiations. Instead of coming to the Court with a proposed resolution of the case, the Tulks seek the Court's imprimatur, via designation as class counsel for the settlement class, in order to attempt to negotiate a class-wide settlement with Amtrak.

b.    Certification Standard

To successfully certify a class, the class must satisfy the prerequisites of Federal Rule of Civil Procedure 23(a) and one of the three subparts of Rule 23(b). *See In re Hydrogen Peroxide Antitrust Litig.* As discussed above, the standards for class certification apply equally to settlement class certification. *See GM Trucks* ("We do not believe that Rule 23 authorizes separate, liberalized criteria for settlement classes.").

The parties contest the appropriate standard for certification under these atypical circumstances. The Consolidated Plaintiffs argue that the *In re Hydrogen Peroxide* standard—requiring "rigorous analysis" with proof of each element by a "preponderance of the evidence"—is appropriate in this matter. The Tulks disagree. While their initial certification motion was not explicit as to its request for preliminary certification or the appropriate standard of review, the Tulks have clarified that they are seeking preliminary settlement class certification. The Tulks maintain that preliminary certification is governed by a standard similar to that used by courts in granting "conditional certification" under the pre-2003 version of Rule 23. The Tulks go on to say that "based on the pleadings, materials available, this Court's prior judicial experience, and undisputed facts, this Honorable Court is *permitted* to make a determination that the requirements of Rule 23 have been met, and grant preliminary class certification for purposes of facilitating settlement negotiations with Amtrak on a global basis." Tulks'

The Court agrees with the Tulks that a settlement class can be preliminarily certified based on a less rigorous analysis than that necessary for final certification. Courts may conduct a less demanding review at the preliminary certification stage.

However, this does not cure the problems with the settlement class proposed here. A review of the case law makes clear, however, that although courts may conduct a less rigorous analysis, the party moving for class certification must still demonstrate that the requirements of Rule 23 are met. Furthermore, in all instances of preliminary class settlement certification this Court has reviewed, the courts approving a preliminary settlement class are doing so after extensive settlement discussions have occurred and the parties have reached a proposed resolution. Finally, the Court is mindful of the Supreme Court's admonition that "the moment of certification requires 'heightened attention,' to the justifications for binding the class members." *Ortiz v. Fibreboard Corp.* (quoting *Amchem Prods., Inc. v. Windsor*). "This is so because certification of a mandatory settlement class, however provisional technically, effectively concludes the proceeding save for the final fairness hearing." That concern is implicated here, as preliminary approval would include an injunction preventing other plaintiffs from pursuing individual claims.

## IV. ANALYSIS

At this stage of the litigation, the Tulks have not shown that the proposed settlement class satisfies Rule 23(b)(1)(B). Meeting the requirements of Rule 23(b) is necessary for class certification whether preliminary or final. Accordingly, the Court will not address whether the requirements of Rule 23(a) are met here.

### a.    Rule 23(b)(1)(B)

Rule 23(b)(1)(B) provides for the certification of a class action if the requirements of Rule 23(a) are met, and in these types of actions, "the shared character of rights claimed or relief awarded entails that any individual adjudication by a class member disposes of, or substantially affects, the interests of absent class members." *Ortiz*. The limited fund class action is one of the "classic examples" or "traditional varieties" of these representative actions, "aggregating claims made by numerous persons against a fund insufficient to satisfy all claims."

The Tulks contend that their motion to certify a settlement class is appropriate under Rule 23(b)(1)(B) because the FAST Act's liability cap establishes a limited fund. The motion postulates that the statutory cap on Amtrak's liability for this derailment effectively limits funds available here for awards of compensatory and punitive damages. In the Tulks' view, the limited fund is $295 million—the potential, aggregated sum of Amtrak's liability for all individual death, personal injury, and property damage claims, and punitive damage claims.

### i.    The Supreme Court's Decision in *Ortiz*

The starting point for analysis of Rule 23(b)(1)(B) is the Supreme Court's ruling in *Ortiz*. The Supreme Court distilled the history of limited fund class actions into three characteristics "presumptively necessary" to ensure that the mandatory Rule 23(b)(1)(B) settlement class device is limited to appropriate circumstances. *Ortiz*. The three benchmarks are:

(1)   "The totals of the aggregated liquidated claims and the fund available for satisfying them, set definitely at their maximums, demonstrate the inadequacy of the fund to pay all the claims."

(2)   "The whole of the inadequate fund [is] to be devoted to the overwhelming claims."

(3)   "The claimants identified by a common theory of recovery [are] treated equitably among themselves."

Accordingly, only when these characteristics are present, is it justified to bind class members under Rule 23(b)(1)(B). Actions that depart from these traditional norms bear the burden of justification, and "the greater the leniency in departing from the historical limited fund model, the greater the likelihood of abuse."

ii.   Existence of Inadequate Fund

The first characteristic requires a determination of 1) the amount of damages in the case, and 2) the upper limit of the fund in question. Unlike the fund presented in *Ortiz*, the upper limit here is fixed: the $295 million liability cap set by Congress. The key question is whether the total amount of damages will exceed that amount. The Tulks argue, citing *Ortiz*, that this Court "can 'make a sufficiently reliable determination of the probable total' " based on "prior judicial experience." Tulks' The Tulks point to the deaths and serious injuries in the case, along with plaintiffs' claims to punitive damages, as sufficient to allow a determination that the maximum value of the claims exceeds $295 million. The Tulks' projections are not based on evidence as to any particular victims in this case.

At this stage of the litigation, the Court cannot possibly make such a finding. Unlike every other request for settlement class certification this Court has seen, the contemplated settlement is based on speculation. The Tulks' motion provides no evidence, outside of the basic facts of this case, to support their contention that the damages here will exceed the $295 million limit. Calculating the damages in this case is not a simple process, unlike cases which involve liquidated damages. Amtrak has stated that they are in the process of disseminating and completing damages questionnaires as a first step to assess the injuries suffered by each plaintiff. This process is ongoing, and no reasonable estimate of the damages is possible at this juncture. Therefore, without any basis to find that damages exceed the statutory limit, the Court will not resort to broad speculation. *See In re Diet Drugs* (denying class certification and finding Rule 23(b)(1)(B) not met where the court had "no reasonable method by which to calculate, or even estimate with comfortable certainty the total value of plaintiffs' claims").

iii.   Fund Wholly Devoted to Claims

The second necessary component requires that the settlement fund at issue be wholly "devoted to the overwhelming claims." In essence, this aspect reflects the purpose of a limited fund action, which is to ensure "that the class as a whole is given the best deal" and the defendant is not given "a better deal than *seriatim* litigation would have produced."

The Tulks argue that any settlement they negotiate would exhaust all available funds, and that the money saved by the potential settlement will result in a better deal for the plaintiffs. As explained above, without evidence of the value of the claims, any finding by this Court that the putative settlement would exhaust the fund and be the best deal for the victims is hypothetical and inappropriate at this time. This is especially true given the potential inequities that granting class certification could have on the litigation, as will be more fully discussed below.

### iv.  Equitable Treatment

The third and final necessary element of Rule 23(b)(1)(B) actions is that "the claimants identified by a common theory of recovery are treated equitably among themselves." Primary equity considerations are the inclusiveness of the class and the fairness of distributions to those within it. The Tulks argue that these factors are met here, because as compared to seriatim litigation, settlement would result in more equitable treatment for the class. They also emphasize that through class treatment, all passengers on the train would be included and protected in any settlement they reach. The Tulks' proposed allocation plan describes the process they would use to reach an equitable result for the victims in this litigation.

As there is no actual plan before the Court, we cannot reasonably assess whether the proposed settlement class would meet this element of Rule 23(b)(1)(B). While the allocation plan filed by the Tulks includes specific details about their envisioned settlement plan and provides insight into what the Tulks seek, it only represents one half of the equation. All parties, including Amtrak and the other plaintiffs, have a voice in settlement. A unilateral plan for attempting to reach settlement is not a settlement agreement. Further, because the nature of this litigation does not allow for simple pro rata distribution of any existing fund, which is often customary in limited settlement fund class actions, the Court is even less inclined to assume that this factor will be met. *See Ortiz* ("Fair treatment is characteristically assured by straightforward pro rata distribution of the limited fund."). Thus, the Tulks have not shown that their proposed settlement class satisfies Rule 23(b)(1)(B).

### b.  Management of the Litigation

A fundamental aspect of class action practice and MDL proceedings is the potential for courts and parties to work together to manage litigation in the most efficient and fair way possible. This ruling is consistent with Federal Rule of Civil Procedure 23, which is derived from equity practice, and those origins remain relevant today. *See Amchem.* The Supreme Court has recognized that "the certification of a nationwide class, like most issues arising under Rule 23, is committed in the first instance to the discretion of the district court." This discretion is reflected in the language of the rules, and ties into "the inherent power of a trial court to manage and control its own pending litigation." In their role, district court judges are entrusted to ensure that class action certification is appropriate, and in harmony with the Federal Rules of Civil Procedure. In addition, a court presiding over an MDL proceeding has "broad discretion to determine the course and scope of pretrial proceedings." At this juncture, the Court finds that the MDL procedures are preferable.

Of primary importance to this Court is facilitating a swift and efficient process that will work towards a fair and appropriate result for the victims of this derailment. Prior judicial experience has shown that when the parties to an action work cooperatively together, better results are achieved. Only one represented party is in favor of settlement class certification, the Tulks. Counsel for nearly all of the plaintiffs in the MDL have expressed vehement opposition to their motion. Any current grant of class certification would likely ensure that this litigation will drag on, raising legal costs and reducing the funds available to the victims in this matter.

The present MDL structure provides a good starting point for putting this litigation on the path to resolution. Through the MDL structure, the parties and the Court may pursue a myriad of procedural options designed to ensure that a fair process takes place, including establishing a framework to promote settlement discussions at any time during the course of the litigation. While the Tulks have brought up many important points about the potential savings a class action would bring, pushing the litigation in that direction is premature and currently unnecessary. Here, the individual personal injury claims have not been proven or liquidated, and it is impossible to make any findings as to the aggregate value of those claims. The existing MDL procedures are not only adequate to assess these claims, the MDL procedures are the superior method. If the claims are sent into mediation, the Court may never have the record or ability to determine their value or the limit and insufficiency of the fund. Would-be class plaintiffs and their counsel have not satisfied any of the requirements for an exceptional mandatory class action.

In fact, the Court has observed that the necessary predicates to efficient resolution are already underway between the parties. The absence of any dispute over liability renders this litigation one primarily concerned with determining each plaintiff's individual damages and ensuring the fairest and most just result under the FAST Act. In this vein, Amtrak and counsel for plaintiffs have already developed a damages questionnaire that is being used to estimate the amount of damages outstanding in this action. As it stands, the Court believes it may be possible for a settlement to be achieved, avoiding the prospect of seriatim litigation. Preliminarily certifying a settlement class at this juncture would stop the forward progression being made, break the bonds between plaintiffs and their chosen counsel, and elevate one particular counsel above all others in this matter—with the obvious side effect of ensuring greater attorney's fees for those counsel representing the Tulks. Thus, in addition to not meeting the requirements of Rule 23, preliminary settlement class certification is not the best method to move this litigation forward.

## V.   CONCLUSION

For the foregoing reasons, plaintiffs Mark and Nicola Tulks' Motion for Settlement Class Certification is denied.

# CHAPTER 8

---

# MASS TORT SETTLEMENT CLASS ACTIONS POST-*AMCHEM* AND *ORTIZ*

■ ■ ■

## A. SETTLEMENT CLASSES REPUDIATED

### IN RE KATRINA CANAL LAND BREACHES LITIG.

United States Court of Appeals for the Fifth Circuit, 2010.
628 F.3d 185.

Appellants, objecting members of a proposed settlement class of plaintiffs damaged or injured by Hurricanes Katrina or Rita, seek review of the district court's certification of a limited fund mandatory class under Federal Rule of Civil Procedure 23(b)(1)(B) and its approval of a final class settlement. We hold that the Supreme Court's opinion in *Ortiz v. Fibreboard Corp.* requires decertification of the mandatory class because the settlement fails to provide a procedure for distribution of the settlement fund that treats class claimants equitably amongst themselves. We further hold that the settlement is not fair, reasonable and adequate because its proponents fail to show that the class members will receive some benefit in exchange for the divestment of their due process rights in a mandatory class settlement. We therefore reverse.

### I. BACKGROUND

In the wake of Hurricanes Katrina and Rita, a plethora of lawsuits were filed against public and private entities by residents of the greater New Orleans area who were harmed by the catastrophic flooding caused by levee and floodwall failures. These complaints were consolidated in the District Court for the Eastern District of Louisiana as *In re Katrina Canal Breaches Consolidated Litigation,* and divided for case management purposes into several categories. This appeal involves the "Levee" and "MRGO" categories.

Following the dismissals of various defendants, the Levee and MRGO plaintiffs sought certification of a limited fund mandatory settlement class under Rule 23(b)(1)(B) and concomitant approval of a settlement with the defendant levee districts, their respective Boards of Commissioners, and their insurer, St. Paul Fire and Marine Insurance Company. The putative class consisted of all Persons (a) who at the time of Hurricane Katrina and/or Hurricane Rita (i) were located, present or residing in the Hurricane Affected Geographic Area (Jefferson, Orleans, Plaquemine, and St.

Bernard Parishes), or (ii) owned, leased, possessed, used or otherwise had any interest in homes, places of business or other immovable or movable property on or in the Hurricane Affected Geographic Area, and (b) who incurred any losses, damages and/or injuries arising from, in any manner related to, or connected in any way with Hurricane Katrina and/or Hurricane Rita and any alleged Levee Failures and/or waters that originated from, over, under or through the Levees under the authority and/or control of all or any of the Levee Defendants.

The class was further divided into three geographical subclasses corresponding to the particular levee defendant that allegedly caused its damages. A claimant could be a member of more than one subclass by virtue of some overlap among these three areas.

Under the relevant terms of the settlement, the class would receive roughly $21 million—representing the limits of the available insurance proceeds, plus interest—in exchange for releasing all claims against the settling defendants related to the hurricanes and/or levee failures. The levee districts themselves would not contribute to the settlement. The settlement fund would be administered and distributed by a special master under the court's supervision. Finally, class counsel would waive their attorneys' fees, while retaining the right to seek "enhanced costs."

The district court issued a preliminary order of certification for settlement purposes, to which Appellants—two groups of dissenting class members—objected. First, Appellants argued that the proposed class did not qualify as a Rule 23(b)(1)(B) class under the standards established by the Supreme Court in *Ortiz v. Fibreboard Corp.* Second, Appellants averred that certifying a mandatory settlement class in a mass tort damages action violates due process. Finally, Appellants opposed the settlement on the grounds that the content of the notice was deficient and misleading, and that the settlement itself provided no benefit to the class while allowing counsel to seek an enhancement of costs.

Following the subsequent class certification and settlement fairness hearing, the district court certified the class and approved the settlement. In certifying the class, the court first determined that the Rule 23(a) prerequisites for all class actions had been met. The court next analyzed whether the class complied with the "stringent standards" for 23(b)(1)(B) classes set by the Supreme Court in *Ortiz*. Noting that the Supreme Court had explicitly refrained from deciding the constitutionality of a mandatory mass tort class certification, the district court held that certification under Rule 23(b)(1)(B) was proper because all three *Ortiz* requirements—a fund demonstrably insufficient to satisfy all claims, devotion of that fund to the payment of claims, and intra-class equity in distribution of the fund—had been met. Finally, the district court approved the settlement based on its determination that notice was reasonable and that the settlement was fair, adequate, and reasonable under this circuit's six-factor test: the court found no evidence of fraud or collusion behind the settlement; litigation would be immensely complex; the cases had been proceeding for nearly four years; success on the merits would be difficult; plaintiffs were settling for the maximum amount they could win through litigation; and class counsel and class representatives all agreed to the settlement.

In this consolidated appeal, Appellants renew their challenges to the district court's class certification and approval of the settlement.

## II. DISCUSSION

### A. Certification of the Class Under Rule 23(b)(1)(B)

We review a district court's decision to certify a class for abuse of discretion. A district court abuses its discretion, inter alia, when it "rests its legal analysis on an erroneous understanding of governing law."

In addition to satisfying the prerequisites of Rule 23(a), a class must also meet the requirements of one of the subdivisions of Rule 23(b) in order to be certified. At issue here is subdivision (b)(1)(B). A "limited fund" action, which aggregates numerous claims against a fund insufficient to satisfy them all, is one type of class action traditionally encompassed by Rule 23(b)(1)(B).

The nub of this case, as it was in *Ortiz,* is the certification of the class under Rule 23(b)(1)(B) on a limited fund rationale. We do not decide the general constitutional question, left open in *Ortiz,* whether a mandatory limited fund rationale could—under some circumstances—be applied to a settlement class of tort claimants. Such circumstances do not exist here because the settlement does not "seek equity by providing for procedures to resolve the difficult issues of treating differently situated claimants with fairness as among themselves," and thereby fails to satisfy one of "the essential premises of mandatory limited fund actions."

*Ortiz* involved a large class of asbestos claimants suing a manufacturer, Fibreboard, which had in turn sued its two insurance carriers for funds to pay the claimants. Eleventh hour negotiations between class counsel, Fibreboard and the two insurance companies produced a settlement fund of $1.525 billion, funded nearly entirely by the insurance companies and contingent on certification under Rule 23(b)(1)(B) as a mandatory limited fund class. The district court certified the class under Rule 23(b)(1)(B). We affirmed. On remand for further consideration in light of *Amchem Products, Inc. v. Windsor*, we again affirmed.

The Supreme Court reversed. The Court expressed "serious constitutional concerns that come with any attempt to aggregate individual tort claims on a limited fund rationale." First, the certification of a mandatory class followed by settlement of its action for money damages obviously implicates the Seventh Amendment jury trial rights of absent class members. Second, and no less important, mandatory class actions aggregating damages claims implicate the due process "principle of general application in Anglo-American jurisprudence that one is not bound by a judgment *in personam* in a litigation in which he is not designated as a party or to which he has not been made a party by service of process," it being "our 'deep-rooted historic tradition that everyone should have his own day in court.'"

In light of these concerns, the Court counseled against "adventurous application of Rule 23(b)(1)(B)," stressing that a limited construction of the Rule, "staying close to the historical model avoids serious constitutional concerns raised by the mandatory class resolution of individual legal claims." The Court described this "historical model" of a limited fund as "a 'fund' with a definitely ascertained limit, all of which would be distributed to satisfy all those with liquidated claims based on a common theory of liability, by an equitable, pro rata distribution." From its discussion of the historical model, the Court identified three "presumptively necessary" characteristics of a traditional limited fund. Those characteristics are:

(1) the totals of the aggregated liquidated claims and the fund available for satisfying them, set definitely at their maximums, demonstrate the inadequacy of the fund to pay all the claims,

(2) the whole of the inadequate fund is to be devoted to the overwhelming claims," and

(3) the claimants identified by a common theory of recovery are treated equitably among themselves.

The Court's phrasing and discussion of this third requirement differs noticeably from the other two requirements in that it departs from a strict interpretation of the traditional limited fund. To cleave to the traditional model of a true limited fund, the third element of intra-class equity should require that the class claims be capable of liquidation and pro rata distribution. However, the Court contemplated that the unattainability of straightforward pro rata distribution would not necessarily disqualify a class action from adhering to the historical model, as long as the settlement otherwise provided for fair distribution amongst the claimants in the class.

The settlement proponents argue, and we agree, that this class does not suffer from the particular defects that led the *Ortiz* Court to find the "procedures to resolve the difficult issues" unsatisfactory in that settlement. The Court identified two structural conflicts obstructing the fairness of distributions within that class. The first conflict was between present claimants—whose interest was in generous immediate payments—and future claimants, whose interest was to ensure an ample fund for the future. This type of temporal conflict between present and future classes is not applicable in this case, which involves an identified class that has suffered a presently identifiable harm. The other conflict in *Ortiz* was between class members whose claims accrued before the lapse of the insurance policy providing the bulk of the insurance funds, giving them more valuable rights to the insurance proceeds, and those who were injured after this policy lapsed. The settlement before us avoids this second concern through the creation of sub-classes providing that the funds from one insurance policy providing coverage to a particular levee district will not be available to any class member who does not have a claim against that levee district. Nevertheless, freedom from the particular infirmities identified in *Ortiz* is insufficient to issue a clean bill of health for intra-class equity here.

The class members in this case suffered a wide variety of injuries, ranging from property damage to personal injury and death, and no method is specified for how these different claimants will be treated vis-á-vis each other. The district court acknowledged that fairness of distribution was a significant concern in this settlement. The issue was addressed during the fairness hearing, where the court received testimony from a class action expert who suggested the use of grids or matrices to differentiate between the various class members, using factors such as the particular kind of damage suffered—death, personal injury, property damage—to create, in essence, subclasses of claimants. The expert suggested that these categories could be further subdivided; for example, by partitioning the category of property damage according to the extent of damage, as measured by the depth of water that caused the damage. While opining that such a method would be fairly inexpensive given the existence of certain data already available to the court, he also stated that, should the administrative costs associated with this differentiation threaten to consume the fund, the court might find that the class would benefit more from a *cy pres* distribution that was related in some way to the levees, such as levee protection or beautification.

None of these procedures made their way into the settlement agreement. Instead, the settlement provides for the appointment of a special master to "provide to the Court a recommended disposition and protocol with regard to the remaining settlement fund, and treatment of Claims of Class members." This arrangement simply punts the difficult question of equitable distribution from the court to the special master, without providing any more clarity as to how fairness will be achieved. The lack of any "procedures to resolve the difficult issues of treating such differently situated claimants with fairness as among themselves," leads us to reverse the district court's order certifying this class. By failing to meet one of the three "essential premises of mandatory limited fund actions" identified by the Supreme Court in *Ortiz,* this settlement class strays too far from the historical model to avoid the Court's constitutional concerns.

## B.  Approval of the Settlement under Rule 23(e)

The objecting class members separately challenge the district court's approval of the class action settlement on the grounds that the settlement does not benefit the class, allows counsel to seek an enhancement of actual costs, and provided inadequate and misleading notice to the class members. We review the district court's approval of the settlement for an abuse of discretion.

### 1.  Benefit to the Class

Rule 23(e)(2) states that a court may approve a settlement proposal that would bind class members "only after a hearing and on finding that it is fair, reasonable, and adequate." Six factors guide our review of a decision to approve a class action settlement agreement:

> (1) evidence that the settlement was obtained by fraud or collusion; (2) the complexity, expense, and likely duration of the litigation; (3) the stage of the litigation and available discovery; (4) the probability of plaintiffs' prevailing on the merits; (5) the range of possible recovery and certainty of damages; and (6) the opinions of class counsel, class representatives, and absent class members.

Based on its wealth of experience in Hurricane Katrina litigation and the evidence it received before and during the certification and settlement hearing, the district court found that all six factors weighed in favor of approving the settlement.

Without quarreling with the district court's findings, we nevertheless conclude that this settlement is not fair, reasonable, and adequate under Rule 23(e) because there has been no demonstration on the record below that the settlement will benefit the class in any way, either through the disbursement of individual checks or through a *cy pres* distribution. "The court must be assured that the settlement secures an adequate advantage for the class in return for the surrender of litigation rights against the defendants" ("Often, the settlement benefits are somewhat speculative in nature and capable of only approximate valuation. Nevertheless, the settlement may be approved *if it is clear that it secures some adequate advantage for the class*").

The settlement provides that the following administrative costs may be paid out of the $21 million settlement fund. No estimate was given as to what these costs might be. Nevertheless, the court recognized that "it is a reasonable fear that the mere cost of adjudicating individual claims may swallow the entire settlement."

The settlement further provides class counsel with the right to seek reimbursement of "enhanced" costs and expenses, and counsel of any class member with the right to seek attorneys' fees. Class Counsel agree to recommend to the Court that no attorneys' fees should be awarded from the settlement fund, and shall oppose any such request(s).

There is no indication in the record as to what these attorneys' costs and expenses will be. At the certification and fairness hearing, class counsel could not provide any estimate of the costs incurred thus far, other than to admit that litigation had been "expensive." Class counsel conceded, and the court accepted, that "a lot of depositions were taken, a lot of costs were incurred, and we don't know what the plaintiffs are going to seek."

We have previously affirmed a district court's approval of a settlement in which costs and attorneys' fees had not been determined as of the date of settlement. However, we were able to definitively state in that case, upon a record that was "exceptionally well-developed," that the class would receive some monetary benefit from the settlement. This was in part because there was a separate sub-fund of $15 million set apart for past and future litigation expenses. Here, we are unable to definitively state, based on the record below, that the class will receive any benefit from the settlement. Moreover, that settlement did not concern a mandatory class. "Because limited-fund classes do not permit opt-outs, certification for settlement imposes particularly stringent standards."

We hold that the district court erred by approving the settlement without any assurance that attorneys' costs and administrative costs will not cannibalize the entire $21 million settlement. In doing so, we express no opinion as to whether such a result would occur; but the burden is on the settlement proponents to persuade the court that the agreement is fair, reasonable, and adequate for the absent class members who are to be bound by the settlement. In our judgment, the settlement proponents have not met this burden because they have failed to provide any basis for their assertion that there will be money remaining after payment of these costs to effect even a *cy pres* distribution, let alone a monetary distribution.

Nor do we consider whether a *cy pres* distribution of the settlement fund, without any monetary distribution, would be fair, reasonable, and adequate under Rule 23(e). That decision would be premature here, where the very possibility of such a distribution is in question. Furthermore, without any specific proposal for a *cy pres* distribution before us, we are unable to determine whether such a distribution would be "for the next best use which is for indirect class benefit," and would be for uses "consistent with the nature of the underlying action and with the judicial function."

### 2.   *Enhancement of Costs*

We agree with Appellants that any "enhancement" of costs is the functional equivalent of a fee. We have repeatedly held that a district court abuses its discretion if it approves a class action settlement without determining that any attorneys' fees claimed as part of the settlement are reasonable and that the settlement itself is reasonable in light of those fees.

As noted above, we have also previously affirmed a district court's approval of a settlement agreement in which attorneys' fees were unknown at the time of approval. In that agreement, as here, attorneys retained the right to request fees and reimbursement of past and future litigation expenses, to be paid from the gross settlement fund upon approval of the district court. Again, however, we were able to definitively state in that case that there would be money remaining in the settlement fund after payment of those costs and fees. Because there is no such assurance here, it was error for the district court to approve the settlement.

### 3. Notice to the Class

Rule 23(e) states that a court must "direct notice in a reasonable manner to all class members who would be bound by the proposal" before approving a settlement. Appellants argue that the notice apprising the class of the proposed certification and settlement was inadequate and misleading because it: (i) failed to provide class members with any way of estimating the amount of money that they could expect to receive in exchange for releasing their claims, nor warned them that it was unlikely that they would receive any recovery at all; (ii) wrongly represented that class counsel would not be seeking attorneys' fees from the settlement fund; and (iii) incorrectly informed class members that they were barred by law from receiving compensation from the levee districts.

Under Rule 23(e), a settlement notice need only satisfy the "broad reasonableness standards imposed by due process." The minimum of due process, as interpreted by the Supreme Court, is that "deprivation of life, liberty or property by adjudication be preceded by notice and opportunity for hearing appropriate to the nature of the case." *Mullane v. Central Hanover Bank & Trust Co.* Notice of a mandatory class settlement, which will deprive class members of their claims, therefore requires that class members be given information reasonably necessary for them to make a decision whether to object to the settlement.

### a. Possibility of Cy Pres Distribution

We have previously held, in the context of non-mandatory class settlements, that a notice "is not required to provide a complete source of settlement information," and that a court does not abuse its discretion by omitting estimates of unit recovery if it concludes that such estimates were "too unreliable to submit," However, we find that the court did not direct reasonable notice to the class here because—assuming that a *cy pres* distribution was permissible and feasible—the notice did not inform class members of the possibility that they would not receive any direct benefit from the settlement. By failing to apprise class members of this information, the notice did not provide interested parties with knowledge critical to an informed decision as to whether to object to class certification and settlement.

Under the heading "Who's Included?" the class notice described the membership of the proposed settlement class as all those who either lived or had property in the greater New Orleans area and were harmed by Hurricanes Katrina and Rita. Under the heading "What Does the Settlement Provide?" the notice then stated:

> A settlement fund that includes all insurance money available to the Settling Defendant will be established in the amount of $20,839,115 (plus any additional interest) for the benefit of the Settlement Class, as well as to cover costs, and expenses. The settlement fund (plus any interest) will be divided among the Subclasses as follows: Subclass 1—$2,371,467; Subclass 2—$5,924,284; and Subclass 3—$12,543,363.

> If the settlement receives final Court approval, an independent "Special Master" appointed by the Court will recommend how to administer the settlement fund for the benefit of the Settlement Class. The Court may request that a second notice be issued to Settlement Class members explaining how the settlement fund will be used or administered.

This language does not clearly inform class members of the real possibility, acknowledged by all parties, that there may be a *cy pres* distribution in lieu of any direct distribution of funds to the class members. This is particularly problematic because no estimate is given of the costs and expenses that will be paid out of the settlement fund, a sum that may greatly reduce the amount available for distribution to the class. Stating that the fund will be administered "for the benefit of the Settlement Class," and hinting that the settlement fund may be "used" rather than "administered," is insufficient to communicate the possibility of a *cy pres* distribution, which is a key aspect of the settlement that might have led more members to object. Therefore, contrary to the district court's judgment, the notice did not contain "all necessary information for any class member to become fully apprised and make any relevant decisions."

b.   Attorneys' Fees

We also find that the notice was misleading insofar as it informed class members that class counsel and other counsel for class members would not seek any attorneys' fees from the settlement. Under the heading "How will the lawyers be paid?" the notice stated:

> Class counsel will not request any attorneys' fees from the settlement fund. However, Class Counsel may ask the Court for reimbursement of their costs and expenses out of the settlement fund. Other counsel for Settlement Class members may also request costs and expenses. Requests for costs and expenses will be made after the settlement is granted final approval by the

Court. The Court may award more or less than the actual costs and expenses.

The settlement agreement, however, provides both class counsel and other counsel with the right to seek "enhanced" costs. As explained above, an enhancement of actual costs and expenses is essentially a fee, and unless class counsel will not seek any such "enhanced" costs, it is inaccurate to assert that they will not request any attorneys' fees from the settlement fund. Moreover, it is unfaithful to the settlement agreement to omit the fact that all counsel may *seek* such fees; simply stating that the court "may award more than the actual costs and expenses" implies that any such action would be entirely *sua sponte*.

c.    Legal Limits to the Fund

In the same section describing the settlement fund, the class notice stated: "Please note that, under law, the Settlement Class can get no additional money or property in this settlement because the Settling Defendants are governmental bodies."

Appellants are correct that this statement is slightly misleading, although in our judgment the district court's approval of this language does not rise to the level of abuse of discretion. As political subdivisions of the State of Louisiana, the levee districts' assets are statutorily exempt from seizure to satisfy a judgment against them. Nor are the levee districts subject to a writ of mandamus requiring them to appropriate additional funds to satisfy potential judgments in this case. However, Louisiana law does not *prevent* the levee districts from appropriating additional money to contribute to the settlement. Therefore, perhaps a more precise statement would have been that, "under law, the Settlement Class can *exact* no additional money or property from the Settling Defendants in this settlement because the Settling Defendants are governmental bodies."

However, the statement as written is accurate in its essential point: that $21 million is the most that the class can expect to receive in the settlement. The choice of words, while less than one hundred percent accurate, does not render the notice so clearly misleading that the district court abused its discretion in approving this portion of the notice.

III. CONCLUSION

For the reasons stated above, we reverse the district court's order certifying this mandatory limited fund class and approving the class settlement.

# B. SETTLEMENT CLASSES APPROVED

## IN RE DEEPWATER HORIZON

United States Court of Appeals for the Fifth Circuit, 2014.
739 F.3d 790.

This is an interlocutory appeal from the district court's order certifying a class action and approving a settlement under Rule 23 of the Federal Rules of Civil Procedure. The ongoing litigation before the district court encompasses claims against British Petroleum Exploration & Production, Inc. (BP) and numerous other entities. All these claims are related to the 2010 explosion aboard the *Deepwater Horizon,* an offshore drilling rig, and the consequent discharge of oil into the Gulf of Mexico.

Several of the original appellants in this case have moved to dismiss their appeals voluntarily, and we have granted those motions. The three groups of appellants remaining before us—the Allpar Objectors, the Cobb Objectors, and the BCA Objectors—all filed objections with the district court opposing class certification and settlement approval based on various provisions of Rule 23. The Objectors' arguments were each addressed and rejected by the district court. The Objectors have now appealed the district court's order and ask this court to remand with instructions to decertify the class and withdraw approval from the Settlement Agreement.

BP also now asks this court to vacate the district court's order, although BP is not formally an appellant and, in fact, BP originally supported both class certification and settlement approval before the district court. In addition to its own set of new arguments under Rule 23, BP also raises additional arguments regarding the Article III standing of certain class members to make claims under the Settlement Agreement. Unlike the Objectors, however, BP argues that the Settlement Agreement can be salvaged if "properly construed and implemented." In BP's view, all of the problems that invalidate the class settlement under Article III and Rule 23 result from two Policy Announcements issued by the Claims Administrator, Patrick Juneau, who was appointed under the Settlement Agreement by the district court.

We cannot agree with the arguments raised by the Objectors or BP. The district court was correct to conclude that the applicable requirements of Rule 23 are satisfied in this case. Additionally, whether or not BP's arguments are correct as a matter of contract interpretation, neither class certification nor settlement approval are contrary to Article III in this case. Accordingly, the district court's order is affirmed.

I.

The factual background of this case is described in more extensive detail in the district court's opinion, *In re Oil Spill by Oil Rig Deepwater Horizon in Gulf of Mexico, on April 20, 2010* and in a previous decision by a different panel of this court. As explained in *Deepwater Horizon I*, BP leased the *Deepwater Horizon* drilling vessel to drill its Macondo prospect off the Louisiana coast. On April 20, 2010, an exploratory well associated with the drilling vessel blew out. After the initial explosion and during the ensuing fire, the vessel sank, causing millions of barrels of oil to spill into the Gulf of Mexico. Numerous lawsuits were filed against a variety of entities, and many of these lawsuits were transferred by the Judicial Panel on Multidistrict Litigation to the United States District Court for the Eastern District of Louisiana pursuant to 28 U.S.C. § 1407.

To satisfy its obligations under the Oil Pollution Act (OPA), BP initially established its own claims process and later funded the claims process administered by the Gulf Coast Claims Facility (GCCF) in order to begin paying out claims immediately rather than at the conclusion of litigation. BP then began negotiating a class settlement in February 2011 and jointly worked with the Plaintiffs' Steering Committee (PSC) to transfer claims from the GCCF to a program supervised directly by the district court.

On April 16, 2012, the PSC filed an Amended Class Action Complaint and a proposed Settlement Agreement for the district court's preliminary approval. In accordance with the terms of the Settlement Agreement, the district court appointed Patrick Juneau as Claims Administrator of the settlement program. Although the Settlement Agreement had not yet received the district court's final approval under Rule 23 of the Federal Rules of Civil Procedure, the Claims Administrator began reviewing claims left unresolved by the GCCF and processing new claims in June 2012 as provided for in Section 4 of the parties' Settlement Agreement, entitled "Implementation of the Settlement."

On August 13, 2012, after a preliminary hearing and the distribution of notifications to the absent members of the proposed class, BP and the PSC moved for final approval of the Settlement Agreement and certification of the class defined in the Amended Class Action Complaint. The Allpar, Cobb, and BCA Objectors all filed objections with the district court opposing class certification and settlement approval based on various provisions of Rule 23. After conducting a fairness hearing to consider the views of these Objectors and numerous others in accordance with Rule 23(e), the district court issued a final order certifying the class and approving the parties' Settlement Agreement on December 21, 2012. The district court emphasized in particular that the "uncapped compensation" available under the Settlement Agreement would "ensure that a benefit paid to one member of the class will in no way reduce or interfere with a benefit obtained by another member." The Objectors appealed.

BP supported the Settlement Agreement during the proceedings leading up to and including the district court's order. BP now argues that two Policy Announcements issued by the Claims Administrator regarding the interpretation and application of the Settlement Agreement—both of which were adopted in orders by the district court—have subsequently brought the Settlement Agreement into violation of Rule 23, the Rules Enabling Act, and Article III of the U.S. Constitution.

The second Policy Announcement by the Claims Administrator addresses the interpretation and application of Exhibit 4B of the Settlement Agreement, entitled "Causation Requirements for Businesses Economic Loss Claims." Exhibit 4B set forth criteria for prospective claimants to demonstrate to the Claims Administrator that their losses were caused by the *Deepwater Horizon* oil spill. In the Policy Announcement, the Claims Administrator explained:

> The Settlement Agreement does not contemplate that the Claims Administrator will undertake additional analysis of causation issues beyond those criteria that are specifically set out in the Settlement Agreement. Both Class Counsel and BP have in response to the Claims Administrator's inquiry confirmed that this is in fact a correct statement of their intent and of the terms of the Settlement Agreement. The Claims Administrator will thus compensate eligible Business Economic Loss and Individual Economic Loss claimants for all losses payable under the terms of the Economic Loss frameworks in the Settlement Agreement, without regard to whether such losses resulted or may have resulted from a cause other than the Deepwater Horizon oil spill provided such claimants have satisfied the specific causation requirements set out in the Settlement Agreement.

BP argued that the lawfulness of the Settlement Agreement was equally threatened by both Policy Announcements' effects on the interpretation and application of Exhibits 4B and 4C. According to BP, these Policy Announcements by the Claims Administrator permit claimants without any actual injuries caused by the oil spill to participate in the class settlement and receive payments. According to BP, this result brings the class settlement into violation of Rule 23, the Rules Enabling Act, and Article III.

## II.

Before we reach the questions regarding class certification and settlement approval under Rule 23, we must resolve the Article III question as a threshold matter of jurisdiction. Questions of law relating to constitutional standing are reviewed *de novo*. "Facts expressly or impliedly found by the district court in the course of determining jurisdiction are reviewed for clear error."

The abuse-of-discretion standard governs this court's review of both the district court's certification of the class and its approval of the settlement under Rule 23. This court exercises *de novo* review as to whether the district court applied the correct legal standard. Importantly, "Rule 23 grants courts no license to engage in free-ranging merits inquiries at the certification stage. Merits questions may be considered to the extent—but only to the extent—that they are relevant to determining whether the Rule 23 prerequisites for class certification are satisfied."

### III.

The crux of BP's standing argument is that Article III "precludes certification of a settlement class that includes members that have suffered no injury" or "who suffered no harm caused by the *Deepwater Horizon* incident." In BP's view, because an unidentified number of such individuals have received and may continue to receive payments under the class settlement, Article III requires this court to reverse the district court's order of December 21, 2012.

In two respects, BP is correct. First, the elements of Article III standing do indeed include both an injury in fact and a causal connection to the defendant's conduct. Second, under the previous decisions of this circuit, both of these elements must be present as a threshold matter of jurisdiction whenever a district court certifies a class under Rule 23.

It is striking, however, that BP makes no attempt to identify a standard that we should apply to determine whether these elements are satisfied in this case. The frequent references in BP's briefs to the "vast numbers of members who suffered no Article III injury" are disconnected from any discussion of pleading requirements, competent evidence, or the standards of proof by which the parties' contentions are evaluated during different stages of litigation. In particular, BP's arguments fail to explain how this court or the district court should identify or even discern the existence of "claimants that have suffered no cognizable injury" for purposes of the standing inquiry during class certification and settlement approval.

The relevant authorities suggest two possible approaches to Article III questions at the class certification stage, both of these approaches require us to reject BP's standing argument. Whichever test is applied, therefore, Article III does not mandate reversal in this case.

### B.

It is clear that the class action survives Article III because the named plaintiffs have each alleged injury in fact, traceability to the defendant's conduct, and redressability by the relief requested. The named plaintiffs set forth their allegations in the operative pleading in this case. The Amended Class Action Complaint explains that "Plaintiffs are individuals and/or entities who have suffered economic and property damages *as a result of the Deepwater Horizon Incident.*" This document thereafter identifies each of the fifteen named plaintiffs individually and explains in detail how each has suffered economic damages due to the "lack of adequate supplies of seafood to process and sell," a "severe reduction in tourist-related bookings," a drop in "demand for marine tourism," "a loss on the sale of residential property," and numerous other types of economic injury and property damage.

Each one of these named plaintiffs satisfies the elements of standing by identifying an injury in fact that is traceable to the oil spill and susceptible to redress by an award of monetary damages. Under the [relevant] test, that is the end of the inquiry. As we explained in *Cole v. General Motors Corp.*, which addressed the Article III standing of named plaintiffs during class certification under Rule 23, we found it "sufficient for standing purposes that the plaintiffs seek recovery for an economic harm that they *allege* they have suffered." At the Rule 23 stage, *Cole* provides that "a federal court must assume *arguendo* the merits of each named plaintiff's legal claim." Indeed, BP has never argued that any of the named plaintiffs lack Article III standing. Accordingly, there is no question that the test is satisfied in this case.

Although *Cole* addressed the standing of named plaintiffs rather than absent class members, it would make no sense to apply a higher evidentiary standard to absent class members than to named plaintiffs. We also stated that even the absent class members are "linked" under Rule 23 to the "common complaint, and the possibility that some may fail to prevail on their individual claims will not defeat class membership." Therefore, we find that Article III and the Rules Enabling Act are satisfied in this case.

### C.

In concluding this analysis, we note the possibility that the application of a stricter evidentiary standard might reveal persons or entities who have received payments and yet have suffered no loss resulting from the oil spill. But courts are not authorized to apply such a standard for this purpose at the Rule 23 stage. Without ever saying so explicitly, BP implies that we should also resolve Article III questions at the Rule 23 stage by looking to evidence of certain prospective claimants' standing. That is, BP cites to items of evidence—in particular, a series of declarations by economists. These economists' declarations, in BP's view, demonstrate that the Claims Administrator has awarded payments under his interpretations to persons and entities that likely were not injured by the *Deepwater Horizon* incident.

BP has cited no authority—and we are aware of none—that would permit an evidentiary inquiry into the Article III standing of absent class members during class certification and settlement approval under Rule 23. It is true that a district court may "probe behind the pleadings" when examining whether a specific case meets the requirements of Rule 23, such as numerosity, commonality, typicality, and adequacy. But the Supreme Court cautioned in *Amgen Inc. v. Connecticut Retirement Plans & Trust Funds* that "Rule 23 grants courts no license to engage in free-ranging merits inquiries at the certification stage. Merits questions may be considered to the extent—but only to the extent—that they are relevant to determining whether the Rule 23 prerequisites for class certification are satisfied."

Relevant circuit authority confirms the inappropriateness of reviewing evidence of absent class members' standing at the Rule 23 stage. Our older decision in *Cole* confirms that it would be improper to look for proof of injuries beyond what the claimants identified in the class definition can "*allege* they have suffered" at this stage. Despite BP's urging, therefore, even a district court could not consider the evidence regarding absent class members' standing at the Rule 23 stage.

Of course, had the class in this case been certified under Rule 23 for further proceedings on the merits rather than for settlement, the district court might ultimately have had occasion to apply a stricter evidentiary standard. As the district court said explicitly, "certain causation issues would have to be decided on an individual basis were the cases not being settled," including "for example, the extent to which the *Deepwater Horizon* incident versus other factors caused a decline in the income of an individual or business." As early as October 6, 2010, the district court anticipated that "issues relating to damages" could and would be "severed and tried separately" from other issues relating to liability, in accordance with this court's previous case law and Rule 23(c)(4). In its submissions to the district court, BP also contemplated the possibility of "a trial of an economic damage test case" and "presentations of proof and comparative responsibility." Such proceedings would have provided opportunities for BP to inquire more deeply into individual claimants' evidence of Article III standing under the applicable evidentiary standards. In the absence of any motion for summary judgment or trial predicated upon the Article III standing of those absent class members, however, it would be premature and improper for a court to apply evidentiary standards corresponding to those later stages of litigation.

Indeed, it would make no practical sense for a court to require evidence of a party's claims when the parties themselves seek settlement under Rule 23(e). Logically, requiring absent class members to prove their claims prior to settlement under Rule 23(e) would eliminate class settlement because there would be no need to settle a claim that was already proven. Such a rule would thwart the "overriding public interest in favor of settlement" that we have recognized "particularly in class action suits." The legitimacy of class settlements is reflected not only in Rule 23(e) but also in the special regime that Congress has created to govern class settlements. Through the procedural mechanism of a class settlement, defendants "are entitled to settle claims pending against them on a class-wide basis even if a court believes that those claims may be meritless, provided that the class is properly certified under Rules 23(a) and (b) and the settlement is fair under Rule 23(e)." By entering into class-wide settlements, defendants "obtain releases from all those who might wish to assert claims, meritorious or not" and protect themselves from even those "plaintiffs with non-viable claims who do nonetheless commence legal action."

The evidentiary standard to be applied by the Claims Administrator, however, is not a matter of Article III standing. It is a question of interpreting the Settlement Agreement and applying it to each individual claim, and we are not called upon to address those issues in this appeal.

## IV.

We turn now to examine the Rule 23 arguments raised by BP and the Objectors. In addressing Rule 23, BP and the Objectors have made nearly identical arguments. They challenge class certification and settlement approval under a variety of provisions of Rule 23 based on the same central premise discussed above in the context of Article III—that a class cannot be certified when it includes persons who have not actually been injured. The Cobb Objectors also expressly adopt BP's arguments by reference and add only a single additional argument. According to the Cobb Objectors, the named plaintiffs did not adequately represent the class under Rule 23(a)(4) because there were no subclasses formed to represent residents of different states, particularly residents of Texas, and no subclass formed to represent those potential claimants who would have been "better off under the GCCF claims process." As explained below, the objections of the Allpar and Cobb Objectors and BP have no merit.

## A.

BP and the Allpar and Cobb Objectors have all challenged certification of the class under Rule 23(a)(2), which requires a demonstration that "there are questions of law or fact common to the class." These arguments rest entirely on a selective quotation from *Wal-Mart Stores, Inc. v. Dukes* and must be rejected. As the Supreme Court stated in *Wal-Mart,* "commonality requires the plaintiff to demonstrate that the class members 'have suffered the same injury.'" Based on this single sentence, it is now suggested that either the diversity of the class members' economic injuries or the inclusion of members who "have suffered no injury at all" might preclude class certification.

When quoted in its entirety, however, the relevant passage from *Wal-Mart* demonstrates why both of these arguments are meritless:

> Commonality requires the plaintiff to demonstrate that the class members "have suffered the same injury." This does not mean merely that they have all suffered a violation of the same provision of law. Title VII, for example, can be violated in many ways—by intentional discrimination, or by hiring and promotion criteria that result in disparate impact, and by the use of these practices on the part of many different superiors in a single company. Quite obviously, the mere claim by employees of the

same company that they have suffered a Title VII injury, or even a disparate-impact Title VII injury, gives no cause to believe that all their claims can productively be litigated at once. Their claims must depend upon a common contention—for example, the assertion of discriminatory bias on the part of the same supervisor. That common contention, moreover, must be of such a nature that it is capable of classwide resolution—which means that determination of its truth or falsity will resolve an issue that is central to the validity of each one of the claims in one stroke.

As this passage shows, the Supreme Court's use of the phrase, "the same injury," in *Wal-Mart* does not support BP's argument. To satisfy the commonality requirement under Rule 23(a)(2), class members must raise at least one contention that is central to the validity of each class member's claims. But this contention need not relate specifically to the damages component of the class members' claims. Even an instance of injurious conduct, which would usually relate more directly to the defendant's liability than to the claimant's damages, may constitute "the same injury." This is confirmed by the example given by the Supreme Court in the above passage from *Wal-Mart,* "discriminatory bias on the part of the same supervisor," which is itself not a type of damages, but an instance of injurious conduct that violates Title VII. Later in the same decision, the Supreme Court stated that another type of injurious conduct on the part of the defendant, "a companywide discriminatory pay and promotion policy," would also have satisfied the "same injury" test for commonality under Rule 23(a)(2).

Accordingly, as these two examples from *Wal-Mart* demonstrate, the legal requirement that class members have all "suffered the same injury" can be satisfied by an instance of the defendant's injurious conduct, even when the resulting injurious effects—the damages—are diverse. As we indicated, the principal requirement of *Wal-Mart* is merely a single common contention that enables the class action "to generate common *answers* apt to drive the resolution of the litigation." These "common answers" may indeed relate to the injurious effects experienced by the class members, but they may also relate to the defendant's injurious conduct. "Even a single common question will do."

The above passage from *Wal-Mart* also demonstrates that district courts do not err by failing to ascertain at the Rule 23 stage whether the class members include persons and entities who have suffered "no injury at all." As the Supreme Court explained, a "contention" regarding the class members' injury is sufficient to satisfy Rule 23, so long as the party seeking certification can show that this contention is "common" to all the class members, is "central" to the validity of their claims, and is "capable" of classwide resolution. There is no need to resolve the merits of the common contention at the Rule 23 stage or to attempt prematurely the "determination of its truth or falsity." Although Rule 23 "does not set forth a mere pleading standard" and a court may need to "probe behind the pleadings before coming to rest on the certification," Rule 23 does not therefore become a dress rehearsal for the merits. As the Supreme Court repeated last term in *Amgen,* "merits questions may be considered to the extent—but only to the extent—that they are relevant to determining whether the Rule 23 prerequisites for class certification are satisfied." In other words, to satisfy the commonality requirement under Rule 23(a)(2), the parties may potentially need to provide evidence to demonstrate that a particular contention is common, but not that it is correct.

The district court's certification of this class, therefore, did not violate Rule 23(a)(2). After reviewing expert evidence, the district court found that numerous factual and legal issues were central to the validity of all the class members' claims. These included "whether BP had a valid superseding cause defense," "whether BP used an improper well design that unreasonably heightened the risk," "whether the cement mixture was unstable, and, if so, whether BP should have prevented its use," "whether BP took appropriate and timely steps to stop the release of hydrocarbons from the well," "whether these decisions (individually or collectively) constitute negligence, gross negligence, or willful misconduct," "whether BP is a responsible party under OPA," "whether BP could limit its liability under OPA," "whether punitive damages are available as a matter of law," and whether BP "failed to mitigate the damages of the class." Neither BP nor the remaining Objectors find fault with any of the items on the district court's long list of common issues. Because "even a single common question will do" under *Wal-Mart,* this list was more than sufficient.

Accordingly, the commonality arguments raised by BP and the Objectors do not require decertification of the class. Although all of the factual and legal questions identified by the district court are more closely related to BP's injurious conduct than to the injurious effects experienced by the class members, they nonetheless demonstrate that the class members claim to have suffered the "same injury" in the sense that *Wal-Mart* used this phrase. Additionally, the district court did not err by failing to determine whether the class contained individuals who have not actually suffered any injury, because this would have amounted to a determination of the truth or falsity of the parties' contentions, rather than an evaluation of those contentions' commonality. This was not required by *Wal-Mart,* and was expressly ruled out in *Amgen.* We therefore reject the challenges raised by BP and the Objectors under Rule 23(a)(2).

## B.

BP and the Objectors also challenge class certification and settlement approval under Rule 23(a)(4), which requires a demonstration that "the representative parties will fairly and adequately protect the interests of the class." According to this argument, an impermissible "intra-class conflict" is created by the Claims Administrator's interpretation because the claimants now include some persons and entities that have suffered injuries, and other persons and entities that allegedly have not. As it has been interpreted, BP argues, the Settlement Agreement "would almost necessarily make injured members worse off than they might have been had non-injured members been excluded from the class." According to BP, had the injured class members been represented by named plaintiffs negotiating exclusively on their behalf, they could have used their increased bargaining power during settlement negotiations to demand a more favorable formula for awarding payments.

The district court must be upheld, however, unless its decision constituted an abuse of discretion. In this case, the district court found that the named plaintiffs were "clearly adequate" to protect the interests of the class as they included "individuals and businesses asserting each category of loss" and were assisted by adequate counsel. After reviewing declarations by each of the named plaintiffs, the district court found that they had "participated in the settlement negotiations" and taken "an active role in the prosecution of this class action." After reviewing expert testimony, the district court also found that the class action was structured to assure adequate representation of all interests within the class and to prevent intra-class conflict. Finally, the district court concluded that the "uncapped compensation" available under the Settlement Agreement would "ensure that a benefit paid to one member of the class will in no way reduce or interfere with a benefit obtained by another member."

Although BP made no objection to the district court's order certifying the class and approving the Settlement Agreement, BP asks this court to find an intra-class conflict of interest because the claimants allegedly include persons and entities that have suffered no injury. In support of this allegation, BP presents us with a series of economists' declarations that had not been provided to the district court when the class was certified. But our previous decisions prevent us from considering this evidence for the first time on appeal. Moreover, even if we were to accept BP's contention that the class does include uninjured persons, *Mims* and *Rodriguez* would foreclose decertification of the class on this basis. As we stated in *Mims* in the context of the Rule 23 requirements, "class certification is not precluded simply because a class may include persons who have not been injured by the defendant's conduct." As we stated in *Rodriguez,* "the possibility that some absent class members may fail to prevail on their individual claims will not defeat class membership."

By contrast, we can consider the argument that the Cobb Objectors have raised under Rule 23(a)(4), which was passed upon by the district court. The Cobb Objectors argue that "class members from Texas, Louisiana, Alabama, Florida and Mississippi" should have been divided into their own subclasses, as should those class members who "were better off under the GCCF claims process."

Although the creation of subclasses is sometimes necessary under Rule 23(a)(4) to avoid a "fundamental conflict," there is no need to create subclasses to accommodate every instance of "differently weighted interests." In this case, because the class members' claims arise under federal law rather than state law, we are not persuaded that there is any fundamental conflict between the "differently weighted interests" of class members from different geographical regions. Although geographical criteria were indeed incorporated into the Settlement Agreement, the reason for this is both obvious and acknowledged in the Cobb Objectors' brief. That is, "causation becomes more difficult" for a claimant to establish "the further one moves from the coast" and, in particular, the further one moves from the Macondo reservoir where the *Deepwater Horizon* incident occurred.

As the district court expressly found, the differences between the formulas applicable in the different geographic zones were "rationally related to the relative strengths and merits of similarly situated claims." The identification of objective, geographically-based criteria therefore easily distinguishes this case from *In re Katrina Canal Breaches Litigation* in which the district court improperly approved a class settlement that sought simply to "punt the difficult question of equitable distribution from the court to the special master, without providing any more clarity as to how fairness will be achieved." The district court's rigorous consideration of the expert evidence demonstrates that it did not abuse its discretion in declining to require subclasses for claimants based in Texas, Louisiana, Alabama, Florida, and Mississippi.

We also must reject the Cobb Objectors' argument that an intra-class conflict exists between class members who were "better off under the GCCF claims process" and those who were not. Most critically, the Cobb Objectors have failed to provide any details about the cause of these claimants' current disadvantage. In their brief, the Cobb Objectors repeat several times that some number of claimants are now "forced to meet arbitrary loss and recovery benchmarks" under the Settlement Agreement, whereas these same claimants apparently could have recovered under the GCCF without doing so. After considering substantial expert testimony, however, the district court found explicitly that the Settlement Agreement's compensation criteria were not arbitrary, but "detailed" and "objective." Nothing in the Cobb Objectors' arguments demonstrates that the district court's conclusions on this question constituted an abuse of discretion. Finally, even if some claimants were practically disadvantaged by the procedures of the court-administered claims process in comparison to the procedures of the GCCF, this mechanical discrepancy is only another example of "differently weighted interests" rather than a "fundamental conflict" of interests. As the Sixth and Third Circuits have held, "each class member naturally derives different amounts of utility from any class-wide settlement" based on his or her unique circumstances, but this does not put all such class members in fundamental conflict with one another. Without a more detailed description of the disadvantage experienced by the group that was supposedly "better off" under the GCCF, we cannot agree with the Cobb Objectors that the district court's certification of this class was an abuse of discretion.

C.

BP and the Objectors also argue that class certification was improper under Rule 23(b)(3), which requires that "the questions of law or fact common to class members predominate over any questions affecting only individual members." According to BP and the Objectors, the Supreme Court's recent decision in *Comcast Corp. v. Behrend*—which was decided three months after the district court certified the class—precludes certification under Rule 23(b)(3) in any case where the class members' damages are not susceptible to a formula for classwide measurement.

This is a misreading of *Comcast,* however, which has already been rejected by three other circuits. As explained in greater detail below, *Comcast* held that a district court errs by premising its Rule 23(b)(3) decision on a formula for classwide measurement of damages whenever the damages measured by that formula are incompatible with the class action's theory of liability. As the court explained, "the first step in a damages study is the translation of the legal theory of the harmful event into an analysis of the economic impact of that event." This rule may reveal an important defect in many formulas for classwide measurement of damages. But nothing in *Comcast* mandates a formula for classwide measurement of damages in all cases. Even after *Comcast,* therefore, this holding has no impact on cases such as the present one, in which predominance was based not on common issues of damages but on the numerous common issues of liability. In the present case, the district court did not include a formula for classwide measurement of damages among its extensive listing of the "common issues" that weighed in favor of certification. The district court always recognized that the class members' damages "would have to be decided on an individual basis were the cases not being settled," as would "the extent to which the *Deepwater Horizon* incident versus other factors caused a decline in the income of an individual or business." The holding of *Comcast* cited by BP and the Objectors, therefore, is simply inapplicable here.

As recalled above, the district court set forth a considerable list of issues that were common to all the class members' claims. Nearly all of these issues related to either the complicated factual questions surrounding BP's involvement in the well design, explosion, discharge of oil, and cleanup efforts or the uncertain legal questions surrounding interpretation and application of the OPA. Accordingly, BP and the Objectors are quite correct to suggest that, although the analysis of BP's injurious conduct gives rise to numerous common questions, the class members' damage calculations give rise primarily to individual questions that are not capable of classwide resolution.

But this is not fatal to class certification. As we stated in *Bell Atlantic Corp. v. AT&T Corp.,* "even wide disparity among class members as to the amount of damages" does not preclude class certification "and courts, therefore, have certified classes even in light of the need for individualized calculations of damages." Accordingly, as we recognized in *Steering Committee v. Exxon Mobil Corp.,* it is indeed "possible to satisfy the predominance requirements of Rule 23(b)(3) in a mass tort or mass accident class action" despite the particular need in such cases for individualized damages calculations. On this basis, therefore, we have previously affirmed class certification in mass accident cases, as in other cases in which "virtually every issue prior to damages is a common issue."

In particular, as we explained in *Madison v. Chalmette Refining, LLC,* predominance may be ensured in a mass accident case when a district court performs a sufficiently "rigorous analysis" of the means by which common and individual issues will be divided and tried. In many circuits, this has been accomplished by means of multi-phase trials under Rule 23(c)(4), which permits district courts to limit class treatment to "particular issues" and reserve other issues for individual determination. Accordingly, *Chalmette Refining* instructed district courts to consider rigorously how they plan to "adjudicate common class issues in the first phase and then later adjudicate individualized issues in other phases" of the multi-phase trial before the final decision is made to certify a class.

Heeding our instruction in *Chalmette Refining,* therefore, the district court planned "to manage such litigation by breaking it down into separate phases, as the district court was prepared to do prior to the parties' reaching a settlement." From the beginning of the litigation, the district court had anticipated that "issues relating to damages" would be "severed and tried separately" from other issues relating to liability. The initial phases of this litigation would therefore have focused on common questions, including which defendants bore responsibility for the well blowout, how much oil escaped from the Macondo reservoir, who bore responsibility for the inability of the defendants to contain the flow earlier, where the oil finally came to rest, and how the efforts to disperse the oil were conducted. "Absent the Settlement," the district court would then have been obliged to determine in later phases how "responsible party status would translate into compensation" under the OPA.

The district court was well aware, therefore, that the class members' damages "would have to be decided on an individual basis were the cases not being settled," as would "the extent to which the *Deepwater Horizon* incident versus other factors caused a decline in the income of an individual or business." Accordingly, the district court did not list the calculation of the claimants' damages either in its list of "common questions of fact" or in its list of "common questions of law." But even without a common means of measuring damages, in the district court's view, these common issues nonetheless predominated over the issues unique to individual claimants. As the district court explained, "the phased trial structure selected by the Court prior to the parties' arrival at a settlement agreement reflected the central importance of common issues to this case."

In rendering this conclusion, the district court did not abuse its discretion. The phased trial of common issues in this case would undoubtedly prevent the repetitious re-litigation of these common issues by each individual claimant in thousands of separate lawsuits. In accordance with our directive in *Chalmette Refining,* the district court also rigorously analyzed how it would adjudicate "common class issues in the first phase" and "individualized issues in other phases." As required by *Amchem Products, Inc. v. Windsor,* this class action would indeed "achieve economies of time, effort, and expense, and promote uniformity of decision as to persons similarly situated, without sacrificing procedural fairness or bringing about other undesirable results." This class action therefore satisfies Rule 23(b)(3).

This analysis is not changed by the Supreme Court's recent decision in *Comcast.* BP and the Objectors suggest that, three months after the district court certified the class and approved the settlement, *Comcast* brought about a revolution in the application of Rule 23(b)(3). According to this argument, *Comcast* declared "that certification under Rule 23(b)(3) requires a reliable, common methodology for measuring classwide damages." This reading is a significant distortion of *Comcast,* and has already been considered and rejected by the Seventh Circuit, the Sixth Circuit, and the Ninth Circuit in the months since *Comcast* was decided.

The principal holding of *Comcast* was that a "model purporting to serve as evidence of damages must measure only those damages attributable to the theory" of liability on which the class action is premised. "If the model does not even attempt to do that, it cannot possibly establish that damages are susceptible of measurement across the entire class for purposes of Rule 23(b)(3)." In this case, however, the district court's inquiry into predominance was never premised on such a formula. As our three fellow circuits have already concluded, we agree that the rule of *Comcast* is largely irrelevant "where determinations on liability and damages have been bifurcated" in accordance with Rule 23(c)(4) and the district court has "reserved all issues concerning damages for individual determination." Even after *Comcast,* the predominance inquiry can still be satisfied under Rule 23(b)(3) if the proceedings are structured to establish "liability on a class-wide basis, with separate hearings to determine—if liability is established—the damages of individual class members." As explained above, this is precisely how the district court planned to calculate the claimants' damages, which "would have to be decided on an individual basis were the cases not being settled." The principal holding of *Comcast* therefore has no application here.

As an additional matter relating to the predominance inquiry, we also address BP's suggestion that *Comcast* prohibits class certification in the present case because payments are made to claimants "who have suffered no injury." In BP's view, payments made under such a formula are not "attributable" to the class action's theory of liability and therefore violate *Comcast*. In support of this argument, BP also has cited our decision in *Bell Atlantic*, which stated (very similarly to *Comcast*) that the predominance inquiry under Rule 23(b)(3) cannot be satisfied when it is premised on a formula for classwide measurement of damages that "is clearly inadequate."

This argument must also be rejected. Neither *Comcast* nor *Bell Atlantic*, nor any other decision that BP has identified, has suggested that predominance under Rule 23(b)(3) can be defeated by a formula for making voluntary payments under a settlement agreement. Both *Comcast* and *Bell Atlantic* addressed formulas for measuring damages in class actions that had been certified for further proceedings on the merits, and neither made any mention of a settlement agreement. The *Amchem* decision, moreover, which did involve a settlement class proposed for certification under Rule 23(b)(3), explained that the predominance inquiry "trains on the legal or factual questions that qualify each class member's case as a genuine controversy, *questions that preexist any settlement*." Indeed, as stated elsewhere in *Amchem*, the existence of a settlement agreement allows the district court to dispense altogether with considering at least one of the Rule 23(b)(3) concerns: "the likely difficulties in managing a class action." Under *Amchem*, when "confronted with a request for settlement-only class certification, a district court need not inquire whether the case, if tried, would present intractable management problems, see Fed. Rule Civ. Proc. 23(b)(3)(D), for the proposal is that there be no trial."

We cannot therefore conceive of why or how a formula for making voluntary payments under a settlement agreement could threaten the predominance of common questions over individual questions in litigation. Indeed, the reason that BP has identified no authority for this proposition is that it is nonsensical. A question of law or fact that is "common" under Rule 23 is one that enables the class action "to generate common answers apt to drive the resolution of the litigation." But after a class action has been settled, by definition the litigation has been resolved and the questions have been answered. For the commonality and predominance inquiries to have any meaning at all, therefore, they must be considered independently from the resolution provided in a settlement—which is precisely what *Amchem* instructs. The arguments raised by BP and the Objectors regarding Rule 23(b)(3) must therefore be rejected.

### D.

BP and the Objectors have also argued that, by virtue of the Class Administrator's interpretations, the class notice distributed to absent class members has been rendered deficient. Under Rule 23(c)(2)(B), "the notice must clearly and concisely state in plain, easily understood language the nature of the action," "the definition of the class certified," "the class claims, issues, or defenses," and other items of information relating to opting out, making objections, and the consequences of the judgment. Without tying their argument to any particular provision of Rule 23(c)(2)(B), BP and the Objectors contend that class members should have been informed of the likelihood that the prospective claimants would include uninjured persons and entities.

In our circuit, however, "it is not required that class members be made cognizant of every material fact that has taken place prior to the notice." Moreover, as we held and as at least four of our fellow circuits have agreed, the class notice must describe the proceedings in "objective, neutral terms." The contention that BP and the Objectors now suggest should have been incorporated into the class notice is neither "objective" nor "neutral" but is an adversarial position that would have been inappropriate for inclusion in a class notice.

Additionally, in *Katrina Canal Breaches,* in which we found a statement in a class notice to be "slightly misleading" regarding a point of Louisiana law, we held that the notice was not rendered deficient because "the statement as written was accurate in its essential point." Here, the class definition was explained in the notice to include persons and entities with economic loss and property damage "arising out of the 'Deepwater Horizon Incident.'" Accordingly, even if we were to accept that the class notice could have been improved by adding the word, "allegedly," this minor legal ambiguity would not be enough to render the class notice deficient. The district court therefore did not abuse its discretion in finding the class notice sufficient under Rule 23(c)(2)(B).

### E.

BP and the Objectors also argue that the Claims Administrator's interpretations preclude approval of the Settlement Agreement under Rule 23(e), which requires a district court to ensure that all class settlements are "fair, reasonable, and adequate." Even the cases cited by BP, however, emphasize that the purpose of Rule 23(e) is "to protect the nonparty members of the class." No case cited by BP or the Objectors suggests that a district court must also safeguard the interests of the defendant, which in most settlements can protect its own interests at the negotiating table. As we stated "the gravamen of an approvable proposed settlement is that it be fair, adequate, and reasonable and is not the product of collusion between the parties." As is abundantly clear from the current controversy surrounding the proper interpretation of Exhibits 4B and 4C, and as the district court expressly found, the Settlement Agreement was concluded in an arms-length negotiation that was free of collusion.

BP also makes a novel argument regarding our decision in *Reed v. General Motors Corp.,* in which we explained that the application of Rule 23(e) should hinge on the analysis of six factors. These factors are: (1) the existence of fraud or collusion behind the settlement; (2) the complexity, expense, and likely duration of the litigation; (3) the stage of the proceedings and the amount of discovery completed; (4) the probability of plaintiffs' success on the merits; (5) the range of possible recovery; and (6) the opinions of the class counsel, class representatives, and absent class members. In the present case, the district court conducted a lengthy and detailed analysis of the proposed settlement under each of the six *Reed* factors. In the district court's view, none of the *Reed* factors counseled against approving the settlement.

BP's argument ignores the six *Reed* factors altogether. Rather, BP relies on a short quotation from *Reed* to suggest that district courts should also ensure that settlement agreements are based on a "fair approximation of class members' relative entitlement." This quotation is clearly taken out of context. No other decision by our court or by any district court has ever cited *Reed* for such a proposition. Nor can any of the six *Reed* factors be easily related to the "fair approximation" analysis that BP proposes. Even attempting to analyze BP's argument under the fifth factor discussed in *Reed,* "the range of possible recovery," BP has identified no reason to believe that the payments made under the Settlement Agreement fall outside the class members' range of "possible" recovery in litigation.

## F.

Last of all, BP and the Objectors have argued that, by virtue of the Class Administrator's interpretations, Rule 23's implicit "ascertainability" requirement is not satisfied. As we held: "In order to maintain a class action, the class sought to be represented must be adequately defined and clearly ascertainable." According to this argument, the Claims Administrator's two Policy Announcements render the class definition irrational and therefore violate the ascertainability requirement. However, as we found in *Rodriguez,* "the possibility that some claimants may fail to prevail on their individual claims will not defeat class membership" on the basis of the ascertainability requirement. Accordingly, this final argument by BP and the Objectors is rejected. In the absence of any other arguments addressing this implicit component of Rule 23, we find that the district court did not abuse its discretion in finding that the settlement class satisfies the ascertainability requirement.

V.

To conclude, the numerous arguments that BP and the Objectors have raised with respect to each of the provisions of Rule 23 are variants, for the most part, of a single argument. Based on our previous decisions, we would reject this argument even if we could consider BP's evidence and accept its factual premise, which we cannot. Under *Mims* and *Rodriguez,* "class certification is not precluded simply because a class may include persons who have not been injured by the defendant's conduct." The result is no different, moreover, under Article III. As we wrote in *Cole,* "it is sufficient for standing purposes that the plaintiffs seek recovery for an economic harm that they *allege* they have suffered," because we "assume *arguendo* the merits" of their claims at the Rule 23 stage.

For the foregoing reasons, therefore, we affirm the district court's order of December 21, 2012.

EMILIO M. GARZA, CIRCUIT JUDGE, DISSENTING:

II.

In addition to straying beyond Article III jurisdictional constraints, the Claims Administrator's interpretation, by eliminating the causation requirement, violates at least two aspects of Rule 23, and runs afoul of the Rules Enabling Act, 28 U.S.C. § 2702(b).

A.

Rule 23(a)(2) requires, as a necessary prerequisite to class certification, that "there are questions of law or fact common to the class." In *Wal-Mart Stores, Inc. v. Dukes*, the Supreme Court interpreted this provision to require that the members of the class have "suffered the same injury." This requires that the class members' claims "depend upon a common contention," the "truth or falsity of which will resolve an issue that is central to the validity of *each one of the claims* in one stroke." The majority asserts that the commonality requirement is satisfied by myriad questions of law and fact about BP's injurious conduct. Certainly, these contentions are central to *many* class member's claims. But Rule 23(a)(2) and *Wal-Mart* require more—the common contentions must go to the validity of *each one of the claims*. Because this class includes a segment of claimants whose injuries need not have been caused by the oil spill, this cannot be so. For example, "whether BP used an improper well design that unreasonably heightened the risk of an incident" says nothing about the validity of a claim for economic injuries caused by factors other than the oil spill. As long as the class impermissibly aggregates those whose injuries were purportedly caused by the oil spill with those without any arguable claim of such causation, questions concerning BP's liability are insufficient to satisfy Rule 23(a) commonality.

The same argument applies with full force to the Rule 23(a)(3) requirement that "the claims or defenses of the representative parties are typical of the claims or defenses of the class." The Supreme Court has observed that the "commonality and typicality requirements of Rule 23(a) tend to merge." *Wal-Mart*. The majority holds that typicality is satisfied because "the class representatives—like all class members—allege economic and/or property damage stemming directly from the Deep water Horizon spill." This disregards the unavoidable fact that causation, initially alleged in Section 1.3.1.2, has been effectively written out by the Claims Administrator. Given the Claims Administrator's controlling interpretation, all class members do not allege injury "stemming directly" from the oil spill.

Rule 23 certification requires that the proposed class meets all the prerequisite requirements of Rule 23(a). Commonality and typicality are absent here.

### B.

The Rules Enabling Act requires that that the rules of procedure "shall not abridge, enlarge or modify any substantive right." 28 U.S.C. § 2702(b). The class action rules must be applied in keeping with this mandate. *See Amchem*. It follows that Rule 23's aggregation function cannot be used to "create new rights and then settle claims brought under them." *Deepwater Horizon I*; *see* (Jordan, J. dissenting) ("Rule 23 serves to efficiently handle claims recognized by law, not to create new claims.").

This Settlement Agreement resolves claims arising under General Maritime Law (tort principles of federal common law) and the Oil Pollution Act. Each of these claims contains some sort of causation element. In order to prevail in a negligence action, a plaintiff must establish that the defendant's breach of duty is the but-for and proximate cause of the injury complained of. Under the Oil Pollution Act, a plaintiff must demonstrate that the costs and damages sought "result from" an oil spill incident. Thus, under the controlling substantive law, there is no right to recover damages for injuries not caused by the defendant's breach. This settlement, however, allows individuals and entities whose injuries were not caused by the oil spill to claim and receive damage payments. That is, the set of eligible claimants is not congruent with the set of actual (those injured by the spill) claimants, the latter being merely a subset of the former. Thus, the settlement eliminates an essential component of the underlying cause of action, creating a legal right for some class members where none exists at law. This violates the Rules Enabling Act—by bringing claimants without causally related injuries into the class, Rule 23's aggregation function has been improperly used to expand substantive rights.

### III.

What makes this case unique, perhaps, is that causation is contemplated on the face of the core documents—the Amended Complaint, Class Definition, and the Settlement Agreement—but eliminated in application by the Claims Administrator's interpretation. In evaluating whether Article Ill's causation requirement for standing has been properly demonstrated at the settlement class certification stage, I would look to the class definition as it has been authoritatively interpreted, not simply as it is ostensibly written. Today, the majority takes another path, turning a blind eye to the Claims Administrator's interpretation.

The concerns identified in this dissent each stem from a common problem: causation has been eliminated for a broad swath of Business Economic Loss claimants. For the foregoing reasons, this requires that the class be decertified. However, this does not necessarily mean that a Settlement Agreement, writ large, is entirely unworkable or that Rule 23 is inapplicable. I simply observe that this attempted global settlement fails in a narrow, but significant, regard. I would vacate the class certification and Settlement Agreement, and remand to allow the parties and the district court to design a solution that complies with Article III, Rule 23, and the Rules Enabling Act.

## IN RE NATIONAL FOOTBALL LEAGUE PLAYERS CONCUSSION INJURY LITIG.

United States Court of Appeals for the Third Circuit, 2016.
2016 WL 1552205.

### I.    INTRODUCTION

The National Football League (NFL) has agreed to resolve lawsuits brought by former players who alleged that the NFL failed to inform them of and protect them from the risks of concussions in football. The District Court approved a class action settlement that covered over 20,000 retired players and released all concussion-related claims against the NFL. Objectors have appealed that decision, arguing that class certification was improper and that the settlement was unfair. But after thorough review, we conclude that the District Court was right to certify the class and approve the settlement. Thus we affirm its decision in full.

### II.    BACKGROUND

#### A.    Concussion Suits Are Brought Against the NFL

In July 2011, 73 former professional football players sued the NFL and Riddell, Inc. in the Superior Court of California. The retired players alleged that the NFL failed to take reasonable actions to protect them from the chronic risks of head injuries in football. The players also claimed that Riddell, a manufacturer of sports equipment, should be liable for the defective design of helmets.

The NFL removed the case to federal court on the ground that the players' claims under state law were preempted by federal labor law. More lawsuits by retired players followed and the NFL moved under 28 U.S.C. § 1407 to consolidate the pending suits before a single judge for pretrial proceedings. In January 2012, the Judicial Panel on Multidistrict Litigation consolidated these cases before Judge Anita B. Brody in the Eastern District of Pennsylvania as a multidistrict litigation (MDL). Since consolidation, 5,000 players have filed over 300 similar lawsuits against the NFL and Riddell. Our appeal only concerns the claims against the NFL.

To manage the litigation, the District Court appointed co-lead class counsel, a Steering Committee, and an Executive Committee. The Steering Committee was charged with performing or delegating all necessary pretrial tasks and the smaller Executive Committee was responsible for the overall coordination of the proceedings. The Court also ordered plaintiffs to submit a Master Administrative Long-Form Complaint and a Master Administrative Class Action Complaint to supersede the numerous then-pending complaints.

The Master Complaints tracked many of the allegations from the first lawsuits. Football puts players at risk of repetitive brain trauma and injury because they suffer concussive and sub-concussive hits during the game and at practice (sub-concussive hits fall below the threshold for a concussion but are still associated with brain damage). Plaintiffs alleged that the NFL had a duty to provide players with rules and information to protect them from the health risks—both short and long-term—of brain injury, including Alzheimer's disease, dementia, depression, deficits in cognitive functioning, reduced processing speed, loss of memory, sleeplessness, mood swings, personality changes, and a recently identified degenerative disease called chronic traumatic encephalopathy (commonly referred to as CTE).

Because CTE figures prominently in this appeal, some background on this condition is in order. It was first identified in 2002 based on analysis of the brain tissue of deceased NFL players, including Mike Webster, Terry Long, Andre Waters, and Justin Strzelczyk. CTE involves the build-up of "tau protein" in the brain, a result associated with repetitive head trauma. Medical personnel have examined approximately 200 brains with CTE as of 2015, in large part because it is only diagnosable post-mortem. That diagnosis requires examining sections of a person's brain under a microscope to see if abnormal tau proteins are present and, if so, whether they occur in the unique pattern associated with CTE. Plaintiffs alleged that CTE affects mood and behavior, causing headaches, aggression, depression, and an increased risk of suicide. They also stated that memory loss, dementia, loss of attention and concentration, and impairment of language are associated with CTE.

The theme of the allegations was that, despite the NFL's awareness of the risks of repetitive head trauma, the League ignored, minimized, or outright suppressed information concerning the link between that trauma and cognitive damage. For example, in 1994 the NFL created the Mild Traumatic Brain Injury Committee to study the effects of head injuries. Per the plaintiffs, the Committee was at the forefront of a disinformation campaign that disseminated "junk science" denying the link between head injuries and cognitive disorders. Based on the allegations against the NFL, plaintiffs asserted claims for negligence, medical monitoring, fraudulent concealment, fraud, negligent misrepresentation, negligent hiring, negligent retention, wrongful death and survival, civil conspiracy, and loss of consortium.

After plaintiffs filed the Master Complaints, the NFL moved to dismiss, arguing that federal labor law preempted the state law claims. Indeed, § 301 of the Labor Management Relations Act preempts state law claims that are "substantially dependent" on the terms of a labor agreement. The NFL claimed that resolution of plaintiffs' claims depended upon the interpretation of Collective Bargaining Agreements (CBAs) in place between the retired players and the NFL. If the CBAs do preempt plaintiffs' claims, they must arbitrate those claims per mandatory arbitration provisions in the CBAs. Plaintiffs responded that their negligence and fraud claims would not require federal courts to interpret the CBAs and in any event the CBAs did not cover all retired players.

## B.    The Parties Reach a Settlement

On July 8, 2013, while the NFL's motion to dismiss was pending, the District Court ordered the parties to mediate and appointed a mediator. On August 29, 2013, after two months of negotiations and more than twelve full days of formal mediation, the parties agreed to a settlement in principle and signed a term sheet. It provided $765 million to fund medical exams and offer compensation for player injuries. The proposed settlement would resolve the claims of all retired players against the NFL related to head injuries.

In January 2014, after more negotiations, class counsel filed in the District Court a class action complaint and sought preliminary class certification and preliminary approval of the settlement. The Court denied the motion because it had doubts that the capped fund for paying claims would be sufficient. It appointed a Special Master to assist with making financial forecasts and, five months later, the parties reached a revised settlement that uncapped the fund for compensating retired players.

Class counsel filed a second motion for preliminary class certification and preliminary approval in June 2014. The District Court granted the motion, preliminarily approved the settlement, conditionally certified the class, approved classwide notice, and scheduled a final fairness hearing. Seven players petitioned for interlocutory review. In September 2014, we denied the petition, later explaining over a dissent that we lacked jurisdiction because the District Court's order preliminarily certifying the class was not an "order granting or denying class-action certification."

Following preliminary certification, potential class members had 90 days to object or opt out of the settlement. Class counsel then moved for final class certification and settlement approval. On November 19, 2014, the District Court held a day-long fairness hearing and heard argument from class counsel, the NFL, and several objectors who voiced concerns against the settlement. After the hearing, the Court proposed several changes to benefit class members. The parties agreed to the proposed changes and submitted an amended settlement in February 2015. On April 22, 2015, the Court granted the motion for class certification and final approval of the amended settlement, that grant explained in a 123-page opinion. Objectors filed 12 separate appeals that were consolidated into this single appeal before us now.

C. The Proposed Settlement

The settlement has three components: (1) an uncapped Monetary Award Fund that provides compensation for retired players who submit proof of certain diagnoses; (2) a $75 million Baseline Assessment Program that provides eligible retired players with free baseline assessment examinations of their objective neurological functioning; and (3) a $10 million Education Fund to instruct football players about injury prevention.

1.    *Monetary Award Fund*

Under the settlement, retired players or their beneficiaries are compensated for developing one of several neurocognitive and neuromuscular impairments or "Qualifying Diagnoses." By "retired players," we mean players who retired from playing NFL football before the preliminary approval of the class settlement on July 7, 2014. The settlement recognizes six Qualifying Diagnoses: (1) Level 1.5 Neurocognitive Impairment; (2) Level 2 Neurocognitive Impairment; (3) Alzheimer's Disease; (4) Parkinson's Disease; (5) Amyotrophic Lateral Sclerosis ("ALS"); and (6) Death with CTE provided the player died before final approval of the settlement on April 22, 2015. A retired player does not need to show that his time in the NFL caused the onset of the Qualifying Diagnosis.

A Qualifying Diagnosis entitles a retired player to a maximum monetary award:

| Qualifying Diagnosis | Maximum Award |
|---|---|
| Level 1.5 Neurocognitive Impairment | $1.5 Million |
| Level 2 Neurocognitive Impairment | $3 Million |
| Parkinson's Disease | $3.5 Million |

| Alzheimer's Disease | $3.5 Million |
| Death with CTE | $4 Million |
| ALS | $5 Million |

This award is subject to several offsets, that is, awards decrease: (1) as the age at which a retired player is diagnosed increases; (2) if the retired player played fewer than five eligible seasons; (3) if the player did not have a baseline assessment examination; and (4) if the player suffered a severe traumatic brain injury or stroke unrelated to NFL play.

To collect from the Fund, a class member must register with the claims administrator within 180 days of receiving notice that the settlement has been approved. This deadline can be excused for good cause. The class member then must submit a claims package to the administrator no later than two years after the date of the Qualifying Diagnosis or within two years after the supplemental notice is posted on the settlement website, whichever is later. This deadline can be excused for substantial hardship. The claims package must include a certification by the diagnosing physician and supporting medical records. The claims administrator will notify the class member within 60 days if he is entitled to an award. The class member, class counsel, and the NFL have the right to appeal an award determination. To do so, a class member must submit a $1,000 fee, which is refunded if the appeal is successful and can be waived for financial hardship. A fee is not required for the NFL and class counsel to appeal, though the NFL must act in good faith when appealing award determinations.

The Monetary Award Fund is uncapped and will remain in place for 65 years. Every retired player who timely registers and qualifies during the lifespan of the settlement will receive an award. If, after receiving an initial award, a retired player receives a more serious Qualifying Diagnosis, he may receive a supplemental award.

### 2. Baseline Assessment Program

Any retired player who has played at least half of an eligible season can receive a baseline assessment examination. It consists of a neurological examination performed by credentialed and licensed physicians selected by a court-appointed administrator. Qualified providers may diagnose retired players with Level 1, 1.5, or 2 Neurocognitive Impairment. The results of the examinations can also be compared with any future tests to determine whether a retired player's cognitive abilities have deteriorated.

Baseline Assessment Program funds will also provide Baseline Assessment Program Supplemental Benefits. Retired players diagnosed with Level 1 Neurocognitive Impairment—evidencing some objective decline in cognitive function but not yet early dementia—are eligible to receive medical benefits, including further testing, treatment, counseling, and pharmaceutical coverage.

The Baseline Assessment Program lasts for 10 years. All retired players who seek and are eligible for a baseline assessment examination receive one notwithstanding the $75 million cap. Every eligible retired player age 43 or over must take a baseline assessment examination within two years of the Program's start-up. Every eligible retired player younger than age 43 must do so before the end of the program or by his 45th birthday, whichever comes first.

### 3. Education Fund

The Education Fund is a $10 million fund to promote safety and injury prevention in football. The purpose is to promote safety-related initiatives in youth football and educate retired players about their medical and disability benefits under the CBA. Class counsel and the NFL, with input from the retired players, will propose specific educational initiatives for the District Court's approval.

### 4. The Proposed Class

All living NFL football players who retired from playing professional football before July 7, 2014, as well as their representative claimants and derivative claimants, comprise the proposed class. Representative claimants are those duly authorized by law to assert the claims of deceased, legally incapacitated, or incompetent retired players. Derivative claimants are those, such as parents, spouses, or dependent children, who have some legal right to the income of retired players. Even though the proposed class consists of more than just retired players, we use the terms "class members" and "retired players" interchangeably.

The proposed class contains two subclasses based on a retired players' injuries as of the preliminary approval date. Subclass 1 consists of retired players who were not diagnosed with a Qualifying Diagnosis prior to July 7, 2014, and their representative and derivative claimants. Put another way, subclass 1 includes retired players who have no currently known injuries that would be compensated under the settlement. Subclass 2 consists of retired players who were diagnosed with a Qualifying Diagnosis prior to July 7, 2014, and their representative claimants and derivative claimants. Translated, subclass 2 includes retired players who are currently injured and will receive an immediate monetary award under the settlement. The NFL estimates that the total population of retired players is 21,070. Of this, 28% are expected to be diagnosed with a compensable disease. The remaining 72% are not expected to develop a compensable disease during their lifetime.

Class members release all claims and actions against the NFL "arising out of, or relating to, head, brain and/or cognitive injury, as well as any injuries arising out of, or relating to, concussions and/or sub-concussive events," including claims relating to CTE. The releases do not compromise the benefits that retired players are entitled to receive under the CBAs, nor do they compromise their retirement benefits, disability benefits, and health insurance.

Of the over 20,000 estimated class members (the NFL states that the number exceeds 21,000), 234 initially asked to opt out from the settlement and 205 class members joined 83 written objections submitted to the District Court. Before the fairness hearing, 26 of the 234 opt-outs sought readmission to the class. After the District Court granted final approval, another 6 opt-outs sought readmission. This leaves 202 current opt-outs, of which class counsel notes only 169 were timely filed.

### III. JURISDICTION AND STANDARD OF REVIEW

We review the decision to certify a class and approve a classwide settlement for abuse of discretion. It exists "if the district court's decision rests upon a clearly erroneous finding of fact, an errant conclusion of law or an improper application of law to fact." *In re Hydrogen Peroxide Antitrust Litig.*

This appeal principally presents two questions—whether the District Court abused its discretion (1) in certifying the class of retired NFL players and (2) in concluding that the terms of the settlement were fair, reasonable, and adequate. Objectors (95 in all) have filed 11 separate briefs totaling some 500 pages addressing these questions. We address each of these arguments, but refer to objectors collectively throughout our opinion rather than cross-referencing particular objectors with particular arguments.

### IV. CLASS CERTIFICATION

Rule 23(a) lays out four threshold requirements for certification of a class action: (1) numerosity; (2) commonality; (3) typicality; and (4) adequacy of representation. "The parties seeking class certification bear the burden of establishing by a preponderance of the evidence that the requirements of Rule 23(a) have been met." If that occurs, we consider whether the class meets the requirements of one of three categories of class actions in Rule 23(b). This is a Rule 23(b)(3) class action under which we consider whether (1) common questions predominate over any questions affecting only individual class members (predominance) and (2) class resolution is superior to other available methods to decide the controversy (superiority). Fed.R.Civ.P. 23(b)(3).

#### A. Numerosity

Rule 23(a)(1) requires that a class be "so numerous that joinder of all members is impracticable." Fed.R.Civ.P. 23(a)(1). There is no magic number of class members needed for a suit to proceed as a class action. We have set a rough guidepost in our precedents, however, and stated that numerosity is generally satisfied if there are more than 40 class members.

The District Court found that a class of 20,000 retired players would be sufficient for numerosity. No objector challenges this finding on appeal.

## B. Commonality

"A putative class satisfies Rule 23(a)'s commonality requirement if the named plaintiffs share at least one question of fact or law with the grievances of the prospective class." "Their claims must depend upon a common contention that it is capable of classwide resolution—which means that determination of its truth or falsity will resolve an issue that is central to the validity of each of the claims in one stroke." *Wal-Mart Stores, Inc. v. Dukes.* Meeting this requirement is easy enough: "We have acknowledged commonality to be present even when not all members of the plaintiff class suffered an actual injury, when class members did not have identical claims, and, most dramatically, when some members' claims were arguably not even viable."

The District Court concluded that "critical factual questions" were common to all class members, including "whether the NFL Parties knew and suppressed information about the risks of concussive hits, as well as causation questions about whether concussive hits increase the likelihood that retired players will develop conditions that lead to Qualifying Diagnoses." It also found common legal questions, including the "nature and extent of any duty owed to retired players by the NFL Parties, and whether labor preemption, workers' compensation, or some affirmative defense would bar their claims."

Some objectors argue that commonality was lacking. Citing the Supreme Court's decision in *Wal-Mart,* they contend that the retired players do not share common issues of fact or law because they were injured in different ways and over different periods of time. For example, the claims of a lineman who played fifteen seasons in the NFL, so goes the argument, will share little in common with those of a back-up quarterback who played two seasons.

These objections miss the mark. In *Wal-Mart,* the Supreme Court held that commonality was lacking when a putative class of 1.5 million female employees alleged sex discrimination by their local supervisors. The local supervisors had discretion in making employment decisions and the class of female employees faced different managers making different employment decisions (some presumably nondiscriminatory). The proposed class thus could not identify common questions capable of classwide resolution.

The concerns in *Wal-Mart* do not apply here because the NFL Parties allegedly injured retired players through the same course of conduct. Even if players' particular injuries are unique, their negligence and fraud claims still depend on the same common questions regarding the NFL's conduct. For example, when did the NFL know about the risks of concussion? What did it do to protect players? Did the League conceal the risks of head injuries? These questions are common to the class and capable of classwide resolution.

## C. *Typicality*

Rule 23(a)(3) requires that the class representatives' claims be "typical of the claims of the class." Fed.R.Civ.P. 23(a)(3). This "ensures the interests of the class and the class representatives are aligned 'so that the latter will work to benefit the entire class through the pursuit of their own goals.'" (quoting *Barnes v. Am. Tobacco Co.*). We also have set a "low threshold" for typicality. "'Even relatively pronounced factual differences will generally not preclude a finding of typicality where there is a strong similarity of legal theories' or where the claim arises from the same practice or course of conduct."

The class representatives, Shawn Wooden and Kevin Turner, were named in the class action complaint and were selected by class counsel. Wooden is a retired player with no Qualifying Diagnosis. Like other retired players without a current diagnosis, he sought a baseline assessment examination to determine whether he had shown signs of cognitive decline and, in the unfortunate event that he developed one of the Qualifying Diagnoses, he would seek a monetary award. Turner was a retired player living with ALS. Like other retired players with currently known injuries, he sought a monetary award. The District Court concluded that the claims of Wooden and Turner were "typical of those they represent." We agree.

Some objectors argue that the claims of the class representatives are not typical because of factual differences between the representatives and other class members, including the number of seasons played and injuries caused by head trauma. But class members need not "share identical claims," and "cases challenging the same unlawful conduct which affects both the named plaintiffs and the putative class usually satisfy the typicality requirement irrespective of the varying fact patterns underlying the individual claims." What matters is that Wooden and Turner seek recovery under the same legal theories for the same wrongful conduct as the subclasses they represent. Even if the class representatives' injuries are unique to their time in football, the NFL's alleged fraudulent concealment of the risks of head injuries is the same.

## D. *Adequacy of Representation*

Rule 23(a)(4) requires class representatives to "fairly and adequately protect the interests of the class." Fed.R.Civ.P. 23(a)(4). It tests the qualifications of class counsel and the class representatives. It also aims to root out conflicts of interest within the class to ensure that all class members are fairly represented in the negotiations. Several objectors challenge the District Court's adequacy-of-representation finding, but we conclude that it was not an abuse of discretion.

*1.   Class Counsel*

When examining settlement classes, we "have emphasized the special need to assure that class counsel: (1) possessed adequate experience; (2) vigorously prosecuted the action; and (3) acted at arm's length from the defendant." Rule 23(g) also sets out a non-exhaustive list of factors for courts to consider when appointing class counsel. They include counsel's work in the pending class action, experience in handling class actions or other complex litigation, knowledge of the applicable law, and the resources available for representing the class.

When class counsel and the NFL began mediation, there was only one proposed class of all retired players. Class counsel, in consultation with members of the Steering Committee and the Executive Committee, decided early in the negotiations that creating two separate subclasses "would best serve all class members' interests and meet with Due Process." To that end, class counsel designated lawyers from the Steering Committee to serve as subclass counsel.

In its final certification and approval order, the District Court found that class counsel and subclass counsel were experienced in litigating mass torts and personal injury actions, vigorously prosecuted the action at arm's length from the NFL, and were able to extract substantial concessions in the process. The Court thus concluded that class counsel adequately protected the interests of the class. No objectors challenge the experience or qualifications of class and subclass counsel. They do make two related arguments regarding the adequacy of the subclass representation, though neither convinces us that the District Court abused its discretion.

Objectors first assert that the procedure for selecting subclass counsel did not ensure adequate representation because subclass counsel came from the team of lawyers already negotiating with the NFL. We agree that class counsel could have gone to the District Court and asked it to appoint counsel from the outside. Yet objectors point us to no precedent requiring such a procedure. Moreover, the District Court assured itself that counsel were adequate representatives. They were selected early in the negotiations, had already been approved by the District Court to serve on the Steering Committee, and were by all accounts active participants in the settlement negotiations. In these circumstances, the District Court did not abuse its discretion in accepting subclass counsel as adequate representatives.

Objectors next press that the subclass counsel for future claimants, Arnold Levin, was not an adequate representative, as he represented nine players who alleged current symptoms in two lawsuits against the NFL. Levin disclosed to the District Court in an application for the Steering Committee that he has agreed to fees in these cases on a one-third contingency basis. Objectors argue to us that Levin's representation of these players created a conflict with his duties to represent the subclass of retired players with no Qualifying Diagnoses. Yet objectors failed to raise this contention in the District Court and did not meaningfully assert it on appeal until their reply brief. If they had raised concerns over Levin's representation of other players, we have no doubt the District Court could ably have addressed this argument. This is part of the reason why we do not normally consider arguments not raised in the District Court—even in class actions—and deem them waived.

That said, some courts have relaxed the standards for waiver in class actions ("Class members were not obliged, on penalty of waiver, to search on their own for a conflict of interest on the part of a class representative."). We agree that the usual waiver rules should not be applied mechanically in class actions. We have an independent obligation to protect the interests of the class, and in many instances class members are far removed from the litigation and lack the information and incentive to object. *See GM Trucks* ("The court plays the important role of protector of the absentees' interests, in a sort of fiduciary capacity, by approving appropriate representative plaintiffs and class counsel."). Accordingly, we retain discretion to consider arguments that go to the heart of the class settlement's adequacy and fairness. Out of caution, we decline to apply the penalty of waiver in this instance.

Turning to the merits, we do not see how representation by Levin created a conflict of interest. He disclosed his representation of the players to the District Court, and it was still satisfied that he was an adequate representative. Beyond this, there is no evidence in the record before us that the players named in the complaints have a current Qualifying Diagnosis. Rather, they simply allege current symptoms that are not themselves Qualifying Diagnoses, including memory loss, headaches, mood swings, and sensitivity to light. Many players without a current Qualifying Diagnosis presumably have similar symptoms. Accordingly, this is not a situation where subclass counsel has clients in both subclasses and there is a risk of a conflict.

### 2.  Class Representatives

A class representative must represent a class capably and diligently. "A minimal degree of knowledge" about the litigation is adequate. The District Court found that the class representatives ably discharged their duties by closely following the litigation, authorizing the filing of the Class Action Complaint, and approving the final settlement.

Some objectors argue that the Court abused its discretion in approving Wooden as representative for the subclass of players with no Qualifying Diagnoses because he did not claim the risk of developing CTE. This is incorrect. In the Class Action Complaint Wooden alleged that he is "at increased risk of latent brain injuries caused by repeated traumatic head impacts." This allegation covers the risk of CTE, which is associated with repeated head impacts. Moreover, what matters more than the words

Wooden used to describe his current health are the interests he would have in representing the subclass. Given what we know about CTE, Wooden, and all retired NFL players for that matter, are at risk of developing the disease and would have an interest in compensation for CTE in the settlement.

### 3.   Conflicts of Interest

"The adequacy inquiry under Rule 23(a)(4) serves to uncover conflicts of interest between named parties and the class they seek to represent." *Amchem Prods.* The "linchpin of the adequacy requirement is the alignment of interests and incentives between the representative plaintiffs and the rest of the class." But not all intra-class conflicts are created equal. If they concern "specific issues in controversy," they are called "fundamental." This hits the heart of Rule 23(a)(4) and will defeat a finding of adequacy.

A recurring fundamental conflict is the divide between present and future injury plaintiffs identified in *Amchem.* Counsel in that case sought to approve a class settlement and certify a nationwide class of persons— numbering between 250,000 and 2,000,000—who shared an unfortunate fact in common: they were all exposed to asbestos-containing products manufactured by 20 companies. The class settlement purported to resolve the claims of persons who had already sustained injuries as a result of asbestos exposure (those with present injuries) and those who had been exposed to asbestos but had not yet developed any injury (those with future injuries, if any injury at all). The District Court approved the settlement and certified the class, but we reversed because, among other things, conflicts of interest within the class precluded a finding of adequacy. Judge Becker explained that the "most salient" conflict of interest was between those with present and future injuries:

> As rational actors, those who are not yet injured would want reduced current payouts (through caps on compensation awards and limits on the number of claims that can be paid each year). The futures plaintiffs should also be interested in protection against inflation, in not having preset limits on how many cases can be handled, and in limiting the ability of defendant companies to exit the settlement. Moreover, in terms of the structure of the alternative dispute resolution mechanism established by the settlement, they should desire causation provisions that can keep pace with changing science and medicine, rather than freezing in place the science of 1993. Finally, because of the difficulty in forecasting what their futures hold, they would probably desire a delayed opt out
>
> In contrast, those who are currently injured would rationally want to maximize current payouts. Furthermore, currently injured plaintiffs would care little about inflation-protection. The delayed

opt out desired by futures plaintiffs would also be of little interest to the presently injured; indeed, their interests are against such an opt-out as the more people locked into the settlement, the more likely it is to survive. In sum, presently injured class representatives cannot adequately represent the futures plaintiffs' interests and vice versa.

The Supreme Court affirmed on this point and agreed that "the interests of those within the single class are not aligned." *Amchem.*

To overcome a conflict of interest within a proposed class, there must be "structural protections to assure that differently situated plaintiffs negotiate for their own unique interests." A common structural protection is the creation of discrete subclasses, each with its own independent representation. *See Ortiz v. Fibreboard Corp.* ("A class divided between holders of present and future claims requires division into homogenous subclasses with separate representation to eliminate conflicting interests of counsel.").

The District Court found no fundamental conflict of interest in this class. It explained the incentives of class members were aligned because they "allegedly were injured by the same scheme: the NFL negligently and fraudulently de-emphasized the medical effects of concussions to keep retired players in games." Moreover, the two subclasses of players guarded against any *Amchem* conflict of interest. Turner, the representative for those with current injuries, "is interested in immediately obtaining the greatest possible compensation for his injuries and symptoms." Wooden, the representative for those who may develop injuries that manifest in the future, "is interested in monitoring his symptoms, guaranteeing that generous compensation will be available far into the future, and ensuring an agreement that keeps pace with scientific advances while compensating as many conditions as possible." The District Court also cited other structural protections, including uncapped and inflation-adjusted monetary awards, the guarantee of a baseline assessment examination, and the presence of a mediator and special master.

The Court's analysis was on point. Some objectors argue that this class action suffers from a conflict of interest between present and future injury plaintiffs. But simply put, this case is not *Amchem.* The most important distinction is that class counsel here took *Amchem* into account by using the subclass structure to protect the sometimes divergent interests of the retired players. The subclasses were represented in the negotiations by separate class representatives with separate counsel, and, as discussed, each was an adequate representative. This alone is a significant structural protection for the class that weighs in favor of finding adequacy.

Moreover, the terms of the settlement reflect that the interests of current and future claimants were represented in the negotiations. The Monetary Award Fund will start paying out claims immediately, providing relief to those currently living with injuries. The Fund is uncapped and inflation-adjusted, protecting the interests of those who worry about developing injuries in the future. The NFL and class counsel must meet every ten years and confer in good faith about "prospective modifications to the definitions of Qualifying Diagnoses and/or the protocols for making Qualifying Diagnoses, in light of generally accepted advances in medical science." This allows the settlement to keep pace with changing science regarding the existing Qualifying Diagnoses. As observed, these are the sorts of settlement terms that rational actors from both subclasses would be interested in when negotiating the resolution of their claims.

Finally, one of the principal concerns driving *Amchem's* strict analysis of adequacy of representation was the worry that persons with a nebulous risk of developing injuries would have little or no reason to protect their rights and interests in the settlement. We have evidence that in this case the concern is misplaced because many retired players with no currently compensable injuries have already taken significant steps to protect their rights and interests. Of the 5,000 players who sued the NFL in the MDL proceedings, class counsel estimated that 3,900 have no current Qualifying Diagnosis. These 3,900 players are represented, in turn, by approximately 300 lawyers. And with so many sets of eyes reviewing the terms of the settlement, the overwhelming majority of retired players elected to stay in the class and benefit from the settlement. We thus have little problem saying that their interests were adequately represented.

Objectors further claim that the settlement's treatment of CTE demonstrates a fundamental conflict of interest between present and future injury class members. Under the settlement, retired players who died before final approval of the settlement and received a post-mortem CTE diagnosis are entitled to an award. For any player who died after final approval, a post-mortem CTE diagnosis is not compensable. Objectors cite this difference in recovery as evidence that the subclass of players with a Qualifying Diagnosis may have bargained away the CTE claims of other players. *GM Trucks* ("A settlement that offers considerably more value to one class of plaintiffs than to another may be trading the claims of the latter group away in order to enrich the former group.").

This argument misunderstands the role of the monetary award for CTE. As the District Court noted in discussing the fairness of the settlement, the monetary award "serves as a proxy for Qualifying Diagnoses deceased retired players *could* have received while living." Retired players who were living with symptoms associated with one of the other Qualifying Diagnoses, but died before approval of the settlement, may not have had sufficient notice of the need to be diagnosed. To provide some compensation to these players, the parties created an award for the post-mortem diagnosis of CTE. The NFL's own estimate is that 46 players out of a class exceeding at least 20,000 will fall into this category and will receive an average award, after offsets, of $1,910,000. The monetary award for CTE is thus an attempt to compensate deceased players who would otherwise be unable to get the benefits available to the class going forward. It is not evidence of a debilitating conflict of interest in the class settlement.

### E.  Predominance

Turning to the additional requirements for certifying a class action under Rule 23(b)(3), the class may be maintained if "the court finds that the questions of law or fact common to class members predominate over any questions affecting only individual members." Predominance "tests whether proposed classes are sufficiently cohesive to warrant adjudication by representation." *Amchem*. "We have previously noted that the Rule 23(b)(3) predominance requirement, which is far more demanding, incorporates the Rule 23(a) commonality requirement."

The District Court found that this class action presented predominate factual questions regarding the NFL's knowledge and conduct as well as common scientific questions regarding causation. The negligence claims "depend on establishing that the NFL knew of the dangers of concussive hits, yet failed to modify the rules of NFL Football to mitigate them, or even to warn retired players that they were risking serious cognitive injury by continuing to play." *Id.* at 380. The fraud claims "suggest a similarly far-reaching scheme, alleging that the MTBI Committee repeatedly obfuscated the link between football play and head trauma." We agree with the District Court that predominance is satisfied in this case.

Objectors argue that damage claims in a mass-tort class action such as this are too individualized to satisfy the requirements of predominance. They cite to *Amchem* where, as we have discussed, a nationwide class of persons exposed to asbestos could not meet the predominance requirement. But *Amchem* itself warned that it does not mean that a mass tort case will never clear the hurdle of predominance. ("Even mass tort cases arising from a common cause or disaster may, depending upon the circumstances, satisfy the predominance requirement."). Moreover, this class of retired NFL players does not present the same obstacles for predominance as the *Amchem* class of hundreds of thousands (maybe millions) of persons exposed to asbestos.

### F.  Superiority

Rule 23(b)(3)'s superiority requirement "asks the court to balance, in terms of fairness and efficiency, the merits of a class action against those of alternative available methods of adjudication." We consider the class members' interests in individually controlling litigation, the extent and nature of any litigation, the desirability or undesirability of concentrating the litigation, and the likely difficulties in managing a class action. The District Court found superiority satisfied because "the settlement avoids thousands of duplicative lawsuits and enables fast processing of a multitude of claims."

No objectors challenge this conclusion, and we have no disagreements with the District Court's analysis. At the time the settlement was reached, 5,000 players had filed over 300 lawsuits in the MDL. Assuming the retired players' claims survived the NFL's motions to dismiss, the resolution of so many individual lawsuits would have presented serious challenges for the District Court. Given our experience with similar MDLs, we expect the proceedings would result in years of costly litigation and multiple appeals, all the while delaying any potential recovery for retired players coping with serious health challenges.

## VI.  CLASS SETTLEMENT

A class action cannot be settled without court approval based on a determination that the proposed settlement is fair, reasonable, and adequate. Fed.R.Civ.P. 23(e)(2). The inquiry into the settlement's fairness under Rule 23(e) "protects unnamed class members from unjust or unfair settlements affecting their rights when the representatives become fainthearted before the action is adjudicated or are able to secure satisfaction of their individual claims by a compromise." *Amchem*.

"The decision of whether to approve a proposed settlement of a class action is left to the sound discretion of the district court." It "bears the important responsibility of protecting absent class members, 'which is executed by the court's assuring that the settlement represents adequate compensation for the release of the class claims.'" In cases of settlement classes, where district courts are certifying a class and approving a settlement in tandem, they should be "even 'more scrupulous than usual' when examining the fairness of the proposed settlement."

### A.  *Presumption of Fairness*

We apply an initial presumption of fairness in reviewing a class settlement when: "(1) the negotiations occurred at arms-length; (2) there was sufficient discovery; (3) the proponents of the settlement are experienced in similar litigation; and (4) only a small fraction of the class objected." The District Court found each of these elements satisfied and applied the presumption. Objectors argue that the presumption should not have applied at all because class counsel did not conduct formal discovery into the fraud and negligence claims against the NFL before reaching the settlement. We conclude that the Court did not abuse its discretion in finding class counsel's informal discovery to be sufficient.

By the time of the settlement, class counsel had undertaken significant informal discovery. For instance, they had obtained a comprehensive database of the claims and symptoms of retired players and had enlisted the assistance of medical experts. They also had a grasp of the legal hurdles that the retired players would need to clear in order to succeed on their fraud and negligence claims, in particular the potentially dispositive issue of federal labor law preemption. Thus, in negotiations with the NFL class counsel "were aware of the strengths and weaknesses of their case." To the extent objectors ask us to require formal discovery before presuming that a settlement is fair, we decline the invitation. In some cases, informal discovery will be enough for class counsel to assess the value of the class' claims and negotiate a settlement that provides fair compensation.

### B.   Girsh & Prudential *Factors*

In *Girsh v. Jepson,* we noted nine factors to be considered when determining the fairness of a proposed settlement:

> (1) the complexity, expense and likely duration of the litigation; (2) the reaction of the class to the settlement; (3) the stage of the proceedings and the amount of discovery completed; (4) the risks of establishing liability; (5) the risks of establishing damages; (6) the risks of maintaining the class action through the trial; (7) the ability of the defendants to withstand a greater judgment; (8) the range of reasonableness of the settlement fund in light of the best possible recovery; and (9) the range of reasonableness of the settlement fund to a possible recovery in light of all the attendant risks of litigation.

"The settling parties bear the burden of proving that the *Girsh* factors weigh in favor of approval of the settlement." A district court's findings under the *Girsh* test are those of fact. Unless clearly erroneous, they are upheld. Later, in *Prudential Insurance* we held that, because of a "seachange in the nature of class actions," it might be useful to expand the *Girsh* factors to include several permissive and non-exhaustive factors:

> [1] the maturity of the underlying substantive issues, as measured by experience in adjudicating individual actions, the development of scientific knowledge, the extent of discovery on the merits, and other factors that bear on the ability to assess the probable outcome of a trial on the merits of liability and individual damages; [2] the existence and probable outcome of claims by other classes and subclasses; [3] the comparison between the results achieved by the settlement for individual class or subclass members and the results achieved—or likely to be achieved—for other claimants; [4] whether class or subclass members are accorded the right to opt out of the settlement; [5] whether any provisions for attorneys' fees are reasonable; and [6] whether the procedure for processing individual claims under the settlement is fair and reasonable.

"Unlike the *Girsh* factors, each of which the district court must consider before approving a class settlement, the *Prudential* considerations are just that, prudential."

The District Court in our case went through the *Girsh* factors and the relevant *Prudential* factors in great detail before concluding that the terms of the settlement were fair, reasonable, and adequate. Objectors try to challenge the District Court's analysis in several ways, but none convinces us.

### 1.   Complexity, Expense, and Likely Duration of the Litigation

"The first factor 'captures the probable costs, in both time and money, of continued litigation.'" The District Court concluded that the probable costs of continued litigation in the MDL were significant and that this factor weighed in favor of approving the settlement. Some objectors assert that the District Court overestimated the costs of continued litigation because the negligence and fraud claims were "straightforward." This is not the case. Over 5,000 retired NFL players in the MDL alleged a multi-decade fraud by the NFL, and litigating these claims would have been an enormous undertaking. The discovery needed to prove the NFL's fraudulent concealment of the risks of concussions was extensive. The District Court would then resolve many issues of causation and medical science. Finally, if the cases did not settle or were not dismissed, individual suits would be remanded to district courts throughout the country for trial. We agree with the District Court that the expense of this process weighs strongly in the settlement's favor.

### 2.   Reaction of the Class to the Settlement

"The second *Girsh* factor 'attempts to gauge whether members of the class support the settlement.'" As noted, the case began with a class of approximately 20,000 retired players, of which 5,000 are currently represented by counsel in the MDL proceedings. Notice of the settlement reached an estimated 90% of those players through direct mail and secondary publications (in addition to the extensive national media coverage of this case). As of 10 days before the fairness hearing, more than 5,200 class members had signed up to receive additional information about the settlement and the settlement website had more than 64,000 unique visitors. With all this attention, only approximately 1% of class members objected and approximately 1% of class members opted out. We agree with the District Court that these figures weigh in favor of settlement approval.

Some note that the percentage of objectors was even lower in *GM Trucks,* a case where we declined to approve a settlement. There, "of approximately 5.7 million class members, 6,450 owners objected and 5,203 opted out." But in *GM* we looked past the low objection rate because there were "other indications that the class reaction to the suit was quite negative," including our concern that the passive victims of a product defect lacked "adequate interest and information to voice objections." Those concerns are not present here. By the time of the settlement, many of the retired players in this class already had counsel and had sued the NFL, suggesting that their claims were valuable enough to pursue in court and that the players were informed enough to evaluate the settlement.

### 3.    Stage of the Proceedings and Amount of Discovery Completed

"The third *Girsh* factor 'captures the degree of case development that class counsel had accomplished prior to settlement. Through this lens, courts can determine whether counsel had an adequate appreciation of the merits of the case before negotiating.' "

The District Court concluded that class counsel adequately evaluated the merits of the preemption and causation issues through informal discovery, and, after ten months of settlement negotiations, the stage of the proceedings weighed in favor of settlement approval. Objectors claim that the lack of formal discovery in this matter should have weighed more heavily against settlement. As with the presumption of fairness, formal discovery is not a requirement for the third *Girsh* factor. What matters is not the amount or type of discovery class counsel pursued, but whether they had developed enough information about the case to appreciate sufficiently the value of the claims. Moreover, requiring parties to conduct formal discovery before reaching a proposed class settlement would take a valuable bargaining chip—the costs of formal discovery itself—off the table during negotiations. This could deter the early settlement of disputes.

### 4.    Risks of Establishing Liability and Damages

"The fourth and fifth *Girsh* factors survey the possible risks of litigation in order to balance the likelihood of success and the potential damage award if the case were taken to trial against the benefits of an immediate settlement." We concur with the District Court that this factor weighed in favor of settlement because class members "faced stiff challenges surmounting the issues of preemption and causation."

To start, if the NFL were to prevail in its motion to dismiss on the issue of federal labor law preemption, "many, if not all," of the class members' claims would be dismissed. Objectors claim the District Court misjudged the risks of establishing liability and damages on this front. They argue that the NFL's preemption defense would not apply to all class members because there were no CBAs in effect before 1968 and between 1987 and 1993. But even if there were a small subset of players unaffected by the preemption defense, the defense still had the capability of denying relief to the majority of class members and this weighs in favor of approving the settlement.

As for causation, the District Court noted that retired players would need to show both general causation (that repetitive head trauma is capable of causing ALS, Alzheimer's, and the like), and specific causation (that the brain trauma suffered by a particular player in fact caused his specific impairments). With general causation, the Court found that even though "a consensus is emerging that repetitive mild brain injury is associated with the Qualifying Diagnoses," the "available research is not nearly robust enough to discount the risks" of litigation. And specific causation would be even more troublesome because a player would need to distinguish the effect of hits he took during his NFL career from the effect of those he received in high school football, college football, or other contact sports. Objectors argue that the District Court put too little faith in the ability of the class to show causation because the NFL has admitted that concussions can lead to long-term problems and formal discovery could disclose that it fraudulently concealed the risks of concussions. But neither of these points is particularly helpful for overcoming the general and specific causation hurdles the District Court identified.

### 5.  Risks of Maintaining Class Action Through Trial

The District Court found that the likelihood of obtaining and keeping a class certification if the action were to proceed to trial weighed in favor of approving the settlement, but it deserved only minimal consideration. This was correct. In a settlement class, this factor becomes essentially "toothless" because " 'a district court need not inquire whether the case, if tried, would present intractable management problems, for the proposal is that there be no trial.' "

### 6.  Ability of Defendants to Withstand a Greater Judgment

The seventh *Girsh* factor is most relevant when the defendant's professed inability to pay is used to justify the amount of the settlement. In the case of the NFL, the District Court found this factor neutral because the NFL did not cite potential financial instability as justification for the settlement's size. In fact, it agreed to uncap the Monetary Award Fund and is thus duty bound to pay every compensable claim.

Some objectors complain that the settlement, which may cost the NFL $1 billion over its lifetime, represents a "fraction of one year's revenues." Even so, that does not change the analysis of this *Girsh* factor. Indeed, " 'in any class action against a large corporation, the defendant entity is likely to be able to withstand a more substantial judgment, and, against the weight of the remaining factors, this fact alone does not undermine the reasonableness of the settlement.' "

### 7.  Range of Reasonableness of the Settlement in Light of the Best Possible Recovery and All Attendant Risks of Litigation

In evaluating the eighth and ninth *Girsh* factors, we ask "whether the settlement represents a good value for a weak case or a poor value for a strong case." "The factors test two sides of the same coin: reasonableness in light of the best possible recovery and reasonableness in light of the risks the parties would face if the case went to trial." "The present value of the damages plaintiffs would likely recover if successful, appropriately discounted for the risk of not prevailing, should be compared with the amount of the proposed settlement."

If the retired players were successful in their fraud and negligence claims, they would likely be entitled to substantial damages awards. But we must take seriously the litigation risks inherent in pressing forward with the case. The NFL's pending motion to dismiss and other available affirmative defenses could have left retired players to pursue claims in arbitration or with no recovery at all. Hence we agree with the District Court that the settlement represents a fair deal for the class when compared with a risk-adjusted estimate of the value of plaintiffs' claims. Objectors claim that the District Court should have taken into account the costs to class members of the registration and claims administration process because they decrease the "real value" for the class. But these costs are not relevant to the eighth and ninth *Girsh* factors. And in any event the Court assured itself that the claims process was "reasonable in light of the substantial monetary awards and imposes no more requirements than necessary."

### 8.   *Prudential Factors*

The District Court found that the relevant *Prudential* factors also weighed in favor of approving the settlement. No objectors engage with the Court's findings on this front. But briefly, we agree that class counsel was able to assess the probable outcome of this case, class members had the opportunity to opt out, and the claims process is reasonable. The provision of attorneys' fees was a neutral factor because class counsel has not yet moved for a fee award.

### C.   *Settlement's Treatment of CTE*

Objectors raise other arguments about the fairness of the settlement that do not necessarily fall neatly within one of the *Girsh* factors. The most common of those arguments is that the exclusion of CTE as a Qualifying Diagnosis for future claimants is unfair. Objectors note that CTE, the "industrial disease of football," was at the center of the first concussion lawsuits and argue that claims for CTE compensation are released by the settlement in return for nothing. The District Court carefully considered this argument before deciding that the settlement's treatment of CTE was reasonable. It made detailed factual findings about the state of medical science regarding CTE—findings that we review for clear error—in support of this conclusion.

The Court first determined that "the study of CTE is nascent, and the symptoms of the disease, if any, are unknown." Surveying the available medical literature, it found that researchers have not "reliably determined which events make a person more likely to develop CTE" and "have not determined what symptoms individuals with CTE typically suffer from while they are alive." At the time of the Court's decision, only about 200 brains with CTE had been examined, and the only way currently to diagnose CTE is a post-mortem examination of the subject's brain.

Citing studies by Dr. Ann McKee and Dr. Robert Stern, objectors argued that CTE progresses in four stages. In Stages I and II, the disease affects mood and behavior while leaving a retired player's cognitive functions largely intact. Headaches, aggression, depression, explosive outbursts, and suicidal thoughts are common. Later in life, as a retired player progresses to Stages III and IV, severe memory loss, dementia, loss of attention and concentration, and impairment of language begin to occur. The District Court explained, however, that these studies suffer from several limitations and cannot generate "predictive, generalizable conclusions" about CTE. The studies suffered from a selection bias because they only examined patients with a history of repetitive head injury. They had to rely on reports by family members to reconstruct the symptoms patients showed before death. And they did not take into account other potential risk factors for developing CTE, including a high Body Mass Index (BMI), lifestyle change, age, chronic pain, or substance abuse.

With this science in mind, the Court next determined that certain symptoms associated with CTE, such as memory loss, executive dysfunction, and difficulty with concentration, are compensated by the existing Qualifying Diagnoses. And many persons diagnosed with CTE after death suffered from conditions in life that are compensated, including ALS, Alzheimer's disease, and Parkinson's disease. Relying on expert evidence, the Court estimated that "at least 89% of the former NFL players" who were examined in CTE studies would have been compensated under the settlement.

To be sure, the mood and behavioral symptoms associated with CTE (aggression, depression, and suicidal thoughts) are not compensated, but this result was reasonable. Mood and behavioral symptoms are common in the general population and have multifactor causation and many other risk factors. Retired players tend to have many of these risk factors, such as sleep apnea, a history of drug and alcohol abuse, a high BMI, chronic pain, and major lifestyle changes. Class members would thus "face more difficulty proving that NFL Football caused these mood and behavioral symptoms than they would proving that it caused other symptoms associated with Qualifying Diagnoses." The District Court also reviewed the monetary award for post-mortem diagnoses of CTE. It found "sound reasons" for limiting the award to players who died before final approval of the settlement. As we have summarized elsewhere, this compensation for deceased players is a proxy for Qualifying Diagnoses a retired player could have received while living. After final approval, players "should be well aware of the settlement and the need to obtain Qualifying Diagnoses," and "there no longer is a need for Death with CTE to serve as a proxy for Qualifying Diagnoses."

Finally, the Court addressed the potential development of scientific and medical knowledge of CTE. Objectors argued that the settlement's treatment of CTE was unreasonable in light of the expected developments in CTE research. But even if a diagnosis of CTE during life will be available in the next five or ten years, "the longitudinal epidemiological studies necessary to build a robust clinical profile will still take a considerable amount of time." The Court also noted that the settlement has some mechanism for keeping pace with science, in that the parties must meet and confer every ten years in good faith about possible modifications to the definitions of Qualifying Diagnoses.

Objectors have not shown any of the District Court's findings to be clearly erroneous, which exists when, "although there is evidence to support the finding, the reviewing court, based on the entire evidence, concludes with firm conviction that a mistake has been made." Objectors argue that the Court overlooked certain expert evidence, but the record does not support this contention. They also complain that it failed to weigh the credibility of the different experts when the objectors' experts were not paid for their services. We do not see how the Court could have made a proper credibility determination on the basis of written declarations alone, and, in any event, we have never required those determinations when considering the fairness of a settlement.

Others claim that the expert evidence on CTE should have been analyzed under *Daubert v. Merrell Dow Pharmaceuticals, Inc.*, which established threshold standards for the admissibility of expert scientific testimony at trial. Objectors failed to present this argument to the District Court, and we deem it waived. Moreover, we have never held that district courts considering the fairness of a class action settlement should consider the admissibility of expert evidence under *Daubert*. And at least one court of appeals has rejected the argument objectors are making because, "in a fairness hearing, the judge does not resolve the parties' factual disputes but merely ensures that the disputes are real and that the settlement fairly and reasonably resolves the parties' differences."

Finding no clear errors in the District Court's findings on CTE, we are also convinced that the Court was well within its discretion in concluding that the settlement's treatment of this condition was reasonable. Most importantly, objectors are not correct when they assert that CTE claims are released by the settlement in return for "nothing." A primary purpose of the settlement is to provide insurance for living players who develop certain neurocognitive or neuromuscular impairments linked to repetitive head trauma (in addition to the benefits provided by the Baseline Assessment Program). Given what we know about CTE, many of the symptoms associated with the disease will be covered by this insurance. And compensation for players who are coping with these symptoms now is surely preferable to waiting until they die to pay their estates for a CTE diagnosis. Moreover, we agree with the District Court that it would be an uphill battle to compensate for the mood and behavioral symptoms thought to be associated with CTE.

Before concluding, we address developments during the pendency of this appeal. In a March 2016 roundtable discussion on concussions organized by the House Energy & Commerce Subcommittee on Oversight & Investigations, the NFL's Executive Vice President cited the research of Dr. McKee and agreed that there was a link between football and degenerative brain disorders like CTE. The NFL's statement is an important development because it is the first time, as far as we can tell, that the NFL has publicly acknowledged a connection between football and CTE. On the other hand, the NFL is now conceding something already known. The sheer number of deceased players with a post-mortem diagnosis of CTE supports the unavoidable conclusion that there is a relationship, if not a causal connection, between a life in football and CTE.

Objectors cite the NFL's concession as further evidence that this settlement should be rejected. They argue that the NFL has now admitted there is a link between football and CTE, yet refused to compensate the disease. Again, we note that the settlement does compensate many of the impairments associated with CTE, though it does not compensate CTE as a diagnosis (with the exception of players who died before final approval of the settlement). Moreover, even if the NFL has finally come around to the view that there is a link between CTE and football, many more questions must be answered before we could say that the failure to compensate the diagnosis was unreasonable. For example, we still cannot reliably determine the prevalence, symptoms, or risk factors of CTE. The NFL's recent acknowledgment may very well advance the public discussion of the risks of contact sports, but it did not advance the science. Accordingly, the NFL's statement is not a ground for reversal of the settlement's approval.

In the end, this settlement was the bargain struck by the parties, negotiating amid the fog of litigation. If we were drawing up a settlement ourselves, we may want different terms or more compensation for a certain condition. But our role as judges is to review the settlement reached by the parties for its fairness, adequacy, and reasonableness. And when exercising that role, we must "guard against demanding too large a settlement based on our view of the merits of the litigation; after all, settlement is a compromise, a yielding of the highest hopes in exchange for certainty and resolution." *GM Trucks*. This settlement will provide significant and immediate relief to retired players living with the lasting scars of a NFL career, including those suffering from some of the symptoms associated with CTE. We must hesitate before rejecting that bargain based on an unsupported hope that sending the parties back to the negotiating table would lead to a better deal. Accordingly, we conclude that the settlement's treatment of CTE does not render the agreement fundamentally unfair.

## VIII.    CONCLUSION

It is the nature of a settlement that some will be dissatisfied with the ultimate result. Our case is no different, and we do not doubt that objectors are well-intentioned in making thoughtful arguments against certification of the class and approval of this settlement. They aim to ensure that the claims of retired players are not given up in exchange for anything less than a generous settlement agreement negotiated by very able representatives. But they risk making the perfect the enemy of the good. This settlement will provide nearly $1 billion in value to the class of retired players. It is a testament to the players, researchers, and advocates who have worked to expose the true human costs of a sport so many love. Though not perfect, it is fair.

In sum, we affirm because we are satisfied that the District Court ably exercised its discretion in certifying the class and approving the settlement.

# CHAPTER 9

---

# THE QUASI CLASS ACTION, MDL LITIGATION, AND ATTORNEY FEES

■ ■ ■

## A. HISTORICAL ANTECEDENTS: THE ATTORNEY FEE PROBLEM

### IN RE AGENT ORANGE PROD. LIAB. LITIG. (APPEAL OF DAVID DEAN)

United States Court of Appeals, Second Circuit, 1987.
818 F.2d 216.

This portion of the Agent Orange appeal concerns the district court's approval of a fee sharing agreement entered into by the nine-member Plaintiffs' Management Committee (PMC) in December of 1983. Under the agreement, each PMC member who had advanced funds to the class for general litigation expenses was to receive a three-fold return on his investment prior to the distribution of other fees awarded to individual PMC members by the district court. In result, the agreement dramatically increased the fees awarded to those PMC members who had advanced funds to the class for expenses, and concurrently decreased the fees awarded to non-investing PMC members, who performed legal services for the class.

David Dean, lead trial counsel for the plaintiff class and a non-investing member of the PMC, challenges the validity of the agreement, to which he was a signatory, contending that it violates DR 5–103 and DR 2–107(A) of the ABA Code of Professional Responsibility.

Because we find that the agreement before us violates established principles governing awards of attorneys' fees in equitable fund class actions and creates a strong possibility of a conflict of interest between class counsel and those they are charged to represent, we reverse the district court's approval of the agreement. Accordingly, the fees originally allocated by the district court, based on the reasonable value of the services actually rendered, will be distributed to the members of the PMC.

The ultimate inquiry, therefore, in examining fee agreements and setting fee awards under the equitable fund doctrine and Fed.R.Civ.P. 23(e), is the effect an agreement could have on the rights of a class. Because we find that the agreement here conflicts substantially with the principles of reasonable compensation in common fund actions and that it places class counsel in a potentially conflicting position in relation to the interests of the class, we reverse. [The court then discussed the fee sharing agreement in light of lodestar formula precedents, and concluded that the any fee distributions must bear some relationship to services rendered—*ed.*]

In our view, fees that include a return on investment present the clear potential for a conflict of interest between class counsel and those whom they have undertaken to represent. "Whenever an attorney is confronted with a potential for choosing between actions which may benefit himself financially and an action which may benefit the class which he represents there is a reasonable possibility that some specifically identifiable impropriety will occur. The concern is not necessarily in isolating instances of major abuse, but rather is 'for those situations, short of actual abuse, in which the client's interests are somewhat encroached upon by the attorney's interests.'" Such conflicts are not only difficult to discern from the terms of a particular settlement, but "even the parties may not be aware that they exist at the time of their settlement discussions." This risk is magnified in the class action context, where full disclosure and consent are many times difficult and frequently impractical to obtain.

The district court recognized that the agreement provided an incentive for the PMC to accept an early settlement offer not in the best interests of the class, because "an attorney who is promised a multiple of funds advanced will receive the same return whether the case is settled today of five years from now." Given the size and the complexity of the litigation, it seems apparent that the potential for abuse was real and should have been discouraged. Unlike the district court, however, we conclude that the risk of such an adverse effect on the settlement process provides adequate grounds for invalidating the agreement as being inconsistent with the interests of the class. The conflict obviously lies in the incentive provided to an investor-attorney to settle early and thereby avoid work for which full payment may not be authorized by the district court. Moreover, as soon as an offer of settlement to cover the promised return on investment is made, the investor-attorney will be disinclined to undertake the risks associated with the continuing litigation. The conflict was especially egregious here, since six of the nine PMC members were investing parties to the agreement.

The district court's factual finding, that the adequacy of the settlement demonstrated that the agreement had no effect on the PMC's conduct, is not dispositive. The district court's retrospective appraisal of the adequacy of the settlement cannot be the standard for review. The test to be applied is whether, at the time a fee sharing agreement is reached, class counsel are placed in a position that might endanger the fair representation of their clients and whether they will be compensated on some basis other than for legal services performed. Review based on a fairness of settlement test would not ensure the protection of the class against potential conflicts of interest, and, more important, would simply reward counsel for failing to inform the court of the existence of such an agreement until after a settlement.

We also reject the district court's finding that its authority to approve settlement offers under Fed.R.Civ.P. 23(e) acts to limit the threat to the class from a potential conflict of interest. At this late stage of the litigation, both class counsel and defendants seek approval of the settlement. The court's attention properly is directed toward the overall reasonableness of the offer and not necessarily to whether class counsel have placed themselves in a potentially conflicting position with the class. Given this focus and other administrative concerns that may come to bear, we find approval authority, in this context, to be insufficient to assure that the ongoing interests of the class are protected.

Equally unpersuasive is the district court's determination that the potential incentive to settle early is offset by an incentive, fostered by the lodestar formula, to prolong the litigation. While a number of commentators have asserted that use of the lodestar formula encourages counsel to prolong litigation for the purpose of billing more hours. Moreover, the court's authority in reviewing fee petitions and approving or disapproving hours billed in an equitable fund action works as a substantial and direct check on counsel's alleged incentive to procrastinate. Consequently, we do not view the lodestar system as countervailing the clear interest in early settlement created by the private agreement.

Additionally, potential conflicts of interest in class contexts are not examined solely for the actual abuse they may cause, but also for potential public misunderstanding they may cultivate in regard to the interest of class counsel. While today we hold that the settlement reached here falls within the range of reasonableness permissible under Fed.R.Civ.P. 23(e), we are not insensitive to the perception of many class members and the public in general that it does not adequately compensate the individual veterans and their families for whatever harm Agent Orange may have caused. To be sure, the settlement does not provide the individual veteran or his family substantial compensation. Given the facts of this settlement, the potentially negative public perception of an agreement that awards an investing PMC member over twelve times the amount the district court has determined to be the value of his services to the class provides additional justification for invalidating the agreement and applying the lodestar formula.

We find the various additional rationales for approving the fee sharing agreement set out in the district court's decision equally unpersuasive. First, the fact that the returns on the advanced expenses did not directly affect the class fund is of little consequence, since we have already determined that the district court's responsibility under applicable lodestar precedents, as well as under Fed.R.Civ.P. 23(e), goes beyond concern for only the overall amount of fees awarded and requires attention to the fees allocated to individual class counsel. Second, while we sympathize with counsel regarding the business decisions they must make in operating an efficient and manageable practice and agree that a certain flexibility on the court's part is essential, we are not inclined to extend this flexibility to encompass situations in which the bases for awarding fees in an equitable fund action are so clearly distorted. Third, whether this class action would have collapsed without an agreement calling for a threefold return is a matter of speculation. Any such collapse, however, would have been due to the pervasive weaknesses in the plaintiffs' case. Fourth, we find wholly unconvincing the district court's suggestion that the investors could have made a sizeable return on their funds if they had invested them in other ventures. We take note of the fact that a threefold return on one's money is a rather generous return in any market over a short period of time. Fifth, while the effect of this fee sharing agreement might have been dwarfed to the point of insignificance if the fees awarded to counsel had been much greater, this simply is too speculative to defend the agreement as not affecting the interest of the class. Finally, we do not find class counsel to have formed an ad hoc partnership. They merely are a group of individual lawyers and law firms associated in the prosecution of a single lawsuit, and they lack the ongoing relationship that is the essential element of attorneys practicing as partners.

## B.  MDL FIDUCIARY DUTIES TO THE CLASS

### KENTUCKY BAR ASSOCIATION V. CHESLEY

Supreme Court of Kentucky, 2013.
393 S.W.3d 584.

The Board of Governors of the Kentucky Bar Association has recommended to this Court that Respondent, Stanley M. Chesley, be permanently disbarred for committing eight counts of professional misconduct as charged. Chesley was admitted to the practice of law in Kentucky on November 29, 1978, and maintains a bar roster address of Fourth and Vine Tower, Suite 1513, Cincinnati, Ohio 45202.

The Board found that Respondent had violated the following provisions of SCR 3.130, the Kentucky Rules of Professional Conduct:

a)  SCR 3.130–1.5(a)—a lawyer's fee shall be reasonable. Attorney's fee of over $20 million exceeded amount established by client contract and contract with co-counsel, and was otherwise unreasonable;

b)  SCR 3.130–1.5(c)—contingent fee agreement. Attorney and co-counsel failed to provide clients with a written statement stating the outcome of the matter and showing the remittance to the client and method of its determination;

c)   SCR 3.130–1.5(e)(2)—division of fees among lawyers of different firms. Attorneys dividing fees without the consent of clients confirmed in writing;

d)   SCR 3.130–5.1(c)(1)—responsibility for partners. Attorney knowingly ratified specific misconduct of other lawyers.

e)   SCR 3.130–1.8(g)—conflict of interest. Attorney representing two or more clients participated in making an aggregate settlement of the claims of the clients without consent of clients and without disclosure of the existence and nature of all the claims and of the participation of each person included in the settlement;

f)   SCR 3.130–3.3(a)—candor to the tribunal. Attorney knowingly made a false statement of material fact or law to a tribunal; Attorney failed to disclose a material fact to the tribunal to avoid a fraud upon the tribunal;

g)   SCR 3.130–8.1(a)—disciplinary matters. Attorney made a false statement of a material fact in connection with a disciplinary matter; and

h)   SCR 3.130–8.3(c) (now codified as SCR 3.130–8.4(c))—Attorney engaged in conduct involving dishonesty, fraud, deceit, or misrepresentation following the initial distribution of client funds and concealed unethical handling of client funds by others.

The Board recommended the permanent disbarment of Respondent and further requests an order of this Court awarding restitution to the affected former clients in the amount of $7,555,000.00. We permanently disbar him from the practice of law in the Commonwealth of Kentucky. We decline to order restitution, as that remedy is not appropriate in a case of permanent disbarment, and the claims are being litigated in separate, civil litigation.

## I.   FACTUAL AND PROCEDURAL BACKGROUND

In March 2006, the Inquiry Commission, acting under rules established by this Court for the adjudication of attorney disciplinary actions, formally began an investigation of Respondent, Stanley Chesley, for his conduct in the settlement of the case of *Darla Guard, et al. v. A.H. Robins Company, et al*, (the *Guard* case) in the Boone Circuit Court, Boone County, Kentucky, including his conduct in the disbursement of funds generated by the settlement of that case. The Inquiry Commission had already been investigating the conduct of other lawyers in connection with that case, namely William Gallion, Shirley Cunningham, Melbourne Mills, and David Helmers, an employee of the Gallion firm. In December 2006, the Inquiry Commission issued formal charges against Respondent.

The *Guard* case began in 1998. Gallion, Cunningham, and Mills had contingent fee contracts with some 431 persons who claimed to have been injured by the diet drug commonly known as "fen-phen." Mills, because of his aggressive advertising, had secured the great majority of those clients and his contingent fee contracts provided for an attorney's fee of 30% of the sum recovered for the client; Cunningham's contracts provided a 33% fee, and the Gallion/Helmers contracts provided for a contingent fee of 33 1/3%. The Boone Circuit Court certified the case as a class action on behalf of the 431 individually-named Kentucky residents and others similarly situated who had been injured by fen-phen. The manufacturer of fen-phen, American Home Products, was the principal defendant in the action.

When the *Guard* case was filed, other similar claims against American Home Products were being pursued in other jurisdictions. A vast number of such claims were consolidated into a single "national" class action pending in a Pennsylvania federal district court. Respondent served as a member of the management committee in the Pennsylvania litigation and participated in the negotiations that reached a settlement of that case. As a result of his involvement in that case, Respondent became familiar with American Home's settlement policies and he became acquainted with its settlement personnel. All of the *Guard* case plaintiffs opted-out of the national settlement with the hope of achieving a more favorable settlement in the Kentucky litigation.

Independently of his involvement in the national case, Respondent initiated a fen-phen lawsuit on behalf of his own clients in the Boone Circuit Court, which he promptly attempted to have consolidated with the *Guard* case. The *Guard* case plaintiffs' counsel voiced strong objections to Respondent's effort to merge the cases. Eventually, however, they relented and accepted the consolidation. Respondent's national reputation and his experience in the national fen-phen settlement was a factor that induced them to drop their opposition to his intrusion into their case.

With the claims of their clients merged, Respondent, Gallion, Cunningham, Mills, and Richard Lawrence, an attorney from Cincinnati who also represented a few individual fen-phen claimants, entered into a collaborative agreement outlining the role each attorney was to perform in the litigation. They also agreed upon a method of dividing the attorneys' fees earned in the case. Gallion would serve as lead trial counsel in the event the case was tried, and would prepare the case accordingly. Cunningham and Mills would enroll clients and maintain client contact information. Respondent would act as "lead negotiator" in the effort to secure a settlement of the claims. Originally, the agreement provided that Respondent would take 27% of the total attorney's fee earned from any of the individual claims he might settle and from an aggregate settlement that resolved all of the claims.

The fee-apportionment agreement was reduced to writing and it expressly provided that "all parties to this agreement shall have the right to review all contracts between themselves and any other parties that may affect the fees earned and *all clients shall be advised of this agreement.*" The agreement also stated clearly that "all parties to this agreement shall be identified as co-counsel in the class action styled *Guard v. American Home Products* in Boone Circuit Court in Kentucky." The agreement provided that it could be terminated by any of the attorneys on December 31, 2000. Respondent, Gallion, Cunningham, Mills, and Lawrence all signed the agreement. Respondent did not inform any clients of the agreement and he undertook no effort to determine whether any of his "co-counsel" informed the clients of the division of effort and fee-sharing arrangements. None of the clients were so informed. Respondent attempted to negotiate a collective settlement of all the *Guard* claims before the December 31 termination date, but he was not successful. He did, however, achieve individual settlements of a few cases. In those cases, the attorney's fees taken were based upon the specific contingency fee agreement with that client.

In late 2000, Respondent corresponded with his co-counsel about extending the arrangement. As a result, a new agreement was reached. The new agreement was similar in all material aspects to the original agreement except that it reduced Respondent's fee for negotiating a settlement of the claims to 21% of the total attorney fees earned. The new agreement contained the same express provisions requiring that *all* clients receive notice of the fee agreement and that *all* of the attorneys be "identified as co-counsel in the class action styled *Guard v. American Home Products* in Boone Circuit Court in Kentucky."

The *Guard* case trial was scheduled to begin in the summer of 2001. A pretrial mediation conference was scheduled. Respondent suggests that his ongoing discussions with opposing counsel actually settled the case before the mediation conference, and that the mediation itself was merely for show. Regardless, a settlement agreement was announced on the second day of the mediation.

The settlement agreement provided that plaintiffs' counsel would obtain the decertification of the *Guard* case as a class action and the dismissal of all claims. American Home Products would pay an aggregate sum of $200 million to be divided among the 431 individual clients who had fee contracts with Mills, Cunningham, Gallion, and Lawrence. Those claims would be dismissed *with* prejudice. The remaining members of the class who had joined the action, approximately 143 individuals, were not included in the financial settlement. Their claims would be dismissed *without* prejudice. The agreement was reduced to writing and was signed by Gallion, Cunningham, Mills, and Lawrence. Respondent claims that he did not sign the agreement because, as he contends, he did not represent any of the individual clients. In his view, he had been employed by the attorneys and had no professional responsibility to the individual clients.

American Home left it for the plaintiffs' attorneys to determine how much of the settlement fund to allocate to each of their clients. However, under the terms of the agreement, plaintiffs' counsel had to provide American Home with a schedule listing each of the settling clients and how much of the settlement money would be allocated to each client. A signed release from each client was also required. The agreement also provided that the settlement would not take effect unless plaintiffs' counsel obtained a specific number of signed client releases before a specified deadline. Two preconditions of the agreement required approval of the Boone Circuit Court. First, the class action could be decertified only by court order. Second, the claims of the individual *Guard* clients could not be dismissed with prejudice without court approval.

The settlement agreement also incorporated a "side letter" which outlined an agreement by which the plaintiffs' attorneys agreed to indemnify American Home up to a total of $7.5 million for any new fen-phen claims that might arise from individuals who were eligible to be members of the decertified class. In other words, $7.5 million of the aggregate settlement would have to be reserved to cover potential claims, at least until the applicable statute of limitations brought the subject to repose. Thereafter, any part of the reserve remaining would be subject to disposition by order of the court.

On May 9, 2001, Respondent, along with Gallion, Helmers, Cunningham, and David Schaefer, an attorney for American Home Products, appeared before the presiding judge, Joseph Bamberger, and tendered for his consideration the "Order Decertifying the Class and Dismissing Action" as required by the settlement. Judge Bamberger expressed concern about decertifying the class and dismissing the individual claims, especially when he realized that the settling clients and the members of the class had not been given notice of the settlement or of the impending dismissal of their claims. Respondent carefully explained to the judge that the settlement resolved only the claims of the client group (the 431); the claims of the members of the decertified class were dismissed without prejudice and they would have other avenues for redress, if they wanted to pursue them. Despite his misgivings, Judge Bamberger signed the "Order Decertifying the Class and Dismissing Action" which was entered into the record on May 16, 2001.

Respondent argues that the entry of that order terminated his responsibility in the case. He had negotiated the settlement pursuant to his agreement with Gallion, Cunningham, and Mills, and he had secured the entry of an order putting the settlement into effect.

None of the clients were informed of the decertification of the class action or the dismissal of their claims. At that point, none of the clients had even agreed to a settlement of the claim against American Home Products. Gallion, Cunningham, Mills, and Helmers then began the process of collecting the necessary releases before the deadline. They promptly set up a meeting with each client. At each meeting, the client was falsely informed that American Home had offered a specific amount for his or her claim, which the attorneys then encouraged the client to accept. Upon the acceptance of an "offer" and the signing of a release, each client was informed that the amount of his settlement must be kept secret and severe sanctions would follow any breach of that confidentiality. In each case, the amount of the "offer" was substantially less than the amount listed on the schedule provided to American Home. The clients were not informed that American Home had agreed to an aggregate settlement of $200 million. The clients were shown none of the actual settlement documents, and they were not informed that the "offer" was coming from their own attorneys, not American Home.

While we do not agree with Respondent's position that his responsibility to the clients ended with the entry of the settlement order, we note at this point that he did not participate in the process of contacting clients to secure the releases. He did not meet directly with any of the clients to effectuate the settlement and it is not shown that he had specific knowledge of the deception practiced upon each client to secure the signed release.

When the releases, sufficient in number to trigger the release of settlement money, were obtained, Respondent advised Helmers on the most effective way to get the releases to American Home and secure its payment of the first installment of settlement money. Upon receipt of the releases, American Home made an initial payment of $150 million to a client trust account in Cunningham's name. Shortly thereafter, on June 19, 2001, Respondent received a check from that trust account in the amount of $12,372,534.37. He received additional checks on July 5, 2001 and August 14, 2001, which corresponded with the dates on which American Home paid additional installments on the $200 million settlement. On November 5, 2001, American Home paid the final installment on the settlement, bringing the total amount paid to $200,450,000.00. Respondent had been paid $16,497,121.87, and he would soon receive more. The payout to the clients totaled only $46 million.

In early 2002, questions about the *Guard* case settlement began to surface. The fee distribution had attracted the attention of Michael Baker, a law partner of Gallion, and of David Stuart, a law partner of Mills. Neither Baker nor Stuart had been actively involved in the fen-phen case, but each one became suspicious about the way the law firm income generated by that case was being handled in his respective law firm. Each of them alerted the Kentucky Bar Association of the potential misconduct in the handling the settlement proceeds, and each filed suit against his respective partner for an accounting of law firm funds.

On January 30, 2002, the Office of Bar Counsel served notice that it was requesting subpoenas for Gallion, Mills, Cunningham, and Bank One relating to the matter. At the same time, Stuart's lawsuit led to Mills' discovery that the settlement amount was *not* the $150 million as he had been told, but was instead $200 million. On February 6, 2002, Mills angrily confronted Gallion about the deception and demanded that more money be distributed to the clients. That evening, or shortly thereafter, Gallion, Cunningham, Respondent, and Mark Modlin, a professional "jury consultant" and friend of the judge, arranged for an off-the-record meeting with Judge Bamberger.

At the meeting with Judge Bamberger, Respondent used his expertise in major class action lawsuits and mass tort settlements to persuade Judge Bamberger that a charitable organization should be established, using the *cy pres* doctrine, to administer the residual funds that might remain after all known claims against the settlement money were paid. Respondent also persuaded the judge that he should award attorney's fees in the decertified and dismissed class action equal to 49% of the gross settlement, using the *Grinnell* factors for awarding attorneys' fees in a successful class action. No consideration was given to the fact that each of the settling clients had a contingency fee agreement setting the allowable fee at 30%, 33%, or 33 1/3% of the amounts recovered.

Judge Bamberger approved the 49% attorney fee and authorized the use of a charitable trust for any excess funds. He also agreed to counsel's suggestion that 50% of the then-remaining undistributed settlement money be paid to the clients on a *pro rata* basis, and that 50% be retained by the attorneys for "indemnification or contingent liabilities." The judge was not informed what dollar amounts were represented by those percentages. The written order agreed upon at that meeting was signed a few days later, but it was not entered in the case record until June 6, 2002, at which time Judge Bamberger also ordered that the record of the case be sealed. It is worth noting that the written order does not reveal the attorney fee percentage allowed by the judge, nor does it disclose any absolute dollar amounts. By its omission of the specific attorney fee percentages, and the absolute dollar amounts, the written order preserves the secret of the fees claimed by the attorneys. Judge Bamberger restricted the clerk's certificate of service on that order to only Mills, Gallion, Cunningham, Helmers, and Respondent. From that point forward, all subsequent orders were sent to only those individuals. Respondent received the order following its June 6, 2002 entry, and other orders that followed, but denies that he read any of them.

Judge Bamberger's February order in effect approved retroactively, or ratified, the disbursement of millions of dollars in attorneys' fees that had already been taken by the attorneys. There is no doubt that the purpose of the February meeting with the judge, when several investigations were beginning to gather steam, was to cover the fee distribution with a thin veil of legitimacy, and to create a legitimate-looking repository in the form of a charitable trust in which to place the undistributed money.

On February 11, 2002, the Inquiry Commission of the Kentucky Bar Association issued the requested subpoenas for bank records and other documents relating to the disbursement of the *Guard* case settlement money. That same afternoon, five wire transfers totaling some $59 million were made by Gallion and Cunningham from several personal accounts to an out-of-state bank account owned jointly by Gallion, Cunningham, and Mills.

After the successful meeting with Judge Bamberger on or about February 6, Respondent and Gallion contacted Helmers to enlist his help in making the second round of disbursements to the clients that had been approved by the judge. Respondent's office provided Helmers with a document to present to each client for his or her signature. In the spring of 2002, with the documents signed, the *Guard* clients received a second distribution of settlement money.

The attorneys also received an additional distribution. On April 1, 2002, Respondent received a check for $4 million, drawn on the same out-of-state bank account of Gallion, Cunningham, and Mills, to which the remaining settlement money had been moved. Respondent testified that he had no expectation of receiving an additional $4 million fee. He testified that he did not know why the check was issued or how the amount was calculated. He made no inquiry to determine the source of the payment or the reason for the payment, or the manner in which the payment was calculated. His firm simply deposited the check, and asked no questions.

That final distribution of attorneys' fees brought Respondent's total to more than $20 million, which he argues is a reasonable fee for a case of such magnitude. The total attorney's fee payable, based upon the contingent fee contracts in effect, using for illustrative purposes the contingent fee of 33 1/3%, or one-third, and the $200,450,000.00 settlement, was $66,816,667.00. Respondents 21% share of that fee would equal $14,031,500.00.

Stuart, in his continuing effort to discover the extent of Mills' wrongful diversion of law firm funds, sought and obtained a commission from the Fayette Circuit Court authorizing the out-of-state deposition of Respondent, an Ohio resident. Before the deposition was taken, however, Stuart and Mills were ordered to attempt to settle their dispute by mediation. Respondent sent word through a Mills-employee attending the mediation conference that, if the settlement talks stalled, he would be willing to contribute money to get the case resolved. Initially, the mediation was unsuccessful because Stuart would not accept the highest amount

Mills would offer. Respondent, who was not a party to the Stuart-Mills lawsuit, then agreed to sweeten the settlement pot by the sum of $500,000.00 to get the case settled and avoid his pending deposition. With that inducement, Stuart settled. Later, Gallion and Cunningham reimbursed Respondent $250,000.00, as their contribution to the Stuart-Mills settlement.

As the Inquiry Commission's investigation proceeded, Mills hired attorney William E. Johnson to represent him. Gallion and Cunningham hired Whitney Wallingford for the same purpose. Respondent, who at the time was not subject to a Kentucky bar disciplinary inquiry, attended a meeting with Mills, Gallion, and Cunningham, and their respective attorneys. At the meeting, Respondent urged all of the attorneys then subject to the KBA investigation to agree upon representation by the same counsel. As a result, Wallingford agreed to withdraw as counsel for Gallion and Cunningham. Before he did so, he submitted a set of documents in response to the Inquiry Commission subpoenas. The response included a client payment spreadsheet that grossly overstated the amounts of money that had been paid to the clients. Before filing the response and the spreadsheet, Wallingford asked Respondent to review the response and provide input. Respondent did so and voiced no disapproval. Respondent claims he had no way to know that the spreadsheet was inaccurate.

Respondent helped Judge Bamberger prepare for his 2005 appearance before the Kentucky Judicial Conduct Commission that was examining the judge's misconduct in the *Guard* case, including his involvement in the creations of the Kentucky Fund for Healthy Living, and his salary for serving as a member of its governing board. Respondent also appeared at the Judicial Conduct Commission meeting and spoke in support of the judge.

In 2005, problems for the *Guard* counsel developed on yet another front when several of the *Guard* case clients filed suit against Respondent, Gallion, Cunningham, Mills, and the Kentucky Fund for Healthy Living alleging misconduct and misappropriation of the settlement funds. The case, styled *Abbott v. Chesley*, is currently pending review before this Court. Respondent initially admitted to being part of the *Guard* case class counsel in initial pleadings, but in subsequent pleadings denied he acted in that capacity.

In preparing a defense for the *Abbott* case, Respondent hired Kenneth Feinberg, a nationally-recognized specialist in handling large aggregate case and class action settlements. At Respondent's behest, and based largely upon information provided by Gallion, Feinberg prepared an affidavit supporting the actions of the *Guard* case counsel in the disbursement of the *Guard* case money. In this disciplinary proceeding, however, and after learning more of the details, Feinberg disavowed the opinion he expressed in the affidavit and withdrew his approval.

After the formal KBA investigation of Respondent began in 2006, Respondent asked Jack Vardaman, the attorney for American Home Products who had negotiated the *Guard* case settlement with Respondent, to write a letter based upon Respondent's notes stating that the *Guard* case had been "settled as a class action" and that "decertification was not relevant to the collateral issues of attorneys' fees or administration of the settlement proceeds and process." Vardaman refused to do so because the statements suggested in Respondent's notes were false.

On December 4, 2006, the Inquiry Commission issued its Complaint of Misconduct against Respondent. After an extensive hearing including the testimony of some forty-three witnesses and the review of dozens of exhibits, the Trial Commissioner, Judge William Graham, issued a report finding that Respondent had violated [multiple rules of professional conduct].

In light of the number and severity of the violations, the Trial Commissioner recommended Respondent be permanently disbarred from the practice of law in Kentucky. In addition, the Trial Commissioner recommended that Respondent pay $7,555,000.00 in restitution to the *Guard* case clients. The Trial Commissioner calculated that amount based on the attorney fees Respondent actually received minus the amount he was contractually allowed to receive.

The matter was presented to Board of Governors at a hearing, with oral arguments, on June 14, 2011. By a vote of eighteen to zero the Board adopted the Trial Commissioner's report and his recommendations. Respondent filed a notice of review with this Court.

## II.  CHARGES AGAINST RESPONDENT

A. SCR 3.130–1.5(a)

SCR 3.130–1.5(a) states in pertinent part:

a lawyer's fee shall be reasonable. Some factors to be considered in determining the reasonableness of a fee include the following: (1) The time and labor required, the novelty and difficulty of the questions involved, and the skill requisite to perform the legal service properly; (2) The likelihood that the acceptance of the particular employment will preclude other employment by the lawyer; (3) The fee customarily charged in the locality for similar legal services; (4) The amount involved and the results obtained; (5) The time limitations imposed by the circumstances; (6) The nature and length of the professional relationship with the client; (7) The experience, reputation and ability of the lawyer or lawyers performing the services; (8) Whether the fee is fixed or contingent.

The Respondent violated SCR 3.130–1.5(a) because the fee he accepted, over $20 million, was unreasonable under the circumstances of this case, and the factors cited in the rule above. Respondent argues that his fee was' reasonable because his personal take from the case was merely 10% of the total amount recovered. He presents with his argument examples of other class actions where greater percentages were approved. He cites, among others, the expert opinion given by Professor Geoffrey C. Hazard:

> When you are talking about this kind of money involved in the settlement lawyer fees in the order of 18, up to 24, 25 percent are within what courts have approved in class actions.

Professor Hazard is referring to the total attorney's fee to be allocated for the case. Here, Respondent's request to Judge Bamberger for a total fee of 49% well exceeds the normal limit suggested by Professor Hazard. Respondent argues that the reasonableness of his personal fee must be judged independently of the total amount taken by all of the attorneys, lest we convict him of guilt by association. However, we disagree. The lawyers agreed among themselves to share the work, and to share the fee. Respondent cannot disavow the excessiveness of the 49% fee ($99,220,500.00) that he requested simply because he did not personally receive all of it.

We also conclude that, given the factors cited in the rule, Respondent's $20,497,121.87 share of the fee was unreasonable, especially in light of his professed ignorance and lack of responsibility for any aspect of the litigation except showing up at the mediation and going through the motions of announcing the agreement. The factors listed in the rule above do not weigh in Respondent's favor. He has shown nothing to demonstrate that he expended a great deal of time and labor on the case. The issues of liability were not particularly difficult or novel, and even if they were, Respondent did not do the heavy-lifting on that aspect of the case. Gallion and Helmers did most of that. We do not see that Respondent forfeited other profitable employment because of his involvement in the *Guard* case. In our view, $20 million does indeed exceed "the fee customarily charged in the locality for similar legal services." The only "time limitation" was to complete his negotiation before the trial a few months away. His "professional relationship" with the clients was by his own admission extremely limited. The only factors that weigh favorably toward a large fee are "skill requisite to perform the legal service properly" and the "experience, reputation and ability of the lawyer."

The more critical factor here, however, is the existence of the contingent fee agreement, the eighth factor listed in SCR 3.130–1.5(a). Respondent argues that his right to a reasonable fee for settling the case was not subject to the contingency fee contracts of his co-counsel because he was not party to those contracts and because the case was settled as a class action. He reminds us that attorney fees payable for the successful prosecution of a class action lawsuit are determined by the trial court, and that his fee was consistent with what was allowed by the trial court in this case. Aside from the fact that the trial judge was disbarred for his collusion with the plaintiffs' attorneys, we reject Respondent's argument that the contingent fee contracts were immaterial to the determination of whether his fee was reasonable.

Respondent cannot claim that the reasonableness of his fee should be based upon class action standards when he himself negotiated the agreement that required the decertification of the class action and the dismissal without any compensation of all pending claims, except those with fee contracts. The fact is that Respondent did not obtain the settlement of a class action; he secured the dismissal of the class action and the settlement of the some 431 individual claims that were subject to contingent fee contracts.

When Respondent sought the judge's approval for an attorney's fee, the class action was long-since dismissed. All of the members of the plaintiff class, except the 431 that had contingent fee contracts with Respondent's co-counsel, were cut loose and left to fend for themselves.

As for the 431 with contracts, none of the claimants had notice that his claim was settled and his case was dismissed. None of them had forfeited his rights under the contingent fee agreement. Each client was entitled to the full measure of compensation allocated to him, less the contingent fee he had agreed to pay.

Respondent argues that he had no duty to the individual clients, because he was hired by none of them and had no knowledge of their fee agreements with Mills, Gallion, and Cunningham. We do not accept that ignorance is an excuse, nor do we find it credible that Respondent was unaware of the fee arrangement. When he entered into his agreement with the other attorneys, Respondent signed on as co-counsel with Mills, Cunningham, and Gallion, and he was one of the lawyers "representing the plaintiffs in the litigation pending or anticipated against American Home Products," as stated in the fee-division agreement. The plaintiffs in the case were his clients, and he assumed the same ethical responsibilities that he would have with any other clients. He had the duty to know his fee responsibilities to them. He had in the fall of 2000 successfully settled some of the individual cases and taken a fee based upon the contingency fee agreement.

By his own testimony, he received the first installments of $16 million in fees without any idea of the authority under which those payments had been made. If he was ignorant of the means by which his fee was being paid, he had a duty to the clients to find out. His later effort to obtain the court's retroactive approval of his fees demonstrates his knowledge that the earlier payments were improperly disbursed to him. The fee for Respondent's work on behalf of the *Guard* clients was governed by fee contracts, and the attorneys' agreement. At most he was entitled to 21% of one-third of the $200,450,000.00 recovered, or $14,031,500.00.

An attorney's fee in a contingency fee case that so grossly exceeds the fee provided for in the fee agreement is unreasonable per se. Respondent's fee was subject to the limitations of the contingent fee agreements so we conclude that he violated SCR 3.130–1.5(a). Moreover, even without the fee contracts with the clients, as shown above, the 49% fee was unreasonable and Respondent's $20 million share of it taken without notice to the client was unreasonable, and constitutes a violation of SCR 3.130–1.5(a).

B. SCR 3.130–1.5(c).

SCR 3.130–1.5(c) states in pertinent part:

> a fee may be contingent on the outcome of the matter for which the service is rendered, except in a matter in which a contingent fee is prohibited by paragraph (d) or other law. Such a fee must meet the requirements of Rule 1.5(a). A contingent fee agreement shall be in writing and should state the method by which the fee is to be determined, including the percentage or percentages that shall accrue to the lawyer in the event of settlement, trial or appeal, litigation and other expenses to be deducted from the recovery, and whether such expenses are to be deducted before or after the contingent fee is calculated. Upon recovery of any amount in a contingent fee matter, the lawyer shall provide the client with a written statement stating the outcome of the matter and showing the remittance to the client and the method of its determination.

It was established in the preceding section the contingent fee agreements governed the fees properly payable to the *Guard* case attorneys. It necessarily follows from that ruling that SCR 3.130–1.5(c) is applicable. The $200 million settlement fund was justified by the cumulative total of individual settlements prepared by the *Guard* counsel and submitted to American Home Products. The cumulative fee of 49% taken collectively by the attorneys obviously exceeded the amount payable under the contingent fee contracts.

The evidence established that none of the clients were provided with an honest "written statement stating the outcome of the matter and showing the remittance to the client and the method of its determination." Instead, the clients were given a falsified statement showing, not the true amount submitted to American Home for the settlement of that individual claim, but a reduced amount, purportedly reduced by the contingent fee stated in the contract.

Respondent argues that he had absolutely no responsibility to the individual case clients because he was only hired by the *Guard* counsel to negotiate the settlement. He contends he had no contractual obligation to the members of the class and that he reasonably relied upon his co-counsel to comply with this Rule.

However, Respondent was a signatory to a fee splitting agreement, which stated that *all* clients were to receive notice of the fee splitting agreement and that *all* of the attorneys are to be "identified as co-counsel in the class action styled *Guard v. American Home Products* in Boone Circuit Court in Kentucky." The plain language of the agreement rebuts Respondent's argument that he assumed no responsibility to inform the clients he had undertaken to represent. We note that he does not rely upon express representation of his co-counsel that they had undertaken to comply with SCR 3.130–1.5(c). Each attorney had an independent duty to see that the clients received the required notice. It is not enough to assume without inquiring that someone else did it. Moreover, had Respondent chosen to exercise his responsibility and determine if the clients were being properly notified, he may have been able to prevent the violations that were later uncovered by Mills' and Gallion's law partners. We agree with the Trial Commissioner and Board of Governors that Respondent violated SCR 3.130–1.5(c).

C. SCR 3.130–1.5(e)

SCR 3.130–1.5(e) provides in pertinent part:

a division of a fee between lawyers who are not in the same firm may be made only if: (1)(a) the division is in proportion to the services performed by each lawyer or, (b) By written agreement with the client, each lawyer assumes joint responsibility for the representation; and (2) The client is advised of and does not object to the participation of all lawyers involved; and (3) The total fee is reasonable.

SCR 3.130–1.5(e)(2) clearly states that the clients must be advised of the fee splitting agreement and given the opportunity to object to the participation of any attorney. Respondent and the other lawyers joining the fee splitting agreement failed to comply. No client was given notice of the agreement, and no client was informed of Respondent's participation as co-counsel and none were given an opportunity to object. That failure casts doubt upon the validity of the agreement from its inception. Respondent's failure to comply includes the facts that he failed to ascertain whether any of his co-counsel had provided the required notice to clients.

Accordingly, we conclude that Respondent violated SCR 3.130–1.5(e).

D. SCR 3.130–1.8(g)

SCR 3.130–1.8(g) provides in pertinent part:

a lawyer who represents two or more clients shall not participate in making an aggregate settlement of the claims of or against the clients unless each client consents after consultation, including disclosure of the existence and nature of all the claims and of the participation of each person in the settlement.

The evidence established that none of the clients included in the *Guard* case settlement were consulted about the aggregate settlement reached with American Home before, during, or after the mediation, and none were notified or consulted before the cases were dismissed by the Boone Circuit Court. No notice of the decertification of the class action and the dismissal of the lawsuit was given to the class and its potential members. Even though Respondent did not sign the final settlement document with American Home, and thus was not expressly identified as a "settling attorney," he was co-counsel for the plaintiffs and shared the responsibility of assuring that the rule was followed.

We agree that Respondent is guilty of violating SCR 3.130–1.8(g). Respondent's argument that he was hired solely to procure a negotiated settlement of the case, and that his responsibility extended no further is simply unavailing. The lawyers were free to divide among themselves the work required to successfully prosecute the claims of their clients, but they may not delegate their ethical responsibilities to another.

When Respondent signed on as co-counsel, he undertook the ethical responsibilities attendant thereto. He was *not,* as he suggests, brought into the case for the purpose of negotiating a settlement, although because that is his forte, he may have taken on that role. We have not forgotten that he was the lawyer for the plaintiffs in a separate case, and that upon his request over the objection of the original *Guard* attorneys, his case was consolidated with the *Guard* case. We do not accept his assertion that he did not represent the *Guard* case clients. He had the same responsibility to the clients as his co-counsel to comply with SCR 3.130–1.8(g). The failure of compliance with the rule was his failure, as well as theirs.

Thus, we agree that Respondent violated SCR 3.130–1.8(g).

E. SCR 3.130–3.3(a)

SCR 3.130–3.3(a) provides in pertinent part:

a lawyer shall not knowingly: (1) make a false statement of material fact or law to a tribunal; (2) Fail to disclose a material fact to the tribunal when disclosure is necessary to avoid a fraud being perpetrated upon the tribunal.

The charge for Respondent's violation of this rule is based upon his appearances before Judge Bamberger in the Boone Circuit Court.

First, when Respondent argued to the court that the *Grinnell* factors should be used to justify an attorneys' fee of 49%, Respondent never disclosed the existence of the contingent fee contracts that limited the total attorney fees to only 33 1/3%, or less (30%). The Trial Commissioner found that Respondent was aware of the contractual fee agreements with the

*Guard* class of the total settlement and thus purposefully withheld that important information.

We understand Respondent's legal position that such contracts are not controlling when a case is settled as a class action. But we find it difficult to believe that Respondent was unaware that the clients he was representing had contingent fee contracts. When he first undertook the effort to negotiate a "global" settlement, he successfully resolved a few of the cases individually and took the contingent fee payable in them. He may have believed when the class action was decertified that the fee agreements were not controlling, but he could not have believed they did not exist.

As we said above in connection with the reasonableness of the attorney's fee, when Respondent began receiving large fee payments without an accounting to explain them, he had a duty to the clients to determine how the fee was being calculated. Had he exercised that duty to the client, he would have learned of the fee agreements. His argument to the judge for an attorney's fee of 49%, without referencing the contingent fee contracts, deprived the court of information material to the issue before the court. That constitutes a violation of the rule.

Second, the Trial Commissioner found that Respondent deceived Judge Bamberger about the use of the *cy pres* doctrine to create the Kentucky Fund for Healthy Living. The Trial Commissioner found that Respondent *knew* the *cy pres* doctrine could not be applied to the aggregate settlement reached in the *Guard* action. Upon review of the matter, however, we conclude that Respondent's advocacy on that point falls into the realm of opinion, and it is far from certain that the *cy pres* doctrine had no place here, especially with the $7.5 million indemnity provision required by the contract.

Finally, the Trial Commissioner found Respondent violated Rule 3.3(a) by "misleading" Judge Bamberger with the argument that decertifying the class and dismissing the case without notifying the *Guard* class members was appropriate. The substantive question in this proceeding is not whether such notice was, or was not, necessary; and we decline to resolve that issue. The question is whether the attorney breached an ethical obligation by advocating a position. In his report, the Trial Commissioner acknowledged some legal disagreement on whether notice is required before decertification. We have not established this rule to punish lawyers for advocating unsound or unconventional legal positions. Its purpose is to deter dishonesty before the courts. We may doubt Respondent's motives for securing the order that allowed for the creation of the charitable trust, but we do not find from the evidence before us that his argument to the court, in that respect, was dishonest or misleading.

We find Respondent guilty of violating SCR 3.130–3.3(a) for the reason set forth above.

F. SCR 3.130–8.1(a)

SCR 3.130–8.1(a) provides in pertinent part:

> . . . a lawyer . . . in connection with a disciplinary matter, shall not: knowingly make a false statement of material fact.

The Trial Commissioner found that Respondent violated this rule by providing incomplete, misleading, and false answers to the interrogatories made by the Inquiry Commission. In particular, the Trial Commissioner found Respondent guilty because he denied having communicated with Judge Bamberger regarding the establishment of the charitable or non-profit entity to disburse residual funds from the *Guard* case. We agree.

The Trial Commissioner also found that Respondent provided false information to the Inquiry Commission by denying knowledge about the second distribution to the *Guard* clients prior to his receipt of additional attorney fees, and by denying he met with his co-counsel and Judge Bamberger to discuss the distribution. From our review of the evidence, we conclude that Respondent was not truthful in that regard.

Respondent is therefore guilty of violating SCR 3.130–8.1(a).

G. SCR 3.130–8.3(c), now codified as SCR 3.130–8.4(c)

SCR 3.130–8.4(c) states that a lawyer may not "engage in conduct involving dishonesty, fraud, deceit, or misrepresentation." The Trial Commissioner found Respondent guilty of violating this rule because Respondent "must have been fully aware of the fraud perpetrated by his accepting fees far in excess of what he was entitled to under his contractual agreement," that Respondent knew that the *Guard* class members did not receive an accurate accounting of the settlement proceeds, and that because of this knowledge Respondent "acted with dishonesty, deceit, and misrepresentation in assisting his co-counsel in their efforts to conceal what had transpired."

Respondent complains that this charge lacks specificity. Based upon our review of the record, we agree with the Trial Commissioner's assessment. The vast amount of evidence compiled and presented in this matter demonstrates convincingly that Respondent knowingly participated in a scheme to skim millions of dollars in excess attorney's fees from unknowing clients. He may have kept himself at arm's length from Mills, Cunningham, and Gallion; and, he may not have known the details of the direct deception that, with Helmers' assistance, they perpetrated upon the clients: But no reasonable person familiar with the evidence could doubt that he received and retained fees that he knew were improperly taken at the client's expense. No reasonable person familiar with the evidence could doubt that he purposefully attempted to avoid conversation and correspondence that would expose his knowledge of the nefarious schemes of his co-counsel. We conclude that Respondent violated SCR 3.1308.4(c), formerly codified as SCR 3.130–8.3(c).

H. SCR 3.130–5.1(c)(1)

SCR 3.130–5.1(c)(1) states in pertinent part:

> a lawyer shall be responsible for another lawyer's violation of the Rules of Professional Conduct only if: The lawyer orders or, with knowledge of specific conduct, ratifies the conduct involved. . . .

The Trial Commissioner found Respondent violated this rule by "orchestrating" the attempt to cover up the unethical conduct of Cunningham, Gallion, and Mills. To ratify another attorney's conduct a person must have actual knowledge of the conduct. However, SCR 3.130–1.0(f) states: "A person's knowledge may be inferred from circumstances." In our review of Respondent's conduct, we have looked not only at direct evidence of his knowledge of his peers' unethical conduct, but also for circumstances that indicate he had such knowledge.

We find several such circumstances, which when taken together, convincingly establish that Respondent was aware of the misconduct of Mills, Cunningham, and Gallion, and that he actively aided in its concealment to prevent or delay discovery of the excessive funds he had enjoyed.

Those circumstances include the following:

a.  He provided $250,000.00 of his own money to assure that David Stuart's suit against Mills would be settled, so that Respondent would not be deposed in that action and Stuart's effort to unravel the truth about the *Guard* case fees would be halted. Respondent was not a party to the dispute between Stuart and Mills. The evidence did not indicate he had a special relationship with either Mills or Stuart that would explain his strong concern about their disagreement, yet he met with Mills to encourage him to settle the lawsuit with Stuart. He actively resisted the effort to depose him. He kept himself apprised through one of Mills' employees of the attempt to mediate a settlement;

b.  He reviewed the deceptive documents that Gallion had given to Wallingford to submit to the KBA investigators. One of those documents was the phony list of *Guard* case clients that documents the greatly exaggerated amount of money each one received from the settlement;

c.  Although he claimed his responsibility in the case was over, he attended at least two meetings before Judge Bamberger to obtain retroactive approval of attorneys' fees and to create the charitable trust that would hide a large part of the purloined cash; and,

d.   After Mills's angry demands to distribute more of the lawsuit proceeds, he recruited Helmers to meet with clients for the second round of payments, and provided him with documents for the clients to sign.

While none of these facts alone is conclusive, all of them together complete the picture of Respondent's effort to conceal or hinder the disclosure of the misdeeds of Cunningham, Mills, Gallion, and Helmers, and thereby protect the improper payments he had accepted. We conclude that Respondent violated SCR 3.130–5.1(c)(1).

I. SCR 3.130–1.7

Respondent was initially charged by the Inquiry Commission with violating SCR 3.130–1.7 which in pertinent part provides that "a lawyer shall not represent a client if the representation of that client will be directly adverse to another client." The Trial Commissioner could not find a clear violation of SCR 3.130–1.7 and found Respondent not guilty of violating this rule. The Board of Governors reached the same conclusion. We regard the matter of this charge as resolved in Respondent's favor and no further action is required.

We now turn to what the appropriate punishment should be for Respondent's numerous ethical violations.

### III.  DISCIPLINE

Based on Respondent's ethical violations, the Trial Commissioner and Board of Governors recommended to this Court that he be permanently disbarred from the practice of law in the Commonwealth and pay restitution in the amount of $7,500,000.00. For the reasons discussed below, we agree with the recommendation to permanently disbar Respondent, but do not order him to pay restitution.

A.   Disbarment

SCR 3.380 provides the following:

Upon finding of a violation of these rules, discipline may be administered by way of a private reprimand, suspension from practice for a definite time with or without conditions as the Court may impose, or permanent disbarment.

Citing to the American Bar Association, *Standards for Imposing Lawyer Sanctions,* Rule 9.2, the Trial Commissioner found that permanent disbarment was the appropriate sanction for Respondent. ABA Standard 9.2 states:

9.2  Aggravation

9.21 Definition. Aggravation or aggravating circumstances are any considerations, or factors that may justify an increase in the degree of discipline to be imposed.

9.22 Factors which may be considered in aggravation. Aggravating factors include:

(a)  prior disciplinary offenses;

(b)  dishonest or selfish motive;

(c)  a pattern of misconduct;

(d)  multiple offenses;

(e)  bad faith obstruction of the disciplinary proceeding by intentionally failing to comply with rules or orders of the disciplinary agency;

(f)  submission of false evidence, false statements, or other deceptive practices during the disciplinary process;

(g)  refusal to acknowledge wrongful nature of conduct;

(h)  vulnerability of victim;

(i)  substantial experience in the practice of law;

(j)  indifference to making restitution.

Based on the record and all of the violations Respondent committed, we find that all of the factors apply except for (a), (e), and (f). We also find that prior case law supports the sanction of a permanent disbarment in this case.

Respondent presents evidence that is supportive of mitigation. His most persuasive mitigation evidence is that he has never previously been disciplined by the KBA. He also presented several character witnesses who testified about his prominence in the Cincinnati legal community and his service to various charitable organizations. We are aware of Respondent's reputation and we do not doubt the veracity of the witnesses that attested to his character. While, the good reputation he has enjoyed and his generosity serves to exacerbate the tragedy of his fall, they cannot atone for the serious misconduct he has committed in connection with this matter. Therefore, we find that permanently disbarring Respondent is an appropriate penalty for his ethical violations.

## B.  *Payment of Restitution*

The Trial Commissioner and the Board of Governors requested that we order Respondent to pay over $7 million in restitution to the *Guard* case clients. We decline to do so. We agree with Respondent's argument that our Supreme Court Rules do not allow for us to order restitution when a disciplinary action leads to a permanent disbarment. SCR 3.380 in pertinent part states: "discipline may be administered by way of a private reprimand, suspension from practice for a definite time with or without conditions as the Court may impose, *or permanent disbarment*." The plain language of the rule indicates that while this Court may order an attorney disciplined by either a temporary suspension from the practice of law, public reprimand, or private reprimand to comply with any conditions imposed by the Court, a permanent disbarment stands alone—separated from the language allowing us to impose conditions by the word "or."

A disbarred attorney is no longer a member of the Kentucky Bar Association and no longer subject to our direct supervision. Moreover, the affected clients have brought a civil action to recover any appropriate damages they sustained, and the determination of their remedy is more appropriately addressed in that forum.

Thus it is ordered that:

1)   Respondent, Stanley M. Chesley, is hereby permanently disbarred from the practice of law in Kentucky. Respondent thusly, may never apply for reinstatement to the Bar under the current rules;

2)   Respondent shall notify all Courts in the Commonwealth of Kentucky or other tribunals in which he has matters pending, and all clients, of his inability to represent them and of the necessity and urgency of promptly retaining new counsel. The Respondent shall simultaneously provide a copy of all such letters of notification to the Office of Bar Counsel;

3)   Respondent shall immediately cancel and cease any advertising activities in accordance with SCR 3.390; and

4)   In accordance with SCR 3.450, Respondent has paid all costs associated with these disciplinary proceedings in the amount of $88,579.62.00.

# C.  THE QUASI CLASS ACTION AND ATTORNEY FEES

## IN RE ZYPREXA PRODS. LIAB. LITIG.

United States District Court for the Eastern District of New York, 2006.
424 F.Supp.2d 488.

### I.   INTRODUCTION

By this order the court exercises its power to control legal fees in a coordinated litigation of many individual related cases-in effect, a quasi-class action. Limiting fees is particularly appropriate in the instant litigation since much of the discovery work the attorneys would normally have done on a retail basis in individual cases has been done at a reduced cost on a wholesale basis by the plaintiffs' steering committee.

## II.  PROCEDURAL HISTORY

In April 2004, pre-trial proceedings were consolidated in actions against defendant Eli Lilly & Company for injuries alleged to have been caused by the prescription drug Zyprexa. After discovery and negotiations overseen by the court-appointed special discovery master and four special settlement masters, in November 2005 the defendant entered into a partial settlement covering some 8,000 individual plaintiffs. Under court supervision, a complex claims administration process was developed. It will be administered by the special settlement masters. Three different "tracks" for recovery are provided. The track selected depends on the nature of each plaintiff's injury and the estimated monetary value of the claim. Track A provides for a lump sum of $5,000. Tracks B and C allow substantially higher recoveries.

## III.  FEE ALLOCATION

On January 3, 2006, the four settlement special masters were directed to consult with the parties in order to arrive at a recommended fee schedule cap and allocation of expenses. They were to suggest fees which were "the lesser of the maximum reasonable fee schedule they recommend, the fee agreed upon between the client and the attorney in an individual case, and the maximum amount permitted under the applicable local state rules or statutes."

Upon consultation with counsel and with members of the plaintiffs' steering committee, the special masters proposed that the court: (1) cap all legal fees for "Track A" settlements ($5,000) at no more than 20%, with a maximum of $500 for costs and expenses to come off the top before computation of fees; (2) cap all other fees at 37.5% of recovery; and (3) work with the firms representing the settling plaintiffs to conduct case-by-case evaluations that might result in further changes in fee caps or allocation of expenses because of "unique circumstances." *See* letter of March 7, 2006 from special settlement master Kenneth R. Feinberg on behalf of the four special settlement masters.

After careful consideration of the complicated and exceptional circumstances posed by this case, this court now adopts the special masters' proposal with two main modifications. First, the court reduces the cap from 37.5% to 35%. Second, in order to guarantee that all attorneys receive adequate but not excessive compensation, the special masters will have the power to vary fee caps upwards to a maximum of 37.5% and downward to 30% in individual cases on the basis of special circumstances; clients and attorneys may appeal to the court from any such adjustments. The special settlement masters will supervise the allocation of costs and expenses in individual cases; they will be limited to those incurred in individual cases, except for Track A cases where there is a cap of $500 as stated above.

The costs of the plaintiffs' steering committee in conducting general discovery and making documents and depositions available to all litigants, whether in federal or state courts, shall be paid out of the general settlement fund, not by individual plaintiffs. This allocation is particularly apt in the present case since all litigants, whether in federal or any state court, have access to the materials obtained in pretrial discovery. The amount to be paid to the plaintiff's steering committee for its discovery and other work shall be approved by the special settlement masters.

In carrying out their duties under this order, the special settlement masters shall act as a group, not individually.

## IV.  BASIS OF AUTHORITY IN FEDERAL COURTS

### A.  Analogy to Class Actions

A district court has the explicit power to require reasonable fees in class actions. *See* Fed.R.Civ.P. 23(g)(1)(C)(iii); Fed.R.Civ.P. 23(h); *cf.* Fed.R.Civ.P. 23(e)(1)–(2) (dealing with approval of terms of settlement). While the settlement in the instant action is in the nature of a private agreement between individual plaintiffs and the defendant, it has many of the characteristics of a class action and may be properly characterized as a quasi-class action subject to general equitable powers of the court. *See* Fed.R.Civ.P. 23(g)(C)(iii); Fed.R.Civ.P. 23(h); Fed.R.Civ.P. 1 ("just determination of every action"); *cf.* Fed.R.Civ.P. 23(e)(1)(2) (dealing with approval of terms of settlement). The large number of plaintiffs subject to the same settlement matrix approved by the court; the utilization of special masters appointed by the court to control discovery and to assist in reaching and administering a settlement; the court's order for a huge escrow fund; and other interventions by the court, reflect a degree of court control supporting its imposition of fiduciary standards to ensure fair treatment to all parties and counsel regarding fees and expenses.

No one except the trial judge, assisted by special masters, can exercise this ethical control of fees effectively. Many of the individual plaintiffs are both mentally and physically ill and are largely without power or knowledge to negotiate fair fees; plaintiffs' counsel have a built-in conflict of interest; and the defendant is buying peace and is generally disinterested in how the fund is divided so long as it does not jeopardize the settlement.

### B.  General Ethical Supervision

#### 1.  Law

The judiciary has well-established authority to exercise ethical supervision of the bar in both individual and mass actions. ("It is extremely desirable that the respectability of the bar should be maintained, and that its harmony with the bench should be preserved. For these objects, some controlling power, some discretion ought to reside in the Court"). This authority includes the power to review contingency fee contracts for fairness. ("This does not remove the suspicion which naturally attaches to such contingency contracts, and where it can be shown that they are obtained by any undue influence of the attorney over the client, or by any fraud or imposition, or that the compensation is clearly excessive, so as to amount to extortion, the court will in a proper case protect the party aggrieved").

A federal court may exercise its supervisory power to ensure that fees are in conformance with codes of ethics and professional responsibility even when a party has not challenged the validity of the fee contract. Supervision includes the power to determine that the fee contract was not obtained through undue influence or fraud and that the amount of the fee is not unfair or excessive under the circumstances of the case.

The explication of the reasons for reviewing contingency contracts in *Farmington Dowel* is persuasive. This was an antitrust suit filed under the Clayton Act. After plaintiff Farmington Dowel Company prevailed on its claims, the district court determined that $85,000 was a reasonable attorney's fee pursuant to section 4 of the Act. Upon examining the existing fee contract between Farmington Dowel and its attorneys, however, the district court refrained from awarding counsel any additional fee, in spite of the award required by section 4. It believed any increase in fee beyond that agreed upon in the contract would be unethical.

On appeal, the Court of Appeals concluded that the Clayton Act's fee award was statutorily mandated. Nonetheless, the court noted that the American Bar Association Canons of Professional Ethics place ethical limitations on attorney's fees; it recognized the district judge's authority to determine the maximum fee that would be appropriate within those limits. Accordingly, the court remanded the issue, instructing the district court to award the statutorily mandated "reasonable fees," while using its discretion to restructure the terms of the original agreement so that the total fee would be in accordance with the Canons of Ethics.

The *Farmington Dowel* court explained that a client's willingness to abide by his original fee contract "is relevant but not controlling, for the object of the court's concern is not only a particular party but the conformance of the legal profession to its own high standards of fairness." Excessive fees would adversely reflect on the courts and the bar, providing judges with strong reason to ensure that any fee contract meets reasonable standards.

Those courts that have considered the matter agree that their supervisory power does not imply a duty to examine every attorney's fee contract. The Court of Appeals for the Seventh Circuit, for example, advocates a case-by-case determination of the need for review. In

*Farmington Dowel,* the Court of Appeals for the First Circuit explained that a court's exercising of its supervisory power-an "ethical judgment" requiring the court "to arrive at a figure which it considers the outer limit of reasonableness"-must be "reserved for exceptional circumstances."

### 2.  Application of Law to Facts

While the plaintiffs' attorneys in the present case are highly skilled and have achieved an exceptional result for their clients, there is a danger that adherence to any previously negotiated contingency fee contracts might result in excessive fees. The total settlement amount held in escrow is large, and the over 8,000 individual plaintiffs involved in the settlement are represented by only a handful of firms, all of whom can be expected to gain substantial fees from their numerous clients' combined recoveries. Yet these firms all benefitted from the effectiveness of coordinated discovery carried out in conjunction with the plaintiffs' steering committee and from other economies of scale, suggesting a need for reconsideration of fee arrangements that may have been fair when the individual litigations were commenced.

The risk of excessive fees is a matter of special concern here because of the mass nature of the case. As the *Farmington Dowel* court recognized, excessive fees can create a sense of overcompensation and reflect poorly on the court and its bar. ("Courts have a stake in attorney's fees contracts; the fairness of the terms reflects directly on the court and its bar."). Public understanding of the fairness of the judicial process in handling mass torts-and particularly those involving pharmaceuticals with potential widespread health consequences-is a significant aspect of complex national litigations involving thousands of parties. These considerations are enhanced where, as here, the Judicial Panel on Multidistrict Litigation has assembled all related federal cases "for coordinated or consolidated pretrial proceedings to *promote the just and efficient conduct of such actions.*" 28 U.S.C. § 1407. Litigations like the present one are an important tool for the protection of consumers in our modern corporate society, and they must be conducted so that they will not be viewed as abusive by the public; they are in fact highly beneficial to the public when adequately controlled.

### V.   PARALLEL STATE LAW

Since this is a series of diversity jurisdiction cases, it is particularly useful to examine state law on fees. The obligation of a federal court to guard against excessive fees is reflected in state law. California, Connecticut, Florida, Illinois, Michigan, New Jersey, New York, Tennessee, Texas, and Wisconsin, among others, have rules or statutes limiting the percentage amounts of contingent fees. Connecticut, Illinois, Massachusetts, Pennsylvania, West Virginia, and other states have recognized that courts have the general authority to reduce a particular contingent fee if it is found to be "excessive," or in violation of the rules of professional conduct.

New York common law, as an example, permitted judges to modify contingency agreements prior to the enactment of that state's modern fee structure, even in cases in which the plaintiffs had executed enforceable contingency contracts. *Gair v. Peck* was an action against the Justices of the New York Supreme Court, Appellate Division, seeking a ruling that the Appellate Division lacked the power to adopt a rule regulating contingent fees in personal injury and wrongful death claims and actions. The rule at issue in *Gair* employed a sliding scale, ranging from 50% on the first $1,000 recovered to 25% on any amount over $25,000, or in the alternative, a percentage not in excess of 33 1/3% of the total sum recovered. The rule also provided that the receipt, retention, or sharing of fees in excess of those prescribed would constitute the exaction of unreasonable and unconscionable compensation, in violation of Canons 12 and 13 of the Canons of Professional Ethics of the New York State Bar Association. The New York Court of Appeals rejected the challenge, confirming the power of the court to control attorneys within its bar, and finding that "contingent fees may be disallowed as between attorney and client in spite of contingent fee retainer agreements, where the amount becomes large enough to be out of all proportion to the value of the professional services rendered." Noting that the Appellate Division rule provided the court with the option to authorize a larger fee upon an application showing that the prescribed fee would be inadequate, the *Gair* court concluded that the rule was a permissible procedural shortcut, enabling New York courts to effectively prevent the enforcement of exorbitant fees.

The trend in the states is to limit contingent fees in substantial cases to 33 1/3% or less of net recovery where fees are large. *See* Cal. Bus. & Prof. Code § 6146(a) (limiting contingency fees in medical malpractice suits to 40% of the first $50,000 recovered; 33 1/3% of the next $50,000; 25% of the next $500,000; and 15% of any amount of recovery over $600,000); Conn. Gen. Stat. Ann. § 52–251c(b) (sliding scale limiting contingent fees in personal injury, wrongful death or damage to property suits to 33 1/3% of the first $300,000; 25% of the next $300,000; 20% of the next $300,000; 15% of the next $300,000; and 10% of any amount exceeding $1,200,000); Fla. Bar Reg. R. 4–1.5(f)(4)(B)(i) (schedule limiting contingent fees in personal injury, products liability, and property damage suits to 40% of any recovery up to $1 million; 30% of any portion of the recovery between $1 million and $2 million; and 20% of any portion of the recovery exceeding $2 million in cases where the defendant has filed an answer to the complaint); Fla. Stat. Ann. § 73.092 (limiting contingent fees in eminent domain proceedings to 33% of any benefit up to $250,000; 25% of the benefit between $250,000 and $1,000,000; and 20% of any benefit exceeding $1,000,000); Mich. Gen. Ct. R. 8.121 (imposing a maximum 33 1/3% limit of recovery on contingency fees in personal injury or wrongful death suits); N.J. Ct. R. 1:21–7 (providing a sliding scale limiting contingent fees in all tort suits to 33 1/3% of the first $500,000 net sum recovered; 30% of the next $500,000 recovered; 25% of the next $500,000 recovered; and 20% of the next $500,000 recovered; on all amounts recovered in excess of $2 million, counsel must make an application to the judge for reasonable fee in accordance with the limiting scheme; where the amount recovered is for the benefit of a client who was a minor or mentally incapacitated when the contingent fee arrangement was made, the fee on any amount recovered by settlement without trial shall not exceed 25%); 22 N.Y. Comp. Codes R. & Regs. tit. 22, § 691.20 (capping contingency fees in any personal injury or wrongful death suit at either 50% of the first $1,000 net recovery; 40% of the next $2,000 net recovery; 35% of the next $22,000 net recovery; and 25% of any net recovery over $25,000, or, if the initial contractual arrangement between the client and attorney so provides, 33 1/3% of any net recovery); Tenn. Code Ann. § 29–26–120 (limiting contingent fees in medical malpractice suits to 33 1/3% of all damages awarded); Tex. Lab. Code Ann. § 408.221 (capping contingent fees in worker's compensation lawsuits to 25% of the plaintiffs' recovery); Wis. Stat. § 655.013 (limiting contingent fees in medical malpractice suits to 33 1/3% or 25% of the first $1 million, depending on whether the liability is stipulated within a statutory deadline, and 20% of any amount over $1 million).

Because the court recognizes the exceptional and complicated nature of this important case, the skilled work of the able attorneys involved in it, and the exceptional result achieved, fees in the present case have not been capped at 33 1/3%—almost a national norm—but rather at 35%, with the power in the special masters to depart upwards to a maximum of 37.5% and downwards to a minimum of 30% on the basis of special circumstances in individual cases.

It should be emphasized that the applicable fee under many state laws is less than the maximum fixed by this order. Nevertheless, the imposed cap is considerably less than the 40% or more insisted upon plaintiffs' attorneys in their discussion with the special masters. This order is likely to save tens of millions of dollars for the clients.

## VI. CONCLUSION

Fees in all settling actions in this multidistrict litigation shall be determined as follows: (1) all legal fees for "Track A" claims ($5,000) shall be capped at no more than 20%, with a maximum of $500 for costs and expenses to come off the top before computation of fees; (2) all other legal fees shall be capped at 35% of the client's recovery, regardless of whether the underlying retainer agreement or state law permits for a higher fee; (3) the special masters shall have discretionary authority to conduct case-by-case evaluations and to order reductions or increases of maximum fees down to 30% or up to 37.5% on the basis of special circumstances in individual cases; (4) the special masters shall have authority to ensure that costs and disbursements charged to individual plaintiffs are restricted to those reasonably allocated to the individual case and that they come off the top of the recovery before fee computation; (5) the costs, disbursements and fees of the plaintiffs' steering committee shall be paid out of the general settlement fund rather than by individual plaintiffs and the amount of this payment shall be approved by the special settlement masters; (6) the special settlement masters are only to act as a group and not individually; and (7) clients and attorneys may appeal to the court from any decision of the special settlement masters. Should state law or the private fee arrangement between client and counsel provide for a lesser fee than that provided under this order, the least fee shall be the one enforced.

## IN RE ZYPREXA PRODS. LIAB. LITIG.

United States District Court for the Eastern District of New York, 2006.
433 F.Supp.2d 268.

### I.   INTRODUCTION AND SUMMARY

This mass tort action on behalf of over 8,000 private individuals against the pharmaceutical manufacturer Eli Lilly and Co. was transferred to this court by the Judicial Panel on Multidistrict Litigation on April 14, 2004. *See* 28 U.S.C. § 1407. A Final Settlement of the bulk of the cases was approved by the court and parties on November 22, 2005. Over 99% of the "settling plaintiffs" filed consents and releases. A large sum has been deposited in escrow to pay plaintiffs' individual claims when approved by the four Special Settlement Masters appointed by the court. The amounts of the payments will be determined by the Special Settlement Masters according to matrixes approved by the court.

The proceeding now requires the court to exercise its equitable and inherent powers to ensure that all settling litigants are treated fairly.

In large part because of inadequate documentary support, only about half of the claims have been approved for payment by the Special Settlement Masters. No money can be paid to any claimant under the terms of the settlement until some 86% of the claims have been so approved.

For the reasons indicated below, the court now orders that by July 17, 2006 all settling plaintiffs who have not yet done so must have filed documents necessary to support their claims, conforming to the guidelines agreed upon in the Final Settlement Protocol, so that all pending settled cases can be approved for payment by the Special Settlement Masters by August 1, 2006. Any plaintiff who fails to comply—either by submitting an inadequately supported claim, or by failing to submit necessary documents—will be deemed to have abandoned the claim; the complaint will be dismissed with prejudice and the case reinstated only upon submission of affidavits showing good cause for the delay and a substantial basis for the renewed claim.

## II.  FACTS

Members of the Plaintiffs' Steering Committee (PSC) and other plaintiffs' attorneys reached an agreement with Eli Lilly and Co. in principle to settle a significant number of Zyprexa personal injury cases pursuant to a June 8, 2005 Memorandum of Understanding. Special Settlement Masters were appointed by the court to assist the parties in effectuating the settlement. A Final Settlement Protocol was approved by the court after consulting with the PSC, other parties, and the Special Settlement Masters. A large sum has been deposited in an escrow fund, subject to court order, where it collects interest. No money has been paid to any claimant.

It has been almost one year since the original Memorandum of Understanding was issued, and six months since the Final Settlement Proposal was approved. Some 99.6% of eligible plaintiffs—representing 8,362 individuals—have tendered releases to Lilly. *See* Letter of Christopher A. Seeger dated May 17, 2006. The Special Settlement Masters report that 4,087 claims have been approved by them for payment.

Pursuant to the settlement agreement, no payment can be made to any of the more than 8,000 individuals who are participating in the settlement until at least 7,193 claims have been properly filed and approved by the Settlement Masters; 6,474 of these claims must be diabetes-related. According to the Special Masters, only 3,737 diabetes-related claims have been approved to date. That means an additional 3,106 claims—2,737 of them diabetes-related—must be approved before the Special Settlement Masters can authorize payments to anyone or the court can release any money from the escrow fund.

The delay appears to be due in large part to the failure of some participating attorneys to provide the Settlement Masters promptly with appropriate documents supporting their claims.

At a Status Conference held June 1, 2006, Special Settlement Master Kenneth Feinberg reported that approximately one-third of potential claimants had delivered supporting documents that did not conform with the instructions for claim submission, while many others have not even filed claim forms.

Those attorneys who have failed to meet their obligation to support their clients' claims promptly and properly cannot be allowed to imperil their own and every other attorney's clients by needless delay, placing unjust and unnecessary obstacles in the way of prompt payment of valid claims. The public interest and that of the parties, as a matter of law and equity, require prompt payment to those who have properly filed and supported valid claims.

## III.  LAW

### A.   Quasi-Class Action

While the settlement in the instant action is in the nature of a private agreement between individual plaintiffs and the defendant, it has many of the characteristics of a class action; it may be characterized properly as a quasi-class action subject to the general equitable power of the court. *See* Fed.R.Civ.P. 23(g)(1)(C)(iii); Fed.R.Civ.P. 23(h); Fed.R.Civ.P. 1 ("just determination of every action"); *cf.* Fed.R.Civ.P. 23(e)(1)–(2) (dealing with approval of terms of settlement). The large number of plaintiffs subject to the same settlement matrix approved by the court, the utilization of special masters appointed by the court to control discovery and to assist in reaching and administering a settlement, the court's order approving and controlling a huge escrow fund, other interventions by the court in controlling discovery for all claimants, the employment of a multidistrict reference, and cooperation among many federal and state courts, reflect a degree of court control that supports the imposition of fiduciary standards to ensure fair treatment to all parties and counsel regarding issues such as settlement procedures. In addition, the viability of an effective pharmaceutical industry and public health considerations necessitate efficient and fair control by the courts of cases of this kind.

In situations involving the aggregation of masses of individual cases in the form of one quasi-class action, "there is a strong interest in allowing the transferee court to manage the consolidated action in the way that it believes will serve best the interests of justice and efficiency." American Law Institute, *Complex Litigation Project*: Appendix B, *Reporter's Study: A Model System for State to State Transfer and Consolidation*, § 6, cmt. c. Recognizing the special difficulties presented by mass tort quasi-class actions, the Federal Judicial Center has advised that "although the 'just, speedy, and inexpensive determination of every action' requirement applies to all cases, the difficult and sometimes contradictory demands posed by mass torts make case management both challenging and critical. The absence of precedent or of legislative or rule-making solutions *should not foreclose innovation and creativity*." MANUAL FOR COMPLEX LITIGATION, FOURTH, § 22.1.

Individual courts are obligated to rely on the "innovation and creativity" allowed by inherent equitable power when confronting the novel challenges of aggregate litigation. "The desire for consistency and efficiency that underlies the normal application of law of the case is outweighed in complex aggregative litigation by the need to ensure that the litigation in its consolidated form is handled fairly." ALI Draft, § 6, cmt. c.

Many of the same considerations that necessitate close judicial supervision of plaintiffs' counsel and proposed settlements in the class action context—such as protecting absent or disinterested litigants, and dealing with plaintiffs' practical inability to monitor their attorneys, some of whom represent hundreds of clients within the same litigation—apply to quasi-class actions such as the instant one. Some of the conventions *required* when a class is certified are *appropriate* in quasi-class actions involving large aggregations of claims. In both contexts, the primary goal of the court is to "ensure that similarly situated individuals receive equal fairness protections regardless of how the courts aggregated the litigation."

### B.  Equitable Estoppel

In a broad sense, equitable estoppel is "a bar that prevents one from asserting a claim or right that contradicts what one has said or done before or what has been legally established as true." It is "grounded on notions of fair dealing and good conscience and is designed to aid the law in the administration of justice where injustice would otherwise result." Equitable estoppel can be "invoked successfully against a party who has occasioned a loss through an obvious lack of care or an affirmative act fairly identified as the cause of the loss."

### IV.  APPLICATION OF LAW TO FACTS

Inaction on the part of almost half the plaintiffs who agreed to be bound by the Final Settlement Agreement thwarts the ability of the remainder of claimants—some of whom have established serious illness and who are in need of prompt compensation—to recover. To avoid continued frustration by the few of the many, those plaintiffs who accepted the Final Settlement Protocol must submit proper claims to the Special Settlement Masters by July 17, 2006; the court finds that this requirement can be readily met. If a claim is not properly supported by that date, it will be deemed abandoned and will be involuntarily dismissed with prejudice. Subject to a motion to reopen, accompanied by affidavits of good cause for the delay and a showing of substantial merit to the claim, a plaintiff with such an abandoned claim will be considered equitably estopped from withdrawing from participation in the Final Settlement Protocol or pursuing the claim independently.

Once 90% of the plaintiffs joined in the original multidistrict litigation ratified the settlement via a signed release, the agreement was to become effective and binding on all parties to the settlement, pursuant to the terms of the original Settlement Proposal. When 8,362 plaintiffs to this quasi-class action (99.6%) agreed to be bound by the Final Settlement agreement, each knew that the ultimate success of the settlement hinged on each one's compliance with the settlement terms. Each plaintiff recognized that each would rely on the good-faith participation of every other.

Unnecessary delay in receiving compensation because of lack of required attention to their responsibilities by fellow claimants warrants application of equitable estoppel. A plaintiff who has "assumed a leading role in creating a very complex lawsuit . . . should not now be allowed to upset the recovery of the other plaintiffs" by inaction. Delinquent plaintiffs (and their attorneys) should be deemed equitably estopped from disrupting a settlement beneficial to all the plaintiffs who have agreed to it if they fail to follow the procedure to which they formally committed themselves when they bound themselves to the settlement. There is no "opt-out" escape from the obligation of plaintiffs and attorneys who have already explicitly agreed to settle.

## V.    CONCLUSION

The claim of any plaintiff who fails to promptly submit acceptable supporting documentation to the Special Settlement Masters by July 17, 2006 will be dismissed on the merits, subject to a motion to reinstate.

Plaintiffs' counsel, the PSC, the Special Settlement Masters, and Defendant's counsel shall confer and, if possible, arrive at a new minimum threshold for payment based on the number of claims approved by the Special Settlement Masters, so that those plaintiffs who have submitted approved claims may be promptly paid. If such an agreement is made, Special Settlement Master Feinberg has assured the court that checks to those claimants whose claims have been approved can be distributed within days. That will put millions of dollars in the hands of plaintiffs who need succor now.

## IN RE VIOXX PRODS. LIAB. LITIG.
United States District Court for the Eastern District of Louisiana, 2009.
650 F.Supp.2d 549.

On August 27, 2008, the Court issued an Order and Reasons capping contingent fee arrangements for all counsel representing claimants in the Vioxx global settlement program at 32% plus reasonable costs. On December 10, 2008, a group of five attorneys, identified as the Vioxx Litigation Consortium (VLC), filed a Motion for Reconsideration/Revision of the Court's Order Capping Contingent Fees and Alternatively for Entry of Judgment. The Court appointed the Tulane Civil Litigation Clinic (Clinic) to represent the interests of claimants whose settlement awards will be affected by the Court's Capping Order. After reconsideration, it is ordered that the VLC's Motion for Reconsideration/Revision of the Court's Order Capping Contingent Fees and Alternatively for Entry of Judgment is granted in part and denied in part.

### I.    FACTUAL BACKGROUND

To put this matter in perspective, a brief review of this litigation is appropriate. This multidistrict products liability litigation involves the prescription drug Vioxx, known generically as Rofecoxib. Merck, a New Jersey corporation, researched, designed, manufactured, marketed and distributed Vioxx to relieve pain and inflammation resulting from osteoarthritis, rheumatoid arthritis, menstrual pain, and migraine headaches. On May 20, 1999, the Food and Drug Administration approved

Vioxx for sale in the United States. Vioxx remained publicly available until September 20, 2004, when Merck withdrew it from the market after data from a clinical trial known indicated that the use of Vioxx increased the risk of cardiovascular thrombotic events such as myocardial infarction (heart attack) and ischemic stroke. Thereafter, thousands of individual suits and numerous class actions were filed against Merck in state and federal courts throughout the country alleging various products liability, tort, fraud, and warranty claims. It is estimated that 105 million prescriptions for Vioxx were written in the United States between May 20, 1999 and September 30, 2004. Based on this estimate, it is thought that approximately 20 million patients have taken Vioxx in the United States.

On February 16, 2005, the Judicial Panel on Multidistrict Litigation conferred multidistrict litigation status on Vioxx lawsuits filed in federal court and transferred all such cases to this Court to coordinate discovery and to consolidate pretrial matters pursuant to 28 U.S.C. § 1407. One month later, on March 18, 2005, this Court held the first status conference in the Vioxx MDL to consider strategies for moving forward with the proceedings. Shortly thereafter, the Court appointed committees of counsel to represent the parties and to meet with the Court once every month to review the status of the litigation.

One of this Court's first priorities was to assist the parties in selecting and preparing certain test cases to proceed as bellwether trials. In total, the Court conducted six Vioxx bellwether trials. The first of the bellwether trials took place in Houston, Texas, while this Court was displaced following Hurricane Katrina. The five subsequent bellwether trials took place in New Orleans, Louisiana. Only one of the trials resulted in a verdict for the plaintiff. Of the five remaining trials, one resulted in a hung jury and four resulted in verdicts for the defendant. During the same period that this Court conducted six bellwether trials, approximately thirteen additional Vioxx-related cases were tried before juries in the state courts of Texas, New Jersey, California, Alabama, Illinois, and Florida. With the benefit of experience from these bellwether trials, as well as the encouragement of the several coordinated courts, the parties soon began settlement discussions in earnest.

On November 9, 2007, Merck and the NPC formally announced that they had reached a Settlement Agreement. The private Settlement Agreement establishes a pre-funded program for resolving pending or tolled state and federal Vioxx claims against Merck as of the date of the settlement, involving claims of heart attack (MI), ischemic stroke (IS), and sudden cardiac death (SCD), for an overall amount of $4.85 billion. The Settlement Agreement is a voluntary opt in agreement and expressly contemplates that this Court shall oversee various aspects of the administration of settlement proceedings, including appointing a Fee Allocation Committee, allocating a percentage of the settlement proceeds to a Common Benefit Fund, approving a cost assessment, and modifying any provisions of the Settlement Agreement that are otherwise unenforceable. Accordingly, this Court has consistently exercised its inherent authority over the MDL proceedings in coordination with its express authority under the terms of the Settlement Agreement to ensure that the settlement proceedings move forward in a uniform and efficient manner.

The Settlement Agreement provides a schedule for the disbursement of interim payments to certain eligible claimants. In order to qualify for interim payments, eligible claimants must fulfill specific registration and filing obligations. Pursuant to the terms of the Settlement Agreement, eligible MI claimants who timely fulfill all of their filing obligations may qualify to receive interim payments beginning on August 1, 2008, or the date on which the Claims Administrator has determined pre-review points awards for at least 2,500 MI claimants, whichever is later. The schedule for distributing interim payments to claimants is conditioned on Merck's decision to waive its walk away privileges.

On July 17, 2008, Merck formally announced that it was satisfied that the thresholds necessary to trigger funding of the Vioxx Settlement Program would be met. Merck further advised that it intended to waive its walk away privileges and that it would commence funding the Vioxx Settlement Program by depositing an initial sum of $500 million into the settlement fund, clearing the way for distribution of interim payments to eligible claimants. On August 20, 2008, the Claims Administrator reported to the Court that it had successfully reviewed approximately 2,750 claims for interim payments.

Against this backdrop, the Court ordered "that contingent fee arrangements for all attorneys representing claimants in the Vioxx global settlement shall be capped at 32% plus reasonable costs." The Court concluded that its authority to implement a fee cap derived from three sources.

First, any court presiding over a mass tort proceeding possesses equitable authority to examine fee arrangements. The Federal Rules of Civil Procedure expressly grant this power to district courts in class actions. *See* Fed.R.Civ.P. 23(g)(1)(C)(iii); Fed.R.Civ.P. 23(h); *see also* MANUAL FOR COMPLEX LITIGATION (FOURTH) § 22.927. While an MDL is distinct from a class action, the substantial similarities between the two warrant the treatment of an MDL as a quasi-class action. Accordingly, this Court found that "the Vioxx global settlement may properly be analyzed as occurring in a quasi-class action, giving the Court equitable authority to review contingent fee contracts for reasonableness." *Id.* at 9; *see also In re Guidant Corp. Implantable Defibrillators Prods. Liab. Litig.,* (relying on the quasi-class action nature of an MDL proceeding and the court's equitable authority to implement a reasonable cap on contingent fees); *In re Zyprexa Prods. Liab. Litig.,* (exercising the court's inherent power to "impose fiduciary standards to ensure fair treatment to all parties and counsel regarding fees and expenses.")

Second, the Court recognized that inherent authority, and a concomitant duty, exists to review contingent fee arrangements *sua sponte,* especially where there is a built in conflict of interest. In the instant case, the Court recognized that the claimant's attorneys were unlikely to question the propriety of their own fees, and the defendant had no incentive to jeopardize the settlement agreement by raising the issue. Accordingly, the Court found it necessary to exercise its inherent authority to protect the large number of elderly Vioxx claimants by capping contingent fee agreements.

Finally, the Court held that the terms of the Vioxx Settlement Agreement voluntarily entered into by the parties in this case provided a further source of authority to examine the reasonableness of the contingent fee contracts. Unlike a traditional settlement agreement, which the parties execute without the assistance of the Court, the parties in this case clearly contemplated that this Court would be heavily involved in the administration of the Settlement Agreement. Furthermore, the parties expressly granted the Court authority to affect the distribution of the settlement fund. Further, the parties gave the Court express authority to modify any provision of the Agreement under certain circumstances (allowing modification if a provision "is prohibited or unenforceable to any extent or in any particular context but in some modified form would be enforceable."). Thus, the parties have invoked the jurisdiction of this Court to act in administering the Settlement Agreement and to ensure the enforceability of that agreement. Accordingly, the Court held that:

> To the extent that the Settlement Agreement would be unenforceable if it resulted in excessive or unreasonable attorneys' fees that threaten the public interest and reflect poorly on the courts, this Court may address those fees in order to ensure fairness to all parties. As a result, the Court finds that it may examine the reasonableness of contingent fee contracts in order to protect the claimants and enforce the Settlement Agreement.

Thus, the power to cap contingent fee contracts inheres in the Court and has also been invoked by the parties in this case.

After concluding that the Court possesses the authority to act, the Court examined the contingent fee contracts in this case and set a reasonable limit on the amount that individual attorneys may charge claimants enrolled in the global settlements, regardless of whether their cases were filed in state or federal court. In making this assessment, the Court weighed a number of factors, including past fee caps implemented by MDL courts facing global settlement agreements. *See In re Guidant* (capping contingent fees at 20% subject to appeal to a special master for an upward departure based on certain limiting factors); *In re Zyprexa* (capping contingent fees at 35% but allowing for departure in either direction based on the unique facts of a given case); *In re Silicone Gel Breast Implant Prods. Liab. Litig.* (capping contingent fees at 25% of a $4.2 billion settlement fund). The Court also considered state law caps on contingent fee agreements in both products liability actions and other cases. *See* N.J. R. Ct. 1:21–7 (providing that an attorney in a products liability action "shall not contract for, charge, or collect a contingent fee in excess of the following: (1) 33 1/3% on the first $500,000 recovered; (2) 30% on the next $500,000 recovered; (3) 25% on the next $500,000 recovered; (4) 20% on the next $500,000 recovered."); Cal. Bus. & Prof. Code § 6146(a) (providing a sliding scale framework for limiting contingent fees in actions against healthcare providers); Tex. Lab. Code Ann. § 408.221 (limiting contingent fee arrangements in worker's compensation lawsuits to 25% of the plaintiff's net recovery). Finally, the Court considered the unique contours of the Vioxx litigation with which the Court is intimately familiar. The Court recognized that without the work of the attorneys from across the country involved in this litigation a global settlement would not have been possible. Further, the Court was mindful that certain attorneys may have expended a great deal of time and effort on behalf of their clients. However, the Court ultimately pointed to the many economies of scale which benefitted attorneys across the board, which meant that "instead of pursuing individual discovery, filing individual motions, engaging in individual settlement negotiations, or preparing individual trial plans, attorneys for eligible claimants who wished to participate in the settlement needed only to enroll the claimants in the settlement and then carefully monitor their progress through the claims valuation process."). Since the efficiency of the MDL process leads to substantial economies of scale, the Court reasoned that justice requires that the claimants enjoy some of this benefit. Accordingly, the Court held that a contingent fee cap of 32% allowed attorneys to be fairly compensated for their hard work while also providing a benefit to the claimants.

At the most recent status conference, held on July 31, 2009, the Claims Administrator reported that interim payments totaling $1,231,091,500 had been issued to 14,977 MI claimants. Additionally, payments totaling $64,260,521 had been issued to 2,086 IS claimants. Accordingly, payments are on track to be completed by the end of September, 2009. As these payments continue to be disbursed, the VLC's Motion for Reconsideration/Revision of the Court's Order Capping Contingent Fees and Alternatively for Entry of Judgment is ripe for decision.

### III.  LAW AND ANALYSIS

After reconsideration, and in light of the extensive briefing, evidence, and oral argument provided by the VLC and the Clinic, the Court finds that its reasoning in the initial Order capping contingent fees was sound.

Accordingly, the Court finds that it has the authority to implement a reasonable cap on contingent fee agreements *sua sponte*. Further, the Court finds that it is fair and reasonable to cap contingent fees at 32% plus reasonable costs based on the unique contours of this litigation. However, the Court also recognizes the possibility that extraordinary circumstances may exist which could warrant a departure (in either direction) from the 32% cap in individual cases. At this time, the Court will address the arguments presented by the VLC in opposition to the initial Order capping contingent fees.

### A.   This Court has subject matter jurisdiction to consider the reasonableness of contingent fee agreements

The VLC first argues that no claimant has challenged the reasonableness of any contingent fee agreement prior to the Court's capping order, and thus, no Article III "case" or "controversy" exists and the Court therefore lacks subject matter jurisdiction to consider the issue.

Where the parties to a lawsuit have invoked the jurisdiction of a district court to preside over a settlement agreement or the distribution of funds in the court registry, the Fifth Circuit has held that courts have subject matter jurisdiction to examine the reasonableness of contingent fee contracts. (holding that subject matter jurisdiction existed to consider reasonableness of contingent fee agreements where the plaintiff had filed a motion for the disbursement of funds in the court's registry); Further, past MDL courts have deemed it appropriate to cap contingent fees even though no claimants had challenged the reasonableness of their agreement. *In re Guidant Corp. Implantable Defibrillators Prods. Liab. Litig.,* ("This Court has the inherent right and responsibility to supervise the members of its bar in both individual and mass tort actions, including the right to review contingency fee contracts for fairness."); *see also In re Zyprexa Prods. Liab. Litig.* ("A federal court may exercise its supervisory power to ensure that fees are in conformance with codes of ethics and professional responsibility even when a party has not challenged the validity of the fee contract.").

In this case, the parties have done more than simply ask the Court to approve a settlement agreement or move for a disbursement of funds. In fact, this Court is expressly authorized to be the Chief Administrator of the Settlement Agreement. In this capacity, the Court is empowered to determine the amount and allocation of common benefit fees, which has a direct impact upon the overall level of attorney compensation. In addition to these powers, the Court has been highly involved in the day-to-day administration of the Settlement Agreement and continues to entertain motions, issue orders, and hold monthly status conferences. Thus, there is no doubt that the parties in this case, who involved the court in dispersing funds and overseeing a settlement, have invoked the jurisdiction of this

Court. Therefore the Court has subject matter jurisdiction to consider the reasonableness of fee agreements.

### B.     This Court has authority to review contingent fee contracts for reasonableness

In the initial capping Order, as discussed above, the Court identified three independent sources of its authority to implement a cap on all contingent fee agreements: 1) the Court's equitable powers; 2) its inherent supervisory authority; and 3) its express authority under the terms of the Settlement Agreement. The VLC challenges all three of these asserted sources.

### 1.     In light of the nature of MDL proceedings, treatment of the Vioxx MDL as a quasi-class action is appropriate

The VLC argues that even if this Court has subject matter jurisdiction to consider the reasonableness of contingent fee contracts, the Court lacks the authority to alter the terms of the VLC's fee arrangements. In mounting this challenge, the VLC attacks each of the asserted justifications propounded by the Court in its initial Order. First, the VLC challenges the Court's equitable authority by arguing that classifying an MDL as a quasi-class action is inappropriate. Focusing on the differences between a class action and an MDL, the VLC points out that the underlying actions in an MDL remain individual in nature while a class action is a representative proceeding. This difference, they maintain, is the reason that fee capping is appropriate in a class action but not in an MDL.

Admittedly, the Federal Rules of Civil Procedure expressly provide that district courts may require reasonable fees in class actions while the MDL statute lacks an analogous provision. *Compare* Fed.R.Civ.P. 23(g)(1)(C)(iii), *and* Fed.R.Civ.P. 23(h), *with* 28 U.S.C. § 1407. This statutory difference, however, is not the end of the story. First, the MDL statute requires that transferee courts "promote the just and efficient conduct of such actions." 28 U.S.C. § 1407(a). In the context of contingent fee arrangements, implementing a reasonable cap promotes justice for all parties by allowing claimants to benefit (as their attorneys have) from the economies of scale and increased efficiency that an MDL provides. Certainly, this statutory language lends support to the proposition that MDL courts, like class action courts, can exercise equitable authority to examine the reasonableness of fees.

Furthermore, several previous MDL courts have considered the issue and have accepted the classification of an MDL as a quasi-class action and proceeded to exercise their equitable powers to cap contingent fees. *See In re Zyprexa; see also In re Guidant.* In *Zyprexa,* for example, the court noted that an MDL "has many of the characteristics of a class action and may be properly characterized as a quasi-class action subject to general equitable powers of the court." The court went on to point out a number of factors which favored this classification, including the payment of claimants out a massive escrow fund, the universal applicability of a uniform settlement matrix, the court's use of special masters in discovery and settlement administration, and other elements of court control.

The global settlement in this case bears a significant resemblance to the global settlement in *Zyprexa*. First, there are approximately 50,000 eligible claimants currently enrolled in the Vioxx Settlement Program. These claimants, like those in *Zyprexa,* are all subject to a universal settlement matrix for awarding points and valuating claims. Second, in order to administer the Vioxx Settlement Program, this Court, like the court in *Zyprexa,* has control over a large settlement fund. Finally, both *Zyprexa* and the Vioxx MDL have made use of special masters throughout the litigation process. Given these similarities, and § 1407's mandate of just and efficient treatment, it is correct to consider this MDL a quasi-class action. Accordingly, it is appropriate for the Court to exercise its equitable authority to examine fee agreements for reasonableness.

*2.    This Court's exercise of its inherent authority to inquire into the reasonableness of fee agreements was justified*

While the VLC recognizes that certain powers inhere in district courts, they challenge the notion that these powers allow an MDL court to implement a reasonable cap on contingent fee agreements. Arguing that "a federal court's inherent powers consist of those necessary for the courts to manage their affairs," the VLC asserts that this Court has failed to justify the use of inherent power to act in this case. Memorandum in Support, at 9. While the VLC is correct that the exercise of inherent power is limited and requires justification, their argument fails because the exercise of inherent authority to inquire into the reasonableness of fee agreements in this case was justified.

Contingent fee contracts have long been accepted in the United States because "they provide many litigants with the only practical means by which they can secure legal services to enforce their claims." While permissible, these contracts are subject to a requirement of reasonableness. Model Rules of Prof'l Conduct R. 1.5(a). Courts that have considered the issue have nearly unanimously concluded that the power to consider the reasonableness of contingent fees is inherent in a federal court. In the context of mass tort litigation, "a court that exercised inherent power to prevent a violation of the lawyers' professional responsibility to charge only reasonable rates would be acting within the parameters of inherent authority as described by the Supreme Court." *See In re Guidant* ("This Court has the inherent right and responsibility to supervise the members of its bar in both individual and mass tort actions, including the right to review contingency fee contracts for fairness.").

Several justifications exist for the exercise of inherent authority to implement a reasonable cap on attorneys' fees. First, when it comes to the percentage or amount of the contingency fee, a conflict of interest necessarily exists between the claimants and their attorneys who both seek to maximize their own percentage of an award. Accordingly, court supervision is necessary. *In re Guidant* ("As for the representative counsel involved, Plaintiffs' counsel have a built-in conflict of interest that is directly opposed to that of their clients."); *In re Zyprexa* ("Plaintiffs' counsel have a built-in conflict of interest; and the defendant is buying peace and is generally disinterested in how the fund is divided so long as it does not jeopardize the settlement."). In this case, like in *Guidant* and *Zyprexa,* the plaintiffs' attorneys had no incentive to challenge the reasonableness of their own fees on behalf of their clients. In fact, there is a strong monetary incentive for the attorneys to remain silent. Had this Court not stepped in, the issue would therefore have gone unaddressed.

Additionally, the magnitude of these MDL proceedings and the resulting publicity creates a concern that disproportionate results and inconsistent standards would damage the public's faith in the judicial process. *In re Zyprexa* ("Litigations like the present one are an important tool for the protection of consumers in our modern corporate society, and they must be conducted so that they will not be viewed as abusive by the public; they are in fact highly beneficial to the public when adequately controlled."). Accordingly, exercising inherent powers to maintain public faith in the judicial process would be justified. In this case, with 50,000 claims from all over the country, and a $4.85 billion settlement in place, public scrutiny is particularly intense. Accordingly, this Court was compelled to act to maintain the confidence of the public.

Finally, where the claimants in a particular case are vulnerable, courts have used their inherent power to examine contingency fees to protect them (capping fees where many of the claimants were mentally or physically ill); *In re Guidant* (capping fees to protect physically ill and aging claimants). In order to qualify for the Vioxx Settlement Agreement, a claimant must have suffered a heart attack, ischemic stroke, or sudden cardiac death. Accordingly, like the elderly and physically ill claimants in *Zyprexa* and *Guidant,* Vioxx claimants have all suffered some form of physical injury and many are elderly. Accordingly, the Court was justified in exercising its inherent authority and responsibility to examine contingent fee contracts for fairness and consistency.

*3.   The parties to the Vioxx Settlement Agreement implicitly authorized this Court to review their fee agreements for reasonableness*

Finally, the VLC challenges the contention that the Vioxx Settlement Agreement authorizes this Court to implement a reasonable cap on contingent fees. Arguing that no provision in the agreement "purports to regulate the fee contracts at issue," the VLC goes as far as asserting that the agreement expressly divests this Court of the authority to act. For support, they point to Section 9.1, which states in part:

Any division of any Settlement Payment with respect to, and as between, any Enrolled Program Claimant, any Executing Derivative Claimants and/or his or their respective counsel is to be determined by such Persons and any such division, or any dispute in relation to such division, shall in no way affect the validity of this Agreement or the Release or Dismissal With Prejudice Stipulation executed by Such Enrolled Program Claimant (and any related executing Derivative Claimants) or his Counsel, as applicable.

However, the VLC's argument misstates the nature of the Settlement Agreement as a whole and Section 9.1 in particular.

The Vioxx Settlement Agreement is replete with examples of the parties' desire to grant authority to this Court. First, the agreement contemplates that this Court will act as the "Chief Administrator" of the Settlement Program, and will "preside over the Program in the capacities specified herein." Acting as the Chief Administrator, the Court is given express authority to make decisions affecting the amount and allocation of attorneys' fees. Pursuant to Section 9.2, the Court is responsible for determining the amount and allocation of common benefit fees for services performed for MDL administration and for the general benefit of all claimants. Furthermore, these common benefit fees are to be paid out of the aggregate attorneys' fees. Accordingly, this Court is expressly authorized to alter the amount of fees paid under individual contingency arrangements.

Further, the Settlement Agreement provides that this Court has the express authority to modify any provision of the Agreement in certain limited circumstances if the Court determines that the provision "is prohibited or unenforceable to any extent or in any particular context but in some modified form would be enforceable." To the extent that the Settlement Agreement would be unenforceable if it resulted in excessive or unreasonable attorneys' fees that threaten the public interest and reflect poorly on the courts, this Court may address those fees in order to ensure fairness to all parties.

While Section 9.1 also deals explicitly with "Individual Counsel Attorneys' Fees," it refers only to the responsibilities of Merck and the Claims Administrator regarding these fees. This provision serves only to require that Merck and other released parties will not be liable for claimant's attorney's fees, to dictate that any dispute over payment of attorney's fees shall not jeopardize the Settlement Agreement, and to outline a procedure for the Claims Administrator to make payments. In fact the only reference to this Court contained in section 9.1 is to say that attorney's fees are subject to reduction based on the Court's determination of common benefit fees and reimbursement of costs. In no way can this provision be construed to limit the authority of the Court to examine unreasonable contingent fee agreements.

Accordingly, the VLC has failed to persuade this Court that it lacks the authority to examine individual fee arrangements and implement a reasonable universal cap. Given the need for efficiency, fairness, and uniformity, the Court finds that it is both necessary and desirable to have a single court consider the issue of reasonableness of fees. In light of this Court's involvement with the proceedings in this MDL and the administration of the Vioxx Settlement Program, the Court will now proceed to consider the VLC's arguments regarding the reasonableness of a universal fee cap of 32%.

### C.   *The Court applied the proper methodology in determining that a universal fee cap of 32% was reasonable*

The VLC next argues that, even if the Court had authority to examine the fee contracts at issue, the methodology used in the Court's inquiry was faulty. Because the Vioxx MDL consists of diversity jurisdiction cases from all fifty states, the VLC asserts that after this Court determined that an inquiry into the reasonableness of fees was necessary, the Court should have undertaken a separate analysis of reasonableness for each and every state. Further, they claim that the reasonableness analysis should have been conducted *ex ante* instead of *ex post*. In addition to being judicially impractical, the VLC's methodological suggestions are squarely at odds with the mandate of justice and efficiency established by the MDL statute. *See* 28 U.S.C. § 1407.

As previously mentioned, the MDL statute requires that transferee courts "promote the just and efficient conduct of such actions." In part, this outcome can be achieved simply through the consolidation of pretrial and discovery proceedings, which leads to tremendous economies of scale for the lawyers who would otherwise be responsible for preparing thousands of individual cases for trial. In the Vioxx MDL, for example, a comprehensive discovery depository was created for the benefit of all plaintiffs' attorneys. Attorneys did not have to pursue individual discovery, nor did they have to file individual motions, engage in individual settlement negotiations, or prepare individual trial plans. Instead, many of the plaintiffs' attorneys in the Vioxx MDL were able to simply wait while a $4.85 billion settlement was negotiated and then do no more than enroll their clients in the settlement and monitor their progress through the claims valuation process.

Because the attorneys in this case benefitted greatly from the efficiency provided by the MDL structure, the justice mandate of the MDL statute requires that the claimants receive a similar benefit, in the form of reasonable attorneys' fees. Furthermore, the claimants' attorneys were all tasked with navigating their clients through an identical settlement matrix and in accomplishing this they all faced similar challenges, regardless of in which state their fee arrangement was consummated. Accordingly, the MDL statute's mandate of fairness requires a uniform, consistent result for all attorneys and their clients. Any other result would be impractical from the standpoint of judicial economy. Conducting fifty independent analyses of reasonableness would drain judicial resources and would eliminate the efficiency that the MDL was designed to create.

In the interests of justice, previous MDL courts have also determined the reasonableness of fees by conducting an *ex post* analysis. *In re Guidant* ("Although the fee arrangements may have been fair when the individual litigations were commenced, the Court concludes that many of the fee arrangements are likely not fair now because of the common benefit work and economies of scale noted above."); *see also In re Guidant Corp.* ("It is apparent that many of the Claimants' attorneys expended additional hours of work that the Court did not anticipate at the time of this initial fee cap. Thus, what was a fair cap then is no longer fair now."); *In re Zyprexa* ("These firms all benefitted from the effectiveness of coordinated discovery carried out in conjunction with the plaintiffs' steering committee and from other economies of scale, suggesting a need for reconsideration of fee arrangements that may have been fair when the individual litigations were commenced."). While the contingent fee arrangements at issue here may or may not have been fair at the time they were entered into, the great weight of authority in MDL proceedings suggests that an *ex post* analysis is proper. To ensure a consistent and fair result for all plaintiffs, the fee agreements must be reexamined in light of the economies of scale and other efficiencies afforded by consolidation into an MDL.

Accordingly, the Court is not persuaded that the methodology employed to determine the reasonableness of fees in the initial capping order was in error. In examining the reasonableness of contingent fees in an MDL, it is appropriate to consider several factors. First, past fee caps implemented by MDL courts facing global settlement agreements are relevant. State law caps on contingent fee agreements in both products liability actions and other cases are also relevant. Finally, in light of these other factors, the unique contours of a particular MDL will ultimately determine what is reasonable in that case.

Of course, this Court is mindful of the substantial contributions made by the plaintiffs' attorneys in the Vioxx litigation. The VLC and the rest of the plaintiffs' attorneys involved are some of the finest lawyers in the country, and without their contribution the Vioxx Settlement Agreement would not have been possible. Nonetheless, based on this Court's intimate knowledge of the Vioxx litigation, along with the briefing and evidence presented by the VLC in conjunction with their Motion to Reconsider, the Court finds that a 32% cap on contingent fee agreements is reasonable and appropriate in most, if not all, of the cases. After all, in a 4.85 billion dollar settlement, a 32% attorney fee means that the fee is over 1.5 billion dollars. This should be adequate compensation for the attorneys.

However, upon further reflection this Court recognizes that, simply because of the large number of claims in this case, in theory and perhaps in reality there may be one or more cases in which special treatment might be justified. In this particular case there are over 50,000 claims originating in all fifty states. Accordingly, it is not unreasonable to conclude that certain rare circumstances might exist which would warrant a departure, in either direction, upwards or downwards, from the universal fee cap. If an attorney believes that such a departure is appropriate in a particular case, it will be incumbent upon that attorney to file an objection with the Court on or before September 15, 2009, and to serve the involved client. The Court, in due course, will set the matter for hearing and will appoint a special master who will take evidence at the hearing and make recommendations to the Court. Of course, the client will be advised of the hearing date and also allowed to present contrary evidence. If the Court determines that a departure is warranted in a particular case, either upward or downward, the Court will determine a reasonable fee based on the unique circumstances presented after deducting the cost associated with this process.

## IV. CONCLUSION

For the above stated reasons, as well as those expressed in the initial capping order, the VLC's Motion for Reconsideration is granted in part and denied in part. Accordingly, it is ordered that contingent fee arrangements for all attorneys representing claimants in the Vioxx global settlement shall be capped at 32% plus reasonable costs. It is further ordered that in the rare case where an individual attorney believes a departure from this cap is warranted, he shall be entitled to submit evidence to the Court for consideration.

## IN RE OIL SPILL BY THE OIL RIG DEEPWATER HORIZON IN THE GULF OF MEXICO, ON APRIL 20, 2010

United States District Court for the Eastern District of Louisiana, 2012.
2012 WL 2236737.

On May 2, 2012, the Court granted preliminary approval to the Economic and Property Damages Settlement and the Medical Benefits Settlement. On June 4, 2012, the Court Supervised Settlement Program, the facility implementing the Settlements, commenced operation. In light of these events, it is an appropriate time to address the issue of individual attorneys' fees. For reasons expressed below, the Court orders that contingent fee arrangements for all attorneys representing claimants/plaintiffs that settle claims through either or both of the Settlements will be capped at 25% plus reasonable costs. The Court also orders that an individual attorney who believes a departure from this cap is warranted will be permitted to submit evidence to the Court for consideration.

In reaching these conclusions, the Court agrees with, relies upon, and incorporates by reference the reasons set forth by Judge Fallon in *In re Vioxx Products Liability Litigation*. The Court will not repeat all of the points made by Judge Fallon, which built upon an earlier order, but it will mention some that are of particular relevance.

*In re Vioxx* is a multidistrict litigation; the settlement before Judge Fallon was not a class action settlement. However, Judge Fallon found— as had other courts—that MDLs are analogous to class actions, referring to them as "quasi-class actions." *In re Vioxx* (citing *In re Guidant Corp. Implantable Defibrillators Prods. Liab. Litig.*); *In re Zyprexa Prods. Liab. Litig.* Thus, in concluding that he had authority to regulate individual attorneys' fees, Judge Fallon relied in part on the fact that Rule 23 expressly authorizes courts overseeing class actions to examine fee arrangements. Like *In re Vioxx,* this Court is also overseeing an MDL. However, unlike *In re Vioxx,* the instant Settlements are structured and preliminarily certified as class action settlements. Thus, because Rule 23 directly applies to the Settlements, there is no need to analogize MDLs to class actions. In this respect, there is an even stronger argument for the Court's authority to cap attorneys' fees than existed in *In re Vioxx.*

Judge Fallon also noted that "a conflict of interest necessarily exists between the claimants and their attorneys who both seek to maximize their own percentage of an award," which made court supervision necessary. Furthermore, the consolidation of pretrial and discovery proceedings create "tremendous economies of scale for the lawyers who would otherwise be responsible for preparing thousands of individual cases for trial." Thus, because the attorneys reaped a great benefit from the MDL structure, Judge Fallon concluded that "the justice mandate of the MDL statute requires that the claimants receive a similar benefit, in the form of reasonable attorneys' fees." It was also noted that "the magnitude of these MDL proceedings and the resulting publicity creates a concern that disproportionate results and inconsistent standards would damage the public's faith in the judicial process." The Court emphatically agrees with these statements and finds them particularly relevant here.

Judge Fallon also relied on the fact that the Vioxx settlement agreement implicitly authorized the court to review fee arrangements for reasonableness. Similarly, here the Settlements give the Court "continuing and exclusive jurisdiction over the Parties and their Counsel for the purpose of enforcing, implementing and interpreting this Agreement, including jurisdiction over all Economic Class Members, and over the administration and enforcement of the Agreement and the distribution of its benefits to Economic Class Members."

Judge Fallon concluded that 32% was a reasonable contingent fee. The Court agrees with the reasons expressed by Judge Fallon for reaching this number. Nevertheless, the Court deviates from 32% because, unlike the circumstances in *In re Vioxx,* no portion of the individual attorneys' contingent fee will be "held back" to create a common benefit fund. Instead, all common benefit fees and costs will be paid by the BP Defendants. Thus, the 25% cap imposed here is nearly equivalent to the cap in *In re Vioxx* after the deduction for common benefit work. *See In re Vioxx.*

Obviously, 25% is only a *ceiling* for contingent fees. Attorneys and their clients are free to agree to amounts lower than 25%. Attorneys have an ethical responsibility to charge only reasonable fees. *See* Model Rules of Prof'l Conduct R. 1.5(a). In many cases, a reasonable fee may be less than 25%, particularly for a relatively simple claim by an individual. This Order is not intended to allow or encourage attorneys to charge more than a reasonable fee under any circumstance.

Finally, because "it is not unreasonable to conclude that certain rare circumstances might exist which would warrant a departure, in either direction, upwards or downwards, from the universal fee cap," attorneys are permitted to file an objection with the Court. *In re Vioxx.* Attorneys must serve the objection on the involved client, who will be permitted to submit contrary evidence. The Court may choose to appoint a special master to take evidence and make a recommendation to the Court. If the Court determines that a departure is warranted in a particular case, either upward or downward, the Court will determine a reasonable fee based on the unique circumstances presented after deducting the cost associated with this process.

Accordingly,

It is ordered that contingent fee arrangements for all attorneys representing claimants/plaintiffs that settle claims through either or both of the Settlements will be capped at 25% plus reasonable costs. The Claims Administrator is directed to require a certification by the attorney that his or her fees comply with this Order. The Claims Administrator shall not make any disbursements until the attorney provides this certification.

It is further ordered that an individual attorney who believes a departure from the 25% cap is warranted will be permitted to object and submit evidence to the Court for consideration.

## D.  THE QUASI CLASS ACTION AS AN END-RUN AROUND RULE 23

### MCFARLAND V. STATE FARM FIRE & CASUALTY

United States District Court for the Southern District of Mississippi, 2006.
2006 WL 2577852.

Before the Court is Plaintiffs' complaint filed on May 9, 2006. There are hundreds of Plaintiffs joined in a single lawsuit, each asserting claims that arise out of damage to property caused by Hurricane Katrina. The Court *sua sponte* raised the issue of whether to sever each of the claims for damaged property into a separate cause of action. On July 13, 2006, the Court entered a Show Cause Order permitting the parties an opportunity to brief the issue of whether the Court should enter an order severing the Plaintiffs' claims into individual lawsuits. The parties have filed responses.

Generally, permissive joinder of plaintiffs under Fed.R.Civ.P. 20 is at the option of the plaintiffs, assuming that they meet the requirements set forth in Rule 20. Under Rules 20 and 21, the district court has the discretion to sever an action if it is misjoined or might otherwise cause delay or prejudice. The central purpose of Rule 20 is to promote trial convenience and expedite the resolution of disputes, thereby eliminating unnecessary lawsuits. The Supreme Court has instructed lower courts to employ a liberal approach to permissive joinder of claims and parties in the interest of judicial economy. *See United Mine Workers v. Gibbs.*

A party seeking joinder of claimants under Rule 20 must establish (1) a right to relief arising out of the same transaction or occurrence, or series of transactions or occurrences, and (2) some question of law or fact common to all persons seeking to be joined. *See* Fed.R.Civ.P. 20(a). The Court may consider the following factors when deciding whether claims should be severed pursuant to Rule 21: (1) whether the claims arise out of the same transaction or occurrence; (2) whether the claims present some common questions of law or fact; (3) whether settlement of the claims or judicial economy would be facilitated; (4) whether prejudice would be avoided if severance were granted; and (5) whether different witnesses and documentary proof are required for separate claims.

The Court concludes that the Plaintiffs should be required to file separate complaints. Although there may be some common issues of law and fact, the Court finds that the Plaintiffs have not met the same transaction or occurrence prong of Rule 20(a). In a superficial sense, the hurricane was a common occurrence; however, the storm was vastly different in its effect depending on the specific geographic location of each particular home. Although Plaintiffs each held basically the same standard homeowner's policy, each insurance contract is a separate transaction.

Likewise, any alleged negligent or fraudulent misrepresentations by insurance agents constitute separate transactions or occurrences.

In essence, Plaintiffs have filed what amounts to a quasi-class action lawsuit but without regard for the rigid requirements for class certification. This Court recently denied an attempt to certify class for Hurricane Katrina cases in *Guice v. State Farm Fire & Casualty Co.* In denying class certification, U.S. District Judge L.T. Senter, Jr. stated that

> this Court's insurance docket can be described as a variety package with respect to such factors as the number of lawyers involved, the theories of recovery being pursued, or the geographical location of the loss. A number of removed cases include miscellaneous allegations against local agents for negligence and other actionable conduct, and these cases may be subject to remand to state court because of a lack of diversity jurisdiction.

In another opinion, Judge Senter wrote that "each property owner in Mississippi who had real and personal property damaged in Hurricane Katrina is uniquely situated. No two property owners will have experienced the same losses. The nature and extent of the property damage the owners sustain from the common cause, Hurricane Katrina, will vary greatly in its particulars, depending on the location and condition of the property before the storm struck and depending also on what combination of forces caused the damage." The undersigned finds that the same considerations apply to the instant case as well.

Accordingly, the Court finds that the Plaintiffs' individual claims should be divided into separate lawsuits requiring separate complaints. Each complaint should correspond to a single damaged property. In other words, if more than one person owns a particular property, there will be one complaint for that property, even though there may be multiple individual plaintiffs pursuing the claim on that property.

The Court recognizes that even though it is requiring separate complaints to be filed, the Court may consolidate issues for trial pursuant to Fed.R.Civ.P. 42. The Court will continue to explore this avenue in an attempt to streamline the litigation process.

# CHAPTER 10

---

# MASS TORTS AND MULTIDISTRICT LITIGATION

■ ■ ■

## A. THE MDL STATUTE AND PROCEDURE

### MULTIDISTRICT LITIGATION
28 U.S.C.A. § 1407

(a)  When civil actions involving one or more common questions of fact are pending in different districts, such actions may be transferred to any district for coordinated or consolidated pretrial proceedings. Such transfers shall be made by the judicial panel on multidistrict litigation authorized by this section upon its determination that transfers for such proceedings will be for the convenience of parties and witnesses and will promote the just and efficient conduct of such actions. Each action so transferred shall be remanded by the panel at or before the conclusion of such pretrial proceedings to the district from which it was transferred unless it shall have been previously terminated: *Provided, however,* That the panel may separate any claim, cross-claim, counter-claim, or third-party claim and remand any of such claims before the remainder of the action is remanded.

(b)  Such coordinated or consolidated pretrial proceedings shall be conducted by a judge or judges to whom such actions are assigned by the judicial panel on multidistrict litigation. For this purpose, upon request of the panel, a circuit judge or a district judge may be designated and assigned temporarily for service in the transferee district by the Chief Justice of the United States or the chief judge of the circuit, as may be required, in accordance with the provisions of chapter 13 of this title. With the consent of the transferee district court, such actions may be assigned by the panel to a judge or judges of such district. The judge or judges to whom such actions are assigned, the members of the judicial panel on multidistrict litigation, and other circuit and district judges designated when needed by the panel may exercise the powers of a district judge in any district for the purpose of conducting pretrial depositions in such coordinated or consolidated pretrial proceedings.

(c)  Proceedings for the transfer of an action under this section may be initiated by—

(i)   the judicial panel on multidistrict litigation upon its own initiative, or

(ii)   motion filed with the panel by a party in any action in which transfer for coordinated or consolidated pretrial proceedings under this section may be appropriate. A copy of such motion shall be filed in the district court in which the moving party's action is pending.

The panel shall give notice to the parties in all actions in which transfers for coordinated or consolidated pretrial proceedings are contemplated, and such notice shall specify the time and place of any hearing to determine whether such transfer shall be made. Orders of the panel to set a hearing and other orders of the panel issued prior to the order either directing or denying transfer shall be filed in the office of the clerk of the district court in which a transfer hearing is to be or has been held. The panel's order of transfer shall be based upon a record of such hearing at which material evidence may be offered by any party to an action pending in any district that would be affected by the proceedings under this section, and shall be supported by findings of fact and conclusions of law based upon such record. Orders of transfer and such other orders as the panel may make thereafter shall be filed in the office of the clerk of the district court of the transferee district and shall be effective when thus filed. The clerk of the transferee district court shall forthwith transmit a certified copy of the panel's order to transfer to the clerk of the district court from which the action is being transferred. An order denying transfer shall be filed in each district wherein there is a case pending in which the motion for transfer has been made.

(d)   The judicial panel on multidistrict litigation shall consist of seven circuit and district judges designated from time to time by the Chief Justice of the United States, no two of whom shall be from the same circuit. The concurrence of four members shall be necessary to any action by the panel.

(e)   No proceedings for review of any order of the panel may be permitted except by extraordinary writ pursuant to the provisions of title 28, section 1651, United States Code. Petitions for an extraordinary writ to review an order of the panel to set a transfer hearing and other orders of the panel issued prior to the order either directing or denying transfer shall be filed only in the court of appeals having jurisdiction over the district in which a hearing is to be or has been held. Petitions for an extraordinary writ to review an order to transfer or orders subsequent to transfer shall be filed only in the court of appeals having jurisdiction over the transferee district. There shall be no appeal or review of an order of the panel denying a motion to transfer for consolidated or coordinated proceedings.

(f)   The panel may prescribe rules for the conduct of its business not inconsistent with Acts of Congress and the Federal Rules of Civil Procedure.

(g)  Nothing in this section shall apply to any action in which the United States is a complainant arising under the antitrust laws.

(h)  Notwithstanding the provisions of section 1404 or subsection (f) of this section, the judicial panel on multidistrict litigation may consolidate and transfer with or without the consent of the parties, for both pretrial purposes and for trial, any action brought under section 4C of the Clayton Act.

# B.  HISTORICAL ANTECEDENTS

## IN RE ASBESTOS PRODS. LIAB. LITIG.

Judicial Panel on Multidistrict Litigation, 1991.
771 F.Supp. 415.

On January 17, 1991, the Panel issued an order to show cause why all pending federal district court actions not then in trial involving allegations of personal injury or wrongful death caused by asbestos should not be centralized in a single forum under 28 U.S.C. § 1407. Because of the difficulty in serving this order on the enormous number of parties in this docket, the Panel relied on the clerks of all district courts to serve the parties to actions in their respective districts. As a result, the parties to the 26,639 actions pending in 87 federal districts and listed on the following Schedule A are subject to the Panel's order. More than 180 pleadings have been filed in response to the Panel's order, and a four hour hearing on the question of transfer was held on May 30, 1991 in New York City, at which time 37 counsel presented oral argument. In many instances the attorneys filing these pleadings or participating in oral argument were representing the views of large groups of parties.

Supporting transfer are plaintiffs in approximately 17,000 actions (including a core group of more than 14,000 plaintiffs represented by over 50 law firms) and 30 defendants (24 of which are named in more than 20,000 actions). Opposing transfer are plaintiffs in at least 5,200 actions and 454 defendants. The positions of those parties that have expressed a preference with respect to transferee district are varied. Many parties suggest centralization in what amounts to their home forum. The Eastern District of Pennsylvania is the district either expressly favored or not objected to in the greatest number of pleadings. The Eastern District of Texas, which is the choice of the aforementioned core group of 14,000 plaintiffs, is also the district that has generated the most opposition from defendants. Other suggested districts that go beyond the home forum approach are the District of the District of Columbia, the Eastern District of Louisiana, the Northern District of Ohio, and the Eastern District of New York. Some parties' forum recommendations are expressed in the forum of a suggested individual transferee judge or transferee judge structure.

On the basis of the papers filed and the hearing held, the Panel finds that the actions in this litigation involve common questions of fact relating to injuries or wrongful death allegedly caused by exposure to asbestos or asbestos containing products, and that centralization under § 1407 in the Eastern District of Pennsylvania will best serve the convenience of the parties and witnesses and promote the just and efficient conduct of this litigation.

## DISCUSSION

Any discussion of § 1407 transfer in this docket must begin with the recognition that the question does not arise in a vacuum. Indeed, the impetus for the Panel's order to show cause was a November 21, 1990 letter signed by eight federal district judges responsible for many asbestos actions in their respective districts. These judges, citing the serious problem that asbestos personal injury litigation continues to be for the federal judiciary, requested that the Panel act on its own initiative to address the question of § 1407 transfer. Furthermore, as the title of this docket suggests, this is the sixth time that the Panel has considered transfer of asbestos litigation. On the five previous occasions (1977, 1980, 1985, 1986 and 1987) that the Panel considered the question, it denied transfer in each instance.

The Panel's constancy is not as dramatic as a mere recitation of the denials might suggest, however. The 1986 and 1987 dockets considered by the Panel involved only five and two actions, respectively. The 1985 Panel decision pertained not to personal injury/wrongful death asbestos actions but rather to property damage claims of school districts that incurred significant costs in removing asbestos products from school buildings. The denial in the 1980 Panel docket was based almost exclusively on the movants' failure to offer any distinctions that would warrant a disposition different from the Panel's first asbestos decision in 1977.

It is only in the 1977 decision, pertaining to 103 actions in nineteen districts, that the Panel offered any detailed analysis of its asbestos litigation reasoning with respect to asbestos personal injury/wrongful death actions. In that decision, the Panel first listed the primary arguments of the responding parties that unanimously opposed transfer: advanced stage of proceedings in many of the actions; use of voluntary coordinating arrangements in several districts; lack of commonality among defendants and plaintiffs; circumstances of exposure predominantly unique to each action; individual questions of causation in each action; predominantly individual questions of the liability of each defendant in each action; local issues predominating in the discovery process; absence of possibility of inconsistent or overlapping class certifications; and the readily discernible nature of the principal area common to all actions, the state of medical and scientific knowledge at a particular time regarding the health hazards posed by exposure to asbestos.

In denying transfer in the 1977 decision, the Panel recognized the existence of some common questions of fact among the actions. For in that docket, as in the matter currently before the Panel, all actions contained allegations of personal injury or death as a result of exposure to asbestos or asbestos containing products. The Panel nevertheless held that the other criteria for § 1407 transfer were not satisfied. In relevant part, the Panel stated:

> Many factual questions unique to each action or to a group of actions already pending in a single district clearly predominate, and therefore transfer is unwarranted. . . . Furthermore, many of these actions already are well advanced. Some of the actions have been pending for up to four years, and trial dates or discovery cutoff dates have been set in several actions. Under these circumstances, transfer would not further the purposes of Section 1407.

Many of the parties presently opposing transfer in this docket rely on the facts and reasoning of the Panel's 1977 transfer decision. They insist that the situation that warranted denial then not only still prevails but has been magnified by the greatly increased number of actions and parties in federal asbestos personal injury/wrongful death litigation—more than 30,000 pending federal actions now, as opposed to the 103 actions subject to the Panel's 1977 decision. In our view, it is precisely this change that now leads us to conclude that centralization of all federal asbestos personal injury/wrongful death actions, in the words of 28 U.S.C. § 1407(a), "will be for the convenience of parties and witnesses and will promote the just and efficient conduct of such actions." In short, we are persuaded that this litigation has reached a magnitude, not contemplated in the record before us in 1977, that threatens the administration of justice and that requires a new, streamlined approach.

The Panel is not the first to reach such a conclusion. Just this past March 1991, the Judicial Conference Ad Hoc Committee on Asbestos Litigation, whose members were appointed by Chief Justice William H. Rehnquist, stated as follows:

> The committee has struggled with the problems confronting the courts of this nation arising from death and disease attributable to airborne asbestos industrial materials and products. The committee has concluded that the situation has reached critical dimensions and is getting worse. What has been a frustrating problem is becoming a disaster of major proportions to both the victims and the producers of asbestos products, which the courts are ill-equipped to meet effectively.

After extensive study, the Institute for Civil Justice of the Rand Corporation in 1985 observed, with respect to how the civil justice system handles asbestos claims, that—

The picture is not a pretty one. Decisions concerning thousands of deaths, millions of injuries, and billions of dollars are entangled in a litigation system whose strengths have increasingly been overshadowed by its weaknesses.

The ensuing five years have seen the picture worsen: increased filings, larger backlogs, higher costs, more bankruptcies and poorer prospects that judgments—if ever obtained—can be collected.

It is a tale of danger known in the 1930s, exposure inflicted upon millions of Americans in the 1940s and 1950s, injuries that began to take their toll in the 1960s, and a flood of lawsuits beginning in the 1970s. On the basis of past and current filing data, and because of a latency period that may last as long as 40 years for some asbestos related diseases, a continuing stream of claims can be expected. The final toll of asbestos related injuries is unknown. Predictions have been made of 200,000 asbestos disease deaths before the year 2000 and as many as 265,000 by the year 2015.

The most objectionable aspects of asbestos litigation can be briefly summarized: dockets in both federal and state courts continue to grow; long delays are routine; trials are too long; the same issues are litigated over and over; transaction costs exceed the victims' recovery by nearly two to one; exhaustion of assets threatens and distorts the process; and future claimants may lose altogether. REPORT OF THE JUDICIAL CONFERENCE AD HOC COMMITTEE ON ASBESTOS LITIGATION, 1–3. The Committee pointed out that presently in the federal system nearly two new asbestos actions are being filed for every action terminated, and that at the current rate, there will be more than 48,000 actions pending in the federal courts at the end of three years.

The Committee also discussed the ongoing change in the demographics of asbestos litigation in the federal courts:

In 1984, when the Federal Judicial Center held its first asbestos conference, asbestos litigation in the federal courts was largely concentrated in only four district courts. Since that time, however, asbestos cases have infiltrated virtually every federal district. Asbestos litigation must therefore be viewed as a national problem rather than merely a local or regional one, especially with the number of Americans affected.

Conclusions similar to those of the Judicial Conference Asbestos Committee have also been reached by judges actively involved in asbestos litigation. In perhaps the most recent comprehensive review of asbestos litigation, Judge Jack B. Weinstein (E.D.N.Y.) observed:

The large number of asbestos lawsuits pending throughout the country threatens to overwhelm the courts and deprive all litigants, in asbestos suits as well as other civil cases, of meaningful resolution of their claims. Several commentators have recounted the inefficiencies and inequities of case-by-case adjudication in the context of mass tort disasters.

The heyday of individual adjudication of asbestos mass tort lawsuits has long passed. *See* ASBESTOS COMMITTEE REPORT ("one point on which plaintiffs' counsel, defense counsel and the judiciary can agree is that the present way in which we have attempted to resolve asbestos cases has failed"). The reasons are obvious: the complexity of asbestos cases makes them expensive to litigate; costs are exacerbated when each individual has to prove his or her claim de novo; high transaction costs reduce the recovery available to successful plaintiffs; and the sheer number of asbestos cases pending nationwide threatens to deny justice and compensation to many deserving claimants if each claim is handled individually. The backlog is eroding a fundamental aspiration of our judicial system to provide equality of treatment for similarly situated persons (recent wave of asbestos litigation marked by high concentration of claims, dominance of characteristics of individual asbestos cases, behavior of parties, lawyers and the attributes of judges "created a situation in which dispositions are slow, costs are high, and outcomes are variable").

Overhanging this massive failure of the present system is the reality that there is not enough available from traditional defendants to pay for current and future claims. Even the most conservative estimates of future claims, if realistically estimated on the books of many present defendants, would lead to a declaration of insolvency—as in the case of some dozen manufacturers already in bankruptcy.

Given the dimensions of the perceived problem in federal asbestos litigation, it is not surprising that no ready solution has emerged. The Judicial Conference Asbestos Committee concluded that the only true solution lies in Congressional legislation. Nevertheless, it stressed that "at the same time, or failing congressional action, the federal judiciary must itself act now to achieve the best performance possible from system under current law." ASBESTOS COMMITTEE REPORT. The Committee also noted that the Panel's order to show cause was pending at the time of the issuance of the Committee's report. The Committee observed that "this committee, by its recommendations, does not intend to affect or restrict in any way the actions of the Panel under 28 U.S.C. § 1407 or reduce the Panel's jurisdiction or authority."

It is against this backdrop that the Panel's decision and role in this litigation must be understood. First of all, our decision to order transfer is not unmindful of the fact that the impact of asbestos litigation varies from district to district, and that in some courts asbestos personal injury actions are being resolved in a fashion indistinguishable from other civil actions. It is not surprising, therefore, that parties and courts involved in such actions might urge that inclusion of their actions in multidistrict proceedings is inappropriate. The Panel, however, must weigh the interests of all the plaintiffs and all the defendants, and must consider multiple litigation as a whole in the light of the purposes of the law. It is this perspective that leads us to conclude that centralization in a single district of all pending federal personal injury and wrongful death asbestos actions is necessary.

Much of the argument presented to the Panel in response to its order to show cause is devoted to parties' differing (and often inconsistent) visions of § 1407 proceedings: 1) some plaintiffs see centralized pretrial proceedings as a vehicle leading to a single national class action trial or other types of consolidated trials on product defect, state of the art and punitive damages, while many defendants staunchly oppose such a trial, favor a reverse bifurcation procedure where actual damages and individual causation are tried before liability, and hope to use § 1407 proceedings to effect the severance of claims for punitive damages through a transferee court order directing that, upon the return of any case to its transferor district, such claims not be tried until claims for compensatory damages have been resolved in all federal cases; 2) some parties hope to persuade the transferee court to establish case deferral programs for plaintiffs who are not critically ill, or who have been exposed to asbestos but do not presently show any signs of impairment (i.e., pleural registries), while many plaintiffs assert that such procedures are unfair or unconstitutional; 3) in response to the pressing concern about transaction costs in this litigation, some defendants consider § 1407 transfer necessary in order to provide a single federal forum in which limits on plaintiffs' contingent fees can be addressed, while some plaintiffs maintain that transfer is necessary to prevent the depletion of defendants' limited insurance coverage by defense costs incurred in multiple districts; 4) some plaintiffs and defendants urge that transfer is necessary in order to develop through discovery proceedings nationwide product data bases on all asbestos products and corporate histories of all asbestos defendants, while other plaintiffs and defendants contend that such efforts would be of no utility and are simply designed to shift liability; 5) some plaintiffs are suggesting that defendants' finances are so fragile as to require limited fund class action determinations pursuant to Fed.R.Civ.P. 23(b)(1)(B), while other plaintiffs resist any attempt to restrict their right to pursue punitive damages; 6) some parties anticipate that a single transferee court would speed up case disposition and purge meritless claims, while others expect a system of spacing out claims so as not to overwhelm currently solvent defendants' cash flow and drive them into bankruptcy; and 7) some parties contend that single transferee court is necessary for the purpose of exploring the opportunities for global settlements or alternative dispute resolution mechanisms, while other parties assert that such hopes are utopian at best as long as i) more than twice as many asbestos cases remain pending in state courts as in federal courts, and ii) currently stayed claims against bankrupt defendants cannot be addressed by the transferee court.

We cite these issues only as illustrations of 1) the types of pretrial matters that need to be addressed by a single transferee court in order to avoid duplication of effort (with concomitant unnecessary expenses) by the parties and witnesses, their counsel, and the judiciary, and in order to prevent inconsistent decisions; and 2) why, at least initially, all pending federal personal injury or wrongful death asbestos actions not yet in trial must be included in § 1407 proceedings. For example, if, as some courts, parties and commentators have suggested, there are insufficient funds to fairly compensate all deserving claimants, this should be determined before plaintiffs in lightly impacted districts go to trial and secure recoveries (often including punitive damages) at the possible expense of deserving plaintiffs litigating in districts where speedy trial dates have not been available. Similarly, if there are economies to be achieved with respect to remaining national discovery, pretrial rulings or efforts at settlement, these should be secured before claims against distinct types or groups of defendants are separated out of the litigation. Finally, because many of the arguments of parties seeking exclusion from transfer are intertwined with the merits of their claims or defenses and affect the overall management of this litigation, we are unwilling, on the basis of the record presently before us, to carve out exceptions to transfer. We prefer instead to give the transferee court the opportunity to conduct a substantive review of such contentions and how they affect the whole proceedings.

It may well be that on further refinement of the issues and close scrutiny by the transferee court, some claims or actions can be remanded in advance of the other actions in the transferee district. Should the transferee court deem remand of any claims or actions appropriate, the transferee court can communicate this to the Panel, and the Panel will accomplish remand with a minimum of delay. We add that for those parties urging that resolution of this litigation lies primarily in the setting of firm, credible trial dates, § 1407 transfer may serve as a mechanism enabling the transferee court to develop a nationwide roster of senior district and other judges available to follow actions remanded back to heavily impacted districts, for trials in advance of when such districts' overburdened judges may have otherwise been able to schedule them.

We remain sensitive to the concerns of some parties that § 1407 transfer will be burdensome or inconvenient. We note that since § 1407 transfer is primarily for pretrial, there is usually no need for the parties and witnesses to travel to the transferee district for depositions or otherwise. Furthermore, the judicious use of liaison counsel, lead counsel and steering committees will eliminate the need for most counsel ever to travel to the transferee district. And it is most logical to assume that prudent counsel will combine their forces and apportion their workload in order to streamline the efforts of the parties and witnesses, their counsel, and the judiciary, thereby effectuating an overall savings of cost and a reduction of inconvenience to all concerned. Hopefully, combining such practices with a uniform case management approach will, in fact, lead to sizeable reductions in transaction costs (and especially in attorneys' fees).

In a docket of this size and scope, no district emerges as the clear nexus where centralized pretrial proceedings should be conducted. The Panel has decided to centralize this litigation in the Eastern District of Pennsylvania before Judge Charles R. Weiner. We note that: 1) more asbestos personal injury or wrongful death actions are pending in that district than any other; 2) the court there has extensive experience in complex litigation in general and asbestos litigation in particular; and 3) the court has graciously expressed its willingness to assume the responsibility for this massive undertaking. Furthermore, in the person of Judge Weiner the Panel finds a judge thoroughly familiar with the issues in asbestos litigation, a track record of accomplishment and successful innovation, and, on the basis of the pleadings before the Panel in which an opinion was expressed, a selection to which the majority of responding plaintiffs and defendants either expressly agree or are not opposed.

Many parties have suggested that the dynamics of this litigation make it impractical, if not impossible, for one single judge to discharge the responsibilities of transferee judge, while other parties have emphasized that more than a single transferee judge would dilute the judicial control needed to effectively manage the litigation. Varying suggestions have been made that the Panel appoint additional transferee judges to handle specific issues (e.g., class or limited fund determinations, discovery, settlement, claims administration, etc.), to deal with separate types of claims or defendants (e.g., maritime asbestos actions, railroad worker actions, friction materials actions, tire workers actions, etc.), or to divide the litigation along regional or circuit lines (helping to insure uniformity of decisions within each circuit pertaining, inter alia, to state law questions involved in the actions). Each of these suggestions has merit, as long as one judge has the opportunity to maintain overall control.

Section 1407(b) contemplates that multidistrict litigation may be conducted by "a judge or judges." It further expressly provides that "upon request of the panel, a circuit judge or a district judge may be designated and assigned temporarily for service in the transferee district by the Chief Justice of the United States of the United States or the chief judge of the circuit, as may be required, in accordance with the provisions of chapter 13 of this title." And the Panel has long expressed its willingness to appoint additional transferee judges in litigants whose size and complexity make it difficult for the original transferee judge to handle § 1407 proceedings alone. We emphasize our intention to do everything without our power to provide such assistance in this docket. Before making any specific appointments, however, we deem it advisable to allow the transferee judge to make his own assessment of the needs of this docket and communicate his preferences to us.

The Panel is under no illusion that centralization will, of itself, markedly relieve the critical asbestos situation. It offers no panacea. Only through the combined and determined efforts of the transferee judge and his judicial colleagues, of the many attorneys involved in asbestos matters, and of the parties, can true progress be made toward solving the "asbestos mess." This order does offer a great opportunity to all participants who sincerely wish to resolve these asbestos matters fairly and with as little unnecessary expense as possible.

## C.  MODERN PRACTICE: MDL TRANSFERS AND BELLWETHER TRIALS

### IN RE OIL SPILL BY THE OIL RIG DEEPWATER HORIZON IN THE GULF OF MEXICO, ON APRIL 20, 2010

United States Judicial Panel on Multidistrict Litigation, 2010.
731 F.Supp.2d 1352.

Before the entire Panel: Before the Panel are four motions that collectively encompass 77 actions: 31 actions in the Eastern District of Louisiana, 23 actions in the Southern District of Alabama, ten actions in the Northern District of Florida, eight actions in the Southern District of Mississippi, two actions in the Western District of Louisiana, two actions in the Southern District of Texas, and one action in the Northern District of Alabama, as listed on Schedule A.

The background of this docket is well known. On April 20, 2010, an explosion and fire destroyed the Deepwater Horizon offshore drilling rig approximately 130 miles southeast of New Orleans and approximately 50 miles from the Mississippi River delta. The explosion killed eleven of the 126 workers on the rig, which eventually sank in approximately 5,000 feet of water. Through mid-July, crude oil gushed from the site in unprecedented amounts. Although the leaking well is now capped, the spill's effects are widespread, with oil reported to have come ashore in Louisiana, Mississippi, Alabama, Florida, and, most recently, Texas. Its full impact on the lives and livelihoods of tens of thousands of Americans, especially those living in or near the Gulf of Mexico, is as yet undetermined.

I.

Plaintiffs in the Eastern District of Louisiana *Cooper* and *Rodrigue* actions have separately moved, pursuant to 28 U.S.C. § 1407, to centralize these actions in the Eastern District of Louisiana, while plaintiff in the Eastern District of Louisiana *Nova Affiliated* action and common defendant BP Exploration & Production Inc. (BP) have separately moved for centralization in the Southern District of Texas.

Dozens of parties submitted responses to the four motions. Almost all responding parties support centralization. Responding defendants all favor centralization in the Southern District of Texas, whereas the positions of responding plaintiffs are more varied with respect to an appropriate transferee district. While many plaintiffs support centralization in the Eastern District of Louisiana, other plaintiffs argue in favor of selection of the Northern District of Alabama, the Southern District of Alabama, the Middle District of Florida, the Northern District of Florida, the Southern District of Florida, the Western District of Louisiana, the Southern District of Mississippi, the District of South Carolina, or the Southern District of Texas. In addition, a small number of other plaintiffs variously argue in favor of other approaches: that the Panel centralize the docket in the Eastern District of Louisiana, but assign it to Judge Shira Ann Scheindlin of the Southern District of New York, who would then sit in the Eastern District of Louisiana by designation; that the Panel divide the docket among three districts; or that the Panel appoint a judge from one of the Florida districts to "ride circuit" among the various involved localities.

Some responding plaintiffs, while supporting centralization generally, argue against including any of the relatively few personal injury/wrongful death actions in an MDL that might be comprised largely of putative class actions seeking recovery for property damage and other economic losses. Of the 77 constituent actions, two are wrongful death actions and one is a personal injury action. Plaintiffs in *Roshto* and *Williams* submitted briefs supporting inclusion of the personal injury/wrongful death actions in centralized proceedings, as did responding defendants, but plaintiff in *Jones* opposes such inclusion.

A few responding parties oppose centralization altogether. They essentially argue that the involved actions are all subject to dismissal for failure to comply with the Oil Pollution Act's (OPA) presentment requirement; and that, in any event, because the OPA is a strict liability statute, the only issue in dispute (at least as to the BP defendants) is the amount of damages to which each claimant is entitled, which, they argue, requires an inherently individualized inquiry and is thus inappropriate for MDL treatment. These parties argue that, at the very least, the Panel should carve out the OPA claims from centralized proceedings.

The briefing and oral argument have contributed greatly to the Panel's deliberations. This is a reminder that although the Panel tries to reach its decisions in a timely fashion, it does so only after affording the parties sufficient time to present their views, both through written submissions, and, in the case of motions seeking the creation of new MDLs, through oral argument. Even in the face of catastrophic circumstances such as these, little is to be gained from hasty decision-making.

## II.

The actions before the Panel indisputably share factual issues concerning the cause (or causes) of the Deepwater Horizon explosion/fire and the role, if any, that each defendant played in it. Centralization under Section 1407 will eliminate duplicative discovery, prevent inconsistent pretrial rulings, including rulings on class certification and other issues, and conserve the resources of the parties, their counsel, and the judiciary. Centralization may also facilitate closer coordination with Kenneth Feinberg's administration of the BP compensation fund. In all these respects, centralization will serve the convenience of the parties and witnesses and promote the more just and efficient conduct of these cases, taken as a whole.

We also conclude that it makes sense to include the personal injury/wrongful death actions in the MDL. These actions do overlap factually with the other actions in this docket, and, indeed, plaintiffs in two of the three constituent personal injury/wrongful death actions specifically argue in favor of such inclusion, as do responding defendants. While these actions will require some amount of individualized discovery, in other respects they overlap with those that pursue only economic damage claims. The transferee judge has broad discretion to employ any number of pretrial techniques—such as establishing separate discovery and/or motion tracks—to address any differences among the cases and efficiently manage the various aspects of this litigation.

Similarly, we do not find any strong reasons for separate treatment of claims brought under the OPA. In our judgment, carving out the OPA claims would only complicate matters, and denying centralization altogether is not a viable option. To the extent that non-compliance with the OPA's presentment requirement becomes an issue, failure to include OPA claims in centralized proceedings would raise the prospect of multiple inconsistent rulings on that issue.

Finally, the limitation proceeding brought by certain Transocean entities and currently pending in the Southern District of Texas is a potential tag-along action in this docket, and will be included on a forthcoming conditional transfer order (CTO). Although our preliminary assessment is that the action should be included in the centralized proceedings, we do not prejudge the matter. Once the CTO issues, the parties are free to object to the action's transfer.

## III.

The parties have advanced sound reasons for a large number of possible transferee districts and judges. Upon careful consideration, however, we have settled upon the Eastern District of Louisiana as the most appropriate district for this litigation. Without discounting the spill's effects on other states, if there is a geographic and psychological "center of gravity" in this docket, then the Eastern District of Louisiana is closest to it. Considering all of the applicable factors, we have asked Judge Carl J. Barbier to serve as transferee judge. He has had a distinguished career as an attorney and now as a jurist. Moreover, during his twelve years on the bench, Judge Barbier has gained considerable MDL experience, and has been already actively managing dozens of cases in this docket. We have every confidence that he is well prepared to handle a litigation of this magnitude.

Some parties have expressed concern that recusals among Eastern District of Louisiana judges unduly limit our choices, and that even Judge Barbier may be subject to recusal. Notwithstanding these concerns, the Panel is quite comfortable with its choice. Judge Barbier is an exceptional jurist, who would be a wise selection for this assignment even had those other judges in the district been available. Moreover, the Fifth Circuit recently denied the petition of certain defendants for a writ of mandamus directing Judge Barbier to recuse himself.

Other parties have made the related suggestion that certain suggested transferee districts (including the Eastern District of Louisiana and the Southern District of Texas) might not present a level playing field for all parties and that we should search elsewhere for a "neutral" judge. With all due respect, we disagree with the premise of this argument. When federal judges assume the bench, all take an oath to administer justice in a fair and impartial manner to all parties equally. That oath applies just as much to a multidistrict litigation involving hundreds (or thousands) of actions and scores of parties as it does to a single civil action between one plaintiff and one defendant. Our experience is that transferee judges impartially carry out their duties and make tough decisions time and time again, and that they uniformly do so without engaging in any location-specific favoritism.

In selecting Judge Barbier, we also decline the suggestion that, given the litigation's scope and complexity, we should assign the docket to multiple transferee judges. Our experience teaches that most, if not all, multidistrict proceedings do not require the oversight of more than one able and energetic jurist, provided that he or she has the time and resources to handle the assignment. Moreover, Judge Barbier has at his disposal all the many assets of the Eastern District of Louisiana, which include magistrate judges and a clerk's office accustomed to handling large MDLs. Judge Barbier may also choose to employ special masters and other case administration tools to facilitate certain aspects of the litigation.

It is therefore ordered that, pursuant to 28 U.S.C. § 1407, the actions listed on Schedule A and pending outside the Eastern District of Louisiana are transferred to the Eastern District of Louisiana and, with the consent of that court, assigned to the Honorable Carl J. Barbier for coordinated or consolidated pretrial proceedings with the actions pending in that district and listed on Schedule A.

## IN RE GENERAL MOTORS LLC IGNITION SWITCH LITIG.

United States District Court for the Southern District of New York, 2016.
2016 WL 1441804.

This multi-district litigation relates to highly publicized defects in certain General Motors branded vehicles and associated vehicle recalls. The MDL includes putative class actions seeking to recover for economic losses allegedly sustained by certain GM car owners and approximately 3,000 individual personal injury or wrongful death claims. As is common in litigation of this scale and complexity, early on in the process, the Court appointed plaintiffs' lawyers to leadership positions, including three lawyers as Co-Lead Counsel—Steve W. Berman, Elizabeth J. Cabraser, and Robert C. Hilliard—and ten other lawyers to an Executive Committee. The Court directed Berman and Cabraser to focus on economic class claims and Hilliard to focus on personal injury and wrongful death claims, but the three have, in most respects, acted as a team. As a team, they and the plaintiffs' lawyers answering to them have accomplished a massive amount in a relatively short amount of time: In little more than a year and a half, they have taken or defended over three hundred depositions; reviewed or produced millions of pages of documents; briefed dozens of discovery-related issues; and brought or opposed close to fifty *in limine*, summary judgment, and *Daubert* motions for two trials held in January and March of this year.

All appeared to be going smoothly for the MDL plaintiffs until January, when the first "bellwether" personal injury case went to trial. On January 22, 2016, after it came to light that the Plaintiff in that case, Robert Scheuer, may have committed perjury and fraud, the case was voluntarily dismissed. The next business day, a handful of plaintiffs represented by attorney Lance Cooper, one of the lawyers appointed to the Plaintiffs' Executive Committee, filed a Motion To Remove Lead Counsel, initially seeking to remove all three Lead Counsel, but later clarifying that they sought the removal only of Hilliard. A few days later, the Cooper Plaintiffs followed with a Motion for Reconsideration of the Order Approving the Establishment of the 2015 New GM Ignition Switch Qualified Settlement Fund, essentially seeking to undo an agreement between Hilliard and General Motors LLC to settle the claims of approximately 1,380 plaintiffs represented by Hilliard. In their motions, the Cooper Plaintiffs made a number of serious allegations against Hilliard, accusing him of, at best, mismanagement and, at worst, self-dealing.

On February 10, 2016, the Court issued a "bottom-line" Order denying the Cooper Plaintiffs' motions on the ground that they were "patently untimely," fell "short of meeting the rigorous standards applicable to motions for reconsideration," and ultimately amounted to little more than "'Monday morning quarterbacking'" that did "not even come close to providing a legal basis for the drastic step of removing Lead Counsel." In its Order, the Court promised to issue an opinion providing "a more detailed analysis" of the issues raised by the Cooper Plaintiffs' motions "in due course." This is that Opinion. It provides a more detailed explanation of why the Cooper Plaintiffs' attacks missed their mark and why their motions were denied. It also addresses a related motion that was not fully briefed when the Court issued its bottom-line Order—namely, a motion filed by Hilliard and co-counsel seeking entry of a protective order prohibiting Cooper and others from contacting their clients "in violation of Rule 4.2 of the New York Rules of Professional Conduct." For the reasons explained below, that motion is also denied.

BACKGROUND

### A.    Plaintiffs' Counsel Leadership Appointments and Duties

Soon after the establishment of this MDL, the Court issued Order No. 5 establishing a leadership structure for plaintiffs' counsel and inviting applications for those positions. On August 15, 2014, following a review of the applications and an opportunity for the applicants to be heard, the Court appointed Berman, Cabraser, and Hilliard as Co-Lead Counsel; appointed Robin L. Greenwald and Dawn M. Barrios as Plaintiff Liaison Counsel and Federal/State Liaison Counsel, respectively; and appointed ten attorneys—including Cooper—to the Plaintiffs' Executive Committee. That Order expressly noted that the "appointments are personal in nature. That is, although the Court anticipates that appointees will draw on the resources of their firms, their co-counsel, and their co-counsel's firms, each appointee is personally responsible for the duties and responsibilities that he or she assumes." Order No. 8 also directed counsel to confer and submit a proposal with respect to an order delineating the duties of the leadership positions.

Thereafter, the responsibilities of counsel were discussed at the September 4, 2014, status conference, and memorialized in Order Nos. 12 and 13. In particular, Order No. 13 detailed the respective duties of Co-Lead Counsel, the two Liaison Counsels, and the Executive Committee. That Order stated that "Lead Counsel will be responsible for prosecuting any potential common benefit claims, as well as coordinating the pretrial proceedings conducted by counsel for the individual Plaintiffs." Such responsibility included the duty to "coordinate the initiation and conduct of discovery on behalf of the Plaintiffs"; "delegate specific tasks to other counsel in a manner to ensure that pretrial preparation for the Plaintiffs is conducted effectively, efficiently and economically"; and "organize themselves and agree on a plan for conducting the MDL on behalf of all Plaintiffs." "In performing these duties as Lead Counsel," Order No. 13

continued, "Mr. Berman and Ms. Cabraser will focus on economic class claims and Mr. Hilliard will focus on individual Plaintiffs" (that is, personal injury and wrongful death claims). To the extent relevant here, the Order also enumerated various "duties and responsibilities" of the Executive Committee, including the need to assist Lead Counsel in various ways.

Order No. 13 further reminded counsel that "all attorneys have an obligation to keep themselves informed about the litigation so that they can best represent their respective clients." Order No. 12 memorialized the process, discussed at the September 2014 status conference, for any plaintiffs' counsel to raise issues with the Court if counsel felt that Lead Counsel was unable adequately to represent his or her views at any status conference. The Order made clear that Lead Counsel was expected to take the lead in speaking on behalf of all plaintiffs and that, barring permission, would be the only counsel to speak at conferences on behalf of plaintiffs. Nevertheless, the Order provided a means by which any other plaintiffs' counsel could be heard. Specifically, if counsel did "not feel that Lead Counsel could adequately represent their views," counsel was invited either to put issues on the agenda for a particular status conference via Lead Counsel and counsel for Defendants or to submit a letter motion to the Court requesting permission to be heard.

### B.   The Bellwether Trial Selection Process and Discovery

The parties' agenda for the October 2, 2014 status conference included a proposal for the selection of cases to be tried as "bellwethers." Thereafter, following submissions on proposed bellwether orders, the Court issued Order No. 25 on November 19, 2014. That Order set forth the bellwether trial plan for MDL cases involving personal injury and wrongful death claims. The Order laid out the eligibility criteria and selection process for choosing what would ultimately be six bellwether cases to be tried. The process involved an initial selection of eighteen cases as to which the parties would engage in case-specific fact discovery; the selection of five of those cases by each party to be potential "Early Trial Cases"; and the exercise of two strikes by each party on the other's list, resulting in six Early Trial Cases to proceed to expert discovery and, presumptively, trial. In accordance with that process, Lead Counsel and New GM each submitted their initial lists of cases on February 17, 2015; narrowed the pool on June 24, 2015; and exercised their respective strikes on July 1, 2015, leaving six bellwether cases selected by New GM.

Of the six cases selected as bellwethers, Hilliard represented the plaintiff or plaintiffs in five. The only exception was *Yingling*, in which the Plaintiff is represented by Victor Pribanic, a lawyer from Pittsburgh, Pennsylvania. In advance of the bellwether selection, Hilliard had approached Pribanic at least twice (once through an associate) about Hilliard's participating in any trial in *Yingling*, and there was some discussion about sharing fees, but Pribanic demurred. On July 27, 2015—

with Pribanic still representing the Plaintiff in *Yingling*—Lead Counsel and New GM proposed that the cases be tried in the following order: *Yingling, Barthelemy/Spain, Scheuer, Reid, Cockram,* then *Norville.* By memorandum endorsement entered the next day, the Court adopted that ordering.

That same day, Hilliard flew to Pittsburgh and met Pribanic for dinner. According to Pribanic, they "discussed the merits of *Yingling*," but Hilliard "never broached the notion" of trying the case together. In a telephone call a few days later, on August 1, 2015, however, Hilliard told Pribanic "he was thinking how they could handle the lawyers' fee if they tried the case together" and proposed that they divide the fees—Pribanic "understood equally"—if the case went to trial. On August 3, 2015, Pribanic sent a letter to Hilliard via e-mail stating, in relevant part as follows:

> I have been thinking of your kind offer to try this case with me. First, I want to thank you for, however it occurred, putting it first in line. It is obviously a tremendous opportunity for our client and a case that I absolutely relish the prospect of trying, albeit it with a bit of trepidation.

> I trust that I can count on you as lead counsel for the personal injury cases in this MDL to assist in any way possible and after meeting you I am confident that I can do so but I am at a complete loss as to how both of us could try this case—I cannot see me second seating you anymore than you would want to second seat me in a trial. I have agonized over some way to split it up and I have no solution short of going it alone, with your good help, and that of my colleagues here at the office and putting my head down and getting to work immediately.

Two days later, Lead Counsel filed a letter requesting that *Yingling* be moved to fifth in the bellwether trial schedule, and *Scheuer* be moved to the first trial spot. The Court, unaware that there might be any backstory behind what appeared to be a routine request, adopted this proposal on August 7, 2015.

Pribanic and Lead Counsel continued to discuss the order of the bellwether trials. Pribanic objected to placing *Yingling* so late in the bellwether trial order, and indicated that he would lodge his objections with the Court. Pribanic went so far as to prepare a motion requesting that the Court move *Yingling* back to the first bellwether slot, but he did not file the motion because Lead Counsel, "at his request, ultimately agreed to ask this Court to move *Yingling* to position number three." On November 11, 2015, Lead Counsel made that request, asking to swap *Yingling* and *Cockram* to make *Yingling* trial three. At the status conference on November 20, 2015 the Court granted Lead Counsel's request over New GM's objection, making the final order of bellwether cases *Scheuer, Barthelemy/Spain, Yingling, Reid, Cockram,* then *Norville.*

In preparation for the bellwether trials (and as part of pretrial discovery for the MDL cases generally), the parties conducted a tremendous amount of discovery in less than a year and a half. As of the close of briefing on these motions—which fell in between the first and second bellwether trials—the parties had reviewed and produced millions of pages of documents; taken or defended over three hundred depositions, including thirty-eight expert depositions; attended and presented arguments at thirteen status conferences; and participated in over two hundred meet and confers. (Since the motions were fully briefed, those numbers have only increased.) With respect to the *Scheuer* and *Barthelemy/Spain* cases alone—the only ignition switch cases to go to trial thus far—the parties filed and briefed over forty motions *in limine*, two substantial summary judgment motions, two *Daubert* motions, two motions (or the equivalent) with respect to the admissibility of "Other Similar Incident" evidence, and a motion for judgment as a matter of law, resulting in approximately twenty opinions of the Court.

## C.   *Settlement Negotiations*

As the parties engaged in pretrial discovery and motion practice, some settlement discussions were, unsurprisingly, proceeding on a parallel track. On September 17, 2015, New GM, Hilliard Munoz Gonzalez LLP, and Thomas J. Henry Injury Attorneys filed a joint letter notifying the Court that they had "entered into a Confidential Memorandum of Understanding in which approximately 1,380 post-Bankruptcy personal injury and wrongful death claimants represented by Hilliard and Henry may be eligible to participate in an aggregate settlement." The settlement was discussed on the record at the October 9, 2015 status conference. And on October 14, 2015, the involved parties filed a motion to appoint two Special Masters to oversee the settlement. On October 20, 2015, the Court held a conference call with the parties to discuss the Special Masters and the settlement fund generally, in preparation for which the parties submitted their Memorandum of Understanding (MOU) under seal for the Court's review. The parties filed a motion to establish a Qualified Settlement Fund (QSF) to facilitate the settlement on December 4, 2015. On December 11, 2015, the Court granted both motions, appointing the Special Masters and establishing the QSF.

## D.   *The First Bellwether Trial and the Instant Motions*

The *Scheuer* trial began as scheduled on January 11, 2016. Before and during the trial, the Court developed various procedures for addressing disputes and ruled on disputes with respect to demonstratives, deposition designations, and key pieces of evidence, among others. On January 18, 2016, New GM filed a motion (originally under seal) to introduce new evidence and witnesses, and to recall Lisa Scheuer, in light of allegations that her husband, Plaintiff Robert Scheuer, had altered a check and given misleading testimony regarding, among other things, the connection between his crash and his inability to move into his family's "dream house." On January 21, 2016, after the conclusion of Scheuer's case-in-chief, the Court granted the motion in part. The next day, Scheuer filed a notice of voluntary dismissal of his case with prejudice. On January 25, 2016—the next business day—the Cooper Plaintiffs filed their Motion To Remove Co-Lead Counsel. Two days later, they followed with their Motion for Reconsideration of the Order Approving the Establishment of the 2015 New GM Ignition Switch Qualified Settlement Fund. Following briefing on the Cooper motions, Lead Counsel filed a motion for a protective order on February 9, 2016, seeking to prohibit Cooper—or any other attorney in the MDL—from communicating with Hilliard's and Henry's clients in violation of Rule 4.2(a) of the New York Rules of Professional Conduct.

### E.   Subsequent Developments

The second bellwether trial, *Barthelemy and Spain v. General Motors LLC*, took place between March 14 and 30, 2016. The Court granted summary judgment for New GM on some of its claims; granted judgment as a matter of law in favor of New GM on Spain's fraudulent misrepresentation claim; and submitted Plaintiffs' claims under the Louisiana Products Liability Act to the jury. On March 30, 2016, the jury found that Plaintiffs had proved by a preponderance of the evidence that the car at issue was unreasonably dangerous because it deviated from manufacturing standards, and because General Motors Corporation failed to provide an adequate warning of a dangerous characteristic of the car; the jury did not find, however, that any unreasonably dangerous characteristic caused the injuries of either Plaintiff and thus returned its verdict for New GM. Accordingly, on April 5, 2016, the Court entered judgment in New GM's favor. Two days later, the parties advised the Court that they had reached a settlement in *Yingling* and the case (which had been scheduled for trial beginning on May 2, 2016) was removed from the trial calendar. The following day, with no explanation or warning, the *Reid* case—the fourth bellwether trial—was voluntarily dismissed with prejudice.

### DISCUSSION

As noted, this Opinion addresses three motions: the Cooper Plaintiffs' Removal Motion and QSF Motion and the Hilliard and Henry motion for a protective order. The Court will begin with its explanation for the denial of the Cooper motions, first with a discussion of why the motions are untimely and, second, with a discussion of each motion on the merits. The Court will then turn to the motion for a protective order. Finally, the Court will address Cooper's own continuing, albeit nominal, membership on the Plaintiff's Executive Committee.

## B.  The Cooper Plaintiffs' Contentions

In any event, even putting aside the rigorous deadlines and standards for reconsideration or the common-sense concerns of timeliness, the Cooper Plaintiffs do not have sufficient basis for the relief they seek. Throughout their motions, the Cooper Plaintiffs assert that Hilliard owes all plaintiffs in the MDL fiduciary duties. Notably, however, they cite no legal authority for that proposition. They also fail to cite—and the Court has not found—any legal authority addressing the standard to be used in evaluating whether lead counsel in multi-district litigation consolidated proceedings (or their equivalent) should be removed. In the absence of such authority, it is tempting to look to the Rule 23 class action context, where courts have generally held that lead counsel should be removed only in "exceptional circumstances." *In re "Agent Orange" Prod. Liab. Litig. MDL No. 381* (denying a request to remove lead counsel where the movant had "failed even to suggest, much less establish, any exceptional circumstances" that warranted removal, and instead "suggested nothing more than a difference of opinion"); *see, e.g., Pigford v. Veneman* (rejecting a motion to remove class counsel despite counsel's "poor performance and missed deadlines"); *Lazy Oil Co. v. Wotco Corp.* (declining to remove class counsel despite class members' dissatisfaction with a settlement because the plaintiffs had "failed to identify 'any concrete act of impropriety' ") *cf. In re Am. Exp. Anti-Steering Rules Antitrust Litig.* (denying final class settlement approval where class counsel had improperly disseminated the defendant's confidential information and disclosed privileged work product); *Schoenbaum v. E.I. DuPont De Nemours* (removing class counsel who had been indicted for paying kickbacks to plaintiffs in other cases).

But the duties owed by lead counsel in the class action context are undoubtedly stronger than the duties owed by Hilliard here. In the class context, lead counsel serve as counsel for all members of the class. Significantly, absentee class members do not have their own separate counsel; instead, they rely on counsel for the class to represent their interests (noting fiduciary duties of class representatives and class counsel towards other members of the class); ("Both class representatives and class counsel have responsibilities to absent members of the class."). Here, by contrast, Hilliard does not serve as counsel for all personal injury and wrongful death plaintiffs in the MDL; instead, each of those plaintiffs is represented by counsel of his or her choice, whether Hilliard or someone else (such as Cooper). That is not to say that Hilliard does not have significant authority vis-à-vis all personal injury and wrongful death plaintiffs. He plainly does, as he speaks on their behalf (to both New GM and the Court) and has the authority to make any number of decisions that are binding, either literally or effectively, on all personal injury and wrongful death plaintiffs. But, in contrast to absentee members of a class action, the personal injury and wrongful death plaintiffs in this MDL (at least those who are not independently represented by Hilliard) have their own counsel. Those counsel not only can, but are required to, monitor the progress of the litigation. And those counsel have various means at their disposal to ensure that the rights and interests of their clients are protected in the event that they believe Hilliard has taken steps that are not in their clients' interest. It follows that, while the duties Hilliard owes to personal injury and wrongful death plaintiffs represented by other counsel are significant, they are not as strong as the duties that lead counsel owes to absentee members of a class action. From that premise, it follows further that the standard for removal of counsel is at least as demanding here as in the Rule 23 context, and probably even more demanding.

Ultimately, the Court need not resolve whether or to what extent the standard for removal here is more demanding than the standard for removal in the Rule 23 context because the Cooper Plaintiffs fail to meet even the Rule 23 standard. Specifically, their (sometimes wild) accusations do not withstand scrutiny, and certainly do not rise to the level that would justify the drastic relief that they seek. Notably, the force of their arguments is significantly undermined by the fact that they no longer seek to remove all three Lead Counsel. As noted, in their reply, they make clear that they levy their charges only at Hilliard, in his capacity as Lead Counsel with primary responsibility for personal injury and wrongful death cases, and do not seek to remove Berman and Cabraser. In doing so, they implicitly concede that there is no basis to accuse Berman and Cabraser of violating their duties to plaintiffs writ large. Yet Berman, Cabraser, and Hilliard were appointed as *Co*-Lead Counsel and have acted together throughout the litigation. Although Hilliard has taken primary responsibility for personal injury and wrongful death cases, the three Co-Lead Counsel have closely coordinated their efforts throughout the litigation, submitting joint letters and briefs, working together to complete discovery, appearing at all conferences, and participating in the trial of the first bellwether. Had Hilliard breached his duties to the MDL plaintiffs, Berman and Cabraser would undoubtedly have known about it and arguably would have had their own duty to bring the breach to the Court's attention. The fact that they did not—and the fact that the Cooper Plaintiffs do not even argue that they should have—is, in and of itself, reason to doubt, if not reject, the Cooper Plaintiffs' charges.

With that, the Court turns to the Cooper Plaintiffs' allegations. They attack Lead Counsel's conduct on three fronts: (1) pretrial discovery and management of the MDL; (2) bellwether trial selection; and (3) the QSF settlement.

### 1.   Discovery and MDL Management

First, the Cooper Plaintiffs allege that Lead Counsel failed to include Executive Committee members in discussions about important issues in the MDL, limited state court counsel's ability to participate at MDL depositions, "siloed" Executive Committee members with respect to depositions and document discovery, and "consistently attempted to thwart efforts by the state court lawyers to coordinate the prosecution of the coordinated actions." Again, the Cooper Plaintiffs provide no evidence other than Cooper's own say-so that such behavior occurred—a say-so that is even harder to credit given that Cooper, by his own admission, has been largely uninvolved with the work of the MDL since at least April 2015. Tellingly, not one of the hundreds of other lawyers representing plaintiffs in the MDL or in parallel state proceedings—and none of the other nine members of the Executive Committee—joined Cooper in making his motions or submitted affidavits in support of his factual allegations. That silence is deafening.

Additionally, Cooper's allegations are contradicted by Federal/State Liaison Counsel Dawn Barrios, who attests that significant efforts have been made to coordinate discovery and information with counsel in Coordinated Actions, including a system for sharing documents and deposition schedules; that state counsel were invited to participate at depositions; and that Lead Counsel have done nothing to obstruct the coordination of state proceedings, but rather had been helpful and supportive. Cooper's allegations are further belied by several other facts: by the fact that no lawyers, including counsel in state-court actions, raised any concerns with the Court despite the mechanisms available to do so; by the fact that Boies Schiller, a firm not affiliated with Lead Counsel (but one of whose partners, David Boies, is a member of the Executive Committee), took the lead in trying the *Barthelemy/Spain* bellwether; and by the sheer amount of work counsel has accomplished, much of which was performed by members of the Executive Committee or their firms: over a hundred depositions; review and production of millions of pages of documents; and the legal research for, and briefing of, forty-plus motions *in limine*, two summary judgment motions, and multiple *Daubert* motions. Indeed, as of the date Cooper's motions were fully briefed, Executive Committee members and Liaison Counsel had spent approximately fifty thousand hours on document review, depositions, and trial preparation; since then, that time has no doubt grown substantially.

It is inevitable in litigation of this size and complexity that there will tensions among plaintiffs' counsel—whose interests are mostly aligned, but sometimes competing. Given that, and with the benefit of 20/20 hindsight, it is no doubt easy to criticize some decisions that Lead Counsel have made in this complex and multi-faceted litigation and to present select examples of the push and pull among high-powered plaintiffs' counsel that could appear unseemly. In the final analysis, however, the Court is not persuaded that the tensions and conflicts here were anything more than the "normal give and take of any MDL." Notably, Cooper himself seems to acknowledge as much, stating that his allegations about the general management of the MDL "were not the reason for filing the Motion to Remove but were provided as background to give this Court context as to what led up to the selection of the bellwether trials" and to the events of *Scheuer*. Even as background alone, however, his unsupported claims are no more persuasive in suggesting there was anything improper in the bellwether selection process, discussed below.

### 2.   The Bellwether Trial Selections

The heart of the Cooper Plaintiffs' Removal Motion is that Lead Counsel violated their presumed fiduciary duties to the MDL plaintiffs by not choosing the "best" cases to be bellwethers and, then, by switching the order of the cases so that *Yingling* was not first. Many of the parameters of the bellwether selection process, however, were put in place by the Court. For example, the Cooper Plaintiffs criticize Lead Counsel for selecting the bellwethers before the Feinberg Claims Facility had run its course, but the deadline for choosing the cases was set by Orders of this Court. Additionally, the Cooper Plaintiffs allege that one of the failings of the bellwether selections was the failure to include any state cases. But they offer no authority—and the Court is not aware of any—for the proposition that a case pending in state court could be tried as a bellwether case in a federal MDL. In any event, other than trying to ensure that the first ignition switch case tried would be one in the MDL (to allow for this Court to take the lead on deciding big picture issues that would be applicable to numerous cases), this Court has not discouraged state courts from setting trial dates in ignition switch cases—precisely on the theory that such trials serve as the functional equivalent of bellwethers. Notably, as of February 10, 2016, there were at least *twenty* more trials relating to the ignition switch defect scheduled to begin before December 4, 2017, in state courts—one of which involves Cooper and *none* of which involve Lead Counsel. In light of the fact that New GM faces twenty-five some odd trials (and counting), against a wide array of plaintiffs' lawyers and with different facts, to focus on the outcome of a single trial in the MDL—as the Cooper Plaintiffs largely do—is to myopically miss the forest for a single tree.

More specifically, the Cooper Plaintiffs' accusations of self-dealing on Hilliard's part in selecting and ordering the bellwether trials miss their mark. The Cooper Plaintiffs criticize Hilliard for the fact that five of the six bellwethers involved his own clients. In doing so, however, they overlook the fact that the percentage of Hilliard's clients that he proposed as early trial candidates (namely, three of the five plaintiffs' picks, or 60%) was *lower* than the percentage of plaintiffs that Hilliard represents in the MDL as a whole (approximately 75%). The Cooper Plaintiffs also criticize the selection of *Scheuer* as a bellwether trial and the decision to try it first, asserting that "it is axiomatic that plaintiffs' counsel always want to try their best case first in MDL litigation." But if by "best," the Cooper Plaintiffs mean "most likely to result in a large plaintiff's verdict," that proposition is by no means "axiomatic." After all, because the primary purpose of bellwether trials is to provide data points for settlement discussions with respect to the universe of cases, the goal is to select the "best" representatives of the universe of cases, not outliers likely to result in victory for one side or the other. To that end, the Order setting up the bellwether selection process dictated that the bellwether selections be "representative" claims. *See* MANUAL FOR COMPLEX LITIGATION (FOURTH) § 22.315 (noting that if bellwether trials "are to produce reliable information about other mass tort cases, the specific plaintiffs and their claims should be representative of the range of cases"); Rothstein, Managing Multidistrict Litigation in Products Liability Cases: A Pocket Guide for Transferee Judges (Fed. Judicial Ctr.) ("If bellwether trials are to produce reliable information about the other cases in the MDL, the specific plaintiffs and their claims should be representative of the range of cases."); Fallon, *Bellwether Trials in Multidistrict Litigation* (arguing that the random selection method should be disfavored for bellwether trials because "if cases are selected at random, there is no guarantee that the cases selected to fill the trial-selection pool will adequately represent the major variables").

From that perspective, putting aside the problems that ultimately resulted in its dismissal (problems, as the Court has made clear elsewhere, for which Lead Counsel bears some blame), *Scheuer* was arguably just as good as, if not a better, bellwether candidate than *Yingling*, the only case the Cooper Plaintiffs cite as an comparator. Among other things, *Scheuer* (a personal injury case) appears to have been more representative of cases in the MDL than *Yingling* (a wrongful death case)—perhaps a result of the number and types of cases that were resolved through the Feinberg Claims Facility. Moreover, even if *Scheuer* was a "weaker" case than some others, Lead Counsel could have reasonably calculated that a win in such a case would provide an even stronger inducement to New GM to settle the rest of the cases. And finally, in the Court's view, it is not inappropriate for Lead Counsel to consider as a factor in selecting the bellwethers—and in moving *Scheuer* to the first trial position—Hilliard's involvement at trial, given his greater familiarity with discovery (including depositions of experts and New GM witnesses), with the Court, and with opposing counsel. In fact, the Court would have been somewhat surprised had Hilliard *not* been trial counsel in the first bellwether given his deep knowledge of the case and greater familiarity with the Court and its procedures. Ultimately, despite the unforeseen end to the *Scheuer* trial, the case provided value in the progress that was made with respect to the bellwether trials generally: the Court's rulings on motions *in limine*, which will apply in future trials, the preparation of expert reports and *Daubert* motions, and the development of procedures for handling evidentiary disputes.

To be sure, *Scheuer* was not originally chosen as the first bellwether—*Yingling* was—and the Cooper Plaintiffs' allegations about why and how Hilliard proposed to switch the order are somewhat troubling. That is, Hilliard could have—and probably should have—handled the situation more deftly, if only to avoid the appearance of impropriety (and exposure to allegations of the sort that Pribanic made and Cooper is now making). But the evidence does not ultimately support the Cooper Plaintiffs' aggressive accusations of self-dealing. Hilliard and Pribanic plainly had discussions with respect to trying *Yingling* together, and it is apparent that fees formed a part of that discussion. But from the contemporaneous evidence, it appears that Hilliard's principal "request" was to try the case together, not for a share of the fees. In particular, Pribanic declined proposals to share fees with Hilliard as early as August 2014 and certainly by April 2015. In spite of that refusal, however, Lead Counsel still selected *Yingling* as one of the bellwether cases and, indeed, initially positioned it first.

By contrast, the communications between Hilliard and Pribanic in the summer of 2015—which may well have precipitated Lead Counsel's request to switch the order of *Scheuer* and *Yingling*—focused on whether the two lawyers would try the cases together, not on fees. As discussed, however, it would not be improper to switch the bellwether order to ensure that Lead Counsel was involved in trying the first case, and the evidence does not support that anything more than that, let alone anything invidious, took place. And notably, the alternative, "maximizing fee" theory advanced by the Cooper Plaintiffs and their expert, Professor Charles Silver—that Hilliard moved *Yingling* out of the first trial slot because he would not share in the trial fees from that case—makes little sense given that *Scheuer* would have been tried regardless. That is, for Hilliard's purposes, there would be little or no real financial difference between scheduling *Scheuer* first or third (or even fifth), as he was effectively guaranteed the fees from that trial whenever it happened. (In fact, Pribanic himself noted as much in his August 3, 2015 letter to Hilliard declining Hilliard's request to try the case together.)

In short, the Cooper Plaintiffs provide an insufficient basis for their attack on the selection of the bellwether cases and fail to justify disrupting the bellwether trial schedule that has been in place for many months. Further, to disrupt that schedule now would prejudice the parties— including the Cooper Plaintiffs—given the extensive discovery and planning that have already gone into the remaining two cases.

### 3.  The QSF

That leaves the QSF Motion, in which the Cooper Plaintiffs contend that the Hilliard-New GM settlement harmed the other MDL plaintiffs and ask the Court to "conduct an inquiry into the settlements and Mr. Hilliard's potential conflicts related to these settlements, including the decision by Mr. Hilliard and GM to enter into the high-low agreements in the bellwether cases." As an initial matter, the Cooper Plaintiffs point to no authority suggesting, let alone holding, that a lead counsel outside of the Rule 23 class action context cannot freely settle his or her own cases. It would be one thing if the QSF were tied to a limited fund. That was the issue in *Ortiz v. Fibreboard Corp.* In a limited fund situation, the potential conflict of interest between lead counsel's own clients and other plaintiffs could be a significant issue and the court may well have a role to play. *See, e.g., Ortiz.* That may even be the case outside the Rule 23 context, to ensure that a race to the courthouse door (or, more precisely, to the settlement table), does not leave some litigants out in the cold. But there is no suggestion here that New GM's ability to satisfy any and all potential judgments is limited. To the contrary, evidence at the *Scheuer* trial indicated that New GM's net worth is $35.4 billion, which is presumably more than enough to satisfy any judgments entered against it in the MDL.

Notably, the Court directly asked Lead Counsel and counsel for New GM at the October 9, 2015 status conference—a conference held after the fact of the settlement had been public for almost a month—whether anyone else should be given an opportunity to be heard and whether there was any potential prejudice to non-settling parties. Counsel assured the Court that there was no issue of limited resources, and New GM reiterated its willingness to discuss settlement with all plaintiffs. Presumably, if there had been any legitimate concern that the settlement could prejudice non-settling parties, Berman and Cabraser would have had every incentive to raise the issue given that the damages sought by the economic loss plaintiffs for whom they have primary responsibility exceed the claims of any individual personal injury or wrongful death plaintiff by a large margin; yet, they raised no concern, let alone objection, to the settlement. Given all that, there is no basis to conclude that the settlement caused any prejudice to non-settling plaintiffs. And given *that*, there is no law or logic for the proposition that Lead Counsel cannot settle their own cases—or alternatively, as Professor Silver suggests, to require them to step down as Lead Counsel if they desire to settle some of their own cases. Indeed, if anything, such a rule would be a serious disincentive for any lawyer to seek a lead counsel position in the first instance and would do a disservice to the interests of plaintiffs as a whole.

The Cooper Plaintiffs' final salvo is that Hilliard "cut a secret deal with GM" by negotiating high/low agreements in Hilliard's five bellwether cases in exchange for settlement of the rest of his cases. The fact of the settlement, however, was anything but secret; it was announced in a public letter and press release, and Hilliard notified the Executive Committee about it directly. And while most terms of the settlement have not been made public, that is because *the Court* granted leave to keep the terms under seal (without opposition, it should be noted, from the Cooper Plaintiffs or anyone else); that is, when Hilliard and New GM negotiated their settlement, they did not necessarily know whether its terms would remain confidential. More specifically, the fact that Hilliard and New GM entered into high/low agreements with respect to the bellwether cases, and carved them out of the settlement, is hardly a "stunning revelation." Lead

Counsel (including Berman and Cabraser) and New GM informed the Court of the agreements *in camera* on November 20, 2015. And given the amount of work the parties had done to prepare the bellwether cases for trial, and the fact that those trials were ultimately intended to benefit the MDL process as a whole, it is hardly surprising that counsel would have left them out of the settlement.

More fundamentally, the Cooper Plaintiffs cite (and the Court has found) no authority for the proposition that high/low agreements—agreements that are not unusual in American litigation—are improper. Nor do the Cooper Plaintiffs cite any authority for the proposition that, even if there were evidence that the high/low agreements were part of some larger *quid pro quo* (and there is no such evidence), the Court would have had a basis to disapprove the parties' private settlement or deny the QSF motion. Notably, while the Cooper Plaintiffs stress the benefits of the high/low agreements to New GM, they ignore the countervailing benefits to the plaintiffs who entered them—namely, that the agreements presumably guarantee them some recovery, even if they were to lose at trial (as Barthelemy and Spain did). They also ignore why such agreements are particularly sensible in the MDL bellwether context: By minimizing the risks to both sides of going to trial, they increase the probability that the chosen cases will actually go to trial and yield useful data for purposes of settling other cases in the MDL. That is, a jury verdict in such a case would still accurately reflect the case's "value," even if that value is not the amount the plaintiff takes home or New GM has to pay. In short, the Cooper Plaintiffs present no basis to undo the voluntary settlement between Hilliard and New GM as they fail to articulate any way in which they, or any other plaintiffs in the MDL, were harmed by it. To the contrary, the settlement is likely only to benefit other plaintiffs, as New GM has repeatedly expressed its willingness to negotiate settlements with other counsel, and the settlement provides a template and a benchmark for settlement of other cases with New GM.

### D.   Cooper's Membership on the Executive Committee

One final issue demands the Court's attention: Cooper's membership on the Plaintiffs' Executive Committee. If anyone has abdicated or violated his fiduciary duties to the MDL plaintiffs in this case, it is Cooper himself. To be clear, that is not because he filed his motions (although his wild accusations have arguably done as much, if not more, harm to plaintiffs' cause than the collapse of the first bellwether, which was an embarrassing but temporary setback), but because—by his own admissions—he has flagrantly failed to satisfy his "duties and responsibilities" as an Executive Committee member. Cooper applied for a position on the Executive Committee, was appointed, and assumed the duties set forth in Order No. 13, including assisting Lead Counsel with pretrial work and working to conduct the MDL on behalf of all plaintiffs. By his own admission, he has not fulfilled any of those duties for at least a year—and, until his motions, failed to share that with the Court, let alone seek the Court's permission to step down from the Committee. (It should be noted, neither did Lead Counsel or other members of the Committee). Whether or not Cooper announced his "formal resignation," it was not for him to decide that his neglect was for the "best" because "nine law firms were still on the EC and working on the GM litigation" and their work was sufficient. Order No. 8 made clear that leadership appointments were personal, not on behalf of law firms, and they were made pursuant to the Orders of this Court.

In the Court's view, it is plainly contrary to the interest of plaintiffs for someone who has abdicated his own responsibilities to remain in a leadership role or occupy a leadership position, even if only in name. Accordingly, and to resolve any doubt about his involvement going forward, the Court hereby formally removes Cooper from the Executive Committee to the extent that he nominally remains associated with it. To be clear, Cooper's removal is *not* a sanction for filing his motions, even if those motions were ultimately without merit; it is based on his own admitted failure to fulfil the basic duties and responsibilities of his position. (That said, it is important to ensure that counsel in leadership roles can work together; Cooper's motions speak for themselves in making clear that he cannot work with Hilliard.) Lead Counsel shall confer with the remaining members of the Executive Committee and advise the Court no later than April 18, 2016, whether they believe that Cooper's vacancy should be filled. If so, Lead Counsel should propose a process for such appointment and should be prepared to address the issue at the next status conference, scheduled for April 20, 2016.

## CONCLUSION

Multi-district litigation of this sort is a complex affair. With so much at stake—in terms of money, ego, and otherwise—it is hardly surprising that conflicts would erupt among counsel, even counsel who are ostensibly on the same "side" and share a common adversary. Nevertheless, the Court finds it regrettable that Cooper levied his broadsides against Lead Counsel in the way he did, rather than taking steps in a more measured and productive (not to mention timely) manner to address or raise any problems that he perceived. In other words, assuming there is any merit to his allegations, he did himself—and, by extension, the plaintiffs in the MDL— a disservice by waiting to raise them until after the (admittedly embarrassing) collapse of the Plaintiff's case in the *Scheuer* trial and then raising them in the way he did. Through its bottom-line Order and this more detailed Opinion, the Court hopes that any clouds of uncertainty hovering over the status of Lead Counsel, the bellwether trial schedule, and the pending settlement have been lifted, thereby promoting the orderly management of the MDL and additional settlements. The Court also hopes that plaintiffs' counsel will stop litigating their grievances with one another and return to focusing on their common adversary, New GM, and on obtaining relief for their respective clients. That is, the Court hopes that counsel—and their clients—can return to focusing on what is truly at stake in this litigation: determining whether and to what extent the plaintiffs in these proceedings are entitled to relief for injuries caused by the acknowledged ignition switch defect in millions of General Motors cars.

# D.  MDL NON-CLASS AGGREGATE SETTLEMENTS

## IN RE WORLD TRADE CENTER DISASTER SITE LITIG.

United States District Court for the Southern District of New York, 2009.
598 F.Supp.2d 498.

In the months following September 11, 2001, thousands of workers participated in New York City's effort to clean up the vast destruction caused by terrorists. The airplane crashes and explosions at the World Trade Center left acres of twisted metal and crumbled concrete. Noxious dust blanketed the rubble and hung in the air for weeks, producing an acrid smell throughout downtown Manhattan. Those who helped in the search and rescue operations, and in the effort to clear the mountains of debris, had to breathe this air as they worked. According to the allegations, protective masks, when worn, filtered this air in varying degrees.

Overlapping government agencies managed the workers, as did private contractors engaged by the City's Department of Design and Construction. Nine thousand and ninety of these workers have filed suits in this court claiming various respiratory injuries and cancers resulting from their exposures to worksite contaminants. They claim inadequate safety procedures and supervision.

### I.   PROCEDURAL HISTORY

Most of the cases were initiated in the New York Supreme Court and then removed to this court. They were assigned to me as related to docket 21 MC 97, which contained September 11th wrongful death actions that I had grouped into one coordinated proceeding. I denied class status because of the variety of illnesses alleged by the plaintiffs, the varying severity of their illnesses, the transient nature of the worksites, the varying levels of supervision governing plaintiffs' work, the variety of defendants, and the complexity of determining and evaluating pre-existing medical conditions.

I organized the cases into their own master docket, 21 MC 100, and considered the issue of jurisdiction. The aggregate demands of the lawsuits—those already filed and the hundreds more that were expected—promised far to exceed the maximum liability set by the Air Transportation Safety and System Stabilization Act (ATSSSA). ATSSSA capped liability at $350 million or the City's insurance protection, whichever was larger. The latter, at the time, seemed not to exist.

I ruled, in an extensive opinion, that claims arising from the search and rescue operations, extending for two weeks after September 11th, arose from the terrorist-related aircraft crashes and were subject to the district court's exclusive jurisdiction. However, claims arising from work and exposures thereafter were much more akin to the activities and risks of construction worksites and to issues addressed by the New York Labor Law, on which the New York Supreme Court had developed a century of expertise. Accordingly, I remanded these later claims to that court. An appeal followed and, after lengthy consideration, the Court of Appeals ruled that all the cases were to be considered subject to the district court's exclusive jurisdiction.

Following remand of the cases to me, I turned to their organization. I appointed Liaison Counsel for plaintiffs and for defendants. At plaintiffs' request, I ordered master pleadings to be filed that alleged the issues common to all plaintiffs. And, I ordered the parties to file short form complaints. These complaints were intended to set out where, when, and for which contractors plaintiffs worked, as well as the causes of their injuries and the defendants' alleged faults.

At the same time, defendants sought to advance their defense that the City and the contractors enjoyed immunity arising from federal and New York State laws. Both sides considered that the prospective substantial litigation expense made it important to clarify the reach and efficacy of this defense at an early time. I ordered discovery on limited issues relevant to the defense. The same discovery also would be relevant to defining the relationships between plaintiffs and the scores of defendant contractors, between defendant contractors and the City, and among the City, the State, and federal agencies that were active at the World Trade Center worksite.

The parties pursued discovery to satisfy both objectives with mixed success. The pleadings were conclusory in their allegations and impossible to understand in relation to essential facts and issues. Remonstrations at conferences and rulings on motions did not seem to advance matters. As happens with discovery confined to limited issues, it proved difficult to define boundaries. Finally, however, defendants made their motions, and I denied the motions in a lengthy opinion, ruling that the issue of immunity hinged on controverted facts. I denied defendants' motion that my order was eligible for immediate review or, alternatively, for certification for interlocutory review, but the Court of Appeals ruled that the appeal could nevertheless be pursued because rulings on immunity sufficiently satisfied an exception for final decisions on severable issues. The Court of Appeals also granted a stay of all proceedings on March 9, 2007, causing a complete stand-still until March 26, 2008, when the stay was dissolved. The Court of Appeals then affirmed my decision.

## II.   THE LITIGATION'S COMPLEXITIES

During the lengthy stay, I considered how these cases should progress were they to be remanded. There were few precedents, perhaps none. These are not typical mass tort claims in which a single product or event injures the victims in a relatively similar way. Here, the victims were injured over a protracted period of time—days, weeks, and months, varying with the hours and dates particular plaintiffs worked in the widespread area (sixteen acres) constituting the World Trade Center site. The exposure to the environment had different medical effects on different individuals. The environment itself varied from one worksite area to another depending on which toxic materials prevailed at which place and time. In aggregate, plaintiffs allege hundreds of different diseases from working among the debris, each of different severity and effects.

The complexity in sorting the plaintiffs' claims is matched by the complex interplay of defendants. Many governmental agencies and scores of contractors were responsible for the World Trade Center work, in varying degrees and with varying overlap. The contractor defendants were engaged in different ways, by different prime contractors, and were supervised and guided by different layers of government agencies. Nor is responsibility clear, for some defendants may be covered by various immunities under federal or state laws and, if found liable, may enjoy a congressional liability cap. Because of such a cap, I would have to carefully administer all settlements and judgments since each plaintiff's recovery would diminish the next plaintiff's potential recovery.

The insurance coverage issues provide additional complexities. Related proceedings clarified the City's insurance coverage and were beginning to disclose the coverage of private contractors. My early concern, that ATSSSA's $350 million liability cap would mean partial and inadequate satisfaction for vast numbers of claimants, had become academic. New York City, in fact, is covered by several layers of private coverage, amounting to approximately $75 million, in excess of the costs of defense, and one billion dollars of coverage through a captive insurance company funded by the Federal Emergency Management Agency. And, beyond that, the private contractors have their own insurance to an extent not yet known.

It would be difficult, perhaps impossible, to obtain and sort all this insurance information in conventional discovery proceedings relating to more than 9,000 cases. While all might have a claim, of possible and varying merit, against the City, it would be necessary to match specific claims of plaintiffs against specific contractors, and to evaluate such claims in relation to different and varying layers of primary, excess, and reinsurance agreements and exclusions.

Finally, all that I and the parties do must be done with an eye towards public accountability. The September 11th litigation stems from an unprecedented national tragedy that impacted New York City, the State, and the Nation in long-lasting ways. The resolutions of these cases must depend on careful and individual evaluations of personal injury and merits in a manner that allows the public to view and understand the results.

### III. Court-Ordered Discovery and Special Masters

The inability of counsel to style useful pleadings, or to proceed with discovery relevant to the immunity defenses without excessive and wasteful disputes, made it necessary to develop an alternative manner of proceeding. Normal discovery to advance 9,090 cases against more than 200 defendants is not possible. But neither is it tolerable to neglect these cases, nor to postpone recoveries for years, nor to allow attorneys motivated in part by their own economics to dictate which cases advance and how. There must be criteria developed to select cases meriting early treatment and capable of serving as models for the rest. Case Management Order No. 8, as amended, sets out a protocol that reflects such criteria. It provides a procedure for selecting appropriate cases for intensive pretrial discovery, motions, and trials on specific dates. I now set out the efforts leading to this order.

I believed that the parties and I needed core discovery to provide the fundamental facts of the cases, the varying responsibilities of government agencies and contractors, and the complex layers of insurance coverage. I required Special Masters, skilled and impartial, to help me devise such discovery, and to develop computer systems to collect the information and make it accessible.

Following the return of the case to my jurisdiction, after the Court of Appeals dissolved its stay, and after vetting the issue with the lawyers, I appointed Professors James A. Henderson, Jr. of Cornell Law School and Aaron D. Twerski of Brooklyn Law School as Special Masters. Professors Henderson and Twerski are distinguished scholars, neutral in relation to the issues of the litigation. Given the assistance of computer experts engaged through competitive bidding, they have the experience and capability to structure and oversee the required exchange of information between the parties and the collection of that information in an efficient and accessible database.

Working with the lawyers, the Special Masters have developed the structure for creating a large database for the litigation. The parties will be required to answer under oath approximately 360 narrowly-tailored questions seeking case-crucial data for each plaintiff: pedigree information, medical history, tobacco use, alleged injuries, medical tests, diagnoses, symptoms, treatments, and any worker's compensation filings and recoveries. Each plaintiff and each defendant will have to detail the hours plaintiffs worked and for which employers, in addition to the safety warnings given, the safety training provided, and the safety precautions taken. Each defendant will disclose his insurance and indemnity protection. The database should promote success because it requires greater detail and specificity than prior efforts at core discovery, operates in a more sophisticated medium, and limits the responses to certain key questions to a list of permissible answers (called a "pick list").

### A.   Traditional Discovery and Trials as Enforcement Mechanisms

The database should provide an enormous amount of relevant discovery information in a functional format. But the information, to be provided by each party, could be self-serving, and needs to be tested for integrity and reliability. While conventional discovery and trials are a court's traditional tools in this regard, there were too many cases to proceed in a traditional manner. Select cases would have to be chosen for discovery and trial.

Deciding which cases adequately represent the field would be difficult. How could information from hundreds of doctors' reports and thousands of examinations be studied for prior conditions and severity of current illnesses? How could one sort the conditions of scores of workplaces and intersecting levels of supervision? Solving such problems—indeed, even enumerating all possible issues—threatened to overwhelm progress. It was critical to establish a set of priorities, and allow those priorities to determine how to proceed.

The first priority was to tend to the most severely injured plaintiffs. Their cases deserved to be tried first, for if they were to prevail, they had the greatest need for a monetary recovery. The second priority was to create a methodology for sampling in relation to the general run of cases, severe, mild, and everything between, in order that rulings on liability, damages, and responsibility might be extended from the particular case in which rulings are made to the rest of the cases. Every case had to be considered as important, for each plaintiff and each defendant deserved rulings on particular merits.

### B.   Determining the Most Severely Injured

Determining who are the most severely injured is not a straightforward task. The 9,090 plaintiffs, in the aggregate, claim approximately 387 diseases ranging from the most life-threatening to the merely irritating. Some plaintiffs have very mild cases of serious diseases while others have very severe cases of less serious diseases. Even permitting trials of only the most severe cases of each disease could mean hundreds of trials, still too many to administer in a reasonable period of time.

To proceed, the Special Masters, in cooperation with Liaison Counsel, looked to a diagnostic system established by the American Medical Association and the American Thoracic Society. The system ranks the severity of an individual's illness among the population suffering from that illness by grading that person's condition from 0 (least severe) through 4 (most severe). The rank corresponds to recorded outcomes of standard medical tests taken by the plaintiff, typically measuring the degree of dysfunction associated with the disease. In consultation with Liaison Counsel, the Special Masters selected six major disease categories that subsumed the generality of illnesses. Although the rankings are specific to each disease category, and severity cannot easily be evaluated across the different categories, the medical criteria do allow a neutral observer to identify a set of the most severely ill in each of the six disease categories. Final selections from this set can be made after considering additional limited criteria considered relevant, for example, plaintiff's length of exposure to hazardous worksite conditions or plaintiff's pre-existing medical conditions.

### IV.  THE RESULTING ORDER

The court proposed and approved Case Management Order No. 8 with modifications suggested by the parties. The amended Order, issued today and attached herein, implements these criteria.

1.  The 9,090 cases are to be divided into five groups of 2,000 cases, according to their filing sequence. Every forty days, one such group of plaintiffs is to populate a subset of the data fields, specifically fields eliciting each plaintiff's disease rankings, the duration of exposure at the World Trade Center, and any pre-existing disorders.

2.  The Special Masters, within ten days following, will identify 200 cases categorized as severe. From these 200, plaintiffs and defendants will each choose two cases.

3.  The Special Masters also will select twenty-five additional cases for diseases not necessarily included in the severity chart.

4.  From this pool of 225 cases, I (with the assistance of the Special Masters) will select two cases, additional to the four selected by plaintiffs and defendants.

5.  The six cases thus identified, from the field of 2,000, will proceed through full pre-trial discovery, to be completed within a set period of time (ranging from 270 days for some of the cases in the first field of 2,000 to 190 days for cases in the fifth field), followed by motions, followed by trial (if dismissal motions are not successful).

6.  Thirty cases will be set for trial, six from each field of 2,000. Despite the sequential process in which these cases will be selected, all trials will begin on a fixed date—May 17, 2010. If one case is resolved, later-filed cases will be tried instead. If more than one case for trial remains, other judges may be

asked to preside over them, or they may be reached in sequence.

7.  Thus, a resolution is in sight for the most severe cases and for representative cases. And one can expect that many of these cases, and many others, will settle either in anticipation of firm trial dates or aided by values gleaned from trials or settlements.

The procedures outlined above were intended swiftly to identify a representative few cases for discovery of all issues and early trials. But the entire field of 2,000 could not be neglected. It was necessary to develop information relevant to all the cases, for otherwise the parties could not share key knowledge about the field of cases, or intelligently discuss the degree to which the cases identified for discovery and trial were representative. Two additional procedures provided for the full field:

8.  The parties are required to populate the entire database for each of the 2,000 cases in the group, according to a fixed schedule. Forty days after the Special Masters choose the 225 cases, the parties are to populate the entire database for these cases. On the same day they select the 225 cases, the Special Masters will identify 400 additional cases (chosen at random) from that group of 2,000. The parties must fully populate the database for these 400 cases 120 days later. Every forty days, this process is repeated for the next group of 2,000 cases. By November 27, 2009, the parties will have fully populated the entire database for 3,125 cases, taken from all five groups (5 multiplied by 625). Finally, the parties will populate the database for each of the 1,375 cases in every group that were not selected as part of the 225-case subgroup or the 400-case subgroup. By January 1, 2011, the entire database for each filed case will be populated.

9.  From each group of 400 randomly selected cases, each party will choose two cases, and I (with the Special Masters' assistance) will select an additional two. These cases will proceed with pre-trial discovery along with the selected "severe" cases. However, trial dates will not be set for these cases, at least not until we know the outcome of the schedule for the "severe" cases.

I recognize that the methodology of Case Management Order No. 8 is extraordinarily complex. It needed to be so because of the number and variety of cases, and to create a consensual agreement for going forward. I recognize also that complexity creates an artificial rigidity that needs adjustment. As further orders may be necessary, they will be made. But the trial and motion schedules will remain firm.

## V.  RATIONALE OF CASE MANAGEMENT ORDER NO. 8

The plan involves three stratagems to bring the thousands of cases before me to resolution. First, since the claims of those most gravely injured commend themselves to highest priority, the plan provides a procedure to identify these cases, a methodology to select a representative sample for full discovery and early trial, and a firm and intensive schedule to begin trials. Full discovery on all issues will assure the integrity of each side's disclosures in the database and a thorough testing of all claims and defenses. A basis for settlement, or valuation by trial, should promote prompt resolution of all such severe cases.

Second, the full population of the database of all remaining cases, first by sample and then in full, enables values to be negotiated for all cases.

Third, the combination of court-established interrogatories for the database and traditional, broad discovery in selected cases will allow the parties vigorously to test their opponents' claims, assuring the integrity and reliability of the parties' disclosures and establishing a procedure that can promote broad resolutions of cases in a fair, efficient, and just manner.

## VI.  CONCLUSION

No general plan for over 9,000 cases can be so wise as to be immutable, or so clever as to foresee all possibilities. However, Case Management Order No. 8 was forged with the experience of earlier failures and frustrations, and with full and intensive cooperation of Special Masters and plaintiffs' and defendants' counsel. It establishes a flexible, fair, and efficient plan to move these cases through discovery and to trial in reasonable time. It remains for the parties to act consistently with its provisions to bring about just such results.

## IN RE WORLD TRADE CENTER LOWER MANHATTAN DISASTER SITE LITIG.

United States District Court for the Southern District of New York, 2015.
2015 WL 3606032.

The terrorist attacks of September 11, 2001 spawned one of the largest and most complex mass tort litigations in history. The final stage in this saga involves the claims of over 1,000 individuals who worked in the buildings surrounding the World Trade Center site and allegedly developed various respiratory and gastrointestinal illnesses as a result of their work. Many of these cases are now settling. *See, e.g., In re World Trade Ctr. Lower Manhattan Disaster Site Litig* (approving settlements between 78 plaintiffs and 98 defendants). This Order deals with another 82 plaintiffs currently represented by the law firms of Gregory J. Cannata & Associates, LLP and Robert A. Grochow, P.C. These 82 plaintiffs have reached a settlement in principle with nearly all of the defendants against whom they brought claims, and seek approval of the settlements and regulation of attorneys' fees. For the following reasons, the Cannata Plaintiffs' motion for approval is granted.

## I.   BACKGROUND

I have previously provided the procedural history of this stage of the September 11th litigation. To reach their settlements, the Cannata Plaintiffs used an approach that was functionally equivalent to that used to reach the settlement with the City of New York and its captive insurer in the previous stage of the September 11th litigation. I approved that settlement in June 2010 as fair and reasonable. More importantly, so did the parties. Over 99% of plaintiffs opted in to the settlement, discharged the defendants, and discontinued their cases. Similarly, all remaining defendants who contributed additional amounts in the end approved the settlement. The total compensation paid to the plaintiffs was over $600 million.

In order to settle these 82 cases, the parties, with the help of Special Masters Aaron Twerski and James Henderson, devised a comprehensive plan for valuing each plaintiff's separate case, taking into consideration the severity of injuries incurred (measured by objective manifestations), the conditions of individual buildings and the scope and scale of work performed, and the number of plaintiffs and defendants associated with each building. The parties then negotiated and agreed, again with substantial assistance from the Special Masters, to aggregate amounts per building to be apportioned to the various plaintiffs who worked in the building and to be paid by the various defendants associated with each building.

The specific allocations to individual plaintiffs are to be calculated according to a "Settlement Plan," developed by the Cannata Plaintiffs. The Settlement Plan awards points to individual plaintiffs based upon the diagnosis of various alleged conditions, the severity of the alleged conditions, and any documented treatment received. Each condition for which points are awarded has been recognized by the National Institute for Occupational Safety and Health as related to exposure to the World Trade Center dust. Adjustments to the points are made based upon an individual plaintiffs' age, smoking history, death, lost earnings, participation in the Captive Settlement, time spent working in individual buildings, and other plaintiff-specific information. The Garretson Resolution Group, a neutral third-party consultant experienced in mass tort settlements, and the neutral administrator appointed by the Court to administer the Captive Settlement, has approved this methodology as "reasonable, objective, fair, and efficient" reflecting the "best practices of modem allocation methodology within aggregate settlements."

The Cannata Plaintiffs retained Garretson to calculate the points attributable to each individual's medical and economic records. In addition, Ball Baker Leake LLP, an independent public accounting firm, has been retained to calculate the specific amounts allocated to each plaintiff based upon the point system and the time individual plaintiffs worked in each building. Ball Baker will also calculate the net amount to be paid to each of the Cannata Plaintiffs, taking into account each plaintiff's share of the common expenses, case specific expenses, and a 25% attorneys' fee.

## II. DISCUSSION

### A. Settlement Methodology and Amount

As I have previously held, Courts confronted with mass tort cases have an obligation to ensure the fairness of settlements entered into by the parties, in the aggregate and as applied to individual plaintiffs. *See In re World Trade Ctr. Lower Manhattan Disaster Site Litig.; see also In re Zyprexa Liability Litig.* Accordingly, I ruled by Order dated July 25, 2014 that all settlements in the 21 MC 102 docket would be subject to review by this Court for fairness and reasonableness, similar to the methodology I used to review fairness and adequacy in the 21 MC 100 litigation.

There is a "strong public policy" in favor of the settlement of complex litigation. Courts reviewing settlement agreements consider two aspects for fairness: the process utilized in reaching the settlement and the substantive terms of the settlement ("A court determines a Settlement's fairness by looking at both the settlement's terms and the negotiating process leading to settlement."). Given the current litigation's similarity to complex class actions, the factors considered by courts in deciding the fairness of class settlements provide a useful guide.

Courts consider several factors in determining the procedural fairness of a settlement. The settlement should be the result of arm's length, hard-fought negotiations rather than the collusion of otherwise adversarial parties. Counsel conducting the negotiations should be experienced in similar cases. Furthermore, settlement should come at a time when sufficient discovery has been conducted, enabling counsel and the parties accurately to assess the strengths and weaknesses of their cases.

Once the proponent establishes that the settlement was reached as a result of a fair process, there is a presumption that the terms of the settlement are also fair and reasonable ("We have recognized a presumption of fairness, reasonableness, and adequacy as to the settlement where a class settlement [is] reached in arm's-length negotiations between experienced, capable counsel after meaningful discovery.") Nonetheless, courts consider several aspects of the substantive terms of a settlement for fairness. These considerations include the complexity, expense, and duration of the litigation; the strengths and weaknesses of the plaintiffs' cases; the attendant risks of bringing the case to trial; and the possible defenses of the defendants. Settlement amounts should not be compared to a "possible recovery in the best of all possible worlds." Rather, "there is a range of reasonableness with respect to a settlement—a range which recognizes the uncertainties of law and fact in any particular case and the concomitant risks and costs necessarily inherent in taking any litigation to completion."

After careful review of both the methodology used in reaching the settlements and the aggregate settlement amount, I conclude that approval of the settlement is appropriate. Gregory J. Cannata & Associates, LLP and Robert A. Grochow, P.C. are competent law firms with considerable experience in mass tort litigations, including the 9/11 litigation since 2005. Their negotiations with the defendants were adversarial, there is no evidence of collusion and resolution came at a time when discovery was sufficiently advanced to permit the parties to fairly evaluate the value of the lawsuits they filed (finding settlement procedurally fair where parties "conducted extensive investigations, obtained and reviewed millions of pages of documents, and briefed and litigated a number of significant legal issues" because parties had the ability to "gauge the strengths and weaknesses of their claims and the adequacy of the settlement").

Because the settlements are the result of a fair process, the consideration to be paid is presumably also fair, adequate, and reasonable. But presumptions are not needed to evaluate the fairness and adequacy of these settlements because the amounts, on their own, are adequate and reasonable.

The aggregate settlement amount is $53,801,796.96. The payments to the plaintiffs range from $25,000 to $1,453,089.72, according to the considerations discussed above. The average settlement amount is $656,119. The precise payment to each plaintiff is set out in a schedule submitted by the Cannata and Grochow law firms and filed under seal.

These cases present difficult complexities regarding the conditions of the workplaces, the safety protections extended, and the causal nexus between the ambient atmosphere and the diseases complained of by the workers. Trial is likely to be risky, long, and expensive, made longer and more complicated by the presence of numerous defendants. Further, the settlement amounts here compare favorably with the Captive Settlement recorded in the 21 MC 100 cases. Accordingly, I find that the settlement terms are well within the "range of reasonableness" reflective of the "uncertainties of law and fact" and the "concomitant risks and costs" of litigating the cases through trial. I therefore approve the settlements and grant Plaintiffs' motion in that regard.

### B.   Attorneys' Fees

Plaintiffs' counsel also seeks approval of a 25% fee after a deduction of common and case-specific expenses. Counsel has reduced their request for fees, from the 33 1/3% provided by their retainer agreements with their clients to 25%, the percentage fee I previously approved in the Captive Settlement. Furthermore, counsel has shown themselves to be competent and zealous advocates for their clients throughout the litigation and, particularly, during the Court-ordered settlement negotiations. Accordingly, I find a fee of 25% to be reasonable and hereby approve it.

### III. CONCLUSION

Plaintiffs' motion to approve the settlements is granted.

# E.  THE AGGREGATE SETTLEMENT RULE: ETHICAL ISSUES

## IN THE MATTER OF NEW YORK DIET DRUG LITIG.

Supreme Court, New York County, New York, 2007.
15 Misc.3d 1114(A).

Parker and Waichman LLP (P & W), on its own behalf and on behalf of its clients, moves for leave to renew or reargue its motion to intervene. In addition to P & W, proposed intervenors referred to as the "Abramova Plaintiffs," also seek leave to intervene. In the event intervention is granted, P & W and the Abramova Plaintiffs seek disclosure of certain documents in support of the amended order which approved the settlement of this action and will then seek to vacate that settlement order.

In this action, known as the *New York Diet Drug Litigation,* plaintiffs asserted claims of personal injury and loss of consortium allegedly due to the ingestion of "fen-phen" diet drugs. Some of those plaintiffs and others are here challenging a settlement approved by our predecessor court which held that the terms of the settlement were fair and reasonable and conformed with all ethical requirements. In that settlement, defendant, American Home Products (AHP), offered a large sum of money to settle virtually all claims.

The ethical issues raised in this case arise out of one of the thorniest areas in tort law—the process to be applied in the settlement of mass tort litigation. Because of the large number of claimants whose cases are settled at one time (in this case over 5,000), mass tort settlements often take the form of collective settlement structures. The alternative to a collective settlement would require the piecemeal analysis of the merits of each claim and individual settlements thereafter, as contemplated when the classic case dominated tort law (one injured plaintiff and one or more allegedly responsible defendants). This would consume the lifetime of many of the claimants themselves when there are thousands of claims to be compromised. As a consequence, counsel and the courts have devised means of settlement expedition, such as the placing of claimants in objective categories of severity of injury, age, gender, economic status, and each claimant's relationship to the acts of the defendant, and then entering into a mass settlement. Because of the large number of clients, great care must be exercised to insure that each client understands the settlement offer and is treated fairly. Ethical rules guide the actions of counsel in these circumstances.

This mass settlement was further complicated by the need to pay a portion of the attorneys' fees earned by settling counsel to other attorneys who referred additional clients. Therefore, claimants who were the original clients of the settling attorneys, Napoli Kaiser & Bern ("Napoli Firm"), would generate greater net legal fees for the firm than would clients who were referred to them by other attorneys.

The record on this motion, which includes a number of previously sealed documents and an affidavit of a former member of the Napoli Firm, has unfortunately raised serious questions regarding the settlement process herein, including claims that:

> (1)  claimants who were Napoli Firm clients were offered disproportionately larger settlements because the firm unfairly inflated settlement offers for its clients so that the attorneys' fees earned by the firm would be greater;

> (2)  unknown to the claimants, their cases were not settled for an amount negotiated for each claimant with AHP, rather their claims were settled based upon the Napoli Firm's own evaluation of the value of each claim in light of a lump sum offer;

> (3)  the Special Master appointed by the settling court did not make individual evaluations of the settlement offers in each case as was represented by the Napoli Firm to its clients and to the settling court; and

> (4)  the ethics opinion submitted in support of the settlement was flawed and based upon less than a full understanding by the expert of the circumstances surrounding the settlement and the applicable law.

Notwithstanding the Napoli Firm's protestations to the contrary, no court, trial or appellate, has ruled on these issues in a contested hearing.

This Court's inquiry into what was disclosed to our predecessor court regarding those objections and allegations of wrongdoing prior to the execution of the order of settlement reveals that that court considered the objections and allegations to be serious, but denied P & W's motion to challenge approval of the settlement, directing that such challenge should be made in either of the companion cases. It should be noted that once these allegations of wrongdoing were disclosed, Justice Freedman unsealed the confidential files in the interests of the public and of the plaintiffs because the only way these plaintiffs could prove the alleged misconduct was by examining the settlement documents. She stated:

> More generally, the interests of justice require that the plaintiffs in *P & W* and *Abramova* have an opportunity to prove their cases.

Finally, the serious charges against Napoli, Kaiser & Bern, if true, would be of concern to both Napoli, Kaiser's clients and the general public.

When the settling court was informed of the claims of ethical and professional misconduct that were asserted by a former associate of the Napoli firm (Mr. Murakami), she referred those claims for later action. This Court now stands in her shoes. She never had the opportunity to adjudicate these claims of misconduct. Clearly, these allegations must be dealt with on the merits as they are much too serious to be pushed aside or further delayed.

*The Nature of the Settlement*

The motion papers direct a great deal of attention to the issue of whether or not this settlement was on an aggregate or collective basis. If the settlement was aggregate, that would automatically trigger the need to disclose conflicts of interest pursuant to Disciplinary Rule, 5–106.

The Rule provides:

A lawyer who represents two or more clients shall not make or participate in the making of an aggregate settlement of the claims of or against the clients, unless each client has consented after full disclosure of the implications of the aggregate settlement and the advantages and risks involved, including the existence and nature of all the claims involved and the participation of each.

Professor Bruce Green was retained by the Napoli Firm to opine on whether or not this was an aggregate settlement and on the ethical standards applicable to this case. He admitted at his deposition that when he was first retained, Paul Napoli referred to the settlement in this case as an "aggregate settlement." The Napoli Firm has nevertheless maintained that this was not an aggregate or collective settlement, and that, therefore, the firm was relieved of the obligation to make full disclosure of conflicts of interest to its clients.

Based upon the hypothetical set of facts presented to Professor Green by the Napoli Firm (in a conversation, not in a written letter of engagement), Professor Green concluded that the proposed settlement agreement was not an aggregate settlement. The Napoli Firm relies on his opinion to contend that the firm had no duty to inform its clients of the true nature of the offer and settlement. This Court cannot agree.

It should be noted that the Rules governing professional conduct do not define what an aggregate settlement is, a fact admitted by Professor Green when he testified that he was unaware of any definition.

But, as Professor Erichson stated:

Nonetheless, in terms of what makes a settlement meaningfully collective, there is no bright line between all-or-nothing settlements and walk-away or tiered walk-away settlements. All of them involve collective conditions and thus present the lawyer-client and client-client conflicts of interest. A settlement with a walk-away provision set at ninety-nine percent, for example, functions almost identically to an all-or-nothing settlement in that the lawyer has a strong self-interest in ensuring that virtually every client accepts the deal, and clients who favor the settlement are pitted against those who do not. The higher the proportion permitted to decline the settlement, the larger the safety valve, but the meaningful line is between settlements with collective conditions and those without.

This Court has read the sealed settlement agreement. It is clearly a lump sum collective or aggregate settlement. The agreement itself is complex (as were the steps leading up to it) but in essence it provides that AHP agreed to pay a lump sum to the Napoli Firm, which sum was described as "the sum of the individual settlement amounts listed in Exhibit 3." One of the keys to understanding why this was an aggregate or collective settlement is that Exhibit 3 which contained the "individual settlement amounts" referred to in the settlement agreement, did not exist at the time the agreement was entered into. The amounts set forth in Exhibit 3 were not amounts negotiated for each client with AHP. The "individual settlement amounts" were not known at the time, they were to be subsequently determined in the process being challenged herein.

The Napoli Firm was to give AHP a rolling series of settlement amounts prior to payment. Section 5(a) of the settlement agreement states:

> The determination of the individual settlement amounts for each of the Settling Claimants will be set forth in Exhibit 3, which (i) will be prepared, signed and notarized by the Settling Attorneys (the Napoli Firm) and (ii) disclosed to AHP in installments before the dates when the Settling Attorneys seek the payments called for in paragraph 13 (the lump sum settlement in installments).

Allegedly, the process being challenged was that the Napoli Firm, without disclosure to its clients, divided up the lump settlement between its clients so that the total of the settling claims equaled the lump sum settlement amount being offered. Therefore, the settlement agreement required the Napoli Firm to "back into" the lump sum settlement amount by having its clients agree to accept individual settlements (determined and offered by the firm) that totaled no more than the lump sum offered. This settlement agreement matched each client against the other clients of the firm because they were each in competition with the others for a share of the lump sum settlement. This triggered conflicts, lawyer-client and client-client.

If the movants are correct, that the Napoli Firm did not disclose to each client that the client was in competition with the firm's other clients, the firm's clients were at a great disadvantage when they sought to decide if they should accept what they mistakenly believed to be a direct settlement offer from the defendant, AHP.

*Conflicts*

Attorney conflicts of interest with very serious consequences can arise out of the joint representation of multiple clients. This problem was highlighted in *Amchem Prods v. Windsor* in which the United States Supreme Court set a "zero tolerance" standard for conflicts in aggregate settlements. The Court held that a group of claims that could not be tried as a class action could not, as an alternative, be settled as a group. The court further held that mass tort cases should be governed by the aggregate settlement rule (which requires complete transparency) because the collective nature of these settlements create lawyer-client and client-client conflicts of interest.

> The most collective settlements are those in which a defendant agrees to pay a lump sum to settle an entire group of claims, leaving the allocation of that sum to the plaintiffs and their lawyer. At the opposite end, the least collective agreements are those in which each plaintiff's settlement amount is negotiated individually.

The nature of the settlement in this case exemplifies the "most collective" or "most aggregate" settlement definition because AHP agreed to pay a lump sum to settle with a group of claimants, with the sum each plaintiff was to receive being determined by plaintiffs rather than by an individual offer to each plaintiff by AHP.

*The Duty to Disclose*

The Napoli Firm seeks to define an aggregate settlement as one that is not just collective, but also one that requires all plaintiffs to agree. The firm argues that because a few clients out of the 5,000 did not agree to settle, disclosure of conflicts was not required. Notwithstanding the arguments of counsel, whether or not the present case fits a particular definition of "aggregate settlement" is not the point. The issue is "was there a duty to fully disclose conflicts of interest and was that duty discharged?" This Court holds that the Napoli Firm's duty to fully disclose conflicts of interest is determined not only by the aggregate settlement rule, but also by the general rule that client consent must be informed consent. The firm had a duty to disclose to its clients what the conflicting interests were. In this mass settlement, the conflict was that all claimants were vying for a share of what was a lump sum offer. They were each in competition with each other.

In his examination before trial, Professor Green confirmed this Court's view that the duty to fully disclose to the client was not to be determined by slavish adherence to the aggregate settlement rule, but rather the duty to insure informed consent when he stated:

> whether or not it was an aggregate settlement or even if it were not, there would be a duty to communicate with the client information that the client could make an informed decision whether to accept the settlement and so in my view, at the time the aggregate settlement rule was really just a specialized application of rules that anyway would be applicable duty to communicate with the client.

The Ethical Considerations also provide some guidance. EC § 5–14 provides:

> Maintaining the independence of professional judgment required of a lawyer precludes acceptance or continuation of employment that will adversely affect the lawyer's judgment on behalf of or dilute the lawyer's loyalty to a client. This problem arises whenever a lawyer is asked to represent two or more clients who may have differing interests, whether such interests be conflicting, inconsistent, diverse, or otherwise discordant.

EC § 5–16 provides:

> In those instances in which a lawyer is justified in representing two or more clients having differing interests, it is nevertheless essential that each client be given the opportunity to evaluate the need for representation free of any potential conflict and to obtain other counsel if the client so desires. Thus before a lawyer may represent multiple clients, the lawyer should explain fully to each client the implications of the common representation and otherwise provide to each client information reasonably sufficient, giving due regard to the sophistication of the client, to permit the client to appreciate the significance of the potential conflict, and should accept or continue employment only if each client consents, preferably in writing. If there are present other circumstances that might cause any of the multiple clients to question the undivided loyalty of the lawyer, the lawyer should also advise all of the clients of those circumstances.

And EC § 5–19 provides.

> Nevertheless, the lawyer should explain any circumstances that might cause a client to question the lawyer's undivided loyalty. Regardless of the belief of a lawyer that he or she may properly represent multiple clients, the lawyer must defer to a client who holds the contrary belief and withdraw from representation of that client.

Finally, Disciplinary Rule DR–5–105 (Conflict of Interest; Simultaneous Representation) provides:

A.   A lawyer shall decline proffered employment if the exercise of independent professional judgment in behalf of a client will be or is likely to be adversely affected by the acceptance of the proffered employment, or if it would be likely to involve the lawyer in representing differing interests, except to the extent permitted under DR 5–105.

B.   A lawyer shall not continue multiple employment if the exercise of independent professional judgment in behalf of a client will be or is likely to be adversely affected by the lawyer's representation of another client, or if it would be likely to involve the lawyer in representing differing interests, except to the extent permitted under DR 5–105.

C.   In the situations covered by DR 5–105 (A) and (B), a lawyer may represent multiple clients if a disinterested lawyer would believe that the lawyer can competently represent the interest of each and if each consents to the representation after full disclosure of the implications of the simultaneous representation and the advantages and risks involved.

Therefore, if it is likely that a conflict exists, as here where the recovery of one client is at the expense of the recovery of another, full disclosure must be made. The aggregate settlement rule can be understood as a particular application of the rule on concurrent conflicts of interest. Both prevent lawyers from trading off client interests against each other without the clients' consent.

In addition, the Napoli Firm made a representation in the settlement agreement itself, that they would comply with the disciplinary rules which require disclosure to clients, specifying New York's aggregate settlement rule as one of the applicable rules. The agreement provides at ¶ 5(c):

To the extent applicable, the Settling Attorneys represent that they have complied, and will comply, with Rule 1.8 of the ABA Model Rules of Professional Conduct, DR 5–106 of the Code of Professional Responsibility, and the counterpart of any other applicable state rule, to the extent such provisions are applicable to this settlement.

In light of the fact that the settlement was an aggregate settlement or at least contained conflicts, full disclosure to the claimants was required. This Court finds that the Napoli Firm had a duty to inform its clients of the full nature of the settlement, particularly: (1) if the specific offers were not offers by AHP, then who was offering them these settlement amounts; (2) if the offers were the Napoli Firm's evaluation of the relative merits of each client's case, then what were the details and the basis for their offer, and (3) if it was true that all clients were to be paid out of one lump sum.

*The Probative Quality of Professor Green's Opinion*

The Napoli Firm seeks to make great use of the opinion letter it obtained from Professor Green. A careful reading of his deposition and his opinion letter reveals a less than clear picture of what Professor Green knew about the proposed settlement. This Court's reading of the settlement agreement and of the affidavits submitted on this motion makes it clear that AHP made no individual settlement offers. Professor Green's deposition casts serious doubt that he was privy to all of the facts and circumstances necessary in forming a probative opinion because he appeared to have a very different view of the facts.

Although these questions were answered over objection (as were almost all of the questions in this extremely difficult deposition), the Napoli Firm's own expert was not approving what is alleged to have occurred here in this settlement. His view, and this Court's view, is that disclosure is required in the circumstance when a finite sum of money is to be divided among a number of clients who are all simultaneously represented by the same attorney.

In addition, Professor Green's opinion letter dated January 9, 2001, sets forth his understanding of the facts as represented to him by the Napoli Firm. This statement of facts as he understood them, which formed the basis of his opinion, differs substantially from the facts as revealed in this record.

His letter states:

For each of the clients individually, you have negotiated a settlement amount. The settlement amount offered to any individual client is not contingent on other claimants' acceptance of their settlement offers. You propose to enter into individual settlements rather than "an 'aggregate' settlement offer to be divided up among all of the plaintiffs." Citing, Roy Simon, *Simon's New York Code of Professional Responsibility*. As Professor Simon discusses in his treatise, an example of an aggregate settlement would be where "a lawyer represents five employment discrimination plaintiffs and the defendant employer makes a lump-sum (i.e. "aggregate") offer of $100,000 for all five plaintiffs." Further, in the event of an aggregate settlement that must then be divided among the claimants, each claimant may have an interest in maximizing his or her share of the aggregate settlement, but the co-claimants' lawyer cannot advocate for one client vis-a vis the others. Nor could the lawyer discourage any one client from accepting the settlement without undermining other clients' interest in accepting it. Here, where the individual amounts are offered to each individual client, these problems are simply not present.

If disclosure of the conflicts was not made, as the plaintiffs contend, there was a violation of the Disciplinary Rules by the Napoli Firm.

This Court is not persuaded that the ethics opinion submitted in support of the settlement is dispositive (or even probative) on the question of whether this was an aggregate settlement or if full disclosure by the Napoli Firm was required for a number of reasons. The opinion was based upon a hypothetical set of facts orally submitted to the expert by the firm before the settlement was entered into. There was no engagement letter setting forth a factual frame of reference. The factual allegations in this case are inconsistent with Professor Green's understanding of the facts as set forth in his opinion letter. And finally, in his deposition Professor Green refused to condone what is alleged to have occurred here, which leaves this Court with the task of determining the true facts. Are the facts as Mr. Murakami states in his affidavit or are they as the Napoli Firm contends?

*Allegations of Affirmative Wrongdoing*

The movants take their challenge of the Napoli Firm's behavior a step further by asserting that in a letter from the firm to each client (the "Letter"), the firm affirmatively misled their clients. Movants contend that not only did the firm fail to inform its clients of the nature of the lump sum offer and that conflicts of interest existed between clients vying for the same piece of the settlement pie, but also that the Napoli Firm made a number of specific misrepresentations as well.

This record reveals that the Napoli Firm sent the Letter in which they represented to each client that the firm sought to settle all or virtually all its cases in the same negotiation, and that the firm was evaluating each offer individually in order to give the client the best estimate of the present value of their individual case. However, the Letter went on to state:

> Our recommendation to accept the settlement offer is based on the final offer made by AHP to settle your case and we believe under all the existing facts and circumstances is fair and reasonable. In light of these factors, we recommend that you accept our recommendation on your behalf. Based on our review of your case, we have negotiated a settlement of $ [a specific amount was set forth].

The acceptance to be executed by the client, prepared by the Napoli Firm, states:

> I also understand that the final settlement offer was evaluated by the Special Master appointed by the court.

This Court finds that a claimant receiving such a Letter and the Form of Acceptance could have a reasonably held belief that the defendant AHP, had made a final offer in negotiations with the Napoli Firm in his/her case, that the final offer had been evaluated by the Special Master and that the Napoli firm was recommending that the client accept the final offer. A sufficient showing has been made by the movants that none of the representations set forth above were true. These allegations require further inquiry and a hearing.

This record (which is not the trial) does not reveal any offers (final or otherwise) to settle any individual claims. The Napoli Firm appears to have been offered one lump sum of money to settle all of its clients' cases who agreed to settle, provided a sufficient percentage agreed (it is also not denied by the Napoli Firm that the number of clients increased after the offer, further diluting the sum available for each claimant). In the affidavit of Stephen Murakami, he states that the Napoli Firm did its own evaluation of the value of each claim in order to increase its own legal fees and then recommended that the client accept its (the Napoli Firm's) offer as if the offer had been made by the defendant AHP.

The representation to a client that a specific dollar amount was offered in a negotiation with the defendant to settle the client's case, when in fact the settlement offer was by the client's own attorney made upon the attorney's evaluation, if true, represents a serious breach of duty to the client.

In addition, it is unclear on this record to what extent the Special Master evaluated each offer (as was represented by the firm in the form of Offer of Acceptance to be signed by the client). Our predecessor court appointed the Special Master, but did not require him to evaluate each offer for fairness. The Special Master was charged with, *inter alia,* the task of determining if the settlement process was fair. In that context, he would not be expected to evaluate each settlement offer. Instead, he would use a strategy, such as random sampling, so that he could opine on the process generally.

In contrast, the Murakami affidavit denies the evaluation was performed in all cases. The testimony of Professor Green is vague but suggests that the Special Master did not perform the evaluations. The affidavits submitted by the Napoli Firm and the Special Master in support of the settlement are also less than clear as to what the Special Master did.

However, on this record it is unclear if the Napoli Firm ever informed its clients that the evaluation by the Special Master was merely "a random review of a sampling of the records." This proved to be troubling to Professor Green.

The Murakami affidavit is more direct. It states:

The Firm also told each client that the "settlement" amount being offered by AHP was evaluated and mediated by a retired judge who had experience and knowledge of the fen-phen litigation. For almost all of the firms' clients, all of that was a misrepresentation!

From a reading of the conflicting factual affidavits and affirmations, this Court is left with the same ambiguous reaction Professor Green expressed. In addition, the Napoli Firm's affirmations do not appear to support either the representation in the Letter nor the statement in the Form of Acceptance that each offer was evaluated by the Special Master.

The record on this motion is replete with factual disputes on virtually every issue. The affirmation of Paul J. Napoli responding to the supplemental submission of P & W sets forth his version of the facts and his subjective evaluation of their meaning. It is not conclusive and does not refute the allegation that the settlement offers were from the Napoli Firm, nor does it refute the allegation that the Special Master did not review each and every settlement offer.

Accordingly, this Court finds that a sufficient showing has been made that the Napoli Firm may have violated the Disciplinary Rules and may have made material misrepresentations in the Letter and the Form of Acceptance. Therefore, the motion to intervene is granted as the interests of the various plaintiffs lie. The issue of P & W's awareness of the acts of professional misconduct, if any, or if the principles of waiver or estoppel will apply to its claim, must await the trial.

The final determination of the request to vacate (or modify) the prior settlement order will remain an open question to await a trial on the allegations of misrepresentations and of manipulation of the settlement; which includes the allocation of settlement amounts, expenses, and legal fees. The issue of the fairness of any specific allocation of the lump sum settlement offered to the plaintiffs will not be considered until these preliminary matters have been dealt with.

# CHAPTER 11

---

# MASS TORTS: DAMAGE SAMPLING AND STATISTICAL PROOF

■ ■ ■

## A.  HISTORICAL BACKGROUND

### WATSON V. SHELL OIL CO.

United States Court of Appeals for the Fifth Circuit, 1992.
979 F.2d 1014.

Shell Oil Company and Brown and Root, U.S.A., Inc., defendants in this mass-tort class action, have permissibly appealed interlocutory orders in this diversity suit. The orders at issue define the class and class issues, designate class representatives, and set a trial plan. Finding neither error nor abuse of discretion, for the reasons assigned we affirm the proposed trial plan.

### I.  BACKGROUND

This litigation arises out of an explosion at Shell's manufacturing facility in Norco, Louisiana. At approximately 3:30 a.m. on May 5, 1988, failure of a pipe elbow, allegedly fabricated and installed by Brown & Root, permitted the escape of a vapor cloud of combustible gases. The vapor ignited and a massive explosion ripped through the plant, causing extensive damage both on the plant site and in the surrounding communities. That same morning the instant federal class action suit was filed. During the next week class action suits were filed in Louisiana state courts and were removed to federal court. The claims against Shell are founded on Louisiana law theories of negligence, strict liability and intentional tort. Plaintiffs assert claims in negligence and strict liability against Brown & Root. Plaintiffs also seek punitive damages against both defendants.

The actions were consolidated and referred to a magistrate judge with instructions to conduct an evidentiary hearing and to submit a report and recommendation regarding designation of class representatives and subclass definitions. The district court substantially adopted the magistrate judge's recommendations, certified the litigation as a class action under Fed.R.Civ.P. 23(b)(3), defined the plaintiff class, and, pursuant to Fed.R.Civ.P. 23(c)(4), defined the "outside the gate" and "inside the gate" subclasses. Subclass A includes in excess of 18,000 claimants. Subclass B has sixteen Shell employee claimants. The district court established notification and opt-out procedures and approved a Plaintiffs' Legal Committee to represent the class.

The district court identified as liability issues common to both subclasses the determination of fault: (1) as it relates to compensatory damage claims, and (2) whether it is sufficient to warrant imposition of punitive damages. As to Subclass B only, the court identified as additional issues: (1) whether the fault of Shell Oil or any other person claiming benefit of workers compensation immunity was intentional thus obviating the immunity, and (2) whether punitive damages are available if workers compensation is the exclusive remedy. The district court thereafter established a procedure for identifying absent class members and obtaining information relating to their claims.

After extensive briefing by the parties, the district court issued orders detailing a four-phase plan for trial. In Phase 1 a jury would determine common issues of liability. If the jury found punitive damage liability it would then perform the Phase 2 function and determine compensatory damages in 20 fully-tried sample plaintiff cases. Based on the findings in these cases, the jury would then establish the ratio of punitive damages to compensatory damages for each class member. If the jury finds no punitive damage liability in Phase 1, Phase 2 is to be omitted.

In Phase 3, a different jury is to resolve issues unique to each plaintiff's compensatory damage claims, *e.g.* injury, causation, and quantum. Phase 3 calls for trials in waves of five, scheduled according to a format based upon factors, including location of the injured person or property at the time of the explosion and extent and nature of the damages. The district court anticipates that "after several waves are tried, a reasonable judgment value for each category of claims would emerge so as to facilitate settlements." In Phase 4 the district court is to compute, review, and award punitive damages, if any are established in Phase 1, for the plaintiffs awarded compensatory damages.

Shell and Brown & Root timely sought leave for an interlocutory appeal which we granted.

## II.   ANALYSIS

We revisit the problem of mass tort litigation recently addressed. The instant litigation, involving claims by more than 18,000 plaintiffs, starkly presents the nearly insurmountable problems of balancing procedural fairness with judicial efficiency in the management of mass tort litigation. At the threshold we must note that in many respects this appeal presents only the broad outlines of the district court's trial plan and, to a large extent, appellate review must await its implementation. Keenly mindful of the magnitude of the mass litigation problem, its increasing frequency, and the need for innovative solutions, we review the present challenges to the district court's orders.

### A.  The Trial Plan: Punitive Damage Concerns

#### 1.  Applicability of Fibreboard

Shell and Brown & Root first argue that Phase 2 violates principles enunciated in *In re Fibreboard Corp.* In that case the panel reluctantly vacated a trial plan in mass tort litigation involving the claims of 3,031 plaintiffs asserting asbestos-related injuries. The dispute in *Fibreboard* centered on the aspect of the plan that called for a jury to ascertain damages for the entire class on the basis of a trial of the specific claims of eleven class representatives, together with such evidence as the parties presented about the claims of thirty illustrative plaintiffs, and the testimony of experts about damages to the entire class. We found the *Fibreboard* scheme infirm for two reasons. First, the proposed plan failed to require each claimant to prove both causation and damages, as required by Texas law. Second, because the proceeding was to ascertain damages for a group of claimants who suffered widely divergent injuries essentially on the basis of a statistical profile, the plan failed to qualify as a "trial" in the sense contemplated by Article III of the Constitution, and was thus beyond the authority of an Article III court. We find the instant case distinguishable from *Fibreboard* because the Phase 2 jury is to make a determination about punitive damages in a mass-disaster context, rather than compensatory damages in products liability litigation.

The law permits punitive damage awards primarily to punish the defendant guilty of egregious misconduct and to deter such conduct in the future. It need hardly be emphasized that the punitive damages inquiry—unlike that for compensatory damages—focuses primarily on the egregiousness of the defendant's conduct. As the trial court aptly noted, the degree of culpability underlying a single act—and hence the propriety of imposing punitive damages as a result of that act—should not markedly vary in a setting such as is here presented, when considered with respect to different plaintiffs. Because of this minimal variance, assessing the propriety of punitive damages on the basis of the claims of a cross-section of the plaintiff class should not, in the words of *Fibreboard,* require "lifting the description of the claims to a level of generality that tears them from their substantively required moorings." That the Phase 2 jury will consider only punitive damages in a mass tort case materially distinguishes this case from *Fibreboard.*

More importantly, the Phase 2 jury is not to extrapolate punitive damages but, rather, is to determine a basis for assessment of punitive damages in the form of a ratio. One might argue that the logic of *Fibreboard,* if not its narrow holding, prohibits use of the Phase 2 procedure to determine quantitatively the amount of actual punitive damages. But Phase 2 purports to do no such thing. Unlike the plan in *Fibreboard,* Phases 2 and 3 appropriately enforce the Louisiana law requirement that a claimant must prove both causation and damage to recover compensatory and punitive damages.

2.    *Applicability of Haslip*

Shell and Brown & Root also claim that Phase 2 runs afoul of the latest Supreme Court teaching on punitive damages, *Pacific Mutual Life Insurance Co. v. Haslip.* Essentially reiterating their *Fibreboard* arguments, Shell and Brown & Root claim that because the Phase 2 plan determines damages on the basis of class representation and extrapolation it violates the *Haslip* due process requirements. Shell also argues that the Phase 2 plan violates the rule that punitive damages must bear a reasonable relationship to compensatory damages.

Shell and Brown & Root at best present premature *Haslip* concerns. *Haslip,* while not a class action or a case purporting to address the concerns which might arise relative to punitive damages in a case involving more than 18,000 compensatory claims, does stand for the general proposition that a punitive damage award by a properly instructed jury, where there is adequate post-verdict review, will not violate due process. In addition to recognizing the fundamental purpose of punitive damage awards—to punish the defendant and deter future misconduct—*Haslip* appears to require that the award have a reasonable basis in the conduct and degree of fault of the defendant, and an understandable relationship to compensatory damages. We cannot, at this early stage, conclude that the plan at bar will not satisfy these criteria. The proposed procedure does not provide for the precise mechanisms of the Phase 2 punitive damage trial nor does it detail the Phase 4 judicial review. However, the absence in Louisiana law of a scheme for review of punitive damages awards such as that approved in *Haslip* should not impede the district court's Erie-mandated effort to act as a dutiful Louisiana trial court mindful of the Supreme Court's teaching in *Haslip.* We hold that Phase 2 of the instant plan, on its face, adequately satisfies *Haslip's* command.

B.    *Phase 3 Trial Rules and Procedures*

Shell and Brown & Root maintain that the Plan is constitutionally unsound because the district court intends to limit traditional trial rules in Phase 3. The district court indicates that Phase 3 will "not necessarily involve full-blown trials," and that "traditional trial procedures, methods of proof, and evidentiary rules will be abbreviated and simplified to shorten trial time." Further quoting *Newberg on Class Actions,* the trial court states that, in class actions, "pleadings, discovery, and strict application of rules of evidence associated with normal adjudication processes for individual lawsuits are often replaced with greatly simplified, informal procedures, often summary in nature." Appellants insist that this language evinces an intent to limit unduly the application of the Federal Rules of Civil Procedure and Federal Rules of Evidence in Phase 3 proceedings.

At this point we can only speculate about how the district court will fill in the broad outlines of its plan in Phase 3. Such speculative concerns do not, however, present an issue ripe for review at this time. While we do not read the plan, as a whole, as indicating the district court's intent to act impermissibly, we simply remind all that the federal rules have the force of law. The secondary source quoted by the district court offers no credible support for the proposition that our rules of evidence and procedure may be altered or diminished in any manner, in actions of this kind, other than those recognized to be within the sound discretion of the district court. We express our confidence that the district court will adhere to acceptable norms in the shaping of the rules to meet the judicial crisis presented by the instant litigation.

### C.   Class Certification

Brown & Root vigorously opposes litigation of the claims as a class action. Relying on the district court's grant of summary judgment in its favor on the strict liability and punitive damage claims, Brown & Root argues that subject matter jurisdiction concerns militate against maintenance of a class action against it, and that such a class action would violate Fed.R.Civ.P. 23. Brown & Root thus suggests that we should sever it from this class action, and permit it to defend the negligence claims in separate proceedings. These contentions lack merit. We review district court class certification decisions only for abuse of discretion; we find no such abuse here.

### 2.   Numerosity of Subclass B

Pointing to the fact that Subclass B contains only 16 plaintiffs, Brown & Root argues that this subclass fails the numerosity requirement of Rule 23(a)(1). That requirement imposes no mechanical rules, turning instead on the practicability of joining all class members individually. We previously have noted that while the number of claimants is relevant to this determination, a court also may consider other factors, including the nature of the action. In the instant case, the district court's class certification includes Subclass B in a larger class of more than 18,000 plaintiffs for the purposes of litigating liability issues with respect to Shell and Brown & Root. Considering the nature of this action, we cannot say that identifying Subclass B for the purpose of litigating the related issue of Shell's liability for intentional tort, amounted to an abuse of the trial court's broad discretion.

### 3.   Predominant Common Issues

Brown & Root, citing *Jenkins,* urges that the absence of issues common to both defendants requires its dismissal from the class action. Brown & Root misperceives controlling law. The commonality requirement of Fed.R.Civ.P. 23(b)(3) is intended to ensure that the disallowance of individual trials is warranted by a sufficient gain in efficiency. Rule

23(b)(3) accordingly requires that "resolution of the common questions affect all or a substantial number of the *class members*." The commonality requirement focuses on the common issues relevant to claims by or against the class members; it does not require that all issues be common to all parties. In the litigation at bar the claims of all plaintiffs require resolution of Shell's liability for punitive damages and of Brown & Root's liability for negligence, both arising out of the same event. That the plaintiffs assert different theories against Shell and Brown & Root does not obviate the commonality of issues.

Brown & Root further suggests that the class issues thus far identified will not "predominate" as required by Fed.R.Civ.P. 23(b)(3). In the context of mass tort litigation, we have held that a class issue predominates if it constitutes a significant part of the individual cases. The class issues to be determined by the Phase 1 jury form integral elements of the claims asserted by each of the more than 18,000 plaintiffs. There can be no serious contention that the district court abused its discretion in determining that these issues predominate for the purpose of class certification.

### 4.  Superiority

Brown & Root finally contends that class proceedings are not a "superior" means of litigating its negligence liability, as required by Fed.R.Civ.P. 23(b)(3). Pointing to *In re Tetracycline Cases,* Brown & Root argues that the variety of class issues will confuse the Phase 1 jury. It further suggests that because it will seek contribution from other contractors, the class action is not a superior means for litigating its negligence liability. Brown & Root insists that class litigation will not reduce complexity and will not substantially reduce the number of issues left for decision in the Phase 3 trials. These arguments fail to persuade.

The proposed Phase 1 should not unduly confuse the jury. This litigation differs markedly from toxic tort cases such as *Jenkins, Fibreboard,* and *Tetracycline,* in which numerous plaintiffs suffer varying types of injury at different times and through different causal mechanisms, thereby creating many separate issues. The case at bar actually will present fewer and simpler issues to the Phase 1 jury. Further, we cannot find that the trial court abused its discretion in opting to utilize the class action in this case simply because Brown & Root may seek contribution from other contractors. Finally, because of the great import of the class issues to the claims of each plaintiff, we cannot agree with defendants' contention that class litigation will not reduce the number of issues or complexity in the Phase 3 trials. To the contrary, after the Phase 1 resolution, only causation and damages will remain in each plaintiff's claim against Brown & Root. In light of the massive proportions of this litigation, and the need to reduce the systemic burden it will impose, we cannot conclude that the district court abused its discretion in fashioning this class-litigation format.

## III. CONCLUSION

In *Fibreboard* we reluctantly issued a writ of mandamus, vacating a portion of the trial plan in that case. In so doing, however, we closed with a salute to the trial judge:

> We admire the work of our colleague, Judge Robert Parker, and are sympathetic with the difficulties he faces. This grant of the petition for writ of mandamus should not be taken as a rebuke of an able judge, but rather as another chapter in an ongoing struggle with the problems presented by the phenomenon of mass torts.

Judge Parker had 3,031 cases consolidated in one action. Judge Henry Mentz has more than 18,000 plaintiffs in the case now before him. We express our admiration for the manner in which Judge Mentz, aided by a very able magistrate judge and equally able trial counsel, has woven our mass tort case law into an acceptable and workable trial plan. We affirm the district court's orders establishing that trial plan and return this case to the district court for further proceedings.

## MADISON V. CHALMETTE REFINING, LLC

United States Court of Appeals for the Fifth Circuit, 2011.
637 F.3d 551.

Dennis, Circuit Judge, concurring:

I concur in the majority's opinion except as to its dicta questioning the vitality of *Watson v. Shell Oil Co.*, in light of *Amchem Products v. Windsor* and its "progeny."

This circuit has affirmed and relied upon *Watson*'s holding following *Amchem. Steering Comm. v. Exxon Mobil Corp.* ("It is theoretically possible to satisfy the predominance and superiority requirements of Rule 23(b)(3) in a mass tort or mass accident class action, a proposition this court has already accepted." (citing *Watson*)("This court has likewise approved mass tort or mass accident class actions when the district court was able to rely on a manageable trial plan—including bifurcation and/or subclasses— proposed by counsel;"); *Mullen v. Treasure Chest Casino, LLC* (affirming class certification in a case alleging that the casino "improperly maintained its air-conditioning and ventilating system" resulting in the plaintiffs' injuries and citing *Watson* as supporting the court's conclusion that Rule 23(b)(3)'s superiority requirement was satisfied).

Likewise, other circuits continue to positively cite *Watson*. Moreover, numerous district courts continue to rely on *Watson,* particularly to determine whether class certification is proper in a mass tort action. Commentators also continue to cite *Watson* as representative of the case law on class actions.

I believe, consistent with this plethora of precedent, including controlling Fifth Circuit authority, that *Watson* as a source of precedential value remains strong in our circuit.

## HILAO V. ESTATE OF MARCOS

United States Court of Appeals for the Ninth Circuit, 1996.
103 F.3d 767.

IX. METHODOLOGY OF DETERMINING COMPENSATORY DAMAGES

The Estate challenges the method used by the district court in awarding compensatory damages to the class members.

### A.  *District Court Methodology*

The district court allowed the use of a statistical sample of the class claims in determining compensatory damages. In all, 10,059 claims were received. The district court ruled 518 of these claims to be facially invalid, leaving 9,541 claims. From these, a list of 137 claims was randomly selected by computer. This number of randomly selected claims was chosen on the basis of the testimony of James Dannemiller, an expert on statistics, who testified that the examination of a random sample of 137 claims would achieve "a 95 percent statistical probability that the same percentage determined to be valid among the examined claims would be applicable to the totality of claims filed". Of the claims selected, 67 were for torture, 52 were for summary execution, and 18 were for "disappearance".

### 1.  *Special Master's Recommendations*

The district court then appointed Sol Schreiber as a special master (and a court-appointed expert under Rule 706 of the Federal Rules of Evidence). Schreiber supervised the taking of depositions in the Philippines of the 137 randomly selected claimants (and their witnesses) in October and November 1994. These depositions were noticed and conducted in accordance with the Federal Rules of Civil Procedure; the Estate chose not to participate and did not appear at any of the depositions. (The Estate also did not depose any of the remaining class members.)

Schreiber then reviewed the claim forms (which had been completed under penalty of perjury) and depositions of the class members in the sample. On the instructions of the district court, he evaluated:

> (1) whether the abuse claimed came within one of the definitions, with which the Court charged the jury at the trial, of torture, summary execution, or disappearance; (2) whether the Philippine military or paramilitary was involved in such abuse; and (3) whether the abuse occurred during the period September 1972 through February 1986.

He recommended that 6 claims of the 137 in the sample be found not valid.

Schreiber then recommended the amount of damages to be awarded to the 131 claimants. Following the decision in *Filartiga v. Pena-Irala*, he applied Philippine, international, and American law on damages. In the cases of torture victims, Schreiber considered:

> (1) physical torture, including what methods were used and/or abuses were suffered; (2) mental abuse, including fright and anguish; (3) amount of time torture lasted; (4) length of detention, if any; (5) physical and/or mental injuries; (6) victim's age; and (7) actual losses, including medical bills.

In the cases of summary execution and "disappearance", the master considered

> (1) the presence or absence of torture prior to death or disappearance; (2) the actual killing or disappearance; (3) the victim's family's mental anguish; and (4) lost earnings computed according to a formula established by the Philippine Supreme Court and converted into U.S. dollars.

The recommended damages for the 131 valid claims in the random sample totaled $3,310,000 for the 64 torture claims (an average of $51,719), $6,425,767 for the 50 summary-execution claims (an average of $128,515), and $1,833,515 for the 17 "disappearance" claims (an average of $107,853).

Schreiber then made recommendations on damage awards to the remaining class members. Based on his recommendation that 6 of the 137 claims in the random sample (4.37%) be rejected as invalid, he recommended the application of a five-per-cent invalidity rate to the remaining claims. He then performed the following calculations to determine the number of valid class claims remaining:

|  | Torture | Summary Execution | Disappearance |
| --- | --- | --- | --- |
| Claims Filed | 5,372 | 3,677 | 1,010 |
| Facially Invalid Claims | − 179 | − 273 | − 66 |
| Remaining Claims | 5,193 | 3,404 | 944 |
| Less 5% Invalidity Rate | − 260 | − 170 | − 47 |
| Valid Claims | 4,933 | 3,234 | 897 |
| Valid Sample Claims | − 64 | − 50 | − 17 |
| Valid Remaining Claims | 4,869 | 3,184 | 880 |

He recommended that the award to the class be determined by multiplying the number of valid remaining claims in each subclass by the average award recommended for the randomly sampled claims in that subclass:

|                          | Torture | Summary Execution | Disappearance |
|--------------------------|---------|-------------------|---------------|
| Valid  Remaining Claims  | 4,869   | 3,184             | 880           |
| × Average Awards         | $51,719 | $128,515          | $107,853      |
| Class Awards             | $251,819,811 | $409,191,760 | $94,910,640   |

By adding the recommended awards in the randomly sampled cases, Schreiber arrived at a recommendation for a total compensatory damage award in each subclass:

|              | Torture | Summary Execution | Disappearance |
|--------------|---------|-------------------|---------------|
| Class Awards | $251,819,811 | $409,191,760 | $94,910,640 |
| Sample Awards | $ 3,310,000 | $ 6,425,767 | $ 1,833,515 |
| TOTALS       | $255,129,811 | $415,617,527 | $96,744,155 |

Adding together the subclass awards, Schreiber recommended a total compensatory damage award of $767,491,493.

### 1.   Jury Proceedings

A jury trial on compensatory damages was held in January 1995. Dannemiller testified that the selection of the random sample met the standards of inferential statistics, that the successful efforts to locate and obtain testimony from the claimants in the random sample "were of the highest standards" in his profession, that the procedures followed conformed to the standards of inferential statistics, and that the injuries of the random-sample claimants were representative of the class as a whole. Testimony from the 137 random-sample claimants and their witnesses was introduced. Schreiber testified as to his recommendations, and his report was supplied to the jury. The jury was instructed that it could accept, modify or reject Schreiber's recommendations and that it could independently, on the basis of the evidence of the random-sample claimants, reach its own judgment as to the actual damages of those claimants and of the aggregate damages suffered by the class as a whole.

The jury deliberated for five days before reaching a verdict. Contrary to the master's recommendations, the jury found against only two of the 137 claimants in the random sample. As to the sample claims, the jury generally adopted the master's recommendations, although it did not follow his recommendations in 46 instances. As to the claims of the remaining class members, the jury adopted the awards recommended by the master. The district court subsequently entered judgment for 135 of the 137 claimants in the sample in the amounts awarded by the jury, and for the remaining plaintiffs in each of the three subclasses in the amounts awarded by the jury, to be divided pro rata.

## B.  ESTATE'S CHALLENGE

The Estate's challenge to the procedure used by the district court is very narrow. It challenges specifically only "the method by which the district court allowed the validity of the class claims to be determined": the master's use of a representative sample to determine what percentage of the total claims were invalid.

The grounds on which the Estate challenges this method are unclear. It states that to its knowledge this method "has not previously been employed in a class action". This alone, of course, would not be grounds for reversal, and in any case the method has been used before in an asbestos class-action case, the opinion in which apparently helped persuade the district court to use this method. *See Cimino v. Raymark Indus., Inc.*

The Estate also argues that the method was "inappropriate" because the class consists of various members with numerous subsets of claims based on whether the plaintiff or his or her decedent was subjected to torture, "disappearance," or summary execution. The district court's methodology, however, took account of those differences by grouping the class members' claims into three subclasses.

Finally, the Estate appears to assert that the method violated its rights to due process because "individual questions apply to each subset of claims, *i.e.,* whether the action was justified, the degree of injury, proximate cause, etc." It does not, however, provide any argument or case citation to explain how the methodology violated its due-process rights. Indeed, the "individual questions" it identifies—justification, degree of injury, proximate cause—are irrelevant to the challenge it makes: the method of determining the validity of the class members' claims. The jury had already determined that Philippine military or paramilitary forces on Marcos' orders—or with his conspiracy or assistance or with his knowledge and failure to act—had tortured, summarily executed, or "disappeared" untold numbers of victims and that the Estate was liable to them or their survivors. The only questions involved in determining the validity of the class members' claims were whether or not the human-rights abuses they claim to have suffered were proven by sufficient evidence.

Although poorly presented, the Estate's due-process claim does raise serious questions. Indeed, at least one circuit court has expressed "profound disquiet" in somewhat similar circumstances. *In re Fibreboard Corp.* The *Fibreboard* court was reviewing a petition for a writ of mandamus to vacate trial procedures ordered in over 3,000 asbestos cases. The district court had consolidated the cases for certain purposes and certified a class for the issue of actual damages. The district court ordered a trial first on liability and punitive damages, and then a trial (Phase II) on actual damages. In the Phase II trial, the jury was "to determine actual damages in a lump sum for each of 5 disease categories for all plaintiffs in the class" on the basis of "a full trial of liability and damages for 11 class representatives and such evidence as the parties wish to offer from 30 illustrative plaintiffs" (half chosen by each side), as well as "opinions of experts regarding the total damage award." The Fifth Circuit noted that the parties agreed that "there will inevitably be individual class members whose recovery will be greater or lesser than it would have been if tried alone" and that "persons who would have had their claims rejected may recover." The court said that

> the inescapable fact is that the individual claims of 2,990 persons will not be presented. Rather, the claim of a unit of 2,990 persons will be presented. Given the unevenness of the individual claims, this Phase II process inevitably restates the dimensions of tort liability. Under the proposed procedure, manufacturers and suppliers are exposed to liability not only in 41 cases actually tried with success to the jury, but in 2,990 additional cases whose claims are indexed to those tried.

The court granted the petitions for mandamus and vacated the trial court's order, but it did so not on due-process grounds but because the proposed procedure worked a change in the parties' substantive rights under Texas law that was barred by the *Erie* doctrine. On the other hand, the time and judicial resources required to try the nearly 10,000 claims in this case would alone make resolution of Hilao's claims impossible. *See Cimino* ("If the Court could somehow close thirty cases a month, it would take six and one-half years to try these 2,298"). The similarity in the injuries suffered by many of the class members would make such an effort, even if it could be undertaken, especially wasteful, as would the fact that the district court found early on that the damages suffered by the class members likely exceed the total known assets of the Estate.

While the district court's methodology in determining valid claims is unorthodox, it can be justified by the extraordinarily unusual nature of this case. " 'Due process,' unlike some legal rules, is not a technical conception with a fixed content unrelated to time, place and circumstances". In *Connecticut v. Doehr*, a case involving prejudgment attachment, the Supreme Court set forth a test, based on the test of *Mathews v. Eldridge* for determining whether a procedure by which a private party invokes state power to deprive another person of property satisfies due process:

> First, consideration of the private interest that will be affected by the procedure; second, an examination of the risk of erroneous deprivation through the procedures under attack and the probable value of additional or alternative safeguards; and third, principal attention to the interest of the party seeking the procedure, with, nonetheless, due regard for any ancillary interest the government

may have in providing the procedure or forgoing the added burden of providing greater protections.

The interest of the Estate that is affected is at best an interest in not paying damages for any invalid claims. If the Estate had a legitimate concern in the identities of those receiving damage awards, the district court's procedure could affect this interest. In fact, however, the Estate's interest is only in the total amount of damages for which it will be liable: if damages were awarded for invalid claims, the Estate would have to pay more. The statistical method used by the district court obviously presents a somewhat greater risk of error in comparison to an adversarial adjudication of each claim, since the former method requires a probabilistic *prediction* (albeit an extremely accurate one) of how many of the total claims are invalid. The risk in this case was reduced, though, by the fact that the proof-of-claim form that the district court required each class member to submit in order to opt into the class required the claimant to certify under penalty of perjury that the information provided was true and correct. Hilao's interest in the use of the statistical method, on the other hand, is enormous, since adversarial resolution of each class member's claim would pose insurmountable practical hurdles. The "ancillary" interest of the judiciary in the procedure is obviously also substantial, since 9,541 individual adversarial determinations of claim validity would clog the docket of the district court for years. Under the balancing test set forth in *Mathews* and *Doehr,* the procedure used by the district court did not violate due process.

RYMER, CIRCUIT JUDGE, CONCURRING IN PART AND DISSENTING IN PART.

Because I believe that determining causation as well as damages by inferential statistics instead of individualized proof raises more than "serious questions" of due process, I must dissent from Part IX of the majority opinion. Otherwise, I concur.

Here's what happened: Hilao's statistical expert, James Dannemiller, created a computer database of the abuse of each of the 10,059 victims based on what they said in a claim form that assumed the victim's torture. Although Dannemiller would have said that 384 claims should be examined to achieve generalizability to the larger population of 10,059 victims within 5 percentage points at a 95% confidence level, he decided that only 136 randomly selected claims would be required in light of the "anticipated validity" of the claim forms and testimony at the trial on liability that the number of abuses was about 10,000.

He selected three independent sample sets of 242 (by random selection but eliminating duplicates). Hilao's counsel then tried to contact and hold hearings or depositions with each of the claimants on the first list, but when attempts to contact a particular claimant proved fruitless, the same number in the next list was used. When the sample results for the first 137 victims proved insufficient to produce the level of sampling precision desired for the project, Hilao's counsel continued from case 138 to case 145. Eventually, 124 were completed from list A, 11 from list B, and 2 from list C.

The persons culled through this process went to Manilla to testify at a deposition (which Dannemiller thought was "remarkable"). Dannemiller Narrative Statement, p. 6. He opined that "this random selection method in determining the percentage of valid claims was fair to the Defendant" as "a random selection method of a group of 9541 individuals is more accurate than where each individual is contacted." Further, the statistician observed that "the cost and time required to do 9541 would be overwhelming and not justified when greater precision can and was achieved through sampling." Finally, he concluded that "the procedures followed conformed to the standards of inferential statistics and therefore the injuries of the 137 claimants examined are representative of the 9541 victims."

In accordance with the "computer-generated plan developed by James Dannemiller," the Special Master oversaw the taking of the 137 depositions in the Philippines. In accordance with the district court's order, the Special Master was to determine "(1) whether the abuse claimed came within one of the definitions, with which the Court charged the jury at the trial held in Hawaii, of torture, summary execution, or disappearance; (2) whether the Philippine military or para-military was or were involved in such abuse; and (3) whether the abuse occurred during the period September 1972 through February 1986." Special Master and Court Appointed Expert's Recommendations, p. 1. Based on a review of the deposition transcripts of the 137 randomly selected victim claims, and a review of the claims, the Special Master found that 131 were valid within the definitions which the court gave to the jury; the Philippine military or para-military were involved in the abuse of the valid claims; and the abuse occurred during the period 1972 through February 1986. As a result, he recommended the amount of compensatory damages to be awarded to the valid 131 claimants, and for the entire class based on the average awards for torture, for summary execution (including lost earnings, which the Special Master determined should be capped at $120,000 per claimant, and which would be determined by the average for the occupation when a witness did not state the amount of income earned), and disappearance (including lost earnings similarly calculated). His report indicates that "for all three categories, moral damages as a proximate result of defendants' wrongful acts or omissions, were weighed into the compensation."

Thus, causation and $766 million compensatory damages for nearly 10,000 claimants rested on the opinion of a statistical expert that the selection method in determining valid claims was fair to the Estate and more accurate than individual testimony; Hilao's counsel's contact with the randomly selected victims until they got 137 to be deposed; and the Special Master's review of transcripts and finding that the selected victims had been tortured, summarily executed or disappeared, that the Philippine military was "involved," that the abuse occurred during the relevant period, and that moral damages occurred as a proximate result of the Estate's wrongful acts.

This leaves me "with a profound disquiet," as Judge Higginbotham put it in *In re Fibreboard Corp.* Although I cannot point to any authority that says so, I cannot believe that a summary review of transcripts of a selected sample of victims who were able to be deposed for the purpose of inferring the type of abuse, by whom it was inflicted, and the amount of damages proximately caused thereby, comports with fundamental notions of due process.

Even in the context of a class action, individual causation and individual damages must still be proved individually. As my colleagues on the Sixth Circuit explained in contrasting generic causation—that the defendant was responsible for a tort which had the capacity to cause the harm alleged—with individual proximate cause and individual damage:

> Although such generic causation and individual causation may appear to be inextricably intertwined, the procedural device of the class action permitted the court initially to assess the defendant's potential liability for its conduct without regard to the individual components of each plaintiff's injuries. However, from this point forward, it became the responsibility of each individual plaintiff to show that his or her specific injuries or damages were proximately caused by the defendant's conduct. We cannot emphasize this point strongly enough because generalized proofs will not suffice to prove individual damages. The main problem on review stems from a failure to differentiate between the general and the particular. This is an understandably easy trap to fall into in mass tort litigation. Although many common issues of fact and law will be capable of resolution on a group basis, individual particularized damages still must be proved on an individual basis.

There is little question that Marcos caused tremendous harm to many people, but the question is which people, and how much. That, I think, is a question on which the defendant has a right to due process. If due process in the form of a real prove-up of causation and damages cannot be accomplished because the class is too big or to do so would take too long, then (as the Estate contends) the class is unmanageable and should not have been certified in the first place. As Judge Becker recently wrote for the Third Circuit in declining to certify a 250,000-member class in an asbestos action: "Every decade presents a few great cases that force the judicial system to choose between forging a solution to a major social problem on the one hand, and preserving its institutional values on the other. This is such a case." *Georgine v. Amchem Prod. Inc.*

So is this. I think that due process dictates the choice: a real trial. I therefore dissent.

# B. CONTEMPORARY APPLICATIONS

## CIMINO V. RAYMARK INDUSTRIES, INC.
United States Court of Appeals for the Fifth Circuit, 1998.
151 F.3d 297.

Before us are appeals and cross-appeals in personal injury and wrongful death damage suits against several manufacturers of asbestos-containing insulation products and some of their suppliers, the district court's jurisdiction being based on diversity of citizenship and the governing substantive law being that of Texas. This is the same set of cases addressed in *In re Fibreboard*, but the judgments now before us result from a trial plan modified following that decision. Principally at issue on this appeal is the validity of that modified trial plan.

By the time of the phase I trial, many of the defendants had settled and others had taken bankruptcy or otherwise been disposed of, so only five remained, namely appellant Pittsburgh Corning Corporation, Carey Canada, Celotex, Fibreboard, and appellant Asbestos Corporation, Limited (ACL). The case against ACL was tried to the court under the Foreign Sovereign Immunities Act. By the time the amount of the extrapolation case judgments was to be calculated, all defendants except Pittsburgh Corning and ACL had passed out of the case.

Judgment was entered against ACL in only two of the ten class representative cases (and in none of either the phase III sample cases or the extrapolation cases). Judgment was actually entered against Pittsburgh Corning in a total of 157 cases, consisting of 9 of the class representative phase I cases, 143 of the phase III sample cases, and 5 of the extrapolation cases (1 from each of the 5 different diseases included in the class). In these 157 cases, Pittsburgh Corning has been cast in judgment for a total of approximately $69,000,000. Pittsburgh Corning and ACL each appeal the referenced judgments entered against them, and the plaintiffs' cross-appeal as to each. The issues presented in the ACL appeal and cross-appeal are few and narrow, and we address them last.

Pittsburgh Corning's appeal presents essentially two groups of contentions, summarized as follows: first, those challenging the implemented *Cimino* trial plan as a whole, particularly its asserted failure to properly try and determine individual causation and, in the five extrapolation cases, damages also, as to any plaintiffs other than the class representatives, assertedly contrary to our decision in *Fibreboard* and Texas substantive law and in derogation of Pittsburgh Corning's Seventh Amendment and Due Process rights; and second, various other issues of a more particular and traditional sort. We now turn to consider Pittsburgh Corning's appeal, addressing first its attacks on the trial plan.

ANALYSIS

As noted, Pittsburgh Corning attacks the *Cimino* trial plan, as it did at all times below, principally on the basis that it fails to properly try and determine individual causation, and in the extrapolation cases also fails to properly try and determine individual damages, as to any plaintiffs other than the ten class representatives whose individual cases were fully tried in phase I. Pittsburgh Corning asserts in this connection, among other things, that these aspects of the trial plan are contrary to *Fibreboard*, impose liability and damages where they would not be imposed under Texas substantive law, and invade its Seventh Amendment and due process rights. Although we do not separately address the due process contention as such, we conclude that the *Cimino* trial plan is invalid in these respects, necessitating reversal of all the phase III sample case judgments as well as the five extrapolation case judgments before us.

We begin by stating some very basic propositions. These personal injury tort actions for monetary damages are "a prototypical example of an action at law, to which the Seventh Amendment applies." The Seventh Amendment applies notwithstanding that these are diversity cases. But because these are diversity cases, the Rules of Decision Act, 28 U.S.C. § 1652, and *Erie R. Co. v. Tompkins*, with its seeming constitutional underpinning, mandate that the substantive law applied be that of the relevant state, here Texas. Substantive law includes not only the factual elements which must be found to impose liability and fix damages, but also the burdens of going forward with evidence and of persuasion thereon.

None of the foregoing is or can be altered by the utilization of Fed. R. Civ. P. 23(b)(3) or Fed. R. Civ. P. 42(a). As to the Seventh Amendment, the Court in *Ross v. Bernhard* held that in a stockholders' derivative action seeking monetary relief—now provided for in Fed. R. Civ. P. 23.1—although the right of the stockholders to sue on behalf of the corporation was an equitable matter determinable by the court, the monetary claims of the corporation against the defendants were legal claims to which the Seventh Amendment applied. The Court observed that "The Seventh Amendment question depends on the nature of the issue to be tried rather than the character of the overall action," and "nothing turns now upon the form of the action or the procedural devices by which the parties happen to come before the court." It also noted that it was "inclined to agree with the description" of derivative suits "as one kind of 'true' class action," and that "it now seems settled in the lower federal courts that class action plaintiffs may obtain a jury trial on any legal issues they present."

And, this Court has long held that the applicability of the Seventh Amendment is not altered simply because the case is Rule 23(b)(3) class action.

Similarly, use of Rule 23(b)(3) or 42(a) does not alter the required elements which must be found to impose liability and fix damages (or the burden of proof thereon) or the identity of the substantive law—here that of Texas—which determines such elements. We squarely so held in *Fibreboard*. And the rules enabling act, 28 U.S.C. § 2072 likewise mandates that conclusion.

Nor is deviation from these settled principles authorized because these are asbestos cases whose vast numbers swamp the courts. *Fibreboard* clearly so holds.

When, after *Fibreboard*, the district court adopted the present trial plan, it initially justified doing so on the basis of its conclusion that "the Texas Supreme Court, if faced with the facts of this case, would apply a collective liability theory, such as the Court's plan, to an asbestos consolidated action." The court based this conclusion on a passage in *Gaulding v. Celotex Corp.*, stating "We are not to be construed as approving or disapproving alternative liability, concert of action, enterprise liability, or market share liability in an appropriate case." We are compelled to reject the district court's conclusion for each of several independently sufficient reasons. To begin with, it is contrary to *Fibreboard*, which plainly holds that under Texas substantive law causation of plaintiff's injury by defendant's product and plaintiff's resultant damages must be determined as to "individuals, not groups." *Fibreboard*'s determination of Texas law is precedent which binds this panel. *Gaulding* furnishes no basis to depart form *Fibreboard* because it was quoted and relied on therein. No Texas appellate decision or statute subsequent to *Fibreboard* casts doubt on the correctness of its reading of Texas law. In the second place, even were we not bound by *Fibreboard* we would reach the same conclusion it did, namely that under Texas personal injury products liability law causation and damages are determined respecting plaintiffs as "individuals, not groups."

We know of no Texas appellate decision which in that or a similar context has even approved of in dicta, much less adopted, the theories of "alternative liability, concert of action, enterprise liability, or market share liability" which *Gaulding* states it was not "approving or disapproving." "We have long followed the principle that we will not create 'innovative theories of recovery or defense' under local law, but will rather merely apply it 'as it currently exists.'" Consistent with that principle, we have on more than one occasion expressly refused to hold that Louisiana would apply a market share liability theory to asbestos personal injury claims, where no Louisiana appellate decision had either done so or declined to do so. We apply Texas law as it currently exits, which is correctly stated in *Fibreboard*. Finally, it is clear that this case was neither tried nor determined on any of "the collective liability theories" mentioned in *Gaulding*.

Thus, the question becomes: did the implemented trial plan include a litigated determination, consistent with the Seventh Amendment, of the Texas-law mandated issues of whether, as to each individual plaintiff, Pittsburgh Corning's product was a cause of his complained-of condition and, if so, the damages that plaintiff suffered as a result.

We turn first to the phase III plaintiffs. In these cases, the trial plan was adequately individualized and preserved Seventh Amendment rights with respect to each individual's actual damages from an asbestos-related disease. However, it was not designed or intended to, and did not, provide any trial or any determination of whether a Pittsburgh Corning product was a cause of that disease. It was strictly a damages trial as to those individual plaintiffs. The stipulation—not entered into until midway through phase III—established merely that "some" individuals working in each of the listed crafts, "during" each of the four decades 1942–1982 and at each of the twenty-two worksites, "were exposed to asbestos" with "sufficient length and intensity to cause pulmonary asbestosis of varying degrees" and that "an asbestos-containing product of Pittsburgh Corning Corporation was present during the decades 1962–1982 at the specified worksites." It was *expressly not* stipulated "that any members of the various crafts at the various worksites had the same exposure to any products," *or* "that any such individuals had the same susceptibility to asbestos-related diseases in the various crafts and worksites," *or* that "any individual plaintiff was in fact exposed to injurious quantities of asbestos from the products of any defendant." Phase III did not litigate or determine whether or to what extent any of the one hundred sixty individual plaintiffs was exposed to Pittsburgh Corning's—or any other defendant's—asbestos, or was exposed to asbestos at any of the twenty-two worksites, or whether any such exposure was in fact a cause of that plaintiff's illness or disease. Nor did phase III litigate or determine either any individual plaintiff's past connection with any particular worksite or craft, or whether or to what extent such individual was exposed to asbestos otherwise than at any of the specified worksites. Indeed, for the most part exposure evidence was not allowed and the jury was instructed to assume sufficient exposure. Nor did phase III either litigate or determine whether or to what extent asbestos exposure, either generally or to the product of any particular defendant, was uniform or similar for members of any given craft at any one or more of the specified worksites.

We note that at least two of the twenty-two sites actually each involved two plants, and another involved "the facilities" of a company "including" its powerhouse. Further, Pittsburgh Corning tendered evidence that a typical refinery covers several square miles and indicating that at refineries, shipyards, and other installations asbestos exposure levels were not uniform at the site or throughout a craft or within a decade or between decades, and that most individuals employed at the twenty-two worksites did not have sufficient exposure to cause asbestosis. Also so tendered was evidence indicating that exposure to asbestos below some level would not produce asbestosis and even above that level risks remain very low until a multiple of five or ten or twenty times the threshold level is reached; that not all those exposed to asbestos in substantial quantities and for protracted periods of time develop asbestosis; that asbestosis develops in "a relatively small percentage of patients with significant asbestos exposure"; and, that although there is a dose response relationship—the more exposure the more risk, the less, the less risk—respecting asbestosis, nevertheless the effect of the same exposure is not the same as between different individuals and "two similarly exposed asbestos workers with exactly the same asbestos historical exposure can go on to have in one case asbestosis and the other case no lung problems." Moreover, we have held, in a Texas law diversity case, that "the appropriate test for a plaintiff's *minimum* showing of producing cause in asbestos cases" is that stated in *Lohrmann v. Pittsburgh Corning Corp.*, namely the " 'frequency-regularity-proximity' test" under which "a motion for summary judgment cannot be defeated merely by alleging work at a shipyard in which defendants' asbestos products had somewhere been present. Rather, there must be proof of frequent and regular work in an area of the shipyard in proximity to some specific item of defendants' asbestos containing product." It is important to note that this is merely a *minimum* showing; *Slaughter* makes clear that making such a showing *merely* gets a plaintiff *to* the jury, it does not entitle him to judgment as a matter of law. Further, it is obvious that for these purposes a shipyard is not considered as a single, undifferentiated, and uniform mass.

We have noted that the district court, in the order in which it initially adopted the present plan, stated that for purposes of the then-contemplated phase II trial it would "make a non-jury determination as to which Plaintiffs or Plaintiffs' decedents worked for a sufficient period of time at each worksite so as to be a proper member of that worksite's group and which Plaintiffs were proper members of each of the crafts at these worksites." As previously observed, after phase I the case proceeded directly into phase III without any phase II, and the stipulation was not entered into until phase III was half complete. It is not clear that the district court ever determined that any (or, if so, which) of the tried one hundred sixty phase III plaintiffs, or that any (or if so, which) of the unsevered extrapolation plaintiffs, actually did work at the worksites "for a sufficient period of time" to be "proper members of each of the crafts at these worksites." And, if such determinations were made, it is not clear what criteria were employed and what source or sources of information were utilized either in selecting or in applying the criteria. In any event, it *is* clear not only that any such determination was made non-jury, but further that it was made without either any evidentiary (or other) hearing or any summary judgment procedure (or Fed. R. Civ. P. 50 motion).

Accordingly, no such determination can serve to justify or sustain the trial plan as implemented.

With one exception, noted below, we are aware of no appellate decision approving such a group, rather than individual, determination of cause in a damage suit for personal injuries to individuals at widely different times and places.

Nor do we consider that *In re Chevron U.S.A., Inc.* justifies the instant trial plan. That action involved claims by approximately 3,000 neighboring property owners for personal injury and property damage allegedly caused contamination from Chevron's former crude oil storage waste pit. Apparently no form of class action was involved, although some cases were consolidated. The district court directed that thirty individual plaintiffs be chosen, fifteen by the plaintiffs and fifteen by the defendants, and that there be "a unitary trial on the issues of 'general liability or causation' on behalf of the remaining plaintiffs, as well as the individual causation and damage issues of the thirty selected plaintiffs." Apparently, the individual causation and damage issues of the remaining *un*selected plaintiffs would be determined subsequently in individual trials (if the unitary trial established "liability on the part of Chevron for the pollutants that, allegedly, give rise to all of the plaintiffs' claims"). Chevron sought mandamus, contending "that the goal of the 'unitary' trial was to determine its liability, or lack thereof, in a single trial and to establish bellwether verdicts to which the remaining claims could be matched for settlement purposes." We stated that the thirty selected plaintiffs were not shown or chosen so as to be representative of the other plaintiffs, and observed that "a bellwether trial designed to achieve its value ascertainment function for settlement purposes or to answer troubling causation or liability issues *common* to the universe of claimants has as a core element representativeness." We granted mandamus prohibiting "utilization of the results obtained from the trial of the thirty (30) selected cases for any purpose affecting issues or claims of, or defenses to, the remaining untried cases." While the majority opinion (one judge specially concurred) contains language generally looking with favor on the use of bellwether verdicts when shown to be statistically representative, this language is plainly *dicta*, certainly insofar as it might suggest that representative bellwether verdicts could properly be used to determine *individual* causation and damages for other plaintiffs. To begin with, no such question was before this Court, as the trial plan contemplated that individual causation and damages issues would not be controlled by the thirty individual bellwether verdicts, which would be used to encourage settlement. Moreover, what we did—our *holding*—was to prevent *any* preclusive use of the unitary trial results (whether for general causation *or* individual causation or otherwise) in cases other than those of the thirty selected plaintiffs. And, we concluded that if the district court carried out another, different trial plan, that would present "matters for another panel to consider in the event those decisions are subject to appellate review." Finally, the majority opinion in *In re Chevron U.S.A.* does not even cite *Fibreboard*, or the Seventh Amendment (or discuss the right to jury trial), and does not refer to the Texas substantive law elements of liability and damages in the matter before it. Clearly, *In re Chevron U.S.A.* does not control the result here, and this panel is not bound by its dicta.

In *Hilao v. Estate of Marcos* a divided panel of the Ninth Circuit in a rule 23(b)(3) class action permitted recoverable tort damages to be determined in a lump sum for the entire class. *Hilao* was a suit under the Alien Tort Claims Act, and the Court essentially applied substantive principles of federal or international "common law." The majority distinguished *Fibreboard* on the basis that there "the proposed procedure worked a change in the parties' substantive rights under Texas law that was barred by the *Erie* doctrine." By the same token, *Hilao* is distinguishable here; it did not operate under the constraints of the Rules of Decision Act or *Erie*; the present case, by contrast, does operate under those constraints. If *Hilao* is not thus distinguishable it is simply contrary to *Fibreboard*, which binds us and which in our opinion is in any event correct. Further, *Hilao* did not address—and there was apparently not presented to it any contention concerning—the Seventh Amendment. Finally, we find ourselves in agreement with the thrust of the dissenting opinion there. ("Even in the context of a class action, individual causation and individual damages must still be proved individually").

In sum, as *Fibreboard* held, under Texas law causation must be determined as to "individuals, not groups." And, the Seventh Amendment gives the right to a jury trial to make that determination. There was no such trial determination made, and no jury determined, that exposure to Pittsburgh Corning's products was a cause of the asbestos disease of any of the one hundred sixty phase III plaintiffs. Nor does the stipulation determine or establish that. Accordingly, the judgments in all the one hundred forty-three phase III cases before us must be reversed and remanded.

We turn now to the extrapolation cases. As to the matter of individual causation, it is obvious that the conclusion we have reached in respect to the phase III cases applies *a fortiori* to the extrapolation cases. In the extrapolation cases there was no trial and no jury determination that any individual plaintiff suffered an asbestos-related disease. Indeed, in the extrapolation cases there was no trial at all—by jury or otherwise—and there was no evidence presented. So, our holding as to the phase III cases necessarily requires reversal of the judgments in the five extrapolation cases before us.

As to the matter of actual damages, the extrapolation cases are likewise fatally defective. Unlike the phase III cases, in the extrapolation cases there was neither any sort of trial determination, let alone a jury determination, nor even any evidence, of damages. The district court considered that these deficiencies were adequately compensated for by awarding each extrapolation case plaintiff who alleged an asbestos-related disease an amount of actual damages equal to the average of the awards made in the phase III cases for plaintiffs claiming the same category of disease. This plainly contravenes *Fibreboard*'s holding that under the substantive law of Texas recoverable damages are the "wage losses, pain and suffering, and other elements of compensation" suffered by each of the several particular plaintiffs as "individuals, not groups." We also observe in this connection that none of the experts at the extrapolation hearing purported to say that the damages suffered by the phase III plaintiffs in a given disease category (whether as disclosed by the phase III evidence or as found by the jury) were to any extent representative of the damages suffered by the extrapolation plaintiffs in the same disease category. The procedure also violates Pittsburgh Corning's Seventh Amendment right to have the amount of the legally recoverable damages fixed and determined by a jury. The only juries that spoke to actual damages, the phase I and III juries, received evidence *only* of the damages to the particular plaintiffs before them, were called on to determine *only*, and *only* determined, each of those some one hundred seventy particular plaintiffs' actual damages individually and severally (not on any kind of a group basis), and were *not* called on to determine, and did *not* determine or purport to determine, the damages of any other plaintiffs or group of plaintiffs. We have held that "inherent in the Seventh Amendment guarantee of a trial by jury is the general right of a litigant to have only one jury pass on a common issue of fact." This requires that if separate trial are ordered, the separately tried issues must be "distinct and separable from the others." *Id. See also Matter of Rhone-Poulenc.* By the same token, where the issues to be separately tried *are* separable and distinct, the Seventh Amendment rights of the parties are preserved as to *both* sets of issues. As the cited cases demonstrate, these principles are fully applicable in class actions for damages. It necessarily follows from these principles that the jury's phase III findings of the actual damages of each of the individual phase III plaintiffs cannot control the determination of, or afford any basis for denial of Pittsburgh-Corning's Seventh Amendment rights to have a jury determine, the distinct and separable issues of the actual damages of each of the extrapolation plaintiffs.

We conclude that the extrapolation case judgments, as well as the phase III judgments, are fatally flawed, are contrary to the dictates of *Fibreboard*, and contravene Pittsburgh-Corning's Seventh Amendment rights. We do not act in ignorance or disregard of the asbestos crises. In *Amchem Products, Inc. v. Windsor*, the Supreme Court called attention to the report of the Judicial Conference's Ad Hoc Committee on Asbestos Litigation, stating that "Real reform, the report concluded, required federal legislation creating a national asbestos-dispute resolution scheme." The

Court also observed, "The argument is sensibly made that a nationwide administrative claims processing regime would provide the most secure, fair, and efficient means of compensating victims of asbestos exposure. Congress, however, has not adopted such a solution." Nevertheless, the Court refused to stretch the law to fill the gap resulting from congressional inaction. As we said in *Fibreboard*, federal courts must remain faithful to *Erie* and must maintain "the separation of powers between the judicial and legislative branches." "The Judicial Branch can offer the trial of lawsuits. It has no power or competence to do more."

We accordingly reverse the judgments before us in all the one hundred forty-three phase III cases and in all the five extrapolation cases, and those one hundred forty-eight cases are remanded for further proceedings not inconsistent herewith.

REYNALDO G. GARZA, CIRCUIT JUDGE, specially concurring:

I write separately to concur in the excellent opinion in this case, but also to add some of my own comments and thoughts about these consolidated cases, which have burdened our judicial system for so many years. In particular, I wish to express my concerns raised by Pittsburgh Corning's attack on Judge Parker's ingenious but, unfortunately, legally deficient trial plan. This case is a striking example of the crisis presented by the state of asbestos litigation in our judicial system; therefore, I am also writing separately to further urge upon Congress the wisdom and necessity of a legislative solution.

Texas law simply provides no way around Pittsburgh Corning's right to a jury trial as to causation or the requirement that causation and damages be determined as to individuals and not groups. *See In re Fibreboard Corp.* (stating that policy choices of State of Texas in defining "the duty owed by manufacturers and suppliers of products to consumers are reflected in the requirement that a plaintiff prove both causation and damage. These elements focus upon individuals, not groups."). If Judge Parker had conducted phase II according to his plan, however, rather than replacing phase II with the phase II stipulation, the only issue before us today would be the propriety of the phase III damages determinations. Of course, the majority opinion correctly explains that these damages determinations were fatally deficient under Texas law and the Seventh Amendment as to the more than 2,000 "extrapolation" cases; however, these "extrapolated" damages determinations are valuable in and of themselves as indications of an appropriate settlement range for each of the five disease categories involved.

It is clear that the enigma of asbestos litigation is not readily susceptible to resolution under the standards and practices representative of traditional tort litigation. *See Jenkins v. Raymark Industries* ("Courts, including those in our own circuit, have been ill-equipped to handle this 'avalanche of litigation.' Our numerous opinions in asbestos-related cases have repeatedly recognized the dilemma confronting our trial courts, and expressed concern about the mounting backlog of cases and inevitable, lengthy trial delays."). In 1991, the Judicial Conference Ad Hoc Committee on Asbestos Litigation, whose members were appointed by Chief Justice Rehnquist, issued a report noting that:

> What has been a frustrating problem is becoming a disaster of major proportions to both the victims and the producers of asbestos products, which the courts are ill-equipped to meet effectively.
>
> The most objectionable aspects of asbestos litigation can be briefly summarized: dockets in both federal and state courts continue to grow; long delays are routine; trials are too long; the same issues are litigated over and over; transaction costs exceed the victims' recovery by nearly two to one; exhaustion of assets threatens and distorts the process; and future claimants may lose altogether.

The history of this case, up to and including our resolution of this appeal (which is dictated by binding authority) is a perfect illustration of the incompatibility of asbestos litigation and traditional tort litigation procedures.

As the majority opinion convincingly establishes, the trial plan which the district court implemented below was legally deficient. As to the 160 phase III "sample" plaintiffs, who tried their cases to a jury regarding damages, the trial plan was inconsistent with the requirement of Texas law that determinations of causation be made as to "individuals, not groups." *See Fibreboard*. The stipulation that replaced phase II established only that "some" individuals working in each of the listed crafts during each of the relevant time periods at each of the 22 work sites were "exposed to asbestos with sufficient length and intensity to cause pulmonary asbestosis of varying degrees," and that a Pittsburgh Corning asbestos product was present at those sites during two of the relevant time periods. As such, the stipulation was not sufficiently individualized, as it would have been if Pittsburgh Corning had stipulated that "all" of the plaintiffs were so exposed.

As to the "extrapolation" plaintiffs, the same rationale applies with respect to the issue of causation. Additionally, however, the extrapolation cases were deficient with regard to the determination of actual damages. In contrast to the "sample" phase III cases, no jury ever considered the "extrapolation" cases, and neither the court nor a jury made any individualized determinations of actual damages, as required by Texas law. *See Fibreboard*. It is for these reasons that we are reversing the judgments in the phase III "sample" cases and the "extrapolation" cases.

It appears, however, that Judge Parker's phase II plan would have been sufficient if he had implemented the plan rather than disposing of it with the phase II stipulation. Under the plan, phase II would have addressed exposure on a craft and work site basis during the relevant time periods. A jury would have made exposure findings regarding specific work sites, crafts, and time periods. The jury would have heard evidence regarding the presence of the defendants' asbestos products and asbestos dust at each work site. The jury would also have heard evidence about the nature of the different crafts at each work site and the relationship of those crafts to asbestos. Additionally, the jury would have heard evidence regarding working conditions at each work site and the relationship of those conditions to the defendants' products.

The presentation of such evidence would clearly be sufficient for a reasonable jury to conclude that the presence of the defendants' products caused injuries to individuals working in certain crafts at certain work sites during certain time periods, and how long of a time period would be sufficient to support such causation. The jury would have also heard evidence regarding the presence of the defendants' products at the relevant work sites during the relevant time periods. Based on that evidence, the jury would have apportioned responsibility among the settling and non-settling defendants. The court would then make a determination of which plaintiffs worked for sufficient periods of time at each work site and which plaintiffs were members of each craft at those work sites.

The evidence, if presented as the plan anticipated, would satisfy the plaintiffs' burden of proof, and would support a reasonable jury's determination of causation specific to craft, work site, and relevant time period. Such evidence would also support a determination of the length of time on the job required to support causation. As such, the court's task of simply plugging each plaintiff into a craft, work site, and time period would be a sufficiently individualized determination of causation for the district court to grant judgment as to the causation issue.

The question of damages, however, is another story. The inescapable reality is that Texas law requires that determinations of damages be made as to individuals, not as to groups, and this Court is powerless to alter that reality. As stated, the Ad Hoc Committee's report concluded that the only real solution to the problems posed by the asbestos litigation crisis lies with Congress, but the Ad Hoc Committee continued that "at the same time, or failing congressional action, the federal judiciary must itself act now to achieve the best performance possible from the system under current law." Judge Parker made a valiant and admirable effort to take such action. Unfortunately, however, this Court is without the power to sanction or condone his approach.

Although resolution of these cases, under the current state of law, would require an inordinate number of damages trials, the parties involved should not lightly cast aside the figures that Judge Parker arrived at in phase III as representative of actual damages in each category of disease.

In arriving at these figures, Judge Parker tried 160 individual "sample" cases from each of the five disease categories represented by the pool of plaintiffs. The two juries that tried those 160 cases determined only whether each particular "sample" plaintiff suffered from an asbestos-related disease or injury and, if so, the amount of damages incurred. Following the trials, Judge Parker held a one day hearing after which he determined that the "sample" cases within each disease category were reliably representative of the more than 2,000 remaining "extrapolation" cases. Judge Parker then assigned each "extrapolation" case to a disease category and awarded actual damages equal to the average of the awards in the "sample" cases involving the same disease.

In sum, the judiciary's utter inability to adequately address the seemingly insurmountable problems posed by asbestos litigation further underscores the need for legislative action. Nevertheless, although the procedure outlined above does not satisfy the demands of Texas law requiring individual determinations of damages, the parties should take notice of these figures as representative of an appropriate settlement range within each disease category. Such notice is particularly advisable for Pittsburgh Corning, against whom the phase I jury awarded a three to one punitive damages multiplier (i.e., $3.00 of punitive damages for every $1.00 of actual damages).

I tend to agree with Judge Thomas F. Hogan's Separate Dissenting Statement to the Ad Hoc Committee's report. Judge Thomas acknowledged the "national crisis involving asbestos litigation," but expressed concern with the Ad Hoc Committee's recommendation that, if Congress chose not to accept the Committee's recommendation of a national legislative scheme to deal with asbestos claims, Congress should consider legislation to expressly authorize the consolidation and collective trial of asbestos cases in order to expedite disposition of cases in federal courts with heavy asbestos personal injury caseloads. Judge Hogan stated:

> My concern is the underlying premise of the report regarding the use of class action "collective" trials (trials by aggregation of claims) of asbestos cases. It is a novel and radical procedure that has never been accepted by an appellate court. It has been challenged as being constitutionally suspect in denying defendants their due process and jury trial rights as to individualized claimants, as well as conflicting with the court's obligations to apply state law.

This recommendation, aside from the constitutional question, as a practical matter may well prove impossible to execute. Trial by aggregation of claims and then the extrapolation of the damages by the court has been recognized by the Committee itself as being "the most radical solution." As mentioned, it has never been approved by any appellate court.

Our decision in this case shows that Judge Hogan's prophecy rang true. Judge Hogan did agree that "a national solution is the only answer." He continued, however, that "since the aggregation or collective trial method is highly questionable, a logical and viable solution would be the passage by Congress of an administrative claims procedure similar to the Black Lung legislation." Judge Hogan concluded: "There already exists a model to follow in the Black Lung program. If there is to be any Conference action, it is hoped the Conference would suggest that Congress consider such an approach."

I agree with Judge Hogan's comments. Obviously, the type of consolidation attempted in this case is unworkable in practice. *Fibreboard* and the majority opinion in this case make that abundantly clear. As I have discussed, it is also apparent that the federal judiciary has not been able to formulate an appropriate response to the asbestos litigation crisis. In fact, this case suggests that we may be without the power to do so.

As such, there must be some alternative solution. The power to devise such a solution lies solely in the halls of Congress. Although I do not express any opinion on the strengths and weaknesses of the Federal Black Lung Program as implemented, the underlying concept of setting up an administrative claims procedure to handle a massive amount of claims for disabling employment-related impairments makes sense in the context of dealing with claims for asbestos-related injuries. Congress promulgated the Black Lung Program to rectify the historical lack of adequate state compensatory schemes for miners suffering from pneumoconiosis. Similarly, asbestos-related injuries have presented the courts with an unmanageable situation, which has resulted in an inadequate method of compensation for such injuries, both from the plaintiffs' and defendants' point of view. As such, I join Judge Hogan in urging Congress to formulate an administrative claim procedure for dealing with claims for asbestos-related injuries modeled on the Black Lung legislation.

In conclusion, I agree with the rationale and the result which the majority opinion has reached. Our hands are tied by the United States Constitution. We must respect Texas law and the Seventh Amendment. As the Ad Hoc Committee noted: "The picture is not a pretty one. Decisions concerning thousands of deaths, millions of injuries, and billions of dollars are entangled in a litigation system whose strengths have increasingly been overshadowed by its weaknesses."

This statement still holds true; however, the picture is much worse today. I implore Congress to heed the plight of the judiciary and the thousands of individuals and corporations involved. Congress alone has the power to devise a system to alleviate these most pressing of concerns. Congress utilized this power in response to the plight of the coal miners. Simply stated, it is Congress' duty and responsibility to do the same in response to the asbestos litigation crisis.

# IN RE FORD MOTOR CO. IGNITION SWITCH PRODS. LIAB. LITIG.

United States District Court for the District of New Jersey, 2000.
194 F.R.D. 484.

## I.   INTRODUCTION

In this consolidated Multi-District Litigation class action suit, plaintiffs claim that they own or owned vehicles manufactured by defendant Ford Motor Company; that their vehicles came equipped with defective ignition switches manufactured by defendant United Technologies Corporation (UTC); that defendants knew that the switches were defective and nonetheless persisted in selling the affected cars and trucks; and that vehicles were damaged by fires caused by short circuits in the defective switches.

Presently before the Court is the renewed motion of the *Snodgrass* plaintiffs for class certification. This Court's jurisdiction is based upon diversity of citizenship, and the laws of nearly 50 states give rise to the various causes of action asserted by members of the proposed classes and subclasses. The main issue for decision is whether plaintiffs' amended class definition satisfies the prerequisites for class certification set forth in Fed.R.Civ.P. 23(b)(3). For the reasons discussed below, the Court concludes that even under plaintiffs' revised proposed class definition, this case is not appropriate for class action treatment, and will deny plaintiffs' application.

## II.   BACKGROUND

In brief, *Snodgrass* plaintiffs' predecessors' initial motion for class certification in this case sought to certify a class of "all persons or entities who purchased or who leased, other than for purposes of resale or leasing, one or more Ford vehicles in model years 1984 through 1992 and who owned Ford vehicles from model year 1993 with ignition switches manufactured before October 1992, and whose vehicles caught on fire as a result of a defective ignition switch." No personal injury or wrongful death claims were asserted.

This Court denied plaintiffs' motion for class certification without prejudice to later renewal of such motion. Plaintiffs now claim that they have cured the deficiencies which impaired the original certification motion, and once again move the Court to approve the plaintiffs' request for class action treatment.

## III.   DISCUSSION

For reasons discussed below, the court holds that common issues of law and fact do not predominate even these elaborately restricted proposed subclasses, that class action is not a superior means of litigating plaintiffs' claims, and that class certification is not appropriate under Rule 23(b)(3).

Accordingly, the court need not and does not reach the question whether plaintiffs have satisfied the threshold Rule 23(a) requirements.

### C. *Whether Individual Issues Predominate Even Under Plaintiffs' Revised Class Definitions*

The Supreme Court has noted that the predominance requirement is not met when there exist a greater number of questions peculiar to the several categories of class members, and to individuals within each category, where such uncommon questions are significant. *Amchem Prods.* In the context of the massive class certified by the district court in the *Georgine* asbestos litigation, the Supreme Court held that the class cohesion that might emerge from the common issues of fact regarding the consequences of asbestos exposure was undermined by the disparities among class members in the means of exposures to different asbestos-containing products, for various lengths of time, resulting in disparities in injury ranging from no physical injury to lung cancer or mesothelioma, with complications of causation arising from cigarette smoking.

That common issues must be shown to "predominate" does not mean that individual issues need be non-existent. All class members need not be identically situated upon all issues, so long as their claims are not in conflict with each other. The individual differences, however, must be of lesser overall significance and they must be manageable in a single class action, as discussed further below.

Here, plaintiffs have proposed a two-stage trial for adjudication of the vehicle owners' claims. Stage One would involve a "class trial" during which competing experts would present classwide statistical and mechanical evidence tending to prove that the fires were caused by the faulty ignition switches. Plaintiffs argue that their evidence at this stage would establish a "rebuttable statistical presumption" of causation. Plaintiffs recognize that statistical evidence of causation would include some "false positives"—fires that fall within the statistical boundaries but were not actually caused a faulty ignition switch. Nevertheless, plaintiffs assert that Stage Two would account for such non-ignition fires. To this end, plaintiffs propose that, once the Stage One proofs are completed, Stage Two would allow defendants the opportunity to rebut this statistical proof.

During Stage Two, defendants would be permitted to show on a case-by-case basis that the ignition switches were not the cause of the fire at issue. At this point, defendants would attempt to persuade the jury that certain individual fires were caused by something other than the defective switch. Alternative causes could include the installation of after-market equipment or simple negligence on the part of the owner.

For the reasons next discussed, the Court holds that under plaintiffs' proposed two-stage litigation plan, class-wide issues do not predominate over issues involving only individual plaintiffs. The Court's holding results from the following four conclusions: (1) even under the revised proposed class definitions, there exist disparate legal standards that would complicate efforts to prove that common issues predominate the proposed subclasses; (2) the proposed subclasses are not amenable to plaintiffs' proposed *prima facie* proof of causation through statistics; (3) the causation issues in this case are inherently individual in nature and will depend on facts particular to each individual plaintiff; and (4) owing to the abundant legal and factual issues that would have to be determined on a case by case basis, *en masse* litigation is not a superior method for addressing the vehicle owners' individual incident claims.

### 2.  *Whether Common Factual Issues Predominate*

It is axiomatic that individual causation remains a prerequisite to class membership. Resolution of the "general causation" question of whether the subject switches are capable of causing the damage alleged by the vehicle owners does not show commonality under Rule 23(a)(2). The question is not whether the switches have the capacity to cause harm, but rather the highly individualistic inquiry of whether it did cause harm and to whom. *Id.* citing *In re "Agent Orange" Product Liability Litigation.* In other words, there can be no inclusion of individuals in either of plaintiffs' proposed subclass unless that person can show that the subject switches caused damage to their vehicle.

A review of the history of this litigation demonstrates the need for individual causation investigation. The original lead plaintiff in this case, Michael Wilks, was dropped from the case after it came to light that he had himself set fire to his car. Likewise, plaintiff Doreen Giddings's claim was voluntarily dismissed after an investigation revealed that the fire in her car was not related to the ignition switch.

Furthermore, investigations by plaintiffs' fire investigation expert, William Hagerty, led to the voluntary dismissal of two of the eight plaintiffs whose cars he investigated. As shown by the events surrounding Mr. Hagerty's work for the plaintiffs, there is much uncertainty over whether the ignition switches themselves caused the fires, even among persons named as individual plaintiffs and class representatives. Other proposed causes include the installation of after-market equipment, which equipment appears to have increased the likelihood of fire.

Plaintiffs have not alleged that the subject switches *always* cause the type of harm alleged by the vehicle owners. Indeed, the very definition of plaintiffs' revised proposed subclasses admits that individual causation remains a critical part of class membership. Under the revised class definition, individuals would not be included unless they are an owner of a vehicle that has been "burned or been damaged by fire because of a defective Fox ignition switch". Thus, as recognized by plaintiffs, it is a threshold requirement for class membership that any fire or smoke damage must actually have been *caused* by one of the subject switches. As shown by a review the language of plaintiffs' proposed subclass definitions, then, class membership is earned by demonstrating a common thread of causation of the particular vehicle fire linked to the ignition switch to the exclusion of other causes. Fundamentally, this raises a problem that one is unable to know who is a member of the class (and thus bound by the court's processes) until a uniform basis of demonstrating causation emerges.

a.  Plaintiffs' Proffer of Statistical Evidence of Ignition Switch Failure Rates

This Court noted in its earlier opinion denying class certification that "there exist troublesome issues of causation that may require special case-by-case measures rendering the *Snodgrass* plaintiffs' claims unsuitable for class certification." Mindful of this observation, plaintiffs now have attempted through use of statistics to answer the Court's call for evidence showing causation on a subclass basis. The data and statistical analysis performed for these purposes by the *Snodgrass* experts and counsel reflect much hard work and expense in attempting to refine the analysis to show coherence of the class. For reasons now discussed, the Court finds that plaintiffs' statistical evidence of causation at most may support a rebuttable presumption that the subject switches caused fires in a significant number of vehicles, but that this presumption still will require case-by-case litigation of whether each putative plaintiff's damages actually were caused by defendants' switches. While statistical analysis may greatly aid the proof of individual incidents through the use of inferential evidence, the continued need for individual litigation of causation makes this case unsuitable for class action treatment.

b.  Whether Plaintiffs Have a Legal Basis for Their Statistical Proffer

Even if the Court were to assume that the plaintiffs' database was sufficiently reliable to create a presumption that the majority of the proposed subclass members owned vehicles with faulty ignition switches, such an assumption would not obviate the need for detailed claimant-specific investigations and jury trials in order to determine whether the subject switches actually caused the damage alleged. This is because rather than direct proof that the subject switches caused the fires, plaintiffs' statistical proofs are geared only towards creating a "rebuttable presumption" of causation.

Defendants assert that, even assuming that plaintiffs' statistical presumptions are valid, this statistical analysis of Ford vehicles' fire rates could at most suggest to a jury that a putative plaintiff—an owner of a given model/year Ford complaining of a steering column-area fire—*might* have experienced an ignition fire. Defendants also maintain that the fact that there is an increased statistical likelihood that an ignition switch caused a fire is not conclusive. Because the proffered statistical evidence cannot by itself establish individual causation, defendants argue, an analysis of the statistical likelihood of causation is an exercise in futility.

As further support for their argument that statistics cannot establish causation in this case, defendants cite the Third Circuit's recent decision in *Barnes v. American Tobacco* for the proposition that even if plaintiffs are able to narrow the field of potential plaintiffs through statistics, the individual plaintiffs still would have to demonstrate that they suffered compensable damages on account of a Fox ignition switch.

In *Barnes,* a group of plaintiffs pursued a class action lawsuit against the tobacco companies on the theory that defendants intentionally enhanced the addictive characteristics of their products. Plaintiffs argued that a Surgeon General's report conclusively established that cigarette smoking is a major cause of three different diseases, and that this evidence more than satisfied their burden of showing that addiction to tobacco caused them harm. The court rejected this argument, stating that "plaintiffs cannot prove causation by merely showing that smoking cigarettes causes cancer and other diseases. They must demonstrate that defendants' nicotine manipulation caused each individual plaintiff to have a significantly increased risk of harm." The *Barnes* court agreed with the District Court's decision to reject plaintiffs' effort to resolve the issue of individual causation by having each class member answer a questionnaire, stating that the questionnaire would at most establish a *prima facie* case of causation. Even after a showing of *prima facie* evidence of causation, the court held, defendants must be allowed the opportunity to cross-examine each individual plaintiff and other witnesses on the plaintiff's behalf, and offer expert testimony about each person's specific circumstances. The Third Circuit agreed with the District Court's conclusion that, owing to the need for individual cross-examination of each individual plaintiff, plaintiffs were proposing an impossible litigation plan.

Plaintiffs argue that statistical proof of causation has been approved by other courts, and that the holding in *Barnes* is inapposite and should be confined to the particular facts of that case. The Court disagrees. The similarities between *Barnes* and this case are manifest. In both cases, the plaintiffs present indirect evidence of causation, and propose a system of rebuttal trials.

This Court finds that *Barnes* counsels that any proffer of *prima facie* proof of causation must be viewed with skepticism because it fails to resolve any individual claim without more evidence, and that a threshold requirement for certification is a realistic litigation plan for resolution of individual causation.

c. An Analysis of Plaintiffs' Statistical Proffer

Plaintiffs claim to have created a database of specific model/years of Ford vehicles that have a far greater statistical likelihood of ignition switch fires than do most models. This database is derived from an updated collection of vehicle owners' complaints contained within Ford's Master Owner Relations System (MORS II). The individual MORS II complaint entries were created by Ford customer service personnel taking down individual customers' complaints sent by way of letter or telephone, and include the model/year of the owner's vehicle, and the owner's stated complaint. These reports are terse, often unverified, and inconclusive. For example, MORS II entry 19.03.52 involves a November 1995 complaint by an owner of a 1989 Ford Probe, and states only that:

Customer says:

The vehicle caught on fire under the dashboard of the vehicle while he was at a stop sign

The inside of the vehicle filled with smoke and the vehicle burst in to flames in the interior of the vehicle

Under the hood of the vehicle is fine. Was not touched by fire

Beginning with a collection of 14,000 MORS complaints involving Ford vehicles with Fox ignition switches, Charles Adams & Associates— litigation consultants retained on behalf of plaintiffs—reviewed the collection for MORS complaints coded as "visible flame", "smoke", or "burnt" in the passenger cabin. From this initial set of 14,000, Adams eliminated those complaints which he concluded could not involve ignition switch fires, because, for example, the report stated that the fire originated in the engine compartment or backseat area. If the MORS entry mentioned an ignition switch, then Adams concluded that the alleged fire was "very likely" caused by one of the subject switches. If the MORS report did not specify the origin of the fire, but only said it started in the steering column, Adams classified such fires as "more probable than not as being ignition switch related." To this list of potential ignition switch fires derived from the MORS II reports, plaintiffs added all incidents in Ford's "ASES" database reported as "alleged steering column fires," together with the vehicles of insurance policyholders involved in the State Farm and CSAA subrogation claims, and the *Snodgrass* named plaintiffs. Apparently, the MORS II reports comprise approximately 47.3% of the total claims. Based on the data just described, the plaintiffs arrived at a figure which has been reduced through a series of eliminations to a putative class of 6,098.

Plaintiffs have performed an elaborate statistical analysis of the above-described database aimed at creating a statistical presumption that any fire in a class vehicle was caused by one of the subject switches. In this analysis, plaintiffs' expert Dr. Jack Moshman, a statistician, examined the Adams-created fire database and broke down the models/years of vehicles included therein, limiting the class to those vehicles to those model/years having statistically homogeneous fire rates of between 2.702 and 3.304 per 10,000 vehicles. Plaintiffs have further refined this large class to arrive at two subclasses: Subclass I, which includes seventeen models with an average fire rate of 2.386 per 10,000, and Subclass II, a three model group with a fire-rate of 6.210 per 10,000. Under this analysis, therefore, the proposed subclasses of vehicle owners include those who own vehicles, which, according to Moshman, have roughly similar chances of catching on fire. By plaintiffs' view, Moshman's analysis makes it possible to have two large subclasses of vehicle owners who have in common a similar statistical likelihood of ignition switch fires.

Moshman's statistical analysis has been attacked by defendants, who claim that there exist no good grounds for plaintiffs' conclusions, chiefly because Moshman's report is based on untested allegations rather than actual ignition switch fires. Defendants also have employed their own statistical expert, Dr. William E. Wecker, who states that the Adams-created database is unreliable and overstates the number of ignition switch-related incidents, and that Moshman's analysis is therefore a parsing of non-probative data. Wecker also contradicts Moshman's finding of statistical homogeneity within the subclasses, asserting that the reported incident rates vary greatly among the model/years. Further, by Wecker's view, Moshman's conclusions are undermined by the fact that he and plaintiffs' counsel selected the model/years to be included in the subclasses in order to achieve the desired result, a technique which Wecker claims runs counter to accepted statistical norms. Wecker concludes that because Moshman's study is premised on unreliable data, and because his proposed subclasses do not include vehicles with statistically homogeneous fire rates, the worth of plaintiffs' statistical proffer is doubtful at best.

Even beyond the concerns raised by defendants, this Court has concerns over the reliability of the Adams/MORS II database as a blueprint for defining classes and subclasses, as well as a basis for proving the homogeneity of the claims within a subclass. At the January 7, 2000 hearing in this case, defendants argued that the database included too many unverified and vague allegations to be reliable. Consequently, the Court questioned how many of the complaints included in the database were backed by substantiation of actual ignition switch fires, and asked the parties to submit a random sample of the MORS II reports so that the Court could form its own impressions as to the quality of the information contained in the MORS II reports. On January 14, 2000, the parties responded by submitting 72 randomly selected MORS II reports—the first report identified on every 10th page of plaintiffs' database.

The randomly selected reports show that, of the 72 reports selected, 19 reports (26%) of the random subset do not even mention the words "ignition switch." Instead, these reports are ambiguous and allege that fires started in various areas of the vehicle, such as the "inside the cab," or within the steering column, the dashboard, or the instrument panel. One of the selected reports, that of Mr. Horn, states that the vehicle owner had replaced the ignition switch several times before the subject fire. Thus, it is unclear in Mr. Horn's case whether his car was even equipped with a Fox switch when it caught fire. Defendants argue that the large number of ambiguous reports shows that the MORS II entries are not probative of ignition switch fires and that the random sample refutes plaintiffs' claim that the database is sufficiently reliable to serve as *prima facie* proof that the proposed subclasses share in common that they had an ignition switch fire.

Plaintiffs have responded to defendants' critique of the random sample by contacting twelve of the nineteen individual vehicle owners (the others apparently were unavailable) whose reports Ford cited as ambiguous and non-probative. Plaintiffs' counsel argues that in many instances, an interview of the vehicle owner led to additional information that, once reviewed by plaintiffs' expert Mr. Hagerty, provides additional support for the theory that the alleged fire originated with the ignition switch. In other instances, plaintiffs claim that once contacted, the complaining owner "verified" that the fire was caused by the ignition switch, either through his own observations or those of service personnel. Apparently, this verification is either based on lay observation or the statements of a third party. Were this case to go to trial, therefore, such verification would likely be the subject of vigorous cross-examination.

Based on the foregoing, the Court finds that, while plaintiffs have arguably rebutted defendants' challenge to several of the MORS II reports, there remain countless other entries that will be subjected to similar scrutiny. As exemplified by the debate on these contested reports in the 72-entry subset, further record development will be required of many, if not all of the MORS II reports. Defendants undoubtedly will refuse to concede that the subject switches caused the damages alleged in every ambiguously worded report, thus necessitating further interviews and expert witness review. In sum, it remains doubtful that all of the MORS II reports included in the database actually represent actual ignition switch fires.

The Moshman analysis of the incidents reported in the underlying database is thus not a suitable basis upon which subclasses for trial could be defined because there is not a reliable basis upon which to conclude that all members of the identified subclasses have in fact sustained an ignition switch fire. Based on the foregoing, the Court questions whether plaintiffs' database is sufficiently reliable to serve even as a *prima facie* showing that certain vehicle owners have in common that they suffered ignition switch fires.

3.  *Plaintiffs Have Not Shown That Class Action is Superior to*
    *Other Available Methods for the Fair and Efficient*
    *Adjudication of This Controversy*

This matter will not be certified for class action treatment for the additional reason that the Court is not satisfied that plaintiffs have set forth a workable plan for resolution of the abundant individual issues in this case. For reasons discussed above, the Court found that common issues of law and fact do not predominate over individual concerns in this matter. Moreover, this Court now finds that plaintiffs' proposed a two-stage trial for litigating vehicle owners' fire-related claims is unworkable.

Plaintiffs have proposed a two-step litigation plan. In the first stage, the Court would hold a "class trial" wherein plaintiffs would present evidence tending to show defendants sold vehicles equipped with defective ignition switches, in violation of implied warranties and deceptive trade practice laws. In the second stage, defendants would be given the opportunity to address the issue of causation, and rebut the statically created presumption that individual plaintiffs' vehicle were actually damaged by an ignition switch fire.

Defendants vigorously criticize plaintiffs' proposed bifurcated trial, arguing that a method of "mini-trials" proposed for stage two would be inefficient for the Court and unfair to the defendants. The Court agrees.

In general, it is desirable to litigate similar, related claims in one forum. On the other hand, efficiency-based arguments on this point begin to lose their force as one contemplates the post-certification trial of plaintiffs' claims. As discussed previously, there are numerous factual issues in this case that cannot be adjudicated on a class-wide basis, and each individual vehicle owner and his/her witnesses would be subject to cross-examination on the particular facts and circumstances surrounding that vehicle owner's purported ignition switch fire. In addition, the second stage of the trial would necessarily involve individual consideration of each of the predictably numerous disputed claims. For example, even if the presumption of causation were available from plaintiffs' successful pursuit of the first phase trials for the various classes and subclasses, individual proofs would have to tie that presumption to the facts of the individual claims, and defense experts, or perhaps fact witnesses, could be expected to testify that the fire did not start in the relevant area of the car, or that it had a separate cause. Thus, each mini-trial could be expected to involve the direct and cross-examination of at least three witnesses: the vehicle owner and a fact witness for plaintiff (such as the mechanic or dealer who diagnosed the fire's origin) to overcome problems of hearsay, and one or two experts. The geographical logistics of such a trial would be formidable, and perhaps prohibitive, for individual claimants from around the country to travel to this Court to try their claims.

Even assuming that the number of contested claims could—as plaintiff suggests—through discovery be narrowed to 3,000, and that the individual "rebuttal trials" were to average just four hours each (a conservative estimate), the second phase of the trial would take approximately twelve years of judicial time. This would not serve the public well, nor would it provide relatively prompt remediation of the valid claims that exist.

Upon consideration of the realities of plaintiffs' proposed system of mini-trials following the establishment of a *prima facie* case of causation, the Court holds that class wide adjudication is not a superior method of adjudication. Plaintiffs' claims do not present a case where common issues predominate. Faced with the realities of plaintiffs' proposed litigation plan, the Court finds that individual litigation of plaintiffs' claims is a superior plan of action than the class action alternative facing the Court: a years-long trial process of rebutting a statistical presumption.

## CONCLUSION

The Court declines to certify these cases as class actions under Rule 23(b)(3). Certification under this provision is inappropriate here because plaintiffs have failed to demonstrate that, in these cases, "questions of law or fact common to the members of the class predominate over any questions affecting only individual members, and that a class action is superior to other available methods for the fair and efficient adjudication of the controversy." Accordingly, plaintiffs' petition for class certification is denied, and the representative plaintiffs' class-based claims will be dismissed without prejudice to the named plaintiffs' rights to pursue their individual claims remaining in this case.

## MCLAUGHLIN V. AMERICAN TOBACCO CO.

United States Court of Appeals for the Second Circuit, 2008.
522 F.3d 215.

While redressing injuries caused by the cigarette industry is "one of the most troubling problems facing our Nation today," not every wrong can have a legal remedy, at least not without causing collateral damage to the fabric of our laws. Plaintiffs' putative class action suffers from an insurmountable deficit of collective legal or factual questions. Their claims are brought as based in fraud under the Racketeer Influenced and Corrupt Organizations Act, but under RICO *each* plaintiff must prove reliance, injury, and damages. Moreover, some undetermined number of plaintiffs' claims are time-barred. Rule 23 is not a one-way ratchet, empowering a judge to conform the law to the proof. We therefore reverse the order of the district court and decertify the class.

## BACKGROUND

Plaintiffs, a group of smokers allegedly deceived—by defendants' marketing and branding—into believing that "light" cigarettes ("Lights") were healthier than "full-flavored" cigarettes, sought and were granted class certification. *Schwab v. Philip Morris USA, Inc.* Plaintiffs' suit is brought under RICO, with mail and wire fraud as the necessary predicate acts. The gravamen of plaintiffs' complaint is that defendants' implicit representation that Lights were healthier led them to buy Lights in greater quantity than they otherwise would have and at an artificially high price, resulting in plaintiffs' overpayment for cigarettes. Plaintiffs allege claims arising from their purchase of Lights from 1971, when defendants first introduced Lights, until the date on which trial commences.

We pause in our narrative briefly to explain the history of Lights, as that history bears on plaintiffs' claims. In 1955, the Federal Trade Commission adopted the "Cigarette Advertising Guides," which proscribed "any implicit or explicit health claims in cigarette advertising except claims that a cigarette was 'low in nicotine or tars' provided it had 'been established by competent scientific proof that the claim was true, and if true, that such difference or differences were significant.'"

Several years later, in 1967, the FTC introduced the "Cambridge Filter Method" for calculating tar and nicotine yield. The Cambridge Filter Method, however, which relies upon a machine to test the tar and nicotine content of cigarettes, is quite unreliable. Most smokers who smoke Lights obtain just as much tar and nicotine as they would if they smoked full-flavored cigarettes, principally by "compensating"—that is, either by inhaling more smoke per cigarette (e.g., by covering ventilation holes, drawing more deeply with each puff, etc.) or by buying more cigarettes, neither of which a machine is capable of doing. Cigarette manufacturers have apparently been aware of this phenomenon for some time. But some smokers continued at least until 2000 to believe that Lights were healthier than full-flavored cigarettes. As the district court noted, citing a 1977 Brown & Williamson Internal Marketing Study, "almost all smokers agree that the primary reason for the increasing acceptance of Lights is based on the health reassurance they seem to offer."

In 2001, however, the National Cancer Institute published a report, "Monograph 13," that "reviewed evidence on the FTC method for measuring tar and nicotine yields and the disease risks of machine-measured low-tar cigarettes." The stated objective of the report was "to determine whether the evidence taken as a whole shows that the cumulative effect of engineering changes in cigarette design over the last 50 years has reduced disease risks in smokers." Monograph 13 discussed the introduction and marketing of low-yield cigarettes, the growing use of these cigarettes, and the practice of compensatory smoking. Ultimately, it concluded that there was "no convincing evidence that changes in cigarette design between 1950 and the mid-1980s have resulted in an important decrease in the disease burden caused by cigarette use either for smokers as a group or for the whole population." The publication of Monograph 13 sparked both this suit, filed in May 2004, and a parallel civil RICO action brought by the federal government.

Plaintiffs seek $800 billion in economic damages (trebled) stemming from their purchases of Lights. On September 25, 2006, the district court certified their proposed class of Lights smokers. On November 16, 2006, this court stayed the proceedings below and granted defendants leave to take an interlocutory appeal under Federal Rule of Civil Procedure 23(f). We now reverse the district court's class certification order and decertify the class.

## DISCUSSION

We review the district court's certification order for abuse of discretion. We will "exercise even greater deference when the district court has certified a class than when it has declined to do so." However, as we recently made clear, "a district judge may not certify a class without making a *ruling* that each Rule 23 requirement is met and all evidence must be assessed as with any other threshold issue," whether or not any such assessment also bears on the merits of the case.

## II.   CALCULATION OF DAMAGES

The district court concluded that plaintiffs could prove collective damages on a class-wide basis, and individual plaintiffs would then claim shares of this fund:

First, defendant's aggregate liability is determined in a single, class-wide adjudication and paid into a class fund. Second, "individual class members are afforded an opportunity to collect their individual shares," usually through a simplified proof of claim procedure. Third, any residue remaining after individual claims have been paid is distributed to the class' benefit under cy pres or other doctrines.

But such "fluid recovery" has been forbidden in this circuit since *Eisen v. Carlisle & Jacquelin* ("No 'fluid recovery' procedures are authorized by the text or by any reasonable interpretation of amended Rule 23"). And while the fact that damages may have to be ascertained on an individual basis is not, standing alone, sufficient to defeat class certification, it is nonetheless a factor that we must consider in deciding whether issues susceptible to generalized proof "outweigh" individual issues.

We reject plaintiffs' proposed distribution of any recovery they might receive because it offends both the Rules Enabling Act and the Due Process Clause. The distribution method at issue would involve an initial estimate of the percentage of class members who were defrauded (and who therefore have valid claims). The total amount of damages suffered would then be calculated based on this estimate (and, presumably, on an estimate of the average loss for each plaintiff). But such an aggregate determination is likely to result in an astronomical damages figure that does not accurately reflect the number of plaintiffs actually injured by defendants and that bears little or no relationship to the amount of economic harm actually caused by defendants. This kind of disconnect offends the Rules Enabling Act, which provides that federal rules of procedure, such as Rule 23, cannot be used to "abridge, enlarge, or modify any substantive right." 28 U.S.C. § 2072(b).

Roughly estimating the gross damages to the class as a whole and only subsequently allowing for the processing of individual claims would inevitably alter defendants' substantive right to pay damages reflective of their actual liability (rejecting a fluid recovery argument because "allowing gross damages by treating unsubstantiated claims of class members collectively significantly alters substantive rights," in violation of the Rules Enabling Act); *Eisen* ("Possible recoveries run into astronomical amount and generate more leverage and pressure on defendants to settle"); *Schwab* ("A question under the Rules Enabling Act is posed by the danger of overcompensation inherent in the plaintiff's fluid distribution plan. It is possible that some claimants will benefit from the plaintiff class' recovery despite the fact that they did not rely on defendants' alleged misrepresentations regarding 'light' cigarettes and were not, therefore, injured in their business or property by defendants' actions."). We disagree with the district court's conclusion that "the risk of overcompensation can be limited by requiring proof through claim forms from claimants concerning the extent of their reliance during the distribution stage." Given that any residue would be distributed to the class's benefit on the basis of cy pres principles rather than returned to defendants, defendants would still be paying the inflated total estimated amount of damages arrived at under the first step of the fluid recovery analysis. Thus, even if defendants were able to avoid overcompensating *individual* plaintiffs, they would still be overpaying in the aggregate.

Moreover, in this case, the district court determined that "evidence of the percentage of the class which was defrauded and the amount of economic damages it suffered appears to be quite weak." It further concluded that "determining]the impact of the fraud on the size of the market and its nature for damage purposes is a daunting enterprise even with the many proffered experts holding up their statistical lanterns to help in the search for the truth." Nevertheless, the district court believed that "the proof of acts of defendants and the various experts' opinions permit a finding of damages to the class with sufficient precision to allow a jury award." For the reasons stated above, we disagree, and we further note our skepticism that if statistical experts cannot with accuracy estimate the relevant figures, a jury could do so based on the testimony of those experts.

The district court's distribution scheme also raises serious due process concerns. As we explained in *Eisen,*

> if the 'class as a whole' is or can be substituted for the individual members of the class as claimants, then the number of claims filed is of no consequence and the amount found to be due will be enormous. Even if amended Rule 23 could be read so as to permit any such fantastic procedure, the courts would have to reject it as

an unconstitutional violation of the requirement of due process of law.

When fluid recovery is used to permit the mass aggregation of claims, the right of defendants to challenge the allegations of individual plaintiffs is lost, resulting in a due process violation. The Third Circuit properly observed in *Newton v. Merrill Lynch, Pierce, Fenner & Smith, Inc.* that "actual injury cannot be presumed, and defendants have the right to raise individual defenses against each class member." To be sure, this does not mean that defendants are "constitutionally entitled to compel a parade of individual plaintiffs to establish damages." However, when fluid recovery is used, as here, to mask the prevalence of individual issues, it is an impermissible affront to defendants' due process rights.

In sum, because we find that numerous issues in this case are not susceptible to generalized proof but would require a more individualized inquiry, we conclude that the predominance requirement of Rule 23 has not been satisfied. We recognize that a court may employ Rule 23(c)(4) to certify a class as to common issues that do exist, "regardless of whether the claim as a whole satisfies Rule 23(b)(3)'s predominance requirement." Nevertheless, in this case, given the number of questions that would remain for individual adjudication, issue certification would not "reduce the range of issues in dispute and promote judicial economy." Certifying, for example, the issue of defendants' scheme to defraud, would not materially advance the litigation because it would not dispose of larger issues such as reliance, injury, and damages. We therefore decline plaintiffs' request for issue certification.

## CONCLUSION

For the foregoing reasons, we reverse the judgment of the district court and order the class decertified.

# CHAPTER 12

## MASS TORT LIMITED ISSUES CLASSES AND MULTIPHASE TRIALS

∎ ∎ ∎

### A. LIMITED ISSUES CLASSES

#### GOOD V. AMERICAN WATER WORKS CO., INC.

United States District Court for the Southern District of West Virginia, 2015.
310 F.R.D. 274.

#### I.

##### A. *The Incident*

On January 9, 2014, approximately 300,000 residents in the Charleston and surrounding area are alleged to have suffered an interruption in their water supply. The interruption was caused by a spill into the Elk River of a coal processing chemical mixture sold and distributed exclusively by Eastman. The mixture was being stored in a facility owned and operated by Freedom Industries, Inc.

The chemical, 4-methylcyclohexane methanol, along with other chemicals, is commonly referred to as "Crude MCHM." Crude MCHM infiltrated WV American's water treatment plant in Charleston. Plaintiffs assert that both Eastman and the water company defendants could have prevented or avoided the incident by taking better precautionary measures, complying with applicable regulations, and using reasonable care.

The vast majority of the plaintiffs and putative class members are residents of dwellings whose water supply was interrupted, employees who lost wages during the Do Not Use order or businesses that lost revenue due to the interruption. All are alleged to have incurred costs for water replacement, travel, and other associated expenses.

##### B. The First Amended Consolidated Class Action Complaint

On December 9, 2014, the First Amended Consolidated Class Action Complaint became the operative pleading in the case. The operative pleading alleges the following:

Count One: Negligence against the defendants;

Count Two: Negligence as to the water company defendants specifically arising out of their failure to address the foreseeable risk posed by the Freedom Industries facility, the failure to adequately warn the class members, the failure to design, maintain, and operate the water treatment plant according to industry standards, negligently and unreasonably delivering and placing on plaintiffs' property the Crude MCHM, and failing to ensure that certain water tankers used to supply residents with replacement water were not filled with contaminated water;

Count Three: Negligence against Eastman for knowingly or negligently delivering its product to a facility without the capacity to safely store it, failing to properly warn of foreseeable risks, including in its MSDS sheets, failing to warn the putative class members of the adverse health effects of Crude MCHM, and failing to properly warn when putative class members were being exposed to Crude MCHM;

Count Seven: Gross negligence against the water company defendants for recklessly ignoring threats to class members both in design and maintenance of their operations, their warnings and attempts to deliver water. They also allege gross negligence against Eastman for failing to properly characterize the risk and provide proper warnings about Crude MCHM and recklessly and wantonly selling that waste product to a suspect facility located on a river bank in the middle of a highly populated area;

Count Eight: Prima facie negligence against the water company defendants for failing to adopt a source water protection plan;

Count Ten: Breach of warranties against the water company defendants inasmuch as they informed customers their water would be safe following flushing and charged their customers the regular rate for the impure water, in violation of the warranties that the water pass without objection in the water utility trade and that the water be suitable for the ordinary purposes for which tap water is commonly used;

Count Eleven: Negligent infliction of emotional distress against the water company defendants arising out of, *inter alia,* their failure to establish an alternative water supply, which failure caused affected individuals to reasonably fear harmful effects from the contaminated water. They also allege negligent infliction of emotional distress against Eastman for failing to warn the putative class members of the health risks presented by Crude MCHM despite the fact that Eastman knew the substance could foreseeably come in contact with human receptors;

Count Twelve: Strict products liability against the water company defendants for failure to warn concerning the contamination until hours after it occurred and for providing incorrect information that it was safe to drink the water when Crude MCHM was at one part per million;

Count Thirteen: Strict products liability against Eastman for, marketing, packaging, selling and distributing unreasonably dangerous and defective Crude MCHM to Freedom Industries, when Eastman knew or should have known of its adverse health effects and risk of harm and failing to adequately warn about the substance, such as using proper practices in its storage and handling and providing adequate Material Safety Data Sheet (MSDS) information concerning it;

Count Fourteen: Strict liability against Eastman for conducting an ultra-hazardous activity by manufacturing and then distributing Crude MCHM to an ill-equipped facility in close proximity to the Elk River and WV American's intake;

Count Fifteen: Public nuisance as to the water company defendants and Eastman;

Count Seventeen: Trespass as to the water company defendants and Eastman;

Count Eighteen: Breach of contract as to the water company defendants and Eastman;

Count Nineteen: Medical monitoring as to the water company defendants and Eastman.

Count Twenty-one: Violation by Eastman of the Toxic Substance Control Act for failing to disclose to government agencies certain information concerning Crude MCHM.

C.   The Certification Requests

In their July 6, 2015 motion to certify, plaintiffs identify the following issues for collective determination:

(1)  certifying this action to be maintained as a class action with respect to particular issues pursuant to Federal Rule of Civil Procedure 23(c)(4), with respect to the overarching common issues of whether Defendants are liable and whether exemplary damages should be awarded as a multiplier of compensatory damages; and

(2)  certifying a single Class of affected businesses and West Virginia American Water customers pursuant to Federal Rule of Civil Procedure 23(b)(3), to adjudicate the issue of damages suffered by the Class resulting from the loss of use of tap water during the period of the "Do Not Use" (DNU) order.

The plaintiffs seek class certification for issues of liability and exemplary damages under Rule 23(c)(4) and for damages to affected residents and businesses under Rule 23(b)(3).

## III.

### B.   Class Certification

2.   *The Proposed Rule 23(c)(4) Liability Issues Class Consisting of Fault, Comparative Fault, and Punitive Damages*

Plaintiffs crystallize the factual underpinnings for the fault portion of their Rule 23(c)(4) liability issue certification (fault issue) as follows:

> Defendants could have prevented or avoided the crisis with better precautionary measures, compliance with applicable regulations, and the use of reasonable care. Specifically, among other things, Eastman failed to avoid the foreseeable harm posed by Crude MCHM by commercializing a waste product and selling it to Freedom Industries without appropriate oversight, reasonable instructions, or warnings, including that Crude MCHM should be stored in non-corrosive, stainless steel tanks. Moreover, both Eastman and WVAW failed to guard against the risk presented by Freedom Industries' facility just upstream from the Charleston area's sole water source. In flagrant violation of industry standards, WVAW was completely unprepared for a spill affecting its sole source of supply and lacked sufficient water reserves to withstand a shutdown of its sole intake for any length of time. WVAW should have determined what chemicals were stored or processed at the site, assessed and planned for the risk they presented to the water supply, maintained sufficient water reserves at all times, and secured an alternate water supply to use in the event of foreseeable emergency.

Plaintiffs also mention certification of the issue of comparative fault. It appears this proposed issue is more aptly characterized as apportionment of fault as to Freedom, as opposed to defendants, respecting liability for the events leading to the Do Not Use order. Plaintiffs also appear to seek certification to determine the issue of impracticability, which is an affirmative defense by the water company defendants to plaintiffs' claim for breach of contract. These apparent requests are consolidated under the heading of "comparative fault issue."

The third component of the proposed liability certification is as follows: "The request for certification as to liability issues under Rule 23(c)(4) includes determining whether exemplary damages   should be imposed." ("Here, the particular common issues of liability, comparative fault, and the ratio of punitive damages to actual harm are common to all claimants in the litigation as a whole, no matter what type of injury was suffered.").

It is unnecessary to undertake the Rule 23 analysis respecting the proposed class punitive damages multiplier. In response to the defendants' substantial, joint attack on the proposal, plaintiffs' two-page reply cites but two unpublished district court cases, presenting dissimilar circumstances. Plaintiffs have failed to explain with supporting legal authority, how they overcome the challenge that their proposal violates due process inasmuch as it would prevent the jury, and then the court, from determining whether compensatory and punitive damages bear a reasonable relationship to one another. The court accordingly declines the plaintiffs' request to include the punitive damages issue as a component of class certification.

The court examines satisfaction of the Rule 23(c)(4) and 23(b)(3) analysis surrounding the proposed issue certification.

### b. The Rule 23(c)(4) Analysis

Our court of appeals has noted that the Rule 23(a), (b) and (c) analysis need not be conducted sequentially ("In sum, in its two most recent class action decisions, *Ortiz* and *Amchem*, the Supreme Court eschewed the dissent's suggested approach of reading each of Rule 23's provisions sequentially."). The court thus turns to analysis of the proposed liability issues of fault and comparative fault under Rule 23(c)(4).

Consistent with the text of Rule 23(c)(4), one commentator recently observed as follows: "Although traditional claims brought under Rule 23(b) involve 'an all-or-nothing decision to aggregate individual cases,' Federal Rule of Civil Procedure 23(c)(4) allows litigants to resolve *specific issues* in a case on a class-wide basis."

There is no impediment to certifying particular issues in a case as opposed to entire claims or defenses. That is the very approach urged by the authoritative MANUAL FOR COMPLEX LITIGATION:

> Rule 23(c)(4)(A) permits a class to be certified for *specific issues or elements of claims* raised in the litigation. This provision may enable a court to achieve the economies for a portion of a case, the rest of which may either not qualify under Rule 23(a). Certification of an issues class is appropriate only if it permits fair presentation of the claims and defenses and materially advances the disposition of the litigation as a whole.

> An issues-class approach contemplates a bifurcated trial where the common issues are tried first, followed by individual trials on questions such as proximate causation and damages. A bifurcated trial must adequately present to the jury applicable defenses and be solely a class trial on liability.

If otherwise compliant with Rule 23, the proposed liability issue certifications provide an orderly means to resolve some of the central issues in the case. That is an approach that is encouraged by our court of appeals.

*See In re A.H. Robins* (noting the need to "take full advantage of the provision in Rule 23(c)(4) permitting class treatment of separate issues to reduce the range of disputed issues" in complex litigation).

The court thus concludes that the proposed liability issue certification is appropriate under Rule 23(c)(4).

### c. The Rule 23(b)(3) Analysis

As noted by our court of appeals, "Rule 23(b)(3) has two components: predominance and superiority."

At its heart, the "predominance inquiry tests whether proposed classes are sufficiently cohesive to warrant adjudication by representation." *Amchem Prods., Inc. v. Windsor.* In other words, to satisfy Rule 23(b)(3), "common questions must predominate over any questions affecting only individual members; such that a class action would achieve economies of time, effort, and expense, and promote uniformity of decision as to persons similarly situated."

A principle often forgotten is that the balancing test of common and individual issues is qualitative, not quantitative. Common liability issues may still predominate even when individualized inquiry is required in other areas. At bottom, the inquiry requires a district court to balance common questions among class members with any dissimilarities between class members.

While courts have denied certification when individual damage issues are especially complex or burdensome, where the qualitatively overarching issue by far is the liability issue of the defendant's willfulness, and the purported class members were exposed to the same risk of harm every time, such as where a defendant violates a statute in the identical manner on every occasion, individual damages issues are insufficient to defeat class certification under Rule 23(b)(3). The same principle would apply here to the alleged liability in negligence.

Turning to analysis of the first and second Rule 23(b)(3) factors, there is apparently little interest among the putative class of a quarter million members in controlling and pursuing litigation on their own. There have been less than 100 cases filed to date respecting the chemical leak cases. Additionally, all of the cases surrounding the chemical leak are presently centered in this forum. It is obviously desirable to keep them in place to the extent feasible.

Finally, there will undoubtedly be management issues that arise in the event the two liability issues are certified. It is difficult to imagine those management concerns approaching some that have been encountered in other certified mass tort contexts. The court is confident that those matters will be addressed in due course as they arise. In making that observation, the court is cognizant of the inefficient, costly and time consuming alternative. Absent the proposed liability issues certification, the issue of fault, for one, would have to be tried seriatim in every case for which a jury is empanelled. That consideration alone tips the balance heavily toward the limited issue certification sought by plaintiffs. ("Proving these issues in individual trials would require enormous redundancy of effort, including duplicative discovery, testimony by the same witnesses in potentially hundreds of actions, and relitigation of many similar, and even identical, legal issues.").

Additionally, absence of the class device would surely discourage potentially deserving plaintiffs from pursuing their rights under the circumstances here presented. That is another factor influencing the outcome sought by plaintiffs. *See Gunnells* (noting in that case that "class certification will provide access to the courts for those with claims that would be uneconomical if brought in an individual action. As the Supreme Court put the matter, 'the policy at the very core of the class action mechanism is to overcome the problem that small recoveries do not provide the incentive for any individual to bring a solo action prosecuting his or her rights.'" (quoting *Amchem*).

Surely, the plaintiffs thus receive a benefit from the proposed issues certification. But so, too, do the defendants. As our court of appeals has noted, the focus of Rule 23(b)(3) in the mass tort context is to "ensure that class certification in such cases 'achieve economies of time, effort, and expense, and promote uniformity of decision as to persons similarly situated, without sacrificing procedural fairness or bringing about other undesirable results.'" (quoting *Amchem Products*). As in *Gunnells*, defendants benefit from procedural fairness by certification:

> Furthermore, class certification "provides a single proceeding in which to determine the merits of the plaintiffs' claims, and therefore protects the defendant from inconsistent adjudications." This protection from inconsistent adjudications derives from the fact that the class action is binding on all class members. By contrast, proceeding with individual claims makes the defendant vulnerable to the asymmetry of collateral estoppel: If TPCM lost on a claim to an individual plaintiff, subsequent plaintiffs could use offensive collateral estoppel to prevent TPCM from litigating the issue. A victory by TPCM in an action by an individual plaintiff, however, would have no binding effect on future plaintiffs because the plaintiffs would not have been party to the original suit. Class certification thus promotes consistency of results, giving defendants the benefit of finality and repose.

There are thus many considerations supporting plaintiffs' proposed issues certification. Nevertheless, defendants offer a number of contentions designed to upend the certification request.

First, defendants assert that the law requires a cause of action *as a whole* be factored into analysis of the predominance requirement of Rule 23(b)(3), as opposed to simply considering that requirement after the court isolates a potentially class-worthy issue under Rule 23(c)(4). The argument is based upon the decision of the United States Court of Appeals for the Fifth Circuit in *Castano v. American Tobacco Co.* and, assertedly, our court of appeals' decision in *Gunnells*.

The issue raised by defendants is one of the primary concerns surrounding the application of Rule 23(c)(4) in the mass tort setting, as noted by one of the leading commentators on the class action device:

> Rule 23(c)(4) is controversial because it could be seen as undermining the requirement of Rule 23(b)(3) that for a class to be certified, "the questions of law or fact common to class members must predominate over any questions affecting only individual members."

The weight of authority, however, runs counter to the defendants and *Castano*. *See, e.g., Valentino v. Carter-Wallace, Inc.* One commentator so observes:

> Although it is clear that plaintiffs seeking issue class certification must establish the four components of Rule 23(a), there is less certainty as to what they must establish under Rule 23(b). Moreover, courts have issued varying opinions in this regard. For the most part, appellate courts have agreed that the issue class can proceed under Rule 23(c)(4) even where the predominance requirement of Rule 23(b) has not been satisfied.

Another leading Rule 23 commentator has noted likewise that "most federal courts of appeal hold that a class action may be maintained with respect to a particular issue regardless of whether the claim as a whole satisfies the requirement that common questions of law or fact predominate over questions affecting only individual members." The defendants' contention is thus not meritorious.

Second, defendants assert a contention running through much of their briefing, namely, that the limited liability issues certification is swamped by the individualized issues left to be determined in the wake, such as causation, damages and punitive damages to name a few. The court is not required under Rule 23, however, to sacrifice class adjudication of a driving issue in the case simply because many individualized inquiries will remain thereafter. That is the case here.

Next, the water company defendants alone assert that inasmuch as causation and damages are essential elements of liability for breach of contract and are individualized in nature, the issue of breach is not susceptible to issue certification. As the water company defendants concede, the breach of contract claim they urge as pled by plaintiffs has in actuality been characterized by plaintiffs, with support in the court's memorandum opinion and order on the water company defendants' motion to dismiss, as an affirmative defense upon which the water company defendants have the burden of proof. It thus raises no concerns respecting individualized determination.

## III.

It is ordered as follows: That plaintiffs' motion for class certification be, and hereby is, granted respecting the fault and comparative fault issues set forth and denied in all further respects.

## B.  MULTIPHASE TRIAL PLANS AND SUBCLASSING

### HILAO V. ESTATE OF MARCOS

United States Court of Appeals for the Ninth Circuit, 1996.
103 F.3d 767.

The Estate of Ferdinand E. Marcos appeals from a final judgment entered against it in a class-action suit after a trifurcated jury trial on the damage claims brought by a class of Philippine nationals who were victims of torture, disappearance, or summary execution under the regime of Ferdinand E. Marcos. We have jurisdiction over the appeal and we affirm.

### FACTUAL BACKGROUND

This case arises from human-rights abuses—specifically, torture, summary execution, and "disappearance"—committed by the Philippine military and paramilitary forces under the command of Ferdinand E. Marcos during his nearly 14-year rule of the Philippines.

### PROCEDURAL HISTORY

Shortly after Marcos arrived in the United States in 1986 after fleeing the Philippines, he was served with complaints by a number of parties seeking damages for human-rights abuses committed against them or their decedents. District courts in Hawaii and California dismissed the complaints on the grounds that the "act of state" doctrine rendered the cases non-justiciable. This court reversed in consolidated appeals. The Judicial Panel on Multidistrict Litigation consolidated the various actions in the District of Hawaii.

In 1991, the district court certified the Hilao case as a class action, defining the class as all civilian citizens of the Philippines who, between 1972 and 1986, were tortured, summarily executed, or disappeared by Philippine military or paramilitary groups; the class also included the survivors of deceased class members. Certain plaintiffs opted out of the class and continued, alongside the class action, to pursue their cases directly.

A default judgment was entered in 1991 against Marcos' daughter, Imee Marcos-Manotoc, upon one of the direct plaintiffs' complaints. That judgment was appealed to this court, which affirmed the district court in 1992, rejecting arguments that Marcos-Manotoc was entitled to foreign sovereign immunity and that the district court lacked jurisdiction under the Alien Tort Claims Act and under Article III of the U.S. Constitution. Marcos died during the pendency of the actions, and his wife Imelda Marcos and son Ferdinand R. Marcos, as his legal representatives, were substituted as defendants.

In November 1991, the district court issued a preliminary injunction that prohibited the Estate from transferring, dissipating, or encumbering any of its assets. The Estate appealed from the preliminary injunction, and this court affirmed, rejecting arguments on foreign sovereign immunity, on abatement of the action upon the death of Marcos, on the district court's lack of authority to enter the injunction, and on subject-matter jurisdiction and cause of action under the Alien Tort Claims Act.

The district court ordered issues of liability and damages tried separately. In September 1992, a jury trial was held on liability; after three days of deliberation, the jury reached verdicts against the Estate and for the class and for 22 direct plaintiffs and a verdict for the Estate and against one direct plaintiff. Judgment was entered and the preliminary injunction modified to take account of the verdict.

The district court then ordered the damage trial bifurcated into one trial on exemplary damages and one on compensatory damages. The court ordered that notice be given to the class members that they must file a proof-of-claim form in order to opt into the class. Notice was provided by mail to known claimants and by publication in the Philippines and the U.S.; over 10,000 forms were filed.

In February 1994, the same jury that had heard the liability phase of the trial considered whether to award exemplary damages. After two days of evidence and deliberations, the jury returned a verdict against the Estate in the amount of $1.2 billion.

The court appointed a special master to supervise proceedings related to the compensatory-damage phase of the trial in connection with the class. In January 1995, the jury reconvened a third time to consider compensatory damages. The compensatory-damage phase of the trial is explained in greater detail below. After seven days of trial and deliberation, the jury returned a compensatory-damage award for the class of over $766 million; after two further days of trial and deliberation, the jury returned compensatory-damage awards in favor of the direct plaintiffs.

On February 3, 1995, the district court entered final judgment in the class action suit. The Estate appeals from this judgment.

### B.   Instructions and Procedure

The Estate argues that even if exemplary damages are available against a deceased's estate, the district court violated its rights under the Due Process Clause by holding the exemplary-damage phase of the trial before the compensatory-damage phase and by not instructing the jury that an exemplary-damage award must bear a relationship to compensatory damages.

### 1.   Due Process Claims

The Estate claims that the sequence in which the district court held the damage phases of the trial violated its right to due process. We review *de novo* a claim of a violation of the Due Process Clause. In its most recent discussion of punitive damages, the Supreme Court wrote that "only when an award can fairly be categorized as 'grossly excessive' in relation to a State's legitimate] interests in punishing unlawful conduct and deterring its repetition does it enter the zone of arbitrariness that violates the Due Process Clause." *BMW of North America, Inc. v. Gore. See also TXO Production Corp. v. Alliance Resources Corp.* The *BMW* Court identified three "guideposts" for measuring gross excessiveness: "the degree of reprehensibility of defendant's conduct; the disparity between the harm or potential harm suffered by the plaintiff and his punitive damages award; and the difference between this remedy and the civil penalties authorized or imposed in comparable cases."

The Estate's argument appears to challenge the district court's procedure and instructions as deficient with respect to the second *BMW* "guidepost". The Court's discussion of this issue, however, offers little support to the Estate's argument. The Court noted the "long pedigree" of "the principle that exemplary damages must bear a 'reasonable relationship' to compensatory damages." The Court also pointed out that it had "refined this analysis in *TXO* by confirming that the proper inquiry is " 'whether there is a reasonable relationship between the punitive damages award and *the harm likely to result* from the defendant's conduct as well as the harm that actually has occurred.' " Finally, the Court reiterated its previous caution that a categorical approach to this question must be rejected: "We cannot draw a mathematical bright line between the constitutionally acceptable and the constitutionally unacceptable that would fit every case."

Thus, the Court has not required, as the Estate would have it, that punitive damages be calculated on the basis of the amount of a previous award of compensatory damages. The fact that the excessiveness of a punitive-damage award is to be measured in part by the reasonableness of the relationship between the award and "*the harm likely to result* from the defendant's conduct as well as the harm that actually has occurred" undercuts the Estate's argument that a punitive-damage award *must* in all cases be determined after an award of compensatory damages, since compensatory damages will not include any recovery for harm that was likely to have occurred but did not actually occur. The departure from the usual sequence in this case did not violate the Estate's due-process rights. Certainly the Estate has no persuasive argument that the actual amount of exemplary damages awarded, $1.2 billion, was grossly excessive, given the eventual award of over $750 million in compensatory damages for the human-rights abuses inflicted on the nearly 10,000 class members.

The Estate also appears to argue that the district court's instructions on exemplary damages were erroneous because they granted the jury unrestrained discretion in arriving at its award. While the Supreme Court has indeed suggested that "unlimited" jury discretion in the determination of punitive damages might violate the Due Process Clause, these instructions did not grant the jury unrestrained discretion in its exemplary-damage determination.

The instructions in this case, like those in *Haslip,* "gave the jury significant discretion in its determination of punitive damages, but that discretion was not unlimited." The *Haslip* Court found that the instructions given in that case "enlightened the jury as to the punitive damages' nature and purpose, identified the damages as punishment for civil wrongdoing of the kind involved, and explained that their imposition was not compulsory." The district court's instructions here provided the same information to the jury. Indeed, while the Estate complains that its rights were violated because the jury was not instructed that a reasonable relationship must exist between the amounts of compensatory and exemplary damages, the actual instructions approved by the Supreme Court in *Haslip* contained no such explanation. The district court's instructions did not leave the jury with the unrestrained discretion that might violate the Due Process Clause.

### 2.   *Trifurcation*

A trial court's decision to bifurcate—or, in this case, trifurcate—a trial is reviewed for an abuse of discretion. In the absence of any constitutional problems with the district court's decision to hold the exemplary-damage phase of the trial prior to the compensatory-damage phase, the district court did not abuse its discretion by the sequence in which it conducted the proceedings below. The compensatory-damage phase presented much more complex questions, requiring the presentation of testimony taken in the Philippines before a special master, than did the exemplary-damage phase, which was closely related to the evidence in the liability phase. In addition, of course, the district court retained the authority, until the entry of judgment, to review and require a remittitur of the exemplary-damage award if the award was, in its view, excessive. Indeed, the procedure followed by the district court is not unprecedented in class-action suits. *See Jenkins v. Raymark Industries, Inc.* (affirming plan for trial on punitive damages before actual damages in class-action suit; noting that since punitive damages are intended to create deterrence and protect public interest, focus is on defendant's conduct, and while Texas law bars a punitive-damage award to a plaintiff who does not receive a compensatory award, "the allocation need not be made concurrently with an evaluation of the defendant's conduct" and "the relative timing of these assessments is not critical"). Thus, the order in which the stages of the trial proceeded was not an abuse of the district court's discretion.

## CONCLUSION

The district court had jurisdiction over Hilao's cause of action. Hilao's claims were neither barred by the statute of limitations nor abated by Marcos' death. The district court did not abuse its discretion in certifying the class. The challenged evidentiary rulings of the district court were not in error. The district court properly held Marcos liable for human rights abuses which occurred and which he knew about and failed to use his power to prevent. The jury instructions on the Torture Victim Protection Act and on proximate cause were not erroneous. The award of exemplary damages against the Estate was allowed under Philippine law and the Estate's due-process rights were not violated in either the determination of those damages or of compensatory damages. The judgment of the district court is therefore

Affirmed.

## IN RE WHIRLPOOL CORP. FRONT-LOADING WASHER PRODS. LIAB. LITIG.

United States Court of Appeals for the Sixth Circuit, 2013.
722 F.3d 838.

Gina Glazer and Trina Allison filed a class action lawsuit on behalf of Ohio consumers against Whirlpool Corporation alleging that design defects in Whirlpool's Duet®, Duet HT®, Duet Sport®, and Duet Sport HT® front-loading washing machines (the Duets) allow mold and mildew to grow in the machines, leading to ruined laundry and malodorous homes. This suit and similar suits filed against Whirlpool in other jurisdictions are consolidated in multi-district litigation managed by the district court in the Northern District of Ohio.

The district court certified a liability class under Federal Rules of Civil Procedure 23(a) and (b)(3) comprised of current Ohio residents who purchased one of the specified Duets in Ohio primarily for personal, family, or household purposes and not for resale, and who bring legal claims for tortious breach of warranty, negligent design, and negligent failure to warn. Proof of damages is reserved for individual determination. We granted Whirlpool's request to pursue an interlocutory appeal of the class certification decision, and we affirmed the district court's opinion and order. We denied Whirlpool's petition for rehearing by the panel and for rehearing en banc. Whirlpool filed a petition for a writ of certiorari.

The Supreme Court granted Whirlpool's petition, vacated our prior judgment, and remanded the case to this court for further consideration in light of *Comcast Corp. v. Behrend*. After reconsideration, we affirm the order of the district court certifying a liability class.

## II. FACTS

The named plaintiffs, Gina Glazer and Trina Allison, are Ohio residents. Whirlpool is a Delaware corporation with its principal place of business in Michigan.

Whirlpool began manufacturing Duets in 2002. The plaintiffs' causes of action rest on the central allegation that all of the Duets share a common design defect—the machines fail to clean properly their own mechanical components to eliminate soil and residue deposits known as "biofilm." The development of biofilm on mechanical parts in turn can lead to rapid growth of mold, mildew, and bacteria in places inside the machines that consumers cannot clean themselves.

Allison purchased a Whirlpool Duet HT® washing machine in 2005 and Glazer bought a Duet Sport® washing machine in 2006. Allison used high efficiency (HE) detergent in her washing machine, while Glazer used a reduced amount of regular detergent. Within six to eight months after their purchases, both plaintiffs noticed the smell of mold or mildew emanating from the machines and from laundry washed in the machines. Allison found mold growing on the sides of the detergent dispenser, and Glazer noticed mold growing on the rubber door seal. Although both plaintiffs allowed the machine doors to stand open as much as possible and also used ordinary household products to clean the parts of the machines they could reach, their efforts achieved only temporary relief from the pungent odors.

Allison contacted Whirlpool about the mold she found growing in the Duet. A company representative instructed her to use the washer's monthly cleaning cycle, add an Affresh™ tablet to the cleaning cycle, and manually clean under the rubber door seal. Allison followed this advice, but the problem persisted. She then contacted a service technician who examined the Duet. He could only advise Allison to leave the door open between laundry cycles to allow the machine to air-dry. Glazer also complained to Whirlpool about mold growing in the Duet she purchased. A company representative advised her to switch from regular detergent to HE detergent and Glazer did so. She did not, however, utilize the Duet's cleaning cycle as recommended in Whirlpool's Use and Care Guide.

Both plaintiffs continued to experience mold growth in the Duets. Neither of them knew at the time of purchase that a Duet could develop mold or mildew inside the machine. If Whirlpool had disclosed this information, plaintiffs allege they would have made different purchasing decisions.

According to the evidence presented in support of the motion for class certification, the Duet® and Duet HT® front-loading washing machines are built on the "Access" platform, sharing nearly identical engineering. Although a few functions vary across the Duet models built on the "Access" platform, most model differences are aesthetic. The smaller-capacity Duet Sport® and Duet Sport HT® front-loading washing machines are built on the "Horizon" platform. With a few differences in function or styling, all Duet models built on the "Horizon" engineering platform are nearly identical. In addition, the "Access" and "Horizon" engineering platforms are also nearly identical to each other. The only two differences are that the "Access" platform is slightly larger than the "Horizon" and the "Access" platform is tilted a few degrees from the horizontal axis, while the "Horizon" platform is not. Front-loading machines are designed for use with HE detergent.

While all washing machines can potentially develop some mold or mildew after a period of use, front-loading machines promote mold or mildew more readily because of the lower water levels used and the higher moisture content within the machines, combined with reduced ventilation. Plaintiffs' expert witnesses, Dr. R. Gary Wilson, Whirlpool's former Director of Laundry Technology from 1976 to 1999, and Dr. Chin S. Yang, a microbiologist, opine that the common design defect in the Duets is their failure to clean or rinse their own components to remove soil residues on which fungi and bacteria feed, producing offensive odors. Dr. Wilson emphasized that the Duets fail to self-clean the back of the tub holding the clothes basket, the aluminum bracket used to attach the clothes basket to the tub, the sump area, the pump strainer and drain hose, the door gasket area, the air vent duct, and the detergent dispenser duct.

Plaintiffs' evidence confirms that Whirlpool knew the designs of its "Access" and "Horizon" platforms contributed to residue buildup resulting in rapid fungal and bacterial growth. As early as September 2003, consumers began complaining to Whirlpool about the mold problem at the rate of two to three calls per day. When company representatives instructed the consumers to lift up the rubber door gaskets on their machines, common findings were deposits of water, detergent, and fabric softener, with concomitant growth of mold or mildew. Service technicians who examined consumers' Duets confirmed the existence of residue deposits and mold growing inside the machines. Whirlpool received complaints from numerous consumers who reported breathing difficulties after repair technicians scrubbed the Duets in their homes, releasing mold spores into the air.

In 2004 Whirlpool formed an internal team to analyze the mold problem and formulate a plan. In gathering information about the consumer complaints, Whirlpool engineers learned that both the "Access" and "Horizon" platforms were involved and the mold problem was not restricted to certain models or certain markets. Whirlpool's team also discovered that mold growth could occur before the Duets were two to four years old, that traditional household cleaners were not effective treatments, and that consumer laundry habits, including use of non-HE detergent, might exacerbate mold growth but did not cause it.

In a memorandum directed to other team members dated June 24, 2004, Anthony Hardaway, Whirlpool's Lead Engineer, Advance Chemistry Technology, wrote that mold growth in the Duets "occurs under all/any common laundry conditions" and "data to date show consumer habits are of little help since mold (always present) flourished under all conditions seen in the Access platform." Hardaway further stated: "As both a biologist and a chemist this problem is very troubling in that we are fooling ourselves if we think that we can eliminate mold and bacteria when our HA wash platforms are the ideal environment for molds and bacteria to flourish. Perhaps we should shift our focus to 'handling'/'controlling' mold and bacterial levels in our products."

In public statements about mold complaints, Whirlpool adopted the term "biofilm" to avoid alarming consumers with words like "mold," "mildew," "fungi," and "bacteria." Although Whirlpool contemplated issuing a warning to consumers about the mold problem, plaintiffs' expert evidence indicates Whirlpool failed to warn the public adequately about the potential for mold growth in the Duets.

Later in 2004, Hardaway and other members of the Whirlpool team discussed redesign of the tub used on the "Horizon" platform because pooling of soil and water served as a nucleation site for mold and bacteria growth. They determined that the "Access" platform's webbed tub structure was extremely prone to water and soil deposits, and the aluminum basket cross-bar was highly susceptible to corrosion because of biofilm. A number of design factors contributed to this corrosion, including insufficient draining of water at the end of a wash cycle and water flowing backward through the non-return valve between the tub and the drain pump. Laboratory analyses confirmed that the composition of biofilm found in Duets built on the "Horizon" and "Access" platforms was identical. In light of these findings, Whirlpool made certain design changes to later generations of Duets.

By 2005, Whirlpool began manufacturing Duets with a special cycle intended to clean the internal parts of the machine. Engineers knew, however, that the new cleaning cycle would not remove all residue deposits. They were concerned that the cleaning cycle might not be effective to control mold growth and that consumers' use of bleach in the cleaning cycle—as recommended by Whirlpool in its consumer Use and Care Guides—would increase corrosion of aluminum machine parts. Internal

Whirlpool documents acknowledged by this time that the available data indicated 35% of Duet customers had complained about odor in the Duets and that complaints continued to increase in all markets.

By March 2006 Whirlpool engineers recognized that consumers might notice black mold growing on the bellows or inside the detergent dispenser, and that laundry would smell musty if a Duet was "heavily infected." By late 2006, Whirlpool had received over 1.3 million complaint calls at its customer care centers and had completed thousands of service calls nationwide.

Faced with increasing complaints about mold growth in Duets and fully aware that other brands were not immune from similar problems, Whirlpool decided to formulate new cleaning products for all front-loading washing machines, regardless of make or model. The company expected this "revolutionary" product to produce a new revenue stream of $50 million to $195 million based on the assumption that 50% percent of the 14 million front-loading washing machine owners of any brand might be looking for a solution to an odor problem with their machines.

In September 2007 Whirlpool introduced two new cleaning products to the retail market: Affresh™ tablets for front-loading washing machines in use from zero to twelve months, and Affresh™ tablets with six door seal cleaning cloths for front-loading washing machines in use more than twelve months. To encourage sales of these products, Whirlpool marketed Affresh™ as "THE solution to odor causing residue in HE washers." The company placed samples of Affresh™ in all new HE washing machines that it manufactured and changed its Use and Care Guides to advise consumers to use an Affresh™ tablet in the first cleaning cycle to remove manufacturing oil and grease. Whirlpool believed this advice would encourage consumers to use the cleaning cycle and Affresh™ tablets regularly—like teaching vehicle owners to change the oil in their cars periodically. Whirlpool instructed its service technicians and call centers to recommend the use of Affresh™ to consumers. But as plaintiff Allison learned from experience, even using Affresh™ tablets in the Duet's special cleaning cycle did not cure the mold problem.

Whirlpool shipped 121,033 "Access" platform Duet washing machines to Ohio from 2002 through March 2009. The company shipped 41,904 "Horizon" platform Duet Sport washing machines to Ohio during the period 2006 through March 2009.

In opposing the motion for class certification, Whirlpool asserted that most Duet owners have not experienced mold growth in their washing machines and that the incidence of mold growth in the Duets is actually quite rare. As a result, consumers who have not experienced the mold problem cannot prove injury to establish Whirlpool's tort liability under Ohio law. The company also contended that class certification was inappropriate because the Duets were built on different platforms, representing twenty-one different models over a period of nine model years. According to Whirlpool, the plaintiffs must prove liability as to each separate model—a task that would defeat the class action prerequisites of commonality, predominance, and superiority. Whirlpool also emphasized that consumers' laundry habits and experiences with the Duets are so diverse that the named plaintiffs are not typical of the class; hence, they may not serve as class representatives. In support of these positions, Whirlpool presented deposition excerpts, affidavits from employees and satisfied Duet owners, expert reports, internal company documents, photographs, copies of Use and Care Guides, and various articles from Consumer Reports. Although Whirlpool requested and was granted permission to present live testimony at the class action certification hearing, the company ultimately did not present any testimony at the hearing.

After assimilating the extensive factual record and the parties' oral arguments on the motion to certify a class, the district court determined that the Rule 23(a) and (b)(3) prerequisites were met as to all issues of liability on plaintiffs' claims for tortious breach of warranty, negligent design, and negligent failure to warn. The court certified the following liability class:

> All persons who are current residents of Ohio and purchased a Washing Machine (defined as Whirlpool Duet®, Duet HT®, and Duet Sport® Front-Loading Automatic Washers) for primarily personal, family or household purposes, and not for resale, in Ohio, excluding (1) Whirlpool, any entity in which Whirlpool has a controlling interest, and its legal representatives, officers, directors, employees, assigns, and successors; (2) Washing Machines purchased through Whirlpool's Employee Purchase Program; (3) the Judge to whom this case is assigned, any member of the Judge's staff, and any member of the Judge's immediate family; (4) persons or entities who distribute or resell the Washing Machines; (5) government entities; and (6) claims for personal injury, wrongful death, and/or emotional distress.

Whirlpool promptly appealed the district court's order certifying the liability class.

### III. ANALYSIS

#### 4. *The Rule 23(b)(3) Prerequisites: Predominance and Superiority*

This brings us to the plaintiffs' showing on the Rule 23(b)(3) requirements of predominance and superiority. The analyses in many of the cases discussed above confirm the presence of predominance and superiority in this case, but two recent governing Supreme Court cases on predominance and superiority seal our conviction that this is so: *Amgen*

*Inc. v. Connecticut Retirement Plans & Trust Funds* and *Comcast Corp. v. Behrend.*

In *Amgen,* the Supreme Court affirmed certification of a class in a securities fraud case brought under § 10(b) and Rule 10b–5 premised on the fraud-on-the-market theory of liability. Amgen did not dispute that Connecticut Retirement met all four of the class action prerequisites of Rule 23(a); the case focused on the Rule 23(b)(3) predominance inquiry. Amgen contended that, to demonstrate predominance and insure class certification, Connecticut Retirement was required to prove, not plausibly plead, a central element of its case: the materiality of Amgen's alleged misrepresentations or omissions. The Supreme Court responded to Amgen's position with this holding:

> While Connecticut Retirement certainly must prove materiality to prevail on the merits, we hold that such proof is not a prerequisite to class certification. Rule 23(b)(3) requires a showing that *questions* common to the class predominate, not that those questions will be answered, on the merits, in favor of the class. Because materiality is judged according to an objective standard, the materiality of Amgen's alleged misrepresentations and omissions is a question common to all members of the class Connecticut Retirement would represent.

The Court repeatedly emphasized that the predominance inquiry must focus on common questions that can be proved through evidence common to the class. A plaintiff class need not prove that each element of a claim can be established by classwide proof: "What the rule does require is that common questions *'predominate* over any questions affecting only individual class members.'"

The Court further explained in *Amgen* that an inability of the plaintiff class "to prove materiality would not result in individual questions predominating. Instead, a failure of proof on the issue of materiality would end the case, given that materiality is an essential element of the class members' securities-fraud claims." The plaintiff class before the Court was "entirely cohesive: It will prevail or fail in unison. In no event will the individual circumstances of particular class members bear on the inquiry." For this reason, the Court rejected Amgen's contention that, under Rule 23(b)(3), "Connecticut Retirement must first establish that it will win the fray. The office of a Rule 23(b)(3) certification ruling is not to adjudicate the case; rather, it is to select the 'method' best suited to adjudication of the controversy 'fairly and efficiently.'" Class adjudication in these circumstances is more efficient, the Court also explained, because it avoids a "mini-trial" at certification that if successful must be repeated at trial or if unsuccessful frees the non-named class members to multiply the litigation.

Following *Amgen*'s lead, we uphold the district court's determination that liability questions common to the Ohio class—whether the alleged design defects in the Duets proximately caused mold to grow in the machines and whether Whirlpool adequately warned consumers about the propensity for mold growth—predominate over any individual questions. As in *Amgen,* the certified liability class "will prevail or fail in unison." Rule 23(b)(3) does not mandate that a plaintiff seeking class certification prove that each element of the claim is susceptible to classwide proof. Evidence will either prove or disprove as to all class members whether the alleged design defects caused the collection of biofilm, promoting mold growth, and whether Whirlpool failed to warn consumers adequately of the propensity for mold growth in the Duets.

Whirlpool does not point to any "fatal dissimilarity" among the members of the certified class that would render the class action mechanism unfair or inefficient for decision-making. Instead, Whirlpool points to "a fatal similarity—an alleged failure of proof as to an element of the plaintiffs' cause of action." That contention, the Supreme Court instructs, "is properly addressed at trial or in a ruling on a summary-judgment motion. The allegation should not be resolved in deciding whether to certify a proposed class." Tracking the Supreme Court's reasoning, we conclude here that common questions predominate over any individual ones. Simply put, this case comports with the "focus of the predominance inquiry"—it is "sufficiently cohesive to warrant adjudication by representation." (quoting *Amchem Prods., Inc. v. Windsor*).

The Supreme Court's subsequent decision in *Comcast Corp.* further instructs us on the necessary predominance inquiry, but after carefully considering the precepts discussed there, we conclude that the case does not change the outcome of our Rule 23 analysis. We explain why.

In *Comcast Corp.,* the district court certified a liability *and* damages class under Rules 23(a) & (b)(3) comprised of more than two million current and former Comcast subscribers who sought damages for alleged violations of federal antitrust laws. Although the plaintiffs proposed four different theories of antitrust impact, the district court found that only one could be proved in a manner common to all class plaintiffs: the theory that "Comcast engaged in anticompetitive clustering conduct, the effect of which was to deter the entry of over-builders in the Philadelphia" Designated Market Area (DMA).

The plaintiffs' expert calculated damages for the entire class using a model that failed to isolate the damages resulting from the one theory of antitrust impact the district court had allowed to proceed. The court nonetheless certified the class, finding that the damages related to the allowed theory could be calculated on a classwide basis. The Third Circuit affirmed.

The Supreme Court reversed in a decision that it described as turning "on the straightforward application of class-certification principles." Because the plaintiffs would be entitled to damages resulting only from the allowed liability theory if they were to prevail on the merits, the Court instructed that the "model purporting to serve as evidence of damages must measure only those damages attributable to that theory. If the model does not even attempt to do that, it cannot possibly establish that damages are susceptible of measurement across the entire class for purposes of Rule 23(b)(3)."

Neither the Third Circuit nor the district court had required the plaintiffs to link each liability theory to a damages calculation because, those courts reasoned, doing so would necessitate inquiry into the merits, which had no place in the class certification decision. The Supreme Court rejected that analysis as contradictory to *Dukes* and as improperly permitting plaintiffs to offer any method of damages measurement, no matter how arbitrary, at the class-certification stage, thereby reducing the predominance requirement of Rule 23(b)(3) "to a nullity." Due to the model's inability to distinguish damages attributable to the allowed theory of liability, the Court ruled that the predominance prerequisite of Rule 23(b)(3) did not warrant certification of a class. Accordingly, the Court reversed the certification order.

This case is different from *Comcast Corp.* Here the district court certified only a liability class and reserved all issues concerning damages for individual determination; in *Comcast Corp.* the court certified a class to determine both liability and damages. Where determinations on liability and damages have been bifurcated, *see* Fed.R.Civ.P. 23(c)(4), the decision in *Comcast*—to reject certification of a liability and damages class because plaintiffs failed to establish that damages could be measured on a classwide basis—has limited application. To the extent that *Comcast Corp.* reaffirms the settled rule that liability issues relating to injury must be susceptible of proof on a classwide basis to meet the predominance standard, our opinion thoroughly demonstrates why that requirement is met in this case.

Accordingly, the principles we glean from *Amgen* and *Comcast Corp.* include that to satisfy Rule 23(b)(3), named plaintiffs must show, and district courts must find, that questions of law or fact common to members of the class predominate over any questions that affect only individual members. Both cases are premised on existing class-action jurisprudence. The majority in *Comcast Corp.* concludes that the case "turns on the straightforward application of class certification principles," and the dissent concurs that "the opinion breaks no new ground on the standard for certifying a class action under Federal Rule of Civil Procedure 23(b)(3)." The dissent notes other class action principles that remain unchanged. "When adjudication of questions of liability common to the class will achieve economies of time and expense, the predominance standard is generally satisfied even if damages are not provable in the aggregate." A class may be divided into subclasses, Fed.R.Civ.P. 23(c)(4)–(5), or, as happened in this case, "a class may be certified for liability purposes only, leaving individual damages calculations to subsequent proceedings." Because "recognition that individual damages calculations do not preclude class certification under Rule 23(b)(3) is well-nigh universal," (in "the mine run of cases, it remains the 'black letter rule' that a class may obtain certification under Rule 23(b)(3) when liability questions common to the class predominate over damages questions unique to class members."

Thus, read in light of *Amgen, Comcast Corp.,* and other cases we have discussed, the evidence and the district court's opinion convince us that class certification is the superior method to adjudicate this case fairly and efficiently. Use of the class method is warranted particularly because class members are not likely to file individual actions—the cost of litigation would dwarf any potential recovery. As the district court observed, any class member who wishes to control his or her own litigation may opt out of the class under Rule 23(c)(2)(B)(v).

Once the district court resolves under Ohio law the common liability questions that are likely to generate common answers in this case, the court will either enter judgment for Whirlpool or proceed to the question of plaintiffs' damages. In the latter event, the court may exercise its discretion in line with *Amgen, Comcast Corp.*, and other cases cited in this opinion to resolve the damages issues.

## IV. CONCLUSION

In summary, we uphold the district court's determination that the Rule 23(a) and (b)(3) class certification prerequisites were met. Plaintiffs established numerosity, commonality, typicality, and adequate representation. In addition, they showed that common questions predominate over individual ones and that the class action is the superior method to adjudicate Whirlpool's liability on the legal claims. Because the district court did not clearly abuse its discretion in certifying a class on the issue of liability only, we affirm.

## PETERSEN V. COSTCO WHOLESALE CO., INC.

United States District Court for the Central District of California, 2016.
312 F.R.D. 565.

## I. BACKGROUND

This lawsuit is a putative consumer class action brought by Plaintiffs Jacob Petersen and others against Defendants Costco Wholesale Co., Inc, Townsend Farms, Inc. Purely Pomengranate, Inc. Fallon Trading Co. Inc., and United Juice Corp. Plaintiffs allege injury as a result of the risk of exposure to the hepatitis A virus (HAV) after consuming Townsend Farms

Organic Anti-Oxidant Blend, a frozen berry and pomegranate seed mix purchased at Costco.

### A.   Facts

An outbreak of hepatitis A infections occurred in the Western United States in May 2013. On May 13, 2013, the New Mexico Department of Health notified the Centers for Disease Control and Prevention of two people who were diagnosed with hepatitis A symptoms within one week of each other. The Colorado Department of Public Health identified additional outbreaks soon after. Ultimately, the outbreak was linked to the consumption of Townsend berry mix sold to consumers at various Costco locations in early 2013.

The CDC informed Defendant Costco of this outbreak on or about May 29, 2013. After learning of the outbreak, Costco took immediate steps to limit the harm caused by the product. Costco removed the Townsend berry mix from its retail locations. On or around May 31, 2013, Costco used its customer database to notify "potential Costco customers by telephone and mail regarding the potential outbreak" and specifically "mailed letters to all Costco members who purchased the product."

In addition to directly communicating with its members, Costco executives sent several internal messages regarding the product. Christine Summers, Costco's Director of Food Safety and Corporate Quality Assurance, sent a letter to all warehouse managers notifying them to "pull and hold" the Townsend berry mix and to "wrap and mark the product 'Do Not Sell.' " On May 31, Craig Wilson, the Vice President of Costco, sent a letter to all building managers informing them the "CDC will this afternoon announce an outbreak of hepatitis A in 5 states—Colorado, New Mexico, Nevada, Arizona, and California" and that the outbreak was "potentially associated" with item #5955820, the " 'Townsend Farm Organic Anti-Oxidant Blend.' " That same day, Costco's building managers were told to inform Costco members they should discard the product, and if they had consumed the product in the last two weeks, they should contact their health care providers to inquire about vaccinations.

On June 2, 2013, Townsend Farms "opened a call center for customers to contact Townsend Farms with any questions." The following day, Townsend Farms announced a partial recall of the Townsend berry mix. The announcement stated Townsend was "implementing this voluntary recall after learning that one of the ingredients of the frozen Organic Antioxidant Blend, pomegranate seeds processed in Turkey," was potentially linked to the outbreak. Townsend later expanded its recall efforts "after the FDA and the CDC confirmed that the epidemiological evidence supports a clear association between hepatitis A illness outbreak and one lot of organic pomegranate seeds used in the Frozen Organic Antioxidant blend subject to the voluntary recall." On June 6, 2013, Costco sent a food safety update to its members. The update informed Costco

Members that "if you have eaten the product in the last 10 days the CDC & FDA advice is to visit your personal health care provider or your local health department to receive a Hepatitis A vaccination." The update added that starting on June 6, 2013, "vaccinations will be available at your local Costco Pharmacy at no charge." Costco also offered to reimburse the cost of vaccinations received at other locations. In total, Costco administered approximately 10,316 vaccinations free of charge at its various stores. Costco maintained records of which members received the hepatitis A vaccination at its pharmacies, and sent letters to these members in December 2013 reminding them to get the follow-up hepatitis booster vaccination. Costco initially paid for the vaccinations administered at its pharmacies, but later asked Townsend to reimburse these costs. Wilson sent a letter to Costco's warehouse managers in mid-December stating that "members that chose to get vaccinated at their health care provider will be coming to get a refund for their booster vaccination."

### B.   Named Plaintiffs

Plaintiffs are individuals from nine different states: California, Arizona, Colorado, Idaho, Nevada, Oregon, Washington, New Mexico, and Hawaii.

### C.   Additional Class Allegations

In addition to bringing suit against Costco and Townsend, Plaintiffs have also named Purely Pomegranate, Fallon, and United Juice as Defendants. Specifically, Plaintiffs allege:

> The defendants Purely Pomegranate, Fallon Trading and United Juice variously and respectively imported, manufactured, distributed, or sold the HAV-contaminated pomegranate arils that the defendant Townsend Farms used to manufacture the recalled products. In turn, the defendant Townsend Farms sold the recalled product to Costco for retail sale in its stores, which is where the recalled product that caused injury to the named-plaintiffs and class members was purchased.

Further, Plaintiffs allege that 162 individuals across ten states were infected by the hepatitis A virus. Finally, Plaintiffs note that "CDC and other state and regional agencies advised any purchasers of the recalled product to refrain from consuming the Product, and to obtain HAV (hepatitis A vaccine), or a prophylactic dose of IG (immune globin)."

### D.   Procedural History

Plaintiffs originally filed this lawsuit on June 3, 2013 in Orange County Superior Court. The case was removed to federal court. Plaintiffs filed the instant Motion for Class Certification on July 27, 2015. Defendants Costco, Townsend, and Fallon filed their Opposition on

September 28, 2015. Defendant United Juice filed its Opposition the same day. Plaintiffs filed two separate replies on October 5, 2015.

## III. Discussion

Plaintiffs seek to certify the following class:

> The class that the plaintiffs propose for certification is defined as follows: All residents of Arizona, California, Colorado, Idaho, Hawaii, Nevada, New Mexico, Oregon, or Washington who: (1) consumed the recalled product—that is, Townsend Farms Organic Anti-Oxidant Blend frozen berry-mix purchased at Costco and subject to the recall that was announced in press releases that the Townsend Farms issued on June 4 and 28, 2013, and (2) received preventive medical treatment, including an injection of hepatitis-A vaccine or immune globulin, blood tests, and other associated costs.

In their Motion for Class Certification, Plaintiffs originally proposed the creation of two subclasses. Plaintiffs' first proposed a "Townsend Farms Only Sub-Class," covering residents of Colorado, Idaho, and Washington. In these three states, a seller that does not manufacture the product—Costco in this case—cannot be held strictly liable for the sale of a defective product. Thus, Plaintiffs in the first proposed subclass asserted claims only against Townsend. Second, Plaintiffs proposed a "Costco/Townsend Farms Sub-Class," which consists of "all persons meeting the class-definition who are residents of Arizona, California, Hawaii, Nevada, New Mexico, and Oregon." In these six states, it is possible to hold a non-manufacturing seller liable for the sale of defective products. Thus, Plaintiffs in the second proposed subclass alleged claims against both Townsend and Costco.

In its tentative order, the Court raised concerns that Plaintiffs' two proposed subclasses did not adequately account for variations in state laws and therefore raised significant issues under the predominance inquiry. In the Court's Order for Additional Briefing, the Court asked the parties "whether additional subclasses can account for the variations in state laws." Plaintiffs now propose three subclasses. Specifically, Plaintiffs propose (1) a subclass for residents of Washington and Idaho (Washington and Idaho Subclass), (2) a subclass for residents of Colorado (Colorado Subclass), and (3) a subclass for residents of Arizona, California, Hawaii, Nevada, New Mexico, and Oregon (Costco/Townsend Farms Subclass). In the alternative, Plaintiffs propose the formation of single-state subclasses. ("A subclass could be created for each of the nine states, if material variations are deemed to exist."). As Plaintiffs have clarified for the Court, they are asking "the Court to certify a liability-only class, reserving for a second phase of trial the issue of damages."

Under Federal Rule of Civil Procedure 23(c)(4), "when appropriate, an action may be brought or maintained as a class action with respect to particular issues." Rule 23(c)(5) provides that "when appropriate, a class may be divided into subclasses that are treated as a class under this rule." As the Ninth Circuit has made clear, "each subclass must independently meet the requirements of Rule 23 for the maintenance of a class action."

## IV.  CLASS CERTIFICATION UNDER RULE 23(b)

Because the Court has concluded Plaintiffs satisfied the prerequisites of Rule 23(a), the Court now turns to Rule 23(b). Specifically, Plaintiffs invoke Rule 23(b)(3), under which common questions of law or fact must predominate and the class device must offer a superior means of resolving the dispute. The Court must also consider whether Plaintiffs have shown that damages can be feasibly and efficiently measured—an issue that affects all three of the proposed subclasses.

### A.  Predominance

As noted earlier, Plaintiffs are seeking certification of a "liability-only class, reserving for a second phase of trial the issue of damages." Thus, the Court must evaluate whether the predominance criterion has been met with respect to Defendants' liability for Plaintiffs' strict liability claim. The Court finds that given this suit involves a single product, sold only at Costco, during a limited and defined period of time, there is initially a strong basis for finding that the proposed class action is "sufficiently cohesive to warrant adjudication by representation." *Amchem*. As the Ninth Circuit noted in *Valentino*, "Plaintiffs contend, with considerable justification, that because the case involves only one manufacturer, only one product, only one marketing program, and a relatively short period of time, the case is more manageable for class action purposes than cases that involves multiple manufactures, multiple products, multiple marketing programs, and a longer period of time." ("In addition, *Dalkon Shield* involved multiple defendants and multiple marketing schemes, unlike the present case where a single manufacturer marketed one drug over a limited period of time."). Indeed, there are several significant common issues here, including Plaintiffs' contention that a single, specific lot of allegedly defective organic pomegranate seed has given rise to Plaintiffs' claims. Therefore, evidence concerning the allegedly defective product in this case is likely to be "proved through evidence common to the class." Put differently, determining whether Defendants sold a defective product in this case will not require a searching individualized inquiry; rather, there will be significant common proof at issue in resolving Defendants' liability. Thus, there is "glue holding together" the proposed class. *Wal-Mart*. Further, there are significant common facts related to Defendants' recall of the allegedly defective product, Defendants' communications to Plaintiffs concerning the allegedly defective product, and the class members' subsequent receipt of preventative medical care. This suggests "classwide proof of causation is feasible in these circumstances because the same" product recall and notice from Costco "generally acted in a similar manner on each class member to product a similar effect" (i.e. seek out preventative medical care). Plaintiffs allege Defendants' sale of a defective product and subsequent recall of that product caused them to pay out-of-pocket for preventative care or lost wages—"objectively measurable harm." Further, Defendants have not raised the possibility of unique, individualized "affirmative defenses (such as failure to follow directions, assumption of risk, contributory negligence, and the statute of limitations)" that generally counsel against predominance in products liability cases. *In re N. Dist. of Cal., Dalkon Shield IUD Prods. Liab. Litig.*

Costco argues there are important differences among the Plaintiffs, including whether "they had been consuming the berry blend in different ways (frozen, thawed, uncooked, cooked, blended, alone), with different frequencies (daily, once a week, once in a long while or just once), over different periods of time (days week, or months)." Costco also mentions the "varying medical histories" of the proposed class members. The Court does not find these minor factual variations in individual consumption or medical histories are significant enough to overcome the significant common questions and defeat predominance. Analyzing "the relationship between the common and individual issues in the case," the Court concludes Plaintiffs' claims are "sufficiently cohesive to warrant adjudication" with respect to the core issues in this case.

Defendants devote the majority of their attention to a single argument against predominance: variations in state laws. While there is no "absolute bar to the certification of a multi-state plaintiff class action," the "law on predominance requires the district court to consider variations in state law when a class action involves multiple jurisdictions." When attempting to certify classes that span multiple states, plaintiffs "bear the burden of providing an extensive analysis of state law variations to determine whether there are insuperable obstacles to class certification." While there are no hard and fast rules for what constitutes a "material difference," the guiding inquiry is whether the state law variations would "spell the difference between the success and failure" of Plaintiffs' strict liability claim. Certification "may be appropriate if the class action proponent shows that state law variations can be effectively managed through the creation of a small number of subclasses grouping the states that have similar legal doctrines."

Plaintiffs contend there are few variations in the states' strict liability because "proving a defect is substantially similar in all nine states." In support of this proposition, Plaintiffs cite to strict liability language from state court decisions in the nine relevant states. According to Plaintiffs, these are the "only three subclasses needed to account for the variations in state law governing strict liability claims based on the allegation of an injury-causing manufacturing defect." As noted earlier, Plaintiffs propose the following subclasses: (1) the "Washington and Idaho Subclass," (2) the

"Colorado Subclass," and (3) the "Costco/Townsend Farms Subclass," which consists of residents of Arizona, California, Hawaii, Nevada, New Mexico, and Oregon. In the alternative, Plaintiffs state that "if material variations are deemed to exist," a "subclass could be created for each of the nine states."

Plaintiffs identify and account for two material variations in the states' strict liability laws. Plaintiffs first note that because it is possible to hold a non-manufacturing seller, like Costco, liable for the sale of defective products in only six states, Plaintiffs created the "Costco/Townsend Farms Subclass" for those six states. Second, in the tentative order distributed to the parties, the Court noted that, in Colorado, non-compliance with a government code raises a rebuttable presumption that the product was defective or negligently made. Thus, Plaintiffs now propose the creation of a separate Colorado subclass to account for that important difference.

Defendants reject the notion that these three subclasses account for all the material variations in the state laws; specifically, Defendants argue that several other differences in the states' strict liability standards, presumptions, and burdens overwhelm the common issues. Defendants specifically contend there are important state law differences concerning whether a product needs to be "unreasonably dangerous" or not; states' causation standards and allocation of liability rules; and unique defenses that are only present in certain states.

As an initial matter, the Court notes that a close analysis of these purported differences reveal that many of them "are insignificant, and therefore, they present no hurdle to class certification." For example, Costco repeatedly points to differences in the states' allocation of liability rules, "including applications of the doctrines of joint and several liability and comparative fault." However, the Court is not convinced these allocation of liability differences are material in the sense that they would "spell the difference between the success and failure" of Plaintiffs' claims. As Plaintiffs' counsel persuasively argued at the hearing, this issue is largely not material to this suit because there is a separate, parallel "indemnity and contribution action." Other purported differences Defendants highlight are simply irrelevant. For instance, in its State Law Variation Exhibit, United Juice writes, "New Mexico allows for additional defenses to section 402A claims." But this unique defense has no bearing on this case, as Plaintiffs have alleged Defendants introduced a defective product into "the stream of commerce."

At the same time, Defendants have highlighted other differences that may, in due course prove to be material. Most notably, Defendants have pointed to different state law formulation concerning whether a product has to be both defective and unreasonably dangerous, or just defective. However, the Court need not resolve whether these variation are material because Plaintiffs have alternatively proposed formulating nine single-state subclasses. This proposal "would avoid almost completely the tangled" variations in state law present in other multi-state class action cases. *In re Welding Fume Prod. Liability Litig.* "The smaller breadth of difference between the nine relevant state laws in this case" counsels in favor of this approach. Indeed, given that the strict liability cause of action is "virtually identical" in several of the relevant states, "careful trial planning with the use of jury interrogatories and special will avoid most jury-instruction complexities."

United Juice argues a "multitude of subclasses are not manageable." Indeed, United Juice asserts Plaintiffs' "attempt to mollify predominance concerns predicated on variations in state law, creates manageability issues that are not adequately addressed by plaintiffs." Plaintiffs respond that additional subclasses do not create an overwhelming manageability problem, "especially for a liability theory as relatively simple as one premised on strict liability and single alleged defect." The Court agrees with Plaintiffs. "The 'broad discretion' that a district court enjoys in determining whether to certify a class goes principally to the question of whether the court reasonably concludes it could manage the complexities that class certification carries." *In re Welding.* In this case, the "undersigned believes a court could manage the differences" in strict liability laws among the nine states chosen by Plaintiffs "by holding separate trials for each state-wide class, or perhaps a combined trial for few statewide subclasses, where the law in those states is similar enough to allow creation of jury instructions and a verdict form that is not too complex." *In re Welding* (finding that eight single-state subclasses on medical monitoring law did not present overwhelming manageability problems). By "choosing only the nine states they did, and proposing single-state subclasses," *id.* Plaintiffs have overcome all of the state law variations Defendants have identified. The Court further notes that during the initial round of briefing, Defendant Costco suggested this possibility of adding additional subclasses ("Should the court not be inclined to deny class certification entirely, additional sub-classes be created to better account for the different causes of action and corresponding recoveries within each of the nine states.").

Based on the foregoing, the Court concludes that Plaintiffs' proposed single-state subclasses both overcome the state law variation problems and present a manageable option for the litigation moving forward.

## C. Damages

Finally, the Court will consider Defendants' arguments that Plaintiffs have failed to meet their burden with respect to damages. The Court recognizes that "in this circuit damage calculations alone cannot defeat certification." Still, Plaintiffs "must be able to show that their damages stemmed from the defendant's actions that created the legal liability." Additionally, "plaintiffs must establish at the certification stage that 'damages can feasibly and efficiently be calculated once the common liability questions are adjudicated.' "

Here, Plaintiffs seek three primary forms of damages: (1) economic damages for those class members who paid out-of-pocket for vaccinations, (2) lost wages, and (3) non-economic damages. Plaintiffs have proposed that class members can "provide receipts to prove actual out-of-pocket expenses," offer an approximation of a reasonable lost wages amount, and use past settlement amounts and testimony to adequately measure non-economic damages. Defendants do not directly challenge Plaintiffs' proposal to use receipts, but raise concerns about Plaintiffs' proposed damages model for measuring lost wages and non-economic damages.

This issue need not be resolved, however. In this case, Plaintiffs ask the Court "to certify a liability-only case, reserving for a second phase of trial the issue of damages." Recognizing that "the amount of damages is invariably an individual question," several courts have recently bifurcated liability questions from damages. The Court finds this approach to be appropriate here and therefore "reserves the issue whether damages can be calculated" based on the methods Plaintiff proposes.

As explained by a district court in this Circuit,

> The fact that a class may not be satisfied for purposes of seeking damages does not mean that it cannot be certified at all. In all of the other circuit court decisions cited in *Jimenez*, the courts of appeal concluded that the cases before them fell outside *Comcast's* scope at least in part because the classes were certified only for liability purposes rather than for purposes of considering damages. As the most recent of those cases noted, "the rule of *Comcast* is largely irrelevant 'where determinations on liability and damages have been bifurcated' in accordance with Rule 23(c)(4) and the district court has 'reserved all issues concerning damages for individual determination.'" *In re Deepwater Horizon* (quoting *In re Whirlpool Front-Loading Washer Prods. Liab. Litig.*); *see also Butler v. Sears, Roebuck and Co.* ("a class action limited to determining liability on a class-wide basis, with separate hearings to determine—if liability is established—the damages of individual class members, or homogeneous groups of class members, is permitted by Rule 23(c)(4) and will often be the sensible way to proceed").

As the Ninth Circuit has repeatedly made clear, "damage calculations alone cannot defeat certification." Thus, "since Plaintiff has established that, with the exception of determining damages, all of the required elements of class certification have been met, the Court will exercise its discretion pursuant to Rule 23(c)(4) of the Federal Rules of Civil Procedure to certify the proposed class solely for purposes of determining liability."

## V. DISPOSITION

For the foregoing reasons, the Court grants Plaintiffs' Motion, insofar as it seeks to certify nine single-state subclasses for the purposes of determining liability.

# C. MULTIPHASE TRIALS AND RES JUDICATA

### WALKER V. R.J. REYNOLDS TOBACCO CO.
United States Court of Appeals for the Eleventh Circuit, 2013.
734 F.3d 1278.

This appeal by R.J. Reynolds Tobacco Company of money judgments in favor of the survivors of two smokers requires us to decide whether a decision of the Supreme Court of Florida in an earlier class action is entitled to full faith and credit in federal court. Florida smokers and their survivors filed in state court a class action against the major tobacco companies that manufacture cigarettes in the United States. In the first phase of the class action, a jury decided that the tobacco companies breached a duty of care, manufactured defective cigarettes, and concealed material information, but the jury did not decide whether the tobacco companies were liable for damages to individual members of the class. The Supreme Court of Florida approved the jury verdict, but decertified the class going forward. *Engle v. Liggett Grp., Inc.* Members of the class then filed individual complaints in federal and state courts. The Supreme Court of Florida later ruled that the findings of the jury in the class action have res judicata effect for common issues decided against the tobacco companies and in favor of the smokers and that the only unresolved issues in the individual lawsuits filed afterward involve specific causation and damages. *Philip Morris USA, Inc. v. Douglas.* R.J. Reynolds argues that the application of res judicata in later suits filed by individual smokers violates its constitutional right to due process of law because the jury verdict in the class action is so ambiguous that it is impossible to tell whether the jury found that each tobacco company acted wrongfully with respect to any specific brand of cigarette or any individual plaintiff. After the district court ruled that giving res judicata effect to the findings of the jury in the class action does not violate the rights of the tobacco companies to due process, two juries awarded money damages to the survivors of two smokers in their suits against R.J. Reynolds. Because R.J. Reynolds had a full and fair opportunity to be heard in the Florida class action and the application of res judicata under Florida law does not cause an arbitrary deprivation of property, we affirm the judgments against R.J. Reynolds and in favor of the survivors of the smokers.

### BACKGROUND

In 1994, six individuals filed a putative class action in a Florida court against the major domestic manufacturers of cigarettes, including R.J.

Reynolds, and two tobacco industry organizations. The plaintiffs sought more than $100 billion in damages for injuries allegedly caused by smoking cigarettes. Their complaint asserted claims of strict liability, negligence, breach of express warranty, breach of implied warranty, fraud, conspiracy to commit fraud, and intentional infliction of emotional distress. A Florida court of appeals approved the certification of a plaintiff class of all Florida citizens and residents who have suffered or died from medical conditions caused by their addiction to cigarettes and the survivors of those citizens and residents.

The trial court divided the class action in three phases. Phase I of the class action "consisted of a year-long trial to consider the issues of liability and entitlement to punitive damages for the class as a whole." During that phase, the jury considered only "common issues relating exclusively to the defendants' conduct and the general health effects of smoking," but the jury did not decide whether the tobacco companies were liable to any of the class representatives or members of the class. In Phase II of the trial, the same jury determined the liability of the tobacco companies to three individual class representatives, awarded compensatory damages to those individuals, and fixed the amount of class-wide punitive damages. According to the trial plan, in Phase III of the class action, new juries were to decide the claims of the rest of the class members.

In Phase I of the trial, the plaintiffs presented evidence about some defects that were specific to certain brands or types of cigarettes and other defects common to all cigarettes. For example, "proof submitted on strict liability included brand-specific defects, but it also included proof that the *Engle* defendants' cigarettes were defective because they are addictive and cause disease." "Similarly, arguments concerning the class's negligence, warranty, fraud, and conspiracy claims included whether the *Engle* defendants failed to address the health effects and addictive nature of cigarettes, manipulated nicotine levels to make cigarettes more addictive, and concealed information about the dangers of smoking." The trial plan called for the jury "to decide issues common to the entire class, including general causation, and the *Engle* defendants' common liability to the class members for the conduct alleged in the complaint."

At the conclusion of Phase I, the trial court submitted to the jury a verdict form with a series of questions to be answered "yes" or "no." The trial court instructed the jury that "all common liability issues would be tried before the jury" and that Phase I of the trial "did not address issues as to the conduct or damages of individual members of the Florida class." The first question on the verdict form asked the jury whether "smoking cigarettes causes" a list of enumerated diseases, and the jury found that smoking causes 20 specific diseases, including various forms of cancer. The second question asked the jury whether "cigarettes that contain nicotine are addictive and dependence producing," and the jury found that cigarettes are addictive and dependence producing.

The jury then answered "yes" to each of the following questions for each tobacco company:

- Did the tobacco company "place cigarettes on the market that were defective and unreasonably dangerous";

- Did the tobacco company "make a false statement of a material fact, either knowing the statement was false or misleading, or being without knowledge as to its truth or falsity, with the intention of misleading smokers";

- Did the tobacco company "conceal or omit material information, not otherwise known or available, knowing that the material was false and misleading, or fail to disclose a material fact concerning or proving the health effects and/or addictive nature of smoking cigarettes";

- Did the tobacco company "enter into an agreement to misrepresent information relating to the health effects of cigarette smoking, or the addictive nature of smoking cigarettes, with the intention that smokers and members of the public rely to their detriment";

- Did the tobacco company "enter into an agreement to conceal or omit information regarding the health effects of cigarette smoking, or the addictive nature of smoking cigarettes, with the intention that smokers and members of the public rely to their detriment";

- Did the tobacco company "sell or supply cigarettes that were defective in that they were not reasonably fit for the uses intended";

- Did the tobacco company "sell or supply cigarettes that, at the time of sale or supply, did not conform to representations of fact made by the tobacco company, either orally or in writing";

- Did the tobacco company "fail to exercise the degree of care which a reasonable cigarette manufacturer would exercise under like circumstances";

- Did the tobacco company "engage in extreme and outrageous conduct or with reckless disregard relating to cigarettes sold or supplied to Florida smokers with the intent to inflict severe emotional distress."

The final question asked the jury whether "the conduct of each tobacco company rose to a level that would permit a potential award or entitlement to punitive damages," and the jury answered "yes" for each tobacco company.

The tobacco companies unsuccessfully objected to the verdict form that the trial court submitted to the jury in Phase I. They argued that the verdict form did not "ask for specifics" about the tortious conduct of the tobacco companies, "rendering the jury findings useless for application to individual plaintiffs." They requested that the trial court submit to the jury a more detailed verdict form that would have asked the jury to identify the brands of cigarettes that were defective and the information the companies concealed from the public. The trial court rejected that proposed verdict form as too detailed and impractical.

In Phase II of the trial, the same jury determined that the defendants were liable to three named plaintiffs. The jury awarded compensatory damages of $12.7 million to those three named plaintiffs, and the jury awarded punitive damages of $145 billion to the class.

Before Phase III of the trial began, the tobacco companies filed an interlocutory appeal of the verdicts in Phases I and II, and the Supreme Court of Florida approved in part and vacated in part the verdicts. The court concluded that the trial court did not abuse its discretion when it certified the *Engle* class for purposes of Phases I and II of the trial, but that the class must be decertified going forward so that members of the class could pursue their claims to finality in individual lawsuits. The court explained that "problems with the three-phase trial plan negate the continued viability of this class action" and that "continued class action treatment for Phase III of the trial plan is not feasible because individualized issues such as legal causation, comparative fault, and damages predominate." The court held as follows that most findings of the jury in Phase I should have "res judicata effect" in the ensuing individual trials:

> The pragmatic solution is to now decertify the class, retaining the jury's Phase I findings other than those on the fraud and intentional infliction of emotional distress claims, which involved highly individualized determinations, and the finding on entitlement to punitive damages questions, which was premature. *Class members can choose to initiate individual damages actions and the Phase I common core findings we approved above will have res judicata effect in those trials.*

The court concluded that the findings about fraud and misrepresentation and intentional infliction of emotional distress cannot have preclusive effect because "the non-specific findings in favor of the plaintiffs" on those questions were "inadequate to allow a subsequent jury to consider individual questions of reliance and legal cause." The court also vacated the finding about civil conspiracy-misrepresentation because it relied on the underlying tort of misrepresentation. But the court stated that the other findings, now known as the approved findings from Phase I, have res judicata effect. The court also vacated the award of punitive damages on the ground that it was excessive and premature, affirmed the damages award in favor of two of the named plaintiffs, and vacated the judgment in favor of the third named plaintiff because the statute of limitations barred his claims.

After the decision of the Supreme Court of Florida, members of the *Engle* class filed thousands of individual cases in both state and federal courts. A central issue in these cases is whether plaintiffs may rely on the approved findings from Phase I to establish the "conduct" elements of their claims against the tobacco companies. The dispute concerns the meaning of the ruling in *Engle* that the approved findings from Phase I "will have res judicata effect." The plaintiffs interpreted the ruling to mean that the tobacco companies could dispute only specific causation and damages in the individual lawsuits. The plaintiffs argued that the approved findings from Phase I establish that the tobacco companies breached a duty of care and failed to disclose material information to every member of the *Engle* class. The tobacco companies argued that, although the jury in Phase I found that they acted negligently in some way or concealed some information, the findings are not specific enough to establish that they acted negligently in connection with any particular brand of cigarette or concealed material information from any particular plaintiff.

We were the first appellate court to consider the res judicata effect of the approved findings from Phase I, and we concluded that the findings have preclusive effect in a later case only when the plaintiff can establish that the jury in Phase I actually decided that a tobacco company acted wrongfully regarding cigarettes that the plaintiff smoked. We explained that, when the Supreme Court of Florida stated in *Engle* that the approved findings from Phase I "were to have res judicata effect," the court "necessarily referred to issue preclusion" and not claim preclusion because "factual issues and not causes of action were decided in Phase I." We explained that issue preclusion applies only to issues that were "actually decided" in a prior litigation, and we remanded the matter for the district court to consider in the first instance whether the approved findings from Phase I establish that the tobacco companies acted wrongfully toward each plaintiff. We explained that, to determine whether a specific factual issue was determined in favor of the plaintiff, the district court should look beyond the face of the verdict and consider "the entire trial record." The tobacco companies argued in that appeal that "using the findings to establish facts that were not decided by the jury would violate their due process rights," but we avoided that question because, "under Florida law, the findings could not be used for that purpose anyway."

Several Florida courts of appeal then held that the approved findings from Phase I establish the conduct elements of the each class member's claims against the tobacco companies, and they rejected our decision in *Brown* that smokers must establish from the trial record that an issue was actually decided in his or her favor. In *Martin,* the court disagreed with our decision in *Brown* that "every *Engle* plaintiff must trot out the class action trial transcript to prove applicability of the Phase I findings." The court held, "No matter the wording of the findings on the Phase I verdict form, the jury considered and determined specific matters related to the defendants' conduct. Because the findings are common to all class members, the plaintiff was entitled to rely on them in her damages action against R.J. Reynolds." For example, the plaintiff in *Martin* brought a claim for fraudulent concealment, and the court held that the Phase I finding about concealment "encompassed all the brands" and that R.J. Reynolds could not relitigate whether it had concealed any material information.

Because federal courts sitting in diversity are bound by the decisions of state courts on matters of state law, those decisions of the Florida courts of appeal supplanted our interpretation of Florida law in The tobacco companies could no longer argue that the approved findings from Phase I have no preclusive effect as a matter of Florida law. Instead, they argued that giving the approved findings preclusive effect would violate their federal rights to due process. The tobacco companies raised that argument in each of the cases filed in the district court, which consolidated those cases in *Waggoner v. R.J. Reynolds Tobacco Co.*

The district court in *Waggoner* held that giving preclusive effect to the approved findings from Phase I does not violate a right of the tobacco companies to due process of law. The district court concluded that "a state's departure from common law issue preclusion principles does not implicate the Constitution unless that departure also violates 'the minimum procedural requirements of the Fourteenth Amendment's Due Process Clause.'" And the district court concluded that the decisions of the Florida courts of appeal do not violate those procedural requirements because those decisions do not arbitrarily deprive the tobacco companies of property and because the tobacco companies had a full and fair opportunity to litigate the conduct elements at Phase I of the class action.

After the district court decided *Waggoner,* the Supreme Court of Florida in *Douglas* held, as a matter of Florida law, that the approved findings from Phase I establish the conduct elements of the claims brought by members of the *Engle* class. The court acknowledged that "the *Engle* jury did not make detailed findings for which evidence it relied upon to make the Phase I common liability findings." But the court explained that, "no matter the wording of the findings on the Phase I verdict form, the jury considered and determined specific matters related to the *Engle* defendants' conduct." The court explained that, although the proof submitted at the Phase I trial included both general and brand-specific defects, "the class action jury was not asked to find brand-specific defects in the *Engle* defendants' cigarettes," but only to "determine like all common liability issues' for the class." The court concluded that the approved findings from Phase I concern conduct that "is common to all class members and will not change from case to case," and that "the approved Phase I findings are specific enough" to establish some elements of the plaintiffs' claims.

The Supreme Court of Florida also held in *Douglas* that giving preclusive effect to the approved findings from Phase I does not violate a right of the tobacco companies to due process. The court stated that the tobacco companies had notice and an opportunity to be heard and were not arbitrarily deprived of property. The court explained that, when it stated in *Engle* that the approved findings have "res judicata effect," it addressed claim preclusion, not issue preclusion. The court stated that claim preclusion "prevents *the same parties* from relitigating *the same cause of action* in a second lawsuit," *id.*, while issue preclusion "prevents *the same parties* from relitigating the same issues that were litigated and actually decided in a second suit involving *a different cause of action*." "Because the claims in *Engle* and the claims in individual actions like this case are *the same causes of action* between *the same parties*," the court concluded that "res judicata (not issue preclusion) applies." The court stated that "to decide here that we really meant issue preclusion even though we said res judicata in *Engle* would effectively make the Phase I findings regarding the *Engle* defendants' conduct useless in individual actions."

The tobacco companies had argued that, based on *Fayerweather v. Ritch,* they had a constitutional right to have issue preclusion apply to the approved findings from Phase I, but the Supreme Court of Florida rejected this argument. The court stated that, "as a constitutional matter, the *Engle* defendants do not have the right to have issue preclusion, as opposed to res judicata, apply to the Phase I findings." The court explained that "claim preclusion, unlike issue preclusion, has no 'actually decided' requirement but, instead, focuses on whether a party is attempting to relitigate the same claim, without regard to the arguments or evidence that were presented to the first jury that decided the claim." The court concluded that, because it was applying claim preclusion instead of issue preclusion, the "decision in *Fayerweather* does not impose a constitutional impediment against giving the Phase I findings res judicata effect."

In this appeal, R.J. Reynolds challenges the decision of the district court in *Waggoner* and appeals the jury verdicts in favor of two plaintiffs, Alvin Walker and George Duke III. Walker filed an amended complaint in federal court for the death of his father, Albert Walker, and Duke filed an amended complaint in federal court for the death of his mother, Sarah Duke. Walker and Duke asserted claims for strict liability, negligence, fraudulent concealment, and conspiracy to fraudulently conceal. The juries decided those cases after the district court decided *Waggoner,* but before the Supreme Court of Florida decided *Douglas.* In both cases, the district court instructed each jury that, under the decision in *Waggoner,* the jury in Phase I conclusively established the tortious-conduct elements of the plaintiffs' claims. The district court instructed the juries that R.J. Reynolds "placed cigarettes on the market that were defective and unreasonably dangerous" and that R.J. Reynolds "was negligent." The only issues for those juries to resolve were whether the decedents were members of the *Engle* class, causation, and damages. The juries in both cases returned split verdicts. The jury found in favor of Walker on the claims of strict liability and negligence, allocated 10 percent of the fault to R.J. Reynolds and 90 percent of the fault to Walker, and entered a judgment of $27,500. The jury found in favor of Duke only on the claim of strict liability, allocated 25 percent of the fault to R.J. Reynolds and 75 percent of the fault to Duke, and entered a judgment of $7,676.25.

## III. DISCUSSION

The Full Faith and Credit Act, 28 U.S.C. § 1738, requires federal courts to "give preclusive effect to a state court judgment to the same extent as would courts of the state in which the judgment was entered." But the Act, like all statutes, is "subject to the requirements of the Due Process Clause." And the law of preclusion is also "subject to due process limitations." Although "state courts are generally free to develop their own rules for protecting against the relitigation of common issues or the piecemeal resolution of disputes, extreme applications of the doctrine of res judicata may be inconsistent with a federal right that is fundamental in character." These principles require that we give full faith and credit to the decision in *Engle,* as interpreted in *Douglas,* so long as it "satisfies the minimum procedural requirements" of due process. R.J. Reynolds argues that this appeal is governed by the Due Process Clause of the Fifth Amendment, but in the district court they argued that the case was governed by the Due Process Clause of the Fourteenth Amendment. Our analysis is the same under either clause because "the reaches of the Due Process Clauses of the Fourteenth and Fifth Amendments are coextensive."

Our inquiry is a narrow one: whether giving full faith and credit to the decision in *Engle,* as interpreted in *Douglas,* would arbitrarily deprive R.J. Reynolds of its property without due process of law. R.J. Reynolds argues that we should conduct a searching review of the *Engle* class action and apply what amounts to *de novo* review of the analysis of Florida law in *Douglas,* but we lack the power to do so. Our task is not to decide whether the decision in *Douglas* was correct as a matter of Florida law. *See Erie R.R. Co. v. Tompkins.* And we cannot refuse to give full faith and credit to the decision in *Engle* because we disagree with the decision in *Douglas* about what the jury in Phase I decided.

The decision of the Supreme Court of Florida to give preclusive effect to the approved findings from Phase I did not arbitrarily deprive R.J. Reynolds of property without due process of law. The Supreme Court of Florida looked through the jury verdict entered in Phase I to determine what issues the jury decided. Based on its review of the class action trial plan and the jury instructions, the court concluded that the jury had been presented with arguments that the tobacco companies acted wrongfully toward all the plaintiffs and that all cigarettes that contain nicotine are addictive and produce dependence. Although the proof submitted to the jury included both general and brand-specific defects, the court concluded that the jury was asked only to "determine 'all common liability issues' for the class," not brand specific defects. The Supreme Court of Florida was entitled to look beyond the jury verdict to determine what issues the jury decided. We sanctioned a similar inquiry in *Brown*, where we stated that, although the jury verdict in Phase I was ambiguous on its face, members of the *Engle* class should be allowed an opportunity to establish that the jury in Phase I actually decided particular issues in their favor. We ordinarily presume that a jury followed its instructions, and the Supreme Court of Florida did not act arbitrarily when it applied this presumption and concluded that the jury found only issues of common liability.

The decision of the Supreme Court of Florida in *Douglas* is consistent with its earlier decision in *Engle*. In *Engle*, the Supreme Court of Florida explained that the approved findings from Phase I "will have res judicata effect" in the later individual cases. But the court did not approve all of the findings from Phase I. Instead, the court stated that the findings of the jury in Phase I about fraud and intentional infliction of emotional distress cannot have preclusive effect because "the non-specific findings in favor of the plaintiffs" on those questions were "inadequate to allow a subsequent jury to consider individual questions of reliance and legal cause." That the court in *Engle* denied preclusive effect to those findings on the ground that they were not specific enough suggests that the court determined that the jury findings about the other claims were specific enough to apply in favor of every class plaintiff. *See Douglas* (explaining that, "by accepting some of the Phase I findings and rejecting others based on lack of specificity, this Court in *Engle* necessarily decided that the approved Phase I findings are specific enough").

R.J. Reynolds had a full and fair opportunity to litigate the issues of common liability in Phase I. "The opportunity to be heard is an essential requisite of due process of law in judicial proceedings." During Phase I, R.J. Reynolds had an opportunity to contest its liability and challenge the verdict form that the trial court submitted to the jury. After the trial court declined to adopt the jury verdict form proposed by the tobacco companies and the jury decided against the tobacco companies on the issues of common liability, R.J. Reynolds challenged those decisions before the Supreme Court of Florida, but that court rejected its arguments. And R.J.

Reynolds petitioned the Supreme Court of the United States to review the decision of the Supreme Court of Florida, but the Supreme Court of the United States denied its petition.

R.J. Reynolds also has had an opportunity to contest its liability in these later cases brought by individual members of the *Engle* class. Although R.J. Reynolds has exhausted its opportunities to contest the common liability findings of the jury in Phase I, it has vigorously contested the remaining elements of the claims, including causation and damages. The modest sums received by the plaintiffs in this appeal—less than $28,000 for Walker and less than $8,000 for Duke—suggest that the juries fairly considered the questions of damages and fault.

R.J. Reynolds argues that "traditional practice provides a touchstone for constitutional analysis" under the Due Process Clause, and that the decision in *Douglas* extinguishes the protection against arbitrary deprivations of property embodied in the federal common law of issue preclusion, which bars relitigation only of "issues *actually decided* in a prior action." R.J. Reynolds fails to identify any court that has ever held that due process requires application of the federal common law of issue preclusion. Nor does R.J. Reynolds identify any other court that has declined to give full faith and credit to a judgment of a state court as later interpreted by the same state court on the ground that the later state court decision was so wrong that it amounted to a violation of due process.

R.J. Reynolds argues that the Supreme Court held in *Fayerweather* that parties have a right, under the Due Process Clause, to the application of the traditional law of issue preclusion, but we disagree. The Supreme Court stated in *Fayerweather* that the Due Process Clause is implicated when a party argues that a court has given preclusive effect to an issue that was not actually decided in a prior litigation. But the Supreme Court held that no violation of the Due Process Clause had occurred because the issue had been actually decided in the prior litigation. The Supreme Court had no occasion in *Fayerweather* to decide what sorts of applications of issue preclusion would violate due process.

R.J. Reynolds next argues that it is impossible to tell whether the jury determined that it acted wrongfully in connection with some or all of its brands of cigarettes because the plaintiffs presented both general and brand-specific theories of liability, but the decision of the Supreme Court of Florida forecloses that argument. Whether a jury actually decided an issue is a question of fact, and the Supreme Court of Florida looked past the ambiguous jury verdict to decide this question of fact.

If due process requires a finding that an issue was actually decided, then the Supreme Court of Florida made the necessary finding when it explained that the approved findings from Phase I "go to the defendants underlying conduct which is common to all class members and will not change from case to case" and that "the approved Phase I findings are specific enough" to establish certain elements of the plaintiffs' claims. Labeling the relevant doctrine as claim preclusion instead of issue preclusion may be unorthodox and inconsistent with the federal common law about those doctrines, but the Supreme Court has instructed us that, "in determining what is due process of law, regard must be had to substance, not to form." "State courts are free to attach such descriptive labels to litigations before them as they may choose and to attribute to them such consequences as they think appropriate under state constitutions and laws, subject only to the requirements of the Constitution of the United States." Our deference to the decision in *Douglas* does not violate the constitutional right of R.J. Reynolds to due process of law. Whether the Supreme Court of Florida calls the relevant doctrine issue preclusion, claim preclusion, or something else, is no concern of ours.

We must give full faith and credit to the decision of the Supreme Court of Florida about how to resolve this latest chapter of the intractable problem of tobacco litigation. For several decades, R.J. Reynolds and the other major companies of the tobacco industry have "remained under the long shadow of litigation, that chronic potential spoiler of their financial well-being." "The tobacco industry was primed to meet these ever larger challenges as a cost of doing business, and it did not lack for plausible, even persuasive, defenses." Courts, after all, long ago recognized the inherent risks of cigarette smoking. And physicians "suspected a link between smoking and illness for centuries." In 1604, King James I wrote "A Counterblaste to Tobacco," that described smoking as "a custom loathsome to the eye, hateful to the nose, harmful to the brain, dangerous to the lung, and the black stinking fume thereof, nearest resembling the horribly Stygian smoke of the pit that is bottomless." And popular culture too recognized those risks. So juries often either discounted or rejected the claims of smokers who sought to hold tobacco companies liable for the well-known harms to their health caused by smoking. But a "wave of suits, brought by resourceful attorneys representing vast claimant pools." We cannot say that the procedures, however novel, adopted by the Supreme Court of Florida to manage thousands of these suits under Florida law violated the federal right of R.J. Reynolds to due process of law.

## IV. CONCLUSION

We affirm the judgments against R.J. Reynolds and in favor of Walker and Duke.

# CHAPTER 13

---

# THE CLASS ACTION FAIRNESS ACT (CAFA) AND MASS ACTIONS

■ ■ ■

## A. DEFINING A MASS ACTION

### ABREGO v. THE DOW CHEMICAL CO.
United States Court of Appeals for the Ninth Circuit, 2006.
443 F.3d 676.

The recently enacted Class Action Fairness Act of 2005 (CAFA) alters the landscape for federal court jurisdiction over class actions. In addition to traditional class actions, CAFA covers certain other cases involving large numbers of plaintiffs, denominated "mass actions." Dow Chemical Company brings this interlocutory appeal, pursuant to 28 U.S.C. § 1453(c)(1), from the district court's order remanding this purported "mass action."

Dow maintains that under CAFA and contrary to preexisting removal jurisdiction law: (1) plaintiffs bear the burden of refuting the district court's removal jurisdiction; (2) a "mass action" is removable regardless of whether there is jurisdiction over all plaintiffs whose claims are necessary to qualify the action as a mass action; and (3) the district court *must* allow jurisdictional discovery to determine the amount in controversy. The disputes between the parties on these discrete issues reflect a larger disagreement over whether the changes wrought by CAFA generally are limited to those enunciated in CAFA's text, or whether courts should infer a broader transformation of jurisdictional principles than the statutory language indicates.

We hold that CAFA did not shift to the plaintiff the burden of establishing that there is no removal jurisdiction in federal court and that Dow did not meet its burden. We therefore affirm the district court's remand of this action to state court. We save for a later day detailed consideration of CAFA's muddled "mass action" provisions.

I.

One thousand one hundred and sixty Panamanian banana plantation workers ("the workers") filed a complaint asserting claims stemming from their alleged exposure to 1, 2-dibromo-3-chloropropane ("DBCP"), a chemical pesticide sold under the brand names "Nemagon" and "Fumazone." The operative complaint alleges that although the

Environmental Protection Agency banned almost all DBCP use in the United States in 1979, the defendants continued to distribute and use the pesticide on plantations in Panama. The workers allege that they suffered "sterility and other serious injuries" as a result of exposure to the pesticide and seek an unspecified amount of special, general, and punitive damages, pre- and post-judgment interest, and attorneys' fees and costs.

On May 13, 2005, three weeks after the state court suit commenced, Dow filed a notice of removal with the district court and, ten days later, an amended notice of removal, both pursuant to CAFA. Dow invoked § 1332(d)(11), which provides for federal jurisdiction over "mass actions." For the purposes of CAFA, a "mass action" is "any civil action in which monetary relief claims of 100 or more persons are proposed to be tried jointly on the ground that the plaintiffs' claims involve common questions of law or fact, except that jurisdiction shall exist only over those plaintiffs whose claims in a mass action satisfy the jurisdictional amount requirements under" § 1332(a). § 1332(d)(11)(B). Section 1332(a), in turn, requires that the amount in controversy exceed $75,000. Under subsection (d)(11)(A), an action that qualifies as a mass action will be "deemed to be a class action removable under § 1332(d)(2)–(10) if it otherwise meets the provisions of those paragraphs." § 1332(d)(11)(A). Prominent among the requirements in these specified paragraphs are that the aggregate amount in controversy must exceed $5,000,000, and that the action must satisfy CAFA's new minimal diversity requirements between plaintiffs and defendants. § 1332(d)(2).

The district court ordered Dow to show cause as to whether "the amount in controversy does not exceed $5,000,000, exclusive of interest and costs, and/or the amount in controversy for each plaintiff does not exceed $75,000." Dow responded, arguing that: (1) CAFA shifted the burden of establishing whether jurisdiction is proper from the removing defendants to the plaintiffs seeking remand; (2) as long as the action prior to removal involved the claims of more than 100 plaintiffs and more than $5,000,000 in the aggregate, the "mass action" subsection provides for removal jurisdiction and calls for subsequent remand only of the claims of those plaintiffs who do not meet the $75,000 jurisdictional amount requirement; and (3) there should be limited discovery related to the amount in controversy, as "contemplated by Congress in enacting CAFA."

On October 11, 2005, the district court issued a brief remand order:

> The Court finds that Defendant has failed to meet its burden of showing that the action constitutes a "mass action," as defined by the applicable statute (i.e., there are 100 or more plaintiffs over which this court has jurisdiction that can be proposed to be tried jointly). As such, the Court determines that it lacks subject matter jurisdiction over this case, and remands the action to state court.

Dow appeals this order, reasserting the same arguments presented to the district court.

A little over a year ago, CAFA became law, amending § 1332 and adding § 1453 to title 28 of the United States Code. These new provisions govern this case. To understand them, however, one must first understand the statutory scheme to which they were added. We therefore begin with a review of those background principles and then proceed to describe the amendments.

Section 1332(a), a preexisting section, vests the district courts with "original jurisdiction of all civil actions where the matter in controversy exceeds the sum or value of $75,000, exclusive of interest and costs, and is between" diverse parties as defined by subsections (a)(1)–(4).§ 1332(a). Although the statute does not so require explicitly, the Supreme Court has repeatedly held, and recently reiterated, that § 1332(a) requires complete diversity, whereby "in a case with multiple plaintiffs and multiple defendants, the presence in the action of a single plaintiff from the same State as a single defendant deprives the district court of original diversity jurisdiction over the entire action."

Under § 1441, another preexisting section, "civil actions brought in a State court of which the district courts of the United States have original jurisdiction," may be removed by the defendant or defendants to federal district court. § 1441(a). Cases removed from state court under § 1441 are ordinarily subject to a stricter diversity standard than applies where original federal jurisdiction is invoked:

> While § 1332 allows plaintiffs to invoke diversity jurisdiction, § 1441 gives defendants a corresponding opportunity. The scales are not evenly balanced, however. An in-state plaintiff may invoke diversity jurisdiction, but § 1441(b) bars removal on the basis of diversity if any "party in interest properly joined and served as a defendant is a citizen of the State in which the action is brought."

In addition, all defendants must agree to removal and removal must occur within one year of the commencement of the action, § 1446(b).

2.

Section 1332(d), added by CAFA, vests the district court with "original jurisdiction of any civil action in which the matter in controversy exceeds the sum or value of $5,000,000, exclusive of interest and costs, and is a class action in which" the parties satisfy, among other requirements, minimal diversity. Section 1332(d) thus abandons the complete diversity rule for covered class actions.

Of particular import here, § 1332(d) does not apply only to traditional class actions. Section 1332(d)(11)(A), provides that "for purposes of this subsection and section 1453, a mass action shall be deemed to be a class action removable under paragraphs (2) through (10) if it otherwise meets the provisions of those paragraphs." The wording of this subsection is clumsy. On its face, § 1332(d)(2)–(10) vests the district courts with *original* jurisdiction over certain class actions, *see* § 1332(d)(2) ("The district courts shall have *original jurisdiction*"), but subsection (d)(11)(A) refers to actions "*removable* under paragraphs (2) through (10)."

> The confusion is not alleviated by the statutory reference to "mass action," which reads:

> Any civil action in which monetary relief claims of 100 or more persons are proposed to be tried jointly on the ground that the plaintiffs' claims involve common questions of law or fact, except that jurisdiction shall exist only over those plaintiffs whose claims in a mass action satisfy the jurisdictional amount requirements under subsection (a).

Section 1332(d)(11)(B)(i). To "otherwise meet" the provisions of § 1332(d) "paragraphs (2) through (10)," the amount placed into controversy by a mass action must—when the "claims of the individual class members are aggregated"—exceed $5,000,000, exclusive of interests and costs. Section 1332(d)(2), (6). The statute does not explain the relationship between the 100 or more persons and $5,000,000 aggregate amount in controversy requirement on the one hand, and the limitation of jurisdiction to "those plaintiffs whose claims in a mass action satisfy in excess of $75,000 jurisdictional amount requirement," on the other.

The final CAFA amendment relevant here is § 1453, which addresses the removal of class actions. Section 1453(b) exempts qualifying actions from the § 1446(b) prohibition of removal "more than 1 year after commencement of the state court action," and overrides the judge-created requirement that each defendant consent to removal. Section 1453(b), moreover, unlike § 1441, allows for removal of actions "without regard to whether any defendant is a citizen of the State in which the action is brought."

3.

Meshing the existing jurisdiction and removal statutory sections with the CAFA "mass action" amendments is far from straightforward. The confusion revolves around the definition of a "mass action" and the relationship of the individual jurisdictional requirement of § 1332(a) to that definition. The problem is best illustrated by looking at the text of the statute:

> The term "*mass action*" means any civil action in which monetary relief claims of 100 or more persons are proposed to be tried jointly on the ground that the plaintiffs' claims involve common questions of law or fact, *except that jurisdiction* shall exist only over those

plaintiffs whose claims in a *mass action* satisfy the jurisdictional amount requirements under § 1332(a).

§ 1332(d)(11)(B)(i) (emphases added). Is the proviso part of the definition of "mass action" or an independent provision? The mystery deepens when considering how the individual jurisdictional requirement relates to § 1332(d)(2)–(10): What happens if individual remands under the § 1332(a) proviso bring the aggregate amount in controversy below $5,000,000, or the number of plaintiffs below 100, or destroys minimal diversity? The text of the statute does not specify whether each of these requirements looks to "plaintiffs in a mass action" or to "plaintiffs in a mass action over whom the district court has jurisdiction." Finally, Congress's use of the word "removable" in the text of § 1332, a statute establishing original jurisdiction, blurs what had previously been a clear distinction between jurisdiction and removal statutes, and thus obscures the reach of jurisdiction over mass actions. Because Congress did not refer to original jurisdiction in either the mass action provision itself, or in § 1453, the text does not answer the important question of when there is original federal jurisdiction over mass actions, and what the scope of that original jurisdiction might be. This gap casts into doubt the interaction between the mass action provision and a host of other statutes that assume original jurisdiction as a starting point.

It is against this complex background that Dow stakes out its position that (1) CAFA shifted the burdens normally applicable in the removal context; (2) under CAFA's mass action provisions, removed mass actions remain in federal court even if the plaintiffs alleging claims in excess of $75,000 do not meet the numerosity or aggregate total amount in controversy requirement of § 1332(d); and (3) CAFA *requires* the district court to allow post-removal jurisdictional discovery. Because we disagree with Dow's position on the first and third issues, we have no reason, on the facts of this case, to resolve the second, and thorniest, question, and do not do so.

C.

We now turn to the merits of the jurisdictional question—that is, whether Dow has established that the workers' action is a "mass action" removable under §§ 1332 and 1453. We conclude that under *any* formulation of the bewildering language of § 1332(d)(11)(B)(i), remand was proper because Dow has failed to meet its burden to establish jurisdiction over even one plaintiff. We therefore need not and do not endorse any particular construction of the mass action provisions of § 1332(d)(11).

Dow maintains that "CAFA expands the district court's *removal* jurisdiction to include actions where the aggregate amount in controversy exceeds $5,000,000, but leaves in place the rule that the court's *subject matter* jurisdiction extends only to those individual plaintiffs who are seeking at least $75,000." On this view, a case in which the aggregate amount in controversy is more than $5,000,000 and which involves in state court more than 100 plaintiffs proposed to be tried together may be removed as a mass action. The claims of any plaintiffs with damages less than $75,000 would then be subject to remand for want of subject matter jurisdiction.

Dow's interpretation of the statute rests upon the conclusion that the mass action provision is ambiguous and is part of a statutory scheme that hardly qualifies as "coherent and consistent," alongside a "clearly expressed legislative intention" that gives shape to key provisions in the statute. Under this view, the mass action provision falls within the rule that "extrinsic materials have a role in statutory interpretation only to the extent they shed a reliable light on the enacting Legislature's understanding of otherwise ambiguous terms."

Dow urges that the Committee Report addresses the problematic clause directly:

> Subsequent remands of individual claims not meeting the section 1332 jurisdictional amount requirement may take the action below the 100-plaintiff jurisdictional threshold or the $5 million aggregated jurisdictional amount requirement. But, so long as the mass action met the various jurisdictional requirements at the time of removal, it is the Committee's view that those subsequent remands should not extinguish federal diversity jurisdictional over the action.

This clarification is consistent with a logical reading of the statute, as a committee report is entitled to considerably greater weight than comments made during floor debate.

In sum, relying on this legislative history, Dow urges that a "mass action" be defined as "any civil action in which monetary relief claims of 100 or more persons are proposed to be tried jointly on the ground that the plaintiffs' claims involve common questions of law or fact," § 1332(d)(11)(B)(i), and removable from state court to federal court if it "otherwise meets the provisions of" paragraphs § 1332(d)(2)–(10), including the $5,000,000 aggregate amount in controversy requirement and minimal diversity. § 1332(d)(11)(A). Once in federal court, the court would exercise jurisdiction only over those plaintiffs whose individual claims meet the $75,000 threshold. Remands of individual claims under $75,000 might take the action below 100 plaintiffs and $5,000,000, but would not extinguish federal jurisdiction over the existing mass action.

The workers' reading of § 1332(d)(11), in contrast, is grounded in the understanding that § 1332(d) is, in general, a grant of original jurisdiction to the district court, and stresses that the "except" clause provides that "*jurisdiction* shall *exist* only over those plaintiffs whose claims in a mass action satisfy the in excess of $75,000 jurisdictional amount."

§ 1332(d)(11)(B)(i) (emphasis added). On this view, the jurisdictional limitation to plaintiffs asserting claims in excess of $75,000 is applicable at the time of removal and to the action as a whole. Both original and removal jurisdiction, then, would depend on establishing § 1332(a) jurisdiction over *each* plaintiff's claims, as well as on meeting the "mass action" requirements with regard to the plaintiffs over whom there is original jurisdiction. This position acknowledges the ambiguity of the statutory language. It stresses, however, that the legislative history Dow relies upon is entitled to exceptionally little weight, because it was, as noted by the minority views in the Committee Report, not available for consideration or discussion before enactment of CAFA.

The workers also urge that Dow's interpretation of the statute disregards the purposes of the "mass action" provision. Dow's interpretation, the workers maintain, could leave in federal court an action with very few plaintiffs, while remanding the "mass" part of the mass action. This result, the workers argue, conflicts with the reason "mass actions" were added to the statute—that they closely resemble the large class actions of national importance to which the statute otherwise applies. *See* CAFA, § 2(b)(2) (noting that CAFA was intended to "restore the intent of the framers of the United States Constitution by providing for Federal court consideration of interstate cases of national importance under diversity jurisdiction").

Resolving which of these two positions is correct is not necessary in this case. To paraphrase the Supreme Court:

> CAFA has made some radical changes in the law regulating jurisdiction and removals. Important questions of practice are likely to arise under it, which, until the statute has been longer in operation, it will not be easy to decide in advance. For the present, therefore, we think it best to confine ourselves to the determination of the precise question presented in any particular case, and not to anticipate any that may arise in the future.

Regardless of the correct construction of the "mass action" provisions, we conclude, Dow has not carried its burden of establishing jurisdiction on removal.

The deference owed to district courts in managing jurisdictional discovery is tempered by concern regarding the time pressure imposed by the general removal provisions of § 1446(b). This concern does not plague us here, as the parties in this case will not be prejudiced in their opportunity to develop the record with regard to the amount in controversy by return to state court. Under CAFA, class actions and mass actions may be removed at any point during the pendency of litigation in state court, so long as removal is initiated within thirty days after the defendant is put on notice that a case which was not removable based on the face of the complaint has become removable. *See* § 1446(b) (setting forth the one-year limitation); § 1453(b) (one-year time limitation of § 1446(b) does not apply to the removal of class actions); § 1332(d)(11)(A) (mass actions are to be treated as class actions under § 1453).

Moreover, by lifting the one year bar, CAFA clearly contemplates that state courts may be burdened, for longer than was previously possible, with cases that ultimately will be removed. As a result, there is also sufficient time to develop in state court the facts necessary to support federal jurisdiction. Also, as state court class action and mass action plaintiffs now run the risk that their case can be removed at any stage of the litigation, there is no longer an incentive for them to remain cagey about the amount in controversy until the one-year window of § 1446(b) has closed.

Finally, we emphasized the importance of "guarding against premature and protective removals and minimizing the potential for a cottage industry of removal litigation." Dow removed this action to district court a mere seven days after the workers filed their First Amended Complaint, and less than a month after the case was filed. Once in federal court, Dow failed to present to the district court any pleading, evidence, or admission that establishes that it is more likely than not that jurisdiction lies. On these facts, it is well within the court's discretion to remand to state court rather than ordering jurisdictional discovery, with the knowledge that later-discovered facts may prompt a second attempt at removal. Doing so avoids encouraging the sort of premature removal presented to us here. We therefore hold that the district court did not abuse its discretion under CAFA by declining to order jurisdictional discovery in this case.

CAFA's legislative history does not alter our conclusion. In arguing that the district court must provide for jurisdictional discovery, Dow points us to yet another a portion of the same Senate Judiciary Committee Report, which states:

> The Committee understands that in assessing the various criteria established in all these new jurisdictional provisions, a federal court may have to engage in some fact-finding, not unlike what is necessitated by the existing jurisdictional statutes. The Committee further understands that in some instances, limited discovery may be necessary to make these determinations. *However, the Committee cautions that these jurisdictional determinations should be made largely on the basis of readily available information. Allowing substantial, burdensome discovery on jurisdictional issues would be contrary to the intent of these provisions to encourage the exercise of federal jurisdiction over class actions.*

This statement is untethered to any statutory language. Moreover, this passage confirms that any decision regarding jurisdictional discovery is a discretionary one, and is governed by existing principles regarding post-removal jurisdictional discovery, including the disinclination to entertain "substantial, burdensome discovery on jurisdictional issues." Applying those established principles, the district court's refusal to accept the proposal that 1,160 plaintiffs located in and around Panama answer contention interrogatories while the case is otherwise put on hold was not an abuse of discretion.

## III.

Nothing in CAFA's language purports to shift the burdens normally applied to removal of a state action to federal court. Dow has failed to meet its burden in demonstrating that the jurisdictional requirements of CAFA are satisfied. For these reasons, we affirm the district court's remand of this action to state court.

## IN RE WELDING FUME PRODS. LIAB. LITIG.

United States District Court, N.D. Ohio, Eastern Division, 2007.
245 F.R.D. 279.

### III. JURISDICTION

The parties agree, and the Court concludes, that it has federal subject matter diversity jurisdiction over the *Steele* action, pursuant to 28 U.S.C. § 1332, as amended by the Class Action Fairness Act of 2005 (CAFA).

Under CAFA, federal courts have jurisdiction in diversity, with exceptions not at issue here, over (1) cases filed as class actions (2) with one hundred or more class members, (3) in which any member of the plaintiff class is a citizen of a state different from that of any defendant (known as "minimal diversity"), and (4) where the amount in controversy exceeds $5 million. In the instant case, the number of welder plaintiffs in the proposed class numbers in the tens of thousands; most of the defendants have citizenship different from most of the plaintiffs; and the aggregate cost of the medical monitoring program and other relief requested by the plaintiffs could easily exceed $5 million by a factor of 400 or more. Thus, federal jurisdiction attaches to the *Steele* case and its proposed multi-state plaintiff class.

Indeed, for reasons discussed later, it is notable that this Court would likely have jurisdiction over even a single-state class action brought by plaintiff welders. For example, if the same case had been filed only by plaintiffs who were citizens of Utah (instead of all eight states recited), the above-listed jurisdictional requirements would still be met. And federal jurisdiction would obtain even if this hypothetical case were filed in Utah state court, as the case would almost surely be removed successfully to federal court. These circumstances differ from the pre-CAFA world, when federal jurisdiction required *complete* diversity between plaintiffs and defendants, even in class actions.

Further, there are serious implications in light of CAFA. As noted above in this opinion, the likelihood that federal jurisdiction will attach to even a single-state class action is much higher after passage of CAFA. To the extent that "some areas of state substantive law are only adjudicated in the form of class actions," CAFA will thus work to preclude state courts from any opportunity to address certain areas of law. More to the point at issue here, CAFA will also remove from state courts the chance even to apply their own civil *procedural* rules to determine the threshold question of whether certification of a medical monitoring class is appropriate. The upshot of CAFA, then, is to move questions of medical monitoring class certification out of state courts and into federal courts—a move, which, based on existing precedent, favors defendants.

## CORBER V. XANODYNE PHARMACEUTICALS, INC.

United States Court of Appeals for the Ninth Circuit, 2014.
771 F.3d 1218.

We must decide whether removal is proper under the "mass action" provision of the Class Action Fairness Act of 2005 (CAFA), 28 U.S.C. § 1332(d)(11)(B)(i), when plaintiffs in several actions moved for coordination in the state trial court pursuant to California Code of Civil Procedure section 404 "for all purposes" and justified their request in part by asserting a need to avoid inconsistent judgments. CAFA extends federal removal jurisdiction for certain class actions and for mass actions in which "monetary relief claims of 100 or more persons are proposed to be tried jointly on the ground that the plaintiffs' claims involve common questions of law or fact." 28 U.S.C. § 1332(d)(11)(B)(i). Because we conclude that all of the CAFA requirements for a removable mass action are met under the totality of the circumstances in these cases, we reverse the district court's remand orders.

### I.

Defendants-Appellants Teva Pharmaceuticals USA, Inc. and Xanodyne Pharmaceuticals, Inc. appeal from the district court's orders remanding these cases to state court. These cases were two of twenty-six pending before the district court alleging injuries related to the ingestion of propoxyphene, an ingredient found in the Darvocet and Darvon pain relief drugs, as well as in generic pain relievers. There are additional propoxyphene cases pending in multidistrict litigation in the Eastern District of Kentucky.

Propoxyphene is a pain reliever that was used in the United States to treat mild to moderate pain from 1957 through November 2010, when drugs containing propoxyphene were taken off the market because of safety concerns. Teva held the rights to the generic form of Darvocet and Darvon, and Plaintiffs allege that Teva was involved in all aspects of the creation, distribution, and sale of generic propoxyphene products. Xanodyne acquired the rights to Darvocet and Darvon in 2007.

To date, more than forty actions have been filed in California state courts regarding propoxyphene pain relievers. On October 23, 2012, a group of attorneys responsible for many of the propoxyphene actions against Teva, Xanodyne, and other defendants filed petitions asking the California Judicial Council to establish a coordinated proceeding for all California propoxyphene actions under section 404 of the California Code of Civil Procedure. California Code of Civil Procedure section 404.1, which sets out the standards for coordination, states:

> Coordination of civil actions sharing a common question of fact or law is appropriate if one judge hearing all of the actions for all purposes in a selected site or sites will promote the ends of justice taking into account whether the common question of fact or law is predominating and significant to the litigation; the convenience of parties, witnesses, and counsel; the relative development of the actions and the work product of counsel; the efficient utilization of judicial facilities and manpower; the calendar of the courts; the disadvantages of duplicative and inconsistent rulings, orders, or judgments; and, the likelihood of settlement of the actions without further litigation should coordination be denied.

Plaintiffs asked for coordination of their lawsuits for reasons consistent with the above factors, including concerns that there could be potential "duplicate and inconsistent rulings, orders, or judgments," and that without coordination, "two or more separate courts may render different rulings on liability and other issues." Plaintiffs argued in their petitions and the supporting memoranda that the cases should be coordinated before one judge "hearing all of the actions for all purposes," to address "the same or substantially similar" causes of action, issues of law, and issues of material fact. After these petitions for coordination were filed, Teva and Xanodyne removed the cases to federal district court under CAFA's mass action provision.

CAFA provides federal district courts with original jurisdiction over "mass actions" if the actions meet all of the statutory requirements. 28 U.S.C. § 1332(d). CAFA defines a mass action as:

> Any civil action in which monetary relief claims of 100 or more persons are proposed to be tried jointly on the ground that the plaintiffs' claims involve common questions of law or fact, except that jurisdiction shall exist only over those plaintiffs whose claims in a mass action satisfy the jurisdictional amount requirements under subsection (a).

28 U.S.C. § 1332(d)(11)(B)(i). The parties dispute only whether Plaintiffs' petitions for coordination constitute proposals for the cases "to be tried jointly" under CAFA.

The district court held that it lacked jurisdiction under CAFA because Plaintiffs' petitions for coordination were not proposals to try the cases jointly, and it remanded the cases back to state court. The district court distinguished these cases from the Seventh Circuit's decision in *In re Abbott Laboratories, Inc.,* and held that Plaintiffs' petitions were sufficiently different from *Abbott's* consolidation request because the petitions filed in this case focused on pre-trial purposes, while the petition filed in *Abbott* explicitly sought consolidation "through trial."

Defendants sought permission to appeal the district court's remand orders, which we granted. A three-judge panel affirmed. A majority of non-recused judges voted to rehear the case en banc. We review the district court's remand order *de novo.*

## II.

The controlling issue before us is whether Plaintiffs' petitions to coordinate actions under California Code of Civil Procedure section 404 constitute proposals for these actions to be tried jointly, making the actions a "mass action" subject to federal jurisdiction under CAFA. The statutory issue for us is whether the petitions filed in this case, seeking coordination of the California propoxyphene actions, were in legal effect proposals for those actions to be tried jointly. This is a question of first impression in the Ninth Circuit.

Congress enacted CAFA in 2005 to "curb perceived abuses of the class action device which, in the view of CAFA's proponents, had often been used to litigate multistate or even national class actions in state courts." *Tanoh v. Dow Chem. Co.* CAFA further extends federal jurisdiction over "mass action" cases when several requirements are met, although only the "proposed to be tried jointly" requirement is at issue here. *See* 28 U.S.C. § 1332(d)(2), (6), (11)(A).

We have said that CAFA's mass action provision is "fairly narrow," given that it applies only if there is an aggregate amount in controversy of $5 million or more, at least one plaintiff who is a citizen of a state or foreign state different from that of any defendant, and when "monetary relief claims of 100 or more persons are proposed to be tried jointly," 28 U.S.C. § 1332(d)(11)(B)(i). *Tanoh v. Dow Chemical Co.* holds, consistent with the plain language of CAFA, that the proposal to try claims jointly must come from the plaintiffs, not from the defendants. Further, *Tanoh* correctly holds that if the mass action provision's requirements are not met, we cannot ignore its terms based on general statements in CAFA's legislative history or the theory that plaintiffs should not be able to "game" jurisdictional statutes to remain in state court.

*Tanoh* also holds that plaintiffs are the "masters of their complaint" and do not propose a joint trial simply by structuring their complaints so as to avoid the 100-plaintiff threshold. Under this view, plaintiffs can structure actions in cases involving more than 100 potential claimants so as to avoid federal jurisdiction under CAFA. That is not surprising, and it is analogous to the fact that individuals and corporations can structure transactions so as to avoid statutory prohibitions or terms. Amici Chamber of Commerce of the United States of America and PhRMA urge us to conclude that the Supreme Court's decision in *Standard Fire Insurance Co. v. Knowles* fatally "undermines Tanoh's reasoning and holding." We reject this interpretation of *Knowles*, which itself reiterates that plaintiffs are the "masters of their complaints" who may structure those complaints to avoid federal jurisdiction in some circumstances.

But while plaintiffs are the masters of their complaints, they are also the masters of their petitions for coordination. Stated another way, when we assess whether there has been a proposal for joint trial, we hold plaintiffs responsible for what they have said and done. California Code of Civil Procedure section 404 allows the coordination of "all of the actions for all purposes" and presents a factor-based test to determine whether coordination is appropriate. Plaintiffs voluntarily asked for coordination under section 404, and they submitted memoranda in support of their petitions for coordination. We will carefully assess the language of the petitions for coordination to see whether, in language or substance, they proposed a joint trial.

We conclude that Plaintiffs' petitions for coordination are proposals for joint trial. First, the petitions say that Plaintiffs seek coordination "for all purposes." "All purposes" must include the purposes of trial. So reading the petitions literally, Plaintiffs, who in total number far more than 100, were seeking a joint trial. Second, the specific reasons given for coordination also support the conclusion that a joint trial was requested. For example, Plaintiffs listed potential issues in support of their petitions that would be addressed only through some form of joint trial, such as the danger of inconsistent judgments and conflicting determinations of liability.

Our conclusions here are consistent with *Tanoh,* where we held that "the decision to try claims jointly and thus qualify as a 'mass action' under CAFA should remain with plaintiffs." Unlike the plaintiffs in *Tanoh,* who merely filed separate actions that the defendant sought to try jointly, Plaintiffs' filing of the petitions for coordination was a voluntary and affirmative act that we conclude was a proposal to try the cases jointly.

Plaintiffs contend that they were simply reciting the section 404.1 factors, but we find this argument unpersuasive given the language of the petitions and the supporting memoranda. Plaintiffs did not simply recite the factors for coordination. They asserted that "the inevitability of realizing the inconsistency and duplication factor of California Code of

Civil Procedure Section 404.1 weighs heavily in favor of coordination." Plaintiffs further asserted that "issues pertaining to liability, allocation of fault and contribution, as well as the same wrongful conduct of defendants," would require coordination. None of these particular arguments is listed in the section 404 factors, and achieving consistency in these areas would almost certainly require a joint trial. Plaintiffs' petitions requested more than pre-trial coordination. Plaintiffs repeatedly stated that the factors catalogued in section 404.1 all supported coordination, including the fact that "one judge hearing all of the actions for all purposes in a selected site or sites will promote the ends of justice." In the application of a jurisdictional rule, as well as in its establishment, we agree with the Supreme Court's observation that "simplicity is a virtue." Looking at the plain language of Plaintiffs' petitions and memoranda, we must conclude that Plaintiffs proposed a joint trial in asking that "all of the actions" be coordinated "for all purposes."

This is not to say that all petitions for coordination under section 404 are *per se* proposals to try cases jointly for the purposes of CAFA's mass action provision. We can envision a section 404 petition that expressly seeks to limit its request for coordination to pre-trial matters, and thereby align with the mass action provision's exception for "any civil action in which the claims have been consolidated or coordinated solely for pretrial proceedings." 28 U.S.C. § 1332(d)(11)(B)(ii)(IV). It is not clear whether the California Judicial Council would grant coordination for less than "all purposes." However, if Plaintiffs had qualified their coordination request by saying that it was intended to be solely for pre-trial purposes, then it would be difficult to suggest that Plaintiffs had proposed a joint trial. But where, as here, plaintiffs petition for coordination by arguing that "hearing all of the actions" together "for all purposes" would promote the ends of justice, they propose a joint trial, triggering federal jurisdiction as a mass action under CAFA.

We reject the rule urged by Plaintiffs that a petition to evoke CAFA must expressly request a "joint trial" in order to be a proposal to try the cases jointly. Although such a rule would be easy to administer, it would ignore the real substance of Plaintiffs' petitions. *See Abbott* ("A proposal for a joint trial can be implicit").

Two of our sister circuits have reached similar conclusions when examining petitions for consolidation. In *Abbott,* the Seventh Circuit reasoned that the plaintiffs' petition for consolidation "through trial" and "not solely for pretrial proceedings" was a proposal to try jointly their separately filed cases. The Seventh Circuit concluded that, contrary to the plaintiffs' assertion that they did not specifically ask for a joint trial, the language of the plaintiffs' petition for consolidation could be construed only as an implicit proposal for joint trial. Plaintiffs here seek to distinguish their own "for all purposes" language from the "through trial" language present in *Abbott,* but the differences between the two phrasings are superficial, and we are not persuaded.

The Eighth Circuit adopted *Abbott's* reasoning, concluding that plaintiffs proposed a joint trial when they filed motions asking for special assignment "to a single judge *for both pretrial and trial matters,*" and then argued at the motions hearing that the special assignment made sense "for consistency of rulings, judicial economy, and administration of justice." *Atwell.* The Eighth Circuit decided that "the motions for assignment to a single judge, combined with plaintiffs' candid explanation of their objectives, required denial of the motions to remand" the cases to state court. Plaintiffs further attempt to distinguish their own petitions for coordination from *Atwell* on the basis that "there is no such explicit language in Plaintiffs' petition," but again we find this distinction unpersuasive given the language of Plaintiffs' memoranda in support of their petitions, which both sought coordination "for all purposes" and gave reasons that likely would be satisfied only by a joint trial of some sort.

Asking for coordination or consolidation "for all purposes" or "through trial" to address common issues of law or fact is a proposal to try the cases jointly and creates federal jurisdiction under CAFA's mass action provision. To hold otherwise would ignore the plain language, as well as the substance, of Plaintiffs' section 404 petitions and supporting memoranda.

### III.

Because we conclude that Plaintiffs' petitions for coordination each constitute a proposal to try the cases jointly, we reverse the district court's orders granting Plaintiffs' motions to remand.

RAWLINSON, CIRCUIT JUDGE, with whom JUDGE BERZON joins, dissenting:

This is admittedly a fairly close case but, upon reflection, I respectfully dissent from the conclusion of my esteemed colleagues that this case fits within the parameters for removal under the Class Action Fairness Act of 2005 (CAFA).

I start from the well-established premise that removal is disfavored when determining federal jurisdiction, and that any doubt that exists when considering removal statutes should be construed against removal. As we also recognized in *Tanoh,* CAFA's mass action provision is "fairly narrow."

With those principles firmly in mind, I reach a different conclusion than that of the majority. The plain language of the Class Action Fairness Act, 28 U.S.C. § 1332(d)(11)(B)(i), confers jurisdiction upon federal district courts to try a "mass action." A mass action is defined as: "any civil action in which monetary relief claims of 100 or more persons are *proposed to be tried jointly* on the ground that the plaintiffs' claims involve common questions of law or fact."

The majority concludes that the Plaintiffs proposed their cases "to be tried jointly" by filing a petition for coordination pursuant to California Code of Civil Procedure § 404.1. That section provides:

> Coordination of civil actions sharing a common question of fact or law is appropriate if one judge hearing all of the actions for all purposes in selected site or sites will promote the ends of justice taking into account whether the common question of fact or law is predominating and significant to the litigation; the convenience of parties, witnesses, and counsel; the relative development of the actions and the work product of counsel; the efficient utilization of judicial facilities and manpower; the calendar of the courts; the disadvantages of duplicative and inconsistent rulings, orders, or judgments; and the likelihood of settlement of the actions without further litigation should coordination be denied.

The plaintiffs' petition for coordination stopped short of requesting a joint trial as contemplated by the plain language of the statute. *See* 28 U.S.C. § 1332(d)(11)(B)(i) (defining a mass action as one in which claims of 100 or more persons "are proposed to be tried jointly").

On page 6 of the Memorandum of Points and Authorities in support of the petition, plaintiffs gave the following explanation for seeking coordination:

> Petitioners' counsel anticipates that the actions will involve *duplicative requests for the same defendant witness depositions and the same documents related to development, manufacturing, testing, marketing, and sale of the Darvocet Product.* Absent coordination of these actions by a single judge, *there is a significant likelihood of duplicative discovery,* waste of judicial resources and possible inconsistent judicial rulings on legal issues.

It is a stretch to parse a proposal for a joint trial from this language. Rather, the obvious focus was on pretrial proceedings, *i.e.,* discovery matters.

On page 7 of the memorandum, plaintiffs informed the court that coordination was also sought because "*use of committees and standardized discovery in a coordinated setting* will expedite resolutions of these cases, avoid inconsistent results, and assist in alleviating onerous burdens on the courts as well as the parties." Again, we see a focus on pretrial proceedings, with no mention of a joint trial.

On page 8, the plaintiffs urged coordination on the following bases:

One judge hearing all of the actions for all purposes in a selected site or sites will promote the ends of justice; Common questions of fact or law are predominating and significant to the litigation; Coordination may serve the convenience of parties, witnesses and counsel the relative development of the actions and the work product of counsel; Coordination may facilitate the efficient utilization of judicial facilities and manpower; Coordination may enhance the orderly calendar of the courts; Without coordination, the parties may suffer from disadvantages caused by duplicative and inconsistent rulings, orders or judgments.

Plaintiffs also stated: "In light of the similarity of the actions, there will be *duplicate discovery obligations* upon the common defendants *unless coordination is ordered. Coordination before initiation of discovery in any of the cases* will eliminate waste of resources and will facilitate economy." Unlike the cases from the Seventh and Eighth Circuits cited in the majority opinion, not once does the Petition For Coordination mention "joint trial" or even "trial." Rather, the continued focus is on pretrial matters.

The majority opinion isolates the phrases "duplicate and inconsistent rulings, orders, or judgments," "two or more separate courts may render different rulings on liability and other issues," and "hearing all of the actions for all purposes" to support its conclusion that the plaintiffs sought a joint trial. In doing so, the majority completely ignores all references to discovery, including on the same page containing the reference to liability, where Plaintiffs stated: "In light of the similarity of the actions, there will be *duplicate discovery obligations* upon the common defendants *unless coordination is ordered. Coordination before initiation of discovery in any of the cases* will eliminate waste of resources and will facilitate economy." A fair reading of the entire petition for coordination reflects a decided focus on pretrial matters.

Reliance by the majority on the quoted portions of the petition to the exclusion of all else is inconsistent with the command that any doubt about federal jurisdiction be resolved in favor of remand. This is especially true where most of the quoted words have little to do with trial. I am not persuaded that a reference to "rulings and orders" evokes the concept of trial rather than pretrial matters. Indeed, the opposite may be true:

An order is the mandate or determination of the court upon some subsidiary or collateral matter arising in an action, not disposing of the merits, but adjudicating a preliminary point or directing some step in the proceedings.

Black's Law Dictionary 1270 (10th ed.2009).

In turn "rulings on motions are ordinarily orders." Consequently, at best, Plaintiffs' reference to rulings and orders is ambiguous, and ambiguity defeats removal.

The majority is also on shaky ground when relying on the plaintiffs' reference to inconsistent judgments, because judgments may be rendered outside the confines of a trial. Default judgments and summary judgments come readily to mind. Indeed, it is not at all uncommon for similar cases to be resolved short of trial.

Plaintiffs' reference to rulings on liability also fit readily within the concept of resolving cases short of trial. Unsurprisingly, the majority's contrary notion that a joint trial is "almost certainly required" to determine liability, is not supported by citation to any California authority. The district court judges who rendered decisions remanding these cases to state court are all seasoned California practitioners, and not one of them interpreted the Petition For Coordination as requesting a joint trial.

The cases from the Seventh and Eighth Circuit relied upon by the majority are easily distinguishable. In this case, the Plaintiffs requested coordination of the cases "for all purposes." The majority reads that phrase as implicitly requesting a joint trial, citing the Seventh Circuit's decision in *In re Abbott Laboratories, Inc.* However, not only did the Seventh Circuit consider a completely different procedure, consolidation as opposed to coordination, the plaintiffs' request in that case explicitly and expressly referenced "consolidation of the cases *through trial* and *not* solely for pretrial proceedings," thereby removing any question of the plaintiffs' intent. In fact, there was really nothing implicit about the *Abbott* plaintiffs' request for a joint trial. Rather, the request for a joint trial was open and notorious.

In a similar vein, the plaintiffs in *Atwell v. Boston Scientific Corp.* requested that their cases be assigned "to a single judge for purposes of discovery *and trial*." None of these cases address the facts of this case, where there was not a single Complaint joining over one hundred plaintiffs, and there was no use of the word "trial" anywhere in the petition seeking coordination.

The California district court judges who considered this issue uniformly distinguished *Abbott*. I am persuaded to the view of these able district court judges.

The conclusion that Plaintiffs implicitly requested a joint trial is not supported by the language of CAFA or by the cases from the Seventh and Eighth Circuits so heavily relied upon by the majority. That conclusion is inconsistent with precedent from the Supreme Court and this circuit that Plaintiffs are the masters of their Complaints, that removal statutes (including CAFA) are to be construed narrowly, that any ambiguity is to be construed *against* removal, and that the plain language of the statute controls. Finally, nothing prevents Defendants from seeking removal if and when Plaintiffs actually request a joint trial. I respectfully dissent.

# B.  LOCAL EVENT OR OCCURRENCE EXCEPTION

## PRESTON V. TENET HEALTHSYSTEM MEMORIAL MEDICAL CENTER, INC.

United States Court of Appeals for the Fifth Circuit, 2007.
485 F.3d 804.

Tenet Health Systems Memorial Medical Center d/b/a Memorial Medical Center (Memorial) moved to remand this class action lawsuit to state court under the "local controversy" exception of the Class Action Fairness Act of 2005, 28 U.S.C. § 1332(d). The district court granted the motion to remand, and LifeCare Management Services, LLC, and LifeCare Hospitals of New Orleans, LLC (LifeCare), timely appealed the order. We affirm the district court's judgment.

### I.   FACTUAL AND PROCEDURAL BACKGROUND

Preston represents a putative class of patients and the relatives of deceased and allegedly injured patients hospitalized at Memorial when Hurricane Katrina made landfall in New Orleans, Louisiana. Memorial owned and operated the hospital, and LifeCare leased the seventh floor of the facility for an acute care center. On October 6, 2005, Preston brought suit against Memorial in the Civil District Court for the Parish of Orleans. Preston asserted claims for negligence and intentional misconduct, "reverse patient dumping" under the Emergency Medical Treatment and Active Labor Act and involuntary euthanization. Preston alleged that Memorial failed to design and maintain the premises in a manner that avoided loss of power in the building. Preston further alleged that Memorial and LifeCare failed to develop and implement an evacuation plan for the patients. According to the petition, Memorial's and LifeCare's failure to maintain the premises and timely evacuate the facility resulted in the deaths and injuries of hospitalized patients. Preston named LifeCare in the Fifth Supplemental Amended Petition for Damages, seeking to certify the following class of persons:

> All patients of Memorial and LifeCare who sustained injuries including death or personal injury as a result of the insufficient design, inspection and/or maintenance of LifeCare and/or Memorial's back-up electrical system, its failure to implement its evacuation plan and/or its emergency preparedness plan and/or its failure to have a plan which would have facilitated the safe transfer of patients out of harm's way, and its failure to have a plan of care for patients in the event of a power outage in the wake of Hurricane Katrina within the property owned by Memorial and

leased and/or operated by LifeCare on or about the time period of August 26, 2005 through and including August 29, 2005 and thereafter, and all persons who sustained personal injury as a result of the deaths or personal injuries to patients of LifeCare and Memorial.

On June 26, 2006, LifeCare filed a timely notice of removal. Memorial never consented to removal from the state court. Preston filed a motion to remand under the local controversy exception of CAFA. On November 21, 2006, the district court remanded the lawsuit to state court under the local controversy exception, home state exception, and the discretionary jurisdiction provision. LifeCare filed a timely petition for appeal pursuant to 28 U.S.C. § 1453. LifeCare only contests the district court's citizenship findings under CAFA's exceptions to federal jurisdiction.

## II. STANDARD OF REVIEW

We review the district court's factual findings as to the citizenship of the parties for clear error (conducting a de novo review of the district court's citizenship determination under CAFA's local controversy exception).

The standard of review for a district court's remand under the discretionary provision constitutes an issue of first impression. We review the district court's remand order for abuse of discretion. In determining the burden of proof to show citizenship under the local controversy exception, courts treating the question in the first instance looked to 28 U.S.C. § 1441(a), the general removal statute).

The local controversy and home state exceptions read that the "district courts *shall* decline to exercise jurisdiction," while the discretionary provision provides that the district court "*may* in the interests of justice and looking at the totality of the circumstances" decline to exercise jurisdiction. Compare §§ 1332(d)(2) & (4) with § 1332(d)(3). LifeCare cogently argues that the local controversy and home state exceptions should be construed narrowly and resolved in favor of federal jurisdiction based on the "shall decline to exercise jurisdiction" language, which represents the classic formulation for abstention. Under the discretionary jurisdiction provision, however, Congress permitted the district court greater latitude to remand class actions to state court. As with supplemental jurisdiction under 28 U.S.C. § 1367(c), the district court does not wield unfettered discretion over whether to remand a case; instead Congress provided a list of factors to guide the district court's consideration.

## III. DISCUSSION

### A.  Statutory Background

Congress enacted CAFA to expand federal jurisdiction over interstate class action lawsuits of national interest. CAFA contains a basic jurisdictional test for removal, which requires the removing defendant to prove minimal diversity and an aggregated amount in controversy of $5,000,000 or more. § 1332(d). CAFA eliminates the standard requirements of unanimous consent among the defendants and the one-year removal deadline. § 1453(b). The district court can decline jurisdiction under three provisions: (1) the home state exception, § 1332(d)(4)(B); (2) the local controversy exception, § 1332(d)(4)(A); and (3) discretionary jurisdiction, § 1332(d)(3).

Pursuant to the local controversy exception, the district court "shall decline to exercise jurisdiction" when the class action meets the following criteria:

(I)   greater than two-thirds of the members of all proposed plaintiff classes in the aggregate are citizens of the State in which the action was originally filed;

(II)  at least 1 defendant is a defendant—

    (aa) from whom significant relief is sought by members of the plaintiff class;

    (bb) whose alleged conduct forms a significant basis for the claims asserted by the proposed plaintiff class; and

    (cc) who is a citizen of the State in which the action was originally filed; and

(III) principal injuries resulting from the alleged conduct or any related conduct of each defendant were incurred in the State in which the action was originally filed; and

    (ii)  during the 3-year period preceding the filing of that class action, no other class action has been filed asserting the same or similar factual allegations against any of the defendants on behalf of the same or other persons.

§ 1332(d)(4)(A). The home state exception provides that the district court "shall decline to exercise jurisdiction" when "two-thirds or more of the members of all proposed plaintiff classes in the aggregate, and the primary defendants, are citizens of the State in which the action was originally filed." § 1332(d)(4)(B).

Under the discretionary jurisdiction provision § 1332(d)(3), a "district court may, in the interests of justice and looking at the totality of the circumstances, decline to exercise jurisdiction over a class action in which greater than one-third but less than two-thirds of the members of all proposed plaintiff classes in the aggregate and the primary defendants are citizens of the State in which the action was originally filed." The district court must consider these factors:

(A) whether the claims asserted involve matters of national or interstate interest;

(B) whether the claims asserted will be governed by laws of the State in which the action was originally filed or by the laws of other States;

(C) whether the class action has been pleaded in a manner that seeks to avoid Federal jurisdiction;

(D) whether the action was brought in a forum with a distinct nexus with the class members, the alleged harm, or the defendants;

(E) whether the number of citizens of the State in which the action was originally filed in all proposed plaintiff classes in the aggregate is substantially larger than the number of citizens from any other State, and the citizenship of the other members of the proposed class is dispersed among a substantial number of States; and

(F) whether, during the 3-year period preceding the filing of that class action, 1 or more other class actions asserting the same or similar claims on behalf of the same or other persons have been filed.

### B.   Discretionary Jurisdiction Provision

The district court remanded this class action lawsuit to state court under all three carve-outs to federal jurisdiction: the local controversy exception, the home state exception, and the discretionary jurisdiction provision. Each CAFA exception requires the court to make an objective factual finding regarding the percentage of class members that were citizens of Louisiana at the time of filing the class petition. The local controversy and home state exceptions to federal jurisdiction are separate and distinct statutory provisions with a common requirement—greater than "two-thirds of the members of all proposed plaintiff classes in the aggregate must be citizens of the State in which the action was originally filed." LifeCare concedes that this class action lawsuit satisfies the distinguishable remaining elements of the two exceptions.

Under CAFA's discretionary jurisdiction provision, the citizenship requirement lowers to require that "greater than one-third but less than two-thirds of the members of all proposed plaintiff classes in the aggregate are citizens of the State in which the action was originally filed." § 1332(d)(3). The movants must satisfy the citizenship requirement as a prerequisite to the district court weighing the additional statutory factors enumerated to guide the court's remand determination. The same legal principles apply to the discretionary jurisdiction provision as apply to the local controversy and home state exceptions. Despite the burden to prove a lesser percentage of class members were citizens of Louisiana, which party bears the burden of proof and the sufficiency of evidence necessary to satisfy the citizenship requirements remains consistent throughout either analysis.

Congress crafted CAFA to exclude only a narrow category of truly localized controversies, and § 1332(d)(3) provides a discretionary vehicle for district courts to ferret out the "controversy that uniquely affects a particular locality to the exclusion of all others." After careful review of the record, the discretionary jurisdiction provision proves to be a particularly well-suited framework for considering the interconnections between the underlying facts giving rise to the alleged legal claims and the extenuating circumstances affecting this preliminary jurisdictional determination. The district court determined that a distinct nexus exists between the forum of Louisiana, the Defendants, and the proposed class. We observe, more specifically, that Preston alleges that LifeCare and Memorial, citizens of Louisiana, committed acts in Louisiana causing injuries and deaths to patients hospitalized in New Orleans, Louisiana, when Hurricane Katrina made landfall. The claims asserted in the petition involve issues of negligence governed by state law. Memorial does not contest that the instant lawsuit fulfills the threshold requirements for removal under CAFA, i.e. the requisite number of proposed class members, minimal diversity, and the necessary aggregate amount in controversy. § 1332(d)(2). Accordingly, we limit our review to whether Memorial presented sufficient evidence to show that a requisite percentage of the putative class members were citizens of Louisiana at the time that the suit was filed.

### 2. Evidentiary Standard for Proving Citizenship

Memorial must prove that greater than one-third of the putative class members were citizens of Louisiana at the time of filing the class action petition. 28 U.S.C. § 1332(d)(7) ("Citizenship of the members of the proposed plaintiff classes shall be determined for purposes of paragraphs (2) through (6) as of the date of the filing of the complaint."). Preston filed this class action lawsuit on October 6, 2005; therefore, Memorial must prove citizenship as of this date. The parties contest the quantum of proof necessary to sustain the moving party's burden. Pursuant to well-settled principles of law, we hold that the party moving for remand under the CAFA exceptions to federal jurisdiction must prove the citizenship requirement by a preponderance of the evidence. This holding means that Memorial, as the movant, must demonstrate by a preponderance of the evidence that at least one-third of the putative class members were citizens of Louisiana.

In the context of diversity jurisdiction, once a person establishes his domicile in a particular state, he simultaneously establishes his citizenship in the same state. Someone acquires a "domicile of origin" at birth, and this domicile presumptively continues unless rebutted with sufficient evidence of change.

Absent specific language in the statute specifying a different evidentiary standard, we employ the time-honored standard routinely applied to the fundamental question of citizenship: proof by a preponderance of the evidence.

### 3. Evidence Adduced to Prove Citizenship Requirement

In an order dated August 22, 2006, the district court acknowledged that "limited discovery is required in order to determine whether it has jurisdiction, particularly in regards to Lifecare's claim that removal is proper under CAFA." Accordingly, the district court ordered that Memorial "shall provide the Plaintiffs and Lifecare with patient information which will permit these parties to identify the patients who suffered personal injuries, including death, during the relevant period; these patients' addresses and phone numbers; as well as next of kin." In a second order, dated August 30, 2006, the district court required Memorial to "provide an affidavit of a Memorial representative attesting to the percentage of patients at issue, both deceased and living, with Louisiana addresses and percentage of those with addresses outside Louisiana."

#### a.   Residency: Medical Records and Current Addresses

Both Memorial and LifeCare submitted evidence in response to the district court's order. Memorial's Medical Records Supervisor, Hal Rome, submitted two affidavits averring to the residency of patients hospitalized when Hurricane Katrina made landfall. In the first affidavit, Rome avers to the following facts:

> That he has reviewed the complete list of all patients hospitalized at Memorial Medical Center at the time that Hurricane Katrina struck on August 29, 2005. That list contains a total of 256 patients. Of that total population of patients, the hospital's records show that 7 of those 256 patients, or 2.83% of the total, provided information to the hospital at the time they registered as patients indicating that they were residents of states other than Louisiana.

In his second affidavit, Rome produced a list showing that thirty-five patients died after the hurricane and records showing that two of the deceased patients gave out-of-state addresses. These same two patients were the only deceased persons that listed emergency contacts with telephone numbers outside of the New Orleans calling area.

LifeCare retained a private investigator, Robert Mazur, to trace the current mailing addresses of potential class members located throughout the country. LifeCare maintained that forty-nine of 146 persons identified as potential class members, more than one-third, currently reside outside of Louisiana. LifeCare's citizenship numbers include patients and surviving beneficiaries. In assessing these documents, the district court noted that "this information presents a valuable indication of the citizenship of the proposed class" but admonished LifeCare's failure to prove "residence and intent, both at the date the suit was filed." The district court reasoned that "LifeCare did not provide information regarding the length of time that these individuals have been residing outside of Louisiana. Additionally, if these individuals were in fact displaced, LifeCare did not indicate whether these individuals intend to remain in their new state of residence."

We agree with the district court's treatment of LifeCare's rebuttal evidence. The pre-Katrina addresses in the medical records, however, only make a prima facie showing of domicile, and citizenship requires residency and the intent to return or remain in the state. A party's residence alone does not establish domicile. We now turn to the evidence establishing intent, the second element of citizenship.

b.   Intent: Statements from Potential Class Members

Memorial presented no evidence from its records to demonstrate that the hospitalized patients not only resided in Orleans Parish at the given addresses but also were domiciled in Louisiana at the time of Hurricane Katrina and at the time of filing suit. As the movant, it relies on the additional evidence filed by the plaintiffs. Preston submitted eight affidavits regarding the intent of potential class members to return to New Orleans, Louisiana, even though they currently resided in a different state. The named plaintiffs provided six of the eight affidavits. For example, the affidavit of Darlene Preston states her former address in New Orleans prior to Hurricane Katrina; her current address in Houston, Texas; and concludes by stating that "she is planning on returning as soon as housing becomes available to her. She is a resident and domiciliary of and has always intended on returning to the City of New Orleans." The affidavit of Aster Abraham, currently residing in Dallas, Texas, states that she and her husband "completed repairs of the family home and she is returning July 2006." Similarly, Terry Gaines-Oden, currently residing in the Colony, Texas, avers that "she has every intention of returning as soon as her house is repaired." These affidavits unequivocally evince the intent of these plaintiffs to not change their domicile.

LifeCare contends that the affidavits should receive little weight under Circuit precedent because the documents show only the subjective intent of the parties. This court gives little weight to statements of intent evidence, however, only when the subjective evidence conflicts with the objective facts in the record. LifeCare points to no objective evidence in the record indicating that the affidavits misrepresented the plaintiffs' intent of returning to New Orleans. To the contrary, in its reply brief to this court, LifeCare accepted the medical records and affidavits as undisputed facts.

In addition to the medical records and affidavits, LifeCare suggests that Memorial should adduce evidence of citizenship in accordance with traditional diversity cases involving one defendant. Prior to CAFA, the removing parties only needed to show citizenship with respect to the named plaintiffs. § 1332(d)(3)–(4). "The factors considered by the district court may include the places where the litigant exercises civil and political rights, pays taxes, owns real and personal property, has driver's and other licenses, maintains bank accounts, belongs to clubs and churches, has places of business or employment, and maintains a home for his family." This suggestion not only affects the moving party but suggests that at this threshold stage of the case, the district court must engage in the arduous task of examining the domicile of every proposed class member before ruling on the citizenship requirement. We decline to adopt such a heightened burden of proof considering the far greater number of plaintiffs involved in a class action as compared to the traditional diversity case. From a practical standpoint, class action lawsuits may become "totally unworkable in a diversity case if the citizenship of all members of the class, many of them unknown, had to be considered." The requisite showing under CAFA prompts this court to reconcile congressional intent, our precedent for determining citizenship, and judicial economy. Thus, the evidentiary standard for establishing the domicile of more than one hundred plaintiffs must be based on practicality and reasonableness.

"The district court has wide, but not unfettered, discretion to determine what evidence to use in making its determination of jurisdiction." Preston admitted the statements of eight potential class members. The district court concluded that the affidavits "suggest that at least some displaced proposed class members intend to return to New Orleans in the near future. Each of these individuals state that they lived in New Orleans at the time of the hurricane, but were forced to evacuate to another state. However, they continue to have every intention of returning to the New Orleans area."

In the wake of Hurricane Katrina, and the compounding effects of the breached levees, nearly eighty percent of New Orleans was engulfed in flood waters rising over twenty feet in lower-lying areas. These cataclysmic events damaged, destroyed, or rendered inaccessible approximately 850,000 housing units. Left with no other option, authorities vested with the responsibility of public safety forced people to evacuate New Orleans in any available mode of transportation. The underlying facts of this lawsuit and the reason for the parties contesting the citizenship issue emanate from a common origin of circumstances: the unmerciful devastation caused by Hurricane Katrina. As an inevitable result of the property damage and evacuation, a great majority of the city's population either temporarily or permanently relocated to habitable areas of Louisiana and other states. In this case, the aftermath of Hurricane Katrina and attendant flooding serves as a common precipitating factor for the mass relocation pertinent to our citizenship determination and threads together the proposed class and many other citizens. The sheer magnitude of this shared catalyst formed an adequate backdrop for the district court's extrapolation that the reasons offered by the affiants for not immediately returning home, i.e. repairing the family home, finding gainful employment, and waiting for the availability of housing units, were probably representative of many other proposed class members.

The Fifth Amended Petition for Damages defines a circumscribed class that includes "all patients of Memorial and LifeCare who sustained injuries and all persons who sustained personal injury as a result of the deaths or personal injuries to patients of LifeCare and Memorial." The eight affidavits in and of themselves are not dispositive proof that at least one-third of the defined putative class were citizens of Louisiana at the time in which the suit was filed. The uncontroverted affidavits of eight beneficiaries stating an intent to return to New Orleans, the emergency contact phone numbers of the deceased patients, and the uncontroverted data gathered from the medical records, however, permitted the district court to make a reasonable assumption that at least one-third of the class members were citizens of Louisiana during the relevant time period regardless of the rebuttal evidence placed in the record. Upon reviewing the medical records, Rome averred that only seven of the 256 patients hospitalized at the time of Hurricane Katrina gave permanent addresses outside the state of Louisiana, which equates to 2.83% of the total number of hospitalized patients. The putative class cannot extend significantly beyond this finite number of persons because in this case, we are not presented with an immeasurably amorphous proposed class. Thus, the discrete number of patients hospitalized at Memorial when Hurricane Katrina made landfall constitutes a reasonable estimate of the total class for determining the preliminary jurisdictional question of citizenship.

Although the actual number of patients and beneficiaries remains an open question, the unequivocal affidavits of eight beneficiaries in conjunction with the residency information gleaned from the emergency contact data of the deceased patients gave the district court a reasonable indication as to the citizenship of these unaccounted for persons. LifeCare identified the current residences of only 146 potential class members to rebut the medical records and affidavits, but LifeCare's evidence fails to demonstrate an intent to change domicile by any of the identified persons. Even though eight affidavits may constitute a small number of statements outside the unique convergence of facts presented in this case, we find that here, the affidavits amplify the court's carefully reasoned conclusion about the probable citizenship of the proposed class of hospitalized patients and their beneficiaries. Therefore, based on the record as a whole, the district court made a reasonable assumption that at least one-third of the class were Louisiana citizens at the time of filing the lawsuit on October 6, 2005, less than two months after the storm hit New Orleans. We do not find the district court's findings of fact clearly erroneous.

### c.    Presumption of Continuing Domicile

Memorial argues that based on the presumption of continuing domicile, LifeCare bears the burden to show that the displaced Hurricane Katrina victims possess no intention of returning to New Orleans, Louisiana. LifeCare contends that its evidence rebuts any presumption that a person residing in the New Orleans area at the time of Hurricane Katrina continued to reside there when suit was filed. Moreover, LifeCare proposes that the presumption is inapplicable in this case due to the massive relocation of over half of the city's population. We find this argument unpersuasive, and further, we find no precedential support for the notion that a forced relocation (especially, a mandatory evacuation prompted by a natural disaster) destroys the presumption of continued domicile.

"There is a presumption in favor of a person's continuing domicile which requires the party seeking to show a change in domicile to come forward with enough evidence to that effect." The law of continuing domicile gains special significance in light of the natural disaster forming the factual basis of this appeal. In a recent case analyzing the citizenship requirement of the local controversy exception, a district court recognized that "given the forced evacuation for several months from several south Louisiana parishes as a result of Katrina, it is reasonable to assume that residents of these parishes might change their addresses in the immediate aftermath of the storm without changing their domiciles." The court described its conclusion as a "common-sense presumption" applied to a "closed-end class."

We agree with the notion that the damage and destruction wrought by Hurricane Katrina warrants the court's incorporation of common-sense as part of the calculus in determining the citizenship of the class members. While cognizant that the patient addresses provided by Memorial do not definitively reflect the patients' domicile at the time of filing suit, as required under traditional diversity standards, we also consider the common genesis of the historically unprecedented exodus from New Orleans in our assessment of the citizenship issue. In light of the vast post-Katrina diaspora and the undisputably slow revitalization in parts of New Orleans, it is unreasonable to demand precise empirical evidence of citizenship in a class action lawsuit filed less than sixty days after the hurricane and related flooding. Many Hurricane Katrina victims may intend to return home yet are still dispersed throughout Louisiana and other states for reasons beyond their control, such as not having shelter and employment in the New Orleans area. Therefore, we find the presumption of continuing domicile relevant in this case.

### d.  Population Survey Data

On appeal, LifeCare cites to a 2006 Louisiana Health and Population Survey Report, conducted by the Louisiana Public Health Institute on behalf of the Louisiana Department of Health and Hospitals. The survey estimated that the 2004 population of 444,515 persons living in Orleans Parish decreased dramatically to 191,139 persons after Hurricane Katrina. Based on surveys returned during June and October 2006, the Louisiana Department of Health and Hospitals published the report on January 17, 2007.

We find this survey to be much too broad to rebut the presumed citizenship of a class member. First, the survey data represents only an initial analysis conducted less than a year after Hurricane Katrina. Second, the published data only account for population decreases in the Orleans Parish area, while CAFA's citizenship requirement looks to citizenship in the state. Third, the submitted survey gives a disclaimer that "a comprehensive final report for all parishes will be produced when the project is completed and all parish specific reports are released." This statement clearly indicates that the project remains a work-in-progress and lends little insight into determining the number of class members no longer located in Louisiana due to the forced evacuation after Hurricane Katrina. Accordingly, we deem the census data as non-probative on whether one-third of the class members were domiciled in Louisiana at the time of filing suit.

### 4.  *Determination of Class Size*

LifeCare argues that Memorial fails to establish the number of people composing the proposed class. Arguably, without knowing the number of persons in the class, the court cannot determine whether one-third of the class members are citizens of Louisiana. LifeCare asserts that the statute requires concrete proof of the number of class members as a prerequisite to ruling on the citizenship requirement. In *Frazier*, the court rejected plaintiff's argument, under the local controversy exception, that the Department of Environmental Quality was a citizen of Louisiana by citing the "long-settled rule that a state has no citizenship for § 1332(a) diversity purposes." Thus, the court never reached the statutory citizenship requirement.

In *Evans*, plaintiffs filed a class action lawsuit in Alabama state court on behalf of a class of persons allegedly injured by the actions of eighteen named defendants and fictitious defendants. The plaintiffs alleged that the defendants operated manufacturing facilities in the Anniston, Alabama area. In their petition, plaintiffs claimed that defendants released various waste substances over an approximately eighty-five-year period, resulting in property damage and personal injury. The attorney introduced evidence of interviews with over 10,000 potential plaintiffs and determined that 5,200 persons qualified for class membership. Of the potential class members, over ninety percent resided in Alabama; therefore, the court could conceivably extrapolate that two-thirds of the entire class were citizens of the state.

The Eleventh Circuit found this evidence insufficient to prove the citizenship requirement under the local controversy exception. The *Evans* court highlighted deficiencies in the evidence, reasoning that the affidavit of the class attorney provided no information "about how she selected the 10,118 people who were considered potential plaintiffs. We know nothing about the percentage of the total class represented by the 10,118 people on which plaintiff's evidence depends." In connecting the evidence to the class definition, the Eleventh Circuit concluded that "the class, as defined in the complaint, is extremely broad, extending over an 84-year period. We do not know if Smith made any effort to estimate the number of people with claims who no longer live in Alabama. We have no way of knowing what percentage of the plaintiff class are Alabama citizens." Notwithstanding the apparently cumbersome investigative work completed by counsel, the Eleventh Circuit "concluded that the evidence adduced by the plaintiffs wholly fails to present a *credible estimate* of the percentage of the plaintiff class who are citizens of Alabama."

Here, we find that the submitted evidence provides an adequate basis for the district court to make a credible estimate of the class members domiciled in Louisiana. CAFA requires the district court to make a threshold jurisdictional determination. Thus, the district court must balance the need for discovery while not unduly delaying the resolution of this preliminary question. The statute compensates for the inability to conduct an in-depth fact finding mission by permitting defendants to remove the case to federal court at any point in the litigation. § 1453(b).

As defined, this proposed class includes patients hospitalized at the time of Hurricane Katrina and their beneficiaries asserting damages for personal injury, wrongful death, and derivative claims. Memorial bears an affirmative burden to establish the domicile of at least one-third of the class members under the discretionary jurisdiction provision, which logically requires determining the size of the putative class. The pre-Katrina addresses in the medical records partially satisfy this burden but provide no basis for determining the total number of potential class members. The district court, however, considered the "addresses and phone numbers of those patients who died at Memorial within the relevant time period, as well as the phone numbers of the patients' emergency contacts listed on their medical forms."

At this preliminary stage, it is unnecessary for the district court to permit exhaustive discovery capable of determining the exact class size to an empirical certainty. Even though a party should take care in defining the putative class, the specificity argued for by LifeCare more appropriately occurs during class certification. Under Fed. R. Civ. P. 23, the district court must "evaluate with rigor the claims, defenses, relevant facts and applicable substantive law in order to make a meaningful determination of the certification issues." At the certification stage, the plaintiff must provide evidence or a reasonable estimate of purported class members. Then, the class size weighs in the district court's certification calculus. Moreover, we are not presented with a situation wherein the district court stymied the parties' efforts to marshal evidence and conduct discovery. Neither Memorial nor LifeCare contends that the district court thwarted their ability to gather relevant information by evidentiary rulings; to the contrary, the district court encouraged the introduction of evidence through two orders of the court.

The defined class clearly involves a finite group of persons: patients hospitalized in Memorial Medical Center at the time that Hurricane Katrina made landfall. We would probably invoke a different analysis if, for example, the class definition included persons trapped in the Ninth Ward in the hours and days following Hurricane Katrina and the levee breach. Under this hypothetical, the ability to quantify such a class, much less parse renters from property owners and other relevant complications, would require more evidence than before the court in this appeal. Here, we know the number of patients. We also know the patients' names, emergency contact information for the deceased patients, and the discrete time period of the episodic event giving rise to the litigation. Moreover, we are not dealing with a class of patients receiving medical care from a national hospital that regularly services out-of-state patients. Memorial Medical Center is a local health care facility primarily servicing the local citizens of New Orleans, as evinced by the local addresses and phone numbers found in the medical records. Only seven patients hospitalized at the time of Hurricane Katrina listed an out-of-state address on their medical forms. The proposed class in this case contemplates a concretely defined group as opposed to the abstractly defined classes ruled on in *Evans* and discussed in the above hypothetical.

Unlike *Evans*, the crux of this case revolves around a narrowly defined class and claims stemming from a localized chain of events. In aligning these circumstances and the adduced evidence, we are not in the position of having to put a square peg in a round hole. Instead, we are dealing with the congruence of fitted pieces. Keeping in mind the measurable bounds of the proposed class, we find that the district court made a reasonable inference regarding the temporary dual residency of the displaced Louisiana citizens at issue in this case. The record reflects that the plaintiffs defined a reasonably confined class and the district court, based on a preponderance of the evidence, made a credible estimate that at least one-third of the class were citizens of Louisiana at the time of filing suit.

5.   *Statutory Factors for Determining the Interest of Justice*

a.    Whether Claims Involve National or Interstate Interest

LifeCare argues that the evacuation of medical and other facilities during disasters such as Hurricane Katrina is an issue of national concern. This broad statement could swallow the rule, however, as many events isolated to one area at any particular time may reoccur in another geographic location in the future. Under CAFA, the terms local and national connote whether the interests of justice would be violated by a state court exercising jurisdiction over a large number of out-of-state citizens and applying the laws of other states. Just because the nation takes interest in Hurricane Katrina does not mean that the legal claims at issue in this class action lawsuit qualify as national or interstate interest. The factual scenario presented in this class action involves two Louisiana businesses operating a local hospital during a natural disaster destroying New Orleans and the compounded devastation of the local levee breach. The evacuation plans, building maintenance, and emergency care procedures are the work product and property of these local entities. Moreover, the district court denied any federal basis for jurisdiction after reviewing the class action petition, and neither party appealed this ruling. For these reasons, although the nation may still be watching the ever-evolving after effects of Hurricane Katrina, this class action lawsuit does not affect national interest as contemplated under the statute.

b.    Whether Claims Are Governed by Louisiana Law and Whether the Class Action Was Pleaded to Avoid Federal Jurisdiction

The plaintiffs in this case assert a variety of negligence claims based on the delayed evacuation of patients from Memorial Medical Center after Hurricane Katrina made landfall. The majority of the claims asserted in the class petition involve negligence issues governed under Louisiana law. Specifically, Memorial and LifeCare argue that the Louisiana Medical Malpractice Act governs the plaintiffs' causes of action.

LifeCare unsuccessfully attempted to remove this case under § 1331, asserting that the plaintiffs' Emergency Medical Treatment and Active Labor Act claim constituted a federal question, which mandated original federal jurisdiction over the lawsuit. The district court concluded that "a viable cause of action under federal law does not exist for 'reverse patient dumping' and thus does not confer jurisdiction under 28 U.S.C. § 1331. Even if it could be argued that federal jurisdiction may exist for the EMTALA claim, the Court finds that the state-law claims predominate over the case in its entirety and thus remand under 28 U.S.C. § 1441(c) is appropriate." Neither party disputes the district court's holding on this issue in their appeal to this court. Moreover, the record does not indicate that the plaintiffs' intentionally pleaded the case in a manner to avoid federal jurisdiction and neither defendant asserts such an allegation.

Accordingly, the class action lawsuit as pleaded satisfies these two requirements.

### c.     Whether a Distinct Nexus Exists between the Forum and the Class Members, Alleged Harm, and the Defendants

The conduct alleged in the class action petition as causing the deaths and injuries of patients hospitalized at Memorial and LifeCare occurred at the defendants' medical facilities in New Orleans, Louisiana. Memorial owned and operated the hospital, and LifeCare leased one floor of the hospital for the operation of an acute care center. Both Memorial and LifeCare are Louisiana corporations organized under the laws of the state, and based on the medical records, nearly ninety-seven percent of the patients permanently resided in Louisiana at the time of admission to these health centers. In light of the localized events giving rise to the alleged negligent conduct and the undisputed residency and citizenship information of the patients and the healthcare providers, we conclude that a distinct nexus exists between the forum of Louisiana and the class members, alleged harm, and the defendants.

### d.     State Citizenship of the Class Members

For the reasons thoroughly discussed in the citizenship analysis, we conclude that the "number of citizens of the State in which the action was originally filed in all proposed plaintiff classes in the aggregate is substantially larger than the number of citizens from any other State, and the citizenship of the other members of the proposed class is dispersed among a substantial number of States." Based on the record, an overwhelming number of patients permanently resided in New Orleans, Louisiana, and the vast majority of the emergency contact phone numbers listed for the deceased patients have the New Orleans area code. After the hurricane, many New Orleans residents were forced to relocate to surrounding areas in Louisiana and other states. As evinced through the affidavits, however, citizens of Louisiana are hindered from immediately acting on their desires to move back home due to employment, housing, and other related issues. Undoubtedly, some evacuees hold no intention of returning to Louisiana but surely are dispersed throughout the nation as opposed to one other state. For these reasons, we determine that the proposed class meets this requirement.

## V.   CONCLUSION

We recognize that Congress crafted CAFA to exclude only a narrow category of truly localized controversies, and the exceptions provide a statutory vehicle for the district courts to ferret out the "controversy that uniquely affects a particular locality to the exclusion of all others." This particular Hurricane Katrina case symbolizes a quintessential example of Congress' intent to carve-out exceptions to CAFA's expansive grant of federal jurisdiction when our courts confront a truly localized controversy.

Based on the medical records, affidavits, and attending factual circumstances, we determine that the district court did not clearly err in finding that one-third of the class members were citizens of Louisiana at the time of filing suit. Accordingly, we affirm the district court's judgment.

# C. AMOUNT IN CONTROVERSY

## THE STANDARD FIRE INS. CO. V. KNOWLES

Supreme Court of the United States, 2013.
___ U.S. ___, 133 S.Ct. 1345, 185 L.Ed.2d 439.

The Class Action Fairness Act of 2005 (CAFA) provides that the federal "district courts shall have original jurisdiction" over a civil "class action" if, among other things, the "matter in controversy exceeds the sum or value of $5,000,000." 28 U.S.C. § 1332(d)(2), (d)(5). The statute adds that "to determine whether the matter in controversy exceeds the sum or value of $5,000,000," the "claims of the individual class members shall be aggregated." § 1332(d)(6).

The question presented concerns a class-action plaintiff who stipulates, prior to certification of the class, that he, and the class he seeks to represent, will not seek damages that exceed $5 million in total. Does that stipulation remove the case from CAFA's scope? In our view, it does not.

I.

In April 2011 respondent, Greg Knowles, filed this proposed class action in an Arkansas state court against petitioner, the Standard Fire Insurance Company. Knowles claimed that, when the company had made certain homeowner's insurance loss payments, it had unlawfully failed to include a general contractor fee. And Knowles sought to certify a class of "hundreds, and possibly thousands" of similarly harmed Arkansas policyholders. In describing the relief sought, the complaint says that the "Plaintiff and Class stipulate they will seek to recover total aggregate damages of less than five million dollars." An attached affidavit stipulates that Knowles "will not at any time during this case seek damages for the class in excess of $5,000,000 in the aggregate."

On May 18, 2011, the company, pointing to CAFA's jurisdictional provision, removed the case to Federal District Court. See 28 U.S.C. § 1332(d); § 1453. Knowles argued for remand on the ground that the District Court lacked jurisdiction. He claimed that the "sum or value" of the "amount in controversy" fell beneath the $5 million threshold. On the basis of evidence presented by the company, the District Court found that that the "sum or value" of the "amount in controversy" would, in the absence of the stipulation, have fallen just above the $5 million threshold. Nonetheless, in light of Knowles' stipulation, the court concluded that the amount fell beneath the threshold. The court consequently ordered the case remanded to the state court.

The company appealed from the remand order, but the Eighth Circuit declined to hear the appeal. *See* 28 U.S.C. § 1453(c)(1)(providing discretion to hear an appeal from a remand order). The company petitioned for a writ of certiorari. And, in light of divergent views in the lower courts, we granted the writ.

## II.

CAFA provides the federal district courts with "original jurisdiction" to hear a "class action" if the class has more than 100 members, the parties are minimally diverse, and the "matter in controversy exceeds the sum or value of $5,000,000." 28 U.S.C. § 1332(d)(2), (d)(5)(B). To "determine whether the matter in controversy" exceeds that sum, "the claims of the individual class members shall be aggregated." § 1332(d)(6). And those "class members" include "persons (named or unnamed) who fall within the definition of the *proposed* or certified class." § 1332(d)(1)(D).

As applied here, the statute tells the District Court to determine whether it has jurisdiction by adding up the value of the claim of each person who falls within the definition of Knowles' proposed class and determine whether the resulting sum exceeds $5 million. If so, there is jurisdiction and the court may proceed with the case. The District Court in this case found that resulting sum would have exceeded $5 million *but for* the stipulation. And we must decide whether the stipulation makes a critical difference.

In our view, it does not. Our reason is a simple one: Stipulations must be binding. The stipulation Knowles proffered to the District Court, however, does not speak for those he purports to represent.

That is because a plaintiff who files a proposed class action cannot legally bind members of the proposed class before the class is certified. *See Smith v. Bayer Corp.* ("Neither a proposed class action nor a rejected class action may bind nonparties"); ("A non-named class member is not a party to the class-action litigation before the class is certified").

Because his precertification stipulation does not bind anyone but himself, Knowles has not reduced the value of the putative class members' claims. For jurisdictional purposes, our inquiry is limited to examining the case "as of the time it was filed in state court." At that point, Knowles lacked the authority to concede the amount-in-controversy issue for the absent class members. The Federal District Court, therefore, wrongly concluded that Knowles' precertification stipulation could overcome its finding that the CAFA jurisdictional threshold had been met.

Knowles concedes that "federal jurisdiction cannot be based on contingent future events." Yet the two legal principles to which we have just referred—that stipulations must be binding and that a named plaintiff cannot bind precertification class members—mean that the amount to which Knowles has stipulated is in effect contingent.

If, for example, as Knowles' complaint asserts, "hundreds, and possibly thousands" of persons in Arkansas have similar claims, and if each of those claims places a significant sum in controversy, the state court might certify the class and permit the case to proceed, but only on the condition that the stipulation be excised. Or a court might find that Knowles is an inadequate representative due to the artificial cap he purports to impose on the class' recovery. Similarly, another class member could intervene with an amended complaint (without a stipulation), and the District Court might permit the action to proceed with a new representative. Even were these possibilities remote in Knowles' own case, there is no reason to think them farfetched in other cases where similar stipulations could have more dramatic amount-lowering effects.

The strongest counterargument, we believe, takes a syllogistic form: First, *this* complaint contains a presently nonbinding stipulation that the class will seek damages that amount to less than $5 million. Second, if the state court eventually certifies that class, the stipulation will bind those who choose to remain as class members. Third, if the state court eventually insists upon modification of the stipulation (thereby permitting class members to obtain more than $5 million), it will have in effect created a new, *different* case. Fourth, CAFA, however, permits the federal court to consider only the complaint that the plaintiff has filed, *i.e., this* complaint, not a new, modified (or amended) complaint that might eventually emerge.

Our problem with this argument lies in its conclusion. We do not agree that CAFA forbids the federal court to consider, for purposes of determining the amount in controversy, the very real possibility that a nonbinding, amount-limiting, stipulation may not survive the class certification process. This potential outcome does not result in the creation of a new case not now before the federal court. To hold otherwise would, for CAFA jurisdictional purposes, treat a nonbinding stipulation as if it were binding, exalt form over substance, and run directly counter to CAFA's primary objective: ensuring "Federal court consideration of interstate cases of national importance." It would also have the effect of allowing the subdivision of a $100 million action into 21 just-below-$5-million state-court actions simply by including nonbinding stipulations; such an outcome would squarely conflict with the statute's objective.

We agree with Knowles that a federal district court might find it simpler to value the amount in controversy on the basis of a stipulation than to aggregate the value of the individual claims of all who meet the class description. We also agree that, when judges must decide jurisdictional matters, simplicity is a virtue. But to ignore a nonbinding stipulation does no more than require the federal judge to do what she must do in cases without a stipulation and what the statute requires, namely "aggregate" the "claims of the individual class members." 28 U.S.C. § 1332(d)(6).

Knowles also points out that federal courts permit individual plaintiffs, who are the masters of their complaints, to avoid removal to federal court, and to obtain a remand to state court, by stipulating to amounts at issue that fall below the federal jurisdictional requirement. That is so. *See St. Paul Mercury Indemnity Co. v. Red Cab Co.* ("If a plaintiff does not desire to try his case in the federal court he may resort to the expedient of suing for less than the jurisdictional amount, and though he would be justly entitled to more, the defendant cannot remove"). But the key characteristic about those stipulations is that they are legally binding on all plaintiffs (federal court, as condition for remand, can insist on a "*binding* affidavit or stipulation that the plaintiff will continue to claim less than the jurisdictional amount"). That essential feature is missing here, as Knowles cannot yet bind the absent class.

Knowles argues in the alternative that a stipulation is binding to the extent it limits attorney's fees so that the amount in controversy remains below the CAFA threshold. We do not consider this issue because Knowles' stipulation did not provide for that option.

In sum, the stipulation at issue here can tie Knowles' hands, but it does not resolve the amount-in-controversy question in light of his inability to bind the rest of the class. For this reason, we believe the District Court, when following the statute to aggregate the proposed class members' claims, should have ignored that stipulation. Because it did not, we vacate the judgment below and remand the case for further proceedings consistent with this opinion.

## DART CHEROKEE BASIN OPERATING CO., LLC v. OWENS

Supreme Court of the United States, 2014.
___ U.S. ___, 135 S.Ct. 547, 190 L.Ed.2d 495.

To remove a case from a state court to a federal court, a defendant must file in the federal forum a notice of removal "containing a short and plain statement of the grounds for removal." 28 U.S.C. § 1446(a). When removal is based on diversity of citizenship, an amount-in-controversy requirement must be met. Ordinarily, "the matter in controversy must exceed the sum or value of $75,000." § 1332(a). In class actions for which the requirement of diversity of citizenship is relaxed, § 1332(d)(2)(A)–(C), "the matter in controversy must exceed the sum or value of $5,000,000," § 1332(d)(2). If the plaintiff's complaint, filed in state court, demands monetary relief of a stated sum, that sum, if asserted in good faith, is "deemed to be the amount in controversy." § 1446(c)(2). When the plaintiff's complaint does not state the amount in controversy, the defendant's notice of removal may do so. § 1446(c)(2)(A).

To assert the amount in controversy adequately in the removal notice, does it suffice to allege the requisite amount plausibly, or must the defendant incorporate into the notice of removal evidence supporting the allegation? That is the single question argued here and below by the parties and the issue on which we granted review. The answer, we hold, is supplied by the removal statute itself. A statement "short and plain" need not contain evidentiary submissions.

## I.

Brandon W. Owens, plaintiff below and respondent here, filed a putative class action in Kansas state court alleging that defendants Dart Cherokee Basin Operating Company, LLC, and Cherokee Basin Pipeline, LLC, underpaid royalties owed to putative class members under certain oil and gas leases. The complaint sought "a fair and reasonable amount" to compensate putative class members for "damages" they sustained due to the alleged underpayments.

Invoking federal jurisdiction under the Class Action Fairness Act of 2005 (CAFA), Dart removed the case to the U.S. District Court for the District of Kansas. CAFA gives federal courts jurisdiction over certain class actions, defined in § 1332(d)(1), if the class has more than 100 members, the parties are minimally diverse, and the amount in controversy exceeds $5 million. § 1332(d)(2), (5)(B). Dart's notice of removal alleged that all three requirements were satisfied. With respect to the amount in controversy, Dart stated that the purported underpayments to putative class members totaled more than $8.2 million.

Owens moved to remand the case to state court. The notice of removal was "deficient as a matter of law," Owens asserted, because it included "no evidence" proving that the amount in controversy exceeded $5 million. In response, Dart submitted a declaration by one of its executive officers. The declaration included a detailed damages calculation indicating that the amount in controversy, *sans* interest, exceeded $11 million. Without challenging Dart's calculation, Owens urged that Dart's amount-in-controversy submission came too late. "The legally deficient notice of removal," Owens maintained, could not be cured by "post-removal evidence about the amount in controversy."

Reading Tenth Circuit precedent to require proof of the amount in controversy in the notice of removal itself, the District Court granted Owens' remand motion. Dart's declaration, the District Court held, could not serve to keep the case in federal court. The Tenth Circuit, as the District Court read Circuit precedent, "has consistently held that reference to factual allegations or evidence outside of the petition and notice of removal is not permitted to determine the amount in controversy."

Ordinarily, remand orders "are not reviewable on appeal or otherwise." § 1447(d). There is an exception, however, for cases invoking CAFA.

§ 1453(c)(1). In such cases, "a court of appeals may accept an appeal from an order of a district court granting or denying a motion to remand." Citing this exception, Dart petitioned the Tenth Circuit for permission to appeal. "Upon careful consideration of the parties' submissions, as well as the applicable law," the Tenth Circuit panel, dividing two-to-one, denied review.

An evenly divided court denied Dart's petition for en banc review. Dissenting from the denial of rehearing en banc, Judge Hartz observed that the Tenth Circuit "had let stand a district-court decision that will in effect impose in this circuit requirements for notices of removal that are even more onerous than the code pleading requirements that federal courts abandoned long ago." The Tenth Circuit was duty-bound to grant Dart's petition for rehearing en banc, Judge Hartz urged, because the opportunity "to correct the law in our circuit" likely would not arise again. Henceforth, Judge Hartz explained, "any diligent attorney would submit to the evidentiary burden rather than take a chance on remand to state court."

Dart filed a petition for certiorari in this Court requesting resolution of the following question: "Whether a defendant seeking removal to federal court is required to include evidence supporting federal jurisdiction in the notice of removal, or is alleging the required 'short and plain statement of the grounds for removal' enough?" Owens' brief in opposition raised no impediment to this Court's review. We granted certiorari to resolve a division among the Circuits on the question presented.

## II.

As noted above, a defendant seeking to remove a case to a federal court must file in the federal forum a notice of removal "containing a short and plain statement of the grounds for removal." § 1446(a). By design, § 1446(a) tracks the general pleading requirement stated in Rule 8(a) of the Federal Rules of Civil Procedure. The legislative history of § 1446(a) is corroborative. Congress, by borrowing the familiar "short and plain statement" standard from Rule 8(a), intended to "simplify the 'pleading' requirements for removal" and to clarify that courts should "apply the same liberal rules to removal allegations that are applied to other matters of pleading."

When a plaintiff invokes federal-court jurisdiction, the plaintiff's amount-in-controversy allegation is accepted if made in good faith. Similarly, when a defendant seeks federal-court adjudication, the defendant's amount-in-controversy allegation should be accepted when not contested by the plaintiff or questioned by the court. Indeed, the Tenth Circuit, although not disturbing prior decisions demanding proof together with the removal notice, recognized that it was anomalous to treat commencing plaintiffs and removing defendants differently with regard to the amount in controversy.

If the plaintiff contests the defendant's allegation, § 1446(c)(2)(B) instructs: "Removal is proper on the basis of an amount in controversy asserted" by the defendant "if the district court finds, by the preponderance of the evidence, that the amount in controversy exceeds" the jurisdictional threshold. This provision, added to § 1446 as part of the Federal Courts Jurisdiction and Venue Clarification Act of 2011, clarifies the procedure in order when a defendant's assertion of the amount in controversy is challenged. In such a case, both sides submit proof and the court decides, by a preponderance of the evidence, whether the amount-in-controversy requirement has been satisfied. As the House Judiciary Committee Report on the JVCA observed:

> Defendants do not need to prove to a legal certainty that the amount in controversy requirement has been met. Rather, defendants may simply allege or assert that the jurisdictional threshold has been met. Discovery may be taken with regard to that question. In case of a dispute, the district court must make findings of jurisdictional fact to which the preponderance standard applies.").

Of course, a dispute about a defendant's jurisdictional allegations cannot arise until *after* the defendant files a notice of removal containing those allegations.

In remanding the case to state court, the District Court relied, in part, on a purported "presumption" against removal. We need not here decide whether such a presumption is proper in mine-run diversity cases. It suffices to point out that no anti-removal presumption attends cases invoking CAFA, which Congress enacted to facilitate adjudication of certain class actions in federal court. *See Standard Fire Ins. Co.* ("CAFA's primary objective" is to "ensure 'Federal court consideration of interstate cases of national importance;' " (CAFA's "provisions should be read broadly, with a strong preference that interstate class actions should be heard in a federal court if properly removed by any defendant.").

In sum, as specified in § 1446(a), a defendant's notice of removal need include only a plausible allegation that the amount in controversy exceeds the jurisdictional threshold. Evidence establishing the amount is required by § 1446(c)(2)(B) only when the plaintiff contests, or the court questions, the defendant's allegation.

## III.

Satisfied that there are indeed "grounds for reversing the Tenth Circuit's decision to deny permission to appeal," we find no jurisdictional barrier to our settlement of the question presented. The case was "in" the Court of Appeals because of Dart's leave-to-appeal application, and we have jurisdiction to review what the Court of Appeals did with that application. Owens, we reiterate, did not contest the scope of our review.

Discretion to review a remand order is not rudderless. A court "would necessarily abuse its discretion if it based its ruling on an erroneous view of the law." This case fits that bill.

There are many signals that the Tenth Circuit relied on the legally erroneous premise that the District Court's decision was correct. In an earlier case, the Tenth Circuit, following the First Circuit's lead, stated considerations that it regards as relevant to the intelligent exercise of discretion under § 1453(c)(1). When the CAFA-related question presented in an appeal from a remand order is "important, unsettled, and recurrent," the First Circuit instructed, a court of appeals should inquire: "Absent an interlocutory appeal, will the question in all probability escape meaningful appellate review." Or, as phrased by the Tenth Circuit, if a district court's remand order remains undisturbed, will the case "leave the ambit of the federal courts for good, precluding any other opportunity for the defendant to vindicate its claimed legal entitlement under CAFA to have a federal tribunal adjudicate the merits." (noting that "the purpose of § 1453(c)(1) is to develop a body of appellate law interpreting CAFA"). Thus, the Tenth Circuit's own guide weighed heavily in favor of accepting Dart's appeal. That the Court of Appeals, instead, rejected Dart's appeal strongly suggests that the panel thought the District Court got it right in requiring proof of the amount in controversy in the removal notice.

In practical effect, the Court of Appeals' denial of review established the law not simply for this case, but for future CAFA removals sought by defendants in the Tenth Circuit. The likelihood is slim that a later case will arise in which the Tenth Circuit will face a plea to retract the rule that both Owens and the District Court ascribed to decisions of the Court of Appeals: Defendants seeking to remove under CAFA must be sent back to state court unless they submit with the notice of removal evidence proving the alleged amount in controversy. On this point, Judge Hartz's observation, dissenting from the Tenth Circuit's denial of rehearing en banc, bears recounting in full:

> After today's decision any diligent attorney (and one can assume that an attorney representing a defendant in a case involving at least $5 million—the threshold for removal under CAFA—would have substantial incentive to be diligent) would submit to the evidentiary burden rather than take a chance on remand to state court.

With no responsible attorney likely to renew the fray, Judge Hartz anticipated, "the issue will not arise again." Consequently, the law applied by the District Court—demanding that the notice of removal contain evidence documenting the amount in controversy—will be frozen in place for all venues within the Tenth Circuit.

Recall that the Court of Appeals denied Dart's petition for review "upon careful consideration of the parties' submissions, as well as the applicable law." What did the parties submit to the Tenth Circuit? Their presentations urged conflicting views on whether a removing defendant must tender prima facie proof of the amount in controversy as part of the removal notice. And what was "the applicable law" other than the rule recited by the Tenth Circuit in *Laughlin* and follow-on decisions, *i.e.,* to remove successfully, a defendant must present with the notice of removal evidence proving the amount in controversy.

From all signals one can discern then, the Tenth Circuit's denial of Dart's request for review of the remand order was infected by legal error. The District Court erred in ruling that Dart's amount-in-controversy allegation failed for want of proof, but that error was driven by the District Court's conscientious endeavor to follow Circuit precedent. The parties trained their arguments in the Tenth Circuit, as they did here, on the question whether Dart could successfully remove without detailing in the removal notice evidence of the amount in controversy (acknowledgment by Owens' counsel that "the issues provided to the Tenth Circuit were very similar to what you see in this Court, with the exception of the question raised by Public Citizen whether this Court has jurisdiction"). Dissenting from the denial of rehearing en banc, Judge Hartz explained at length why the Tenth Circuit "owed a duty to the bench and bar" to correct the District Court's misperception and to state as the Circuit's law: "A defendant seeking removal under CAFA need only allege the jurisdictional amount in its notice of removal and must prove that amount only if the plaintiff challenges the allegation." In this regard, we note, the Tenth Circuit has cautioned against casual rulings on applications like Dart's. "The decision whether to grant leave to appeal" under § 1453(c), the Tenth Circuit stressed, calls for the exercise of the reviewing court's correctly *"informed discretion."*

Recall, moreover, that Owens never suggested in his written submissions to this Court that anything other than the question presented accounts for the Court of Appeals' disposition. If Owens believed that the Tenth Circuit's denial of leave to appeal rested on some other ground, he might have said so in his brief in opposition or, at least, in his merits brief. He said nothing of that order, for he, like Dart, anticipated that the question presented was ripe for this Court's resolution.

In the above-described circumstances, we find it an abuse of discretion for the Tenth Circuit to deny Dart's request for review. Doing so froze the governing rule in the Circuit for this case and future CAFA removal notices, with no opportunity for defendants in Dart's position responsibly to resist making the evidentiary submission. That situation would be bizarre for a decision-maker who did not think that the amount in controversy in diversity cases is a matter a removal notice must demonstrate by evidence, not merely credibly allege. And if the Circuit precedent on which the District Court relied misstated the law, as we hold it did, then the District Court's order remanding this case to the state court is fatally infected by legal error.

Careful inspection thus reveals that the two issues Public Citizen invites us to separate—whether the Tenth Circuit abused its discretion in denying review, and whether the District Court's remand order was erroneous—do not pose genuinely discrete questions. Instead, resolution of both issues depends on the answer to the very same question: What must the removal notice contain? If the notice need not contain evidence, the Tenth Circuit abused its discretion in effectively making the opposing view the law of the Circuit. By the same token, the District Court erred in remanding the case for want of an evidentiary submission in the removal notice. We no doubt have authority to review for abuse of discretion the Tenth Circuit's denial of Dart's appeal from the District Court's remand order, and in doing so, to correct the erroneous view of the law the Tenth Circuit's decision fastened on district courts within the Circuit's domain.

For the reasons stated, the judgment of the U.S. Court of Appeals for the Tenth Circuit is vacated, and the case is remanded for further proceedings consistent with this opinion.

### ROBERTSON V. EXXON MOBIL CORP.
United States Court of Appeals for the Fifth Circuit, 2015.
814 F.3d 236.

This lawsuit alleging personal and property damages stemming from oil pipe-cleaning operations was filed in Louisiana state court and removed to federal court under the Class Action Fairness Act, 28 U.S.C. § 1332(d) (CAFA). The district court allowed jurisdictional discovery and then ordered the case remanded to state court on the ground that Defendants had not met their burden of showing that at least one plaintiff satisfies the individual amount-in-controversy requirement that CAFA applies to so-called "mass actions." Holding that Defendants did make that showing, we reverse.

### I. FACTS AND PROCEEDINGS

Plaintiffs are 189 natural persons who live, work, or own real property in a certain part of Harvey, Louisiana, or formerly did so. They allege that the nearby cleaning of pipes used in the oil industry produced harmful radioactive material that injured their health and property. Defendants are several oil companies, contractors that cleaned pipes for those oil companies, and the owners of property on which the pipe cleaning took place.

Plaintiffs contend that the relevant pipe-cleaning operations began in 1958 and operated continuously through 1992. According to Plaintiffs, the dirty pipes were covered with "pipe scale" that accumulates during drilling and production operations and contains radioactive and otherwise hazardous compounds known to present serious health risks. When the pipe-contractor defendants removed that pipe scale, Plaintiffs submit, they produced radioactive dust that became airborne and settled onto the Plaintiffs' properties, where some of it was absorbed into the ground or surface water. Plaintiffs allege that some of this material remains on their property despite remediation efforts, and will continue to emit harmful radiation for thousands of years. Plaintiffs contend that Defendants long knew or should have known of these hazards, but that Plaintiffs were not on notice of them until 2001, when landowner-defendants the Grefers posted a warning sign. Plaintiffs seek compensation for a wide variety of harms—including physical injuries, contracted diseases, medical expenses, lost wages, emotional distress, and property damage and diminution of value—as well as punitive damages and restitution of part of a nine-figure verdict awarded to the Grefers in a previous lawsuit.

After Plaintiffs filed this lawsuit, Defendants removed it to federal court, claiming that it is a removable "mass action" under CAFA. Plaintiffs then filed a motion to remand, arguing that Defendants had not met their burden of proving CAFA's basic jurisdictional requirements and that, in the alternative, three exclusions or exceptions to CAFA jurisdiction applied. The district court granted that motion, concluding that neither Plaintiffs' complaint nor Defendants' evidence shows that any plaintiff's claim satisfies CAFA's $75,000 individual amount-in-controversy requirement. We granted Defendants' petition for permission to appeal pursuant to 28 U.S.C. § 1453.

## III. DISCUSSION

### A.

CAFA expanded federal district courts' original jurisdiction to include " 'class actions' and 'mass actions' " in which there is minimal diversity and the aggregate amount in controversy exceeds $5 million. A mass action— the category that occupies us here—is "any civil action in which monetary relief claims of 100 or more persons are proposed to be tried jointly on the ground that the plaintiffs' claims involve common questions of law or fact, except that jurisdiction shall exist only over those plaintiffs whose claims in a mass action satisfy the jurisdictional amount requirements under subsection (a)." 28 U.S.C. § 1332(d)(11)(B)(i). That subsection (a), in turn, limits diversity jurisdiction to "civil actions where the matter in controversy exceeds the sum or value of $75,000, exclusive of interest and costs." 28 U.S.C. § 1332(a). Because the party seeking removal bears the burden of establishing federal jurisdiction, we have held that a putative mass action removed under CAFA must be remanded if the defendants cannot establish that (1) the aggregate amount in controversy exceeds $5 million and (2) at least one plaintiff's claim satisfies the $75,000 individual amount in controversy. The district court held that Defendants had not met their burden of showing the individual amount in controversy as to any plaintiff, and did not address the aggregate requirement.

Plaintiffs' state-court complaint alleges no amount in controversy—indeed, Louisiana law prohibits it. Defendants alleged satisfaction of the aggregate and individual jurisdictional amounts in their notice of removal, but Plaintiffs contested those allegations by filing a motion to remand. In such a case, the court must decide by a preponderance of the evidence whether the relevant amount in controversy is met. *Dart Cherokee Basin Operating Co. v. Owens* (citing 28 U.S.C. § 1446(c)(2)(B)). A removing defendant can meet its burden of demonstrating the amount in controversy by showing that the amount is "facially apparent" from the plaintiffs' pleadings alone, or by submitting summary-judgment-type evidence. The required "demonstration concerns what the plaintiff is claiming (and thus the amount in controversy between the parties), not whether the plaintiff is likely to win or be awarded everything he seeks").

Contrary to Plaintiffs' argument, that the removing party bears the burden of proving the amount in controversy does not mean that the removing party cannot ask the court to make common-sense inferences about the amount put at stake by the injuries the plaintiffs claim. In *De Aguilar v. Boeing Co.,* for example, we found it facially apparent that claims for "wrongful death, terror in anticipation of death, loss of companionship, and funeral expenses" exceeded $50,000 per plaintiff (the individual amount in controversy for diversity jurisdiction at that time), even though the complaint did not specify an amount of damages and the plaintiffs' attorney had submitted an affidavit stating that no plaintiff's damages exceeded $49,000. And in *Allen v. R & H Oil & Gas Co.,* we held that a complaint supported federal jurisdiction because "a court, in applying only common sense, would find that" hundreds of plaintiffs who sought punitive damages for "a wide variety of harm allegedly caused by wanton and reckless conduct" would collect more than $50,000 if they were successful. With this in mind, we turn to Defendants' showing here.

Whether or not the amount in controversy is facially apparent from Plaintiffs' complaint, Defendants submitted evidence that satisfies their burden of showing that at least one plaintiff's claim exceeds $75,000. Defendants filed in opposition to the motion to remand Plaintiffs' interrogatory responses—which constitute summary-judgment-type evidence. In response to one interrogatory, Plaintiffs produced a chart detailing each individual plaintiff's claimed damages. Plaintiffs assert that Defendants' conduct has caused them to suffer a wide variety of specific harms, some of which, common sense dictates, place more than $75,000 at stake: for example, (1) Eddie Ashley claims that she has suffered, among other harms, emphysema and the wrongful death of her husband from lung cancer; and (2) Tommie Jones avers that he developed prostate cancer and a host of other ailments. We hold that it is more likely than not that these plaintiffs seek to recover more than $75,000. Indeed, Plaintiffs' counsel acknowledged at oral argument that for the plaintiffs who contracted cancer, he would be "asking the jury, come trial, for a whole lot more than $75,000." For these reasons, the district court erred when it ordered this case remanded on the ground that no plaintiff satisfies the individual amount-in-controversy requirement.

## IV. CONCLUSION

We hold that the district court erred when it found that no plaintiff satisfies CAFA's individual amount-in-controversy requirement, and reverse on that basis. We remand this case to the district court to address Plaintiffs' remaining jurisdictional arguments.

# CHAPTER 14

---

# FUND APPROACHES TO RESOLVING MASS TORTS

■ ■ ■

## A.  THE SEPTEMBER 11TH WORLD TRADE CENTER DISASTER FUND

### SCHNEIDER V. FEINBERG
United States Court of Appeals for the Second Circuit, 2003.
345 F.3d 135.

In September 2001, Congress created the September 11 Victim Compensation Fund, Title IV of the Air Transportation and Safety and System Stabilization Act of 2001, which authorizes the Attorney General to issue regulations governing compensation from the Fund and to designate a Special Master to administer it. The stated purpose of the Act is "to provide compensation to any individual (or relatives of a deceased individual) who was physically injured or killed as a result of the terrorist-related aircraft crashes of September 11, 2001." The Attorney General designated Kenneth R. Feinberg (Special Master), and in consultation with him, promulgated a series of regulations to guide and expedite the award of compensation. These regulations created a mechanism by which claimants could either choose to collect presumptive awards based on the victims' income and family status, or they could seek higher compensation upon a showing of "extraordinary circumstances."

The Special Master promulgated presumptive loss tables based on victims' incomes up to the 98th percentile of income. The highest presumptive award, at the 98th percentile, is approximately $4 million. "Extraordinary circumstances" must be adduced in support of claims seeking compensation in excess of the maximum presumed award of approximately $4 million. The measure of compensable economic loss under the regulations also varied by consumption rates—i.e., by the percentage of a victim's income that would have been consumed by the victim and therefore is excluded from the presumed loss suffered by dependents and survivors.

Two sets of plaintiffs brought suit separately challenging the presumed award process. Cheryl Schneider is the wife of Ian Schneider, a partner in the firm of Cantor Fitzgerald, L.L.P., whose income far exceeded the 98th percentile. She alleges that the Special Master has in effect adopted a de facto cap on her award in violation of an asserted statutory mandate that she be compensated for her full economic loss. The Colaio plaintiffs sue on behalf of a class of personal representatives of decedents who died in the attack on the World Trade Center, all of whom are eligible for compensation from the Fund. According to the complaint, this class "comprises a group that includes single and married decedents, decedents with and without children, and decedents whose work experiences and average earnings cover a broad spectrum" The regulations, interpretive methodologies, and policies adopted by the Special Master are challenged under the Administrative Procedure Act.

Defendants moved for judgment on the pleadings pursuant to Fed.R.Civ.P. 12(c), and plaintiffs cross-moved for summary judgment on the basis of accompanying affidavits. The United States District Court for the Southern District of New York (Hellerstein, J.), decided the Colaio and Schneider suits in tandem. Among other rulings, the court found no evidence of a de facto cap on compensation; accorded deference to the regulations and accompanying presumptive award tables; held that they reflected a permissible interpretation of the statute; and dismissed plaintiffs' claims. We affirm for the following reasons.

I

Following the September 11, 2001 attacks, Congress enacted the Air Transportation and Safety and System Stabilization Act of 2001 in order to "preserve the continued viability of the United States air transportation system" from potentially ruinous tort liability in the wake of the attacks. Title IV of the Act deals with liability in a number of ways, two of them relevant to this appeal: (i) it caps tort liability stemming from the attacks at "the limits of the liability coverage maintained by the air carrier," and (ii) it sets up the September 11 Victims Compensation Fund "to provide compensation to victims of the terrorist-related aircraft crashes of September 11, 2001." These measures are made to reinforce each other because eligibility for compensation from the Fund is conditioned upon a waiver by claimants of "the right to file any civil action" in state or federal court except "a civil action to recover collateral source obligations."

In keeping with the goal of expedition, claims must be filed no later than two years after promulgation of procedural rules by the Special Master, and the Special Master is required to "complete a review, make a determination, and provide written notice to the claimant" no later than 120 days from the filing of the claim. In making that determination, "the Special Master shall not consider negligence or any other theory of liability," may not award punitive damages, and "shall reduce the amount of compensation determined by the amount of collateral source compensation."

The Act imposes on the Special Master the affirmative duty to "determine" "the amount of compensation to which the claimant is entitled based on the harm to the claimant, the facts of the claim, and the individual circumstances of the claimant." Regulations promulgated pursuant to the Act define "individual circumstances" to "include the financial needs or financial resources of the claimant or the victim's dependents and beneficiaries." "Harm to the claimant includes any economic and noneconomic loss." And "economic loss" is defined as "any pecuniary loss resulting from harm (including the loss of earnings or other benefits related to employment, medical expense loss, replacement services loss, loss due to death, burial costs, and loss of business or employment opportunities) *to the extent recovery for such loss is allowed under applicable State law.*" Regulations construe the emphasized phrase to mean only that the Special Master must compensate claimants for "categories or types of economic loss compensable under state law," not that he must compensate them in accordance with state tort law in other respects.

The Act vests administration of the Fund in the "Attorney General, acting through a Special Master appointed by the Attorney General" and authorizes them to "promulgate all procedural and substantive rules for its administration." "No later than 90 days after the date of enactment the Attorney General, in consultation with the Special Master" was required to "promulgate procedural regulations" and regulations governing "other matters determined appropriate by the Attorney General."

Following a period of notice and comment, the Attorney General and Special Master timely promulgated several regulations that bear on these appeals. Some of these regulations (referred to above) defined statutory terms. Several others established a "presumed award" scheme; and one of those authorized the Special Master to "develop a methodology and publish schedules, tables, or charts that will permit prospective claimants to estimate determinations of loss of earnings or other benefits."

Compensation for non-economic loss is set at $250,000, with an additional $100,000 for each dependent. The minimum presumptive award is $500,000 for a deceased victim with dependents or spouse, and $300,000 for a single deceased victim.

Presumed award tables are calculated "up to but not beyond the 98th percentile of individual income in the United States for the year 2000," i.e., not exceeding $231,000 per year, a level that yields a presumed award of $3–4 million (depending on variables such as age), minus collateral source compensation.

There is a two-track system for processing claims. In Track A, a claims evaluator determines the claimant's presumed award using the tables and methodology developed by the Special Master, and informs the claimant (within 45 days) as to eligibility and the amount of the compensation. The claimant may accept the presumed award or may seek a hearing to present evidence in support of an individualized determination of compensation to justify an upward adjustment based on "extraordinary circumstances." In

Track B, the claimant can proceed directly to a hearing, receive an eligibility determination in 45 days, present evidence, and receive an individualized determination of compensation greater than the presumptive award upon a showing of "extraordinary circumstances." But because no presumed award tables are calculated for income earners above the 98th percentile (i.e., those who earned more than $231,000) the presumed award is capped at that level ($3–$4 million), and if high income earners seek greater compensation, they have no choice but to seek an individualized determination.

Commentary accompanying the final regulations explain the purpose of the scheme. The restriction on presumed awards to income below the 98th percentile is premised on the notion that "calculation of awards for many victims with extraordinary incomes beyond the 98th percentile could be a highly speculative exercise," "requiring a detailed evaluation of variable and often complex formulae for non-variable income, differing work life expectations, often highly volatile industries or markets, and other factors that are not subject to easy generalization." Moreover, the commentary regards "the purpose of the Act not simply to examine economic and non-economic harm, but also to provide compensation that is just and appropriate in light of the financial needs and resources of the claimants." Compensation under the Act was not intended to "replicate a theoretically possible future income stream" and "the individual circumstances of the wealthiest and highest income claimants will often indicate that multi-million dollar awards out of the public coffers are not necessary to provide them with a strong economic foundation from which to rebuild their lives." Compensation above the 98th percentile level therefore "would rarely be necessary to ensure that the financial needs of a claimant are met," but could be awarded "upon a more detailed record."

Plaintiffs have not filed claims with the Fund; but they have attended informal meetings with the Special Master to discuss their claims (what are referred to as "test cases"). (The plaintiffs' kin all appear to have been employees of Cantor Fitzgerald, and the firm's counsel was present at these meetings). At her meeting with the Special Master, plaintiff Cheryl Schneider presented an expert report explaining that the lost income to the Schneider family was between $28 million and $52 million. The Special Master indicated that his consultant, Price Waterhouse, had calculated the lost earnings at $14–15 million, but the Special Master added that the issue was "moot" since either number was "far north of anything" he would pay. In a subsequent conversation, he told her that he would not give more than $6 million to anyone.

The other Plaintiffs testify to similar conversations in which the Special Master told them that he did not intend to award compensation on the basis of the lost incomes of high-income earners. It does appear that, contrary to the statement he reportedly made to Mrs. Schneider, the

Special Master expressed a willingness to award up to $7 million dollars in later informal conversations.

Some members of Congress advocated a cap on individual compensation award, but Congress did not vote on the proposition; the text references no cap. The statute, which "constitutes budget authority in advance of appropriations and represents the obligation of the Federal Government to provide for the payment of amounts for compensation" by the Fund, seems to be a blank check. Legislative history is equivocal and unhelpful on whether the payout would be subject to considerations of need or proportionality.

## II.

A reviewing court must "set aside agency action" that is "arbitrary, capricious, an abuse of discretion or otherwise not in accordance with the law." We analyze whether an agency's construction of its organic statute comports with the statute's meaning under the two-step test set forth in *Chevron U.S.A., Inc. v. Natural Resources Defense Council.* "The judiciary is the final authority on issues of statutory construction, and must reject administrative constructions which are contrary to clear congressional intent." Courts therefore look first to "whether Congress has spoken to the precise question at issue," and if so "give effect to the unambiguously expressed intent of Congress." "If the statute is silent or ambiguous with respect to the specific issue," a court may consider only "whether the agency's answer is based on a permissible construction of the statute." And if so, the court must defer to the agency's construction of the statute.

Not all agency interpretations of the agency's organic statute are entitled to *Chevron* deference. *Chevron* deference is clearly owed to regulations adopted by formal rule-making after notice and comment. But "interpretations such as those in opinion letters—like interpretations contained in policy statements, agency manuals, and enforcement guidelines, all of which lack the force of law—do not warrant *Chevron*-style deference." The touchstone is whether the agency interpretation is intended to carry "the force of law" (not whether it has been subjected to formal notice-and-comment procedures under the APA). Thus *Chevron* deference applies where the interpretation is "the type of legislative ruling that would naturally bind more than the parties to the ruling."

Interpretive guidelines that lack the force of law but nevertheless "bring the benefit of an agency's specialized experience to bear" on the meaning of a statute, are still entitled to "some deference." ("We consider that the rulings, interpretations and opinions of the Administrator under this Act, while not controlling upon the courts by reason of their authority, do constitute a body of experience and informed judgment to which courts and litigants may properly resort for guidance."). The extent of (so-called) *Skidmore* deference is chiefly the "power to persuade."

The challenged regulations were adopted after a period of notice and comment, and are evidently intended to carry the force of law as to all claims submitted to the Fund. The accompanying tables were not subject to formal rule-making procedures, but they also exert force of law over all claims. Unlike opinion letters, interpretive rulings, agency manuals, and enforcement guidelines, the tables are "the type of legislative ruling that would naturally bind more than the parties to the ruling." They are meant to guide compensation, and they apply equally to all claimants seeking compensation from the Fund. The district court properly held that—to the extent that they do not contradict Title IV's clear and unambiguous meaning—*Chevron* deference is owed to the regulations adopted by formal notice-and-comment procedures and to the presumed-award tables adopted to implement the statute and regulations.

### A.   *De Facto Cap*

The Colaio Plaintiffs and Cheryl Schneider seek a declaration that the Act prohibits the Special Master from imposing a cap on compensation awarded to high earners. It is clear enough that Congress did not place a de jure cap on compensation, and that any cap on compensation would be a direct violation of the statute, and therefore would command no *Chevron* deference. Moreover, defendants acknowledge that any cap would be unlawful. Thus the regulations impose no cap; and the Special Master has disclaimed imposing one. There is no dispute between the defendants and the plaintiffs on the lawfulness of a cap, and there is no need in present circumstances for an "amen" declaration by this Court.

Notwithstanding the parties' agreement that there is no de jure cap, plaintiffs seek to demonstrate that a de facto cap is being imposed. They argue that the Special Master's refusal to promulgate presumed loss tables above the 98th percentile, coupled with the requirement that claimants seeking more than the maximum presumed award of $3–4 million demonstrate "extraordinary circumstances," furnish cover behind which the Special Master will fix awards based on his subjective and necessarily arbitrary impressions of what claimants should need or may deserve. Plaintiffs contend that the Special Master's private criteria are manifested by private statements (made in informal consultations) and by public pronouncements in which the Special Master expresses reluctance or unwillingness to make very large awards to wealthy families of the highest-income victims.

This Court reviews the district court's grant of summary judgment *de novo*. In doing so, we construe the evidence in the light most favorable to the non-moving party and draw all reasonable inferences in its favor. In addition, a court deciding judgment on the pleadings must construe allegations in the pleadings "liberally in favor of the plaintiffs." Defendants have conceded plaintiffs' version of the facts at oral argument before the district court. Nevertheless, we agree with the district court that there is no reliable evidence supporting the existence of a de facto cap.

The record does not show that the cut-off on the presumed-loss tables and the "extraordinary circumstances" requirement for awards exceeding $4 million constitute a sham or pretext. The Special Master plausibly explained that presumptions of loss above the 98th percentile would "require a detailed evaluation of variable and often complex formulae for non-variable income, differing work life expectations, often highly volatile industries or markets, and other factors that are not often subject to easy generalization." As this Court has noted, "the projection of future income at high levels" of earnings is "itself extremely conjectural."

The Special Master's remark that he would pay no claimant more than $6 million does not establish such a cap, since in subsequent informal meetings with other prospective claimants he has proposed awards of up to $7 million dollars. Plaintiffs have produced estimates from private experts showing that their economic losses range as high as $50 million (in the case of plaintiff Schneider). These estimates are, however, implicitly shaped by assumptions about the level of economic loss available in tort litigation. Such assumptions are not compelling because tort claims would be predicated on aggressive theories of liability against entities that enjoy the privilege of bankruptcy, and would therefore be contentious and uncertain—as well as prolonged, and discounted by attorneys' fees. Payment from the Fund, by contrast, is simple, certain, non-contentious, and prompt.

The Special Master's consultant has produced an estimate of economic loss (in the case of Schneider) of $14–15 million. But we do not know what assumptions were made in coming up with this figure. And no statutory provision binds the Special Master to accept the estimate of his consultant, or treat that estimate as a baseline.

In addition, we decline to rule that the record of historical earnings is a sound predictor of high income from businesses that were themselves impacted by the events of September 11, particularly given that some part of the partnership draw may be attributable to ownership of a successful enterprise that has suffered changed circumstances. As noted above, the higher the stream of earned income, the less reliable it may be on a sustained basis. We do not know what should result from the present valuing of an after-tax stream of income vulnerable to such contingencies, but these circumstances can notionally justify proposed awards sharply less than an honest estimate might support.

Finally, plaintiffs also point to public statements by the Special Master that "the individual circumstances of the wealthiest and highest income claimants will often indicate that multi-million dollar awards out of the public coffers are not necessary to provide them with a strong economic foundation from which to rebuild their lives." Such comments fuel an impression that the Special Master has closed his mind to awards that exceed his idea of what is appropriate in the most general sense of the word.

These comments and suggestions do not command *Chevron* deference because they are not binding dispositions that carry the force of law. However, except for promulgated regulations (which do not control the level of awards above the 98th percentile), it appears that Congress has confided each award to the sealed box of a Special Master's mind, has refrained from meaningful prescriptions, and has placed the result beyond the reach of review. ("The Special Master's determination of compensation shall be final and not subject to judicial review."). So while we agree with plaintiffs that the Special Master's comments are hard to square with the text of the Act, we decline to declare what we cannot enforce. ("The two principal criteria guiding the policy in favor of rendering declaratory judgments are (1) when the judgment will serve a useful purpose in clarifying and settling the legal relations in issue, and (2) when it will terminate and afford relief from the uncertainty, insecurity and controversy giving rise to the proceeding.").

## B.  *Interpretive Regulations*

The plaintiffs challenge two regulations promulgated by the Attorney General in consultation with the Special Master: (i) 28 C.F.R. § 104.41, which defines the phrase "individual circumstances" to include the "financial needs and resources of the victim's dependents and beneficiaries"; and (ii) 28 C.F.R. § 104.42, which construes the phrase "to the extent recovery for such loss is allowed under applicable state law" (in the definition of "economic loss") to mean that only the categories of loss compensable under governing state law may be used to calculate economic loss. Plaintiffs argue that these interpretive regulations are contrary to the meaning and purpose of the Act and therefore are not entitled to *Chevron* deference.

According to plaintiffs: the word "compensation," used in the Act to describe the payments made by the Fund to claimants, is a legal term of art denoting a sum that makes one whole; its use evidences Congressional intent to award claimants the full value of their economic loss as it would be formulated under state tort law (less collateral source remuneration); and the regulations represent impermissible readings of the statute because they reduce awards below full recovery for economic loss.

The use of the word "compensation" does not reflect unambiguous Congressional intent to afford the same level of compensation available under the tort law. True (as the plaintiffs point out), the statute borrows other terms of art from tort law, such as "collateral source" and "punitive damages." But that does not compel the inference that "compensation" is used in the Act as a term of art in contradistinction to words that are potentially more general, such as "payment" or "remuneration." The term "compensation" is used elsewhere in the Act as a synonym of "payment," as in the phrase "collateral source compensation," which is used to mean "collateral source payments."

The Special Master is not obliged to read "compensation" as a tort term of art in one place when it has no such meaning elsewhere in the statute. The canons of statutory construction favor the consistent use of terms throughout a statute. ("A term appearing in several places in a statutory text is generally read the same way each time it appears." In other statutes, Congress commonly employs the word "compensation" otherwise than as a term of art, e.g. "workers' compensation," "compensation" for death or disability in wartime, and "compensation" for victims of vaccines.

Further, the plain language of the Act does not compel plaintiffs' interpretation. In certain contexts, Congress has evinced a clear intent to provide tort victims with compensation to make them whole. *See, e.g.,* (providing that any employee who is discharged for bringing to light the fact that employer has filed a false claim of action against the federal government "shall be entitled to all relief necessary to make the employee whole"); (providing that programs receiving funds from the National and Community Service State Grant Program must establish grievance procedures for "displaced employees" empowered to award such relief as will "make the displaced employee whole"). Nowhere in the statute does Congress use the term "make whole," nor does the Act authorize the Special Master to award whatever amount necessary to compensate each victim's *full* economic loss. The weight of commentary on this point is that it was not the purpose of the Act to make the victims of the September 11 attacks whole.

The Act's legislative history reinforces our conclusion. Some members of Congress (arguably) believed that the Act permits the level of recovery sought by the plaintiffs, while others emphatically believed that it did not. The Act does not unambiguously provide for a level of compensation available in tort, and certainly is susceptible to the Special Master's interpretation. Consequently that interpretation is entitled to *Chevron* deference.

We are also unconvinced by the plaintiffs' separate challenges to individual regulations.

The Act requires the Special Master to calculate "compensation based on the harm to the claimant, the facts of the claim, and the individual circumstances of the claimant." Plaintiffs challenge the regulation providing that such "individual circumstances of the claimant may include the financial needs or financial resources of the claimant or the victim's dependents and beneficiaries."

Plaintiffs have failed to demonstrate that this interpretation of the phrase "individual circumstances" is an impermissible reading. The legislative decision to omit a cap on awards does not impliedly foreclose needs-based considerations. Nothing in the explicit statutory language establishes such a bar, and certainly the legislative history indicates that at least some members of Congress felt such considerations were appropriate under the statute.

Need is certainly a consideration in the Special Master's formulation of minimum awards, as everyone agrees. Plaintiffs, who tacitly accept formulation of minimum awards in part on the basis of need, are thereby compelled to argue that the Act unambiguously forecloses a *decrease* in compensation based on needs and resources, while allowing an *increase*. But the provision setting forth the relevant factors for determining compensation requires consideration of certain enumerated factors without such a distinction ("The Special Master *shall determine* the amount of compensation *based on*"). At the very least, the Act is reasonably susceptible to alternative readings, and the Special Master's interpretation is entitled to deference.

Using the phrase "individual circumstances" to prompt consideration of economic needs, the Special Master has said or implied that very large awards justified by economic loss would be unseemly. Thus, to the extent the Special Master is employing a need-based analysis to compute awards, he has introduced some limit on what would otherwise be proper compensation under the Act. Such notion, in our view, would seem to be contrary to what Congress aimed to accomplish in the statute. The overriding purpose of the statute is, of course, fair compensation for economic and non-economic loss. Therefore, even though the Special Master has authority to conduct a thorough analysis, he should take into full account a claimant's economic loss, as specifically required by the statute, before evaluating need-based circumstances. This slight shift in approach has the virtue of more closely reflecting Congress' aim as well as appearing to be more fair to claimants.

The plaintiffs also challenge the Special Master's reading of the Act to borrow categories of compensable economic loss from state law without borrowing state tort law whole to calculate economic loss. The Act defines "economic loss" as "pecuniary loss resulting from harm (including the loss of earnings or other benefits related to employment, medical expense loss, replacement service loss, loss due to death, burial costs, and loss of business or employment opportunities) to the extent recovery for such loss is allowed under applicable state law." The challenged regulation construes the phrase "to the extent recovery for such loss is allowed under applicable state law" to mean "that the Special Master is not permitted to compensate claimants for those categories or types of economic losses that would not be compensable under the law of the state that would be applicable to any tort claims brought by or on behalf of the victim." Plaintiffs contest this interpretation on the ground that the plain meaning of the Act requires calculation of economic loss in the manner prescribed by applicable state tort law.

The provision at issue is ambiguous, because it is unclear whether the phrase "such loss" refers to "pecuniary loss"—as plaintiffs argue—or to the categories of loss in the immediately preceding parenthetical. We owe deference to the interpretation announced in the regulation because it is not an unreasonable reading of the statute.

The greatest disparity at issue is attributable to the tort law rule that uses pre-tax income to calculate economic loss. But the underlying rationale for this rule is that otherwise the tax would be a windfall to the tortfeasor—a rationale that does not apply here, since the federal government is not a tortfeasor and is the tax collector. We cannot presume that Congress intended to create a windfall entitlement of tax-free income.

In any event, Congress could have made the application of state tort law unambiguous if it chose to do so. Congress created an exclusive federal cause of action for any suit for damages arising out of the events of September 11th. That provision stipulated that:

> The substantive law for decision in any such suit shall be derived
> from the law, including the choice of law principles, of the State
> in which the crash occurred unless such law is inconsistent with
> or preempted by Federal law.

In short, Congress has not spoken on the issues addressed by the challenged regulations, and the Special Master has adopted a permissible interpretation of the Act that is entitled to deference. Therefore, the district court properly dismissed the plaintiffs' claims challenging these regulations.

### C. Consumption Rate for Single Childless Decedents

Finally, the Colaio plaintiffs challenge as "arbitrary and capricious" under the APA the disproportionately higher consumption rates used by the Special Master to calculate presumptive losses for single decedents with no children. We lack jurisdiction to decide this issue.

"Agency action is not subject to judicial review to the extent that such action is committed to agency discretion by law." There is no jurisdiction if the governing statute or regulations "are drawn so that a court would have no meaningful standard against which to judge the agency's exercise of discretion." The APA's "arbitrary and capricious" standard does not by itself provide a "meaningful standard" of review. Dismissal for lack of jurisdiction is appropriate where there is "no law to apply."

Here, there is no law to apply because no standard of review—other than the APA's "arbitrary and capricious" standard itself—governs. The Act does not guide or limit the Special Master's discretion on this point: it expressly allows the Attorney General and the Special Master to adopt all substantive and procedural regulations necessary to resolve claims, and places the resolution of claims beyond the reach of judicial review.

Since we have found the regulations, interpretive methodologies and policies to be consistent with the meaning of the Act, calculation of compensation, even if based on disproportionate consumption rates, represents an exercise of the broad discretion given to the Special Master. There is simply no "meaningful standard" against which to judge the exercise of that discretion.

### CONCLUSION

For the foregoing reasons, we dismiss the appeal in part and in remaining part we affirm the district court's dismissal of the complaints in these actions. The mandate shall issue forthwith.

## CRUZ V. MCANENEY

Supreme Court, Appellate Division, Second Department, New York, 2006.
31 A.D.3d 54, 816 N.Y.S.2d 486.

Appeal from an order of the Supreme Court, Kings County, dated July 2, 2004, and entered in an action to recover a monetary award distributed by the federal September 11th Victim Compensation Fund of 2001. The order, in effect, denied defendant's motion to dismiss the complaint.

Plaintiff, the surviving domestic partner of a victim of the September 11, 2001 terrorist attacks on the World Trade Center, stated a cause of action against defendant, decedent's brother, to recover a portion of the $ 531,541.42 award distributed by the federal September 11th Victim Compensation Fund of 2001 (Fund) to defendant as decedent's personal representative (*see* Air Transportation Safety and System Stabilization Act) based upon allegations that the award was enhanced by the sum of $ 253,454 to account for the reality of plaintiff's domestic partnership with decedent. Defendant had a fiduciary duty under federal law to distribute the award to beneficiaries "in a manner consistent" with the applicable state law, and New York law evinces an intent to compensate surviving domestic partners, as family members, for their losses resulting from the terrorist attacks (*see* September 11th Victims and Families Relief Act). In addition, plaintiff also stated viable claims for the imposition of a constructive trust and unjust enrichment.

We are called upon to decide as a matter of first impression whether or not the confluence of the equitable doctrines of constructive trust and unjust enrichment, together with what we perceive to be the intent of New York and federal legislation enacted to compensate the victims and survivors of the September 11, 2001, terrorist attacks, requires that we affirm the denial of this motion to dismiss the complaint for failure to state a cause of action. We find that they do.

Viewed in the light most favorable to the plaintiff, as we must, in the context of this motion to dismiss for failure to state a cause of action, state the following are the relevant facts:

Patricia McAneney died intestate on September 11, 2001, as a result of the terrorist attacks on the World Trade Center. Patricia's brother, the defendant James P. McAneney, as her personal representative, filed a claim on her behalf with the September 11th Victim Compensation Fund of 2001. While the claim was pending, the plaintiff, Margaret Cruz, submitted a statement of financial interest with the Fund, stating that she was entitled to all or part of any award because she was Patricia's loving, domestic partner for more than 15 years. At that time, the Fund's Special Master allegedly told the plaintiff that an award had already been approved in the sum of $278,087.42. This amount allegedly reflected Patricia's pain and suffering, as well as the economic loss of Patricia's survivors analogous to the amount awarded in a traditional wrongful death suit.

On March 10, 2003, the Special Master allegedly explained to the plaintiff that the approved award of the sum of $278,087.42 had been calculated as if Patricia were single and lived in a one-person household. However, the Special Master also expressed a willingness to recalculate the economic loss portion of the award and increase it by the sum of $253,454, to a total sum of $531,541.42, to account for the reality of the plaintiff's domestic partnership with Patricia. Allegedly, the Fund was willing to distribute the full award to the defendant, as personal representative for Patricia, provided he agreed in writing to distribute the increased portion ($253,454) to the plaintiff. However, the Fund was unwilling to mandate that the defendant, as personal representative, distribute the full award of the sum of $531,541.42 to the plaintiff as Patricia's sole survivor and beneficiary.

Additionally, some representatives of the Fund allegedly told the plaintiff that the Fund would not distribute the increased portion of the award to the defendant absent a settlement agreement regarding distribution of the increased portion to her. The parties then attempted to settle this matter. Unfortunately, they were unable to do so.

With negotiations at an impasse, representatives of the Fund allegedly informed the plaintiff on May 23, 2003, that it was in the process of distributing the award to the defendant, but assured her that only the smaller, original award of the sum of $278,087.42 would go to the defendant if a settlement could not be reached. While the plaintiff requested that the Fund mandate that the defendant distribute the increased portion of the award to her, the Fund refused to assist her.

Allegedly, the plaintiff continued her attempts to negotiate with the defendant, but he would not make any decision regarding a settlement before June 23, 2003, when his newly retained litigation counsel would be available for consultation. In the interim, on or about June 12, 2003, the Fund informed the plaintiff that it would soon distribute the larger award of the sum of $531,541.42, despite the absence of a settlement agreement. The alleged rationale for distributing the larger award under these circumstances was that the plaintiff could litigate the dispute in state court.

Ultimately, the defendant, as Patricia's personal representative, received an award of the sum of $531,541.42 from the Fund. He refused further negotiations with the plaintiff and declined to distribute any portion of the award to her. Instead, he distributed the entire award to himself, on the ground that he was Patricia's only surviving blood relative. The plaintiff, therefore, commenced the instant action to compel the defendant to disburse all or part of the award to her.

The complaint asserts three causes of action based on the factual allegations stated above. The first cause of action allege that the plaintiff is entitled, as the surviving domestic partner of the decedent, to the full award or a portion of the award, and the defendant, as the personal representative of the decedent, is under a fiduciary duty to distribute same to her.

Alternatively, in the second and third causes of action, the plaintiff asserts claims under the equitable theories of constructive trust and unjust enrichment. Under these theories, the plaintiff alleges that she is entitled to at least the sum of $253,454 because the Fund intended that this portion be distributed to her. Since this amount was added on to the original award to account for the reality of her domestic partnership with Patricia, the plaintiff alleges that the defendant has an equitable duty to convey, at least, this amount to her.

The defendant moved to dismiss the complaint in its entirety alleging that it failed to state a cause of action. The Supreme Court, in effect, denied the motion. The defendant appeals, and we affirm.

The Fund was created by the federal government as title IV of the Air Transportation Safety and System Stabilization Act. The Fund's purpose is "to provide compensation to any individual (or relatives of a deceased individual) who was physically injured or killed as a result of the terrorist-related aircraft crashes of September 11, 2001. Thereunder, a personal representative may file a claim with the Fund on behalf of a deceased victim of the terrorist attacks.

A special master, appointed by the United States Attorney General, administers the Fund. The special master's tasks include determining the eligibility of claimants and the amount of compensation to be awarded. Once the special master makes a determination regarding amount and eligibility, the special master authorizes payment of the full award to the claimant, who must be the personal representative in cases of deceased victims. Under the Act, the personal representative has the duty to "distribute the award in a manner consistent with the law of the decedent's domicile or any applicable rulings made by a court of competent jurisdiction," which has been interpreted as not precluding an expansive definition of who is entitled to be compensated.

In the instant case, it is undisputed that Patricia's state of domicile was New York and, thus, the defendant, as her personal representative, has a duty to distribute the award "in a manner consistent with the law" of this state. In this instance, the New York State laws enacted for the purpose of providing relief to the victims of the September 11, 2001, terrorist attack evince an intent to compensate surviving domestic partners, as family members, for their losses from this tragedy. Based on the federal statutes and regulations regarding the Fund, a state's intestacy laws, while relevant, do not solely determine the identity of beneficiaries of the award and, notwithstanding the absence of a valid will, a partner in a longstanding domestic relationship may share in any award made by the Fund. Thus, the first cause of action, especially in light of allegations that the award was increased as a result of the plaintiff's application to the fund, stated a cause of action.

It is true that the plaintiff and Patricia were not married under the laws of any state at the time of Patricia's death and, thus, the plaintiff cannot be treated as the surviving "spouse" for purposes of the intestate distribution of the award from the Fund. Nevertheless, the plaintiff may be entitled to some unspecified portion of the award from the Fund, albeit not the entire sum of $531,541.42.

Moreover, under principles of equity, the second and third causes of action also state viable claims for the imposition of a constructive trust and unjust enrichment. The ultimate purpose of a constructive trust is to prevent unjust enrichment and, thus, a constructive trust may be imposed " 'when property has been acquired in such circumstances that the holder of the legal title may not in good conscience retain the beneficial interest' " The usual elements of a constructive trust are "(1) a confidential or fiduciary relationship, (2) a promise, (3) a transfer in reliance thereon and (4) unjust enrichment" Thus, courts can and will impose constructive trusts "whenever necessary to satisfy the demands of justice."

Similarly, to prevail on a claim of unjust enrichment, "a party must show that (1) the other party was enriched, (2) at that party's expense, and (3) that 'it is against equity and good conscience to permit the other party to retain what is sought to be recovered.' " "Unjust enrichment, however, does not require the performance of any wrongful act by the one enriched." "Innocent parties may frequently be unjustly enriched."

Viewing the allegations in the light most favorable to the plaintiff, justice in the instant case could conceivably require the imposition of a constructive trust, and concomitantly show that the defendant, in his personal capacity, would be unjustly enriched if he was also allowed to retain the portion of the Fund's award that was allegedly increased after the plaintiff's application to the Fund and in recognition of the plaintiff's loss of her lifetime partner.

The legislation enacted in our state following the September 11, 2001, terrorist attack also lends support to the argument that the plaintiff may be entitled, at least, to the increased portion of the award as compensation for her loss, such as a law providing same-sex domestic partners with certain rights to compensate for the loss of their loved ones due to this specific, horrific event. The Legislature declared,

> that domestic partners of victims of the terrorist attacks are eligible for distributions from the federal victim compensation fund, and the requirements for awards under the New York State World Trade Center Relief Fund and other existing state laws, regulations, and executive orders should guide the federal special master in determining awards and ensuring that the distribution plan compensates such domestic partners for the losses they sustained.

Although this legislation did not make any changes to this State's intestacy laws, it recognized that domestic partners should be compensated from the Fund for the loss of their loved ones.

Indeed, Governor George Pataki responded to the September 11, 2001, terrorist attacks in a similar fashion by authorizing "Crime Victims Awards" to all persons who could show a sufficient relationship with the victims, including "common ownership of property, common house-holding, shared budgeting and the length of the relationship between such person and the victim" In addition, the legislature enacted section 4 of the Workers' Compensation Law for the specific purpose of providing death benefits to domestic partners of those killed as a result of the September 11, 2001, terrorist attacks.

As Patricia's personal representative, the defendant has a duty to distribute the award to beneficiaries "in a manner consistent" with this State's law. As noted in the  State September 11th Act, this State has recognized that surviving domestic partners should receive compensation for the loss of their loved ones due to the September 11, 2001, terrorist attacks. Thus, if the plaintiff can prove that the Fund increased the award by the sum of $253,454 to account for the reality of her relationship with Patricia, it would be inconsistent with the legislation regarding the September 11, 2001, terrorist attacks to permit the defendant to keep that portion of the award for himself. Under these unique circumstances, if proven, the defendant could not in good conscience retain that sum and, as Patricia's personal representative, he would have a duty to convey such sum to the plaintiff. Accordingly, the plaintiff has succeeded in stating viable causes of action for a constructive trust and unjust enrichment.

In light of the above, there is no merit to the defendant's contention that state law bars the instant action. State law provides that

> *any person* who serves as the personal representative of a victim of the terrorist attacks on September eleventh, two thousand one, and who files a claim with the fund, shall have no liability to any person resulting from any actions *taken reasonably and in good faith* under the act, including but not limited to the payment or distribution of any award received from the fund in accordance with any plan of distribution that has been submitted to and approved by the special master appointed under the act.

Accordingly, state law merely provides a qualified immunity to any personal representative who takes reasonable and good faith actions in distributing the award.

Again, viewing the allegations in the light most favorable to the plaintiff, such qualified protection is not available to the defendant in the instant case. According to the complaint, the defendant seeks to retain for himself the increased portion of the Fund's award that specifically accounts for the plaintiff's relationship with Patricia. Such action cannot be interpreted as having been taken in a reasonable and good faith manner, especially in view of this State's recognition that domestic partners should be compensated for the loss of their loved ones. Moreover, the Fund allegedly distributed the full award of the sum of $531,541.42 to the defendant, as Patricia's personal representative, with the understanding that the plaintiff could pursue any claim to compensation in state court. Accordingly, as the plaintiff alleges, in essence, the plan of compensation was still in dispute when the award was distributed to the personal representative. Under these circumstances, state law does not bar the instant case.

Finally, contrary to the defendant's contention, section 405(b)(3) of the Act likewise does not bar the instant case. That section provides as follows:

> Not later than 120 days after that date on which a claim is filed the Special Master shall complete a review, make a determination, and provide written notice to the claimant, with respect to the matters that were the subject of the claim under review. Such a determination shall be final and not subject to judicial review.

The defendant contends that the plaintiff wrongfully challenges the Special Master's determination by bringing the instant action. Contrary to the defendant's contention, the Act only addresses the special master's determination regarding eligibility of the claimant and the amount of compensation to be awarded on behalf of the claimant. As the United States Attorney General has stated:

Congress did not, however, address who could ultimately receive compensation. Indeed, the 120-day statutory deadline for adjudicating claims on the Fund could in many instances preclude the Special Master from fairly determining how best to disburse awards among family members. Because state laws routinely serve that type of function, it makes the most sense that they generally provide the bases for distribution.

Thus, the special master disburses the full amount of the award to the personal representative, who, in turn, is charged with distributing the award to beneficiaries in a manner consistent with the law of the decedent's domicile.

In light of the above scheme, the plan of distribution is devised by the personal representative, not the special master. While the special master has the discretion to direct the personal representatives to distribute some portion of the award to family members who are not contemplated to be appropriately compensated, the special master is not obligated to do so. Accordingly, the Act and the regulations do not bar an action, like the instant one, when the plaintiff disputes only the personal representative's distribution plan. Under these circumstances, the plaintiff is not challenging any determination made by the special master.

Indeed, the Fund's regulations contemplate that state courts should preside over disputes regarding the personal representative's plan of distribution. For instance, in determining the final amount of the award, the special master "may designate the portions or percentages of the final award that are attributable to economic loss and non-economic loss, respectively, and may provide such other information as appropriate to provide adequate guidance for a court of competent jurisdiction and a personal representative."

Since the plaintiff does not challenge the Special Master's determination regarding eligibility and amount, and only disputes her absence from the personal representative's plan of distribution, her claims are not barred by the Act. Therefore, the motion to dismiss the complaint was properly denied, and the order is affirmed.

## BARRETTO V. GONZALEZ

United States District Court for the Southern District of New York, 2006.
2006 WL 3476787.

The issue raised by this case is whether I have jurisdiction to resolve a dispute between the former wife, and the more recent female companion, of a New York City fireman who died in the World Trade Center collapse of September 11, 2001. The object of the dispute is a Victim Compensation Fund award given by Special Master Kenneth Feinberg to the fireman's surviving daughter. For the reasons that follow, I hold that I lack jurisdiction to hear this dispute, and I remand the case to the New York Supreme Court for Kings County, from which it was removed.

## BACKGROUND

### I.  FACTS

Lieutenant Dennis Mojica of the New York City Fire Department was one of many firefighters who came to the World Trade Center to put out the fires caused by the terrorist-related aircraft crashes of September 11, and was trapped in the towers when they collapsed. Dennis Mojica was survived by his daughter, Allessandria Mojica, a minor. Hortensia Gonzalez is Allessandria Mojica's biological mother and the defendant in this case. Mojica, at the time of his death, had been living with another woman, Maria Barretto, the plaintiff. Maria Barretto and Dennis Mojica had been living together for eight years preceding Mojica's death, together with Allessandria Mojica and Maria Barretto's two daughters. Barretto's complaint alleges that she and Dennis Mojica were engaged to be married.

Shortly after the terrorist attacks, Congress created the September 11th Victim Compensation Fund to provide compensation to the relatives of persons like Dennis Mojica. *See* ATSSSA. Defendant Gonzalez filed a claim on the Fund on behalf of Dennis Mojica as his "personal representative." Special Master Kenneth Feinberg determined that under the regulations and applicable New York law, the entire amount of compensation should be distributed to the unmarried decedent's minor child, Allessandria Mojica. As a minor, however, Allessandria Mojica does not have control of the Victim Compensation Fund award; instead, Hortensia Gonzalez has legal control of the award as Mojica's "Representative Payee." The parties dispute whether Gonzalez has exercised control of the award consistent with her fiduciary duties.

### II.  COMPLAINT AND PROCEDURAL HISTORY

The complaint alleges that defendant breached her fiduciary obligations to plaintiff by collecting compensation from the Fund in excess of that authorized by the Surrogate's Court of New York County and by failing to distribute plaintiff's fair share of the Fund award to plaintiff. In particular, plaintiff alleges that defendant collected an award of $1.7 million from the Fund, an amount she was not authorized to collect. According to the complaint, defendant was not authorized to collect more than $50,000. Plaintiff further alleges that Special Master Feinberg increased the total amount of the award by $520,000 as a consequence of her presence in the Mojica household, and that defendant's refusal to distribute that amount to plaintiff breaches a fiduciary duty.

Plaintiff filed her complaint in the Supreme Court of the State of New York for Kings County. Defendant removed the case to the United States District Court for the Eastern District of New York, which transferred the case to this Court. After reviewing the complaint, I ordered defendant to show cause why this case should not be remanded to state court. Responding to my order, defendant argues that plaintiff's "claim arises from the Special Master's determination that she was not entitled to any portion of the award" and that "this Court has jurisdiction over cases resulting from the events of 9/11." I now turn to the merits of these arguments.

## DISCUSSION

### I. APPLICABLE LAW

#### A. Removal and Remand

A party may remove "any civil action of which the district courts have original jurisdiction founded on a claim or right arising under the Constitution, treaties or laws of the United States." 28 U.S.C. § 1441(b). If the removal action is challenged on motion by a party or by the district court sua sponte, the removing party bears the burden of showing that removal was properly based on federal jurisdiction. If at any time before final judgment it appears that the district court lacks subject matter jurisdiction over a case removed to it from a state court, the district court must remand the case to the state court from which it was removed. 28 U.S.C. 1447(c).

#### B. Federal Jurisdiction Under the Air Transportation Safety and System Stabilization Act

"The United States District Court for the Southern District of New York shall have original and exclusive jurisdiction over all actions brought for any claim resulting from or relating to the terrorist-related aircraft crashes of September 11, 2001." ATSSSA § 408(b)(3). Thus the question before me in this case is whether plaintiff's state law causes of action for breach of fiduciary duty nevertheless arise out of or relate to the events of September 11 within the meaning of § 408(b)(3). A full description of the Court's jurisdiction under the ATSSSA is not appropriate in this case, however. Previous cases have compelled the courts to examine in detail the jurisdictional boundaries of the statute but this case is not one of them.

### II. FEDERAL JURISDICTION TO HEAR BARRETTO'S COMPLAINT

Plaintiff Barretto's case raises no common issues of law or fact involving the events of September 11, 2001, and therefore does not state a federal cause of action under the ATSSSA ("Section 408(b)(3) does not vest the Court with jurisdiction over actions that involve no claim or defense raising an issue of law or fact involving" the events of September 11, 2001).

Plaintiff asserts that an individual, Hortensia Gonzalez, owed her a fiduciary duty; that Gonzalez breached that duty; and that because of that breach, she is entitled to damages. The injury she alleges was not sustained on September 11, 2001, nor did it occur during the ensuing response to the terrorist attacks, or during the debris removal effort. She does not allege that airlines, property managers, municipalities, state agencies, or any other entity that played a role in the events of September 11 is liable for her injuries. The facts pertinent to her case are those facts that would show that defendant, as administrator of Dennis Mojica's estate and his personal representative before the Fund, owed plaintiff a fiduciary duty, and that defendant breached that duty. Thus as part of her case, plaintiff might introduce evidence that decedent died intestate and that she was decedent's partner in a "longstanding domestic relationship." *See Cruz v. McAneney* (holding that allegation that decedent's personal representative breached fiduciary duty to distribute Fund award in manner consistent with New York law states cause of action). The facts of plaintiff's case are not common facts involving the events of September 11, 2001, which is to say, her claim does not arise out of or relate to those events. Therefore, plaintiff does not state a federal cause of action under the ATSSSA.

### CONCLUSION

For all of the foregoing reasons, I hold that this Court lacks jurisdiction to hear plaintiff's case under the ATSSSA. The case is remanded to the New York Supreme Court for Kings County, from which it was removed. No costs are awarded to either party.

## IN RE SEPTEMBER 11 LITIG.

United States District Court for the Southern District of New York, 2009.
600 F.Supp.2d 549.

I write in this opinion to accept the report of the mediator, Sheila L. Birnbaum, Esq., to comment on her invaluable work, and to summarize the proceedings of the ninety-five wrongful death and personal injury cases that led to her appointment. Because of her work, described in her report attached to this opinion, the cases have all but been resolved and master calendar 21 MC 97 has been closed.

On September 11, 2001, terrorists killed 2,752 people and injured scores more. As with every mass tragedy, the victims could sue to recover their damages. However, this tragedy was different, for it seared the nation and threatened its institutions like no other. Hence, just eleven days after the attacks, Congress enacted the Air Transportation Safety and System Stabilization Act which limited the traditional remedy, provided an alternative remedy, and required the claimant to choose between them.

Those who sued had to file in federal court, not state court, and only in one particular federal court, the Southern District of New York. Under ATSSSA, the defendants, primarily the airlines and other aviation-related companies, could not be liable beyond their insurance coverages. As interpreted, the Act provided that neither punitive damages, nor excesses of state-authorized recoveries, would be available. The vast number of claimants and the scope of their claims threatened the integrity of the

American aviation industry and the availability of sufficient resources to satisfy all eligible claimants. An exclusive jurisdiction in a single district court, it was thought, could coordinate all litigation, assure equity among claimants and defendants, and avoid ruin to the American aviation industry. (Senator Hatch: "For those who seek to pursue the litigation route, I am pleased that we consolidated the causes of action in one Federal court so that there will be some consistency in the judgments awarded."); (Senator McCain: "In addition to removing the specter of devastating potential liability from the airlines, and guaranteeing that the victims and their families will receive compensation regardless of the outcomes of the tangle of lawsuits that will ensue, the bill attempts to provide some sense to the litigation by consolidating all civil litigation arising from the terrorist attacks of September 11 in one court").

ATSSSA balanced these limitations with a largely unprecedented right, the right to file a claim with a Special Master appointed to administer a Victim Compensation Fund, and to recover on that claim without having to prove fault or to endure the risks, costs, and travails of a court suit. *see* Department of Justice, Kenneth R. Feinberg, Esq., FINAL REPORT OF THE SPECIAL MASTER FOR THE SEPTEMBER 11TH VICTIM COMPENSATION FUND OF 2001. Five thousand five hundred and sixty claimants participated in the Fund, receiving more than $7.049 billion in full satisfaction of their claims, all within thirty-three months of the attack. The Fund was open only to those victims who died or incurred their injuries within twelve hours after the terrorist crashes on September 11, 2001. Those who filed claims with the Special Master were forbidden to file or pursue a court suit.

Not all families participated in the Victim Compensation Fund. Some, the successors of victims with very high incomes or income potential, believed that the Fund would not compensate them adequately in relation to lost income, and filed suits instead. Others filed suits to avoid having to deduct their life insurance recoveries and other collateral-source payments from awards given by the Special Master—only ATSSSA required such deductions. Still others wanted to tell their stories, participate in forcing facts into the public domain, or avail themselves of traditional remedies for other reasons. And some could not free themselves from the shadows and despair of the September 11 tragedy to do anything on a timely basis, even though the Special Master made special efforts to reach such people and relaxed the Fund's requirements to accommodate such claimants.

In all, ninety-five suits were filed, seeking recoveries for ninety-six claimants. I collected the cases for coordinated management in 21 MC 97. Proceedings began after the Victim Compensation Fund closed, so that the litigation did not compete with the workings of the Fund.

Two parallel, but competing, interests quickly emerged. Some claimants wished to negotiate settlements as quickly as possible, with discovery to be deferred for a reasonable time to allow settlement negotiations to proceed. Others pressed to proceed with discovery expeditiously. I determined that both pursuits should go forward, simultaneously. I set a period during which counsel for defendants could focus on settlement negotiations, but ordered the aviation defendants also to gather responsive documents and ready them for production. I appointed liaison counsel to lead and organize the discovery and arranged executive committees of interested lawyers. I granted the motion of the United States Transportation Security Administration to intervene and to develop a procedure to filter production by the Aviation defendants to avoid making public Sensitive Security Information. Stipulated Protective Order Governing Access to, Handling of, and Disposition of Potential Sensitive Security Information. Under TSA regulations, SSI is information that, if it were to be made public, "would continue to expose vulnerabilities."

I also established procedural rules to govern settlements. Because each settlement recovery would erode a limited pool of insurance resources, a procedure of court approvals was provided to assure fairness. Settlements were to be vetted in groups to guard the privacy interests of the plaintiffs and the contributing defendants (essentially, the Aviation defendants). Contingent fees were to be limited to 15% of recoveries. Litigants and attorneys were told that settlements would be evaluated as to distributive fairness, so that like parties should expect like settlements, without regard to whether they entered into negotiations early or late in the settlement process. Leveraging for higher amounts often paid to those settling first, or last, would not be permitted. Each settlement negotiation would hinge on the case's merits, and not piggy-back on the values of other settled cases.

Thirteen cases were settled within a relatively short space of time, but then settlements stopped. Discovery proceedings also slowed, for it took long periods of time for the TSA to develop protocols for sifting defense-produced information. The TSA had to distinguish between that which properly should be characterized as SSI and that which could be produced in original or in redacted form. The TSA also had to develop procedures to provide security clearances for attorneys who would need to review disclosed information. Rather than the normal manner of rulings by district courts on discovery disputes, discovery disputes with the TSA required administrative procedures leading to final determinations and judicial review by the Courts of Appeals. Then, the discovery proceedings relating to TSA and SSI disputes portended longer than anticipated delays, even for complex lawsuits (discussing number of attorneys who could represent parties at depositions involving SSI). The complexity of discovery and the inevitable long delays prompted me to urge the parties to pursue settlements. I suggested assistance by a Board of Mediators whom I proposed to appoint. I told litigants and counsel that vindication by litigation, in addition to being uncertain and probably unsatisfactory, would consume a very long time because of the problems posed by the TSA filters of SSI.

The parties proposed Sheila L. Birnbaum, Esq., a widely respected practitioner in the field of mass torts and a partner of Skadden, Arps, Slate, Meagher & Flom LLP, to be the mediator. I accepted immediately. Her Report summarizes her work and that of Thomas E. Fox, Esq., also of Skadden, Arps. Their efforts directly led to the settlement of seventy-two cases. Only three cases remain. Without her patience, skill, empathy, and persistence, these results would not have been achieved. I accept her report, and order it to be filed with this opinion and the court records of this litigation.

Ms. Birnbaum's involvement initially led to a spate of settled cases, but negotiations then seemed to stall, just as they had done before her appointment. The attorneys reported sharp differences between the perceived values of cases that their discussions were not able to bridge. Without a way to obtain a more objective assessment, additional settlements became unlikely.

Nevertheless, litigants still wished to settle in preference to the risks and long waits inherent in discovery and trial. I determined that the problems of discovery delay arose in connection with issues of liability, not damages. The liability issues required extensive discovery of witnesses whom the government did not want to produce and of documents and information permeated with SSI. The damages litigation required discovery of limited facts—a decedent's past and potential income, the pain and suffering just prior to death, perhaps the pain and suffering of near relatives, and the reasonable income expectations of successors from decedents. Although also difficult, these issues could be discovered and tried in a relatively short time. I ordered damages-only discovery and damages-only jury trials in six cases, a sample of the field, that were to be identified jointly by plaintiffs and defendants, or by me if the parties could not agree. Both sides objected because of the absence of precedents, but they acquiesced upon reconsideration, and when it became clear that I was determined to proceed.

The experiment was successful. After some discovery, and without the need of any trials, all six cases settled and more followed. The values were moderately higher than previous settlements, but acceptably so. In a few cases, I approved contingent fees of 20% of recoveries in recognition of the additional work that the attorneys performed and the exceptional quality of that work.

One additional problem was encountered. There were, by now, relatively few cases left of the original ninety-five. One law firm, after rejecting the mediator's offer of assistance, succeeded in negotiating settlements for a group of four cases. These settlements were larger than similarly situated earlier cases and higher than the recommendations of the mediator. The law firm, having successfully leveraged on a group settlement that would have left very few cases remaining on the calendar, demanded a fee of 25% citing their success and their clients' written agreements. Defendants were willing to pay these larger sums to settle, I believed, because of significant balance sheet benefits they could obtain by clearing loss reserves set aside for administering trial, given how few cases would have remained against the insurers' loss reserves.

I disapproved the settlements and the fees as disproportionately large. The litigants then accepted the assistance of the mediator and agreed to settlements that were consistent with previous settlements. They also agreed to a 15% contingency fee. I then approved the settlements.

At this point, there are only three cases left of the original ninety-five. I ordered 21 MC 97 closed, and transferred the three wrongful death cases to 21 MC 101, to conduct discovery, and to be tried, according to procedures in relation to all the property-damage cases. Ms. Birnbaum and Mr. Fox have completed their assignment.

Ms. Birnbaum, assisted by Mr. Fox, has performed extraordinary work to settle the September 11 wrongful death and personal injury litigation. In her report, Ms. Birnbaum describes the settlement process and the factors that most influenced settlement values. She allowed each of the plaintiffs' families to express their loss and the quality of the lives lost on September 11. She absorbed their losses and their pain with empathy and brought opposing counsel and high officers of the airlines to sit in their presence and hear their stories. She gained plaintiffs' confidence. Without her assistance, most of these cases, in my opinion, would not have settled.

Equality among similarly situated claimants is a concept difficult to quantify. Ms. Birnbaum describes the effects on settlements of different future earning potentials, of different dependencies among family members, of different laws governing the recovery for pain and suffering, of different relevant state and foreign laws, and of other variables. Plaintiffs' lawyers were vigorous in pressing these differences to the advantage of their clients—that, indeed, was their duty. Defendants' lawyers, just as avidly, resisted. The process was difficult. Fortunately, Ms. Birnbaum and Mr. Fox were suited for the task, for their tireless work produced settlements satisfactory to plaintiffs and defendants, on a consistent, fair, and just basis. Ms. Birnbaum and Mr. Fox merit the great praise expressed by litigants, counsel, and the court.

REPORT OF THE MEDIATOR ON THE MEDIATION AND SETTLEMENT EFFORTS OF THE PARTIES IN THE CASES PREVIOUSLY DOCKETED UNDER 21 MC 97

Comes now Sheila L. Birnbaum, Esquire, a member of the bar of this Court and the mediator agreed to by the parties and approved by the Court, to report to the Court on the mediation efforts of the parties and the resulting settlements in connection with the claims brought against passenger airline carriers, airport security companies, and others for wrongful death because a person was present on one of the various flights or was located at the World Trade Center or the Pentagon at the time of the terrorist attacks on the morning of September 11, 2001. These mediation efforts also included several personal injury claims brought by people who were present in or near the World Trade Center or in the Pentagon at the time of the terrorist attacks on those locations on the morning of September 11, 2001. The terms of the settlements that were negotiated as a result of these efforts are confidential. Therefore, this report cannot go into the specific amounts of the individual settlements that occurred.

### THE CONTEXT OF THESE CASES AND THE MEDIATION

Shortly after the terrorist attacks of September 11, 2001, the Air Transportation Safety and System Stabilization Act, was enacted and signed into law. The Act expressly was intended to preserve the continued viability of the air transportation system in the United States. Among the Act's provisions was the establishment of the September 11th Victim Compensation Fund of 2001 to be administered by a Special Master. The Act established the Fund as an administrative alternative to litigation for the immediate victims of the terrorist attacks of September 11, 2001. As set forth in the Special Master's report, the participation in the Fund included approximately 97% of the claims by families of the victims of the attacks. The Fund paid out approximately $7.049 billion in compensation and completed its operation in about 33 months. Therefore, those participating in the Fund received their compensation payments no later than early in 2004, fulfilling one of the goals of the Act by providing financial assistance to the victims of the attacks without the delay, cost, and uncertainty of traditional litigation.

For those foregoing the administrative alternative of the Fund and choosing traditional litigation, the Act provided a federal cause of action as the exclusive remedy for damages arising out of the September 11, 2001 attacks. The Act also provided that the exclusive jurisdiction for this federal cause of action is the United States District Court for the Southern District of New York. The Act further limited the liability of the air carriers and other aviation defendants to the limits of their insurance coverages. The Act also mandated that the choice of law rules of the state where a particular flight crashed would govern the claims emanating from that flight.

Approximately 3% of the potential claimants filed traditional litigation cases in the United States District Court for the Southern District of New York pursuant to the exclusive federal cause of action created by the Act in lieu of participation in the Fund. These cases formerly were part of docket 21 MC 97. These cases consisted of 95 wrongful death and personal injury cases arising from the death or injury of 96 people. There were 85 wrongful death claims and 11 personal injury claims. Fifteen different law firms represented one or more of the various plaintiffs in these cases.

The 95 cases in total involved decedents on each of the four flights that were the targets of the terrorist attacks and some decedents who had been located on: American Airlines flight 11, which crashed into 1-WTC involved 27 cases, of which six were filed on behalf of people who were located on the ground; American Airlines flight 77, which crashed into the Pentagon involved 30 cases, of which seven were filed on behalf of people who were located on the ground; United Airlines flight 175, which crashed into 2-WTC involved 20 cases, of which six were filed on behalf of people located on the ground; and United Airlines flight 93, which crashed in an open field in Pennsylvania involved 14 cases. In addition, four cases were filed by plaintiffs who allegedly sustained personal injuries in the vicinity of the World Trade Center Towers in New York. One of these cases was previously dismissed by the Court.

As anticipated by the Act, these litigated cases have been subject to extensive delays due in part to broad discovery efforts, costs, and uncertainty not only of that inherent in any litigated matter, but also due to the unique and complex discovery and substantive law issues raised by litigating the events and circumstances surrounding that fateful morning. This Court has issued numerous opinions in these cases over the ensuing years, which provide greater detail of the complex and time consuming issues raised in these litigated cases.

Approximately 13 cases were settled prior to the commencement of these mediation efforts. Thus, 82 cases remained to be mediated. Given the likelihood of continued delays in these litigated cases and the slow pace of the negotiated settlements between the parties, the Court encouraged the parties to engage in mediation efforts. Representatives of both plaintiffs and defendants contacted me in or about January of 2006 to see if I would be willing to serve as a neutral mediator in an effort to facilitate settlements among the parties in these cases. I agreed to do so and my role as mediator was approved by the Court in February of 2006. With the approval of the Court and the parties, I also arranged for Thomas Fox, Esq. of my office and also a member of the bar of this Court to assist me in connection with these mediation efforts.

### THE PROCESS OF THIS MEDIATION

The mediation process began with an orientation session conducted by the parties' counsel to review the issues raised by these unique cases. We became familiar with the substantive legal and factual claims and defenses being raised by the parties. To this end, lawyers for all of the parties to the mediation attended a two-day mediation session in New York in February 2006. Representatives of plaintiffs and defendants discussed the unique substantive legal and factual issues involved in these cases.

In addition, we were provided detailed briefing booklets prepared by the various plaintiffs' counsel providing the personal details of each of the decedents and injured plaintiffs whose cases were included in the mediation process. Without doubt and without exception, the personal stories of the decedents and the circumstances surrounding their deaths were compelling on a personal level and the devastating loss to family and friends surrounding them was quite moving.

Following the initial mediation sessions, we began a series of meetings between representatives of defendants and individual plaintiffs' law firms to mediate specifically the cases represented by that plaintiffs' law firm. In fact, we scheduled multiple tracks of these meetings so that more than one plaintiffs' law firm was involved in mediated settlement discussions during the same general period of time. We employed standard mediation techniques. Often we held a joint meeting of the parties' representatives initially and then met with those representatives separately to discuss the issues and the respective settlement positions of the parties. As the parties' positions narrowed, we sometimes would make recommendations on how a gap should be resolved. In every instance, it was ultimately the choice of the individual clients whether to accept a settlement or not.

Settlements were reached in approximately 12 cases during the period from March through May of 2006. All of these settlements were approved by the Court. However, it became clear following these early mediation sessions that one obstacle to reaching settlements was the sense on the part of many of the families that either (i) they had not had an opportunity to tell the story of their loss and express their feelings to a representative of the Court, and/or (ii) they had not had an opportunity to tell the story of their loss to a representative of the airlines and to personally receive expressions of condolences for their loss from the airlines. In addition, some families had difficulty accepting a monetary settlement to resolve the claims over the loss of their loved ones because of the tendency to equate the amount of any monetary settlement of a legal claim with the value of the actual lives of their family members who were lost.

We decided that if the mediations were to have a better chance of succeeding, the families would have to be present and have an opportunity to express themselves. Mediation sessions were then scheduled and held involving representative of the defendant airlines and security companies and the individual families of those killed or injured in the attacks. These meetings occurred over a period of months and took place in Washington, D.C., New York City, and Boston. Needless to say, the meetings with the families were a heart-wrenching and emotionally draining experience for all involved.

These meetings with the families provided a confidential mechanism to meet some of the needs of the families involved as well as providing an appropriately focused environment within which to resolve cases. Families were able to convey to the mediator and to representatives of the airlines and security companies—both legal counsel and company officers—personal details about their loss and the difficulties they have faced subsequently. Families also were able to personally hear from the mediator and representatives of the airlines and security companies sincere expressions of condolences for their loss on both an official and personal level. In addition, these sessions provided an opportunity for me as the mediator to explain the limitations of our imperfect tort system and how the system of monetary recovery in wrongful death cases does not even try to value a person's life because that simply cannot be done. These lengthy and emotionally draining meetings were critical in being able to reach settlements in many of the cases. Further, as the Court is aware, at my request and with the consent of the parties, the Court itself participated in some of these mediation sessions, which were held at the federal courthouse in Manhattan. Some of the cases involved uniquely difficult issues.

Some of the cases also presented difficult issues concerning the value of the economic claims at issue in the case. Often this involved a decedent who had a high income when he or she died and/or who had a claim of high future earnings. The mediation efforts in these cases at times involved the preparation and discussion of conflicting expert economic reports and analyses in an effort to define more precisely a reasoned value of a plaintiff's economic loss claim in order to permit negotiations to succeed.

These efforts persisted over a period of 19 months and resulted in settlements in 53 cases, including eight cases that were settled during a prolonged mediation session held on September 24, 2007. The settlements reached on September 24, 2007 included cases that had been set for damages-only trials by the Court. Each of these settlements were approved subsequently by the Court. These negotiations also laid the ground work for additional settlements that were reached directly between the parties on October 4, 2007. Following these settlements, additional conference calls and discussions were held separately with representatives of the parties to further assist in the resolution of the remaining cases. However, no further mediation meetings occurred, although representatives of the parties continued discussions and reached some additional settlements outside of the mediation.

The four cases represented by the Azrael Gann & Franz firm that were subject to this Court's Order disapproving the settlements and rejecting a request for higher attorney fees were cases that reached an impasse during the mediation and settlement was attempted subsequently by the parties outside of the mediation. Following the Court's decision to disapprove these settlements, the parties sought my assistance to try to resolve the cases in a manner consistent with the Court's Order dated July 24, 2008. As a result of numerous conference calls and discussions with the lawyers for the parties that occurred from August to October, 2008, new settlements were reached in these four cases consistent with the Court's Order. These settlements were subsequently approved by the Court.

Following these settlements, there remained only 4 unsettled cases out of the original docket. Given all of the prior settlements and the guidance that could be gleaned from the Court's Order, we endeavored to have one last mediation session at the courthouse in Manhattan involving the decision makers in each case. Of these 4 remaining cases, only the decision makers in 1 case had been previously involved in the mediation. The courthouse was selected as the site of the mediation session to facilitate the Court's participation in the mediation of the cases. These 4 cases were mediated over the days of December 3 and 4, 2008. It resulted in the settlement of one of the cases. Productive conversations in good faith occurred in the other 3 cases, but no settlements were reached. It is not my position or the purpose of this report to speculate on or disclose the specific reasons why the 3 remaining cases have not settled.

In summary, there were 95 cases (covering 96 claims) that originally made up the Court's docket. Of these, 72 cases (covering 73 claims) were settled directly as a result of the mediation efforts, 6 cases were settled directly between the parties separately during the period of the mediation, 13 cases were settled prior to the mediation, 1 case was dismissed by motion, and there are 3 remaining cases.

Thus, the 92 cases previously settled involved 93 claims.

### FACTORS AFFECTING SETTLEMENT VALUES

Cases were evaluated and negotiated on an individual basis in the mediation. However, certain demographic factors were often looked at in making rough comparisons among cases with regard to people who were, in a very general sense, similarly situated. These factors included marital status, age, number and age of children and other dependents, income level, and working life expectancy.

Beyond these demographic and income factors, consideration had to be given in each case to other factors. These included, for example, variations in the laws of the various States pertaining to the availability and calculation of damages in wrongful death cases, whether a claim was governed by International Treaty, and the presence of any individualized facts worthy of special consideration.

Under the Act, the substantive law to be applied to a given case would be determined by the choice of law rules of the jurisdiction in which the flight crashed. With respect to the three flights that crashed into New York and Pennsylvania, applicable choice of law rules required an analysis in which the domicile of the victim was an important factor. As a result, the claims of victims on the same flight with differing domiciles could vary depending on the different substantive law that might govern the elements of damage or differing methods of calculating damages. For example, under the law of New York, wrongful death damages are determined by calculating the pecuniary loss suffered by those economically dependent on the decedent. On the other hand, Connecticut law places the decedent's estate into the shoes of the decedent and his or her likely future income would be considered to determine the economic damages under the wrongful death statute without regard to whether there are economic dependents of the decedent. Differences in the various state laws, including disputes over domicile in some cases, is an example of how cases that were similarly situated in terms of basic demographics or income data could nonetheless result in differing settlement amounts.

With respect to American Airlines flight 77 that crashed into the Pentagon, the choice of law rule of the Commonwealth of Virginia applied. Under Virginia law, *lex loci delecti* is the operative choice of law rule. This meant that for cases emanating from American Airlines flight 77, the substantive law of Virginia would apply regardless of the domicile of the decedent. Under the Virginia wrongful death statute, the grief of surviving family members is an independent element of damages, unlike the law of many other states, such as New York for example. While reported cases in Virginia explain that grief damages are subject to an objective standard and are not without reasonable limits, it is an element of damages that introduced a level of uncertainty into the evaluation of these cases, especially given the unique nature of the September 11, 2001 attacks. This substantive law difference in Virginia was somewhat tempered by the inability under Virginia law to recover for pre-impact conscious pain and suffering (even if provable), which is an element of damages recoverable under the laws of other states, including New York.

Again these examples are meant to illustrate how the potential application of the laws of the different States could affect the ultimate valuation of a given case beyond the age, income, and other family demographics of the decedents.

Furthermore, several cases involved victims who were traveling on tickets for international passage and therefore were covered by International Treaty (i.e., the Warsaw Convention and related protocols). Coverage under Treaty provisions raised other issues that affected the value of cases, including strict liability and pre-judgment interest issues.

In addition, beyond the application of different domestic or international laws, there were individual circumstances in cases that simply required different treatment by the parties in settlement negotiations. Examples of some of these special individual factors include: surviving parents or spouses of the decedent having serious health conditions that were going to have required additional support from the decedent; children and/or siblings of the decedent having severe permanent physical or emotional disabilities pre-dating the decedent's death where the decedent offered financial or other valuable support to that child or sibling; and very high incomes and the presence and likely future growth of stock options.

Therefore, cases could legitimately be viewed differently for settlement as a result of the presence of one or more of these factors. This is why each case had to be looked at and negotiated individually in the mediation. However, these individual factors notwithstanding, the age, income and family situation of the decedent provided a basis to make a rough comparison of the range of settlements of decedents who were in a general sense similarly situated as well as permitting the identification of settlements that might seem outside of that range.

The settlements arrived at in this process are confidential. Without disclosing actual numbers, but in order to give some sense of scale of these efforts, the aggregate total of the settlements, both those made previously (as advised by the court) and those reached directly due to the mediation efforts, were approximately $500 million. As indicated previously, some of these cases involved decedents with extremely high earnings and/or other exceptional circumstances, life insurance and other collateral source payments did not have to be (and were not) deducted, and many different aspects of law played significant roles. Therefore, a straight per case average of this amount would be misleading. Furthermore, and ever more importantly, no figure can affect the personal loss and painful anguish suffered by the families who lost loved ones in this national tragedy.

## THE CASES REMAINING

Of the 3 cases remaining that were formerly part of 21 MC 97, 2 cases arise from American Airlines flight 11 and 1 case arises from United Airlines flight 175. All of these remaining cases are wrongful death cases.

## FINAL COMMENTS

The settlement of these cases was made possible only because of the existence of the Fund and the fact that 97% of the claims participated in the Fund. Absent the Fund, the thousands of traditional tort cases that would have been filed likely would have created an enormous burden on the courts. Moreover, those claims may have forced several airline and other companies to file for protection under the bankruptcy law. Absent the Fund, most, if not all, of the thousands of families, would not have received any compensation as a result of litigation even these 7 years later.

One question that invariably will be asked is whether those who chose not to participate in the Fund secured greater compensation than those who participated in the Fund. Even in hindsight, this is an impossible question to completely answer. Those who participated in the Fund obtained recoveries that were without the uncertainty of the litigation and were obtained rapidly. Many of those who participated in the Fund also obtained those recoveries having to pay little or no attorneys' fees.

The reasons families did not choose the Fund, but decided to litigate were varied. Some believed that there would have been substantial reductions in their recovery in the Fund due to collateral sources of recovery (e.g., insurance) or a recovery formula that did not account for very high income levels.

These mediated settlements occurred years after the recoveries were obtained from the Fund and with a great deal of uncertainty along the way. Further, the recoveries here were subject to the payment of attorneys' fees. The families of decedents with very high incomes probably achieved settlements that would have been unlikely achievable through the Fund because of the rules governing the Fund, including deductions for collateral sources of recovery such as life insurance policies. These deductions typically are not made in traditional litigation cases. Therefore, given the lengthier passage of time for these settlements to be negotiated, approved and paid, the added physical burden and emotional toll of the prolonged and uncertain litigation and settlement process, and the delay in achieving some measure of closure and financial security because of the ongoing litigation, it is impossible to judge whether people similarly situated who pursued the traditional litigation track and settled their cases pursuant to mediation did better overall than those who participated in the Fund, regardless of any differences in gross settlement amounts.

This situation nonetheless picks up on a question raised by the Special Master of the Fund. In the event of a future tragic event like that of September 11, 2001, does it make good public policy to have a fund similar to the Fund in this instance? However, if there were to be a fund established in the future in response to such an event, the question also must be asked whether the fund should be the exclusive remedy. Obviously, it only would be by making recovery from such a fund the exclusive remedy that would guarantee the use of consistently applied criteria to value and compensate like claims without the serendipity of factors such as in what state did the fatality occur or the domicile of the decedent. On the other hand, since we live and are governed by the laws of the several states and their variations, the fact that different outcomes— or for that matter different settlement resolutions—can result due to the application of different state laws is an inevitable consequence of our legal system.

I would be remiss if this report did not recognize the outstanding professionalism and good faith exercised by the respective counsel for all of the parties in those cases where settlement was achieved during our mediation efforts. Similarly, the support and cooperation of the Court in the conduct of these mediation efforts was extensive and unfailing. These circumstances combined to enable the mediation efforts to succeed as well as they did. It has been a privilege and honor meeting with the families in this process and working with counsel on both sides and the Court.

### IN RE WORLD TRADE CENTER DISASTER SITE LITIG.
United States District Court for the Southern District of New York, 2011.
769 F.Supp.2d 650.

Plaintiffs' Liaison Counsel, Worby Groner Edelman & Napoli Bern LLP moves under Federal Rule of Civil Procedure 60(b) for an Order vacating my Order of February 7, 2011, appointing Noah H. Kushlefsky, Esq., as special counsel to advise 59 Plaintiffs represented by Napoli Bern, The 59 Plaintiffs were accepted by Napoli Bern as clients even though they had made claims to and received recoveries from the Victim Compensation Fund created by the Air Transportation Safety and System Stabilization Act.

Napoli Bern sued the City of New York, its contractors, and various other entities on behalf of these 59 Plaintiffs, even though these Plaintiffs had given releases of all litigation by making claims to the VCF. When it came time to settle, Napoli Bern removed these Plaintiffs from the list of Plaintiffs eligible to settle—for reasons, it seemed, that preferred their other clients and were against the wishes of some, perhaps all, of these 59 clients, Napoli Bern had previously represented that it would find an independent special counsel to advise these Plaintiffs with regard to their cases in this litigation, but never did so. I therefore appointed Mr. Kushlefsky in relation to what I perceived was a conflict of interest. Napoli Bern now responds that no such appointment is necessary. It was, and is, necessary, and for the reasons that follow, the motion of Napoli Bern is denied.

### I.    BACKGROUND TO THE MOTION

In June 2010, the City of New York and its contractors, the WTC Captive, and Plaintiffs' Liaison Counsel submitted an amended version of the SPA for review. I found the terms of the SPA fair and reasonable and approved them. The SPA required at least 95 percent of the Plaintiffs eligible to settle to choose to do so. If fewer than 95 percent of these Plaintiffs opted into the SPA, it would not be effective, and the 10,000 to 11,000 cases on the Court's docket would proceed toward trial. The SPA provided that Plaintiffs eligible to settle their cases had until September 8, 2010, to choose whether or not to settle, a date later extended to November 8, 2010.

The Plaintiffs eligible to settle were compiled on a list by Plaintiffs' Liaison Counsel, mainly Napoli Bern, and cross-checked and certified by the WTC Captive. Plaintiffs were eligible to settle if they had filed either a complaint or a notice of claim against the City by April 12, 2010. This list, the Eligible Plaintiff List (EPL), was not filed and was considered confidential to the parties. I was given to understand that approximately 10,500 Plaintiffs in the Master Calendars were listed. If 5 percent, approximately 525 eligible Plaintiffs, chose not to opt into the SPA, the settlement would not be effective.

On July 26, 2010, and August 3, 2010, I held public meetings in Staten Island and Queens, respectively, to discuss the SPA with the Plaintiffs themselves, and to answer their questions. The meetings were attended by Plaintiffs' Liaison Counsel; Defendants' counsel; the WTC Captive's counsel; the Allocation Neutral; and the Special Masters. All addressed the people assembled. At these meetings, several Plaintiffs raised the question of their eligibility to settle despite previously making claims to the VCF. These Plaintiffs made clear that they wished to enter the SPA, representing that their injuries had become much more serious and that their recoveries from the VCF reflected an earlier and different state of injuries. At the Queens public meeting, I stopped the discussion of this issue because of the likelihood that it would soon be presented to me for decision:

> There is going to be an issue or there may be an issue with the Victims Compensation Fund and people who have made claims. You needn't say things because they could be relevant in that and I will have to decide. I can't decide that now.

I learned, subsequently, that 59 Plaintiffs were affected, all represented by Napoli Bern, with knowledge, it seemed, of their VCF experiences.

Under ATSSSA, any person who makes claim to the VCF "waives the right to file a civil action (or to be a party to any action) in any Federal or State court for damages sustained as a result of the terrorist-related aircraft crashes of September 11, 2001." The SPA, negotiated by Plaintiff's Liaison Counsel with the WTC Captive, provides that "any Plaintiff who received an award from the September 11th Victim Compensation Fund is ineligible to receive any payment referenced in this Agreement."

Napoli Bern had conflicting obligations. If the 59 Plaintiffs were admitted to the SPA, as many of them requested, the final settlement amount would be spread thinner, affecting in particular the most severely injured Plaintiffs, the "Tier 4" Plaintiffs, whose recoveries were variable and dependent on how much of the fixed settlement amount would remain after the less severely injured Plaintiffs had been paid. Further, litigating the eligibility of the 59 Plaintiffs could have delayed and prejudiced the entire settlement, and therefore prejudiced the expectations of many for timely realization of their settlements, which were to provide funds to pay for medical and other necessities. Finally, if the 59 Plaintiffs opted out of the SPA, the ability of the Plaintiffs to attain the 95 percent threshold, and to attain the higher percentages yielding larger settlement payments, would be jeopardized. On the other hand, Napoli Bern had to make any possible arguments it could on behalf of these 59 Plaintiffs. Any way one looks at it, Napoli Bern's common representation of these 59 Plaintiffs and its thousands of other Plaintiffs put the firm in conflict.

Napoli Bern had additional issues. Napoli Bern, in the expectation of a contingency fee, had advanced over 10,000 cases for nine years without compensation. As I learned later in the litigation, from a motion that Napoli Bern withdrew, the firm was deeply in debt, to the extent of millions of dollars, secured by personal guaranties of the principals of the firm, payable at high, compounding interest rates. Approval of the SPA would produce approximately $150 million for the firm in fees, plus expenses, and would allow the firm to liquidate its debt.

In the first week of September, and before, I raised the issues of conflict with Napoli Bern, and the need for an independent lawyer to consult with the 59 Plaintiffs and to file an appropriate motion. Napoli Bern offered to engage an independent lawyer, in preference to my appointing one, and I deferred to that wish. In the weeks that followed, nothing happened. Thus, in an order setting a status conference for October 5, 2010, I initiated another discussion. At the conference, Mr. Napoli asked for more time to engage such a lawyer:

> THE COURT: Item 4 of the agenda reads: The status of plaintiffs who were not listed as eligible for recovery under the master settlement agreement because they participated in the victim compensation fund, their stated desire to participate in the master settlement, and the need for a judicial determination of these plaintiffs' eligibility.
>
> Mr. Napoli, do you want to report?
>
> MR. NAPOLI: Yes, your Honor.
>
> Our office is in the process, and we asked for the consultation of the Court, of finding special counsel to work on and talk with these clients to work on what is going to happen with these cases, whether it be by motion practice or some other means of resolution, and we would ask that we report back to you on finding special counsel.
>
> THE COURT: I'm anxious to help you, Mr. Napoli. I welcome your report. I received letters from these people, many of them, who complained that they entered the Victim Compensation Fund thinking that their injuries were slight. They say their injuries are now graver. They signed a release in a very broad form giving up all rights to litigate, and they would like to escape the terms of their release. One way or another, we need to have resolution of this issue.

The master settlement process agreement defines eligible plaintiffs in such a way as to exclude these people, but they need to have resolution of their status in the litigation and whether the defense of release is valid or not and to what extent. So I'm very happy that you are exploring the availability of the special counsel to represent this group, and we'll see how this goes.

By late October, Napoli Bern still had not progressed. Mr. Napoli asked for another 30 days, representing that his firm was weighed down with processing settlement paperwork.

I continued to discuss the issue of these 59 Plaintiffs informally with counsel. A number of times, Mr. Napoli represented to the Court and to counsel for the WTC Captive that he would opt out these 59 Plaintiffs— without consulting with his clients, it appeared—but withdrew that purported resolution when counsel for the WTC Captive pointed out that if these 59 Plaintiffs had no right to litigate, then they had no right to accept or reject the settlement, and also that 59 opt-outs would jeopardize the Plaintiffs' ability to obtain a 95 percent approval. Following these discussions, Mr. Napoli simply removed these 59 Plaintiffs from the EPL. Now, he would neither have to opt in or opt out for them. The 59 Plaintiffs thus became non-persons for purposes of the SPA.

In mid-November, the SPA was approved by 95.1 percent of the Plaintiffs listed on the EPL. There are issues with regard to that approval rate as well, but their telling awaits another motion pending before me. Of relevance to the present motion, Mr. Napoli's effort to resolve the issue was not a lawful resolution, for a lawyer cannot derogate any client's interests and prefer another client's interests.

By an agenda item at the status conference held February 2, 2011, I told Mr. Napoli that he had run out of time:

> THE COURT: Number two on the agenda is the status of plaintiffs who obtained compensation from the first victim compensation fund, I issued an order in October but there were discussions well before that. In November Mr. Napoli asked for another 30 days.

> Where are we, Mr. Napoli?

> MR. NAPOLI: Your honor, I think there's two things to discuss on this topic. And one is the Zadroga Bill. There is some question as to whether or not these individuals will be eligible or ineligible for the reopening of the VCF to remedy any inequities in the amount of money they received either because it wasn't enough at the time, they didn't understand the injuries they had or those injuries got so much worse.

> So in that regard on one hand I would ask that your Honor stay this until the regulations come out—

> THE COURT: No.

> MR. NAPOLI: OK. Then, your Honor, on the second hand, your Honor, then 1 would ask that a briefing schedule be made—

THE COURT: The issue is, who gives them advice? They need to be advised whether to try and opt into the settlement, whether to not opt into the settlement, whether to voluntarily dismiss their cases or to proceed with their cases. They need a lawyer to advise them. You have been their lawyer but you are bound under the settlement. As I understand it the terms of the VCF which they all participated in is to bar them from litigation. So someone's got to advise them what to do and I think I've waited enough time.

On February 7, 2011, I engaged Noah H. Kushlefsky, Esq., of Kreindler & Kreindler LLP, to advise these 59 Plaintiffs "of their respective rights and options with regard to continuing in this litigation." I provided that Napoli Bern was to compensate Mr. Kushlefsky for his services, for Mr. Kushlefsky would perform services that Napoli Bern was obligated to perform. The clients would be free, following consultation, to remain with Napoli Bern if both client and law firm, after full disclosure and discussion, agreed that Napoli Bern henceforth would be able to provide zealous and conflict-free representation to each client. Or, these 59 Plaintiffs could choose any other counsel to represent them, or any of them, including Mr. Kushlefsky.

I since have learned that Napoli Bern has refused to cooperate with Mr. Kushlefsky, and has not turned over the files for any of these clients. Instead, Napoli Bern moves under Federal Rules 60(b)(1) and (6) for vacatur of my Order appointing Mr. Kushlefsky. Napoli Bern makes three arguments: (i) that Napoli Bern does not possess a conflict of interest with regard to these 59 Plaintiffs; (ii) that if a conflict does exist, the appointment of Mr. Kushlefsky is too broad a remedy; and (iii) that requiring Napoli Bern to compensate Mr. Kushlefsky is an unfair sanction under Federal Rule of Civil Procedure 11.

## II.   DISCUSSION

In relevant part, Federal Rule 60(b) provides:

On motion and just terms, the court may relieve a party or its legal representative from a final judgment, order, or proceeding for the following reasons:

  (1)   mistake, inadvertence, surprise, or excusable neglect; . . .

  (6)   any other reason that justifies relief.

Federal Rule 60(b)(1) is available for the district court to correct its own legal errors. The point is to provide parties with a mechanism for obtaining corrections of legal error more efficiently than the appeal process. Federal Rule 60(b)(6) motions must be based on some reason other than those enumerated in the other subsections of the rule. The rule is used sparingly, "as an equitable remedy to prevent manifest injustice." To obtain relief, the party must set forth "highly convincing material" in support of the motion.

Napoli Bern's principal contention is that no conflict exists with regard to these 59 Plaintiffs. New York Rule of Professional Conduct 1.7(a) sets forth the relevant rule on conflicts, and it provides that a lawyer "shall not represent a client if a reasonable lawyer would conclude that either the representation will involve the lawyer in representing differing interests; or there is a significant risk that the lawyer's professional judgment on behalf of a client will be adversely affected by the lawyer's own financial, business, property or other personal interests." Comment 1 to Rule 1.7 provides:

> Loyalty and independent judgment are essential aspects of a lawyer's relationship with a client. The professional judgment of a lawyer should be exercised, within the bounds of the law, solely for the benefit of the client and free of compromising influences and loyalties. Concurrent conflicts of interest, which can impair a lawyer's professional judgment, can arise from the lawyer's responsibilities to another client, a former client or a third person, or from the lawyer's own interests. A lawyer should not permit these competing responsibilities or interests to impair the lawyer's ability to exercise professional judgment on behalf of each client.

Comment 24 further notes that "a conflict of interest exists if there is a significant risk that a lawyer's action on behalf of one client will materially limit the lawyer's representation of another client in a different case." At bottom, the consideration is straightforward: the reasonable lawyer should consider if one client "may reasonably fear that the lawyer will pursue his or her case less effectively out of deference to the other client."

Napoli Bern has been in a state of conflict of interest within the meaning of Rule 1.7(a). Napoli Bern took on these 59 Plaintiffs with the promise, implicit in any representation, that it would provide zealous advocacy, free from dilution by concerns about how other clients would be affected. To provide that service, Napoli Bern would have had to advocate that these 59 Plaintiffs should not be barred from suit by the ATSSSA, and that they should be able to settle under the SPA. However, such advocacy by Napoli Bern would have created risk for other Plaintiffs that the settlement would be delayed or defeated, or that many of them would receive smaller recoveries. The interests of Napoli Bern's clients were "differing," as contemplated by Rule 1.7(a), and Napoli Bern's obligation to provide loyal and zealous advocacy for each of its clients was compromised.

Napoli Bern first tried to put the 59 Plaintiffs on the EPL, and then tried to opt them out of the SPA, this suggesting that in time they might be able to overcome the bar of the ATSSSA release. But this stratagem was not a solution desired by the Plaintiffs, for some or all of the 59 Plaintiffs preferred to settle. Indeed, some of the 59 Plaintiffs pleaded to the Court at the public meetings and in letters that they wanted—even needed—to settle. But Napoli Bern did not respond to the problem; instead, it removed these 59 Plaintiffs from the EPL. Having thus been in conflict for months, and having done nothing about it, Napoli Bern failed to give these 59 Plaintiffs the proper representation to which they were entitled. Instead, Napoli Bern favored the needs of the thousands of other clients whom it also represented. That this happened is hardly surprising, especially when one considers the possibility that Napoli Bern had financial motivations for preferring its thousands of settling clients.

Napoli Bern argues that it was not in conflict because these 59 Plaintiffs had no merit to their cases. The merit of these Plaintiffs' cases is not the issue. A lawyer's first obligation is make any and all possible good-faith arguments on behalf of his or her clients—each and all of his her clients—that is, to *advocate* as effectively as possible on their behalves. Napoli Bern indeed has an obligation to make arguments "warranted by existing law or by a non-frivolous argument for extending, modifying, or reversing existing law or for establishing new law," Fed.R.Civ.P. 11(b)(2), but it has made no arguments on behalf of these Plaintiffs. Instead, Napoli Bern has allowed them to become second-class citizens of the Plaintiff population, waiting at the back of the line for all others to resolve their cases before having a chance to be heard. Even today, none of these 59 Plaintiffs knows whether or not his or her case is viable or can be made viable.

Nor is the conflict dissipated because the chance to settle under the SPA is now unavailable. Over 200 cases remain, those of the Plaintiffs who rejected the SPA and those of Plaintiffs who were ineligible. These cases are going to be the subject of rigorous pretrial practice, including motions to dismiss, motions under *Daubert v. Merrell Dow Pharmaceuticals*, and motions *in limine*. Then, there will be trials. Whose cases shall go first? How shall Napoli Bern divide its resources among these remaining cases? Shall these 59 Plaintiffs wait until the end of the process? Does Napoli Bern intend again to subordinate the claims of these clients in favor of others?

From Mr. Napoli's representation at the last status conference, it appears Napoli Bern believes the new VCF created by the James Zadroga 9/11 Health and Compensation Act of 2010, provides a solution to the firm's current problem. The Zadroga Act was not passed to alleviate Napoli Bern's dilemma or provide a relief from its unprofessional conduct. Whether the 59 Plaintiffs, or any of them, may become eligible to enter the new VCF authorized by the Zadroga Act is an open question at this point, and irrelevant to the concerns expressed in this Order.

Napoli Bern has ducked its conflict for months. That delay should not be extended. Napoli Bern's clients are as much entitled to conflict-free advice as any other client. I appointed Noah H. Kushlefsky to provide that consultation and advice, for Napoli Bern cannot do it.

This is a unique litigation, brought by 10,500 individuals, the rescue and clean-up workers who performed heroic service on the World Trade Center pile of smoldering debris. For many of these individuals, the injuries they alleged are seriously debilitating, compromising their lives, their vitality, and the health and well-being of their families. The realities of the cases have required a measure of judicial supervision to ensure that each of these Plaintiffs has been treated fairly. As part of that judicial supervision, I suggested months ago, and Napoli Bern agreed, that these 59 Plaintiffs needed an independent lawyer to consult with them, and, if need be, to represent their interests in a way that would not be influenced by the interests of any other Plaintiffs. Napoli Bern failed to fulfill this obligation, and its clients may well have been seriously prejudiced.

As to the remedy itself, Napoli Bern contends that I have, in effect, sanctioned the firm under Federal Rule 11 by foisting a lawyer on it, at its expense, for the benefit of clients who chose Napoli Bern to represent them. Whether and to what extent Napoli Bern should be sanctioned is another question—one that I do not need to reach in this Order. The issue here is how best to provide conflict-free representation to these 59 Plaintiffs. Mr. Kushlefsky was appointed because Napoli Bern, having asked for and received permission to find its own independent counsel to do the job, failed or was incapable of finding one. It is only fair that Napoli Bern compensate Mr. Kushlefsky, under my supervision, for performing the task that Napoli Bern undertook to do, but could not perform.

### III. CONCLUSION

Napoli Bern's motion is denied. Noah H. Kushlefsky, as special counsel, shall begin contacting each of the 59 Plaintiffs promptly. Napoli Bern is ordered (i) to send a copy of this Order to each of the 59 Plaintiffs, and (ii) to forward a list of names, addresses, index numbers, and phone numbers of each of these 59 Plaintiffs to Mr. Kushlefsky. Napoli Bern shall file a report showing it performed these requirements, by March 16, 2011. Napoli Bern shall further promptly and fully cooperate with Mr. Kushlefsky by turning over files of these 59 Plaintiffs, and otherwise providing its cooperation. Mr. Kushlefsky shall endeavor to complete his consultations, and file a report, by April 15, 2011, making recommendations on how to proceed, including a description of motions that may be appropriate.

# B.  THE GULF COAST CLAIMS FACILITY AS AN EXTRA-JUDICIAL PROCESS

## IN RE OIL SPILL BY THE OIL RIG DEEPWATER HORIZON IN THE GULF OF MEXICO ON APRIL 20, 2010

United States District Court for the Eastern District of Louisiana, 2011.
2011 WL 323866.

Before the Court is Plaintiffs' Motion to Supervise Ex Parte Communications with Putative Class, as well as several responses including BP Defendants' Opposition, Plaintiffs' Reply in Support, Plaintiffs' Supplement, BP Defendants' Supplemental Memorandum in Opposition, the State of Mississippi's Statement of Interest, the State of Louisiana's Notice of Joinder in Motion to Supervise, and the State of Florida's Statement of Interest.

### PROCEDURAL HISTORY AND BACKGROUND

This multi-district litigation consists of hundreds of consolidated cases, with thousands of claimants, presently pending before this Court. These cases arise from the April 20, 2010 explosion, fire and capsizing of the "Deepwater Horizon" mobile offshore drilling unit, which resulted in the release of millions of gallons of oil into the Gulf of Mexico before it was finally capped approximately three months later. The consolidated cases include claims for the death of eleven individuals, numerous claims for personal injury, and various claims for environmental and economic damages.

The Oil Pollution Act of 1990 (OPA) requires BP, as the designated "responsible party" for the Deepwater Horizon oil spill, to "establish a procedure for the payment or settlement of claims for interim, short-term damages." In the initial months after the casualty, BP began to directly receive and pay interim claims arising from the oil spill. To assist in handling claims, BP contracted with one or more claims adjusting firms. Subsequently, on June 16, 2010, the White House issued a Press Release announcing that an "Independent Claims Facility" and a $20 billion escrow fund would be established by BP to fulfill these and other legal obligations of the company. The Claims Facility was to be responsible for developing and publishing standards for recoverable claims, under the authority of Ken Feinberg, who would serve as an independent administrator. BP announced that effective August 23, 2010, the Gulf Coast Claims Facility (GCCF), spearheaded by Mr. Feinberg and his law firm, would replace the original BP claims process and perform BP's obligations under OPA with respect to private economic loss claims. Although a formal Trust Agreement was executed to establish the escrow fund, the nature of the relationship between BP and the GCCF and Mr. Feinberg remains a disputed issue.

In their instant Motion, Plaintiffs request that the Court oversee or supervise communications between the GCCF and putative class members to ensure that communications are neither misleading nor confusing.

### PARTIES' ARGUMENTS

First, Plaintiffs argue that the GCCF is indistinguishable from BP-explaining, for example, that BP created the GCCF, that BP still retains some level of control over the GCCF, and that the GCCF is BP's agent for the purpose of satisfying BP's role as the "responsible party" under OPA. Accordingly, Plaintiffs argue that the Court should require changes to the GCCF communications that Plaintiffs perceive to be misleading and confusing. Specifically, Plaintiffs argue that the Court should order that BP Defendants, Mr. Feinberg, the GCCF, or their representatives:

- Refrain from contacting directly any claimant that BP and/or the GCCF knows or reasonably should know is represented by counsel, including, but not limited to, any person or entity who has filed a lawsuit or submitted a PPF, a Short-Form Joinder, a GCCF Claim, or a BP Claim that reflects representation by an attorney.

- Refrain from referring to the GCCF, Mr. Feinberg, or Feinberg Rozen, LLP (or their representatives), as "independent" or "neutral," and should further:

- Affirmatively state (on the website, Release, and in all communications-written, oral, and electronic) that a lawyer of the claimant's choice should be consulted before accepting a final offer or signing a Release;

- Affirmatively state that punitive damages (and/or additional damages) may be available in litigation, but are not being recognized or paid by the GCCF;

- Affirmatively state (on the website, Release, and in all communications) that they cannot advise as to the value of the claim, merits of the claim, or any legal consequences of the settlement;

- Affirmatively state (on the website, Release, and in all private and public communications) that Mr. Feinberg, Feinberg Rozen, LLP, and the GCCF are BP's agents in performing BP's statutory duties under the Oil Pollution Act of 1990;

- Affirmatively advise claimants (on the website, Release, and in all communications) of the pendency of the MDL 2179 litigation, the availability of Short-Form Joinders (without the need of an attorney or the payment of a filing fee), and the existence of the Liability/Limitation/Test Case Trial in February 2012 in New Orleans;

- Affirmatively advise (on the website, Release, and in all communications) the putative class and claimants that pro bono attorneys or community leaders retained to assist claimants in the GCCF process are being compensated directly or indirectly by BP, and are not "independent."

- Every communication with a putative class member should be prefaced to inform them of the above.

- Further if any communication, public or private, from the GCCF, Mr. Feinberg, or Feinberg Rozen, LLP purports to inform claimants/plaintiffs/putative class members of their right to seek relief from the Oil Spill Trust Fund, such communication shall also advise: (a) that they can also elect to seek relief in a court of law using a Short-Form Joinder in MDL 2179 that can be filed without an attorney and without the payment of a filing free; (b) that some damages or other remedies available in a court of law may not be available from the Oil Spill Trust Fund; (c) that the total funds available from the Oil Spill Trust Fund are limited; and (d) that the Coast Guard (not a court) may determine that they have not satisfied the Coast Guard's presentment requirements.

Plaintiffs maintain that this Court has the duty and the authority to protect members of the putative class, citing Federal Rule of Civil Procedure 23, Federal Rule of Civil Procedure 16, the MANUAL FOR COMPLEX LITIGATION, and *Turner v. Murphy Oil*. Because MDL 2179 includes cases which were initiated as putative class actions, Plaintiffs argue that these proceedings are subject to Rule 23, which allows courts to issue orders "to protect class members and fairly conduct the action" and "impose conditions on represented parties." The MANUAL FOR COMPLEX LITIGATION explains that "the court must protect the interests of absent class members, and Rule 23(d) gives the judge broad administrative power to do so, reflecting the equity origins of class action" which includes the ability to "regulate communications with potential class members, even before certification."

Plaintiffs also urge the Court to adopt analogous reasoning to that of Judge Fallon in *Turner v. Murphy Oil*. There, Judge Fallon decided to supervise communications between defendant Murphy Oil and the putative class members, concluding that Murphy Oil's communications with putative class members was commercial speech not fully protected by the First Amendment (because defendant's economic interest in reducing litigation costs were involved). Accordingly, Judge Fallon ordered certain restrictions on communications by or on behalf of the defendant, Murphy Oil, including (1) the requirement that the Release contain language about seeking independent legal advice, (2) the requirement that Murphy Oil not initiate contact with any individual who had not previously contacted

Murphy Oil, and (3) the requirement that Murphy Oil comply with Rule 4.2 of the Louisiana Rules of Professional Conduct and not communicate with persons already represented by counsel.

BP counters that Plaintiffs' requested relief contravenes the extra-judicial process statutorily mandated by OPA. Because Plaintiffs do not contend that they have exhausted the OPA's claims process (by fulfilling the presentment requirement), BP argues that Plaintiffs cannot bring a valid court action. Next, BP takes the position that Plaintiffs' requested relief is an unconstitutional prior restraint on speech protected by the First Amendment and authorized by OPA. Citing *Bernard v. Gulf Oil Co.,* BP explains that prior restraints are justified only in "exceptional circumstances" and require a showing that judicial intervention is necessary to prevent "direct, immediate and irreparable harm," a standard BP contends Plaintiffs cannot meet. BP argues that Plaintiffs have not provided any evidence that putative class members misunderstood GCCF publications or felt coerced. BP also argues that Mr. Feinberg's and the GCCF's speech is non-commercial expression entitled to full protection under the First Amendment—as Mr. Feinberg and the GCCF are implementing public policy established by Congress and the President and are not acting on behalf of a client. BP draws a distinction between cases that Plaintiffs cite for the proposition that courts can interfere with communications to members of a putative class-in Plaintiffs' cases, defendants were in ongoing business relationships with the defendants; whereas, the GCCF has had no prior relationship with claimants. Rather than monitor Mr. Feinberg's speech, BP urges Plaintiffs to exercise their own First Amendment rights-a step that BP explains Plaintiffs are already taking by airing their concerns through the local and national media.

Furthermore, BP maintains that Mr. Feinberg and the GCCF are independent decision-makers as to OPA claims. Although the GCCF is funded by BP and has a contract with BP, Feinberg Rozen, LLP makes OPA claims decisions subject to the legal parameters of OPA. BP insists that Mr. Feinberg is solely responsible for administering the GCCF, that he developed the protocols and Release, and that he does not report to BP. BP argues that these facts more than satisfy the definition of an independent contractor (which provides that an independent contractor works according to his own methods and without direct supervision).

Additionally, BP insists that Plaintiffs seek a mandatory injunction directing speech by the GCCF on matters either already disclosed on the GCCF website and in its claims and releases or that, under BP's perspective, is clearly inappropriate or untrue. Specifically, BP points to GCCF materials that already inform claimants that: (1) if a claimant has an attorney, he or she should confer with the attorney before submitting a GCCF claim or signing a release; (2) the GCCF is not a law firm and does not give legal advice; (3) claimants have the right to be represented by lawyers of their own choosing; (4) Mr. Feinberg does not report to BP and BP does not control the GCCF in any way-the decisions of Mr. Feinberg are only subject to the GCCF limited appeal authority in the protocol for interim and final claims; and (5) the free legal services program is paid for by a prepaid grant funded by BP.

## DISCUSSION

The Court has the responsibility to ensure that the mandates of OPA are implemented. A responsible party's use of a third party to fulfill its statutory obligations is not only consistent with the intent of OPA but also highly commendable if those claims can be resolved even more efficiently and fairly. The existence of the GCCF does, however, raise issues concerning both its role and its relationship to BP. Is the GCCF completely independent of BP and a neutral arbiter of claims? Is the GCCF actually BP or an agent of BP? Or, is the GCCF another type of hybrid mixture of the traditional plaintiff-defendant adversarial model of dispute resolution and the use of a third party?

OPA contemplates that the responsible party will "establish a procedure for the payment or settlement of claims for interim, short-term damages." If the responsible party decides to have a third party accomplish this obligation, the assumption is that the third party is an extension or agent of the responsible party—as was the situation prior to the creation of the GCCF when BP used claims-adjusting firms to handle claims. If, however, the responsible party decides that an "independent" and "neutral" or other hybrid entity is to fulfill its OPA claims obligation, it is incumbent on the responsible party to disclose the nature of its relationship to this entity and the precise role of the entity. Otherwise, the default assumption applies that the claims are being handled by the responsible party itself.

Full disclosure concerning the relationship between the responsible party and the third party acting in accordance with OPA is consistent with the policy underlying other court-overseen claims-resolution facilities— such as class actions or other settlement funds and bankruptcy trusts— and is consistent with the transparency policies of many defendants. The legitimacy of a third-party claims-resolution facility is derived in no small part from the claimants' ability to learn, comprehend, and appreciate how that facility is operated so that the claimants can fully evaluate the rationale behind the communications made to them by the facility. Full disclosure and transparency can insure that the reality of the operation of a third party will be consistent with any publicity concerning that entity. Full disclosure can also give protection to the responsible party from possible future legal attacks on the validity of the evaluation, payment, and release of claims.

This Court encourages and commends any claims process that will fairly, quickly, and efficiently resolve claims in this litigation. Innovative and thoughtful procedures are to be encouraged. Those procedures must, however, be fully transparent so that claimants can evaluate them appropriately. The Court recognizes and appreciates the enormity of the undertaking of Mr. Feinberg and does not intend to impede or interfere with his ability to fairly and efficiently process claims.

### Mr. Feinberg, Feinberg Rozen, LLP and GCCF Are Not Fully "Independent" of BP

BP argues that since Feinberg Rozen, LLP is not providing legal advice to BP, they are not subject to the ethical rules restricting contact by lawyers with unrepresented persons. But, this argument misses the larger point. As the designated "responsible party" under OPA, it is BP's responsibility to "establish a procedure for the payment or settlement of claims for interim, short-term damages." To fulfill its statutory obligations, BP has created the GCCF, which is administered by Mr. Feinberg and his law firm, Feinberg Rozen, LLP. The fact that BP in this instance has chosen to delegate this responsibility cannot relieve BP of its statutory obligations.

After reviewing the facts and submissions by the parties, the Court finds that BP has created a hybrid entity, rather than one that is fully independent of BP. While BP may have delegated to Mr. Feinberg and the GCCF independence in the evaluation and payment of individual claims, many other facts support a finding that the GCCF and Mr. Feinberg are not completely "neutral" or independent from BP. For example, Mr. Feinberg was appointed by BP, without input from opposing claimants or the Plaintiffs' Steering Committee (PSC), and without an order from the Court. Mr. Feinberg is not a true third-party neutral such as a mediator, arbitrator, or court-appointed special master.

BP pays Mr. Feinberg and his law firm a flat fee each month, pursuant to a written contract which outlines his duties and responsibilities in great detail. This Contract is a private one between only BP and Feinberg Rozen, LLP-the United States is not a party to this Contract. Mr. Feinberg and Feinberg Rozen, LLP provide claim intake, claim review, claim evaluation and claim settlement and payment services. BP decided the amount and manner in which it funded the GCCF through this trust agreement. BP is given monthly reports regarding distributions made to GCCF beneficiaries, and Mr. Feinberg states that in administering the fund, the GCCF has no conflicts of interest; that it will hold all client information in confidence; that it cannot reveal any confidential information relating to the GCCF without giving BP prior notice so that BP can seek a protective order; that all information gathered from claimants will be turned over to BP, with no restrictions as to its use.

Additionally, the Contract provides that BP will "indemnify, defend, and hold harmless" Feinberg Rozen, LLP "from and against any and all threatened or commenced actions that are threatened, asserted, brought, commenced, or sought by any person or entity relating to or arising from the operation of the GCCF." BP may choose to allow Feinberg Rozen, LLP to "use and access certain of its computers, equipment, furniture, and properties", as well as "use and access certain facilities, properties, and offices owned or leased by BP." Under the Contract, BP retains the ability to audit Feinberg Rozen, LLP as long as the firm retains information about claimants. In administering the GCCF, Feinberg Rozen, LLP agrees to comply with BP's Code of Conduct and to refrain from subcontracting its obligations without prior written approval from BP.

Although the Contract has an expiration date of August 13, 2013, the Contract may be terminated earlier: by BP, if Feinberg Rozen, LLP materially breaches its obligations and fails to cure, if Feinberg Rozen, LLP breaches its fiduciary obligations, or if Feinberg Rozen, LLP ceases to devote substantial time to running the GCCF; and by Feinberg Rozen, LLP for any reason whatsoever. The Contract also provides that Feinberg Rozen, LLP's fees will be evaluated after January 15, 2011, and that thereafter the parties will mutually agree on fees in advance of the first day of each successive quarter.

The GCCF is settling claims against BP under OPA, but also attempting to settle claims that fall outside of OPA, such as personal injury and death claims. In their releases of BP, the GCCF requires claimants to release and assign all rights or claims not only against BP, but against any other potentially liable party. Whether or not seeking such broad releases is appropriate, the GCCF is clearly acting to benefit BP in doing so. BP may appeal an award of the GCCF if it exceeds $500,000; appeals are decided by a three-judge panel and are binding only on BP.

Under these circumstances, while Mr. Feinberg appears "independent" in the sense that BP does not control Mr. Feinberg's evaluation of individual claims, Mr. Feinberg and the GCCF cannot be considered "neutral" or totally "independent" of BP.

### Supervision of Communications with Putative Class Members

BP is not only the designated OPA "responsible party," but also a primary Defendant in this MDL and the consolidated putative class actions. Even prior to certification of a class, this Court has both the inherent authority and the responsibility under Rule 23 to supervise or control certain communications with potential class members, especially those who are unrepresented by their own counsel. MANUAL FOR COMPLEX LITIGATION § 21.12. If potential class members have received inaccurate, confusing or misleading communications, the Court may take action to cure the miscommunication and to prevent similar problems in the future. This is long-established law:

> Misleading communications to class members concerning the litigation pose a serious threat to the fairness of the litigation process, the adequacy of representation and the administration of justice generally.

This authority is consistent with the First Amendment, as are many other controls on statements about litigation. In *Kleiner,* the Eleventh Circuit explained that:

> In general, an order limiting communications regarding ongoing litigation between a class and class opponents will satisfy First Amendment concerns if it is grounded in good cause and issued with a "heightened sensitivity" for First Amendment concerns. In ascertaining the existence of good cause, four criteria are determinative: the severity and likelihood of the perceived harm; the precision with which the order is drawn; the availability of a less onerous alternative; and the duration of the order.

Furthermore, the *Kleiner* court noted that district courts are free to prohibit false or misleading speech by a defendant and may restrict a defendant from using methods of speech that are inherently coercive or prone to abuse. BP attempts to distinguish this line of cases by the fact that in several cases there was an ongoing business relationship between the claimants and the defendant. In this case, OPA itself mandates that claimants must first present their claims to BP as the responsible party, thereby requiring ongoing contact between the parties.

Because the Court finds that the hybrid role of Mr. Feinberg and the GCCF has led to confusion and misunderstanding by claimants, especially those who are unrepresented by their own counsel, the Court finds that certain precautions should be taken to protect the interests of claimants—narrowly tailored in accordance with the First Amendment. *Gulf Oil Co. v. Bernard.* The clear record in this case demonstrates that any claim of the GCCF's neutrality and independence is misleading to putative class members and is a direct threat to this ongoing litigation, as claimants must sign a full release against all potential defendants before obtaining final payments. For example, in this case Mr. Feinberg has been quoted on a number of occasions as publicly advising potential claimants that they do not need to hire a lawyer and will be much better off accepting what he offers rather than going to court. A full disclosure of the relationship between Mr. Feinberg, the GCCF, and BP will at least make transparent that it is BP's interests as the OPA responsible party that are being promoted.

The Court finds that not all of Plaintiffs' requested measures are appropriate or necessary, and will tailor a more narrowly focused remedy. The Court finds that the following precautions represent a narrowly-tailored approach, and that "an order any less restrictive would not effect the purposes of Rule 23." Further, the Court specifically finds that this will not unduly burden BP's, Mr. Feinberg's and the GCCF's ability to speak on their own behalf. "Communication can continue with potential claimants, while the interests of putative class members in receiving independent information is protected." *Turner v. Murphy Oil.*

Accordingly, it is ordered that the Motion to Supervise Ex Parte Communications with Putative Class is granted in part, as follows:

It is ordered that Defendant BP, through its agents Ken Feinberg, Feinberg Rozen LLP, and the Gulf Coast Claims Facility, and any of their representatives, in any of their oral or written communications with claimants, shall:

(1)  Refrain from contacting directly any claimant that they know or reasonably should know is represented by counsel, whether or not said claimant has filed a lawsuit or formal claim;

(2)  Refrain from referring to the GCCF, Ken Feinberg, or Feinberg Rozen, LLP (or their representatives), as "neutral" or completely "independent" from BP. It should be clearly disclosed in all communications, whether written or oral, that said parties are acting for and on behalf of BP in fulfilling its statutory obligations as the "responsible party" under the Oil Pollution Act of 1990.

(3)  Begin any communication with a putative class member with the statement that the individual has a right to consult with an attorney of his/her own choosing prior to accepting any settlement or signing a release of legal rights.

(4)  Refrain from giving or purporting to give legal advice to unrepresented claimants, including advising that claimants should not hire a lawyer.

(5)  Fully disclose to claimants their options under OPA if they do not accept a final payment, including filing a claim in the pending MDL 2179 litigation.

(6)  Advise claimants that the "pro bono" attorneys and "community representatives" retained to assist GCCF claimants are being compensated directly or indirectly by BP.

Further, in light of the Court's responsibility to ensure full compliance with the Oil Pollution Act of 1990, and to address various additional concerns that have been raised,

It is further ordered that the parties shall submit additional briefing on the question of whether and how BP as the responsible party is fully complying with the mandates of OPA, for example, in the processing of claims for "interim, short-term damages," or "final damages," methodologies for evaluation of claims, and the release forms required of claimants. Said briefing shall be filed not later than February 11, 2011.

# INDEX

References are to Pages